HABERMAS AND
RELIGION

HABERMAS AND RELIGION

Edited by Craig Calhoun, Eduardo Mendieta, and Jonathan VanAntwerpen

polity

First published in 2013 by Polity Press

Polity Press
65 Bridge Street
Cambridge CB2 1UR, UK

Polity Press
350 Main Street
Malden, MA 02148, USA

ISBN-13: 978-0-7456-5326-6
ISBN-13: 978-0-7456-5327-3(pb)

A catalogue record for this book is available from the British Library.

Typeset in 10 on 12 pt Adobe Sabon by
Servis Filmsetting Ltd, Stockport, Cheshire
Printed and bound by Berforts Ltd, Stevenage.

The publisher has used its best endeavours to ensure that the URLs for external
websites referred to in this book are correct and active at the time of going to
press. However, the publisher has no responsibility for the websites and can
make no guarantee that a site will remain live or that the content is or will
remain appropriate.

Every effort has been made to trace all copyright holders, but if any have been
inadvertently overlooked the publisher will be pleased to include any necessary
credits in any subsequent reprint or edition.

For further information on Polity, visit our website: www.politybooks.com

Contents

〇〇

Abbreviations

The following abbreviations are used for frequently cited works by Jürgen Habermas. Full bibliographical details can be found in the Bibliography. Dates in square brackets are the dates of publication in English.

AWM   *An Awareness of What is Missing* (2008 [2010])
BFN   *Between Facts and Norms* (1992 [1998])
BNR   *Between Naturalism and Religion* (2005 [2008])
CES   *Communication and the Evolution of Society* (1976 [1979])
CEU   *The Crisis of the European Union* (2011 [2012])
DS   *Dialectics of Secularization* (2005 [2006])
DW   *The Divided West* (2004 [2007])
EFK   *Essay on Faith and Knowledge* (n.d.)
EFP   *Europe: The Faltering Project* (2008 [2009])
FHN   *The Future of Human Nature* (2001 [2003])
FWL   "From Worldviews to the Lifeworld" (n.d.)
HE   "History and Evolution" (1976 [1979])
IO   *The Inclusion of the Other* (1996 [1998])
JA   *Justification and Application* (1991 [1993])
JS   "Justice and Solidarity" (1990)
KHI   *Knowledge and Human Interests* (1968 [1971])
KV   *Kritik der Vernunft* (2009)
LC   *Legitimation Crisis* (1973 [1975])
LPS   *The Liberating Power of Symbols* (1997 [2001])
MCCA *Moral Consciousness and Communicative Action* (1983 [1990])
NC   *The New Conservatism* (1985/1987 [1989])
OPC   *On the Pragmatics of Communication* [1998]

PC   *The Postnational Constellation* (1998 [2001])
PDM   *The Philosophical Discourse of Modernity* (1985 [1990])
PF   *The Past as Future* (1993 [1994])
PMT   *Postmetaphysical Thinking* (1988 [1992])
PPP   *Philosophical-Political Profiles* (1981 [1983])
PSI   *On the Pragmatics of Social Interaction* (1984 [2001])
RPS   "Religion in the Public Sphere" (2006)
RR   *Religion and Rationality* (2002)
STPS   *The Structural Transformation of the Public Sphere* (1962
        [1989])
TCA   *The Theory of Communicative Action* (1981 [1984/1987])
TJ   *Truth and Justification* (1999 [2003])
TRS   *Toward a Rational Society* (1958/1968 [1970])

Editors' Introduction

For social and political theorists – both philosophers and social scientists – religion was long an easy subject to ignore. Or, if it wasn't ignored, its importance was minimized. It was treated as a fading phenomenon, a survival from earlier history, not really a part of modernity. Great figures of modern social theory such as Marx, Weber, and Durkheim all expected religion to lose its grip in the face of trends like capitalism, reason and rationalization, the growing complexity of social organization, and cultural pluralism. Religion demanded attention because it held back progress – not least as "the opium of the people" – or because it played a temporarily crucial role in early modern transitions before the process of secularization marked its decline, or because as it disappeared an absence was noticed, a need for new forms of ritual and new sources of social solidarity and cultural integration. These were not just nineteenth-century ideas; they remained prominent throughout the twentieth-century history of political philosophy and social theory. To be sure, there were ebbs and flows of attention to religion. There was something of a flourishing early in the twentieth century and another in the period just after World War II. But the overall pattern remained intact, and indeed religion was particularly off the agenda for philosophy and social science during the last decades of the twentieth century. This coincided with a decline in certain forms of religious practice (a decline meticulously tracked by researchers). Mainline Protestant denominations in the US lost members continuously, while newer forms of religious practice blossomed throughout the world; religious practice plummeted even more markedly in Europe. To be sure, some researchers noticed, and puzzled over, a resurgence of evangelicalism and fundamentalism, not just in the US but throughout the world. It is for this reason that sometimes social analysts refer to this global phenomenon as the "revitalization" of religion. This received attention especially as it shaped politics – a "new religious right" – notably in the US (where, a few observers reminded us, religion hadn't faded as much or as fast as in Europe). But these observations were slow to gain center stage in most of philosophy and social science. They gained more traction in anthropology and history, perhaps, than in other disciplines, but almost everywhere the dominant intellectual framework remained the expectation of secularization.

What was widely called "the secularization *hypothesis*" became instead more of an assumption in most of political philosophy and social theory. If religion mattered, it was because of its influence in the past, and as a survival out of step with the dominant patterns of progress. This was evident not least in the work of Jürgen Habermas, perhaps the most distinguished and enduringly influential figure in these fields during the late twentieth century and to the present day.

Quite remarkably, Habermas has been at the forefront of debates since the early 1960s. He was the foremost representative of the Frankfurt tradition of critical theory, but he also engaged in extended debates and reciprocal learning with Niklas Luhmann, Hans-Georg Gadamer, John Rawls, Robert Brandom, and others of the most influential thinkers in philosophy and social science. He wrote fundamental work in philosophical anthropology and epistemology; he put the idea of the public sphere at the center of thinking about democracy; in his *Theory of Communicative Action*, he produced the most important analysis of reason and rationalization since Weber and the most influential synthesis of action theory and systems analysis since Parsons. And, in keeping with the philosophy and social theory of his era, he did all this with what for a long time seemed like no more than passing attention to religion.

This changed, modestly in the 1990s, then with major emphasis since the beginning of the current century. The change was driven not so much by concern over past neglect or a sense of intra-theoretical need; it was driven by attention to troubling dimensions of contemporary affairs. Throughout his career, Habermas had been actively engaged in political debates, not only offering his theoretical work to help in resolving them but accepting the challenge to innovate in response to shifting public concerns and evident transformation in society. Still, it was impressive to see one of the world's most famous thinkers resist the temptation simply to defend his established views and instead take up issues that posed challenges. And Habermas's engagement with religion has demanded not just the application of his existing theory but innovation of it, and even restructuring of its fundamental assumptions.

First, Habermas was pushed by genetics and other innovations in biotechnology to ask anew about the core nature of the human (*FHN*). This led him to examine the inheritance – often left tacit – of metaphysical notions that understood the human essentially in relationship to the divine and to Creation. Habermas was disturbed most by what he saw as a potential renewal of eugenics, driven by an unchallenged technological impetus and unclarified assumptions concerning individuality and political liberty. Instead, Habermas situated his analysis of the dangers of liberal eugenics in an exploration of the moral nature of the human and human self-development. This built on Habermas's earlier work on communicative action, especially as it related to philosophical anthropology and an evolutionary theory of human capacities for social self-organization and incremental advancement of what in a Hegelian-Marxist vocabulary might be considered "species-being." Centrally, Habermas argued that much of the semantic import of the idea of divine Creation could be and indeed was rendered in secular terms as the idea of human dignity. Religion, Habermas suggested, was a crucial source for convictions at the heart of notions like human rights, but meaning drawn from religious faith could be translated into terms accessible to those without such faith and on the basis of reason.

Second, like many, Habermas was shocked by the 9/11 attacks. He was troubled by the fundamentalist convictions that informed some terrorist actions. This drew him into an unexpected dialogue with Jacques Derrida, a post-structuralist thinker with whom he was in many ways philosophically at odds but with whom he found impressive commonalities in analysis of the ethical and political implications of both terrorism and the US-led War on Terror (see *Philosophy in a Time of Terror*). He was also astonished and disturbed by a US President who invoked religion in framing his response and who made a public point of praying in Congress as he took the country and the world to war. Rather than just condemning what he didn't like, Habermas struggled to articulate a theoretical account that would make sense of sharing citizenship with those who offer reasons rooted more in faith than reason and who sometimes reach troubling, literally terrifying conclusions. He repeatedly engaged Kierkegaard, a central figure in both religious and secular philosophical thinking about faith and knowledge, but even more drew on Kant and a tradition he construed as advancing a procedural approach over the search for prior substantive commonalities as a basis for collective life (*BNR*). Habermas also notably situated the rising prominence of religion in the public sphere in relationship to "the epoch-making historical juncture of 1989–90" as well as more recent events ("Religion in the Public Sphere," *BNR*, 114). It reflected not only age-old questions about faith and knowledge, but also a specific historical period shaped by geopolitical chaos and a weakening of apparent alternatives to capitalist domination.

Third, and at the same time, Habermas was worried by the difficulties of integrating a growing and increasingly visible Muslim minority into the European public sphere. This worry was reinforced by efforts to make official declarations of Europe's Christian identity, for example, in proposals for the Basic Law. It intensified more general concerns over strains in the European Union that had drawn Habermas's attention for several years. A strong supporter of the European project, he called for a constitution that would provide the procedural basis for mutual ethico-political commitments ("Why Europe Needs a Constitution," *New Left Review*, 2001, and widely reprinted). Europe offered a prime example of the kind of "complementary learning process" he thought could drive progress generally, and specifically both overcome animosities that had recurrently driven the continent to war and build institutions that would provide for democracy and social welfare. He was predictably troubled when neo-liberal ideologies brought the hollowing out of such institutions, and he saw in this one reason for the growing fragility of Europe's public sphere. He saw resurgent projects of ethnic identity as threats to Europe's collective learning process and argued for "constitutional patriotism" that would unite Europeans on the basis of commitment to procedural norms for living together and reaching common decisions despite difference (*PC, EFP, CEU*). He was particularly aghast at what he saw as efforts to rehabilitate deplorable dimensions of Germany's past (*NC, PF*). This may help explain his surprisingly harsh response to Charles Taylor's articulation of a politics of recognition (*IO*, 8; see also *BFN*). Habermas's strong commitment to procedural rather than culturally substantive grounding for shared citizenship encouraged him to approach religion in the public sphere mainly as an occasion for -tolerance. But he was to deepen this view and introduce considerable complexity.

Both the influence of religion in American politics and the hostility to Muslims in Europe were for Habermas first and foremost questions about the public sphere. In his theory, mutual public engagement underpinned the capacity to shape forms of social organization and solidarity democratically. For this to be democratic depended on recognizing and hearing the voices of all citizens. Religion thus posed questions about inclusion and exclusion that were already on Habermas's agenda through consideration of other forms of cultural difference (see *IO*). And he was alarmed to find some secularists as intolerant toward religious voices in the public sphere as the fundamentalists they condemned. Religion also renewed questions that had long engaged Habermas about the processes by which reasoned critique and communication oriented to producing common understanding might guide both intellectual and social progress (*MCCA, TCA, JA, BFN*). If religious reasons depended on different intellectual and personal bases from those of others, this was potentially a limit to democratic participation guided by rational-critical discourse. Habermas came to rely on a version of Rawls's notion of translation: the obligation of citizens reciprocally to render their arguments in terms accessible to each other, and to make their best efforts to understand each other on the basis of what was common to their thought. To this he added the idea of complementary learning processes that went beyond mere translation, as citizens gained semantic content from and possibly were changed by their interactions. In each case, thinking about religion pushed Habermas further, partly because he saw more potential for the bridging of other divides through practical reason, and saw the differences between religious and secular reason as more profound.[1]

At the same time, Habermas entered into increasingly prominent public dialogues with religious thinkers – including then Cardinal Ratzinger, who was to become Pope shortly after their much publicized encounter. These actually built on a longer history of discussions, for example, with the theologian Johann-Baptist Metz. Theologians had shown considerable interest in Habermas's work for many years, and their interest solicited response and dialogue.

Habermas's exploration of religion in the public sphere created a stir, and even shocked and disturbed more than a few of his followers. The level of interest – and unease – reflected both Habermas's enormous intellectual stature and the extent to which his work had previously not just been secular but typical of lines of thinking that at first blush seemed to ignore religion. It is in light of his recent and more explicit engagement with the question of religion that his early views on the matter have been discerned and tracked (as Eduardo Mendieta does in some detail in the Appendix to this volume).

This book responds to the rich intellectual debates that have accompanied Habermas's engagement with issues of religion. Its authors are among the most prominent philosophers and social and political theorists in the world. For some, religion is a primary concern. For others, it is a secondary dimension to their interest in ethics, public discourse, social solidarity, or social conflict. They are concerned less with a specialist understanding of religion than with exploring how different understandings of religion should fit into and inform broader perspectives on society and social change, on knowledge and human existence. Some write from perspectives informed by religious belief; some are sharply antagonistic to theocentric theories. What unites them are the convictions that how we think about religion is centrally important today, and that the writings of Jürgen Habermas are exceptionally helpful stimuli to better thinking.[2]

Habermas Takes Up Religion

Habermas has shown a serious interest in religion for at least the last twenty years. To be sure, he gave attention to Weber's account of both the role of religion in producing modernity – especially the Protestant Ethic (see *TCA*, vol. 1, ch. II). And he attended to some religious thinkers like Gershom Sholem (1978 in *PPP*; 1997 in *LPS* and *RR*), and to the religious influence of Jewish philosophers on members of the Frankfurt School, in particular, and German idealism, in general (*PPP*). But religion figured in rather more secondary and subterranean ways in Habermas's core philosophical and sociological analyses. It appeared to be neither an important topic for attention nor an important intellectual source. This assessment is now being revised from the perspective of Habermas's increasing interest in "faith and reason."

Indeed, Habermas produced accounts of the Enlightenment and modernity generally from which religion was remarkably missing. In this he was not entirely out of step with contemporary theorists, but the pattern was striking, especially considering the capacious, encyclopedic nature of his writing and theory-building. It is remarkable that religion is not considered seriously in *The Philosophical Discourse of Modernity*, and that religious thought is not taken up as such in *Knowledge and Human Interests*.

Even Habermas's engagement with Kant, which was formative for his mature work, did not initially address Kant's philosophy of religion – or his complex relationship to religion – with much depth. This did of course change, in the case of Kant most prominently with "On the Boundary between Faith and Knowledge" (chapter 8 of *BNR*). Most of Habermas's early discussions of religion were contained and constrained by the assumptions of secularism; indeed, this personal overcoming of the limits of inadequately reflective secularism may be one of the most basic meanings of his controversial term "postsecular." But not only did Habermas expect more reduction in religion's role through the course of modernity than actually occurred; he also saw less of religion's role in the constitution of modernity throughout its history than we, or perhaps he now, might have wished. We can see early examples of his changing perspective in his considerations of transcendence and anamnestic reason (overcoming forgetting) during the 1990s (reprinted in *RR*).

One of Habermas's most famous early books, namely, *The Structural Transformation of the Public Sphere*, is an example illustrating that perhaps the most central ways in which religion has come to the forefront of contemporary debates – and Habermas's attention – is through challenges to the liberal institutionalization of the public sphere. The nearly 30-year delay before it was published in English translation meant that it had a sort of second life after it appeared in 1989.[3] This not only associated it with new developments in political theory, like the idea of deliberative democracy, but with momentous public events like the crises of communist states, worldwide protest movements like Solidarity in Poland and the Tiananmen Square democracy movement in China, as well as the eventual unification of Germany. And, as newly published, Habermas's intellectual framework became basic to efforts to understand the new roles religion played in contemporary democracies.

Yet religion simply doesn't figure in *The Structural Transformation of the Public Sphere* (1962, 1989b).[4] This is not just a matter of skewed examples, but of the overall structure of the book. An account of the formation and transformation of the European public sphere might very plausibly have begun with the Reformation. This was when print publics first emerged; in many countries this was the first time intellectual debates were conducted in the demotic European languages and galvanized large populations. The Reformation overlapped the Renaissance and both are arguably eras in the history of secularism as well as religion. But the crucial point is simply that a history and social theory of the public sphere that started by recognizing the intertwining of political discourse (and indeed social and economic discourse) with religious debate in early modern Europe would have made for an importantly different perspective on the public sphere.

Something of the same thing could be said for Habermas's major engagements with questions of political legitimacy and institutional change (*LC*) and law and democracy (*BFN*). Religion does get some attention in his magnum opus, *Theory of Communicative Action*. But it appears mainly as central to the enchanted worldview (in Weber's term), a worldview from which communicative action, reason, and social progress free people, not as itself advanced through communicative action; or, following Durkheim, as the precursor to a social solidarity and universalistic moral attitudes, but destined to be assimilated *in toto* in the glue of society. It matters more for motivation than meaning. Religion is, in the sense mentioned at the beginning of this introduction, of *transitional* interest as it figures in early phases of modernity. Part of Habermas's shift in thinking in the last two decades comes with his recognition that religion's significance has remained great and that it includes possibly under-recognized potential.

There is, thus, a certain analogy between Habermas's engagement with religion late in his career and his engagement with the category of the public sphere near its start. In each case, he focused on an aspect of modern society that was dismissed and sometimes even attacked by much of the left (with which he otherwise identified). In the early 1960s, it was common for Marxists to denigrate "mere bourgeois democracy" as at best of tactical utility, possibly helpful in bringing about a transition to socialism, but not valuable in and of itself. And the 1950s did reveal at best a conservative and highly managed version of democracy, not least in the quietist, unreflective Adenauer era in Germany. Yet Habermas argued that even though the public sphere was a category of bourgeois society, limited in its bourgeois forms and distorted by its actual institutional history, it was nonetheless one with great potential for advancing transformative struggles and bringing greater human liberation. The aged Max Horkheimer criticized Habermas's treatment of the public sphere for what he saw as an invitation to renew popular, possibly popul*ist* struggles that he feared (remembering the rise of National Socialism) could be potentially dangerous. Habermas's book was much more positively received by the new left, and it did indeed breathe new life into democratic struggles. At the end of the twentieth century and the beginning of the twenty-first, though, Habermas was increasingly concerned by an apparent exhaustion of these struggles. The left seemed to have lost intellectual creativity as well as momentum. Not just the radical left but democratic liberalism itself needed an infusion of new thinking, new sources of meaning, and better ways of connecting enduring values to new issues. And here Habermas saw semantic potential in religion. Religious ideas and language had been important throughout the history of struggles to improve human life and society. Not only had religious movements been part of that history, but words and concepts, utopian ideals, and habits of solidarity had migrated from purely religious usage to broader and sometimes secular usage. Some in a sense had been "translated." Many had brought new infusions of meaning, with new capacities for creativity and understanding.

Though Habermas's interest in religion had been growing for a decade, the depth and extent of his engagement came as a surprise to many early in the third millenium of the Common Era. More than any other single work, his lengthy essay on "Religion in the Public Sphere" provoked wide-ranging responses. The text appeared in several versions in different contexts, from the European *Journal of Philosophy* to a range of online versions linked to different oral presentations, and inclusion as a chapter in Habermas's book *Between Naturalism and Religion*. Militant atheists decried it as evidence that Habermas was growing soft on religion. Thoroughly secular critical theorists were unsure just what to make of it. Some religious thinkers embraced it as a welcome sign of constructive dialogue, though many were also critical of specifics and some accused Habermas of continuing secularist prejudice against religion. It is possible that Habermas surprised himself. When he began to ask more indepth questions about religion, these raised issues for other themes in his work. Religion pressed him to think further about philosophical anthropology, about the prepolitical bases for democratic politics, about the relationship between personal and cultural identity and citizenship, about procedural ethics and substantive morality, about tolerance, about the relationship between faith and knowledge, and about liberalism and its limits. It entered into his examination of the importance and problems of European unification, of differences between Europe and the US, and of the problems of both terrorism and the War on Terror.

Habermas's work on religion is shaped by both immediate public affairs and deep roots in philosophy and social theory. It informs both areas in important ways. In the remainder of this introduction, we offer an orientation to the contributions of the chapters that follow. In each of these, distinguished contributors take up Habermas's more recent work in relation to their own disciplines, perspectives, and sense of what is vitally important. Together they offer a guide not just to reading Habermas, but to making sense of today's major arguments over the place of religion in philosophy, political theory, and critical social thought.

The Contents of the Book

In the book's opening chapter, sociologist **José Casanova** offers one of the most synoptic and incisive discussions to date of the multiple and contested meanings of secularity and secularization, constructing a typology of the different ways in which they have been and can be understood, to which he correlates a range of senses in which, in turn, the postsecular may be thought. First there is what Casanova calls "mere secularity," in which the secular refers simply to the time before the advent of the kingdom of God. Secularization, from this perspective, refers to two processes: the disenchantment of the temporal and the laicization of the spiritual. Accordingly, the postsecular would imply their reversal: a re-enchantment, or re-spiritualization, of the mundane world as well as a de-laicization of religion. This, however, is not what Habermas means by postsecular, Casanova avers. A second meaning of secularization, then, is what he calls "self-contained secularity," best illustrated, perhaps, by Charles Taylor in *A Secular Age* (2007). For Taylor, religion has become but one among many possible and permissible moral and cognitive orientations within the "immanent frame" of modern society and subjectivity. Corresponding to this version of secularity is a concept of postsecularism that would suggest something like "secularization in reverse." But, as Casanova notes, this is simply not borne out by empirical observation.

Nor does Habermas seem to subscribe to this sense of postsecularism. There is, finally, a third meaning of the secular, Casanova's "secularist secularity," or "secularism as stadial consciousness" – the naturalization of secularity by a philosophy of history that hypostatizes secularization as a universal process of human development, the teleological movement of which culminates in the abandonment of childish belief and the ascension to mature unbelief. It is this understanding of secularity to which Habermas opposes his concept of the postsecular, inasmuch as secularist secularity, qua philosophy of history, is an ideology that relegates "religion" to a primitive stage of human development. Here, postsecularism is a challenge: the ideological insouciance that assures a certain West of its alleged superiority over other cultures, not least within its own borders. In the second section of his chapter, Casanova, with characteristic acuity, advances his case for disaggregating our understandings of secularity and secularization by way of a comparison of the divergent paths toward secularization taken respectively by Europe and the United States. In the third and final section, he turns again to Habermas's affirmation of a postsecular attitude, contextualizing it in relation to some of the most pressing challenges of contemporary global politics.

In chapter 2, **María Herrera Lima** identifies two different ways of reading Habermas's recent work, and seeing it as addressed to two different sorts of problematics. On the one hand, Habermas's work can be seen as addressing a set of political and legal issues, related to the conditions for mutual coexistence of secular and religious communities under conditions of what John Rawls has called "reasonable" pluralism. On the other hand, his work can be read as addressing a series of conceptual and historical issues, and as concerned with tracing a genealogy of modern ideas of justice that combine religious and secular sources, in what Herrera Lima calls Habermas's "new genealogy of faith and reason." Pointing to difficulties in what she refers to as Habermas's "middle way" between the excesses of modern secularists and the anti-modern and anti-liberal bias of some of the contemporary defenders of a religious revival – difficulties she associates with the normative expectations Habermas would place on both religious and secular citizens – Herrera Lima proposes a stronger role for historical studies than the one she finds in Habermas's work. Considering the intertwined traditions of religious and secular thought in European history, as well as reconstructions of that history by both Hans Blumenberg and Charles Taylor, she seeks "to understand the changed historical and social conditions for religious beliefs and practices in our secular age" and to advance an understanding of secularization as a contingent historical process full of local particularities. Emphasizing, as Taylor does, the optionality of contemporary forms of religious belief and practice – that is, the extent to which religion has become one "choice" among others – Herrera Lima argues that the transformations associated with a secular age "make it impossible to appeal to religion *alone* as a remedy for the lack of solidarity and other distortions of contemporary social life, since, as the sociological evidence shows, they are very much part of the *same* cultural formation." She then turns, in closing, to a reconsideration of the relationship between philosophy and religion, and to the place of religion in the public sphere, suggesting that we cannot "single out religion as a privileged source of moral insights" and, indeed, that there is "no distinct body of religious beliefs and practices isolated from the life of society and its interests that we could invoke as an indisputable source of moral insights."

María Pía Lara situates Habermas's work on religion within the rich and variegated history of debates around the religious sources of modernity. The supposition that political modernity is "dependent" on a religious prehistory has become all but taken for granted, she argues, to the neglect of the fact that the modern period has also witnessed "fundamental contributions to politics that had little or nothing to do with religion." According to Pía Lara, the most important moral and political concepts of the modern age cannot be comprehended merely as translations or secularizations of theological antecedents, as both Carl Schmitt and Karl Löwith famously argued. It was on the basis of this philosophical position, she contends, that each assumed a view both pessimistic and conservative in regard to political modernity. Thus, she recurs instead to Hans Blumenberg's rebuttal to Schmitt and Löwith, namely, that, as opposed to a "substantial continuation" of the theologico-political into modernity, the latter rather articulates itself through the "reoccupation" of the conceptual *positions* once, but not inevitably, tenanted by theological concepts. In the subsequent sections of her essay, Pía Lara recalls the influence of Hannah Arendt on Habermas (an influence that the latter has expressly acknowledged). It was Arendt, she writes, who best articulated "the proper conceptual frame of politics by proposing the concept of worldliness as its reference." For Arendt as well as for Habermas, political modernity emerges in particular through a reconceptualization of power, no longer as sovereign authority (Schmitt's exemplar of a secularized theological concept), but as an essentially mundane as well as an essentially collective capacity. At the heart of Pía Lara's rich reconstruction of a major chapter in modern intellectual history, then, is the question of what exactly Habermas means when he says that it is the task of a postmetaphysical philosophy to "translate" the semantic contents of religious concepts. Translation, it is implied, means less the preservation of those semantic contents under the guise of a different discursive register than a generative refunctioning and repositioning of conceptual positions in new constellations, through which the source and target languages, as it were, are rendered incommensurable with one another. Her chapter thus forces us to think more expansively and with added nuance about what it is that Habermas means by "translation."

Nicholas Wolterstorff takes up the themes of postmetaphysical philosophy, religion, and political discourse, three phenomena whose interrelations he sees as a central preoccupation of Habermas's recent writings. Wolterstorff opens his chapter with a reconstruction and brief summary of what Habermas says about religion and secularization, identifying in Habermas's work an understanding of religion as a "sacred complex" of worldview, scripture, and communal ritual. By contrast, postmetaphysical philosophy, as Habermas conceives it, neither incorporates a worldview nor seeks to develop one. Instead, it aims to make explicit the structure of our shared lifeworld. Habermas's project of postmetaphysical philosophy – "the orienting center" of his thought – is also defined both by its secular understanding of reason and by a commitment to a particular form of rationality. Wolterstorff dubs this "Kant-rationality," which he defines as the expectation that a body of thought be "based solely on premises and inferences that all cognitively competent, adult human beings would accept if those premises and reasons were presented to them, if they understood them, if they possessed the relevant background information, and if they freely reflected on them at sufficient length." Postmetaphysical philosophy is conceived as secular, but not "secularistic," and through constructive dialogue with religion, it seeks – in Habermas's words – to "salvage cognitive contents from religious traditions," or to appropriate elements from religious worldviews. Yet Wolterstorff questions the understanding of reason and rationality by which Habermas claims to distinguish postmetaphysical philosophy from religion, suggesting that "every body of philosophical though is limited in its persuasive powers." There is, Wolterstorff argues, "no extant postmetaphysical philosophy," because "there is no substantial body of philosophical thought that satisfies the requirement of Kant-rationality." Indeed, he suggests, there are powerful reasons to believe that there never will be, as "philosophical reflection under conditions of freedom expands the scope of disagreement." Furthermore, Wolterstorff concludes, the requirements of Kant-rationality oversimplify the complex and diverse role of reasons and reason-giving in philosophy, in part because "we do not usually aim our remarks at humanity in general," but rather at a specific audience or readership, and in part because we offer reasons with different aims in mind – at times to persuade, and at other times simply to make explicit the reasons for which we hold the position we do. We do not always expect the reasons we give to be persuasive.

Like Wolterstorff, **Thomas McCarthy** is at pains to emphasize both diversity and persistent disagreement. Attending to Habermas's reconstruction of the critique of reason, which he sees as at the heart of Habermas's "unfinished project of enlightenment," McCarthy calls for Habermas to make "a still sharper descent from the heights of transcendental philosophy." Habermas's demanding notion of discourse, McCarthy argues, is open at multiple points to contestation from both modernized believers and postmetaphysical reasoners, and the "path of reconciliation he proposes" between faith and reason "is rife with dialectical and hermeneutical snares." Reflective believers, for example, may dispute his sharp separation of truth and rightness and goodness, or otherwise reject the accounts of reason and faith that figure in his analysis of cognitive presuppositions and global dialogue. Indeed, McCarthy suggests – drawing on extensive earlier work of his own – Habermas's conceptualization of the distinction between ethical and moral claims gives rise to an "inextricable entwinement" of moral and ethical discourse about the right and the good, and so must face a potentially endless set of disagreements regarding the interpretation and application of moral principles. While Habermas would seek to fix the terms of interpretation by appealing to a general analytical framework, such frameworks are themselves, McCarthy argues, historically and culturally situated, and thereby open to contestation and ongoing disagreements, which reflect different interpretive and evaluative standpoints. Within the human sciences, the notion of "one right answer" may reasonably serve a "regulative" function – forming an indispensable pragmatic presupposition of practices of reasoned disagreement – but the myriad ongoing disagreements we find within these branches of knowledge, frequently keyed to different interpretive starting points, suggest that we cannot reasonably expect to regularly agree upon that "one right answer." Among the perennial contestants for claims to knowledge in these arenas will be religiously imbued interpretations and explanations, and in the penultimate section of his chapter McCarthy considers a set of problematic distinctions in Habermas's work – between cultural and political public spheres, between the "opaque core" and rationalizable periphery of religious faith, and between the accessibility and acceptability of norms – that bear on Habermas's proposed terms of engagement among secular thinkers and religious believers. Putting "dialectical and hermeneutical pressure" on these key analytical distinctions, McCarthy underscores the importance of conceiving of theorizing as a form of reflective participation in the very communicative practices it seeks to understand and inform. "One should not expect the fault lines between faith and reason to be bridged in theory, once and for all," he writes, "but rather repeatedly and variously in a global proliferation of situated practices."

According to **Amy Allen**, Habermas's engagement with religion ought to be understood against the background of his sustained attempt at a "genealogy of postsecular reason." She notes that Habermas himself has taken up the term *genealogy* to refer to his own project of reconstructing the "learning process" that societies undergo in their journeys through secularization, rationalization, and modernization. Adopting Colin Koopman's classification of three distinct modes, or types, of genealogy – "subversive, vindicatory, and problematizing" – she goes on to argue that Habermas, in his genealogical reconstruction of postsecular reason, should be read as combining both vindicatory and problematizing tendencies, while muffling the more subversive registers of the genealogical approach (sounded, by way of contrast, to such reverberating effect by the likes of Nietzsche and Foucault). She contends in particular that Habermas unduly diminishes the critical capacity of his own project by rejecting contextualist philosophical standpoints and insisting instead on the inviolable "context-transcendence of validity claims," which position, she notes, "has long been central to [his] philosophical project, and a principal means by which he has distinguished his way out of the philosophy of the subject from rival approaches." Habermas's avowed opposition to contextualism, moreover, rubs up uncomfortably against not only his stated political positions – particularly his "goal of framing a genuinely open-ended and symmetrical dialogue between religious and secular citizens" – but also his own philosophical genealogy, as it were. Inasmuch, that is, as Habermas acknowledges that the notion of context-transcendence is itself historically situated, and so, however broadly speaking, context-specific, he ought rather to adopt the position of what Allen calls the "principled contextualist," which "maintains that [. . .] we understand claims to normative validity (and also truth) as context-transcending, in the sense that they aim toward transcendence," but not in the sense that transcendence simply appertains, *eo ipso*, to such claims. Hence, Allen puts forth a reading of Habermas's latest project decidedly inflected by the contextualism that he "needlessly demonizes," in her words, but in the interest, nevertheless, of advancing both his genealogical reconstruction of philosophical modernity and the democratic and egalitarian aspirations to which it is conjoined.

J. M. Bernstein's contribution is an original, and potentially upending, critique of Habermas's lately advanced conception of a "postsecular society." Bernstein raises fundamental doubts as to whether the project of "postsecularity" is a coherent and defensible one. If the position that Habermas has taken in recent writings is indeed tenable, he says, it is so only insofar as it is a "radically secularist" one after all. Acknowledging at the outset the "reconciliatory rhetoric and tone" of Habermas's foray into religion, Bernstein nonetheless suspects that his attempt to equalize the "epistemic and attitudinal burdens on secular and religious citizens" is an empty, because misunderstood, gesture – first, because such an equalization can never lead to a suspension of the giving and taking of reasons (such as is implied, according to Bernstein, in the concept of faith) without abrogating the axioms of deliberative democracy, but also because the conditions of political participation to which Habermas would hold the citizens of a democratic state are inherently prejudiced in favor of the unconfessing subject. And "rightly so," Bernstein quips, since faith is that which neither modern subjectivity nor the democratic polity can abide without, in effect, sacrificing themselves. The affirmation of faith, according to Bernstein, bespeaks a performative contradiction, the dissolution of which has been the signal accomplishment of secular reason. As faith is beyond comprehension, what sustains it despite its logical impossibility, argues Bernstein, through a reading of Kierkegaard's *Fear and Trembling*, is its entailment of "the sacrifice of the other," as embodied in Isaac in the story of Abraham, and, more broadly, of "the sacrifice of love of the world as orienting our being in the world." The point, of course, is not that faith commits its confessor literally to perform sacrificial acts, but that it does stand or fall on an abrogation of the demands of deliberative justification, which makes it "incommensurable with worldly ethics." By way of a counterpoint to Kierkegaard, Bernstein proffers a reading of Caravaggio's second version of *The Sacrifice of Isaac* (1603), a painting that exposes us, through the agonized gaze of Isaac, to the inescapability of the interpellating regard of an embodied and suffering other, inexorably making the viewer a witness to Isaac's crucible. The suspension of communication and of reasoned adjudication (exemplified by the silence of Abraham) is, with the advent of secular modernity, no longer an option, Bernstein contends. His essay thus issues in a pointed challenge to apologists for a "postsecular society": "if secular reason is intrinsically a critique of faith, then how could there be a postsecular society that was not a repudiation of reason?"

In the following chapter, **James Bohman** develops two interrelated lines of dialogue with Habermas's ideas, both recent and longstanding. On the one hand, Bohman's engagement with Habermas's conception of postsecular social consciousness clearly can be read as a contribution to the elaboration of the idea of "communicative freedom" first developed in *The Theory of Communicative Action*. On the other hand, he aims to extend Habermas's usage of "postsecularity" as both a descriptive and a normative term by reinscribing it within a broad concept of pluralism. For Bohman as well as for Habermas, "postsecularism" at once describes a social reality and institutes a norm by which to evaluate and to negotiate that reality. Bohman's challenge to Habermas, however, is that his "conception of postsecularism [. . .] is neither descriptively nor normatively rich enough to take up the challenges of pluralism in ways of life" in the context of an emerging transnational society that increasingly overshadows the enclosure of the nation-state. Moving through a range of historical examples, with a particular focus on the activism of transnational organizations, Bohman argues that Habermas's models, first, of a "translation" between religious and secular idioms within a constituted public sphere, and, second, of a change in mentality on the part of religious and secular citizens, making them more hospitable to each other's normative claims, do not suffice to engender the necessary conversion of communicative freedom into communicative *power*, particularly in cases of religious conflict, which pose, perhaps, the greatest threat to the further recognition and affirmation of an actually existing pluralism. At stake here is the transformative function that communicative power can have at the global level. "With an eye to the problem of conflict," he writes, "it is important to analyze communicative freedom less with an eye to formal institutionalization than on a more basic and practical level as the recognition of persons or groups as having a *communicative status*, that is, as someone who is able to address others and be addressed by them in turn." Thus, postsecularity, he concludes, ought to be considered less as a condition of public deliberation in democratic states – one that aims to ameliorate the tension between institutional neutrality and citizens' comprehensive religious doctrines – than as a "critical standard for living with the permanent fact of increasing diversity of forms of life at all levels of international society," and in such a way as to render pluralism a resource for democratization and not merely a hindrance to be overcome.

Hent de Vries also takes up the idea of the "postsecular," exploring what he refers to as "the postsecular challenge." If the concept of the postsecular has something new to offer, de Vries suggests, this has to do with the way in which it forces the concept of the secular and the practices of secularism to "loosen and lighten up," to become less narrow and more historicized and contextualized. Associating the postsecular challenge with a worldwide resurgence of "global religions" that has coincided with an explosion of new media, de Vries seeks to complicate Habermas's account of reason-giving and religion in the public sphere, in part by suggesting that the discourses of such religions "tend not so much to say and state but do and sway things." Global religions are passionate and performative, and "in all they say and do and envision it is the affects that are the most effective." To tap into what de Vries calls the traditional religious and theologico-political "archive," therefore, it will be necessary to be attuned to different models of reasoning and imagining, acting, and judging. While de Vries associates such attunement with the inauguration of a "postsecular" dispensation, he nonetheless sees the term "postsecular" as both tenuously tied to Habermas's understanding of postmetaphysical thinking and problematic in at least some of its articulations. It is difficult to see, he suggests, how postsecular thinking could tap into the deep and immense archives of global religions while at the same time continuing to align itself with a "rational" and "formal-pragmatic" understanding of postmetaphysical thinking. Postsecular thought, as de Vries puts it, "reaches deeper down and further back towards words and things, gestures and powers, sounds and silences" than does postmetaphysical thinking. A different concept of rationality and an alternative to postmetaphysical thinking is called for. Although the "postsecular" remains ill-defined in its central features, then, if it is taken not as yet another attempt at historical periodization but rather as a project to shift perception and a marker for a timely theoretical and pragmatic problem, a new vantage on its interpretation and potential uses opens up, one that might allow for new forms of engagement with religion as an ambiguous and abiding phenomenon in the public domain and globalized world.

Christina Lafont's text is a lucid effort to negotiate between the positions staked out by Habermas and by John Rawls, respectively, as regards the cognitive burdens placed on religious (as well as, for Habermas, secular) citizens for the purposes of public deliberation. The problem is, as Lafont makes clear, fundamental to the ideal of deliberative democracy, for its credibility, she writes, "essentially depends on the ability to provide a plausible account of political deliberation [. . .] under the pluralistic conditions characteristic of liberal democracies in which citizens hold a wide variety of religious and secular outlooks." In recent writings (notably, in "Religion in the Public Sphere"), Habermas has attempted to redress the deficiency of Rawls's controversial "proviso" that policies advanced on the basis of religious reasons be admissible only insofar as they may be corroborated by properly political reasons – namely, that it places an undue "cognitive burden" on religious citizens, by forcing them to articulate their positions in terms that do not reflect their reasons for holding those positions in the first place. According to Lafont, however, Habermas's proposed "institutional translation proviso" does little to alleviate the burden – it only shifts the exclusion of religious reasons from the informal public sphere to the realm of formal political institutions. Her own intervention into the debate effectively re-poses the problem: "Since the discussion of the ethics of citizenship concerns political obligations," she writes, "it seems to me that the obligation to 'take seriously' the views of our fellow citizens on contentious legislative decisions has a specifically *political* rather than merely cognitive meaning." It is on this basis that she puts forth a different proviso, that of what she calls "mutual accountability." For Lafont, in short, the fundamental political principles of liberty and equality ought to function as the arbiters of political deliberation, such that, while religious citizens need not translate their views into an idiom that would belie the religious character of their convictions, they do need to be able to defend those positions in terms of their compatibility with the democratic principles in the benefits of which they, as much as secular citizens, share. While Lafont's proposal, as she herself concedes, may not suffice to resolve some of the more refractory problems that divide contemporary democracies, it nevertheless provides one of the most robust arguments to date for the plausibility of the deliberative-democratic ideal.

In the subsequent chapter, **Maeve Cooke** turns as well to the question of democratic legitimacy. Cooke's starting point is Habermas's view that permitting religious contributions to democratic decision-making within the formal public sphere constitutes a violation of the neutrality of democratic procedure. Habermas's view is based, Cooke argues, on a limited understanding of religious validity claims, which he suggests lack the general accessibility of their secular counterparts and thus must be translated into a secular language if they are to be considered within parliamentary debates and legislative processes (as opposed to being considered in debates within the informal public sphere, where we would allow them). What is the basis for this prohibition? "Religiously rooted existential convictions," Habermas has suggested, refer "to the dogmatic authority of an inviolable core of infallible revealed truths" and thus are not open to "*unreserved* discursive examination." Unpacking and critiquing this claim, Cooke seeks to complicate Habermas's seemingly simplistic understanding of dogmatic religious authority, while attending in particular detail to the question of revelation, which she treats as a form of "disclosure." Habermas, she argues, demonstrates an "insufficient appreciation of the ways in which the rational acceptability of claims to validity may depend on kinds of 'world-disclosure' or 'revelation' that are non-argumentative" and at the same time he over-inflates the power of arguments to change the way we see the world, including the world of politics and morality. Distinguishing between "argumentation-internal" and "argumentation-external" modes of disclosure and change, Cooke argues that non-argumentative forms of lived experience may be relevant when it comes to explaining how "epistemically significant shifts in perception" come about. An effort to right Habermas's neglect of the non-argumentative dimension of rational acceptability, furthermore, has consequences for his understanding of democratic legitimacy. If rational agreement cannot be brought about purely by way of the exchange of arguments, Cooke suggests, Habermas's own theory would seem to call for an alternative to the epistemic-constructivist understanding of democratic legitimacy that he appears to favor. This alternative conception of legitimacy, by Cooke's account, would retain central features of Habermas's approach. Yet it would allow for the possibility that key shifts in perception do not have to come about purely argumentatively, it would acknowledge the importance of the non-argumentative, experiential dimension of practical reasoning, and it would place no barriers, in principle, to the inclusion of religious arguments in processes of democratic deliberation.

In this contribution, **Matthias Fritsch** ambitiously delves into one of Habermas's crucial philosophical projects, namely, his attempt to ground both human freedom and moral responsibility through the reciprocal mediation of the claims of faith and those of reason. Already in *The Theory of Communicative Action*, Habermas had spoken of the "linguistification [*Versprachlichung*] of the sacred"; more recently, this facet of his thinking has found expression in his concern with the "translation" of the semantic content of religious idioms by secular discourse. But, as Fritsch writes, "it has been difficult to translate the origin of morality into a secular context precisely because God combines [. . .] two aspects in such a felicitous but next to impenetrable way: God's gaze addresses all equally, but at the same time each one with infinite care for his soul." Indeed, more than difficult; as he goes on to argue, it is this antithetical bipolarity of the divine idea that we have inherited from the Abrahamic faiths – at once individualizing and universalizing in its instauration of the moral subject – that renders its translation, and so its secularization, definitively incomplete. What nevertheless fascinates in Habermas's – as well as Derrida's – work in this regard is its "attempt to do justice to both aspects, Habermas within the universalist-egalitarian and Derrida from within the phenomenological tradition." The latter, on Fritsch's account, has tended to emphasize the radically individuating dimension of the divine idea, as the source of moral responsibility, at the expense of its universalizing and egalitarian dimension, whereas Habermas has, "perhaps unsurprisingly, emphasized this universal aspect above all." But in the face of contemporary incursions of biogenetic engineering into the sphere of human development – and, concomitantly, of human initiative and action – Habermas has been led "to pose the question of responsibility anew, and in such a way that both the individuating power and the alterity of the preceding and obligating standpoint" increasingly figure as central to his account of the grounds of moral action, "to the point where the standpoint's historically 'divine' origin – and that means the question of 'translating' God – resurfaces." Through a critical reconstruction of Levinasian ethics, as well as of Derrida's account of the "testimonial pledge" implicit in every speech act, Fritsch attempts another sort of translation – but one that insists on the impossibility of ever conclusively dissolving the language of faith in the solvent of secular reason, for the presuppositions of communicative action – upon which Habermas would ground man's moral freedom – themselves rest only upon the groundless ground of faith: "The structure of agency," Fritsch concludes, "is like a promise, and a promise requires faith in its future realizability."

In a rich chapter on memory, solidarity, and the work of translation, **Max Pensky** delves into what Jeffrey Olick has called the "politics of regret," asking how social and political theory might best approach our duty to come to terms with an unjust collective past. Seeking to articulate a third alternative between unsatisfying and strictly secular responses to this question and what Richard Rorty called the "skyhook" of theology, Pensky confronts the challenge and limitations of secularizing translations, and attempts "to change the form and nature of theological concepts to tailor them for philosophical use." A consideration of memory politics – which Pensky deems "the quintessential form of collective ethical-political discourse" – thus becomes the occasion for an extended reflection on the problematic promise of translation. Habermas recognizes, Pensky suggests, that neither an unswervingly secular nor an unambiguously theological answer to "the question of the normative status of the unjust dead" will be persuasive, as his role in the "Historians' Debate" of the 1980s made clear. While thoughtful political theorists such as Pablo de Greiff have sought to offer an account of remembrance of the unjust dead that is articulated in entirely secular or "atheological" terms, Habermas, Pensky argues, refuses to pursue this option, and for good reason, since such deflationary and secular accounts must ultimately regard solidarity with the past – "the sense of someone missing" – as a kind of mistake. Religious accounts of solidarity and memory, on the other hand, illustrate limitations of a different sort. Through a consideration of the work of German Catholic theologian Johann-Baptist Metz, Pensky examines a theological rendering of remembrance that articulates "a familiarly non-negotiable, metaphysical moment of pre-established meaning, a very vivid and in this case almost literal example of Rorty's skyhook." This sets the stage for the sustained attention to the imperfect work of translation with which the chapter concludes. Religious concepts, while in need of translation, are also in some respects resistant to it, and indeed they contain an untranslatable dimension. Thus, translation "always betrays, and always fails." Yet despite "the necessary failure of a translation from religious to moral language," it is nonetheless possible to pursue a form of solidarity with the past that can "bring to collective awareness a sense of *what*, and not just who is missing," an awareness expressed, on rare occasions, "in a language strange and broken, and therefore beautiful."

Drawing on an extended and distinctive reading of Hume, **John Milbank** sets out to offer a critical alternative to Habermas's account of the distance between "discursive reason" and "ineffable faith." Suggesting that "metaphysically agnostic philosophy" – with which he associates Habermas's postmetaphysical project – has "allowed religious extremism to fill a certain void," Milbank argues that a sharp separation of faith and reason implies that faith is "beyond the reach of any sort of argument" and encourages "irrational and purely emotive political movements." By contrast, he argues, faith and reason are in reality always intertwined: "if critical faith has to become a more reflective mode of feeling, then reason has always to some degree to feel its ways forward." Feeling – what Hume called "sympathy" – figures prominently in Milbank's elaboration of this claim. Hume, he argues, went beyond skepticism "in the name of feeling," which can be seen as a sort of middle term between reason and shared faith, with the latter – without which "no arguments would get off the ground" – taken to mean something like "common feeling." Reason, furthermore, may be conceived as a form of "tempered feeling" and thought seen as a "species of feeling," with the strength of trustworthy feeling understood as "what *truly* reveals to us the real." While Habermas would place faith behind an impassable "sublime barrier," then, thereby encouraging faith to become dangerous, Hume, on Milbank's reading, indicates how religion is in fact in continuity with the rest of human natural and cultural existence. From this perspective, Milbank suggests, Habermas's "easy discriminations" between what belongs to the realm of reason and what belongs to the realm of faith become more difficult to sustain. One upshot of this view, Milbank argues, is that Habermas's peculiar account of the possibility of "translation" of religious insights into a secular idiom within the public sphere becomes much less compelling. The reality of religion in the public sphere today, he suggests, is both more bracing and more optimistic than Habermas's account allows. It is, to be sure, a matter of a "clash of rival metaphysics and not one of polite agnostic neutrality." But within the public sphere conceived in Humean terms we also find a "shared horizon of feeling" with an "inherent fluidity" that "permits of many substantive shared outlooks and actually fosters *less* conflict than a situation where we will endlessly debate (as in the history of the United States) whether formal barriers between faith and reason have been transgressed or not."

With his "Reply to My Critics," **Jürgen Habermas** has done a great service to the editors, but above all to the readers, of this volume. One crucial theme in Habermas's reply is the question of the stages in the evolution of religious experience, thought, and institutions. He reasserts his commitment to the principle that human experience (in the broadest of senses) should be analyzed in terms of a process of learning, driven not by an immanent logic – whether of the mind, of history, or of society – but by human beings' coming to terms with contingent circumstances and challenges. What is especially noteworthy in his affirmation of a dialectic of development is that critical thought as much as religious consciousness are said to be intertwined in a process of learning that catalyzes the movement of history, a process that has not yet congealed or exhausted itself, and that shows no signs of doing so. Alongside his reaffirmation of the philosophical task of analytically reconstructing the *Gestalten* of the mind, or the condensations of human experience in comprehensive pictures of the cosmos, Habermas reflects on what he means by a "genealogy" of modern postsecular consciousness. He notes that his genealogy, qua rational reconstruction, should not be taken as the expression of any subversive intention on his part. It is not the case that his reconstructions aim to undermine contemporary mental, moral, or socio-cultural orientations. His genealogy of postmetaphysical thinking and postsecular consciousness ought to be understood, rather, as meant to problematize what he calls the secularist misunderstanding of enlightened secular thought. Postmetaphysical thought must guard against both philosophical orientations that discount *in toto* the cognitive and moral content of religious beliefs and surreptitious attempts to smuggle religious semantics into philosophy in the absence of the radically critical reflection that underwrites the specificity and the autonomy of philosophical thinking.

Perhaps the most remarkable aspect of Habermas's reply is that it is at the same time an autobiographical document, and one that reveals a great deal about his unique philosophical formation as well as his intellectual rapport with both contemporaries and predecessors. It thus helps us to situate his work in relation to a long and still generative tradition of reflection on the discord of faith and reason. In addition to coming to such questions from within an intellectual tradition that has never abjured their exigency, he has also arrived at them as a German who has meditated incessantly and intensely on the issue of German responsibility for the genocide of millions of Jews and other innocent victims. From this position, Habermas has long reflected, not solely on the problem of German responsibility for the Holocaust, but more generally on our responsibility, personal as well as collective, both for the past and to the future. The tone and phrasing of his response, as well as the scrupulous care that it evinces, is indicative of the distinctly personal dimension of Habermas's preoccupation with the sometimes buried but nevertheless unexhausted normative contents of religious thought and experience. But, whatever may be his ultimate position on the questions of religion and modernity, secularization and the postsecular, that are taken up throughout this volume, Habermas continues to manifest a relentlessly reflective and self-critical attitude, and so stands as an exemplar for all who would continue to think, with earnestness, commitment, and humility, under the weight of our history and in the ever enigmatic face of the future.

Part I

Rationalization, Secularisms, and Modernities

1

Exploring the Postsecular

Three Meanings of "the Secular" and Their Possible Transcendence

José Casanova

Jürgen Habermas has been one of the most influential theorists of secular modernity. His theories of societal rationalization and rationalization of the lifeworld, his theory of linguistification of the sacred, and his theory of the public sphere all are grounded in the formulation of a master process of secularization which is, on the one hand, intrinsically related to processes of Western modernization and, on the other, is understood as the latest and most advanced stage within a general stadial and evolutionary process of human development (*TCA*; *STPS*; *HE*). In this respect, "secular" and "modern" had always been coterminous and intrinsically related within his theory.

It is therefore remarkable that Habermas has now initiated a new discourse of "postsecular" societies, the more so if one considers the fact that for decades he had resisted the new discourse of postmodernity, insisting on the need to defend and promote "the unfinished project of modernity" (*PDM*). Since one can assume that Habermas is not yet ready to abandon the discourse or the project of modernity, one must ask what can modern "postsecular" mean? In which way might modern individuals or societies be said to be "postsecular"?

In the following presentation, I would like to proceed by exploring, first, three different meanings of the term "secular," to which would correspond three different understandings of the postsecular. Second, I would like to interrogate the extent to which Habermas's conception of secularization is still too closely linked to particular European patterns of secularization, meaning that as a result he may maintain still too intrinsic a correlation between processes of modernizations and processes of secularization. Finally, I want to offer a few remarks concerning the idea of a postsecular world society.

I   Three Meanings of Secular

I would like to introduce an analytical distinction between three different meanings of the word secular, or three different ways in which one may be said to be secular, to which would correspond three different understandings of the process of secularization.

I.i   Mere secularity: living in the secular world and in secular time

This is the broadest possible sense of the term "secular," which is derived from the medieval Christian theological transformation of the Latin term "*saeculum.*" Originally, the Latin word *saeculum*, as in *per saecula saeculorum*, only meant an indefinite period of time. But, as first used by Augustine, the "secular" referred to a temporal space between the present and the eschatological *parousia* in which both Christians and pagans could come together to pursue their common interests as a civil community.[1] In this respect, the Augustinian use of "secular" is very similar to the modern meaning of a secular political sphere, that of the constitutional democratic state and that of a democratic public sphere, which is neutral with respect to all worldviews, religious as well as non-religious. Such a conception does not equate the secular with the "profane," as the other of the "sacred," nor is the secular the other of the "religious." It is precisely a neutral space that can be shared by all who live in a society that is either not religiously homogeneous or is multicultural, societies which by definition will have different and most likely competing conceptions of what is "sacred" and what is "profane." This was precisely the situation in late antiquity. Judeo-Christian monotheism had led to a de-sacralization or disenchantment of the pagan sacred. Consequently, the Christians' refusal to sacrifice to "pagan" gods or to worship the divine emperor earned them the epithet of "atheists." The Christian sacred was the pagan profane and vice versa.

Eventually, however, with the consolidation of Western medieval Christendom and the hegemonic triumph of the Christian Church, the secular became one of the terms of a dyad, religious/secular, which served to structure the entire spatial and temporal reality of medieval Christendom into a binary system of classification separating two worlds, the religious-spiritual-sacred world of salvation and the secular-temporal-profane world. The sacred-profane and the religious-secular binary systems of classification became superimposed, and the secular became equated with the earthly city while the religious became equated with the heavenly city: thus, the distinction between the "religious" or regular clergy, who withdrew from the world into the monasteries to lead a life of Christian perfection, and the "secular" clergy who lived in the world along with the laity.

It is from this new theological perspective of medieval Christendom that the modern meaning of "secularization" emerges. To secularize means, first of all, to "make worldly," to convert religious persons or things into secular ones, as when a religious person abandons the monastic rule to live in the world, or when monastic property is secularized. This is the medieval Christian theological meaning of the term "secularization" that may serve, however, as the basic metaphor of the historical process of Western secularization. This historical process needs to be understood as a particular reaction to the structuring dualism of medieval Christendom, as an attempt to bridge, eliminate, or transcend the dualism between the religious and the secular world. Even in the West, however, this process of secularization follows two different dynamics.

One is the dynamic of internal Christian secularization which aims to spiritualize the temporal and to bring the religious life of perfection out of the monasteries into the secular world. It tends to transcend the dualism by blurring the boundaries between the religious and the secular, by making the religious secular and the secular religious through mutual reciprocal infusion. This path was initiated by the various medieval movements of Christian reform of the *saeculum,* was radicalized by the Protestant Reformation, and has attained its paradigmatic expression in the Anglo-Saxon Calvinist cultural area, particularly in the United States.

The other different, indeed almost opposite, dynamic of secularization takes the form of laicization. It aims to emancipate all secular spheres from clerical-ecclesiastical control and in this respect it is marked by a laic–clerical antagonism. Unlike in the Protestant path, however, here the boundaries between the religious and the secular are rigidly maintained, but those boundaries are pushed into the margins, aiming to contain, privatize, and marginalize everything religious, while excluding it from any visible presence in the secular public sphere, now defined as the realm of *laïcité,* freed from religion. This is the paradigmatic French-Latin-Catholic path of secularization, but it will find diverse manifestations throughout continental Europe.

With many variations, these are the two main dynamics of secularization which culminate in our secular age. In different ways, both paths lead to an overcoming of the medieval Christian dualism through a positive affirmation and revaluation of the *saeculum,* that is, of the secular age and the secular world, imbuing the immanent secular world with a quasi-transcendent meaning as the place for human flourishing. In this broad sense of the term "secular," we are all secular and all modern societies are secular and are likely to remain so for the foreseeable future, one could almost say *per saecula saeculorum*. Postsecular in this context could only mean a re-sacralization or re-enchantment of modern societies within a sacred immanent frame akin to that of pre-axial societies, something that must be viewed not only as empirically unlikely but as practically impossible. This is certainly not the intended meaning of post-secular in Habermas.

I.ii   Self-contained secularity within the immanent frame of the secular age: to be or not to be religious, that is the question!

There is a second narrower meaning of the term "secular," that of self-sufficient and exclusive secularity, when people are simply "irreligious," that is, devoid of religion and closed to any form of transcendence beyond the purely secular immanent frame. Here, secular is not any more one of the units of a dyadic pair, but is constituted as a self-enclosed reality. To a certain extent, this constitutes one possible end result of the process of secularization, of the attempt to overcome the dualism between religious and secular, by freeing oneself of the religious component.

In his recent work, *A Secular Age*, Charles Taylor has reconstructed the process through which the phenomenological experience of what he calls "the immanent frame" becomes constituted as an interlocking constellation of the modern differentiated cosmic, social, and moral orders.[2] All three orders, the cosmic, the social, and the moral are understood as purely immanent secular orders, devoid of transcendence, and thus functioning *etsi Deus non daretur*, "as if God would not exist." It is this phenomenological experience that, according to Taylor, constitutes our age paradigmatically as a secular one, irrespective of the extent to which people living in this age may still hold religious or theistic beliefs.

The question is whether the phenomenological experience of living within such an immanent frame is such that people within it will also tend to function *etsi Deus non daretur*. Taylor is inclined to answer this question in the affirmative. Indeed, his phenomenological account of the secular "conditions" of belief is meant to explain the change from a Christian society around 1500 CE, in which belief in God was unchallenged and unproblematic, indeed "naïve" and taken for granted, to a post-Christian society today in which belief in God not only is no longer axiomatic but becomes increasingly problematic, so that even those who adopt an "engaged" standpoint as believers tend to experience reflexively their own belief as an option among many others, one moreover requiring an explicit justification. Secularity, being without religion, by contrast tends to become increasingly the default option, which can be naively experienced as natural and, thus, no longer in need of justification.

This naturalization of "unbelief" or "non-religion" as the normal human condition in modern societies corresponds to the assumptions of the dominant theories of secularization, which have postulated a progressive decline of religious beliefs and practices with increasing modernization, so that the more modern a society the more secular, that is, the less "religious," it is supposed to become. That the decline of religious beliefs and practices is a relatively recent meaning of the term "secularization" is indicated by the fact that it does not yet appear in the dictionary of most modern European languages.

The naturalization of "unbelief" or "irreligiosity" as the normal "modern" human condition is a characterization that certainly applies to a majority of Western European societies. But it is not characteristic of the United States, where being religious is still the normal default option, while unbelief is the uncommon option which requires a reflexive commitment and is in need of justification. Indeed, the fact that there are some modern non-European societies, such as the United States or South Korea, that are fully secular in the sense that they function within the same immanent frame and yet their populations are also at the same time conspicuously religious, or the fact that the modernization of so many non-Western societies is accompanied by processes of religious revival, should put into question the premise that the decline of religious beliefs and practices is a quasi-natural consequence of processes of modernization. If modernization per se does not produce necessarily the progressive decline of religious beliefs and practices, then we need a better explanation for the radical and widespread secularity one finds among the population of Western European societies.[3]

The meaning of "postsecular" in this context would be that of individuals as well as societies becoming religious again, undergoing processes of religious revival, which would reverse previous secular trends. Peter Berger has used the expression "de-secularization of the world," while David Martin asks whether "secularization (has) gone into reverse."[4] There is little evidence, however, that individuals or societies in the heartland of secularization, Western Europe, are becoming postsecular. Habermas also does not appear to use "postsecular" in this second meaning of the term.

I.iii Secularist secularity: secularism as stadial consciousness

I would like to maintain that secularization in the sense of being "devoid of religion," does not happen automatically as a result of processes of modernization, but rather needs to be mediated phenomenologically by some other particular historical experience. Self-sufficient secularity, that is, the absence of religion, has a better chance of becoming the normal taken-for-granted position if it is experienced not simply as an unreflexively naive condition, as just a fact, but actually as the meaningful result of a quasi-natural process of development. As Taylor has pointed out, modern unbelief is not simply a condition of absence of belief, nor merely indifference. It is a historical condition that requires the perfect tense, "a condition of 'having overcome' the irrationality of belief."[5] Intrinsic to this phenomenological experience is a modern "stadial consciousness," inherited from the Enlightenment, which understands this anthropocentric change in the conditions of belief as a process of maturation and growth, as a "coming of age" and as progressive emancipation. For Taylor, this stadial phenomenological experience serves in turn to ground the phenomenological experience of exclusive humanism as the positive self-sufficient and self-limiting affirmation of human flourishing and as the critical rejection of transcendence beyond human flourishing as self-denial and self-defeating.

In this respect, the historical self-understanding of secularism has the function of confirming the superiority of our present modern secular outlook over other supposedly earlier and therefore more primitive religious forms of understanding. To be secular means to be modern, and therefore by implication to be religious means to be somehow not yet fully modern. This is the ratchet effect of a modern historical stadial consciousness, which turns the very idea of going back to a surpassed condition into an unthinkable intellectual regression.

The function of secularism as a philosophy of history, and thus as ideology, is to turn the particular Western Christian historical process of secularization into a universal teleological process of human development from belief to unbelief, from primitive irrational or metaphysical religion to modern, rational, postmetaphysical, secular consciousness. Even when the particular role of internal Christian developments in the general process of secularization is acknowledged, it is not in order to stress the particular contingent nature of the process, but rather to stress the universal significance of the uniqueness of Christianity as, in Marcel Gauchet's expressive formulation, "the religion to exit from religion."[6]

I would like to propose that this secularist stadial consciousness is a crucial factor in the widespread secularization that has accompanied the modernization of Western European societies. Europeans tend to experience their own secularization, that is, the widespread decline of religious beliefs and practices among their midst as a natural consequence of their modernization. To be secular is not experienced as an existential or historical choice which modern individuals or modern societies make,

Location	Qty	Item	Description
332 – 002 – 10	1	9780745653273	HABERMAS AND RELIGION

Type OW2   Qty 1   Plan# 30566   Parcel# 127780417

Group# 269056

Seq# 395   **003**

but rather as a natural outcome of becoming modern. In this respect, the theory of secularization mediated through this historical stadial consciousness tends to function as a self-fulfilling prophecy. It is, in my view, the presence or absence of this secularist historical stadial consciousness that explains when and where processes of modernization are accompanied by radical secularization. In places where such secularist historical stadial consciousness is absent or less dominant, as in the United States or in most non-Western postcolonial societies, processes of modernization are unlikely to be accompanied by processes of religious decline. On the contrary, they may be accompanied by processes of religious revival.

Now that we have introduced a distinction between those three different meanings of being secular: (a) that of *mere secularity*, that is, the phenomenological experience of living in a secular world and in a secular age, where being religious may be a normal viable option; (b) that of *self-contained, self-sufficient, and exclusive secularity*, that is, the phenomenological experience of living without religion as a normal, quasi-natural, taken-for-granted condition; and (c) that of *secularist secularity*, that is, the phenomenological experience not only of being passively free, but actually of having been liberated from "religion" as a condition for human flourishing, we may be in a better position to address the question of the meaning of "postsecular" in Habermas's own work.

Within the context of the third meaning of the term "secular," that of secularist secularity, postsecular would imply reflexively abandoning or at least questioning the modern secularist stadial consciousness which relegates "religion" to a more primitive, more traditional, now surpassed stage of human and societal development. This appears to be the sense in which Habermas uses the term "postsecular," not as a change in society itself, as a reversal of secular trends, but as a change in consciousness, as "an altered self-understanding of the largely secularized societies of Western Europe, Canada, or Australia."[7] Postsecular here would mean, first of all, becoming reflexively aware of what Habermas calls a "secularistic self-misunderstanding." But becoming aware in itself should not be sufficient. It should be accompanied, one may assume, with the overcoming, or at least with some correction of the secularististic self-misunderstanding.

There is no doubt that Habermas himself in his later writings has adopted a postsecular reflexive attitude and has corrected the most blatantly secularistic self-misunderstandings built into his own theories. The question I would like to address in the following section is whether Habermas's postsecular correction has gone far enough or whether his position is still tied to European (mis-)understandings of processes of secularization which irremediably tend to link intrinsically contingent patterns of European Christian secularization with general processes of modernization. As Habermas indicates, after several decades of dispute between the European and American paradigms of secularization, it is "still undecided . . . whether the religious USA or the largely secularized Western Europe is the exception to a general developmental trend" (1.1).

But, in my view, it is precisely this way of putting the question, namely, the extent to which any particular supposedly contingent pattern is "exceptional" or resembles some general developmental trend, which has marred the debate between the European and American paradigms of secularization.

We need to reopen the question as to the relationship between particular contingent historical patterns of secularization and particular historical processes of modernization, both in Europe and the United States, so that we may then develop a more open global comparative historical perspective and examine the variable relations between patterns of secularization and patterns of modernization beyond the West.

II   Modernization and Secularization: A Comparison of European and US Patterns

Over a decade ago, I suggested that in order to speak meaningfully of "secularization" we needed to distinguish three different connotations of the term:

(a) Secularization, as *differentiation of the secular spheres* (state, economy, science), from religion, usually understood as the "emancipation," of the secular from ecclesiastical institutions and religious norms and the concomitant differentiation and specialization of religion within a newly emerged religious sphere. In this respect both the religious and the secular are reciprocally and mutually constituted structures which first emerge with modernity.

(b) Secularization, as *decline of religious beliefs and practices* in modern societies, often postulated as a human universal developmental process. This is the most recent but by now the most widespread usage of the term in contemporary academic debates on secularization, although it remains still unregistered in the dictionaries of most European languages.

(c) Secularization, as *privatization of religion*, often understood both as a general modern historical trend and as a normative condition, indeed as a precondition for modern liberal democratic politics. My book, *Public Religions in the Modern World*, put into question the empirical as well as the normative validity of the privatization thesis.[8]

Maintaining this analytical distinction, I argued, should allow us to examine and to test the validity of each of the three propositions independently of each other and thus to refocus the often fruitless secularization debate into comparative historical analysis that could account for different patterns of secularization, in all three meanings of the term, across societies and civilizations. We could distinguish secular differentiation, religious decline, and religious privatization respectively as Secularization I, Secularization II, and Secularization III. But this already points precisely to problems in our definitions and in our categories.

Since it appears that in Europe all three processes of secularization, namely, secular differentiation, religious decline, and privatization of religion, seem to be historically interrelated, they are perceived subsequently as three dimensions of the same general process of secularization. Indeed, European sociologists tend to view Secularization I and II as intrinsically related because they view the two realities, the decline in the societal power and significance of religious institutions, and the decline of religious beliefs and practices among individuals, as structurally related components of general processes of modernization.

American sociologists of religion tend to view things differently and practically restrict the use of the term "secularization" to its narrower more recent meaning of decline of religious beliefs and practices among individuals. It is not so much that they question the secularization of society, but simply that they take it for granted as an unremarkable fact. The United States was born as a differentiated modern secular society. Yet the sociologists see no evidence of a progressive decline in the religious beliefs and practices of the American people. Consequently, many American sociologists of religion tend to discard the theory of secularization, or at least its postulate of the progressive decline of religious beliefs and practices, as a European myth, once they are able to show that in the United States none of the usual "indicators" of secularization, such as church attendance, frequency of prayer, belief in God, and so on, evince any long-term declining trend.[9]

The main disputes between the European and the American paradigms all turn around Secularization II, that is, on the contrast between the undeniable pattern of religious decline in Europe and the undeniable pattern of religious vitality in the United States. These general trends are not in dispute.[10] What is in dispute is the relation between the divergent trends of religious decline in Europe and persistent religiosity in the United States with secular differentiation and with processes of modernization.

The new American paradigm has turned the European model of secularization on its head.[11] In the extreme "supply-side" version of the rational-choice theory of religious markets, American sociologists use the American evidence to postulate a general structural relationship between disestablishment or state deregulation, open free competitive and pluralistic religious markets, and high levels of individual religiosity. What was until now the American exception attains normative status, while the previous European rule is now demoted to being a deviation from the American norm. The low levels of religiosity in Europe are now supposedly explained by the persistence of either establishment or of highly regulated monopolistic or oligopolistic religious markets.[12] But the internal comparative evidence within Europe does not support the basic tenets of the American theory. Monopolistic situations in Poland and Ireland are linked to persistently high levels of religiosity, while increasing liberalization and state deregulation elsewhere are often accompanied by persistent rates of religious decline.[13]

An impasse has been reached in the debate. The traditional European theory of secularization offers a relatively plausible account of European developments, but is unable or unwilling to take seriously, much less to explain, the surprising vitality and extreme pluralism of denominational forms of salvation religion in America. The emerging American paradigm offers a convincing explanation of the US religious market, but is unable to account for internal variations within Europe. In fact, neither of the two theories can offer a plausible account of the significant internal variations within Europe.

Former East Germany, the Czech Republic, and France are probably the most secular of all European societies. These are the societies in which religion as a chain of collective memory is clearly disappearing. But it should be obvious that in all three cases those processes of secularization cannot be understood simply in terms of processes of modernization or in terms of persistent monopolistic conditions. I assume few people would be inclined to attribute the higher levels of secularization of East Germany, compared with those of West Germany, to the fact that East Germany is a more modern society, unless of course one is willing to argue that secularity itself is evidence of modernity.

Indeed, in order to understand the significant internal variations in patterns of secularization throughout Europe, not only between East and West Germany, but also among other European societies which are similar in many other respects, for instance, between Poland and the Czech Republic (two similar Slavic East European Soviet-type Catholic societies), or between France and Italy (two similarly modern Latin Catholic societies), or between the Netherlands and Switzerland (two highly modern bi-confessional Calvinist-Catholic societies), it should be obvious that one should look less at levels of modernization or at persistent monopolies, which explain very little, and more at historical patterns of relations between Church, state, nation, and civil society. Only a comparative historical analysis can help us overcome the impasse.[14]

The drastic decline in church attendance across Europe since the 1950s constitutes the strongest evidence for the defenders of the traditional theory of secularization. Less than 20 percent of the population in the majority of European countries attends church regularly, while in East Germany, Russia, and the Scandinavian countries the proportion of regular churchgoers decreases to the single digits. When compared with the very different evidence of continuing vitality in congregational, associational religion in the United States across all denominations – Protestant and Catholic, Jewish and Muslim, and now Hindu and Buddhist – it is obvious that this is the fundamental difference between American and European religiosity. Secularization in Europe takes primarily the form of "unchurching" (*Entkirchlichung)*, which should be understood as a form of liberation from the type of territorialized confessional religiosity which was the legacy of the Westphalian system. European Christianity, for all kinds of reasons, never made the full historical transition from territorial national churches based on the territorial parish or *Pfarrgemeinde*, to competing denominations of civil society based on voluntary religious associations, a modern form of religious community.

The analytical distinction between "church" and "denomination" is the key to any comparative analysis of religious developments and patterns of secularization in Europe and the United States. Following Max Weber's definition, sociologically, a "church" is an ecclesiastical institution which claims the monopoly of the means of salvation over a territory. The territorialization of religion and the corresponding confessionalization of state, nation, and peoples are the fundamental facts and formative principles of the Westphalian system of sovereign territorial states, which emerged in early modern Europe out of the so-called wars of religion. The principle *cuius regio eius religio* is the general formative principle of such a system, a principle moreover which was already well established before the wars of religion and even before the Protestant Reformation, as shown by the expulsion of Jews and Muslims from Spain by the Catholic monarchs in order to establish a territorial Catholic state ruling over a homogeneously religious Catholic society. What the Peace of Westphalia represented was the generalization of this dual model of confessionalization of states, nations, and peoples and territorialization of ecclesiastical religion among the emerging European territorial states. Every early modern European state (with the exception of the Polish-Lithuanian Commonwealth), was defined confessionally as

Catholic, Anglican, Lutheran, Calvinist, or Orthodox. In this respect, religious homogenization and in many instances ethno-religious cleansing stand at the very origin of the modern European state.

This is the fundamental factor of early modern European history that will determine the various patterns of European secularization. Comparatively speaking, European secularization can be best understood as a process of successive de-confessionalizations of state, nation, and peoples, which was phenomenologically experienced as a process of liberation from confessional identities. This is what determines the historically unique character of European secularization, which is now increasingly being recognized as a form of "European exceptionalism" rather than as a general model of modernization that is likely to be replicated elsewhere. In fact, the European pattern of secularization can hardly be replicated in other contexts in which there was no previous historical pattern of confessionalization of states, nations, and peoples requiring their secularization, that is, their de-confessionalization.

If my assumption is correct, it would imply that the various different patterns of European secularization and the various patterns of civil society formation across Europe are very much related to the various patterns of de-confessionalization of state, nation, and peoples. Those patterns are historically complex and although generally path-dependent, they also traverse recognizable breakthroughs at historical turning points which offer structural opportunities to change course or revise the particular path of secularization.

It is this common phenomenological experience of having passed through stages of de-confessionalization that permeates the typically European stadial consciousness that understands the process of secularization as a process of progressive emancipation from religion.

In fact, without taking into account the *longue durée* European pattern of confessionalization of states, peoples, and territories, it is not possible to understand the difficulties which every continental European state has, irrespective of whether they have maintained formal establishments or are constitutionally secular, and the difficulties which every European society has, the most secular as well as the most religious ones, in accommodating religious diversity, and particularly in incorporating immigrant religions. This is one of the fundamental differences between Europe and the United States, which never underwent a process of confessionalization and developed a radically different model of religious denominationalism.

Paraphrasing Karl Marx's "On the Jewish Question," one could say that if America can be characterized simultaneously as the model of "perfect disestablishment" and the "land of religiosity par excellence," European societies offer by contrast the inverse combination of different forms of "imperfect disestablishment" and "lands of secularity par excellence."[15] The United States never had to undergo a formal process of separation of Church and state, since it never had either a confessional state or an established state Church, from which the state had to separate itself. Unlike most Europeans, Americans also did not need to undergo a process of de-confessionalization from any national ecclesiastical institution, since even the established colonial churches, Congregational, Presbyterian, and Anglican, remained minoritarian institutions and the majority of the population remained unchurched. The American state was born as a modern secular state, without having to undergo any process of de-confessionalization, and the dual constitutional formula of no establishment of religion at the state level and free exercise of religion in society guaranteed the development of denominationalism as a system of free and open religious pluralism in society.

American denominationalism is a system of mutual recognition of de-territorialized voluntary religious institutions and associations within civil society without any state regulation or interference other than through the courts, when there are legal conflicts within or among religious organizations. The American state not only has no office of regulation or registration of religious associations, but does not even have the right to register or survey the religious denomination of its individual citizens.

Tocqueville's remains the classic and still unsurpassed analytical sociological account we have of the modern system of American religious pluralism and its affinities with the model of a pluralist and democratic civil society. Like so many other European visitors, Tocqueville was immediately struck by the vitality of religion in America and by the "innumerable multitude of sects" he found there. But unlike so many later European visitors and professional observers who tended to minimize or explain away the relevance of this phenomenon by referring to "American exceptionalism," as if the vitality of religion in America was simply the exception that confirmed the general rule of European secularization, Tocqueville saw it clearly as a "novel" situation, that is, as the product of modern developments and not simply as a traditional residue that was eventually bound to disappear with progressive modernization, and therefore as a challenge to the premise of European secularization.

Indeed, by tying his explanation of the striking pluralism and vitality of religion in America to a historical theory of modern individualism, to a historical theory of modern civil society, and to a historical theory of modern civil religion, Tocqueville offers a more persuasive institutional theory of the unique vitality of the very particular American system of religious denominationalism than contemporary supply-side theories of the American religious markets. These supply-side theories are based

(a) on dubious anthropological presuppositions of a single and universal type of rational human action based on the utilitarian calculation of costs and benefits; (b) on an ahistorical theory of religious markets according to which the demand for religious commodities is universally constant, while what changes is the supply along with changes in the level of regulation and free competition in the religious market; and (c) on an ahistorical theory of a self-differentiated and self-regulated religious market that appears disembedded from the American state, from the legal-constitutional system, from the American nation, and from American culture, and is therefore a model which presumably can be exported to any society in the world or can naturally flourish once state regulation of religious markets disappears.

It should be obvious that the different models of religious denominationalism within a pluralistic civil society alongside confessional national churches with limited pluralism have important consequences for the constitution of civil society on both sides of the Atlantic, but also for the development of inclusionary, more egalitarian and solidaristic welfare states in Europe, and the weak development of a welfare state in the USA. As the polemical debates around the attempts of the Obama administration to reform the American health system clearly indicate, the very discursive legitimation of what is a taken-for-granted principle in most European nation-states, namely, the principle of a public national health system which guarantees a minimum egalitarian access of health care for all its citizens, is immediately suspect as an etatist, socialist un-American project and susceptible to the most irrational debates. What is surprising is not that conservative Republicans may oppose the Democratic project of reforming the national health system, but that their arguments still find such a resonance within American public opinion.

One can certainly find close elective affinities between the anti-etatist model of state–civil-society relations and the model of free exercise of religion protected from any kind of state regulation or control. But secularist interpretations of the relation between the absence of a welfare state in America and the persistence of religion invert, in my view, the nature of the relationship. It is not, as Norris and Inglehardt tend to argue, that Americans are still so religious because of their existential insecurity due to the absence of a welfare state, but rather that Americans have defeated so far every attempt to institutionalize the welfare state because of the model of a self-organized and privately regulated civil society which is so intrinsically related with their model of religious denominationalism.

Norris and Inglehart have added new dimensions to the dispute between the two competing paradigms of secularization by introducing new global comparative evidence from the World Values Survey, which would seem to support the classic paradigm of secularization by apparently finding a close correlation between levels of socio-economic development and levels of secularization.[16] I find the evidence, however, somewhat unpersuasive.

Empirically, all the evidence for the positive correlation between modernization and secularization comes from Western Christian (that is, post-Christian) societies, primarily Western European countries with the addition of Canada, Australia, and New Zealand (that is, European settler colonial societies). Japan is the only non-Western society that would seem to corroborate Inglehart's thesis. But in the case of Japan, as in the case of China, one could offer a more convincing socio-cultural explanation for what appears to be already inordinate evidence of secularity well before the precipitation of processes of modernization.

For that reason, I find Habermas's reliance on the evidence provided by Norris and Inglehardt, in order to somehow still maintain the thesis of a supposedly intrinsic correlation between levels of modernization and levels of secularization, highly problematic. It may indicate a lingering secularist misunderstanding which is not only dissonant with Habermas's new postsecular reflexivity, but even more so with Habermas's own attention to "The Sacred Roots of the Axial Age Traditions"[17] and to his "Awareness of What is Missing" (*AWM*). Such an awareness or even any attention to any kind of dynamics of religious rationalization are absolutely missing from Inglehart's reductionist and ahistorical account of religion, though one must admit that the account is elegant in its utter positivist and materialist simplicity.

Inglehardt's theory of religion regresses to nineteenth-century positivist genealogies of "primitive" religion, without bothering to consider Durkheim's or Weber's more developed sociological theories. As a socio-psychological phenomenon, "religion" for Inglehardt is simply a response to conditions of existential material insecurity. Given the increasing existential security that accompanies economic development, religion is likely to lose its functional relevance and its *raison d'être*. Thus, the teleological prediction of increasing secularization is likely to accompany increasing modernization and this appears to be confirmed by the World Values Survey. In post-industrial societies, religion that is associated with economics of scarcity and with material existential insecurity is apparently replaced by higher forms of post-materialist spiritual values.

One wonders whether Inglehart would be willing to admit the paradigmatic post-materialist character of the spiritual search of the Buddha or of all the other paths of individual salvation and redemption "beyond human flourishing" associated with the Axial Age. Certainly, individual polytheistic and polyformic religious search has always been an important option, at least for elites and religious virtuosi, within the Hindu,

Buddhist, and Taoist traditions. What Inglehart calls the expansion of post-materialist spiritual values can be understood in this respect as the generalization and democratization of options until now only available to elites and religious virtuosi in most religious traditions. As the privileged material conditions available to elites for millennia are generalized to entire populations, so are the spiritual and religious options that were usually reserved for them. It may not be appropriate, however, to characterize such a process of generalized religious individuation as religious decline, or as secularization.

China and the United States are the two great outliers in Inglehart's global chart of societies along the vertical "traditional/secular-rational" axis and the horizontal "survival/self-expression" axis, which put into question the entire theory albeit in opposite directions. Given the basic assumption that "people who experience ego-tropic risks during their formative years (posing direct threats to themselves and their families) or socio-tropic risks (threatening their community) tend to be far more religious than those who grow up under safer, comfortable, and more predictable conditions,"[18] and given the catastrophic experience of material existential insecurity suffered by broad sectors of the Chinese population throughout the twentieth century, one should expect high levels of religiosity among the Chinese population, particularly among older generations. Yet the evidence tends to point in the opposite direction. China, along with Japan, perhaps for similar reasons, appears to be one of the most secular societies on earth, at least as measured by the Western Christian categories of religiosity used by the World Values Survey.[19]

Both the evidence of a society like China, which may have been both "secular" and economically undeveloped, and the evidence of a society like the United States, which seems to have become progressively more rather than less religious as it became more economically developed, seem to put into question the intrinsic correlation between modernization and secularization. American religion is not a survival from a premodern traditional society, but is a product of American modernity. Thus, the expectation that religiosity will also eventually decline as the material conditions of the American population become more secure, is highly problematic. None of the three explanations of American exceptionalism offered by Norris and Inglehart seem very convincing.

To attribute American high religiosity to the economic insecurity associated with high levels of economic inequality does not sound convincing, when all sectors of the American population, from the most privileged to the most disprivileged, evince inordinately high levels of religiosity, at least in comparison with most Western European societies.[20]

As I have already indicated, Norris and Inglehart's argument that Americans are still so religious because they do not yet have a welfare state inverts, in my view, the more plausible direction of the correlation between the system of American denominationalism and the weakness of the welfare state in America.

As to the argument that Americans may be inordinately religious due to the constant flow of poor immigrants from undeveloped countries, it is empirically equally problematic for several reasons. There is no evidence of any decline of American religiosity from the late 1920s to 1965, when the gates of immigration to America for all practical purposes were closed, a period which also coincides with a limited institutionalization of the welfare state. There is no evidence of an increase in American religiosity after 1965, when the gates of immigration became wide open again. Moreover, the assumption that immigrants may be more religious because they come from undeveloped countries is also problematic, since half of all post-1965 new immigrants tend to have higher levels of education and income than the average American. Moreover, there is compelling historical evidence that immigrants to America in all waves of successive immigration, throughout the nineteenth century as well as in the late twentieth century, become increasingly more religious, not less, as they settle in the new country. In fact, most immigrant groups, Protestants and Catholics, Jews and Muslims, Hindus and Buddhists, today as in the past, claim to be more consciously and reflexively religious in the United States than they were in their old countries before immigration.[21]

I would like to add, in this context, that Habermas's reference to the rapid secularization of post-Franco Spain as evidence of the correlation between modernization and secularization seems to me equally problematic. In my view, the rapid and drastic secularization of Spanish society within one single generation, following the forced confessionalization of the Spanish population under the Franco regime, offers more plausible evidence for correlating processes of European secularization with dynamics of de-confessionalization. In my view, phenomenologically, the Spanish case can be interpreted as evidence of a massive *nach-holende* conversion to secularity of a population that wants to be definitively "modern" and "European" after a long experience of isolated backwardness.[22] Indeed, Spain is one of the few Western European countries (along with Ireland) in which questions of "the postsecular" have not emerged at all.

III   Are We "Still" Secular or Are We Witnessing the Emergence of a "Postsecular World Society"?

Insofar as answering this question requires projecting one's gaze and one's interpretation of what appear to be contemporary trends into the future, one can offer at best some cautiously speculative answers, well aware that the social sciences have a dismal record of historical forecasting, that history remains contingent and therefore unpredictable, and that the future remains therefore fundamentally open.

Concerning the first meaning of the word "secular," that of living phenomenologically within the immanent frame of a secular world, not only are we in the West still secular and likely to remain so for the foreseeable future, but even most non-Western societies are also becoming increasingly secular, in the sense that the cosmic order is increasingly defined by modern science and technology, the social order is increasingly defined by the interlocking of citizenship "democratic" states, market economies and mediatic public spheres, and the moral order is increasingly defined by the calculations of rights-bearing individual agents, claiming human dignity, liberty, equality, and the pursuit of happiness. Indeed, globally one must admit that the whole world is becoming simultaneously both more "religious" and more "secular" alongside the increasing globalization of the Western Christian binary system of classification of religious-secular reality. Indeed, the categories of "religious" and "secular" recently became globalized for the first time in all non-Western cultures.

Concerning the second meaning of "secular," there is little evidence of any significant religious revival among the population of Western European societies, except among immigrant groups. At best, one could say that the rate of religious decline has slowed down or has been halted. Actually, the rate of secularization in many European societies may have reached a point of no return. Religion as "a chain of memory," using the formulation of the French sociologist Danièle Hervieu-Léger, appears broken almost without repair and large generations of young Europeans are growing up without any personal relationship with or even knowledge of the Christian religious tradition.[23] Not only the Christian churches, but most importantly families have lost their role in the process of religious socialization. Barring any unforeseeable religious revival, it is unlikely that the process of European secularization, that is, the unchurching of the European population, may be reversed. In this respect, it is premature to speak of European societies as postsecular.

And yet something fundamental is happening to the European secular zeitgeist. Neither the naive, unreflexive secularity which accepted being without religion as the quasi-natural, modern condition, nor the secularist self-understanding which turned the particular process of European Christian secularization into a universal normative development for all of humanity are simply tenable, that is, can be simply taken for granted without questioning or reflexive elaboration any more.

We are not "religious" again, yet. But we have certainly become obsessed with religion as a question, particularly as a public issue.[24] The fact that we are asking the question of whether we may be entering a postsecular world society is itself evidence that we have crossed a threshold, that we cannot be simply unreflexive secularists any more. As on so many other occasions throughout his exemplary lifework, Habermas is once again reading the "signs of the times" and interpreting the zeitgeist with a prescient accuracy. One could, of course, reassert one's secularism again, even aggressively and militantly. But this in itself is a response to what is viewed as an unwelcome and dangerous return of the repressed, of something we thought we had overcome and left behind. Unlike his defense of modernity against postmodern currents, Habermas is on this occasion ready to reflect upon his own secularism and adopt a postsecular attitude.

There are many reasons for this new reflexive and inquisitive attitude. I will only mention three, which are in line with the same phenomena also analyzed by Habermas:

(A)   Globalization

The first and most obvious reason can be subsumed under the code word "globalization." In our global age, it has become increasingly evident that European secular developments are not a universal norm for the rest of the world; that, as the rest of the world modernizes, people are not becoming more secular like us, but are becoming more religious – or, actually, they are becoming simultaneously both more secular and more religious, which of course only confuses our binary categories. But once it becomes obvious that the secularization of Europe is, comparatively speaking, rather exceptional, the old theory that explained Europe's secularity in terms of its modernity is no longer plausible.

It is no longer only the United States which appears to be an exception to the European rule of secularization, but the rest of the world appears to be equally exceptional, so that we have now reached a point where we are talking of the "European exception." Global media continuously impress upon global subjects not only "the ceaseless role of religion in fostering both conflict and reconciliation," but the unexpected vitality of the world religions under global conditions. It is time to cease viewing these revivals as a survival or persistence of something traditional and to begin asking ourselves the extent to which the very formation of a world society, the very process of globalization, calls for religious responses to which the old world religions are responding in manifold ways. Globalization presents not only new challenges for the old world religions but also new great opportunities.

Moreover, we should be cautious with the new fashionable discourse of European exceptionalism, for two main reasons. First, because when it comes to "religion" and its antonym, "the secular," there is no global rule. We must humbly recognize that many of our received categories, derived from our Christian-secular European developments, fail us when we try to understand developments in the rest of the world, in that rather than facilitating understanding these categories actually lead to a fundamental misunderstanding. None of the categories prove very helpful in trying to understand contemporary religious developments around the world – not the category of religious fundamentalism, as if we were witnessing a single global anti-modern reaction to secular modernity; not the term proposed by Peter Berger, "the desecularization of the world," as if we were witnessing simply a reversal of a previous process of secularization; and not even such expressions as the "return of religion" or "religious revival," as if we were simply witnessing the return of the old traditional religions. We need first a "de-secularization" of our consciousness and of our secularist and modernist categories before we can develop better concepts to understand the novelty and the modernity of these developments.

But, second, the discourse of European exceptionalism is also problematic because even within Europe there is no single European rule of secularization.

It is the secularist self-understanding of European modernization in its global colonial encounter with the other that has constructed such a rule of European secularization. The historical reality is that of multiple and complex patterns of secularization and religious revivals across Europe, many of them also intrinsically implicated with global colonial developments beyond Europe. This brings us to the second main reason for our renewed reflexive and polemical interest in religion.

(B)   European integration

The process of European integration, the expansion to the East, and the possible entry of Turkey have made evident that there is no European rule. None of the national models, the French or the German, the Dutch or the Italian, the Danish or the British can serve as a general European model. The acrimonious debates concerning the preamble to the European Constitution make obvious the confusion about the so-called fundamental European values, the problematic notion that one must choose between Christian and secular values, or between Christianity and the Enlightenment as the source of the supposedly universal European values.

One must add the puzzling prospect of Turkey joining the European Union, of a Muslim democratic Turkey which may well meet all the formal criteria and tests to join the European club and yet cannot be fully European because it is neither Christian nor secular.

(C) Immigration and increasing religious pluralism

Finally, there is the novel reality that European societies, due to interrelated processes of religious individuation and more importantly increasing immigration, are becoming either for the first time or again after many centuries religiously pluralistic. The model of the homogeneous nation-state inherited from the Westphalian system is being put into question. The Westphalian principle *cuius regio eius religio* was not significantly altered either by the critical transition from royal to national or popular sovereignty after the French Revolution, or by the expansion and consolidation of democracy in Western European societies after World War II.

The manifest difficulty which all European societies show in the integration of Muslim immigrants can be viewed as an indication of the problems that the model of the European nation-state has, whether it is formally secular or not, in regulating deep religious pluralism. One must question the problematic notion that the European secular state is de facto a religiously neutral state and therefore already contains within itself the proper solution to the management of religious pluralism in society. Today, in Europe, Islam is indeed the elephant in the room in any discussion of religion and secular modernity.

We need to be more reflexively aware of the complex historical process of Western Christian secularization and its relation to allegedly general processes of modernization. We must avoid the false dichotomies built into our binary categories, either religious or secular, either traditional or modern. Above all, we must be more critically reflexive of the stadial consciousness built into our "secular self-interpretation of modernity." Becoming postsecular does not mean necessarily becoming religious again, but questioning our stadial consciousness, de-stabilizing if not our secular immanent frame, at least the possibilities of transcendence within the immanent frame, and being open, receptive, at least curious, to all the manifold forms of being religiously human.

Habermas wants to resist the relegation of philosophy by positivism and naturalism to an intermediate stage between a religious-theological and a positive-scientific stage of the human mind. His insistent defense of a postmetaphysical form of philosophical thinking that is not superseded or made irrelevant by positivist science is laudable, and particularly necessary at the contemporary moment of global expansion of scientism and technocratic impulses. But when it comes to religion, one cannot avoid the impression that Habermas still holds on to problematic secularist stadial assumptions that relegate religion to a stage of development superseded by postmetaphysical philosophical or scientific thinking. How one is to interpret the insistence that religious discourse to be taken seriously in the public sphere must first be translated to supposedly universal secular rational discourse, as if secular discourses by definition were rational and universal. Habermas seems to want to maintain, at least implicitly, the association of the secular with the rational and the religious with the pre-rational.

Here Bellah's warning that in human cultural evolution no stage is ever forgotten, much less superseded by the next stage, should indeed inform our deliberations. We humans cannot live without rituals and we cannot live without myths. Only then can Arnason's reflection on Patocka, a reflection that Habermas seems to want to make his own in his most recent work, be taken seriously, namely, that "the idea of a self-limiting secularization, reinstated as a regulative principle of modernity would reopen and perpetuate the mutual interrogation of philosophy, science and religion."[25]

2

The Anxiety of Contingency

Religion in a Secular Age

María Herrera Lima

Reason must find its own natural being. This *motif* is not alien to the great religions but it needs "secularization" today not to contribute, isolated and on a higher plane, to the same impoverishment of the world it seeks to exorcise.

T. Adorno, *Stichworte, Kritische Modelle*, 2[1]

Introduction

Among the many subjects Jürgen Habermas has studied in his long intellectual career, he has turned to religion in his recent work. He had written previously on the relations of philosophy and theology and maintained conversations with other thinkers interested in these matters, but what he is proposing today, in the light of a perceived resurgence of religion worldwide, is a more ambitious project of a conceptual reconstruction of the history of philosophy that challenges its received interpretation. He has called the new visibility of religion in public affairs "a challenge for a secular self-interpretation of modernity." Departing from his earlier pronouncements on these questions, Habermas now seems convinced that at this later stage of global modernization religions may provide some resources to counter the lack of solidarity and other deficiencies of a consumer and success-oriented society.

This reading of the present situation questions not only the idea of a diachronic causal link between modernization and secularization, but also introduces the idea of different paths to modernity, or of a world-wide synchronic (or "culturalist") characterization of modernization that is no longer restricted to the European model. Thus, the challenge for Habermas consists in finding a way to make compatible the continued presence of religion (everywhere) with the cognitive advances of modern consciousness postulated by his theory of communicative rationality. His response to this challenge has taken the form of an investigation of what he regards now as the common remote historical origins of "faith and knowledge" as parallel and – in the most controversial aspect of his proposal – as complementary intellectual formations. This new geneal-ogy of faith and reason considers as well the conditions for possible forms of dialogue between philosophy and religion – or, in Habermas's terms, "of mutual learning" – which, in turn, depend on his characteriza-tion of a historically developed reflexivity of both religious and secular consciousness. It is in this area where we find the most significant changes with respect to the emphatic understanding of the secular character of modernity of his earlier work, and it will be one of the main concerns of this chapter (section 1).

In addition to the already mentioned new genealogy of reason, his proposed characterization of a revisionist understanding of the present situation as "postsecular" attempts to overcome received antagonisms and sets a new political program for democratic societies. Habermas agrees with those who want to correct the excesses of modern secularists and considers religion compatible with modernity and its legal and politi-cal institutions – even as a potential candidate for reparation of some of its deficiencies – while maintaining, at the same time, a cautious distance from the anti-modern and anti-liberal bias of some of the contemporary defenders of a religious revival. But the middle way he proposes is not free of difficulties, among other reasons because the "postsecular," as he understands it, is not an empirical description (differences and conflicts persist) and the normative conditions that Habermas assigns to it (asking more than the usual tolerance of religion from secular citizens and the acceptance of liberal pluralism from religious believers) is unlikely to gain generalized acceptance from either side of the controversy it intended to remedy in the first place. (This last group of problems – of religion in the democratic public sphere – will not be considered in this chapter.)

Another possible objection on matters of method or historical research is related to the revised account of secularization, implied rather than explicitly developed, in which this new project rests. In the first place, because different reconstructions can have important con-sequences in the framing of relevant issues, these in turn may have an effect on our understanding and diagnosis of cultural modernity. Second, because long-term conceptual reconstructions (or evolutionary accounts) are internally related to the contingencies of empirical events (historical accounts) those interconnections must be made explicit – in particular, in the case of the history of secularization as a historical event, and, as such, as a problem that is distinct from the more general question of whether religions as cultural practices may be included in the development of modern reason.

Therefore, what I want to propose, to begin with, is a stronger role for historical studies than the one adopted by Habermas. For that, I will take a closer look at the intertwined traditions of religious and secular thought in European history (section 2), and consider other versions (or reconstructions) of that history (Charles Taylor), in order to understand the changed historical and social conditions for religious beliefs and practices in our secular age (section 3). Finally (in section 4), I will turn briefly to Habermas's discussion on philosophy and religion, with the conviction that a secular orientation that expands the reach of discourse ethics beyond the moral-legal domain can be a viable alternative (if not an exclusive one) to the perceived limitations of its present form.

Going back to Adorno's brief remarks in the interview quoted at the beginning, one could see that these debates are more than half a century old, and that the climate of discussion today is not that different for those who want to assume an emphatically secular view on the contingency of human life. What is significantly different from the time Adorno was writing, though, is that since the decline of the dominant political ideologies of the past century many public debates have been recast in religious terms. Thus, it is even more urgent today to resist the temptation of seeing religions as unchanged; we must consider the ways in which they have been affected by the process of secularization in the last phase of economic and cultural modernization. Religions are not isolated, but are complex cultural practices involved as well in mundane concerns; as social institutions they share the dominant interests and general developments of their time, and to understand this is crucial for any debate on the appropriate conditions for participating in the political and cultural public spheres. As Adorno maintained in his time: even the contents of theology will not remain unaltered; everyone must endure the test of entering the secular, the profane, and of dwelling there.[2]

I Secularization and Modernity: A Changed Perspective

Some of the changes in Habermas's view on the development of modernity with respect to his earlier work are rather striking: a new genealogy of reason that *includes* religion and places philosophy as a secular partner of theology rather than as its enlightened successor; as he said recently, "I defend Hegel's thesis that the major world religions belong to the history of reason itself" (*BNR*, 6). According to this new reconstruction, cognitive advances can be detected in traditions of religious thought, even if in order to be generally accessible to largely secular audiences theological motifs must find translation into secular terms. Habermas is convinced that in the present climate of discussion it is possible to look at the legacy of religious traditions, "without effacing the boundary between the universes of faith and knowledge" (211) and thus, without fearing a relapse into metaphysics. According to him, what can be learned from religion is something that may be lacking in the present world dominated by market imperatives and bureaucracies, a "disruptive power" that was assigned to art in his earlier work, "as the medium in which modernity makes contact with the archaic" ("Three Perspectives," *PDM*, 51–74) (for example, by Schlegel or Nietzsche). This Romantic motif, however, is now turned into the recognition of the potential semantic contents of religion, and, thus, for continuing a process of mutual learning with philosophy that challenges its received secular self-understanding.

The problem of the need for compensation for the loss of social integration once provided by religion is not new in Habermas's work. However, in *The Philosophical Discourse of Modernity*, he offered a different interpretation for the loss of unifying power of traditional religions; he maintained there that the proposed rehabilitation of traditional forms of life devalued by modernity was not viable, because, he asked, "How are traditions, for which truly convincing grounds have gone by the boards with the collapse of religious and metaphysical world views, supposed to live on as subjective powers of belief, if only science still has the authority to ground our holding something?" (72). Thus, the idea of a compensatory role, whether assigned to religion or to traditional ethical forces, or even to art, was criticized by Habermas in that book as characterizing the "neo-conservative diagnoses of the age" (71).

Recently (2004), though, he has recovered this theme in connection with the debate on the sources of legitimation of the secular constitutional state ("Prepolitical Foundations of the Constitutional State?", *BNR*, 101–13). In this recent debate, the old theme of the need for compensations of the modern state is reproduced as the question of "whether political authority still even admits of a secular – i.e., a non religious or post metaphysical – justification once law has been completely positivized" (101). These doubts have to do with questions of motivation.[3] Although the problem of (the lack of) motivation for morality is not restricted to questions of public justice, Habermas continues to stress this aspect even if he also includes other problems now, such as the need for solidarity, that suggest greater openness to what was previously assigned to the domain of ethical life. However, this new line of questioning should not be taken as meaning that he accepts the old conservative

thesis of the need for pre-political or traditional compensations as implying [that] "the liberal state is incapable of reproducing the motivations
on which it depends from its own secular resources" (105), but it does
amount to the recognition that the emphatic secular self-assurance of the
modern state and liberal society has been somehow threatened by two
opposing social trends:

First, by what he regards now as the negative effects that result from
"the politically uncontrolled dynamics of the global economy and global
society" (107) that erode civic solidarity at the local or state level and
may be at the root of political conflicts – in other words, as the effects of
a *highly successful secularization* seen as the expansion of a consumer-
oriented society indifferent to the needs of others. In this sense, religions
(and other traditional forms of community) may seem to play a functional role in coping with life's contingencies.

Second, in the opposite direction, by what to some is a *partially failed
secularization*, since the still vital presence of religious practices may be
experienced as yet another threat to the self-reliance of the secular liberal
state.

Habermas is convinced that a new relation with religion (or religions,
in a plural sense) can be proposed, without renouncing the gains of democratic institutions and their political culture (equal respect, impartiality,
freedom of thought). This acknowledgment amounts to a challenge for
him that requires finding a middle ground between conservative (or fundamentalist) appropriations of the theme of an "ambivalent modernity"
on the conservative camp,[4] and skeptical reactions toward the claims of
the universalistic rational morality he defends, voiced by the postmodern
critics of the Enlightenment (see "Equal Treatment of Cultures and the
Limits of Postmodern Liberalism," 270–311).

The revised interpretation of this old theme may be seen, at least in
part, as a move in the direction of making some religious thinkers allies
in the development of communicative rationality, as he did, for example,
in his work on Karl Jaspers, with whom Habermas shares the aspiration
of finding a common basis for the pacific coexistence of different religious
traditions – without suppressing their beliefs – or in his dialogue with
Michael Theunissen, a theologian who had already expressed religious
motifs in philosophical terms (*LPS*, chapters 2 and 7). But his new project
goes beyond the dialogue of philosophers and theologians. It is not just
a question of selective appropriations that can be undertaken from the
(secular) perspective of philosophy, as it has been done in the past in
non-problematic ways. Rather, it seems to address at least two different
problem areas: on the one hand, the political-legal question of the role of
religion in the democratic public space (which deserves a separate treatment) and, on the other, the cluster of problems that arise from the idea

of a reconstruction of the history of philosophy in its relation (or debt) to moral insights from religious traditions. Among those problems, the idea of social learning is of central importance to understand the possible connections and changes of perspective with respect to his earlier work.

II   Learning Processes and the Idea of Social Evolution

Over the years, in the development of his research program, Habermas has incorporated a notion of social evolution in different versions, some already rejected at least in part, while others are still present in different forms. An example of the latter is the idea of collective learning processes that make it possible for cultures to achieve the necessary cognitive conditions to become self-reflective ("Morality, Society and Ethics," *JA*, 157). In an earlier essay (*HE*), in a debate between narrative history and sociological theories of development, Habermas proposed a version of the theory of social evolution as an alternative to functionalist accounts of development and to the then current versions of universal history. There, he criticized historians for their limited search of "general structures and patterns of events" merely as the basis for comparative perspectives in global history, urging them instead "to take the leap from typological, comparative universal history to developmental theory," since the same methods employed in search of those regularities "can also serve in the discovery of societal universals for a theory of development" (*HE*, 6). Taking a stand against what he saw as an empiricist understanding of historical research, he also restricted the writing of history – because of the constraints of the narrative form – to a subordinated role in the division of labor with theoretical accounts.

Without going into the details of that debate, we find in this essay some explicit characterizations of Habermas's notion of social learning, not just as experiments in "construction and reconstruction" in the sense of Piaget's theory, but as evolutionary processes which are dependent on structures of consciousness. In his words, "collectively shared structures of consciousness are understood as learning levels, i.e. as structural conditions of possible learning processes" (29). His alternative concept of a theory of evolution is based on assumptions about universal structures of consciousness and levels of learning scaled according to the logic of development illustrated, at that time, by the example of the transition to the modern age (8).

However, Habermas no longer defends his early formulations exclusively in terms of the development of Western rationalization – as he did, for example, in *Communication and the Evolution of Society* (1976), where it appeared in connection with the project of reconstruction of historical materialism, or in *Moral Consciousness and Communicative Action* (1983), where he related it to stages in the development of moral consciousness in the psychology of Lawrence Kohlberg. In the latter we find, perhaps, the strongest notion of social evolution, even if cautiously dissociated from literal translations of a biological model. There, in the context of debates on the shortcomings and possible insights of neo-evolutionist theories of development (which at that time formed the framework of modernization theories), Habermas maintained that "the heuristic usefulness of the biological model consists in its directing our attention to the evolutionary learning mechanism" (*CES*, 171). Those forms of linguistically mediated shared knowledge amount to *species capacities,* or collective learned abilities that open the way to other cultural and technical achievements, and for Habermas, more importantly, become conditions of possibility for the development of normative structures. But even if the strong Eurocentric implications have been replaced in his recent work by a worldwide study of the development of cultures and civilizations, the idea of learning processes in the practical-moral domain has remained constant in his research program, with differences in formulation, and in the auxiliary sciences or disciplines he has turned to for support.

As he said in connection with the need for confirmation of the hypothetical reconstructions of his discourse theory of ethics (in addition to the internal debates with other moral theories), "a theory of this kind is also open to, indeed dependent upon, *indirect* validation by *other* theories that are consonant with it" (*MCCA*, 117, emphasis in the original). So, one way of reading recent changes in his position is that, at least in part, these are taking place in the domain of indirect forms of validation (revised genealogies of moral thought) rather than as affecting the substance of his philosophical program.[5]

If, at first, one finds some of his writings on religion surprising – because they *do* raise questions about his previous emphatic defense of the Enlightenment and the self-sufficiency of modernity – it is possible to find important elements of continuity as well, both in the core of the philosophical program, and in some specific aspects of the theory of modernity. One of these elements is related to the role that the history of religions has played as a model for cultural development and the idea of European modernization (as in the work of Max Weber). One could say that the idea of evolutionary stages in the historical reconstruction of religion is due in part to the stability of its body of doctrine subjected to institutional and dogmatic controls, as well as to the fact that changes in doctrine and in established ritualized practices require public justification. That is, those changes must be explained to their followers in ways consistent with the doctrine and in accordance with authorized procedures, for they must be seen (by believers) as not merely adaptations to the political and economic needs of the times. In addition, since these changes occur in the form of epochal events (Councils, Edicts), they are ideal markers of stages in the development of new attitudes that may as well be understood as indicators of collective learning processes – even though accepting this would imply the use of a more emphatically historical conception of the idea of social learning than the one usually employed by Habermas.

Max Weber's idea of the "disenchantment of the world" may now have to be adjusted because of the persistent observance of religion, but the thesis of societal rationalization remains valid for Habermas as it was proposed in *The Theory of Communicative Action*: "Weber's theory covers religion and societal rationalization – that is, the universal-historical emergence of modern structures of consciousness, on the one hand, and the embodiment of these rationality structures in social institutions, in the other" (I, 156); so, even if the first part of this assertion is now somewhat revised, the second remains of central importance for his normative theory of democracy.[6] In turn, the idea of a historical reconstruction of modernity – that now explicitly includes rationalized religious traditions – and the history of changes in epistemic attitudes necessary for the kind of reasonable interactions and forms of mutual learning between secular and religious citizens that Habermas proposes, could, still "be defended within the framework of an evolutionary theory" (*BNR*, 144). In other words, the already achieved modern de-centered consciousness, capable of transcending the particularities of concrete situations, is regarded as the end result of a history of learning processes that work as conditions of possibility for a universalistic morality.

However, moving from the idea of evolution in relatively short temporal terms – the history of modern rationalization in Weber's sense – to long-term conceptions of human evolution that mark cognitive advances as species-learning processes, as Habermas understands them, presents some problems: in the early accounts of his theory because of the lack of a clear distinction between empirical history and evolutionary processes; and, in his recent work, because transitions from conceptual reconstructions (or genealogies) of religious and philosophical thought are not always specified, and the idea of learning refers sometimes to the above mentioned long-term evolutionary processes (species learning), and at others to actual interactions among individuals (as in the proposed mutual learning between religious believers and secular citizens). These distinctions are important for moral theory. The idea of moral learning cannot be reduced to the very general level of cognitive capacities; from the perspective of the life of actual persons, it is something that occurs in his or her "century" – that is, in the horizon of the lived experience of each individual – and in that sense it is not cumulative. It starts all over again with the birth of every human being, with all the uncertainties of individual choices. Thus, this form of learning must be distinguished as a different phenomenon, distinct from the received moral wisdom incarnated in shared collective norms and institutions.

However, admittedly, problems related to the empirical basis of philosophical studies are endemic in political philosophy and, in the case of Habermas, it is something that has already been discussed by earlier critics in connection with his work on the public sphere and on the epistemic conditions stipulated by his model of democratic legitimacy.[7]

In connection with these problems, and as a response to the challenge of the re-description of Western secularization that underlies his new research projects, I want to propose, as mentioned earlier, a stronger role for historical studies than the one adopted by Habermas, for example, in the early essay discussed above (*HE*) and as implied in his recent idea of a genealogy of faith and reason. Accepting the need to take into consideration social and historical facts as complementary to political philosophy (but not theoretically blind as interpretations) does not necessarily mean to take sides with a narrow conception of historicism or contextualism, or to be skeptical about any form of normative theory. There is no single formula to determine the appropriate relation between the idealizations of normative theory with the findings of empirical research, or those between "ideal" and "real" theory[8] – it is something that depends on the creative imagination of the theorist for selecting the relevant facts and giving them a convincing articulation. So, we could see in this effort, rather, an attempt to avoid two extremes: on the one hand, of positivistic social and political theories (or "Hobbesian" accounts of political conflicts), and, on the other, of collapsing idealizations with actual descriptions of empirical events.

The question of the history of political relations of organized religions with modern nation-states and societies (now in a global perspective) must be addressed as a development that confronts political theorists at each stage, attending to specific problems and the language in which these could be formulated. Rather than seeing actual historical events as something accidental to the philosophical debate, we could maintain that problems of political and moral theory are shaped as much by the internal constraints of the discussion – as conversations with other texts – as they are by the demands of their historical circumstances.[9]

Secularization – at least in the reading that I want to advance – becomes a contingent and more emphatically historical process with all its local particularities, and as such it loses the character of historical necessity. This changed conception of secularization affects, first, the perceived nature of modern societies, and, second, the institutional functioning and self-image of established religions that had to adapt to changes in the economy and the public culture of capitalist modernization. The process of acquiring an increased reflexivity by monotheistic religions, studied by Habermas, has been accompanied all along by a history of mutual adaptations and negotiations that continue to this day, and that, in some sense, represent the *secularization of religion* itself.

III   Secularization: Two Traditions of Interpretation

In the current revision of the concept of secularization there are a number of contrasting positions: it is not a single theory but a cluster of inter-related concepts and conflicting interpretations. This revision, in turn, is not restricted to the failed predictions of the Enlightenment about the decline or loss of social relevance of religion, but it rather asks whether the concept still has an explanatory value. On the one hand, sociologists and historians of religion[10] make a convincing argument for the con-tinuing usefulness of secularization as an analytic tool for the study of changes in the public role of religions in contemporary societies, with some adjustments and precisions, while other authors find conceptual reasons to question the notion of secularization within the theory of modernity, as in the case of Hans Blumenberg[11] – because of the deriva-tive nature of the concept – or even suggest abandoning it altogether, as Robert Bellah,[12] because of the chaotic picture of its conflicting uses.

The seemingly irreconcilable diversity of uses of secularization, in addition to differences in disciplinary approaches, reveals an old antagon-ism that still resonates in current debates and that is not always explicit or easy to detect. However, the picture is not as chaotic as it may seem at first glance: under closer scrutiny, one may gradually discern at least two rival versions of secularization that also concern themselves with the meaning and direction of history in modern times. These are not unified accounts but they do exhibit some continuity as traditions of interpreta-tion; they are not neutral either; historically, they were undertaken from a partisan perspective. What has been said about the Enlightenment "thesis" of the disappearance of religion[13] could apply as well to the conservative dismissal of secularization as a "myth"; they were not just theories but political and ideological programs. They disagreed not only in their prognosis on the fate of religion in modernity but on their themes and orientation too: the secular version was not restricted to the role of religion in modern society, but had to do mainly with the transformation of a cultural *ethos*; while the religious version was concerned with the assimilation of those changes and the theological answers it could offer them.

Many of the original meanings are still at work in contemporary uses, such as that of the "secular" as a domain of ordinary experience, and of several uses of "secularization." Some of them are quite harmless, or at least not polemical, and others are antagonistic, related in the latter case to the two historic versions of the concept of secularization: (1) the first one, that I will call the ecclesiastical or religious version, that is not just a reaction to the second, but a process with a long history of theological justifications and philosophical debate; and (2) the secular version, also older than the Enlightenment.

III.i   The ecclesiastical or religious version

In the current debate, this version appears in a simplified form as compensation of the harms inflicted by an overzealous Enlightenment, but in fact it conflates two of its historical uses:

(a) Secularization simply as *differentiation* of domains and of religious jurisdiction, for example, as a distinction between monastic rule and secular clergy, or as a *transference* between these two domains, and, by extension, as used to refer to the pastoral work of the Church "in the world" and the "temporal" business of ecclesiastical institutions (economy, political relations, etc.). There is nothing controversial about these uses of the secular or secularization from a religious perspective, and they *do* require the previous idea of a neutral conception of the secular and the separation of domains. They are, rather, supported by theology: the sacred as a qualitatively distinct domain that is eternal as a contrast to the finite, measurable time and the fallible (or "fallen") nature of human existence.

(b) Secularization as *loss* (of spirituality or of the power of the Church). This is the most important of current uses for our topic. It began to be thematized during the Reformation and Counter-Reformation, and received philosophical articulation during Romanticism and the late nineteenth century (and traces of it can be found in post-Romantic utopias). But the controversial sense of *loss* (as an uncritical assumption in need of revision) derives from the idea of *transference as confiscation* of ecclesiastical property, and of the reversal of public functions from religious to civil authorities in the eighteenth and nineteenth centuries. This latter use is the one with negative connotations, perceived as an offense or harm that underlies the anti-Enlightenment feelings of old conservatives and of the so-called New Christian Right.

III.ii   The secular version

The idea of the *secular* as the domain of human experience proper, goes back to Roman times, and later uses of the idea of *secularization* derive from it. Although the version associated with the Enlightenment (in its most vocal and anti-clerical form) is the one usually assumed, it is by no means the only one.

But, first, it is necessary to consider the word "secular" (*saeculum* or century, or "what belongs to the century"). In Roman games (*ludi seculares*),[14] this was used as a measure of the time an individual could count as lived experience. From this meaning were derived other uses: *earthly, worldly,* and later, in the system of medieval oppositions, a whole array of contrasting notions: *earthly, worldly, mundane versus heavenly, otherworldly, celestial;* or as in: *sacred-profane, temporal-eternal,* and so on.

There is a certain advantage in preserving a somewhat neutral sense of the secular for explaining a domain of experience that has possessed some degree of autonomy, since ancient times, as a parallel area of popular culture, and later of science and high culture: irreverent or indifferent to religious beliefs, and rebellious before censorship and conventional social norms. Even if we take into account the relevant historical changes, there is plenty of evidence of this sort of behavior in literature and the arts, even among the clergy, in times of a predominantly religious worldview, as well as in traditions of heterodoxy and religious skepticism.

As for the idea of *secularization* as a recovery of this domain (of the secular) from the control of the clergy, it began explicitly in the humanism of early modernity and centered on the idea of *liberation* (from superstition and censorship) and of *emancipation* (of civil functions from ecclesiastical domination). It also applied in other domains of experience – such as those related to the body and sexuality – as emancipation from a conventional-religious morality, or as gaining independence from doctrinal controls in the case of science and critical thought. But the most contested aspect of what has become known as the "Enlightenment thesis" is the assumption of the *necessary decline of religion* with the advance of modernization (either as a practice or in its social relevance).

What these two versions have in common is that they assume a partisan perspective and dismiss the rival's characterization of the meaning and direction of the historical process, but, more importantly, they ignore their mutual imbrications. It may not be possible to adopt a completely neutral position on these questions – nor are there "pure" versions of these historical interpretations. Rather, what we usually encounter are various combinations and differences of degree in their ideological commitments. Nevertheless, we can attempt to exercise some methodological restraint and, if necessary, make our commitments explicit so as to avoid the extremes of both "secularists" and "religionists" (as the detractors of secularization have been characterized).[15]

In addition, we must take into account the variety of responses to secularization from the two ideological positions. From the religious perspective, secularization was not restricted to the narrow idea of "loss." For example, in the tragic vision of the "hidden God" of Pascal,[16] or in theological elaborations where the obscurity or lack of intelligibility of a secularized culture and history becomes part of a providential design. And it can be seen in the rejection of the involvement of religion in political affairs and material ambitions (not to be corrupted by temporal powers)[17] that led to the defense of a radical separation of Church and state by some religious thinkers and confessions. It would be an unacceptable simplification to assume a single political orientation as guiding the relations between religion and the secular state in the history of modern democracy.[18]

From a secular point of view, overemphasizing the fight against religion obscures the creative side of the emergence of new civil institutions and a system of rights that is not necessarily incompatible with religious freedom, but which is, rather, its condition of possibility in modern pluralistic societies. "Toleration" is, after all, a secular "virtue," one that affects the public behavior of different people in modern societies. Thus, a more tempered version of secularization in the political domain abandons the idea of a "necessary decline" of religion and considers instead that the *distinction and separation of domains and areas of legitimate action* of religious and civic institutions constitutes the core idea of secularization.

Habermas's idea of the secular is consistent with the latter use (the secular constitutional state). Although he follows the received conception of secularization as "expropriation," he opposes the "zero-sum game" between the two sides of the dispute; instead, he maintains that the liberal state, once it has acknowledged the permanence of religion in modern societies, can find a "third way" beyond older antagonisms (*FHN*, 104–5). In that sense, he agrees with revisionist versions of secularization in the sociology of religion that aim to correct the Enlightenment's assumption of a necessary decline of religion in modernity. He calls this new condition "postsecular" in the sense of non-partisan (or refraining from the excesses of "secularism") as the attitude demanded of secular citizens, just as he characterizes as "postmetaphysical" (or reasonable) the required attitude of organized religions in the acceptance of the pluralism of beliefs and non-violence (the rule of law) in modern democratic societies. However, he has expressed some reservations about the idea of a predominantly secular culture these days – because of what he calls "the egocentric exhaustion of solidarity resources" and the weakening of community-based public spheres. For those reasons, he wants to recover from religious traditions some moral or ethical insights that he believes have been neglected (or "repressed") by the secular culture of our time.

Corresponding to the traditions of interpretation described above, there are as well opposing ways to "end" the secularization thesis: on the religious side, the more radical approach suggests abandoning not just the idea of secularization but also the category of "religion." Against the grain of what I have defended here, Robert Bellah,[19] for example, proposes to suppress the distinction of domains extending the idea of religiosity to every form of ritualized behavior. There is a tendency among many of the defenders of a religious revival these days to re-describe religion in terms of a vague idea of religiosity, less dependent on dogmatic or institutional controls and associated to other political concerns such as respect for nature, or vegetarianism, and so on. But such re-descriptions could not support the kind of cohesive ethical communities required to counter the influence of an overwhelming materialistic global modernization. In addition, those ethical and political concerns (as in the case of the ecologists and others) center on specific issues and include a wide variety of secular and religious perspectives, so they could not serve as an example of a return to religion either. There are, however, other alternatives for an understanding of the conditions of a possible recovery of religion in the secular age, as in the case of Charles Taylor, who takes into account the changed historical conditions for religious beliefs.

IV   Religion in a Secular Age

The question of new historical conditions for religious belief in modernity is of central importance to our topic. The sociological fact of the continuing existence and public presence of religion in the public sphere in developed societies, as well as changed attitudes and sensibilities, have produced a reaction in the sociology of religion and in debates on political theory and philosophy with the consequent reactivation of debates on secularism. But it cannot be simply assumed that religions have not suffered profound transformations in their beliefs and actual practices. According to major sociological studies, there is little observable difference between attitudes and forms of public behavior among the majority of citizens in developed societies, whether declaring a religious affiliation or none at all.[20] More importantly, the reasons offered for church attendance and involvement in religion shifted markedly over the course of the twentieth century from obedience to pleasure.[21] This assimilation of the everyday experience of believers to the general *ethos* of the times, dictated by economic imperatives rather than by either religion or philosophy (or "high culture"), is taken for granted even within many religious communities and ecclesiastical authorities. As a consequence, religion in general – with no further specifications on which groups, on what public issues or policies, and so on – could not be assumed to provide an unmistakable ethical or moral orientation.[22] This fact is accepted by religious critics, who recognize the difficulty of making a sharp separation between religious and secular citizens as they acknowledge "the porosity and intermingling of the *civitates*,"[23] and observe that the general trends of modern society (including those that they were supposed to counter) have left their mark on religion: "one will not in general find that religious communities are free of egoism and deficient solidarity."[24]

Under the new description, secularization acquires many meanings but is as inescapable – if not more – as in the older version because it can spread horizontally across cultures, and selectively, through the generalization of practices and habits of the consumer culture and the mass media, parallel to the systemic and technological imperatives of the global economy. As for the effects of these processes on religions around the world, we can see that churches have modernized their internal organization: they function now as transnational corporations, own banks, television and radio stations, hire political lobbyists and are more concerned with their public image.[25] Whether or not these changes are described in terms of an "internal secularization" of religion, as Wilson and others have called it, is not crucial. What is, however, firmly secured is the importance of understanding the institutional history of each religion within the general social and political developments of its time. Thus, whatever terms we use to describe it, religion has not been immune from the effects that led to the "secular age"; in the words of Charles Taylor: "Plainly something important has happened; there has been a decline in something very significant, which many people recognize under the term 'religion.'"[26]

From the standpoint of philosophy, changes in the place that religious beliefs occupy in the economy of knowledge and private experience – in another sense of "privatization," not just in the fact that religion, in sociological terms, became regarded as belonging to the private sphere – are crucial for understanding the kind of dialogue that may take place between philosophy and religion today. The turn to an "inner life" of religion in modernity that placed it in the area of existential choices and concerns – that was already observed by Max Weber – had many consequences for the constitution of new secular forms of identity and for changes in what Charles Taylor has called the "conditions of belief" in modern societies.[27] What is striking about these changes is not merely the transference of functions that previously were administered by the Church or clergy to the new secular professionals, for example, in education or public health institutions, or in the expansion of areas of labor and leisure activities that replaced older forms of community and traditional habits, but rather in the fact that

> a secular age is one in which the eclipse of all goals beyond human flourishing becomes conceivable; or better, it falls within the range of an imaginable life for masses of people. This is the crucial link between secularity and a self-sufficing humanism.[28]

So the idea of the possible *irrelevance* of religion is, then, the most damaging for its survival; even if – as Taylor carefully documents – religious practices have not disappeared, they have often become a mere matter of "choice" for individuals. The move toward this idea of religion as "choice," as a special kind of good for the satisfaction of otherwise unfulfilled needs in a market-like scenario, was prepared by the turn to the anthropological as the only source of meaning after the "disenchantment" of nature and the adoption of a mechanistic idea of the cosmos. Within religion itself, a turn to the expressive could already have been detected in the shift from theological considerations to a concern with the reactions of the believers, as Taylor observes in the case of some Protestant denominations: "[in] Pietism and Methodism, for whom a powerful emotional response to God's saving action was more important than theological correctness."[29] And, on the side of the Catholic Counter-Reformation, this trend toward the expressive was already constitutive of the representations of piety found in Baroque architecture and the visual arts of the period.

Those were powerful changes that affected everyone in many areas of ordinary life during the transition to modern society, for example, "In the transfer of many issues that were considered moral to a therapeutic register"[30] (from sin to illness) that Taylor mentions. But these and other developments in the process of secularization are not only described but also received with ambivalence by Taylor as a critic of this "self-sufficing" (or God-less) humanism. Thus, the question for him is: how did we reach this point? "What exactly is it which has happened, such as that the conditions of belief are altered?"[31] Or in what way can the modern "immanent frame" of subjective experience still be open to some experience of religious transcendence?

Taylor explicitly takes a stand in the field of contested interpretations of secularization that we have been discussing – adopting a religiously committed standpoint – in a way that at least in part accepts the validity of the rival interpretation. According to his description, religious beliefs seem to be restricted in modernity to the domain of existential experiences, characterized in the examples he offers in psychological terms (as *epiphanies*) that could also accept a secular characterization as aesthetic experiences. But it follows that for him the question of the meaning of those experiences also could be interpreted in either direction in the "unquiet frontiers of modernity."[32] That is, from the point of view of secularization, what Taylor calls "the sources of deeper meaning in our lives" shifted to the secular domains of the arts and culture or to individual self-fulfillment (in work, love, leisure, etc.), but conversely, it could still be possible to trace them back to religious sources. This is not, however, something that can be anticipated or that would happen for everyone, so his doubts about how secular is, after all, the "secular age," are not intended as definitive conclusions, but only as indications of the difficult and unresolved sense of incompleteness or "loss" of the modern condition.

Nevertheless, what is crucial for my present discussion as a partial conclusion that can be obtained both from the sociological descriptions of the behavior of modern believers, and from Charles Taylor's characterization of the conditions of religious belief in the present secular age, has to do with the nature of the reasons offered to justify those beliefs. When an idea of personal choice free from doctrinal or ecclesiastic controls is introduced in the practice or observance of present-day religions – or even as a possible choice among different creeds – the structure of arguments for justifying religious affiliation and/or observance changes dramatically. Individual self-fulfillment or self-realization, pleasure instead of obedience, or the rejection of notions of sacrifice or self-denial are unmistakably secular in origin, and the open-ended spirituality advocated by many former members of established religions can only resort to secular reasons – in a strict sense non-religious sources – to decide on those choices. Advocating reasons of this kind, places at the same level decisions for choosing this or that religion (in this or that form) with those for not seeing oneself as committed to any religion at all. In other words, it places those choices at the level of what Habermas calls existential orientations, not susceptible of achieving generalized agreement in pluralistic societies.

The relatively recent radicalization of an individualistic conception of religious affiliation in the course of the late nineteenth and twentieth centuries, and the consequent alteration of the sources of meaning of everyday life, would no longer allow religion to claim the status of a "worldview" valid for everyone, or to consider itself as a "form of life" detached from the rest of society. This understanding makes it impossible to appeal to religion *alone* as a remedy for the lack of solidarity and other distortions of contemporary social life, since, as the sociological evidence shows, they are very much part of the *same* cultural formation.

In a general sense, the state of affairs described in this section presents problems that must be addressed by all the proponents of a religious restoration in the public life of present-day modern societies. An acknowledgment of the continued presence of religious observance – in different degrees and forms in modern societies – is not a sufficient reason to assume that this phenomenon could be assimilated to the beliefs and habits of the past, or that they do not require non-traditional forms of legitimation.

V   Philosophy and Religion as Moral and/or Existential Orientations

Habermas's recent views on religion as a source of possible ethical motives can be read in more than one way: in a non-controversial manner, suggesting that religions may offer an understanding of what life is or should be about – as one existential orientation among many – or in the more problematic sense of claiming a special place for religion in the public sphere and in its proposed relation to philosophy. In the first case, seeing religious views as ethical orientations (and, as such, as a possible source for moral insights) would be a matter of making explicit some of the contents of the traditional teachings of religions that may be possible to rephrase in terms acceptable to secular audiences. In this sense, religions may play a functional role for the community of believers (and even beyond) in helping people "cope with contingency." They could also contribute to the design of public policies through their participation in the public sphere as communities of interpretation – in dialogue and open competition with other groups and their respective proposals. Organized religions and religiously vocal individuals can be regarded in this manner as interested publics, participating in networks of exchange of points of view that contribute to the formation of public opinion and, through their interventions in this social space, participate in what Habermas had described before as the constitution of "cooperatively negotiated interpretations" (*BFN*, 361).

But understanding religion in this way would not justify any special treatment for organized religions, and certainly could not demand of secular subjects (or of any citizen) that they should abstain from criticizing or speaking against anything they may regard as wrong or harmful either in religious doctrine or in the practices of religious institutions. A strong secular critique in many areas of life continues to be necessary to counter the repressive and intolerant aspects of religion as Taylor recognized in the case of the puritanical repression of sexuality, or these days, of abuses of the Catholic Church. It would seem that we cannot single out religion as a privileged source of moral insights after the "expressive turn" in modern history and the fact that the sources of meaning in life have been displaced from religious to secular domains of experience.

However, Habermas has explicitly said that he does not consider religion (only) as an ethical (or existential) orientation, because of the moral (truth) claims advanced by religion. Depending on the way in which we read his recent writings, we could see them as addressing two different kinds of problems: (1) political/legal, related to the investigation of the conditions for mutual coexistence of secular and religious communities under conditions of "reasonable" (Rawls)[33] pluralism, and (2) conceptual/historical, tracing the genealogy of modern ideas of justice that combine religious and secular sources (as he has done in his genealogy of human rights), or as a *single* project, finding an underlying *unity* for both proposals in the idea of a strong program of a (Kantian) deontological conception of practical philosophy.

On an essay on the contemporary importance of Kant's philosophy of religion, Habermas outlines this second program ("The Boundary between Faith and Knowledge," *BNR*, 209–47). Habermas seems to share the doubts already expressed by Kant about the possibility of acting morally on "reason alone," and also follows Kant by finding in religion a supplement of some kind. But the answer to the question "why should we need religion at all?" is not the same for both authors. In Kant's case, it was not to provide morality with "an incentive" but "to satisfy a 'natural need' that would otherwise constitute a 'hindrance' to morality."[34] It was not, then, because "the incentives of the law are not enough" but rather, as the Kantian scholar Susan Meld Shell has read it, intended as "a moral exercise that aims to cultivate our capacity and will to virtue."[35]

Habermas's doubts are more radical than the "moral hesitation" Kant wanted to overcome in his work on religion.[36] [Pure] practical reason, according to Habermas, cannot respond to the pathologies of the modern individualistic and consumer-oriented global culture "armed solely with the insights of a theory of justice" (*BNR*, 211); as a consequence, "today the question [of the need for religion] is posed from the perspective of a threat to the normative content of modernity as it arose in the West" (238). A modern age that saw itself as advancing in "self-consciousness" "self-determination," and "self-realization," as characterized by Hegel, says Habermas, was "also a result of secularization, and thus of the liberation from the constraints of politically powerful religions" (238). But today it has to face different challenges: in addition to "the reactionary longing for a fundamentalist counter-modernity" (from which some of the contemporary religions cannot be excluded), there are also internal

challenges that come "from within the uncontrolled process of modernization itself" (238). So, he asks: "why and in what sense can religious
traditions claim to be not 'superfluous' even for an agnostic, and hence
non-apologetic, philosophy of religion" (212)? But then, in turn, we may
ask, in what ways? And how so, if religions themselves are undergoing
these days a serious crisis of self-identity, and belong, as political actors,
to the same general troubled cultural horizon?

There seems to be some ambiguity between two possible interpretations of the inclusion of religion in the debate on moral motivation: on
the one hand, Habermas wants to retain a conception of the "moral will"
in a way that sounds at times too close to the idea of a "pure" practical
reason (as the improbable assumption that maintains that it is possible
to act for the sake of reasons *alone*) as Kant demanded. In the words of
Susan Meld Shell, "with Kant's discovery of the concept of autonomy
comes an insistence on the executive power of (human) reason – a power
that he [Kant] had previously specifically denied: reason now combines
legislation and execution in a single act."[37] While, on the other hand,
Habermas's recent defense of the need to "supplement" the executive
power of reason by an appeal to religion could lead in the opposite
direction of a diminished or not so "pure" understanding of the rational
moral will. This is the case not only because actually existing religions
would not be likely to accept the sober characterization of "rational religions" as proposed by Habermas (and consequently, affective motives
and other "ends" may also come into play – if we accept an interpretation of religious practices consistent with the sociological evidence), but
also because Habermas could be moving *away* from Kant's ascetic and
critical understanding of religion, including in his program authors from
very different (and even antagonistic) philosophical traditions, such as
Schleiermacher and Kierkegaard (discussed by Habermas in the same
essay on the philosophy of religion).

The exact implications of such inclusions are not altogether clear, but
we may ask, nevertheless: how can a strong Kantian conception of moral
autonomy – about which Habermas is very emphatic in many places –
be retained while *at the same time* making room for Schleiermacher's
anti-Kantian "alternative to the Enlightenment" (*BNR*, 233), or for his
conservative and uncritical defense of religious institutions? How can
a secular moral subject accept the "abdication of reason" (before God)
proposed by Kierkegaard (237)? Is this a recognition of the "limits of
reason"? Or is it moving away from a philosophy of religion (respectful
of the boundaries between faith and knowledge) to the kind of "religious
philosophy" against which, as Habermas also reminds us, Kant's philosophy of religion could be seen as a warning (247)?

Habermas explains this transition from the Kantian philosophy of religion to other authors and philosophical traditions in terms of the reception of Kant's thought, although, of course, this would only open the debate in new directions with no clear conclusion in sight. However, what seems to be one of the main motivations for his recent interest in religion can be found in a motif that runs through the whole discussion: what he calls the "protest against contingency" underlying Kant's defense of Christianity. According to Habermas, it is "the absence of a guarantee of happiness for those who act rightly" – not even in the form of an improvement of the human condition, if not as an individual reward – that led Kant to find (in religion) a supplement for this lack: "Kant supplements moral thought [. . .] to reinforce its confidence in itself and to preserve it from defeatism" (247).

To Habermas, this intuition justifies finding some space for religion in his thought as implying a universalistic moral perspective somehow compatible with the standpoint of his normative political theory. According to his reading of Kant's philosophy of religion, this insight can be taken as a model of what can be learned from actual religious communities and practices, and not only from religion as an abstract ideal. Finally, following a different line of argumentation, religion finds a place in his recent project of a new genealogy of philosophy (in the Hegelian vein of a history of reason) because he regards now the history of moral insights from religious origin and those of a secular morality as parallel (and interconnected) developments. If the first (Kantian) formula suggests forms of cooperation (between secular and religious publics) in philosophy and the civil society of democratic pluralistic states, the second one (from nineteenth-century hermeneutic and existential philosophers), proposes a politically conservative defense of religion that cannot be easily harmonized with the liberal tenor of his theory of justice.

However, Habermas does not want to offer at this point definitive conclusions on this issue. In his words:

> [. . .] whether a different perspective on the genealogy of reason can enable postmetaphysical thinking to deal with the problem specified by Kant – or even lead us to a better understanding in the diagnosis of the breakdown of solidarity – is a question which I deliberately left open. (*AWM*, 69)

Consequently, the problems we have discussed are mostly questions to Habermas about the extent of his changed perspective in his philosophical program.

As a final observation, I want to refer briefly to what seems to be Habermas's main argument so far for the defense of a convergence between the rational universalistic moral perspective of his normative political theory and the moral attitude of the major (rationalized) modern religions; that is, the expected radical transformation of their self-understanding as a consequence of a newly acquired awareness of their shared past. There are only scant observations and suggestions on this issue, rather than a fully developed argument, at this stage of Habermas's project; but, in any case, it would seem that the idea of a common origin of philosophical thought and monotheistic religions (in a remote evolutionary phase) could not be conclusive. To begin with, because the level of generality of those long-term historical processes will make nearly impossible to derive practical consequences from them, and also because philosophical and religious thought, even if they belong to the same historical tradition (and share its cognitive advances) could still be seen as separate "branches" of a common tree, in conflict with one another as existential orientations (directed toward extramundane salvation versus worldly realization, and so on), or confronted as rival moral theories. In other words, a genetic explanation could not prevent conflicts of interpretation or clashes between incompatible beliefs. Thus, we may ask: if the motivational potentials of religious convictions are not to be understood exclusively as existential orientations, as Habermas maintains, in what ways could the recourse to a shared historical tradition serve as a basis for justification (of their validity) to non-believers? Since the sources of justification of religious beliefs are not historical in any case, but rest on arguments of authority (revelation as sanctioned by ecclesiastical authorities), and, from the secular side, religious faith does not belong to the language game of argumentation, the form of rational justification of truth claims available to modern philosophy.

Therefore, we will have to wait for a more detailed explanation of the ways in which Habermas proposes to recover the ethical and moral motifs "buried" in religious traditions from the perspective of a non-apologetic secular philosophy, because, as I have tried to examine in this paper, we cannot assume that religious doctrines and practices have not been contaminated by the same processes of fragmentation and loss of meaning experienced by modern culture as whole. There is no distinct body of religious beliefs and practices isolated from the life of society and its interests that we could invoke as an indisputable source of moral insights. It is not the case, either, that convictions that are not based on religious doctrine are less strong or important for those who hold them than those of religious subjects, as, for example, on issues of distributive justice, equal rights, gender and sexuality, reproductive medicine, animal rights, and so on; nor is it the case that secular or non-religious convictions do not advance claims that are not negotiable. The assumed fallible nature of secular knowledge is only hypothetical; that is, a person may preserve her moral identity and maxims of conduct throughout her entire life, even if, at the same time, she recognizes that there are no absolute certainties to guide her existential and moral choices. Thus, Habermas's refusal to accept a "defeat" of reason can be read as a utopian longing that seeks to recover its lost unity, or taken as an insight into the present state of our human condition, assuming the risks of contingency and individual autonomy, without renouncing the hope for justice.

3

Is the Postsecular a Return to Political Theology?[1]

María Pía Lara

There is no doubt that religion has become a huge concern for those interested in political theory and philosophy. This radical shift in reconsidering the relationship between politics and religion might be due to two major contributions in the academic world: the publication of Charles Taylor's *A Secular Age*,[2] and Habermas's assertion that we must learn to live in a postsecular world (*DS, AWM*). These works have triggered a revision of theories about secularization, about the prevalence of religion in the life of modern communities (peripheral and mainstream), and about the need to thematize the possible or desirable dependence of politics on religion.

If all of these issues are in need of critical reviewing, it is because so much energy has been invested lately in developing a way to bring back the historical connection of religion to politics. However, in my view, efforts also ought to be directed at carefully examining the struggles among different theorists, which entail focusing on how these arguments about religious contents played a major role in politics, and on how this role has been transformed or preserved in Western political theories. By examining how political theorists explain the dependence of politics on religion, we will see that this "dependence" thesis has been almost taken for granted.[3] Furthermore, all these efforts at unveiling the religious sources of political conceptual building are less interested in showing the other side of the coin, namely, that there were fundamental contributions to politics that had little or nothing to do with religion. I propose to reconsider this position not in order to return to more traditional views of secularization, which regard the Western secular tradition of political conceptual coinage as a clear-cut achievement in "the legitimacy of the modern age."[4] Rather, what I wish to highlight instead is that our reflection on differences in translation, and in thinking about how some concept was first coined, can help us draw a more nuanced theoretical approach toward the efforts at translations and innovation (as disclosure) in political conceptual history. This perspective could help us focus on how these innovations helped redesign the territory of politics more progressively, involving inclusionary theories of democracy. These were accomplishments of theorists who understood politics as doing something altogether different from merely following the similarities of both disciplines with regard to finding a common link between their structural basis. Part of those structural differences between them came to light due precisely to how these theorists, who were concerned with secularization, highlighted the historical struggles of the meaning of secularization, and of how the historical process of the emergence of politics led to new designs of conceptual building.

Thus, I wish to introduce this other side of the critical examination of conceptual history. But before doing so, I must first say a few words about my main position for this essay. First, as you can see from the previous paragraph, I will not be debating Habermas's proposal, which claims that we should allow religious contents to find their proper translations in public political debate.[5] Habermas's theory in this regard is dealing with the problem of how to modify our views of deliberation in the public sphere. I think that the issue has been widely discussed, and it has raised some serious objections, as well as needing clarification by the most well-known Habermasian critical thinkers.[6]

My concern, however, is to explain the method I will be using, which is based on what Reinhart Koselleck has called *Begriffsgeschichte*, which he defines as a method that "derive[s] from the sphere of a philosophical history of terminology, historical philology, semasiology, and onomatology."[7] What is unique and illuminating about this method lies in the fact that it deals with concepts that are founded in "politico-social systems that are far more complex than would be indicated by treating them simply as linguistic communities organized around key specific concepts."[8] This method also highlights the feedback between coining concepts and their influence in social practices. Since the debate on secularization first developed among philosophers of history, their work ought to be the proper object of focus in the debate about how to understand *Begriffsgeschichte*. Indeed, the work of thinkers such as Koselleck, Karl Löwith, Hans Blumenberg, and even Hannah Arendt and Jürgen Habermas, were all focused on how the philosophy of history relates to political frameworks. Precisely because the philosophy of history became the discipline that inherited the questions concerning the translation of religious contents into the domain of politics, the question has since its inception involved further questions of secularization. This issue was first raised in relation to the classical thesis developed by Carl Schmitt, who claimed that "all significant concepts of the modern doctrine of the state are secularized theological concepts."[9] Both Löwith and Koselleck agreed in their conceptualization that eschatology had been translated into political concepts. Blumenberg reacted against Löwith's thesis by claiming that the modern age could not be seen as a secularized form with eschatological contents. I will also include in this chapter the work of Hannah Arendt, even though she is not a philosopher of history, since she gave a critical account of how the Western tradition of politics was inextricably connected to Greek philosophy and Western religious traditions. Finally, Habermas will be the last author who is not a philosopher of history,[10] but whose work will help me illuminate how specific categories of deliberative democracy can be considered as politically disclosive ones.

Defining Disclosure

I wish to argue that the most innovative ways of creating political concepts owe little or nothing to religious content. A perfect example of this kind of politically disclosive category is Kant's introduction of the concept of publicity.[11] Kant saw this concept as a basic feature of "sociability" – the disclosive political dimension of communicability – and as an exercise of public freedom because it entailed new definitions of power and action. It was innovative in the sense that it enabled political actors to think of politics not only as being defined through the tasks of the administration of the state (where power was understood as domination, and the ruler established his rule through his hierarchical position as the embodiment of the state), but in actual political interactions among citizens. This Kantian legacy was considered central to Hannah Arendt's work on conceptual coinage as we will see throughout the essay. It was precisely because Kant elaborated his principle of "publicity" initially in the first Appendix to his essay on *Perpetual Peace* – which led him to disclose the territory of political interactions among actors – that Habermas followed Arendt's initiative with his intention to develop further the democratic horizons of communication and action.[12] Both efforts by Arendt and Habermas gave us a completely different view of the political semantics of concepts such as authority and legitimacy in political action, as we will see in the last part of this chapter. In considering how Habermas took some of the key features of Arendt's conception of action (as communicative action), and of power (as enabling citizens to participate politically through acting in concert), we will see that the meaning of disclosure entails configuring a new spatial scenario. Disclosure means here that seeing is also making. Thus, disclosure entails establishing a key relationship between coining a new concept and opening up a new space of political interaction among actors.[13] In the final section of the chapter, we will be able to see how Habermas's theory of the public sphere was intended as an alternative account to the very critical one developed by Koselleck, who claimed in *Critique and Crisis*[14] that "the Enlightenment itself became Utopian and even hypocritical – it saw itself excluded from political-power sharing. The structure of Absolutism, which was rooted in the dichotomy between sovereign and subject, between public policy and private morality, prevented the Enlightenment and the emancipation movement produced by it from seeing itself as a political phenomenon".[15] Habermas's efforts at developing *further* the categories of public deliberation, public opinion, communicative action, and the power of citizens, were intended as a stark refutation of Koselleck's negative diagnosis about modernity and his theory of the period of the Enlightenment as losing its political dimension because of the emergence of an apolitical subject, the civil society.[16] Although Arendt and Habermas give us completely different views of the meaning of concepts such as authority and legitimacy, nevertheless, as I will show later, Habermas's conceptions of action and power, inasmuch as they reflect Arendtian commitments, demonstrate that disclosure in the political realm entails the configuration of a new space of political interaction among actors.[17] In this, Habermas's theory of the public sphere offers an alternative to Koselleck's, that "[t]he structure of Absolutism . . . prevented the Enlightenment and the emancipation movement produced by it from seeing itself as a political phenomenon."[18] Habermas's reconstruction of the emergence of the public sphere was meant to construct a normative category of the public sphere by engaging in its empirical reconstruction to show the new field of agency disclosed through such a category.[19]

Theorizing the Secular as Translation or Creation?

In his book *Meaning in History*, Löwith claims that the so-called modern era was a process of an eschatological translation of religious concepts into politics.[20] Löwith's theory presupposes that translations are done through analogies between religion and politics. Nevertheless, Löwith is critical of the view of eschatology translated into philosophy of history. According to him, those theories of the secular substituted theology with the discipline of "philosophy of history and its quest for a meaning due to the history of salvation."[21] Löwith claimed that, contrary to these

eschatological efforts, the Greeks were more moderate in their speculations, and understood history as "the eternal recurrence of sunrise and
sunset, of summer and winter, of generation and corruption."[22] Thus,
even if he is against the model of secularization as translation, he thinks
that the ancient view of history formulated by the Greeks as *historein*
was finally lost in modernity.

Hans Blumenberg claimed in *The Legitimacy of the Modern Age*,[23]
on the other hand, that not everything was eschatological translation but
that there was a reoccupation of the territory of religion by politics. The
reoccupation theory is an immanent theory about changes in conceptual
coinage due to historical failures to address ancient metaphysical and
religious questions. Thus, the difference, according to Blumenberg, was
due to the fact that the moderns found new answers to old problems
and achieved a different perspective with regard to the practices of social
actors. Briefly put, modernity is a second overcoming of Gnosticism
because medieval thinkers failed to meet the challenge of finding an
answer to the problem of evil in the world. According to Blumenberg,
Marcion, who was the greatest Gnostic thinker of the second century,
tried to give an answer to the problem by devaluing the world and
locating the good outside of it. This dualism of two worlds entailed a
big problem for Christianity, for it questioned the unity of God and
the world. It was Augustine who finally displaced Marcion's dualism
by locating evil in humankind. However, the cost of this solution led
to another challenge. Augustine's revalorization of God's creation led to
conceiving of human guilt as a mode of resignation instead of trying to
find a way out of this immobility through action. Thus, the heritage of
the Gnostics, according to Blumenberg, was only "translated"[24] until
the medieval synthesis began to unravel. This was achieved through the
intervention of William of Ockham, who questioned this synthesis by
engaging in a radical doubt about the intelligibility of the cosmos. For
those nominalists who believed in the unlimited will of God, this task
was impossible. Philosophers could not give a rational account of evil,
irrationality, and chaos.[25] If God was first conceived as responsible for
all evil, the transformation that Blumenberg highlights places evil within
human responsibility.[26]

Blumenberg argues that we need to focus on how the reoccupation
of the territory left void by religion was filled by politics in modernity.
Blumenberg claims that modernity was not a radical break with the past,
but a better resolution of various scholastic problems. In proposing to
look at how modernity found its legitimacy, he is also trying to refute
Löwith's perspective about history as cyclical. Blumenberg also acknowledges that there was a break with the past because of the emergence of
new answers to old questions. It is in trying to ground this last statement

that his theory of the reoccupation assumes that modernity is legitimate because it entailed "a second overcoming of Gnosticism."[27]

So, the complex story told by Blumenberg assumes that while humans lost their religious role in the universe, they started trying to master and control the world in which they had to live. This is the position that Blumenberg calls self-assertion.[28] The full break of the process of self-assertion only came with Immanuel Kant's critical philosophy,[29] which "concentrated all directed, purposeful processes in man's rational action."[30] For Blumenberg, the processes of modernity that we have called "secular" are not the products of gaps between epochs, or a repetition of Christian themes, but an immanent process in which changes occurred when humans were able to distance themselves from previous ways of posing things. The concept of worldliness (*Verweltlichung*) was a functional category that entered the domain of politics, where previously there had been only theological-religious understanding. With the category of worldliness as the space of the reoccupation, we find ourselves entering into new semantic territory.

Blumenberg has a second model that is also related to his main concern with fear, which is found in *The Work on Myth*.[31] According to Blumenberg, myths are the vehicles in which we humans find ways to cope with fear and to kill time. They are stories about what is meaningful to human lives (life, death, the afterlife, men, women, harmony, order, obedience, communities, traditions, etc.). Myths do not explain anything, and they do not make intelligible what is unintelligible; rather, their function is to orient and to console humans. They are a necessary and ineliminable activity of human life. According to Blumenberg, we have to cope with the "absolutism of reality" (*Absolutismus der Wirklichkeit*),[32] the unknown or half-known exterior.

Religious texts – though not all religious myths and stories – are not parts of these narratives since they belong to dogmatic views of how things should be told.[33] So, for Blumenberg, while monotheistic religions depend on the truth of the book, myth appears in the realm of polytheism. Myths have a rational function. This function is not opposed to logos but complementary. In *The Legitimacy of the Modern Age*, Blumenberg argued that there was a new concept of legitimacy achieved in the immanent process of the dynamic of posing and answering questions. In the new theoretical model based on myth, however, Blumenberg claims that our fears are permanent and that we need both mythos and logos. They are not opposed. They complement each other, which is why myth-making is a perspective that stimulates tolerance and plurality as opposed to dogmatism and prejudices. Myths can evolve in the sense that they are rewritten, recreated, but they are also radically *historical*.

Myths are not simply stories; they are also narratives that provide meaning by making this meaning significant (*Bedeutsamkeit*). The work on myth is propelled by the relationship between narrators and receivers of those narratives. Blumenberg argues that "this work presupposes familiarity with what it is done to, not only in those who perform it, but also in those who have to take it in, receptively. It always presupposes a public that is able to respond to the mechanism of reception."[34] Chiara Bottici has called this model an "interrelational model," and it can also be argued that its logic obeys a theory of reception or of spectatorship that functions in a dialogical way.

We have seen how Löwith's model of translation presupposed that the religious views were taken by modern concepts. Löwith views the modern philosophy of history as trying to perform the function of prophets and priests.[35] He radically rejects this modern process of secularization, but his views fortify the main argument expressed in Carl Schmitt's famous dictum of his political theology.

In trying to refute Löwith's thesis, Blumenberg elaborated a complicated story about the process of translation in modernity. For him, "secularization" or *Verweltlichung* cannot be understood in terms of the process of rationalization of religion by an exogenous agency. Rather, it is an immanent historical process in which religion played a major role. He refuted Schmitt and Löwith by using a distinction between the idea of *substantial continuation* of theological contents of thought in modernity and his idea of the *functional reoccupation* of these contents by the latter. His reoccupation (*Umbesetzung*) theory is laid down not by establishing an identity of content between theology and politics, but as the way our consciousness articulates its functions. He is not against eschatology. Rather, he thinks eschatology is only one partial account of what happened. In his theory there are continuities with late medieval thinking and discontinuities. A major accomplishment described in this view is that in this historically immanent process, Blumenberg interprets human responsibility as a gate to think about political action. He also coins the concept of legitimacy to establish what is new about modernity. Finally, his conception of self-assertion is key in considering that humans began to see themselves as agents of change.

His second theory in the work on myth can be taken as a contribution toward understanding how stories can become significant for humans and how they help us cope with deep human concerns. Blumenberg poses a condition for using religious meanings or myths in this theory. Religious myths can and have been used when they are not considered parts of an original single book or a monotheistic account.[36] This is the reason why poets have not taken monotheistic myths into their creative material.[37] What is important for my purposes about this theory is that Blumenberg makes clear how myth can be used for politics.[38] The function of myth could be a useful device because of the significance that it takes in working through the establishing of meaningful features of the identity of people, of classes, and of groups who aim at the emancipation of humankind.

Koselleck, on the other hand, argues that the concepts coined during the period of the Enlightenment – like Kant's concept of publicity and its relation to the public sphere – destroyed the notion of politics and power derived from the absolutist state (and the religious connection between political power and sovereignty). Koselleck thinks that this was due to a perverse connection between critique and the intervention of morality as a frame to politics. According to him, this process of enlightened critique led to a crisis whose outcome was the most relevant transformation of the secular. Like Löwith before him, he thinks that the translation of eschatology into secular theories about progress made philosophy of history the best candidate to replace religion.[39] Likewise, in a similar attempt to the one offered by Blumenberg in *The Legitimation of the Modern Age*, he focuses on the novelties of modernity and attributes to it extraordinary transformations that led to certain new practices struggling against the state and against the autonomy of politics. However, if Blumenberg saw self-assertion as a positive way in which humans gained responsibility, Koselleck interpreted these new attitudes as provoking an intervention from morality that is hypocritical because it regards itself as non-political. He traces the origins of the secular to this battle against religion by political theorists. Hobbes thought that the subordination of ethics to politics was pointless when societies had to face the political alternative of peace and war. Thus, he proceeded to expel the role of "conscience" from the realm of the state. As a result, his views considered the private and the public to be separate spheres.[40]

It was Locke who first coined "the law of opinion" as a third type of law, differentiating it from the realms of divine and legal law.[41] If citizens lacked executive power, they still had the power to perform their moral judgments, albeit in secrecy.[42] The moral character that Hobbes extracted from politics (the state) was brought back by Locke, who broadened it in two ways. On the one hand, the citizens had a morality whose obligatory character was no longer invested in individuals as such, but in society, as "a structure" taking shape in "clubs" and other forms of association.[43] On the other hand, bourgeois ethics, which Koselleck interprets as secret and tacit, moved back into the public domain. What Locke had unleashed was the decisive challenge to the powers of the absolutist state. Koselleck goes back to analyze how in the public sphere citizens and the bourgeois intelligentsia constituted themselves as a new and novel social stratum. They possessed the indirect power to defeat the autonomy of politics. Koselleck charges the secret Masonic lodges, the literati, the illuminati, and the bourgeois society as being responsible for this outcome.[44] Koselleck views "the Republic of letters" as the scenario in which the category of criticism[45] first appeared as a consequence of the fact that collective consciousness had turned these type of exercises into a common task (being the judges of all). What began as the art of judging, a fundamentally non-political criticism, turned out to be a very politically charged task. It was Bayle who turned criticism into an essential function of reason. Critique got its strongest weight in society when it was instituted as the device that allowed its function to be separated from those performed by religion (through revelation). Koselleck argues that criticism gave way to hypocrisy because it was used as a disguised political weapon against power.[46] The bourgeois intellectuals understood power only in terms of its abuse. Enlightenment practices pushed criticism to its utmost limits: the critic saw himself as the king of kings,[47] leading him to identify progress with revolution. From then on, the competing claims between the authority of the state and that of society gave way to varied prognostications of revolutions to come. These theories acquired legitimacy because they were mostly developed as theories of the philosophy of history.[48] With the discipline of the philosophy of history, which now replaced all religious theories about salvation and redemption, the indirect guidance of political events by the internal moral realm expressed in theories would be determined by the course of history.[49] And it is this crisis that would lead in the end to the horrible catastrophes that have occurred from the eighteenth-century revolutions to the atrocities of the present.

Koselleck and Löwith had very negative views about secularization because they encouraged philosophy of history to function as a guide to action. Koselleck developed his criticism against the view of power promoted by a new relationship between morality and politics. He claims that the order of the political was marred by the destruction of the absolutist state. Thus, for him, the categories of publicity (Kant), the law of citizens (public opinion), the intervention of critique by the intellectuals and literati – they all promoted changes and began by building up theories that became the expressions of utopias. They led, ultimately, to inspire actual revolutions, and finally to a long crisis. It is not difficult to see that Koselleck's views are closer to Schmitt's conceptions of sovereignty and power. His views about the public sphere were aimed at trying to show how the activities that were supposedly purely moral were in fact political. He claimed they were hypocritical because these new agents did not have a good opinion of political power, and they saw themselves as the legitimate judges of all.

Koselleck raises his strongest criticism against viewing philosophies of history as providing a prognosis, utopian programs, which ultimately

have been destructive in view of the outcomes of revolutions in the twentieth century. The danger in providing theories about the good society
with closed, finalist endings, is that they become authoritarian. They are
also redemptive, in the religious sense.[50]

Politics as Disclosure

In "What Is Authority?" and in her two main essays about secularization, which are included in her book *On Revolution*,[51] Arendt forcefully
defends the autonomy of politics, distinguishing, however, her position
from the Western tradition. Her analysis describes how Greek philosophy and Christian religion were fused. The difference between this
Arendtian version and Blumenberg's own version of the fusion of the
traditions of Greek and medieval thought is that for Arendt the outcome
was problematic. She questions the notion of authority because this category was used as the result of the fusion between Platonic ideas about
truth and power and the way Christians borrowed them for their own
political purposes. The first step Arendt takes is to claim that authority
was lost in modernity and that there is no need to recover it. Her second
step is to show how Plato was the original designer of the structural
connection between religion and politics. He articulated this connection
by establishing a link between politics and a transcendental frame. This
legacy was taken by Christianity because authority connected politics as
truth with transcendence as divine power. It is this legacy in the Western
tradition that has led modernity into crisis. Arendt was so worried about
the historical effects of the fusion between philosophy, religion, and tradition, that she "propose[s] to reconsider what authority was historically
and the sources of its strength and meaning."[52]

Her strategy was to see how the experiences of the Greeks' political
practices were not taken into account by Plato when he first defined
authority through philosophical means and not in relation to politics.
Plato defined authority not in terms of persuasion or violence, but
transcendentally, grounded in reason and truth. Arendt claimed that if
authority is what makes people obey, Plato used this notion as a way to
establish the legitimacy of reason. Plato had to connect validity to transcendence so as to mitigate violence. Arendt argues that it was Plato's
definition of politics as truth that was later taken by the Christians. This
was how the Western tradition connected authority to religion and, later
on, through the Romans, with the handling of tradition through foundation. This is also the explanation of why the link between politics and
religion became inextricable.

According to Arendt, Plato first approached the concept of authority in his *Republic*, where he thought that the philosopher king should rule with the tools of reason. Plato wanted the philosopher to rule but this was motivated not by his interest in the *polis* but for the sake of philosophy. Plato then thought that truth worked more effectively than coercion or persuasion, but his problem lay in how truth could compel non-philosophers. So, in the end, he was forced to establish the "tyranny of reason" through the device of transcendence. Arendt claimed that Plato "solved [the dilemma of obedience] through the concluding myth of rewards and punishments in the hereafter."[53] For Arendt, it was clear that Plato did not believe in them; he just wanted to make sure that the rest of the citizens did. Plato had to legitimize coercion as a principle of truth, so he drew the connection of transcendence with the models of existing hierarchical relationships, such as the shepherd and his sheep, or the helmsman of a ship and the passengers. This specific connection of an asymmetrical position was what made his conception of authority an authoritarian one.[54] Since these examples were taken from the private life, Arendt claimed, the asymmetry between one and the other was translated to the political position of the ruler and the ruled. Plato used those examples, however, because he wanted to make sure that it was the relationship itself that was the compelling motive for obedience. Hence, the ideas are the truth of the world and they transcend the sphere of the human. Therefore, the connection between truth and transcendence became the definitive solution as they were fused together through the notion of authority. Since ideas become the standards of measures beyond this world, the essential character of authoritarian government legitimates the exercise of power beyond the sphere of power, that is, by using the device of transcendence instead of immanence. Plato discovered that the rewards and punishments granted by obedience worked in a much better way than actual violence, but in establishing the connection of power to transcendence, he ended up by fusing authority (*Herrschaft*) with the sacred (*das Heil*). The semantic identity of domination and authority became fused in the German notion of *Gewalt*. It was due to the usefulness of this fusion that Christianity adopted the concept of authority, which by then was not only a fundamental part of the religious realm but also a necessary device for the justification of political hierarchical power. Arendt believed that it was precisely this historical development that prevented modern politics from being able to provide a different concept of authority.

Arendt claimed that the notion of authority became central to philosophers because it implied the transcendental connection to a hierarchical form of government. It was also the political solution that translated divine power into the rule of one. Therefore, Arendt claimed, modern politics should not be concerned with rescuing a concept of authority because such a theoretical device belongs to the Western perspective we have inherited. Arendt claimed that ideas had "nothing to do with political experience, and the problem of action." Rather, they pertain to the experience of the philosopher in his task of exercising contemplation. Arendt claimed that Plato used the metaphor of seeing instead of doing, and had constructed the political with a philosopher's notion of epistemic truth: "as [if] the interest of the philosopher and the interest of man *qua* man coincide; both demand that human affairs, the result of speech and action, must not acquire a dignity of their own but be subjected to the domination of something outside their realm."[55]

Arendt had a different view about how the Romans conceptualized authority. The Romans thought of authority as a foundation, as an augmentation. Thus, their conception of authority was linked to the founding of the city of Rome and in how the Romans understood the act of augmentation through the religious action of building up a community (*religare*). The identity between Roman politics and Roman religion (polytheism) is key in Arendt's recovery because she wants to highlight that the Romans took the most illuminating myths from the Greeks (the *Iliad*), and translated them into their own narrative, giving them a full significance in their collective recollection of the founding of Rome (Virgil). Finally, Arendt says, authority for the Romans lay in the Senate, while power was embodied by the people.

If Arendt praised the Romans for their polytheism, she was not hostile to religion as such. Religion and narrations could have a place in her theory, albeit not through translations. Indeed, stories played a major role in Arendt's views of politics. She understood that stories have a powerful effect in the identity of collective groups such as those from the Hebrews and the Romans. Arendt, however, had a very special connection to one Christian figure – Jesus – who she took as a source of powerful semantic meanings. She made use of his actions to disclose with them specific politically disclosive *images*. In seeing the previously unseen dimension of the image, we also understand the significance displayed by the symbols of those actions in the field of politics. Thus, Arendt took Jesus' actions of forgiveness and promise to construct and fully disclose those actions as *images*. These images opened up the new scenario for politics through seeing the previously unseen territory of political action. Both actions, to forgive and to promise, are seminal in political narratives because those actions articulate the connection between actions as contingent and the possibility of creating new beginnings. The significance of Jesus' actions crystallizes in images that disclose their potentialities only after they are interpreted as political actions. The space of freedom and contingency now appeared before humans as an effort of making mutual promises (mutuality). Their mutual promises constitute a political contract among them, though it need not be legitimized by God but by each other. Humans are also prone to error; hence the need for forgiveness. No one has full control of the outcome of their actions. Since error is an essential part of human freedom, and contingency a constitutive dimension of action, promise and forgiveness are taken as belonging to the realm of politics.

Arendt went further in her exploration of politics when she connected her ideas of freedom and action to a new, radically modern concept of power, with this new version of power having to do with freedom and contingency. In her texts *On Revolution* – "Foundation I" and "Foundation II"[56] – Arendt goes back once more to the Romans. Here she attempts to give a positive account of the notion of revolution (in contrast to the negative one first given by Koselleck), and by doing so searches for a way out of the theological legacy of a sovereign will, the hierarchical conception of the notion of rule; and for a way to purify politics from violence and non-political phenomena. In this search, she finally connects action to a modern, immanent conception of freedom. With this interconnection, she planned to disclose the nature of action as possessing a double feature: as contingency and as the powerful and innovative way in which humans could change things. It is in these essays about foundation and revolution that she chooses to leave behind the perplexities and "vicious circles" of the constituent power and constituted powers (Sieyés), the notions of the creation and the creator (political theology), and the differentiation between the moments of extraordinary politics from ordinary (Schmitt). At the bottom of this creative process was not only Arendt's concern with a conception of sovereignty and of hierarchical power, there was also her larger quest to ground beginnings and actions immanently. The two main categories that she would use would be freedom and power.

Both essays show how she regarded power as something collective, as emerging from within an immanent process of acting in concert. Her historical example, the American Founding Fathers, was not a mythical description of gods or of a past tradition. Rather, her description is the historical interpretation of how these men were capable of establishing a new country inspired by and through the writing of a constitution and in acting in concert. Power could be the opposite of religious power because the Founding Fathers were inspired by the political foundation of Rome, albeit with one basic difference: "the constitution that derived its general authority [came] from the subordinate authorities" (authorized bodies such as districts, counties, townships, etc.). Contrary to earlier notions of political power relating it to the sovereign God, Arendt interpreted her historical example as a singular political experiment. The Founding Fathers were never tempted to derive law and power from the same origin. The seat of power to them was the people, but the source of law was to become "the Constitution, a written document, an endurable objective thing, which, to be sure, one could approach from many different angles and upon which one could impose many different interpretations, which one could change and amend in accordance with circumstances, but which nevertheless was never a subjective state of mind, like the will."[57]

Thus, Arendt's notion of power is the space where mutual promises take place.[58] The power resides in the people. The task of politics was not to justify the power of one against the others, but rather to enable a way to generate, conceptually speaking, a specific kind of power, one that could be shared by all and be specific only to political action. This notion of power is disclosive because it makes it possible to envision human interactions within a space that was not seen as such before. This space appears as soon as power is shared by agents who have established a collective goal to pursue. This is why we can say that power is like a "miracle" because it enables people to act in concert. The sharing of power with others comes through the possibility of seeing that we can change things if we act together. Power and immanence can then become entangled through these actions. Power is also decentered into different functions or actions. Power, too, can be the object of checks and balances. Power here is not reduced to domination or the administration of the state, but it bears the imprint of a new kind of legitimacy.

Arendt finally is able to give us the proper conceptual frame of politics by proposing the concept of worldliness as its reference. This concept means that we do not need transcendence for politics. Immanence is the proper frame because politics is defined by the power of collective actions, by our capacity to initiate new actions and to create possibilities to transform the *world we live in*. Politics means constructing the world with others. To put it bluntly: politics became an autonomous source of action only when those who were interested in ideas about power and government transformed their questions about authority into a new set of demands about the kinds of actions that legitimate a new beginning. This change was not based on any external justifying authority but on achieving legitimacy through the shared exercise of power and action. This was a historical transformation that turned from an initial hierarchical notion of power (represented by divine power) toward the task of building up an innerworldly government in the sharing of power among equals. Arendt understood that the political quality of power lies in its being self-generating. It will never derive from anything else but itself.

Arendt missed, however, one important element of the political that relates to power and conflict: justice. In her views there are no considerations about how equality among citizens first arises. She thought of citizens deliberating but never defined the kinds of things that they should be deliberating about. It is clear that Arendt was motivated to leave behind what she thought to be the extra-political notion of justice because it pertained to the sphere of morality (and the social). This is the reason why she invests so much time in explaining why the Americans were the only ones to have solved the problem of the social, and in how their past legacy allowed them to qualify as equals despite the obvious problem of the existence of slavery. Her concern for establishing an immanent frame for the political could be one of the reasons why she failed to see that a political notion of justice was needed. Actors can have the chance to question the status quo of their places outside the political order, and they do so precisely because they understand that they are not in the kingdom of heaven, and that on earth, there are things – institutions – that need not be unfair as they are. After all, politics for Arendt is all about constructing a world in common.

Bringing Justice into the Domain of Politics

In this last part, I will focus on Habermas's work, albeit only with reference to his more sociological and political views about secularization and the public sphere. I will also focus on one of his most recent essays on this subject, in which he addresses some of the questions that I have been dealing with in this essay.[59] I think that if we take this political dimension of Habermas's work, we will be able to see how he transformed his empirical understanding of social movements with regard to his elaboration of a political conception of justice as social inclusion.

I have said before that Habermas gave an alternative account of modernity and secularization to the one first given by Koselleck.[60] Habermas took up the challenge of refuting Koselleck's pessimistic and conservative views about the Enlightenment and the public sphere with his book *The Structural Transformation of the Public Sphere*, and in the rest of his work on politics. We can see the similar road taken by both theorists in their explanations of the emergence of the bourgeois public sphere.[61] Habermas's defense, however, was aimed at restoring a positive view about Kant's concept of publicity,[62] and at showing how this disclosure led Kant to coin a category that has become essential to modern politics: the concept of the public use of reason.

Habermas developed a creative historical articulation of the original conception of publicity by framing it in two different steps: the literary public sphere where actors begin by expanding the horizon of the public sphere through their own actions of reading, deliberating, and theorizing about themselves, and the second step, which was the transformation of the political public sphere to which belong deliberations, critique, and public opinion. This political transformation of the public sphere occurs when actors consciously raise their critical claims about general issues. Habermas argued that the public sphere is a collective space that was erected as a political laboratory where people learned to see themselves as exercising new social (literary and dialogical) habits and new political practices (the participatory right to public debate). He envisioned the political qualities of the public sphere because it is there that the flow of information enables citizens to realize what needs to be discussed collectively. Though in its initial conception Habermas left untouched the issue of social exclusions – as feminists critically claimed after his book on the public sphere appeared[63] – in his later revisions, especially in his reply to his critics in *Habermas and the Public Sphere,*[64] and in a much more systematic way in *Between Facts and Norms,*[65] he deals with the question of exclusion, which by now has become a central theme in his work.

When Habermas first focused on the general bourgeois public, he was more interested in documenting the political function of the public sphere as an "organ for the self-articulation of civil society" (*STPS,* 74). The coincidences between his narrative and Koselleck's are striking, although their conclusions are radically different. Wherever we find condemnations of Koselleck's views, we encounter a positive appraisal from Habermas's point of view. Habermas gave a positive definition of public opinion as "a principle opposed to arbitrariness and subject to the laws immanent in a public" (82). Later on, his initial notion of the public sphere as an informal arena underwent a complete process of disclosure. In his deliberative ethics, for example, Habermas often spoke of solidarity as being the other side of justice. This insight can be seen when articulated in the political dimension if we focus on how the public sphere provides the explanation of the interrelationship established between solidarity and hegemony. His concept of solidarity was seen as the valid result of the political process of achieving hegemony and influence through public opinion.[66]

Habermas's conception of the dynamics of the public sphere has evolved through his dialogue with his critics, and he has also developed a more sociological approach to the public sphere versus the constitutional-making with his empirical references.[67] For Habermas, the challenge was to give a better account of the dynamic possibilities of the public sphere as a space of mediation between the state and social actors. It was then that he turned his focus on "new" social movements, which operated within a frame that was immanent rather than socially exclusionary.[68] He detected the mutual influence that politics and publics have on each other. He argued that social movements have two distinctive strategies:

an "offensive" one and a "defensive" one. In the offensive one, "publics" (in the plural) bring issues to an entire society, define ways of approaching problems, propose possible solutions, supply information, and so on. Defensively, these publics also attempt to gain public influence, to generate counter-publics, to consolidate new collective identities, to expand rights, and to reform institutions (*BFN*, 370). However, the main concern of these social movements is in relation to social inclusion and the measures needed to transform institutions and rights of inclusion. This is the reason why I can interpret Habermas's concept of political justice within the dynamic conception of the public sphere as becoming potentially disclosive.

If John Rawls was concerned with defining justice through the traditional device of the social contract, Habermas left this device out of his view precisely because political actors now have the task of redefining justice through their claims for inclusion.[69] Thus, Habermas argues, "a discursive or deliberative model replaces the contract model: the legal community constitutes itself not by way of a social contract but on the basis of a discursively achieved agreement" (*BFN*, 449). The actors have the capacity to identify problems mostly because they are affected by them (365). The participation of counter-publics is fundamental to gaining hegemony through reasons, which generate solidarity.[70] Hegemony is also a product of the immanence of action. Publics are plural and through communication they can become porous to one another. Public opinion is also the result of the successful strategy of deliberating about these problems and of gaining hegemony with their proposed ways of transforming institutions. Thus, Habermas argues that the "boundaries inside the universal public sphere as defined by its reference to the political system remain permeable in principle. The rights to unrestricted inclusion and equality built into liberal public spheres prevent exclusion mechanisms of the Foucauldian type and ground a *potential for self-transformation*" (*BFN*, 374). Therefore, communication and participation are activities that pertain to the political domain because the public sphere is a new space for action and visibility. When processes of social interaction give rise to experiences of injustice, they generate political conflicts. These conflicts are expressed in critical claims among actors until they catalyze into the growth of social movements and generate new subcultures.[71] With their controversial presentation in the media, such publics might reach the larger public and subsequently gain a place on the political agenda. For Habermas, public reason is a pivotal category because our claims must find ways in which the articulation and significance of social needs and demands are expressed as *disclosing* the contents of new ways of envisioning rights of inclusion. As we have seen before, disclosure here means that these rights have been delivered by excluded actors as powerful expressions that begin to unveil previously unseen territories of injustice, exclusion, or domination.[72] However, Habermas's conception of the good society still bears a metaphysical connection to utopian ideals of self-transparency and self-sufficiency. It is this remnant of "utopian ideas" connected to his model of the ideal speech situation that, as Maeve Cooke has argued, became closely linked to notions of redemption associated with the philosophy of history that Koselleck had extensively criticized.[73] In order to get rid of this perspective, which could lead to bad utopianism and finalism, Maeve Cooke has argued that Habermas's theory must acknowledge that one must leave "decisions regarding its material substance to historically situated agents who must respond to specific experiences and exigencies."[74] In my view, however, if we interpret Habermas's more sociological theory of politics, we can see how he attempts to explain the processes of social inclusion vis-à-vis social movements giving these actors full responsibility in the task of disclosing the meaning of justice.

Habermas's recent work also offers his interpretation of Arendt's legacy in his own political theory. He considers that what he described in his theory as the power to mobilize and to influence parliament is inspired by Arendt's notion of power.[75] Its effectiveness is related to how power becomes a source of legitimacy. Recall that Arendt claimed that power is immanent and "no one is really able to possess" it.[76] Habermas further argued that power was "an *authorizing* force expressed in 'jurigenesis'– the creation of legitimate law – and in the founding institutions."[77] By aligning power with law, as Habermas argues, "law joins forces *from the outset* with a communicative power that engenders legitimate law."[78] Morality is filtered through the laws as they express ways that broaden the horizon of inclusion. What Arendt left untouched – namely, the notion of social inclusion as a definition of justice – has been taken up by Habermas in the connection he establishes between lawmaking and this new kind of power connected to the system of rights. Habermas argues that law should become the medium through which communicative power is translated into administrative power. This step will not only stimulate empowerment among actors, as Arendt wanted, but will also frame the empowerment of actors within the framework of statutory authorization. It is this kind of legitimacy that Habermas claims can only be the outcome of a whole process of discursive formation.[79] The subjects of deliberation in the public sphere must find out how their claims of inclusion can reach agreements with what needs to be done as illocutionary obligations. This is a distinctive *political*, self-conscious exercise, which ends up being successful only when the law reflects the outcome of those processes of deliberation as rights of inclusion.

It is here that Habermas solved Koselleck's criticism against civil society. Contrary to Arendt's concern with the concept of sovereignty, he was able to find a definition of it as popular sovereignty. Habermas connected his conception of popular sovereignty with the help of Kant's concept of publicity and with Rousseau's notion of the general will. His conception of rational-will formation was the systematic outcome of this Kantian-Rousseauian theory. The process of deliberating about certain matters and issues related to justice – such as social inclusion – was the result of visualizing how subjects can attain hegemony once their claims are understood by others and are accepted as necessary for transforming social institutions. Habermas took one more step in defining popular sovereignty as a procedural process.[80] He showed that sovereignty could be rescued and translated into *political* terms. His theory – inspired by the work of Julius Fröbel – asserts that there are no immediate relations of identity between the sovereign will and the collective actors. It is in the process of developing public opinion as will formation that "determines when a political will [is] not identical with reason [but] has the presumption of reason on its side" (*BFN*, 475). It is in how the process takes shape that a popular sovereignty is established as its legitimate outcome.

Arendt was not only against sovereignty, as we have seen, but she was also against the authoritarian perspective of politics defined by a notion of epistemic truth. For her, in politics there was no truth, only opinions. Since Habermas was concerned with bringing back a political concept of justice to debates in the public sphere, he had to re-establish the validity of the claims expressed by the actors. When actors can make their claims as rights for inclusion into a larger society, then the contents of the arguments disclose how the results are expressions of the public use of reason. Thus, the concept of public reason is Habermas's solution, inspired by Rawls, to the Arendtian dilemma. This new spatial territory provides a new interrelationship between morality and politics. Habermas's notion of popular sovereignty has another quality to it: sovereignty is not the embodiment of power in a particular person but a subjectless and anonymous process of will formation. If power for Arendt is defined as subjectless, sovereignty for Habermas is also defined as subjectless. As Habermas argues, sovereignty "makes itself felt in the power of the public discourses" (486).

Finally, Habermas understood why Koselleck – like Carl Schmitt – was against civil society as a new emergent collective actor. Even if Habermas accepts Koselleck's views that in modernity society has lost "its politomorphic features" (9), and he observes that this outcome led to a certain degree of "depoliticization," a crucial step was taken by citizens when they turned to the public sphere in order to struggle for their own rights of political participation. This modern process is precisely what changed our historical views about the *meaning* of politics.

Indeed, Habermas clarifies that, in this way, politics "within liberal states [expresses itself in] the substance of sovereign power gradually dissolved in the acid bath of democratic law-making; and legal norms gradually penetrated and decomposed the hard decisionistic core of sovereign discretion" (11). Thus understood, it is the praxis of constitution-making – exercised by the citizens – that "gives their [participation] a political form by means of positive law" (ibid.). As such, civil society is an actor who "now bears the political responsibility for social integration" (ibid.). Therefore, as Habermas concludes, the self-empowerment of citizens "strips the legitimation of political power of its metasocial character, in other words of the reference to the warrant of a transcendent authority operating beyond society" (ibid.).

In the most recent stage of his work, Habermas has been dealing again with problems first posed by Koselleck's critical views. He knows about the dangers of reviving political theology and how political thinkers have used it in their political conceptual coinage to promote a specific view about the *narrow* tasks of politics and the political (17). Nevertheless, in his postsecular position, Habermas seems to be getting away from Arendt's strategy about innovation and disclosure. Habermas claims now that the Enlightenment does not possess enough resources for preserving the normative contents of modernity. This new crisis, he argues, springs from how secular citizens lack the sensibility toward injustice and exclusion. If societies are not completely secularized, and if "secular reason cannot accomplish its task of justifying constitutional principles without getting support from the religious and metaphysical doctrines of the corresponding communities" (19), we need to rethink the place of religion in political conceptual coinage too. This perspective might need one more effort to rethink the frontiers between politics vis-à-vis morality, and ethical value orientations vis-à-vis religion. Does this move mean a return to political theology, or should we aspire to transform "the political" into something new? I am not sure. After all, democratic politics of immanence are only disclosed in a modern age facing problems that no restoration of a presecular past can solve.[81] As Lefort says:

> Should we not conclude that the old transfers from one register to the other were intended to ensure the preservation of a *form* that has since been abolished, that the theological and the political became divorced, that a new experience of the institution of the social began to take shape, that *the religious is reactivated at the weak points of the social*, that its efficacy is no longer symbolic but *imaginary*, and that, ultimately, it is an expression of the unavoidable – and no doubt ontological – difficulty democracy has in reading its own history, as well as of the difficulty political or philosophical thought has in assuming, without making it a travesty, the tragedy of the modern condition?[82]

4

An Engagement with Jürgen Habermas on Postmetaphysical Philosophy, Religion, and Political Dialogue

NICHOLAS WOLTERSTORFF

Among the most prominent themes in the publications of Jürgen Habermas over the past decade is that of the interrelations among post-metaphysical philosophy, religion, and political discourse. The topic of postmetaphysical philosophy goes back a long way in Habermas's writings. What is new is Habermas's preoccupation with the relation of such philosophy to religion, and with the relation of both of these to political discourse. In this chapter I want to engage Habermas on his understanding of these three phenomena and their interrelations.

The first part of this chapter will consist of a summary of Habermas's position on these matters. Since the various components of his thought hang together in an admirable fashion, I think it best, for the most part, not to interrupt my summary with points of critique but to hold off on critique until we have the entire picture before us. Though the summary will be rather extensive, it will still give little sense of the richness of detail in Habermas's discussion.

Habermas holds that a very important contribution to our historical understanding was Karl Jaspers's observation that in the relatively short period between 800 and 200 BCE, independent cognitive revolutions took place that gave rise to the religious and metaphysical worldviews that remain influential to the present. Jaspers called this period the *Axial Age*. Examples of what Jaspers had his eye on are Buddhism, Judaic monotheism, and classical Greek philosophy. Postmetaphysical philosophy, as the term suggests, purports to differ on a fundamental point from the metaphysical worldviews of the Greek philosophers. It is, nonetheless, a descendant of Greek philosophy; and Habermas thinks that to understand the relation between postmetaphysical philosophy and present-day religion, we must keep in mind that both of them had their ultimate origins in that same axial age.

The project of what he calls *postmetaphysical philosophy* is at the center of Habermas's discussion; everything rotates around that project. As we will see in due course, the term "postmetaphysical" is somewhat misleading for identifying the sort of philosophy he has in mind. But since it is the term he himself uses, I will use it as well.

Though the project of postmetaphysical philosophy is the orienting center of Habermas's discussion, I think it best to approach what he has to say about that project by first looking briefly at what he says about religion.

Religion and the Thesis of Secularization

Habermas observes that it was common practice in twentieth-century sociology to think of religion in purely functional terms. Religion was commonly said to serve the function of coping with contingencies of various sorts; that's why it exists. And the common wisdom was that a consequence of modernization is that we now have other and better ways of coping with the relevant contingencies than the ways that religion provided. Hence the once-popular secularization thesis: the modernizing of a society causes the decline, and eventually the disappearance, of religion in that society. Habermas questions this functional understanding of religion; that leads him to reject the accompanying secularization thesis as well.

A prominent dimension of the religions that emerged from the Axial Age, especially of Judaic monotheism and its two offshoots, Christianity and Islam, is the "dimension of infallible truth claims and unconditional obligations" (*EFK*, 1.6), these being supported in good measure by reasons, the totality in each case being an example of what Habermas calls a *worldview*. The emergence of religious worldviews "alters the self-understanding of [the] religious communities in such a way that an unmitigated functionalist conception of religion misses its essential point" (1.5). The role that the truth claims, the obligations, and the supporting reasons play in the life of the adherents of some religion cannot be reduced to whatever observable social function the worldview might serve (1.6).

There is more to the religions that emerged from the Axial Age and their descendants than worldviews, however. "The cognitive breakthrough ... should not obscure the fact that the religious traditions preserve the *connection of worldview and ritual practice*," and the

connection of both of those with sacred scriptures. It is the intertwine-
ment of worldview, ritual, and scripture that constitutes the *proprium* of
post-axial religion; if religion were only a worldview, "it could not affirm
its [unique] distinctiveness over against secular thought" (2.2).

The postmetaphysical philosopher finds that religion's *proprium*
eludes his grasp, rather in the way in which the experience of a work
of art also eludes his grasp. There is nothing like it in postmetaphysical
philosophy. Thus "at best, philosophy *circumscribes* the opaque core of
religious experience when it reflects on the specific character of religious
language and on the intrinsic meaning of faith. This core remains as
profoundly alien to discursive thought as the hermetic core of aesthetic
experience, which likewise can be at best circumscribed, but not penetrated, by philosophical thought" (*BNR*, 143). Philosophy in its origins
belonged to a way of life; and though the core of religious experience
remains alien to philosophy, nonetheless there are affinities between the
way of life of a post-axial religion and that of the ancient Greek and
Roman philosophers. Postmetaphysical philosophy does not even belong
to a way of life.

We saw that functional accounts of religion prove inadequate for
understanding the role of a religion's worldview in the life of its adherents; they prove even more inadequate for understanding the role of the
complex *proprium* of a religion in the life of its adherents. If "the sacred
complex" of worldview, sacred scripture, and communal ritual "is the
true source of the persuasiveness of religion, it must have an *intelligible
intrinsic meaning* for participants completely independently of the function ascribed to it from an observer's perspective" (*EFK*, 2.7).

Habermas's rejection of functionalist understandings of religion in
favor of what one might call the *sacred complex* view has, as its corollary,
his rejection of the standard secularization thesis. Since the attraction for
a religion's adherents of its sacred complex is not to be accounted for
in terms of social function, the claim that something else in modernized
societies plays the function that religion once played has to be rejected as
presupposing a mistaken view of religion.

Rather than religion losing its relevance "as a contemporary intellectual formation, whether in the public sphere and the political culture of
a society or in the life conduct of the individual" (1.13), what normally
happens is that religions adapt themselves to the requirements of modernity. In modernized societies they typically become rationalized and
individualized (1.15). "The major religions are clearly capable of finding
answers to [the challenges of modernization], both cognitively and at the
level of religious experience and practice" (1.15). What we see developing, both in the emerging world society and within national societies, is
"competing self-interpretations of modernity . . . as the various modern-

ization projects draw their sustenance from different world religions" (1.26). We see the emergence of "multiple modernities" (1.19).

What is Postmetaphysical Philosophy?

Let us move on to the orienting center of Habermas's thought, his project of a postmetaphysical philosophy. Habermas speaks in one place of "the collapse of metaphysics" (*RR*, 76), a comment hard to read in any other way than as the declaration that metaphysics is no longer viable. In another place, however, he says that postmetaphysical philosophy "refrains" from making "ontological pronouncements on the constitution of being as such" (*BNR*, 140). To refrain from making metaphysical or ontological pronouncements is obviously different from declaring such pronouncements untenable. My guess as to how these two comments fit together is that while Habermas himself thinks that metaphysics and ontology have collapsed, Kant being the great destroyer, it does not belong to the project of postmetaphysical philosophy as such to claim that they have collapsed. What does belong to the project is refraining from making and assessing metaphysical and comprehensive ontological pronouncements.

Take an example. Suppose that some present-day philosophy student reads the *Enneads* of Plotinus and finds the metaphysical worldview there presented both intellectually compelling and existentially satisfying. Unusual, but not impossible. As I understand Habermas, were he to find himself in dialogue with this student, he would not try to argue the student out of his Plotinianism by insisting, along positivist lines, that no claims were made in the *Enneads* because Plotinus' sentences lack meaning; neither would he try to argue the student out of his Plotinianism by insisting that the metaphysical claims made were false, or lacking in evidential support. He would not even try to persuade the student that his embrace of Plotinianism was "unreasonable." He would indeed argue that Plotinian metaphysics is not rational in a sense of "rational" that I will explain shortly. But to declare that Plotinian metaphysics is not rational in that way is not, for Habermas, to imply that it is unreasonable for a person in the modern world to embrace it.

In short, to embrace the project of *postmetaphysical* philosophy is not to dismiss metaphysical worldviews as untenable for one reason or another. Postmetaphysical philosophy is not *anti*-metaphysical philosophy. If nobody did any longer embrace a metaphysical worldview, then the kind of philosophy Habermas has in mind would in fact be *post*metaphysical. But that would be historical happenstance. It's not of the essence of such philosophy that it be *post*metaphysical; it peacefully coexists with metaphysical worldviews. It's of its essence that it be *non*-metaphysical.

That's to say what it is not. What is it? As I understand the project, postmetaphysical philosophy has three essential characteristics in addition to that of being non-metaphysical. First, postmetaphysical philosophy does not, as such, incorporate a worldview; neither does it aim at developing one.[1] Instead it has a topic, or subject matter, this being our shared lifeworld, and it has a corresponding aim, namely, to give philosophical articulation to that shared lifeworld – to make its structure "explicit" (*EFK*, 2.6).

And what is our shared lifeworld? Let me quote Habermas at some length:

> The "world" of the lifeworld is different from that of worldviews. "World" in this context signifies neither the sublime cosmos or the order of things, nor a sequence of global ages or salvatory events. The lifeworld is not accessible to us as a theoretical object; instead we find ourselves *in* it in a pretheoretical manner. It *surrounds* and *supports* us as we, as finite beings, are *coping* with the things and events we encounter in the world. Husserl speaks of the "horizon" of the lifeworld and of its "function as a basis" for our everyday activities. The lifeworld can be described in an anticipatory way as the insurmountable, only intuitively accompanying horizon and as the unavoidable, implicitly present background of a personal, historically situated, embodied, and communicatively socialized everyday existence. We are aware of ourselves performatively as *experiencing* subjects who are embedded in organic life processes, as *socialized* persons who are involved in their social relations and practices, and as *actors* who intervene in the world. (*FWL*, 2)

Some readers will be aware of my own long-standing interest in the thought of the unjustly neglected eighteenth-century Scots philosopher, Thomas Reid, the fruition of that interest being my *Thomas Reid and the Story of Philosophy*.[2] When I read what Habermas says here about lifeworld, I am immediately put in mind of Reid's doctrine of common sense. What Reid referred to as *common sense* is the same as what Habermas, and his predecessor Husserl, refer to as our *shared lifeworld*; Reid explains it as what we all do and must take for granted in the living of our lives. To Reid belongs the honor of being the first to introduce the idea of our shared lifeworld into modern philosophy. I judge it to have been a grave error on his part to have called it "common sense"; the connotations of the term resulted in near-universal misunderstanding and subsequent dismissal.

Reid thought that the project of articulating what we all do and must take for granted into explicitly stated principles of common sense is an important part of the enterprise of philosophy; philosophy in general has no other soil, he said, than common sense. It's a difficult project, and the results of trying to carry it out, always fallible. Reid would second Habermas's explanation of why that is the case:

> The concept of the lifeworld relies upon the distinction between performative awareness and fallible knowledge. The unique character of the attendant, intuitively certain, yet always implicit background knowledge that accompanies us in our everyday routines can be explained by the fact that the lifeworld is present to us only in a performative manner, in the execution of actions which are always oriented to something else. (*FWL*, 3)

Another defining feature of postmetaphysical philosophy is that it is *rational*. I know of no place in his recent writings in which Habermas explains the concept of *rational* that he has in mind. Of course we knew in advance that he would not follow in Kant's footsteps and explain rationality by developing a more or less elaborate account of the nature of the rational subject – by developing an ontological anthropology. That way is closed to him. His understanding of rationality will have to be a non-ontological, non-metaphysical understanding.

Given that Habermas does not offer an official explanation of what he understands by rationality, we have no option but to extrapolate from hints. He says that in postmetaphysical philosophy, "only 'public' reasons count, hence reasons that have the power to convince also beyond the boundaries of a particular religious community" (*BNR*, 245). He speaks of "the autonomy of a universally shared reason" (*EFK*, 2.2). He says that postmetaphysical philosophy employs a "generally accessible language" (*BNR*, 139). It would be easy to quote a sizable number of other passages to the same effect.

Let's extrapolate from these hints. I suggest that when Habermas describes postmetaphysical philosophical as *rational,* he is employing the term "rational" in the same way that Kant employed it in the passage in *The Critique of Pure Reason* where he distinguished between *revelational* theology (*theologia revelata*) and *rational* theology (A 631=B 659). Rational theology, says Kant, is based "solely upon reason." Though he does not explain what it is for a theology to be based solely upon reason, from his subsequent identification and description of various forms of theology that he regards as based solely upon reason it becomes quite clear what he has in mind.

Theology is based solely upon reason, and is thus rational theology, just in case it is based solely on premises and inferences that all cognitively competent adult human beings would accept if those premises and reasons were presented to them, if they understood them, if they possessed the relevant background information, and if they freely reflected on them at sufficient length. (What constitutes *sufficient* length is, of course, a nice question.) For the sake of convenience, let me henceforth call this sort of rationality, *Kant-rationality*. I suggest that a defining feature of what Habermas calls "postmetaphysical philosophy" is that it possesses Kant-rationality.

Suppose this suggestion is correct. Why does Habermas think the project of developing a philosophy that satisfies the demands of Kant-rationality is important? Why make Kant-rationality one of the defining features of postmetaphysical philosophy?

Again we have to extrapolate from hints. In one of the passages just quoted, Habermas spoke of "a universally shared reason"; in another he spoke of "reasons that have the power to convince also beyond the boundaries of a particular religious community." Habermas acknowledges that religious people use reasons; he is not one to tar all religious people with being irrational. But since the sorts of reasons they use do not convince beyond the boundaries of their own religious communities, their reasons do not actualize the universalizing potential of our "universally shared reason." Habermas would say the same thing about the reasons offered by metaphysical philosophies: they do not realize the inherent universalizing potential of our shared reason. The principle of Kant-rationality is to be understood as articulating what is required if the inherent universalizing potential of our shared reason is to be actualized. Whether our shared reason does in fact have the universalizing potential that Habermas assumes it has is an issue that I will be taking up later.

A fourth defining feature of postmetaphysical philosophy is, strictly speaking, an implication of the preceding feature. Postmetaphysical philosophy is secular – not secular*istic,* but secular. It practices "methodical atheism" (*RR*, 74). Philosophy, says Habermas,

> can draw *rational* sustenance from the religious heritage only as long as the source of revelation that orthodoxy counterposes to philosophy remains a cognitively unacceptable imposition for the latter. The perspectives which are centered *either* in God *or* in human beings cannot be converted into *one another.* Once the boundary between faith and knowledge becomes porous, and once religious motives force their way into philosophy *under false pretenses,* reason loses its foothold and succumbs to irrational effusion. (*BNR,* 242–3)

Postmetaphysical philosophy is *anthropocentric* philosophy. *Theocentric* thinking, by definition, is not postmetaphysical philosophy.

Religion and Postmetaphysical Philosophy

Having considered Habermas's understanding of religion and his project of postmetaphysical philosophy, let us now turn to one of the theses prominent in his writings over the past decade, namely, that postmetaphysical philosophy should engage rather than ignore present-day religion, and that it should do so with what he calls a *dialogical* approach (*BNR*, 245). A dialogical approach is distinct from the *rationalist* approach of the Hegelian tradition, which seeks "to *subsume* the substance of faith into the philosophical concept" (245). It is likewise distinct from an approach that sits in judgment on religious worldviews, either attacking them or undertaking to defend them apologetically. Postmetaphysical philosophy does not presume "to decide what is true or false in religion"; it "leaves the internal questions of the validity of religion to disputes within rational apologetics" (245).

A dialogical approach to religious traditions is "open to *learning* from them" (245).[3] Its aim is "to salvage cognitive contents from religious traditions. All semantic contents count as 'cognitive'" if they "can be translated into a form of discourse decoupled from the ratcheting effect of truth of revelation. In this discourse, only 'public' reasons count, . . . reasons that have the power to convince also beyond the boundaries of a particular community" (245).

Intriguing words, "to salvage cognitive contents." What does Habermas mean? Sometimes he says that the postmetaphysical philosopher aims to *translate* components of religious worldviews into his own philosophical conceptuality; in other passages he speaks of the postmetaphysical philosopher as *appropriating* elements from religious worldviews. My own sense is that if we look at the examples Habermas gives of the activity he has in mind, "appropriation" is the more apt term.

Philosophy, he says, "has long since appropriated biblical motifs" (*EFK*, 1.40); to think of the relation between biblical religion and philosophy as purely "polemical" is to ignore this fact. Here are some examples of appropriation:

> Modern rational natural law was indeed the product of a critical engagement with the Christian natural law. However, a careful examination of the origins of late scholasticism in Spain shows that it could simultaneously draw upon the egalitarian universalism of "man's" creation in God's image. The modern concepts of the individual person and of life history as a medium of individuation borrow their connotations of uniqueness, irreplaceability, and inwardness from the biblical notion of a life for which everybody is responsible before God, confronting him as a second person. Moreover, the secular morality of equal respect for everybody preserves

the categorical aspect of unconditionally valid obligations because the divine standpoint of the Last Judgment survives as a trace of an *inner-worldly* transcendence in the "moral point of view." (1.41)

We have all had the experience, upon listening to someone of a quite different persuasion from our own, of seeing the reality that he was trying to get at even though we ourselves would never put it that way. Though we dissent from the propositions he affirms, we see what he was trying to get at. We then put that in our own words; we *appropriate* it. We don't translate *what he said* into a different language; we appropriate *what he was trying to get at*. Habermas's thought is that appropriation, so understood, is what the postmetaphysical philosopher mainly aims at in his dialogue with religion.

Think of it like this: the postmetaphysical philosopher aims to "make explicit the practical knowledge" of our lifeworld. That goal proves elusive. What he discovers every now and then, in his dialogue with religion, is that the religious person is getting at something in our shared lifeworld that hitherto had eluded his own notice – for example, that every human being has equal and ineradicable worth. The philosopher then appropriates this insight for his own postmetaphysical philosophical purposes. He abstracts the insight from the revelational context in which the religious person placed it and from the theocentric language in which she stated it, and formulates the insight in his own anthropocentric secular language, supported with reasons that satisfy the demands of Kant-rationality.

The philosopher does not insist that the religious person cease setting her insight within a theocentric framework and cease formulating it in theistic language; he does not insist that henceforth she think only the thoughts and employ only the language of postmetaphysical philosophy. His appropriation of insights from the worldview of some religion is not aimed at changing anything whatsoever in the practice of that religion.[4] His aim is only to appropriate whatever may be useful for his own project of constructing a postmetaphysical philosophy. And he does not contend that his appropriation exhausts the meaning of religious concepts (*BNR*, 110).

As we shall see shortly, Habermas holds that the religious person stands to benefit from this appropriation as well as the philosopher. I dare say Habermas believes that the religious person may benefit from the dialogical engagement in ways that have nothing directly to do with the philosopher's activity of appropriation. Presumably something like "the cross-fertilization of Christianity and Greek metaphysics that gave rise . . . to the discipline of dogmatic theology" can still take place today (110). But given that the vision of a postmetaphysical philosophy constitutes the center of Habermas's thought, the outcome of the dialogue that he emphasizes is the philosopher's appropriation. Philosophical appropriation of religious insight is important to the philosopher for the contribution it makes to the project of a postmetaphysical philosophy. It proves important to the religious person for the contribution it makes to her ability to play the role of an office-holder in a liberal democracy. And beyond this, it proves important to all of us for its contribution to an emerging international legal order.

If the dialogue is to take place and be fruitful, both religion and philosophy must "shape up." Both must become self-critical. "The religious side must accept the authority of 'natural' reason as the fallible results of the institutionalized sciences and the basic principles of universalistic egalitarianism in law and morality" (*AWM*, 16). The philosophical side must overcome its loss of interest in the appropriation of religious insight, not to mention its rejection of the assumption that there is no such insight.

On this last point, Habermas observes that "among the philosophers of the second half of the twentieth century" there was "a noticeable waning of philosophical interest in possibly undiscovered treasures from" religion (*EFK*, 1.43). The judgmental attitude implicitly expressed by this waning of interest must be overcome if dialogue is to occur. Philosophy must not "set itself up as the judge concerning truths of faith" (1.43). No dialogue can occur if the philosophical side declares, for example, that the epistemic status of religious convictions is that they are simply *irrational* (*BNR*, 112).[5] Philosophy must overcome "a narrow secularist mindset" (140); it must purge itself of its tendency toward secular*ism*.

> As long as secular citizens are convinced that religious traditions and religious communities are, as it were, archaic relics of premodern societies persisting into the present, they can understand freedom of religion only as the cultural equivalent of the conservation of species threatened with extinction. Religion no longer has any intrinsic justification in their eyes . . . Clearly, citizens who adopt such an epistemic stance toward religion can no longer be expected to take religious contributions to contentious political issues seriously or to participate in a cooperative search for truth to determine whether they may contain elements that can be expressed in a secular language and be justified by rational arguments. (139)

In his recent writings, Habermas seems to me far more stern and emphatic in his insistence that philosophy must shape up if genuine dialogue is to take place than in his insistence that religion must shape up. "When the secular side excludes religious fellow citizens from the circle of modern contemporaries and treats them as specimens to be protected like an endangered species, this corrodes the very substance of a *membership* based on equal rights in the universe of rational persons" (*EFK*, 1.33). Sharp words! As are these:

> the main issue is the distinction between a secular and a secular*istic* understanding of autonomous reason. In this connection, the question arises of how the secular character of postmetaphysical thinking must be understood in relation to religious traditions if there is to be any prospect of an agreement on the legal and political integration of a tension-laden multicultural world society – and, in addition, whether secular reason is even *capable* of understanding itself in such a self-limiting manner in the first place. (33–4)

The fact that Habermas's rhetoric is asymmetrically weighted against the secularistic philosopher should not, however, conceal from us the fact that the "shaping up" on which Habermas insists is asymmetrically weighted against the religious person. The religious person must accept the "basic principles of egalitarianism in law and morality" and must accept the authority of natural reason as manifested in the "results of the 'institutionalized sciences.'" Depending on the particular character of the religion in question, this may well require the religious person to alter her views. What's required of the philosopher is not that he alter his philosophical views but only that he take an interest in religion as a potential source of insights that can be appropriated for his own purposes.

Throughout most of his discussion Habermas is extraordinarily accepting of post-axial religions as they come. When the postmetaphysical philosopher meets a religious person, he not only refrains from offering judgments about the truth or falsehood of the person's religious worldview; he concedes that this worldview may possess some form of rationality or reasonability distinct from Kant-rationality. And he affirms that religious people find meaning in the sacred complex of their religion even though he, the philosopher, proves incapable of fully understanding that meaning or of offering a surrogate. Now suddenly we hear that the religious person must accept the basic principles of egalitarianism in law and morality, and must accept the authority of natural reason as manifested in the institutionalized sciences. Why the shift in tone? Why the implicit critique of certain religions when previously critique was disavowed?

The answer, so I guess, is the following. It's when he is discussing the philosophical project of appropriating insights from religion that Habermas comes across as accepting of post-axial religions as they are. It's when he is discussing the requirements of dialogue – two-way interchange – that he says that whereas philosophers must be willing to listen to religious people so as to appropriate such insights as they may have, religious people may have to alter their views so as to become modern and progressive in their mentality. I find that in his recent writings Habermas has little to say about the understanding of dialogue that he is here employing, nor about the implicit imperative to dialogue.

Postmetaphysical Philosophy, Religion, and Public Political Debate

Habermas regards the construction of a postmetaphysical philosophy as a worthy project in its own right. But he also regards it as playing an important socio-political function. To explain what function that is, let me begin by noting that he expresses his agreement with a point I have made in some of my writings, that many religious people try to conduct their daily lives *on the basis of* their faith rather than *in addition to* their faith, and that many of these find it difficult if not impossible to formulate an alternative cognitive basis for their political convictions, their ecological convictions, their convictions concerning warfare, and the like. But it is incompatible with the idea of a liberal democracy that such people be required, or even urged, to absent themselves from public dialogue on fundamental social issues. As Habermas puts it, "the liberal state, which expressly protects such forms of existence as a basic right, cannot at the same time expect *all* citizens in addition to justify their political positions independently of their religious convictions or worldviews" (*BNR*, 128).

Habermas and I are thus joined in opposition to the position taken by Rawls, Audi, and a good many others on this point. He says that

> We cannot infer from the secular character of the state a direct personal obligation on all citizens to supplement their publicly expressed religious convictions by equivalents in a generally accessible language. And certainly the normative expectation that all religious citizens when casting their vote should *ultimately* let themselves be guided by secular considerations is to ignore the realities of a devout life, an existence *guided* by faith. (129)

It should be obvious that these remarks fit hand-in-glove with Habermas's understanding of religion.

It would be easy to interpret these words as a call for secularists to tolerate religious voices in the public square. Habermas makes it clear that toleration is not what he is calling for.

> What is at stake is not a respectful sensibility for the possible existential significance of religion for some other person . . . but a self-reflexive overcoming

of a rigid and exclusive secularist self-understanding of modernity . . . The admission of religious assertions into the political arena only makes sense if *all* citizens can be reasonably expected not to exclude the possibility that these contributions may have cognitive substance . . . Such an attitude presupposes a mentality on the part of secular citizens that is far from a matter of course in the secularized societies of the West. On the contrary, the recognition by secular citizens that they live in a postsecular society that is also *epistemically attuned* to [the] continued existence of religious communities is a consequence of a change in mentality that is no less cognitively exacting [for the secular person than is] the adaptation of religious consciousness to the challenges of an environment that is becoming increasingly more secular. In line with the standards of an enlightenment endowed with a critical awareness of its own limits, the secular citizens [must] understand their non-agreement with religious conceptions as a *disagreement* that is *reasonable* to expect. Without this cognitive presupposition, [religious] citizens cannot be reasonably expected to make a public use of their reason, at least not in the sense that secular citizens are willing to enter into a political discussion of the content of religious contributions with the intention of translating potentially morally convincing intuitions and reasons into a generally accessible language. (138–9)

Habermas holds that "those who hold a public office or are candidates for such" (128) are required to do what ordinary citizens are not required to do. They "have a duty to remain neutral among competing worldviews" (128). "Every citizen must know and accept that only secular reasons count beyond the institutional threshold separating the informal public sphere from parliaments, courts, ministries, and administration" (130).

Where are the secular reasons to be found that office-holders are to employ? Habermas's answer is that they are to be found in postmetaphysical philosophy. The existence of an adequate postmetaphysical philosophy is the "cognitive precondition under which [a democratic civic ethos] can be reasonably expected of citizens" (144). I feel sure Habermas does not mean that religious citizens must consult the writings of professional philosophers of a postmetaphysical stripe for the reasons they need if they are to serve in public office; he is assuming the existence of a filtering-down process from philosophers to the general public.

With Habermas's full line of thought in mind, it's clear that it is somewhat misleading to describe the reasons that the religious person must use when serving in public office as "secular." To describe them as "secular" is to make them sound alien to religion. But if things go as Habermas thinks they should go, some of these reasons will have become part of postmetaphysical philosophy by the appropriation process described earlier. They are insights of religion couched in the secular language of the postmetaphysical philosopher. Thus it is that Habermas says that "the truth contents of religious contributions can enter into the institutionalized practice of deliberation and decision-making only when the necessary translation already occurs in the pre-parliamentary domain, i.e., in the political public sphere itself" (131).

There is No Extant Postmetaphysical Philosophy

There is much that is worth engaging in the rich and complex line of thought that I have summarized. In this essay I will have to confine myself almost entirely to some critical comments on the orienting center of it all, Habermas's project of a postmetaphysical philosophy. If that project proves not viable, then much of what Habermas says about the relation between religion and philosophy, and some of what he says about the role of religion in the public square, will have to be re-thought.

Recall that postmetaphysical philosophy has four defining character-istics: it is non-metaphysical, it seeks to articulate our shared lifeworld, it is rational in that it possesses what I called "Kant-rationality," and it is secular. And let me remind the reader of my explanation of Kant-rationality: a body of thought possesses Kant-rationality just in case it is based solely on premises and inferences that all cognitively competent, adult human beings would accept if those premises and reasons were presented to them, if they understood them, if they possessed the relevant background information, and if they freely reflected on them at sufficient length.

I submit that there is, at present, no postmetaphysical philosophy, no substantial body of philosophical thought that satisfies the criteria for a postmetaphysical philosophy, the main reason being that there is no substantial body of philosophical thought that satisfies the requirement of Kant-rationality. Habermas obviously regards his own philosophical work as an example of postmetaphysical philosophy. It seems clear to me that it is not. Habermas's philosophy does not enjoy the consensus of those who have read and reflected on what he has written; many reject premises that he employs and inferences that he makes. And it would be extremely implausible to argue that all who have rejected some of his premises and conclusions are either not cognitively competent adults or have not understood those premises and inferences, have not freely reflected on them at sufficient length, or have lacked the requisite back-ground information.

Habermas himself makes this very point, albeit indirectly. At several points he mentions two sorts of philosophical opponents to his own way of thinking: hardbitten naturalists and historicists. Let me quote one passage:

> Reflection on the advances in genetics, brain research, evolutionary biology, and artificial intelligence inspired by naïve faith in science has lent support to a hard boiled naturalism that undermines the personalistic understanding of the human mind and any normatively imbued description of sociocultural forms of life. At the same time, the historical and cultural-anthropological accounts of the particularistic nature of the actual backgrounds of universalistic claims and pretenses has promoted a contextualist critique that strikes at the heart of the humanist project. In my view, serious objections can be raised against both the scientistic radicalization of naturalism and the radicalization of historicism into a self-defeating critique of reason. (*EFK*, 1.40)[6]

It is not clear to me whether Habermas regards naturalist and historicist philosophies as seriously flawed examples of postmetaphysical philosophy or as not examples of postmetaphysical philosophy at all. For our purposes here, it doesn't matter how this question is answered. Habermas thinks that "serious objections" can be raised against both naturalism and historicism; in his writings he has raised those objections. But he is well aware of the fact that while some historicists and naturalists have simply ignored what he has written, others have read and reflected on what he has written on these matters but not found his objections persuasive. They remain historicists or naturalists. There is one passage in which Habermas sounds almost despairing. He remarks that whether or not "a scientistic form of secularism will ultimately win out over the more comprehensive concept of reason underlying postmetaphysical thinking is, for the time being, an open question even among philosophers themselves" (*BNR*, 145). But surely it would be both implausible and arrogant to argue that all historicists and naturalists who have read Habermas are either not cognitively competent adults or have not understood his premises and inferences, have not freely reflected on them at sufficient length, or have lacked the requisite background information.

   Is it no more than a historical accident that there is at present no substantial body of philosophical thought that satisfies the requirement of Kant-rationality, and hence none which qualifies as postmetaphysical philosophy? I think not. The history of philosophy gives us powerful reason to conclude that there never will be a substantial body of philosophical thought which possesses Kant-rationality. Philosophical reflection under conditions of freedom expands the scope of disagreement.

Where Does This Leave Us?

Suppose my claim is correct, that the project of a postmetaphysical philosophy is non-viable because it is highly unlikely that there ever will be a substantial body of philosophical thought which possesses Kant-rationality. Since the project of such a philosophy is the orienting center of the entire line of thought that I have summarized, the conclusion that the project is non-viable has rippling consequences throughout Habermas's thought. Let me call attention to just two.

First, recall what is, for Habermas, one of the fundamental differences between the worldview of a religion and postmetaphysical philosophy: the reasons offered by the former lack the power to convince beyond the boundaries of that particular religion; the reasons offered by the postmetaphysical philosopher are the expression of a universally shared reason. It turns out that every body of philosophical thought, including Habermas's, has the trait that Habermas here ascribes to religious worldviews and not the trait that he ascribes to postmetaphysical philosophy. Every body of philosophical thought is limited in its persuasive powers, and that's how it will always be. There may be good reasons for philosophers to appropriate religious insights for their own purposes; but the reason cannot be that such appropriation will serve the cause of constructing a body of thought that possesses Kant-rationality.

Second, we will have to give up the hope that philosophy can provide us with a stock of Kant-rational reasons that can be used by officials in making political decisions. In principle that leaves open the possibility that something else than philosophy can provide us with such a stock of reasons. But the very same reasons for doubting that philosophy will ever provide us with such a stock are reasons for doubting that such a stock can be found anywhere else. We will have to live with the fact that there is no alternative to some members of parliament using naturalistic considerations in making their decisions, some using humanistic considerations, some using historicist considerations, some using utilitarian considerations, some using libertarian considerations, some favoring economistic considerations, some asking what serves the rational self-interest of themselves and their cohorts, some using religious considerations of one kind and another – along with various combinations of these.

Though there is no way around this hard fact, let me add that, in the United States today, there seem to me to be powerful pressures toward concealing whatever religious or humanistic-justice reasons one might have for favoring some policy and instead trying to find economistic and rational self-interest reasons for that policy, presumably because such reasons are thought to have more appeal for Americans generally than any other sorts of reasons. A depressing thought!

Habermas remarks in one passage that all participants in international discussions concerning justice "must be prepared to use only those arguments that could convince anyone in principle irrespective of their underlying metaphysical or religious commitments" (*EFK*, 1.28). The explanation I proposed of *Kant-rationality* spoke of premises and arguments that all cognitively competent adult human beings *would* accept under conditions of a certain sort; this passage speaks instead of what they all *could* accept. Does this point to a promising alternative understanding of rationality?

An obvious question here is, could accept *if what*? Suppose that a member of parliament of a generally Habermasian orientation offers humanistic-justice considerations in opposition to a human genetic-engineering project proposed by a fellow parliamentarian whose orientation is purely scientistic and naturalistic. Only if the latter gave up his scientistic naturalism *could* he accept the Habermasian arguments. But giving up one's scientistic naturalist orientation in favor of some other orientation is not something one can decide to do. And, in any case, the parliament of a liberal democracy is not closed to those whose orientation is scientistic naturalism.

Habermas sometimes says that religious reasons for political positions are "inaccessible" to secularists; others who write on these matters often say the same thing. The idea seems to be that religious reasons, sooner or later, all go back to faith in the content of revelation and that such faith is certain and unquestionable for the person who has it. But secularists have not been the recipients of revelation; nor can they become recipients by an act of will on their part. Religious reasons are in that way "inaccessible" to them.

I submit that this is a distorted picture of religion and of the reasons that religious people offer. Ever since the High Middle Ages Christian theologians have regularly used revelation, and faith in the content of revelation, as two of their most fundamental categories. But in the orientation of most Christians, not to mention that of other religious people, the pair revelation–faith does not have the looming importance it has had in the history of Christian theology; rarely does one hear someone say, "God told me, so it's true; and that's the end of the discussion."

And note, once again, that the person whose orientation is that of scientistic naturalism can no more decide to adopt a humanistic orientation than he can decide to become a recipient of revelation. Given the understanding of "inaccessible" offered above, a humanistic orientation is inaccessible to him.

Why Kant-rationality Eluded Habermas

In bringing our discussion to a conclusion, let's dig deeper and try to pinpoint why it is that Habermas's own philosophy falls far short of achieving Kant-rationality, and thus of being an example of postmetaphysical philosophy. One can understand why the speculations of the metaphysician fail to achieve Kant-rationality. But take the project of elucidating the structure of our shared lifeworld. Is it not reasonable to expect that when those who possess "universally shared reason" engage in this project, the results will approach Kant-rationality? Habermas emphasizes that since the structure of our shared lifeworld does not lie open before us, we must expect some disagreement. Fair enough. No doubt this explains some of the controversies over Habermas's claims concerning the implications of communicative rationality. But is it not reasonable to expect that we will slowly move in the direction of rational consensus? How then are we to explain the deep disagreements between Habermas, on the one hand, and historicists and scientistic naturalists, on the other? These are not speculative metaphysicians.

Part of the answer is that a good deal of Habermas's philosophy cannot plausibly be viewed as explicating the structure of our shared lifeworld. None of Habermas's understanding of religion that I summarized at the beginning of this chapter can be so viewed; nor can his insistence that the fundamental stance of philosophers toward religion should be that of seeking to appropriate for their own purposes the insights of religion. Our shared lifeworld has nothing to say on such matters.

Another part of the answer is that Habermas's stated philosophical aim, of elucidating the structure of our lifeworld, is itself a highly contested aim for philosophy. Not only would no speculative metaphysicians accept it; few historicists would accept it and no scientistic naturalists would accept it. Of course, it is open to Habermas to declare that, whatever may be their goal, this is the goal he has set himself as a postmetaphysical philosopher. But if he is to have a genuine debate with the naturalist, he cannot simply declare that such-and-such belongs to, or is an implication of, the structure of our shared lifeworld and that it contradicts what the naturalist says. He has to move out of the hermeneutic posture and declare that such-and-such is the truth of the matter. But to make that move is perforce no longer to confine himself to explicating the structure of our shared lifeworld. In short, Habermas in fact does not confine himself to explicating the structure of our shared lifeworld; that was the point of the preceding paragraph. If he wants to debate with those who do not embrace that project, as he does, he cannot so confine himself.

There is a third, and I think more important, reason for Habermas's philosophy not exhibiting Kant-rationality. Habermas says that the postmetaphysical philosopher neither has a worldview nor aims at constructing a worldview. My own view, to the contrary, is that everyone who engages in the practice of philosophy brings to his engagement a worldview and that this colors how he sees things. Nobody comes to the engagement with an empty mind, just drinking in the facts. The worldview one brings to the enterprise may be unarticulated, and it may be woefully incomplete compared to highly developed worldviews. Nonetheless, the philosophical thought of the contemporary naturalist is the result of a complex interaction between a worldview that he brings to the enterprise of philosophy, his own reflection on the philosophical "data," and his engagement with his fellow philosophers.

It's true that postmetaphysical philosophy is not, as such, a worldview; the defining characteristics of postmetaphysical philosophy are purely structural. But it would certainly be possible to write an essay on Habermas's worldview as expressed in his writings. And such an essay would have to raise the question of whether Habermas's worldview is as free of ontology as he presents his philosophy as being, and as he apparently wants it to be. Readers cannot miss noticing that Habermas operates with a certain understanding of the nature of the person – operates with a certain *anthropological ontology*. I think a good deal of Aristotle's philosophy can be understood as an attempt to explicate the structure of our shared lifeworld. But whereas Aristotle is interested in that lifeworld as a whole, Habermas is interested almost exclusively in that part of our lifeworld which pertains to persons and their communicative activities. The difference between Aristotle's philosophy and Habermas's is not that whereas Aristotle's explication of the structure of our lifeworld makes ontological commitments, Habermas's does not; the difference is that Habermas focuses on only a small part of that lifeworld.

If Habermas's philosophy were an example of postmetaphysical philosophy, it would be an extraordinarily distinctive species of philosophy. But it is not. It does not confine itself to explicating our shared lifeworld: it exhibits a worldview; it does not achieve Kant-rationality. So what is it then? One more member of the crowd.

Should Philosophers Aim at Kant-rationality?

The point made above, about the role of worldviews in the practice of philosophy, cries out to be developed and defended. But I must reserve that for another occasion. Let me instead close with a question suggested by Habermas's concept of a postmetaphysical philosophy, namely, should we who are philosophers *aspire* to Kant-rationality in what we say and write qua philosophers, even though we know we will not succeed? Is it the role of the philosopher to persist in bumping his head against the wall, trying to achieve what he knows will not be achieved by himself or anyone else?

Am I, in this present chapter, playing that role? Am I implicitly aspiring to satisfy the requirement of Kant-rationality? If one of my readers offered me a reason for concluding that something I said was mistaken, I would either concede the point or try to find some argument that I think might persuade the objector that he was mistaken. Does this show that I am implicitly aspiring to achieve Kant-rationality?

The role of reasons in philosophy strikes me as considerably more diverse and complex than Habermas acknowledges. For one thing, we offer reasons with different aims in mind. Sometimes we offer reasons for a position we hold with the aim of persuading our listeners or readers of our position; on other occasions we offer reasons for a position we hold with the aim of making clear to others the reasons for which we ourselves hold our position. We may or may not expect that the other person will find those reasons persuasive. And, second, the reasons we offer, whatever be our aim in offering them, are usually audience-specific or readership-specific in their intent. We do not usually aim our remarks at humanity in general. We have in mind a certain kind of audience or a certain kind of readership, and we offer reasons for our position that we hope that audience or readership will find persuasive, or reasons that will make clear to them why we hold the position we do.

In composing this essay, I had in mind a readership composed of philosophers with a certain kind of training and skill; and I had the double aim of showing how I reached the conclusions I did and of persuading my readers of the truth of those conclusions – without any expectation whatsoever that I would be entirely successful in this latter aim. Had I had a quite different readership in mind, I would have tried to find quite different reasons or to present my reasons in a quite different way. Sometimes the historicist philosopher addresses contemporary Western philosophers in general; sometimes she addresses her fellow historicists. The reasons she gives for her positions on these two quite different occasions, whatever her aim in giving those reasons, will be different.

So should we who are philosophers aim at Kant-rationality, knowing all the while that we will come far short of achieving it? Most of us most of the time do not aim at that. Our not doing so is not an indication that we are not "really" philosophers.

Part II

The Critique of Reason and the Unfinished
Project of Enlightenment

5

The Burdens of Modernized Faith and Postmetaphysical Reason in Habermas's "Unfinished Project of Enlightenment"

Thomas McCarthy

> ... to criticism everything must submit. Religion through its sanctity, and law-giving through its majesty, may seek to exempt themselves from it. But they then awaken just suspicion, and cannot claim the sincere respect which reason accords only to that which has been able to sustain the test of free and open examination.[1]

> I have therefore found it necessary to deny *knowledge,* in order to make room for *faith.*[2]

Reviewing Habermas's reflections on faith and reason over the past two decades, I have been struck by the overall continuity of his views, from the exchange with theologians and religious philosophers at the University of Chicago in 1991[3] to the recent exchange with Jesuit scholars at the Hochschule für Philosophie in Munich (*AWM*). At the same time, the changes in context, purpose, and emphasis are unmistakable. His heightened concern with the "derailment" of global modernization processes pervades the later writings (*BNR, AWM, EFK*). This motivates him to take up themes from traditions of thought incited by similar concerns – *Lebensphilosophie* and historicism, phenomenology and hermeneutics. It is also behind the expanded role of historical-comparative methods in his social-evolutionary approach to world religions and civilizations, as well as his offer of alliance to modernized religious communities in the struggle for global justice against the depredations of capitalist modernization. These shifts give his renovated construction of the critique of reason, which is at the heart of his "unfinished project of enlightenment," a somewhat steeper critical gradient than in the 1990s. In what follows, I shall argue that it is not yet steep enough, that certain burdens of reason, which he duly mentions but does not fully develop in these recent writings, call for a still sharper descent from the heights of transcendental philosophy.

I   Prologue

Habermas frequently remarks on the great diversity covered by the deceptively homogeneous rubrics of "faith" and "reason." Attending for present purposes only to the variety of reflective conceptions, the term "faith" has to be sufficiently capacious to accommodate, for instance, both fideism and rationalism, both realism and anti-realism, as well as everything between and beyond – Deism as well as the Reformed tradition, Kierkegaard as well as Aquinas, Wittgenstein as well as Kant, and so on and so forth.

These are not merely so many options in religious self-understanding; they are also conflicts of interpretation and have been articulated as such. Moreover, the diversity within the Christian tradition has its parallels within Hinduism and Buddhism, Confucianism and Daoism, Islam and Judaism. Taking all of this into consideration, it is evident that the category "faith" is meant to include an immense variety of often competing self-understandings of religion at the reflective level, not to mention the varieties of religious experiences themselves.

The same holds, of course, for the term "reason," or in the case at point "secular reason." We have only to survey the history of modern Western philosophy to document this. And lest it seem a thing of the past, we need only glance at contemporary debates concerning "the nature, scope, and limits of reason" among modernists and postmodernists, neo-Kantians and neo-Hobbesians, neo-Humeans and neo-Aristotelians, neo-Hegelians and neo-pragmatists, and so forth.

Now this immense diversity on both sides of the constructed faith/ reason divide presents a prima facie problem for Habermas, one of whose aims in these latest writings is, as he puts it, to examine the cognitive presuppositions of intercultural dialogue about global justice, in light of the growing reflexivity of both religious and secular consciousness (*EFK*). As in Rawls, the dialogue has to accommodate the great variety of "comprehensive doctrines" or "worldviews" within our own culture; and, more so than in Rawls, it must accommodate the immense diversity of reflective views within and between other cultures as well. Habermas argues, correctly I think, that Rawls's treatment of neutrality in his later work is not itself philosophically neutral (*IO*, ch. 3). That is to say, his political liberalism, with its emphasis on overlapping consensus, itself rests on philosophical views that are controversial. Accordingly, Habermas acknowledges from the start the philosophically non-neutral standpoint from which he develops his own argument. It is, of course, the standpoint that he has elaborated at great length in a plethora of books and articles on the theory of communicative action. This acknowledgment does not, however, resolve the tension between the inclusiveness of his vision of global dialogue, on the one hand, and the specificity of his conception of, and his case for, its cognitive presuppositions, on the other. Reflective participants with different views of faith, of reason, and of their relation will typically also have different views of these presuppositions. They will, in short, not simply grant the truth of his theory of communicative action; nor the adequacy of his analytic, comparative, and evolutionary account of the world religions, which, though by no means simply derived from that theory, is expressly framed by it.

Habermas presents global dialogue more or less as an idea of practical reason in the Kantian sense, but one structured by an account of practical reason quite different from Kant's, in that he endeavors to build language and culture, history and society into its core structures. And this "detranscendentalization" inherently opens the projected unity of reason to a diversity of voices, including a diversity of conflicting views on the very presuppositions in question. One move sometimes mentioned by Habermas at this point cannot, I think, end the argument. His evolutionary account of learning processes at the level of cultural development does not preclude ongoing conflicts of interpretation among the most "advanced" participants. Taylor and MacIntyre, for instance, or Plantinga and Wolterstorff reject the accounts of reason and faith that figure in his analysis of cognitive presuppositions, not to mention reflective members of other cultures – which is not to say that he is wrong, but only that his views are themselves controversial.

Another move, which has gotten increasing play in these recent writings, is to point to the structural and functional convergences of the societal modernization processes ineluctably under way across the globe. And these increasingly common "infrastructures" – market economies and state bureaucracies, for instance – are not without their political and cultural consequences. But, as Habermas well knows, we are in no position to predict where this will eventually lead – whether to a new cosmopolitan constitution, for instance, or merely to a rebalancing of international power relations from West to East, or to something entirely unforeseen. In Kantian terms, we have to do here not with "determinant" judgments about the past and future course of history, but with "reflective" judgments, general interpretations consistent with available empirical materials and shaped by ideas and ideals of practical reason, and thus oriented to broad conceptions of futures we might

hope to attain, if we engage ourselves practically to bring them about.[4]
Needless to say, such hopes too will be open to a diversity of responses,
from Benjaminian melancholy to neo-realist scorn. In a word, diversity
and disagreement are reasonably to be expected not only within global
discourse concerning global justice, but also about the very conditions
of possibility, or impossibility, of any such discourse, as I shall further
elaborate.

II   The Burdens of Faith: Dialectic at a Standstill

The preceding remarks merely expand upon aspects of Habermas's
approach that he acknowledges. He is writing as a reflective member of
Western culture with a particular view of secular reason, but as one who
seeks to hold open the possibility of engaging with, understanding, and
learning from other points of view, in particular, from points of view
informed by religious faiths. It is essential to this aim, as he conceives
it, that the religious standpoints in question be "modernized" – that is,
reflexively de-centered and willing to accept, among other things: (a) the
findings of institutionalized science and scholarship in their domains of
competence; (b) the legitimate authority of the modern constitutional
state organized through positive law; (c) the universalist egalitarianism of
modern secular morality, which demands equal respect for the autonomy
of individuals in adopting terms of social cooperation and personal plans
of life; and (d) the ineliminable pluralism of worldviews and forms of
life, thus allowing for reasonable disagreements concerning the ultimate
meaning and value of life (*RR*, 15f.; *BNR*, 136f.). Now this delineation
of the burdens of modernized faith has not been, and may never be,
accepted by all reflective believers or all reflective communities of faith.
Some fideists, for example, might hold that the passionate commitment
faith requires in the face of objective uncertainty is incompatible with the
dispassionate impartiality and commitment to objectivity required of participants in discourse. Other reflective believers might hold that modern
law and secular morality can only ever be of secondary importance in
comparison to the dictates of religious belief, practice, and conscience.

But I am more interested here in the evident tension in Habermas's
account between the way religious faith looks to "us" – in the sense,
roughly, of Hegel's phenomenological observers, that is, to us postmetaphysical thinkers – and to "them," that is, to religious believers
themselves. One may be inclined to see this as a familiar dialectical
tension between two standpoints that are to be superseded in a higher
standpoint; but given the unavailability of the standpoint of absolute

knowledge, and without the movement of the concept underwritten by Hegel's logic, the dialectic comes to a standstill and we are left with two only very partially mediated standpoints.

It is true that, over the centuries, Christian theology has reconciled religious belief with core elements of modern life, so that cognitive dissonances between faith and reason have been much reduced, at least for the sort of modernized faithful with whom Habermas seeks to dialogue. But, as he sees it, there is a "core" of religion – tied to religious experience and practice, ritual and community – that cannot be exhaustively captured or explained in conceptual terms.[5] Rather, it is typically expressed and communicated in symbolic terms alien to the discursive forms of analysis and critique proper to propositionally differentiated speech. And for Habermas – that is, from the perspective of his theory of communication – this is the heart of the tensions between faith and reason. Symbolic expression of this kind relates back to a primordial form of communication in which the reflective differentiation of cognitive, normative, evaluative, and expressive claims is not operative. It relates, as he also puts it, to a mode of mutual understanding in which a "linguistically non-transparent" core of performative meaning can be communicated without the possibilities of semantic articulation afforded by propositionally differentiated speech.[6] In this mode, what we take to be distinct validity claims are embedded in synergistic wholes that are more than the sum of their parts. For us postmetaphysical reasoners, who want to examine the different claims in line with their own independent logics, this synergy gives rise to what we experience as discursive "interference." For us, the claimed "truths of faith" are not discursively decidable validity claims in the ordinary sense; they appeal to different kinds of grounds – to divine revelation, ritual practice, religious experience, and the like – and thus to modes of justification different from ordinary claims to propositional or normative truth. But they take themselves to be making valid truth claims about the way things really are and valid normative claims about the way everyone ought to act. For us, who no longer understand the core meanings of religious language in onto-theological or historico-teleological terms, these purported "truths" can have at bottom only ethical significance – that is, they express existential commitments to ways of life oriented to various basic values and highest goods, and anchored in various religiously imbued identities (*IO*, ch. 3; *BNR*; *EFK*). And since, on Habermas's account of them, ethical claims, unlike claims to propositional truth or moral rightness, are not claims to universal validity, they are not truth claims in the proper sense, the self-understanding of believers to the contrary notwithstanding.

Thus, when Habermas urges us to be open to the "truth contents" (*Wahrheitsgehalte*) of religion, he is not referring to the propositional truths of, say, a religious metaphysics, or even directly to the moral truths of, say, a divine command morality. Rather, he has in mind the ethical values and goods ensconced in religious beliefs and practices, which he wants us to regard as potential candidates for generalization into universal norms. That is to say, they may prove to be "equally good for all." Indeed, as Habermas repeatedly notes, many of the fundamental norms of modern morality are descended, by way of secular reformulation and generalization, from Western traditions of faith – such that, for instance, equality in the eyes of God could be translated into universal norms of equal dignity and equal respect. And his brief for openness to the truth contents of religion is predicated upon the possibility that this potential has not yet been exhausted (*BNR*; *EFK*).

But as far as "truth" in the specific sense of truth about the objective world is concerned, there is nothing further to be expected from religious worldviews. For the cognitive development of worldviews has been a process of advancing objectivation (*Versachlichung*), that is, a progressive stripping of our image of the objective world of lifeworld projections and a progressive de-centering of our objectivating descriptions and explanations of it (*KV*). Thus, we can no longer understand the natural world in terms of the communicative relations and narrative explanations of mythical worldviews; nor in terms of the teleological orders of cosmos and history of traditional monotheism. And we can no longer claim infallibility or any other form of dogmatic certainty for our propositional knowledge of the states of affairs that obtain in the objective world. In this respect, modernized religious consciousness must be at one with secular postmetaphysical consciousness. It is important to note, however, that this growing convergence upon modern forms of consciousness does not entail that "they" must accept Habermas's substantive account of communicative action as the proper framework in which to interpret religious utterances.

As the contemporary state of discussion makes quite clear, there is ample latitude, at this shared level of reflexive modernity, to dispute such matters. In particular, reflective believers may dispute Habermas's sharp separation of truth and rightness and goodness. They may reject his understanding of their truth claims and his way of discoursing about them or, to be more precise, of not discoursing about them; for, from his point of view, many of these purported truth claims may not be decidable in normal discourse. But if the pure, differentiated forms of discourse are unsuited to deciding the truth or falsity of religious claims, and if they refuse to treat the latter merely as evaluative or expressive utterances, then what is the basis for the dialogue that Habermas seeks? As they may not accept his account of its cognitive presuppositions, they may reasonably decline to converse with him on that basis. And this seems to suggest that, if there is to be conversation, "we" and "they" shall have to fashion forms of dialogue based on much thinner presuppositions.

III The Burdens of Reason: Objectivation and Interpretation

While the preceding discussion of the burdens of modernized faith could proceed largely by drawing out some implications of Habermas's own views, my discussion of the burdens of postmetaphysical reason will seek to uncover tensions in his stated views. These tensions are, broadly, of a dialectical and hermeneutical nature; and as I have argued for them at some length in earlier works,[7] I shall here present only a brief restatement of one point and abbreviated arguments for two more.

(a) As my remarks above on Habermas's distinction between ethical and moral claims indicated, the values, goods, and identities central to ethical life cannot, on his account, claim universal validity in a postmetaphysical framework; by contrast, moral discourse precisely considers claims that proposed norms are universally valid, in the sense that they are equally good for all or equally in the interest of all. In my view, this conceptualization of the relation in question gives rise to an inextricable entwinement of moral and ethical discourse about the right and the good.[8] Because the interpretation and weighing of proposed values and goods are intrinsically open to reasonable disagreement, the claim that something is equally good for all is also open to contestation on similar grounds. That is to say, "good" cannot be an inherently contestable concept without "equally good for all" being so as well. This, then, is an irremovable burden of practical reason in a postmetaphysical setting, when we can no longer appeal to a metaphysically framed anthropology to delimit what is good "by nature" for each and every human being "as such." This burden makes itself felt all the more sharply in contemporary political discourse, where deciding what is for the common good of culturally heterogeneous polities regularly runs up against ethical disagreements about basic values, highest goods, and collective identities.

(b) It may well seem that this analysis is of limited significance in view of the host of general proscriptions that have gained cross-cultural acceptance. And it is indeed of critical significance for morality that a number of basic human vulnerabilities are shielded by categorical norms in a great variety of cultures. But any attempt to fix such norms in canonical formulae typically runs into strong disagreements about how concretely to understand and apply them. It is in this vein that Habermas credits Hegel's insight against Kant concerning the substantive emptiness and motivational weakness of abstract universals, and the necessity of their being embedded in some form of ethical life to lend them the specificity and power of concrete universals. But he treats this differently from Hegel, in terms of the complementarity of discourses of justification and discourses of application. On this account, justified moral norms remain unchanged, while problems that arise in applying them to ever changing cases are dealt with according to a distinct logic of application.

However well this analysis may hold up for legal norms with constitutionally anchored formulations and institutionalized practices of adjudication – and even there, I think, it encounters problems – it raises a host of issues in connection with moral norms. In the absence of institutionally secured procedures, moral principles are open to endless disagreements of interpretation and application. They do not, as Habermas himself once phrased it, exist in "transcendental purity" but only as formulated in some language or other; and such formulations will always reflect the contexts and interests of particular historical times and social spaces. Moreover, on a pragmatic theory of meaning, the application of abstract norms to ever-new situations, including situations not envisaged in the heretofore "standard" array of cases, affects the very meaning of the general norm itself. In short, there is a reciprocal influence here between the general and the particular and not just a one-way application of unchanging general norms to changing particular situations. Accordingly, we (postmetaphysical thinkers) must reckon with reasonable disagreements concerning both the meaning and application of general moral norms, disagreements reflecting differences in the situations and worldviews of interpreters, including of course religious differences. What, for instance, does "equal respect" mean in practice, to what situations does it apply, and how?

(c) Another sort of hermeneutical issue arises in connection with Habermas's account of the progressive objectivation of our image of the world in and through the development of scientific inquiry in the modern period. He notes that this objectivation is "bipolar": proceeding on the one side via the growth of the natural sciences from the seventeenth century onwards, and on the other side via the growth of the human sciences from the nineteenth century onwards (*KV*). It is important to note that the German word usually translated as "science," that is, *Wissenschaft*, does not have exactly the same intension or extension as the English term used to translate it. It is closer in meaning to the broader signification of the term "science" prior to the nineteenth century, which was used to render the Latin term *scientia*, which in turn was used to render the Greek *episteme*. Roughly speaking, like these earlier English, Latin, and Greek terms, *Wissenschaft* refers to any branch of organized, disciplined, reasoned knowledge (*Wissen*), rather than only to science in the narrower sense for which the natural sciences are paradigmatic. Thus, in German one can speak of the *Geisteswissenschaften,* where we tend to speak of the humanities. It covers, in short, all organized branches of knowledge from physics to philology.

This is relevant to my main point here, to wit that Habermas's uses of the terms *Wissenschaft* and *Versachlichung* – translated here as objectivation – are not merely bipolar but equivocal in important respects. His own account of the objectivation of world images furnishes the material needed to make this point. The natural sciences objectivate the world by progressively stripping it of the lifeworld projections that pervade our everyday images of the world, displacing them with a rigorously externalist view of quantifiable objects, states, and events in causal relations. But this is not at all how the human "sciences" *versachlichen* the realm of "objective spirit," as Habermas, echoing Hegel, sometimes refers to the realm of historically variable, socio-cultural forms of life. Rather, they do so by making the human world the *Sache* or object (or topic or subject matter) of forms of impartial inquiry aspiring to objectivity. Now the sorts of inquiry in question, Habermas repeatedly emphasizes, are fundamentally different from those in the natural sciences (*KV,* 238f.). As "meaning" is a basic feature of socio-cultural forms of life, access to socio-cultural phenomena must be gained hermeneutically, that is, by way of interpretation. And this requires that investigators also adopt the first- and second-person perspectives of virtual participants rather than exclusively the third-person perspective of outside observers.

When Habermas first made this methodological point against neo-positivists in his 1967 literature review, *Zur Logik der Sozialwissenschaften,* he soon had to resist the subtle inducements of Gadamer to follow him further down the garden path of hermeneutics. In particular, Gadamer wanted to know how Habermas was going to avoid the inherent contextuality of interpretation, its rootedness in the hermeneutic situation of the interpreter, and its constitutional susceptibility to the historical and cultural variability of the latter. To make a long (and very interesting) story very short (and much less interesting), Habermas avoided the specter of relativism to which this gave rise by appealing to the idea of using a theoretical framework to fix the terms of interpretation.[9] He presented as an example the use of psychoanalytic theory to frame depth-psychological interpretations and explanations; and he held out the prospect of reconstructing historical materialism to provide just such a fixed theoretical framework for historical and social interpretation and explanation. That project eventually took the form of his theory of communicative action and the theory of social evolution based on it.

I have argued for some time now that these purported theories

could more accurately be understood as general analytical and interpretive frameworks, the decisive difference being that the latter too are
historically and culturally situated and thus, in the end, essentially contestable.[10] As a result, we cannot reasonably expect in human studies,
as we do in natural science, regularly to agree upon "one right answer"
– even granted that our inquiries are typically structured by the pragmatic presupposition that there is one. In these branches of knowledge,
we must learn to live with reasonable, ongoing disagreements reflecting different interpretive and evaluative standpoints. As evidence of
this, it will have to suffice here to point to the familiar persistence of
epistemological and methodological disputes in all of the human sciences; critical theorists vie with structuralists and functionalists, and
they with symbolic interactionists and rational choice theorists, and they
with historical, institutional, and comparative approaches, and most
of the above with Habermas's theory of communicative action. If one
adds to this mix the myriad of substantive disagreements that persist
in many areas of social and historical inquiry, as well as the competing interpretive frameworks now emerging in modernizing and recently
modernized, non-Western societies, the idea that the "reconstructive
sciences" Habermas favors could freeze the play of difference across
the broad expanse of historical and human studies seems implausible
(*KV*, 260ff.).

This line of argument has particular application to the discussion
of faith and reason. If hermeneutic situatedness is a general burden of
postmetaphysical reason in discourse about the human world, interpretation and explanation of religious phenomena, in particular, should
be susceptible to ongoing reasonable disagreement – as they in fact
appear to be. But the point I want to stress here is that this also gives
"modernized," religiously imbued interpretations of historical, cultural,
social, and political phenomena equal standing in principle with competing interpretations in the global discourse of modernity. As Max
Weber argued over a century ago, the situatedness of social scientific
interpretation includes the *Wertbeziehungen*, the value relations, of the
interpretive standpoints involved. Even if we no longer subscribe to his
neo-Kantian theory of value, it remains that our different hermeneutic
starting points are informed not just by beliefs and practices but also by
values and goods. In consequence, while the development of the branches
of knowledge (*Wissenschaften*) concerned with socio-cultural forms of
life does bring with it levels of reflexivity and de-centration incompatible
with magical, mythical, and onto-theological forms of interpretation, it
by no means produces the sort of convergence on "one right answer"
we have come to expect in the natural sciences. Rather, it gives rise to
forms of discourse that may as well lead to reasonable disagreement as to

reasoned agreement. In these areas, the conversation, however committed to the standards of reasonable discourse and informed by empirical findings, continues. Self-understanding is inherently open-ended.

On the other hand, while the logics of human studies involving interpretive procedures preclude expecting agreement on the one right answer to every well-posed question – an expectation that is, by contrast, not often disappointed in the natural sciences – this does not mean that "anything goes." Rather, in these domains it is often the case that "more than one thing goes," in the sense of being a party to an ongoing reasonable disagreement. Impartiality and objectivity remain, as Habermas stresses, constitutive virtues of the organized, institutionalized practices that comprise these *Wissenschaften*. The careful marshaling and weighing of evidence and argument for and against different positions in the pursuit of reasoned agreement remains a hallmark of the best work in history, sociology, psychology, economics, political science, and other areas of organized knowledge of the human world. It is just that the *einheitsstiftende Idee* that informs and structures it, the idea of a single objective world that is the same for all of us – as Habermas, echoing Kant, characterizes it (*KV*, 261) – functions as a regulative idea in the human sciences in a way different from that in the natural sciences. In the latter, following the maxim to seek one right account of natural events is regularly rewarded with universal agreement on just such an account. In the human sciences, however, pursuit of the truth concerning human affairs frequently leads to disagreement that is reasonable in the sense of being in line with the canons of evidence and argument proper to the discipline in question, and sometimes to disagreement about those very canons.

In these domains, we rarely encounter "proof" or "demonstration" in any strictly logical sense; rather, we normally have to do with more or less cogent arguments, and cogency is a very different sort of relation from logical proof. Assessing cogency involves judging the weight to be given to different kinds of considerations, the force to be credited to different sorts of arguments, and the like. All of this suggests that Habermas cannot reasonably expect to avoid persistent reasonable disagreements, either concerning his prolegomenon to global discourse or in that discourse itself. The institutionalization and inculcation of impartial and objective procedures do not ensure agreement – as the history of philosophy itself illustrates: we are still debating, as impartially and objectively as we can, the same questions that occupied Plato and Aristotle, and are still supposing, in a way that structures our discourse, that there is one right answer to each of them, but are also, obviously, still disagreeing about just which it is.

IV   Faith and Reason in the Public Sphere: Analytic Distinctions and Synergic Realities

What is the practical political significance of Habermas's idealized conception of the relation of faith and reason? On that conception, when believers have reflexively accommodated the inescapable "facts of modernity," including the irreducible plurality of views on the ultimate meaning and value of human life; and when secular reasoners have moved beyond the narrowness of the first Enlightenment and absorbed the lessons of the second; the relations between faith and reason – as well as, of course, among the diversity of views on either side of this constructed divide – will have to be dialogical. No party is authorized to legislate to the others or in a position to predict the future course and eventual outcome of dialogue. Rather, each party has to respect the freedom and equality of all other participants in the global discourse of modernity.

This is meant to be an ideal of (de-transcendentalized) practical reason; the reality to which it relates is obviously in a quite different condition, with perhaps a majority of actually existing believers not yet modernized or not fully modernized in Habermas's sense; and with very many secular thinkers not yet fully enlightened about the nature, scope, and limits of postmetaphysical reason. But I shall not discuss here the pros and cons of the neo-Kantian strategy Habermas follows in interpreting and evaluating historical, cultural, and social realities from this perspective as, for instance, better or worse approximations to the normative ideal. I want instead to put some dialectical and hermeneutical pressure on a few key analytical distinctions that he relies upon when employing it for purposes of normative political theory.

(a) One of them is more often tacit than explicit in these recent writings but was elaborated upon at length in earlier publications: the distinction between cultural and political public spheres. Now this is a notoriously fraught distinction, as earlier discussions of Habermas's scheme (and of Rawls's similar, but not identical, distinction between public reason and background culture) have made evident. When Habermas now requires, for instance, that "in their role as citizens" secular reasoners should abstain from making wholesale judgments about the rationality or irrationality of religious belief, or about the reasonableness or unreasonableness of the ethical orientations they express, he is clearly making recommendations concerning discourse in political public spheres. On the other hand, when he credits the critique of religion offered by philosophical, historical, psychological, and sociological discourse since the eighteenth century with contributing to the modernization of religious consciousness that he endorses, he is speaking primarily of developments within cultural spheres.

Now it would make little sense to recommend that this latter critique be brought to an end, that scholars and intellectuals and publicists suppress their critical thoughts on the origins, sources, traditions, functions, and practices of religion. In particular, it would make no sense in terms of his own account of the critical role of discourse in the cultural learning process. On that account, cultures learn, in large measure, through the discursive formations and processes they institutionalize – in schools and universities, in print and electronic media, and so forth. And, according to Habermas, discourse calls for reciprocal engagement to raise, criticize, defend, and revise claims of all sorts. On his account, this requires a symmetrical positioning of all participants, with no views exempt from the give and take of the exchange of reasons. In such discursive contexts, respect for the integrity and authenticity of interlocutors whose lives are based on religious conviction would not call for "abstention" – as he says it does in political public spheres – but for a certain kind of engagement: we show respect to other discourse participants by critically engaging with them in examining the matters at issue. Openness to other views and an orientation to mutual learning pertain to this process and would be defeated by abstaining from it.

Assuming that Habermas would endorse this view of the encounter between faith and reason in cultural spheres, it becomes imperative to ask how the very different conditions of political discourse he recommends could be realized in practice, given that we are dealing here with an analytical distinction that is by no means descriptive of our much messier, mass-mediated, cultural-political and political-cultural public spheres.

(b) Habermas's distinction between the "core" of religious belief, to which the civic ethic of abstention applies, and those religious beliefs that may be assessed in terms of socially institutionalized, scientific *Weltwissen*, that is, knowledge of the objective world, is also problematic. He recommends that, in our role as citizens, we abstain from criticizing the former but not the latter (*EFK*, 42). So religiously inspired claims about the way things really are in the objective world, or about how everyone should morally conduct themselves, can be contested in the political public sphere using the standards of modern science and modern morality. But, for many religious believers, such "is" and "ought" metaphysical and moral claims are central to or intricated with core tenets of faith. That is, in reality the two types of analytically distinguished beliefs are not neatly demarcated but interpenetrating.

The problems here are exacerbated when we recall that knowledge of the world importantly includes knowledge of socio-cultural worlds, as pursued in history, the social sciences, cultural studies, humanistic scholarship, and the like. Key knowledge claims in broad swaths of these disciplines have proved to be ongoingly contestable, and among the perennial contestants are religiously imbued interpretations and explanations. Whether or not we judge them to be the best available accounts, we cannot rule them out a priori, that is, prior to all discursive examination. So in actual practice, an assessment of which religious beliefs are, to use Habermas's formulations, "over and above" or "beyond" those that can be scientifically settled (*BNR*, 109) – and thus which belong to the core – is itself inherently contestable.

Further, as noted above, Habermas proposes that postmetaphysical thinkers regard the truths of faith that belong to this core from an ethical perspective, that is, as ethical insights and orientations that are potential candidates for translation into a generally accessible language, where they might possibly gain general assent. Now it is important to note here that in Habermas's framework, there can be reasonable disagreements concerning ethical claims too, which may be discussed in what he calls "ethical-existential" and "ethical-political" discourses. But this means that our best efforts at translation of, say, religious strictures on the education or employment of women, or on homosexual unions, might yield ethical recommendations we judge, with reasons, to be not good but bad. The premise that postmetaphysical philosophers can no longer claim to be the final judges of ethical disputes does not entail that postmetaphysical thinkers may not be participants in ethical debates. In short, channeling religious views on to an ethical track doesn't end disagreement: it opens the field to reasonable disagreements about ethical matters. So in this regard, too, it is difficult to see how refraining from critical judgments of religious beliefs might actually be put into practice. Agnosticism concerning religion is evidently not the only way, and may not be the best way, to foster public dialogue and mutual learning between them.

(c) These complications of Habermas's analytical distinctions between cultural and political public spheres, and between the opaque core and rationalizable periphery of religious faith, put additional pressure, in turn, upon his idea of "worldview neutrality" in regard to the foundations of democratic constitutionalism and to the exercise of legitimate state power. He often explains such neutrality in terms of the universal "accessibility" or "intelligibility" – "in principle" – of the language in which the relevant norms are stated and reasons given (*IO*, ch. 3; *BNR*, ch. 5). Now, taken literally, this is a very weak sense of neutrality, for accessibility is not the same as acceptability. Thus, for instance, while neo-Hobbesian and neo-Darwinian positions on international relations are generally intelligible, they are at the same time unacceptable from many particular religious and secular points of view. Worldview neutrality could, it seems, only fill the role that Habermas assigns it – that is, to allow for consensus on matters of political justice across differences in worldviews – if it meant not merely accessibility or intelligibility to all, but rather acceptability or justifiability to all. And, indeed, he uses these latter formulations as well, often in the same paragraphs with the former. But they are generally accompanied by the modal verb "could" – that is, they require that constitutional fundamentals and exercises of legitimate power could be accepted as justified by all. But that formulation only defers puzzlement: what does "could" mean here if, in fact, the norms or decisions in question are being contested from many different interpretive and evaluative points of view?

Habermas sometimes writes of proponents claiming such universal acceptability, but, to paraphrase Hegel, one such claim is as good as another. And he sometimes appeals to Rawls's notion of a "module" of political values, reasons, and norms that fits without cognitive dissonance into competing worldviews and thus may be embraced as more than a modus vivendi from within each (*EFK*, 32f.). But Rawls generally restricts this approach to the ambit of a shared political culture within a single political tradition. Habermas wants to extend it to a global setting, where the shared political culture, such as it is, would be rather thinner, even in the sphere of international law, to which he expressly adverts. As he knows, the interpretation and application even of the human rights conventions that most nations have actually signed are still hotly contested. More generally, some key questions must be asked. Is what I have said above about the logic of interpretive frameworks compatible with supposing that concrete formulations of legal and political norms can be equally acceptable from all points of view? Is it compatible with the idea that a valid norm be justified equally to citizens of all persuasions, and for the same reasons?

V Epilogue

The questions I have raised concerning Habermas's discussion of the relations between a faith that has accommodated itself to irreversible developments in the modern world and a reason that has overcome the narrowness of the original Enlightenment project and recognized modernized religious consciousness as, in Hegelian terms, a contemporary *Gestalt des Geistes*, taken all together, suggest that the path of reconciliation he proposes is rife with dialectical and hermeneutical snares. Far from setting out neutral conditions of dialogue between religious and secular thinkers, his proposal is open at multiple points to contestation not only by "them" – that is, the modernized believers with whom he proposes to dialogue about global justice – but also by "us," that is, the postmetaphysical, secular thinkers in whose name he makes the proposal. The proposal, which he explicitly offers from a particular, philosophically and theoretically informed point of view, cannot in the very nature of the case rise above the very considerable diversity of opinion across and on either side of the great divide. It is in itself a particular view of the contemporary burdens of faith and reason, and of the possibilities and constraints they present for efforts to continue the unfinished project of enlightenment, particularly in regard to the discourse of global justice. Thus, Habermas can do no more than propose it and attempt discursively to weather the storm of objections to be expected from every corner of both sides. Many of them will be to the effect that his proposal is not in fact neutral toward, or equally fair to, all of the competing positions. Its virtues are, rather, those of a well-informed, well-thought out, and well-meaning contribution to the ongoing, reflexive discussion of what the conditions of communication themselves ought to be.

Having said this, I should make clear that I am not questioning the need for intercultural dialogue about global justice; nor the importance of reflecting upon the conditions under which this could come to pass. But I am doubtful that the problems involved can be settled in theory, prior to and as a guide for practice. It seems, rather, that theory in this area functions best when it accompanies and reflects upon difficulties encountered in communicative practices, that is, when it is a form of reflective participation in those very practices. If this is so, one should not expect the fault lines between faith and reason to be bridged in theory, once and for all, but rather repeatedly and variously in a global proliferation of situated practices, only some of which will have the character and meet the conditions of Habermas's demanding notion of discourse. And, even in those cases, the most we can reasonably expect is that participants will be sufficiently aware of the conditioned character of their discourses that, while putting forward their own positions on the matters at issue, they will be willing to listen to and take account of objections raised from other points of view. Very often, they will agree to disagree and, as we may hope, seek reciprocally to accommodate their reasonable disagreements in the institutions and spaces they have to share.

This is, indeed, what one would expect from a reconstruction of Kant's conception of reason in terms of the pragmatics of discourse, such as Habermas proposes in his theory of communicative rationality (*BNR*, ch. 2). Like Kant's transcendental principles, Habermas's pragmatic presuppositions cannot be ignored without damaging our relation to objectivity and truth.[11] Thus, for instance, the supposition that there is one right answer to any well-posed question about the objective world is fundamental to the rational structure of theoretical discourse. Analogously to a Kantian idea of reason, this idealizing presupposition posits a "collective unity" as the goal of rational deliberation, thereby lending systematicity and coherence to its outcomes.[12] In this regard, it is indispensable to learning processes, for reasoned disagreement about just which answer is the right one is a principal motor force driving them.

On the other hand, the goal toward which transcendental ideas direct the understanding, Kant warns us, is a *focus imaginarius*, beyond any given experience. Though we must presuppose and pursue it, we cannot assert its objective reality without succumbing to transcendental illusions.[13] Even after such illusions are detected and their invalidity acknowledged, however, they do not cease to trouble us. For they arise from the most fundamental rules governing the use of our understanding, in that such subjective necessities naturally and inevitably appear to be objective necessities in the things themselves. Correspondingly, while the pragmatic presupposition of "one right answer" is integral to the *Versachlichung* of the *Weltwissen* that institutionalized *Wissenschaften* pursue, we can avoid the illusion it fosters of being in possession of the truth only by reflexively attending to its "regulative," rather than constitutive, function. In terms of the institutionalization of discourses about the human world, this translates into the requirement that they be so organized as to accommodate persistent disagreement about the meaning and value of human life and the reasonable disagreements in the human studies to which this inevitably gives rise.

6

Having One's Cake and Eating It Too

Habermas's Genealogy of Postsecular Reason

AMY ALLEN

☙

Habermas's recent work on religion is motivated, in large part, by a worry about the impotence of a thoroughly secular philosophy in the face of the challenges of twenty-first-century life. As he puts it: "pure practical reason can no longer be so confident in its ability to counteract a modernization spinning out of control armed solely with the insights of a theory of justice. The latter lacks the creativity of linguistic world-disclosure that a normative consciousness afflicted with accelerating decline requires in order to regenerate itself" (*BNR*, 211). Meaning has become an increasingly scarce resource in the modernizing world, and a purely postmetaphysical philosophy cannot generate this resource on its own. Hence, a philosophy suited to our postsecular age relies on religion as a form of world-disclosure that both serves as a rich source of semantic content and offers a critical perspective on the pathologies of Western modernity. Habermas's acknowledgment of this close relationship between the religious traditions of the West and its postmetaphysical philosophical orientation not only raises difficult questions about the boundaries between faith and knowledge, but also presents a significant challenge to the secularistic self-understanding of much of Western philosophy.

In his reflections on religion, as in much of his philosophical work in recent years, Habermas takes a de-transcendentalized reading of Kant as his point of departure. He criticizes Kant for treating religion both as a heritage and as an opponent – in this sense, Kantian reason attempts to have its religious cake and eat it, too – and for failing to recognize the inherent plurality of conceptions of the good. Nevertheless, Kant's notion of the ethical community as a philosophical articulation of the kingdom of God on earth provides a model for the kind of reflective appropriation and translation of religious contents into secular philosophical terms that Habermas believes postmetaphysical thinking needs. Moreover, Kant's cosmopolitan vision inspires Habermas's conception of what remains the best hope for the political organization of a multicultural, religiously pluralistic world society.

As we know from Hegel, de-transcendentalizing Kant in large part means historicizing him; hence, the historical reconstruction of the emergence of a form of reason that is no longer secular, but that must now see itself as *post*secular, is crucial to Habermas's work on religion. Habermas refers to this historical reconstruction as a genealogy of post-secular reason. The aim of this genealogy is to uncover the rootedness of secular Enlightenment normative ideals – including the ideals that guide Habermas's own work – in a particular religious tradition and context, specifically the emergence of the monotheistic religions of the Axial Age. And yet this acknowledgment does not, in Habermas's view, lessen the context-transcendent force of those ideals. Hence, throughout his work on religion, the contextualist is one of Habermas's great foils (the other being the reductive naturalist). On the face of it, however, it is unclear just how the genealogical strand of Habermas's project fits together with his sharp critique of contextualism, especially since some of the great-est genealogists in the philosophical tradition were also contextualists – think of Hume, Nietzsche, and Foucault. In what follows, I attempt to sort out the relationship between Habermas's understanding of the genealogical method and his critique of contextualism, and then briefly consider the implications of these issues for Habermas's political concep-tion of public reason. I start by clarifying Habermas's use of the term "genealogy" and considering the limitations of the particular genealogi-cal method that he employs. This leads me to raise anew some familiar questions about Habermas's critique of contextualism and to suggest a more contextualist interpretation of Habermas's meta-normative project than he is willing to endorse. Finally, I argue that such a contextualist reading of Habermas's meta-normative project not only coheres better with the political aims of his work on religion, but also provides a way of defending Habermas against a version of the very same charge he makes against Kant: that of attempting to have his religious cake and eat it, too.

I   Habermasian Genealogy: Vindicatory or Problematizing?

Habermas has, in recent years, taken to describing certain key aspects of his project as "genealogical" (*IO*, ch. 1). This usage persists in his recent writings on religion (see *BNR*, 6, 143, 146), a principal aim of which is, as Habermas puts it, tracing the "genealogy of secular and postmetaphysical thought" (*EFK*, 3). Getting clear on how Habermas understands genealogical inquiry is crucial for understanding his project on religion, but Habermas, unfortunately, tends to leave this key methodological concept unexplained. In order to shed some light on this issue, I shall distinguish three different modes of genealogical inquiry: subversive, vindicatory, and problematizing.[1] The common core of these three ways of doing genealogy is their attempt to explicate, as Nietzsche puts it in the Preface to *On the Genealogy of Morals*, "a knowledge of a kind that has never yet existed or even been desired," namely, "a knowledge of the conditions and circumstances in which [moral values] grew, under which they evolved and changed."[2] However, each of these three modes of genealogical inquiry uses such knowledge for a distinctive end. Nietzsche's own mode of genealogical inquiry is commonly taken to be subversive; that is to say, it aims not only to raise the question of the value of our values, but also to *call them into question*, by raising doubts about their value for "furthering the advancement and prosperity of man in general (the future of man included)."[3] The danger of a purely subversive genealogy is, as many of Nietzsche's critics have pointed out, that it seems to court the genetic fallacy.[4] Vindicatory genealogy, by contrast, also raises the question of the value of our values but, unlike subversive genealogy, it answers that question in the affirmative. Hence, for example, the genealogies of truthfulness offered in Bernard Williams's *Truth and Truthfulness* are vindicatory in the sense that they are designed to show "why truthfulness has an intrinsic value; why it can be seen as such with a good conscience."[5] The danger of a purely vindicatory mode of genealogy, by contrast, is its tendency to whiggishness. The third mode of genealogical inquiry seeks neither to subvert nor to vindicate the values and concepts whose contingent history it uncovers, but rather to problematize them. Problematizing genealogy aims not at a normative evaluation – either negative or positive – of the practices that it excavates, but rather, as Colin Koopman explains, it attempts "to clarify and intensify the difficulties that enable and disable" the practices it studies.[6]

To be sure, all three of these modes of genealogical inquiry can be present, to greater or lesser degrees, in any one genealogical account. Indeed, one might argue that the best genealogies are those that weave together all three of these modes of genealogical inquiry. That is to say, the most compelling genealogies are able to problematize our current practices, forms of life, and ways of thinking precisely because they have both subversive and vindicatory elements, without being purely subversive or vindicatory, thus avoiding the twin dangers of the genetic fallacy and whiggishness. The thought here is that a genuinely problematizing genealogy enables us to appreciate what is gained and what lost in the historical and conceptual transformations we are charting, and helps us to see how those transformations have given rise both to specific dangers and to potentials for progressive change that are embedded within our forms of life.[7] I shall return to this issue below.

With this tripartite distinction in hand, we can consider: first, whether Habermas's genealogy of postsecular reason is best understood as subversive, vindicatory or problematizing, or some combination thereof; and, second, the limitations of the specific genealogical strategy that Habermas adopts. With respect to the first question, we can easily dispense with the possibility that Habermas's use of genealogy is subversive; clearly, his aim is not to subvert or defeat our contemporary form of postsecular reason. But is his use of the genealogical method best understood as vindicatory or problematizing, or some combination of the two? This is a more difficult question to answer. In one of Habermas's earlier usages of the term, he maintains that genealogical arguments can help to justify the moral point of view by providing necessary support for the principle of universalization (U). As he puts it: "[the] justification strategy, which I have here merely sketched, must be supplemented with genealogical arguments drawing on the premises of modernization theory, if (U) is to be rendered plausible" (*IO*, 45). The justification of (U) relies on genealogical arguments because only such arguments can establish, as William Rehg puts the point, "that a commitment to discourse is somehow most rational or most in concert with the structures of lifeworld communication, or that it is the result of a moral learning process."[8] In this context, it sounds as if Habermas's genealogy of the moral point of view is vindicatory: it aims to vindicate or justify the principle of universalization by making it out to be the outcome of a moral learning process and/or the ongoing process of the rationalization of the lifeworld. According to this interpretation, Habermasian genealogy reconstructs the historically contingent emergence of concepts – such as the moral principle of universalization – but understands such concepts, despite their contingent emergence, as the results of learning processes. This usage of the term "genealogy" is thus closely tied to the project of rational reconstruction.

In the context of his recent work on religion, however, Habermas seems to understand the point of his genealogical inquiry somewhat differently: its aim is to compel "secular thought to engage in a reflection on its own origins" and hence to "break with the self-immunizing mindset that closes itself against any historical reflection on the context out of which it developed" (*EFK*, 3). Such formulations have more of a problematizing ring to them, inasmuch as they suggest that the aim of the genealogy of postsecular reason is to shake secular thought out of its complacency by problematizing its own self-understanding. By revealing the rootedness of putatively secular categories, concepts, and normative ideals in a "heritage of religious traditions that it [i.e., secular thought] has assimilated and transposed" (3), Habermas's genealogy of postsecular reason clarifies the dangers associated with a narrowly secularistic point of view. Hence, the payoff of such a problematizing genealogy would be twofold: not only to provide secular thought with a more accurate self-understanding, but also, from a political point of view, to give the lie to the secularistic assumption that religious believers are so strange and different from "us" that we no longer have to talk to "them" or even take "them" seriously.

Central to the problematizing strand of Habermas's genealogy, then, is his reconsideration of the secularization hypothesis, according to which the process of modernization leads to a corresponding decline in the social and cultural relevance of religion. Although Habermas thinks that empirical data may still be marshaled in support of this hypothesis (10) – and that the worldwide resurgence of religion could be understood as a response to heightened existential insecurity around the globe (11) – the problem with this view is that it uses the concepts of "secularization" and "modernization" imprecisely (12). Proponents of the secularization hypothesis have tended to assume, erroneously, that the declining function of religion in modernity also implies "a *loss of relevance* of religion as a contemporary intellectual formation, whether in the public sphere and the political culture of a society or in the life conduct of the individual" (13). In contrast, Habermas takes note of the emergence of forms of "public religion" even as other aspects of secularization proceed apace.

In light of the continued importance of religion, then, our multicultural world society must be considered not secular but "postsecular." The problematization of our secular self-misunderstanding leads to "the shattering of the secular*istic* confidence in the *imminent disappearance* of religion. The awareness of living in a secular society is no longer bound up with the *certainty* that advancing social and cultural modernization can occur *only* at the cost of the public influence and personal relevance of religion" (18). Habermas reminds us that the secularization hypothesis was originally connected with theories of modernization and social evolution. Hence, the question of the future of religion is inextricably bound up with our judgments about the fate of modernity (19). In his reassessment of the problematic of modernity, Habermas steers a middle path between, on the one hand, a systems-theoretical approach that understands social evolution in terms of systems functionalism and, on the other hand, a culturalist reading that views "modernity" as "a program that is inscribed in western culture alone" (23). The functionalist interpretation "sees only the leveling effects of *universal* evolutionary trends," and as a result is blind to the ways in which different cultures respond to the pressures of heightened social and economic complexity in their own, unique, culturally inflected ways (24); whereas the culturalist interpretation "is blind to the global spread of functional systems that obey their own logic irrespective of context" (23). What is needed is a third, reflexive and comparative conception of modernity, according to which "modernity" represents "the shared arena in which *different civilizations* encounter one another" with the framework of a "globalized social infrastructure" which includes, most prominently, modern science, bureaucratic state institutions, and capitalist markets (25).

From a political point of view, the constitutionalization of international law requires something more than a global social infrastructure. It also requires a level of cultural integration of world society sufficient to enable the intercultural recognition of principles of political justice. Although Habermas acknowledges that such efforts are hampered by the asymmetrical power relations that structure intercultural dialogue among global actors (27), he nevertheless thinks it is possible to articulate the cognitive presuppositions for a fair and open intercultural dialogue about such principles and how best to institutionalize them at the level of a global multicultural society (27). As Habermas notes, the answer, at least in the abstract, is clear:

> all parties to such discourse, irrespective of their cultural backgrounds, must be ready to consider controversial issues simultaneously from their own perspective and from that of each of the other participants; in addition, even in the case of questions of justice, they must be prepared to use only those arguments that could convince anyone in principle irrespective of their underlying metaphysical or religious commitments. The result of these cognitive presuppositions is to single out an ideologically neutralized and, in this sense, secular level of understanding. (28)

I will return in section III to the question of whether or not this way of understanding the framework for intercultural communication does, in fact, as Habermas maintains, distribute the cognitive burdens equally among secular and religious participants. For now, let me just note that Habermas maintains that the ongoing conflict over the fate of "modernity" is now carried on "*exclusively* between modern societies. There is no premodern society left in the global arena" (28). And he insists that the constitutionalization of international law – hence the project of global justice – depends upon the participants in this conflict being able to transform the rich semantic content of their religious (or other strong) traditions into potentially universalizable, secular, "freestanding" norms and concepts, for only the latter can provide the necessary foundations for international law. If either the realists in international relations theory or the postmodern contextualists are right about the incommensurability of competing worldviews and conceptions of justice, then the cosmopolitan project is in serious jeopardy (29).

If a genuinely open intercultural dialogue is to be possible, this will require a modern Western self-understanding of reason that is secular without being secularistic (33). Insofar as the problematizing strand of Habermas's genealogy aims precisely to dislodge and unsettle an overly confident secularism, it plays a crucial role in his work on religion. The secularistic self-understanding of reason, as found in the work of Kant, though it ensures freedom of religion at legal-political level, nevertheless "keeps religion at arm's length" and thus refuses to "encounter the [religious] other as an equal" (38). Kant reserves for philosophy the right to determine which aspects of religious traditions are rational and which are not. As Habermas observes, however, "a religion conceived in such philosophical terms . . . is no longer a religion for true believers . . . [and] it provokes moreover a lingering resentment on the part of religious citizens who no longer recognize their own beliefs and feelings under the new descriptions attributed to them" (38). By rendering the encounter between religion and secular reason in fundamentally asymmetrical and non-reciprocal terms – secular, philosophical reason is able to determine which aspects of religion are rational, but religion has nothing to say in return, and philosophy has nothing to learn from religion – Kant's philosophical critique of religion thus rules out a genuinely dialogical relationship between secular reason and religious tradition (39). A genuine dialogue with religion would have to be open to the possibility that philosophy or secular reason has something to learn from religion also. Such openness requires a rejection of the secularistic self-understanding of reason (39).

Understood in this way, the aim of Habermas's genealogy of postsecular reason seems to be to problematize the overly confident secularistic self-understanding of modernity, by compelling those who hold such a view to acknowledge the formative role that religious traditions and modes of thought have played in the development of their own concepts and categories. The political point of this socio-historical argument is to frame an open-ended, symmetrical and reciprocal dialogue between secular and religious thinkers and citizens, in which each side can learn from the other. Central to accomplishing this goal is the problematization of a certain whiggish and self-congratulatory story that we moderns like to tell ourselves, according to which modern, scientific, secular societies have overcome the naive, traditional worldviews associated with religious beliefs and ways of life.

And yet, alongside and in a somewhat uncomfortable tension with this problematizing strand of Habermas's genealogy of postsecular reason, there is a strong vindicatory current as well. The vindicatory aspect of Habermas's genealogy turns around the idea of the learning process, a process that has long been central to his notion of rational reconstruction. As Habermas puts it at the beginning of his Yale lectures:

> The encounter with religion as a contemporary intellectual formation requires secular thought to engage in a reflection on its own origins that takes the form of a genealogy of secular and postmetaphysical thought within the horizon of the Axial Age and of the discussion of faith and knowledge in the High Middle Ages. Assuming that it understands its own evolution as a learning process, the tradition of humanist Enlightenment thought discovers within itself an heritage of religious traditions that it has assimilated and transposed. (3)

In this passage, Habermas makes it clear that the point of his genealogy of postsecular reason is to reconstruct its own history as a learning process. Through this learning process, a prior religious heritage has been assimilated and transposed into a secular, enlightened, humanist language and form of life. Inasmuch as Habermas assumes that we ought to understand our history as a learning process, he seems to require us to see our present, secular form of life as a developmental advance over a prior religious form of life. Hence it is with his appeal to the notion of a learning process that the vindicatory aspect of Habermas's genealogy of postsecular reason comes to the fore.

Reflecting back on the preceding discussion of the three modes of genealogical inquiry, we can raise two critical questions about Habermas's genealogical project. First, does the strong vindicatory current coupled with the complete lack of a subversive element in Habermas's genealogy lead him to ignore the regressive features of the emergence of postsecular reason, thereby obscuring the dialectical character of the Enlightenment and insufficiently problematizing postsecular reason? In other words, can Habermas's goal of problematizing an overly confident secularistic self-understanding be reached with a genealogy that is devoid of any subversive aspects, that tilts so strongly toward the vindicatory side? And, second, in light of the emphasis on the vindicatory in his mode of genealogical inquiry, can Habermas avoid the charge of whiggishness?

To be sure, Habermas is well aware of the danger of blindness to the dialectical character of the Enlightenment. As he puts it, "the

Enlightenment remained ignorant of the barbaric reverse side of its own mirror for too long. Its universal claims made it easy to overlook the particularistic kernel of its European origin. This immobilized, rigidified rationalism has been transformed into the stifling power of a capitalistic world civilization, which assimilates alien cultures and abandons its own traditions to oblivion" (*RR*, 130). Not only has the Enlightenment been blind to what Thomas McCarthy has aptly called "barbarism at the heart of [its] own civilizing process,"[9] but Christianity has been thoroughly implicated in this barbarism. Habermas continues: "Christianity, which thought it could use this civilization as an 'innocent catalyst for the worldwide transmission of its message of hope', the Church which believed it could send out its missionaries in the wake of the European colonizers, participated unwittingly in this dialectic of disenchantment and loss of memory" (*RR*, 130). Facing up to the barbarism at the heart of European colonialism and its postcolonial, neo-liberal, capitalist legacy rightly has the effect of undermining an overly confident self-understanding of modernity (*EFK*, 39).

Habermas's acknowledgment of the force of the postcolonial critique of the Enlightenment is important, and it serves to complicate somewhat his genealogical account. However, if one of the aims of Habermas's genealogy is to problematize an overly confident modern self-understanding that is blind not only to its own rootedness in a religious tradition but also to its own barbarism, then it seems odd that his genealogical story largely glosses over any discussion of the connections between those religious traditions, practices, and doctrines and relationships of power, constraint, and subordination. Here I am thinking not only of the Church's participation in the "civilizing mission" of colonialism, which Habermas does discuss, but also of the internal practices, rituals, and doctrines of the Christian Church, which he does not. Such doctrinal commitments as the drive for purity, the disdain for the body as a source of impurity, and the focus on self-punishment, self-denial, and self-abnegation in the pursuit of such purity, and their concomitant ritualistic practices – all of which Nietzsche subjected to a trenchant critique in *On the Genealogy of Morals* – play no significant role in Habermas's story. Nor does he thematize the disciplining of the body through confessional practices, the pathologizing of "deviant" sexual practices or "abnormal" individuals, or the invention of an individualizing, pastoral form of power that underlies and makes possible modern forms of governmentality, as explored by Foucault. These are also aspects of the religious heritage of Western modernity, and the semantic content of at least some of these features of our religious heritage has arguably been preserved and translated into our secular philosophical notions of reflexivity, (bad) conscience, and personal and moral autonomy.

To be sure, Habermas likely wants to avoid this kind of approach because he thinks of this mode of genealogical inquiry – a genealogy that not only reveals the contingent emergence of our concepts, norms, and ideals, but also links that emergence to relations of power – as subversive of reason. Hence, such a genealogy would contribute to what he calls the "growing defeatism concerning reason" (*EFK*, 39). What Habermas fails to appreciate is that this subversive story could be one thread of a larger genealogical account that has both subversive and vindicatory elements, but that ultimately aims neither simply to subvert nor to vindicate, but rather to problematize modern, Western, postsecular reason. Whether or not Nietzsche can be read this way, I'm not so sure, but there are many passages in which Foucault indicates that this is precisely the aim of his genealogical project. For instance, he maintains that the aim of a genealogy of the relationship between rationality and power is to ask the following questions: "*What* is this Reason that we use? What are its historical effects? What are its limits, and what are its dangers? How can we exist as rational beings, fortunately committed to practicing a rationality that is unfortunately crisscrossed by intrinsic dangers?"[10] The point is neither to defeat nor to reject reason; even if it were possible to do so without undermining one's own critique, "nothing," as Foucault says, "would be more sterile."[11] Rather, the aim is to interrogate the ways in which specific forms of rationality and rationalization to which we are fortunately committed are unfortunately intrinsically connected to relations of power and modes of subjection.

Furthermore, if it is the case that these relations of power and subjection are also part of the story of the emergence of postsecular reason from out of the Judeo-Christian religious tradition, then the question for Habermas would be this: is it possible to take over the positive elements of the semantic potential of religion – the drive toward transcendence, the redemptive hope for salvation, the solidaristic notions of a universal brotherhood, and so on – without also taking on board the dangerous aspects of that tradition, namely, the drive for purity, the denial and disciplining of the body, and the compulsion toward self-beratement and self-abnegation? If we are to be sufficiently attentive to those dangers, then shouldn't our genealogy of the relation of modern, postsecular reason to its religious roots also include this part of the story? After all, religion may well be a source of social, cultural, and political ideals, as Habermas's work reminds us, but it is also, as we have known at least since Freud, a source of illusions, and powerful and dangerous ones at that. We forget this at our peril.

Habermas's relative lack of attention to this problem in his genealogy of postsecular reason leads us to the second question that I posed above: given the strong vindicatory current in Habermas's genealogy of postsecular reason, can he avoid the charge of whiggishness? This question is connected with deep and difficult problems in the philosophy of history, centering on the notions of development and progress, and whether it is possible to reformulate such ideas even in light of their endemic ideological misuse to justify and rationalize forms of racism, neo-racism, colonialism and neo-imperialism.[12] To put the point schematically, the worry is that any sort of vindicatory genealogy of Western modernity runs the risk of re-enacting Western cultural imperialism by understanding the West as developmentally superior to and hence more advanced than its non-Western counterparts, who are then interpreted as under-developed and cognitively inferior.

Habermas is, of course, well aware of this problem. He has addressed the charge of ethnocentrism as far back as his essays on discourse ethics from the 1980s (*MCCA*, ch. 3).[13] He tends to respond to this sort of objection by appealing to the *inevitability* of the universalizable norms that he invokes. Thus, with respect to the principle of universalization, he argues that it is grounded in the unavoidable presuppositions of a communicative form of life to which there is no coherent alternative, to which the only possible alternatives are "the monadic isolation of strategic action, or schizophrenia and suicide" (102). Similarly, with respect to political modernity, Habermas maintains that there is no viable alternative, since no purely premodern societies remain in our globalized world (*EFK*, 28). And, in his recent work on religion, he makes this claim to inevitability with respect to the emergence of postsecular reason itself (*RR*, 149). But such claims about the inevitability of moral, cultural, and political learning processes don't dispel the worry about whiggishness; instead, they heighten it.

Another option here would be for Habermas to respond to charges of cultural imperialism by saying that the vindicatory aspect of his genealogical account can only be understood from the first-person point of view, that is, it is only for "us," for adherents to or members of modern Western forms of life. On such a reading, the vindicatory thread of Habermas's genealogy of postsecular reason ought not to be construed as making any grand claims about world-historical progress. Rather, it should be understood as pointing out that "we" members of modern Western cultures must inevitably see certain aspects of "our" historical development from "our" own internal first-person point of view as the result of irreversible learning processes. I will return to this point below, but for now, let me note two things: first, this way of understanding the vindicatory aspect of Habermas's genealogy is easier to reconcile with the subversive side of the story of the emergence of modern, Western, postsecular reason, the side that Habermas, for the most part, fails to tell; and, second, as a result, this way of understanding the vindicatory thread of Habermas's genealogical project better serves the overall problematizing aim of his genealogy of postsecular reason. But this way of reconciling the two distinct strands of his genealogical project is made possible by a thoroughly contextualist reading of Habermas's vindicatory genealogical claims. Hence, this discussion leads us into a thorny set of philosophical issues about Habermas's relationship to and critique of contextualism, issues to which I now turn.

II   Contextualism and Context-transcendence

The idea of the context-transcendence of validity claims has long been central to Habermas's philosophical project, and a principal means by which he has distinguished his way out of the philosophy of the subject from rival approaches such as postmodernism (see *PDM*, especially lecture XI). Habermas's recent work on religion not only provides an interesting exemplar of the idea of context-transcendence, but also gives that notion, and Habermas's debate with his contextualist rivals, a new, quasi-religious twist. Habermas's work on religion serves as an exemplar of his claim about context-transcendence in the sense that his genealogy of postsecular reason traces Enlightenment concepts and norms to their rootedness in a particular religious context and yet simultaneously maintains their universal, context-transcendent validity. The new twist in Habermas's critique of contextualism is that he now associates this philosophical position with those magical-mythical worldviews that never made the great cognitive advance characteristic of the Axial Age: the construction of the extramundane standpoint of the divine, the vantage point from which the world could be understood as a whole. Hence, Habermas now describes contextualism as a form of neo-paganism (see, for example, *RR*, 159; *BNR*, 246). After briefly discussing these two aspects of Habermas's work on religion, I want to suggest, first, that Habermas overdraws the contrast between himself and (at least some versions of) contextualism and, second, that he errs by lumping contextualists in with the reductive naturalists as enemies of reason. Not only should Habermas understand his own project in more contextualist terms than he seems willing to accept, but he should also view contemporary contextualists as potential allies in the project of critiquing a technical-scientific reason that is presently running amok.

Habermas characterizes his understanding of the relationship between context and context-transcendence as an attempt to chart a middle course between "the Scylla of a leveling, transcendence-less empiricism and the Charybdis of a high-flying idealism that glorifies transcendence"

(*RR*, 91). The theory of communicative action understands this tension between the transcendent and the immanent as rooted within every-day communicative praxis, but not, for that reason, eliminated. In the context of his work on religion, Habermas's middle path consists in his greater attention to the rootedness of the Enlightenment ideals of freedom, equal respect, autonomy, mutual recognition, and liberation – ideals that are central to his own work – in the particular historical context of Judaic and Christian religious traditions, paired with his insis-tence that such ideals nevertheless transcend their original context. As he puts it: "Universalistic egalitarianism, from which sprang the ideals of freedom and a collective life in solidarity, the autonomous conduct of life and emancipation, the individual morality of conscience, human rights and democracy, is the direct legacy of the Judaic ethic of justice and the Christian ethic of love" (149). And yet this legacy can be the source of universal moral and political ideals, aspirations, and institutions. Hence, Habermas continues, "this legacy, substantially unchanged, has been the object of a continual critical reappropriation and reinterpretation. *Up to this very day there is no alternative to it.* And in light of the current chal-lenges of a postnational constellation, we must draw sustenance now, as in the past, from this substance. Everything else is idle postmodern talk" (149, emphasis added). Similarly, he notes that he does not object to the claim that his conception of communicative action "nourishes itself from the legacy of Christianity"; nor does he reject the contention that his early account of emancipation (in *Knowledge and Human Interests*) "could be 'unmasked' as the secularizing translation of the divine promise of sal-vation" (*RR*, 160). At the same time, Habermas insists that philosophy must translate the semantic contents of those religious ideas into secular terms – that is, it must adhere to a strict "methodological atheism" (160) – in order to meet the peculiar demands of justificatory, argumentative discourse. By performing this translation, philosophy gains access to a mode of discourse that "holds open the dimension of validity-claims which transcend social space and historical time" (134).

Habermas's genealogy of the Axial Age further complicates this story of contextually grounded context-transcendence, for, in that genealogy, he argues that the decisive feature of the Axial Age is the emergence of "a unifying perspective that allowed the new intellectual elites to tran-scend occurrences within the world and to distance themselves from and objectify the latter *as a whole*" ("The Sacred Roots of the Axial Age Traditions," unpublished, ch. 2, p. 3). The distinctive cognitive advance – and here the vindicatory aspect of Habermas's genealogical account shines through once again – of the Axial Age is thus the construction of "a divine standpoint outside the world," for "without such a standpoint or principle the human mind cannot develop a picture of the world, or of the ages of the world, as a whole from a theoretical perspective or a universalistically oriented ethics from a practical perspective" (ibid.). Hence, what emerges in the Axial Age traditions are precisely *the conditions of possibility for the idea of context-transcendence*. This cognitive breakthrough makes it possible to distinguish essence from appearance, which, in turn, enables a progressive de-mythologization of the world. The key features of this cognitive breakthrough include "a widening of perspectives, of an upgrading of reflexivity, and of an increasing awareness of contingency" (ibid., p. 5). Such a cognitive advance already contains *in nuce* the key hallmarks of the postconventional point of view that emerges in full form in Western modernity.

In Habermas's view, the construction of the point of view of the divine – which is later de-transcendentalized and understood as a point of view rooted within the social world, as a transcendence from within (see *RR*, 135) – affords a far greater explanatory power than that of contextualist narratives ("The Sacred Roots of the Axial Age Traditions"). This brings us to Habermas's critique of contemporary philosophical forms of contextualism – represented in the work of neo-Heideggerians, neo-Wittgensteinians, and neo-Nietzscheans – as neo-pagan. Such contextualisms are neo-pagan in that they reject the very notion of the extramundane standpoint, even in its de-transcendentalized version, and the distinction between essence and appearance that such a standpoint makes possible. As such, they recall, according to Habermas, the pagan mythical-magical worldview that predates the great cognitive advance of the Axial Age.

> The historicism of paradigms and world-pictures, now rife, is a second-level empiricism which undermines the serious task confronting a subject who takes up a positive or negative stance towards validity-claims. Such claims are always raised here and now, in a local context – but they also transcend all merely provincial yardsticks. When one paradigm or world picture is worth as much as the next, when different discourses encode everything that can be true or false, good or evil, in different ways, then this closes down the normative dimension which enables us to identify the traits of an unhappy and distorted life. (*RR*, 134)

The central problem with such historicist contextualist positions, then, is that they "imply the rejection of the universalistic significance of unconditioned validity claims" (159).

Although Habermas acknowledges that such versions of contextualism "may initially have the innocently pragmatic sense of sharpening our sensitivity for contexts," he also sharply criticizes "the flat anti-Platonism that circulates so thoughtlessly in today's modish late Heideggerian and late Wittgensteinian currents" (159). Not only that, but he calls them neo-pagan, which, in the context of his writing on religion, does not seem to be intended as a compliment, though I suspect that Nietzsche, Heidegger, and Foucault would have been delighted to take it as one anyway. In any case, Habermas's staunch defense of the context-transcendence of validity claims against the neo-pagan contextualists should give us some pause. As Maeve Cooke has recently argued, Habermas's commitment to context-transcendence is not only in tension with his commitment to the notion of situated rationality, but also opens him up to charges of latent authoritarianism.[14] Cooke argues that one way of ameliorating this tension and alleviating the worry about authoritarianism is to construe such claims as context-transcend*ing* rather than as context-transcend*ent*, thereby construing this idea in a maximally dynamic, open-ended, and essentially contestable way.[15] Habermas's notion of context-transcendent validity must, as Cooke sees it, acknowledge its own historical situatedness in "the social imaginary of Western modernity."[16] As Cooke sees it, this way of taking up Habermas's project marks out a context-transcend*ing* approach to critical theory that is distinct from the radical contextualism that she attributes to Richard Rorty. To be sure, Habermas's genealogy of postsecular reason seems to aim toward just the sort of acknowledgment of its own historicity that Cooke calls for. But given that acknowledging its own historicity entails the recognition on the part of the context-transcending approach that "it is not merely committed to the idea of situated rationality, it also recognizes the historical situatedness of that idea,"[17] it seems to me that such an approach is best understood not as an alternative to contextualism, but rather as a principled form of it.[18] Whatever label one chooses for it, it is much closer to contextualism than Habermas's pointed dismissals of contextualism as neo-paganism would lead one to believe.

Indeed, the principled contextualist could maintain that it is overly tendentious of Habermas to frame the issue as a choice between the notion of context-transcendence, on the one hand, and a shallow immanence, on the other hand. She could agree with Habermas that we must understand claims to normative (and truth) validity as both immanent and transcendent at the same time, but disagree about the best way to construe this both/and. Habermas's standard formulation, repeated in the passage cited above, is to say that "such claims are always raised here and now, in a local context – but they also transcend all merely provincial yardsticks." But this way of putting it might seem, to the principled contextualist, to downplay the immanent, this-worldly aspect of those claims by admitting no more than the trivially true point that such claims must be spoken by some particular person or typed into some particular computer screen in order to be raised. This formulation seems not to do justice to the immanent moment or the *within* of transcendence from within. A more contextualist way to construe transcendence from within would be to say that norms and ideals are *both* transcendently immanent – that is, they have a context-transcend*ing* aim or significance – *and* are immanently transcendent – that is, their transcendence is understood as an aspiration, an "idealizing projection," or a "promissory note,"[19] not as a fait accompli. Such an account does not level out the notion of transcendence from within into a flat empiricist anti-Platonism, nor does it undermine or close down the normative dimension that enables us to view forms of life as distorted, though it does interpret this notion and this dimension differently than does Habermas. Rather than insisting that claims raised from within our context do transcend that context, this principled contextualist position maintains that from within our context, we understand claims to normative validity (and also truth) as context-transcending, in the sense that they aim toward transcendence. Such a modified contextualism could accept many of the same substantive norms that Habermas endorses at a first-order level (such as autonomy, equality, reciprocity, human rights, etc.), but the contextualism would consist in the rejection of the second-order, strongly universalistic, context-transcendent interpretation of Habermas's meta-normative project.

If this is a plausible middle ground between Habermas's strong construal of context-transcendence and the radical form of contextualism that he rejects, then we can see that Habermas need not regard all forms of contextualism as philosophical rivals. Moreover, we can see why it is a mistake for him to lump contextualism together with the reductive forms of naturalism that he rightly criticizes. Habermas equates contextualism with reductive naturalism because he believes that both views deny the standpoint of the divine, the extramundane (but now de-transcendentalized and innerworldly) standpoint. Hence, both movements threaten the self-understanding of Western modernity with "a *growing defeatism concerning reason*" (*EFK*, 39). As a result of these self-defeating critiques of reason, "the self-affirmation of reason as secular, postmetaphysical thought can no longer rely on science and enlightenment *without qualification*. It is compelled to qualify science and enlightenment by, for example, rejecting physicalism or warning against the presumptuousness of a totalizing critique of reason" (39–40). Indeed, in his dialogue with theologians, Habermas indicates that one of his central aims in addressing the issue of the relationship between faith and knowledge is to combat this defeatism: "Postmetaphysical thinking cannot cope on its own with the defeatism concerning reason which we encounter today both in the postmodern radicalization of the 'dialectic of the Enlightenment' and in the naturalism based on a naïve faith in science" (*AWM*, 19–20). In this battle, Habermas believes that postmetaphysical thinking needs religion on its side, as a source of rich semantic content and of the awareness that something is missing, that our form of life is deformed or pathological.

However, as I have argued, the principled contextualist need not reject the very idea of the de-transcendentalized extramundane standpoint. Rather, she can retain a substantive commitment to this idea while, at a meta-normative level, understanding that commitment as itself historically situated. Then the only remaining difference between Habermas and the principled contextualist would be at the level of philosophy of history: Habermas, unlike the contextualist, is committed to seeing this idea as not only historically emergent but also as a cognitive advance, as the result of a learning process. But if, as I discussed at the end of the previous section, this commitment can be understood as the claim that "we" adherents to Western modernity must see the idea of context-transcendence as the result of a learning process, then this insight, too, can be framed in contextualist terms. In that case, the vindicatory aspect of Habermas's genealogy could be understood as a vindication *for* "*us.*"[20] This means not only that learning only counts as learning *for us*, but also that when it counts as such, it really counts as *learning*, that is, as a workable response to a set of historically emergent problems and as an advance over previous responses.[21] On the other hand, if Habermas is committed to the claim that the nineteenth and twentieth centuries' de-transcendentalization of an idea of context-transcendence that emerged with the monotheistic religions and Greek metaphysical traditions of the Axial Age just is a cognitive advance full stop, in the sense of a more developed way of relating to the world, if, that is, the vindicatory aspect of his genealogy is meant as a vindication *tout court*, then I do not see how this claim is compatible with the problematizing aims of Habermas's genealogy of postsecular reason; nor do I see how Habermas can avoid the charge of whiggishness.

Regardless of how this issue gets decided, however, Habermas is wrong to lump reductive naturalism and neo-pagan contextualism together, as twin enemies of reason. Habermas is right, I think, to argue that reductive naturalism reduces the world to a flat anti-Platonism in which human consciousness, morality, and freedom are nothing more than a swirl of neural networks and mechanisms. On the least sophisticated versions of this view, there is nothing about the human being that cannot be "explained" in terms of which regions of the brain light up on an fMRI scan. But many forms of contextualism, like Habermasian critical theory, stand opposed to this sort of naturalism. Contextualists such as Foucault and the historians of science who have been inspired by him – Ian Hacking, Donna Haraway, Bruno Latour, Paul Rabinow, and others – may reject the strong notion of context-transcendence, but their efforts to historicize scientific theories by tracing their connections to contingent relations of power and constraint generate a powerful and productive critique of reductive naturalism. Rather than dismissing them as enemies of reason, Habermas would do better to view these contextualists as allies in his project of critiquing technical-scientific reason.

III   The Cognitive Burdens of Public Reason

The issues I have raised about the vindicatory aspects of Habermas's genealogy of postsecular reason and his commitment to a strong understanding of the context-transcendence of validity claims give rise to a final political objection to Habermas's conception of public reason. Habermas maintains that the cognitive burdens of participating in public, political dialogues are, on his conception of public reason, shared equally and symmetrically between secular and religious citizens. There is, however, a residual asymmetry in Habermas's account of those cognitive burdens, and this asymmetry is connected to his lack of attention to the role that power plays in the historical emergence of postsecular reason and his overly strong understanding of context-transcendence. In other words, Habermas, despite his departure from Rawls's stricter version of the translation requirement (*BNR*, 128), still stacks the deck in favor of secularism, and this is related to the vindicatory character of his genealogy of postsecular reason and his commitment to a context-transcendent understanding of the normative perspective of modernity.

To be sure, Habermas is well aware of this concern. Hence, he maintains that he considers it an "open question . . . whether the revised concept of citizenship that I have proposed still imposes an *asymmetrical* burden on religious traditions and religious communities" (138). Habermas maintains that the cognitive burdens of public reason are not asymmetrical because although the burdens placed on religious citizens are demanding – namely, that in official political institutions they must frame their reasons in secular terms – those placed on secular citizens are equally so, for they must carry out "a self-reflexive overcoming of a rigid and exclusive secularist self-understanding of modernity" (138). In other words, secular citizens cannot treat their religious co-citizens as naive throwbacks to a more primitive form of life; nor can they treat them as an exotic endangered species that must be preserved through a practice of mere toleration. But Habermas's claim about these cognitive burdens is quite strong; he maintains that the change in mentality required of secular citizens is "*no less cognitively exacting* than the adaptation of religious consciousness to the challenges of an environment that is becoming progressively more secular" (139, emphasis added). No doubt the standpoint that Habermas has in mind for secular citizens in a postsecular society is cognitively (not to mention affectively or motivationally) demanding; but is it accurate to say that it is *no less* cognitively demanding or exacting than what is demanded of religious citizens? The cognitive burdens on the religious citizen flow from the cognitive dissonances that result for religious believers under modern conditions of religious pluralism, the rise of modern science, and the emergence of positive law. Accordingly, religious citizens must be able to relate to their religious beliefs in a self-reflexive manner, acknowledge the autonomous progress of a secular science, and grant the priority of secular reasons in the political arena (137). The cognitive demand for the secular person, by contrast, is that she must be self-critically aware of limits of secular reason. In other words, the cognitive burdens of public reason require the religious believer to be quasi-secular – by granting the autonomous status and progressive nature of modern science and positive law and by adopting a self-reflexive posture toward her own religious beliefs – whereas the secular citizen simply needs to be even more reflexive than she already is, by becoming self-reflexive about the limits of her own secularism. It may well be possible to describe these stances as the result of "complementary learning processes" (140), but that does not mean that they are symmetrical and equally demanding.

However, as Habermas admits, even the question of whether and in what sense the transition from religious to secular worldviews and the concomitant changes in mentality just described should be seen as the result of a learning process at all is complex and essentially contested. After all, from what point of view can we assert that the heightened reflexivity required by both secular and religious citizens is the result of a learning process? And, conversely, from what point of view can we assert that the failure to adopt such a reflexive posture on the part of both religious fundamentalists and atheistic secularists results from a "learning deficit" (144)? Habermas concedes that "these changes in mentality count as complementary 'learning processes' only from the perspective of a specific normative self-understanding of modernity" (144). One could try appealing to a theory of social evolution to defend this assumption, but even setting aside the controversial nature of such theories, this would entail the unacceptable implication that religious citizens should understand themselves as cognitively backward. Moreover, Habermas insists that it is up to members of religious communities themselves to decide whether a modernized, reflexive faith is still a genuine faith (138, 145). Hence, Habermas concludes that *from the point of view of political theory*, the question of whether the changes in mentality necessary for public reason should count as learning processes must remain open, and the normative conception of public reason itself must be understood as essentially contested (145).

Habermas's argument turns on the claim that these questions – namely, the question of whether an increasingly modern, reflexive, secular (but not secularistic) mindset should be understood as the result of a learning process and the question of whether the normative conception of public reason is overly demanding of religious citizens – should be left open *politically* even though he does not regard them as *philosophically* open. If I understand Habermas correctly here, however, then he ends up in very much the same place as Kant. To be sure, Habermas rejects Kant's paradoxical stance toward religion – which Kant understands as both a part of his own philosophical heritage and an obscure and dogmatic opponent – hence, he rejects the notion that philosophy can decide the truth and falsity of religious beliefs. "Reason," he notes, "cannot have its religious cake and eat it" (226). And yet, by claiming that, from a philosophical perspective, the secular, reflexive, modern mindset that is demanded by his conception of public reason must be understood as the result of a learning process – even as he leaves this question open politically – Habermas seems to want to do precisely this. Like Kant, Habermas preserves the freedom of religion at a legal-political level, and insists upon the open-endedness and essentially contested nature of political disputes between religious and secular citizens. However, also like Kant, by failing to acknowledge the asymmetrical distribution of the cognitive burdens of public reason, Habermas arguably fails to "encounter the [religious] other as an equal" (*EFK*, 38). Although Habermas does not reserve for philosophy the right to determine which aspects of religious traditions are rational, he does reserve for philosophy the ability to determine which changes in mentality should count as learning processes and which as deficits. Moreover, even if religious citizens are able to assume the cognitive burdens that Habermas proposes, they can only do so by adopting a self-reflexive and epistemically modest mode of religious belief that "is no longer a religion for true believers" (38). Although such an abstract and intellectualized way of understanding one's religious commitments may make sense for theologians, it has little in common with the ways in which most religious believers experience their own faith.

Habermas could avoid this uncomfortable position by adopting a philosophical and normative stance that coheres better with his political stance, one in which questions of whether or not the history of modernity is understood as progress, and whether or not validity claims are actually capable of transcending their contexts, are left open not only *politically* but also *philosophically*. That is, he could offer a genuinely problematizing genealogy of postsecular reason by tempering the vindicatory thrust of his genealogy with a greater appreciation for the subversive aspects of that story, and he could adopt a more contextualist understanding of the claim to context-transcendence. Such a philosophically contextualist and problematizing version of his project would, I submit, cohere better with his political aim of framing an open and symmetrical dialogue with religious believers and evincing a genuine willingness to learn from them.

This question is even more pressing at the intercultural level, since at that level it is not individuals but states that are either secular or religious, hence it is difficult to see how Habermas's institutionalized version of the translation requirement, according to which individuals acting in the public political sphere must translate their religious claims into publicly accessible hence secular terms, will be useful here. Religious states would most likely balk at the idea that they must translate their religious motivations into secular language at the level of international institutions such as the United Nations, even if not at the level of the global public sphere. They would likely view this requirement as an instance of a secular Eurocentric cultural imperialism or of a thinly veiled crusading American Christianity. Habermas himself emphasizes that, in intercultural dialogue, secular Western thinkers "do not want to be perceived as crusaders of a competing religion or as salespeople of instrumental reason and destructive secularization" (*FHN*, 103). And yet, he also maintains that if we are to avoid undermining the tentative steps that have been taken toward a cosmopolitan international political order:

> the West, molded by the Judeo-Christian tradition, must reflect on one of its greatest cultural achievements: the capacity for decentering one's own perspectives, self-reflection, and a self-critical distancing from one's own traditions . . . In a word: overcoming Eurocentrism demands that the West make proper use of its own cognitive resources. (*RR*, 154)

There's a certain irony involved in saying that the way to avoid Eurocentrism is for the West to celebrate its own cultural achievements, to be even more like itself: even more reflexive and self-critical than it already is. This makes it seem as if we can overcome Eurocentrism on the cheap (which is *not* to say that accomplishing what Habermas is recommending here would be *easy*). Presumably, Habermas would agree that whether this cognitive resource should be viewed as a cultural achievement that has resulted from a learning process is a question that must be politically left open and viewed as essentially contestable in the ongoing and intensifying debates about multiple and alternative modernities. I do not wish to take issue with this point. My suggestion, rather, is that Habermas should recapitulate this commitment to openness and ongoing contestation at a philosophical level, and that this would best be accomplished by offering a more problematizing genealogy of postsecular reason – one that combines vindicatory and subversive elements – and endorsing a more contextualist interpretation of his meta-normative project.

Conclusion

Habermas himself acknowledges that the dispute between Habermasians and contextualists is "a domestic dispute over which side accomplishes the detranscendentalization [of reason] in the right way: whether the traces of a transcending reason vanish in the sands of historicism and contextualism or whether a reason embodied in historical contexts preserves the power of immanent transcendence" (*BNR*, 25). Of course, to say that this is a domestic dispute is not to deny that it is a heated and serious conflict. As we all know, family quarrels are often the most intense kinds of conflicts, precisely because your family members know better than anyone else just which of your buttons to push. My aim in this paper has not been to reignite this family conflict but to reframe it from the perspective of Habermas's recent work on religion. In so doing, I have offered a more contextualist way of understanding the power of immanent transcendence, one that understands genealogy as thoroughly problematizing rather than merely subversive or merely vindicatory, and that interprets the notion of context-transcendence as a dynamic context-transcending aim. In so doing, I have attempted a domestic reconciliation, by staking out ways of understanding Habermas's genealogy of postsecular reason project that draw him closer to the contextualist position that he, in my view, needlessly demonizes, but without thereby undermining his commitment to first-order, substantive universalist, context-transcending norms. I have also argued that such a construal of Habermas's normative and meta-normative project fits better with his political goal of framing a genuinely open-ended and symmetrical dialogue between religious and secular citizens at both the national and global levels.

7

Forgetting Isaac

Faith and the Philosophical Impossibility of a Postsecular Society

J. M. BERNSTEIN

Introduction

Despite their reconciliatory rhetoric and tone, Jürgen Habermas's writings on religion are emphatically secularist; and the few arguments meant to soften his secularist stance are either false or so indeterminate as to resolve nothing. For all intents and purposes, he requires the religious citizen to unconditionally accept the moral terms of political modernity. In comparison to these requirements, the demands on the secularist are negligible. That said, in the middle of his Yale lectures, Habermas urges a telling thesis against a narrow secularist conception of autonomous reason:

> When the secular side excludes religious fellow citizens from the circle of modern contemporaries and treats them as specimens to be protected like an endangered species, this corrodes the very substance of membership based on equal rights in the universe of rational persons. Without a reciprocal recognition, however, the formal equality in legal status of state and world citizens can ensure at most a *modus vivendi*. (EFK, 33)

I take the second sentence here as falsely qualifying the problem: even with the kind of untrammeled mutual recognition that derives from the mutual respect of citizens for one another as conscientious subjects, perceiving one another to have the right to live in accordance with the god of their choosing in a constitutional state under universal laws, the secularist might still regard her fellow citizens as living in accord with irredeemably archaic beliefs and social forms. Hence, even with strong mutual respect in place, the way citizens frame one another's substantive beliefs – the "archaic" versus the "unsaved," say – can and does weaken if not utterly dissipate the solidarity necessary for a successful democratic polity. Nothing in Habermas's various arguments seems to me to honestly address this problem; nor, I should concede, do I have any plausible remedies to offer. The religious tearing at the fabric of the secular self-understanding of the state continually threatens to make relations of citizens to one another and hence their relation to the state a modus vivendi.

The first section of this essay will elaborate the claim that Habermas's position is, as it stands, radically secularist – and rightly so. Nothing in Habermas's account truly bends in a postsecularist direction. My one sharp area of disagreement with Habermas concerns his demand that secular reason be agnostic about religious beliefs. Habermas mistakes the issue here; reason can evaluate any content for cognitive goodness – it's what reason does. What secular reason must repudiate is faith itself. In the second section, on the *Cogito*, I shall argue that secular reason is constituted by the discovery that it cannot sacrifice itself to a higher authority, call it the evil demon, call it God. In the following section, on Kierkegaard's account of the nature of faith in *Fear and Trembling*, I argue that faith requires the sacrifice of the other, and hence the repudiation of the authority of moral reason. In the final section, I argue that the movement through which God as the "wholly other" is displaced by intersubjective relations, in the manner Habermas recommends, occurs genealogically through the repudiation of faith. I take the original site of this repudiation of faith to be in Caravaggio's *Sacrifice of Isaac* in 1603; arguably, moral modernity can be dated from that moment. Rational and moral modernity arrive through the destruction of faith itself as a mode of world-relation in radical acts of self-affirmation (Descartes) and recognition of the other (Caravaggio). Secular reason is necessarily and emphatically other to faith. However vital and widespread religious life now is, from this philosophical perspective, the idea of a faith-based, faith-respecting postsecular society is impossible.

It is only faith in its austere understanding, the kind of faith that Kierkegaard unflinchingly urges and that belongs to both fundamentalism and many resurrected religious practices, that challenges the secularist self-understanding of reason and by extension the constitutional framing of religious pluralism. Arguably, it is this conception of faith that is at stake in the actual debates between religious and secular views of the fate of modern society. And it is certainly this radical Kierkegaardian conception of faith that has been used within philosophy for contesting the authority of secular reason, and hence this conception of faith which yields the self-doubt of secular reason in the "post" of the postsecular.

In pointing to the "arguments" of Descartes and Caravaggio against faith, I mean to be highlighting two pivotal moments in the constitution of secular reason; these moments belong to what is indeed a progressive learning process. In the postsecular willingness to repudiate these genea-logical touchstones of Western reason, I hear a self-lacerating doubt. However well intentioned, with respect to these debates, Habermas's pretence of providing a postsecular understanding of reason, politics, and modernity does more harm than good.

Religion within the Limits of Democracy Alone

At least, in the United States, the normative idea of a postsecular society designates something closer to a "tolerant religious society," to borrow Ronald Dworkin's phrasing, in which society as a whole is conceived as broadly committed to lives of faith and worship with tolerance being offered to religious minorities and non-believers.[1] In this setting, liberal-ism is just one more emphatic belief system. Although he did not intend to support a conservative religious position, John Rawls's idea of an "overlapping consensus" goes a long way toward making religious views and their secular counterparts functional equals. In opposing Rawls, Habermas convincingly argues that the resources necessary to determine which comprehensive worldviews are "reasonable," and thus potential candidates for belonging to a freedom-of-religion-preserving overlapping consensus, cannot be secured through the resources of religious world-views themselves; it is "up to philosophical theory to settle the criteria of 'reasonableness' in advance, that is, on the basis of practical reason alone" (*EFK*, 47). Practical reason is another name for autonomous secular reason. Behind Habermas's argument here is the assumption that the only way to guarantee a true plurality of worldviews is derivatively, through affirming the rights of autonomous individuals to pursue their conception of the good life as long as they leave others equally free to pursue their conception of the good life. In one phrasing, this is to say that cultural rights, including the rights of religious groups, are derivative from the inviolability of human dignity, which includes: "the guaran-tee of equal access to the patterns of communication, social relations, traditions, and relations of recognition that are required or desired for developing, reproducing, and renewing their personal identities" (*BNR*, 296). Without liberal democracy, there is no pluralism, only conflicting comprehensive worldviews in a war of all against all.

Rawls's overlapping consensus doctrine is a version of the idea that liberal democracy derives from the long history of the clash of religions;

because none of these religions, each with a claim to absoluteness, could finally prevail over competitors, they agreed to disagree, and adopted liberalism as the mechanism appropriate to that agreement. Rawls, to be sure, intended the overlapping consensus to converge on *substantive* normative principles, and hence for the consensus itself to be substantive; it is this conception of an overlapping consensus that is now being proposed by Charles Taylor. Setting aside that optimistic outcome, two things become unsatisfying about this view of liberalism: first, its role is contingent upon all religions failing to become politically dominant; but this makes agreeing to disagree strategically contingent upon acknowledged political weakness, and the doctrine of agreeing to disagree not a movement to a higher form of reflection but solely a shift from substantive to merely instrumental reasoning – which is one plausible reading of the meaning of the priority of the right over the good. Thus, were political weakness to disappear, then the commitment to liberal pluralism could be rationally dissolved. (This, I take it, is the position of some actual postsecular religious believers.) Second, if the commitment to liberal democracy contains a strategic lining, then the ultimate commitment of religious believers is not to the rights and norms underpinning our life together, but to the revealed deliverances of their chosen god. That this should be so is hardly surprising: if you believe you have an immortal soul, then you will have an infinite self-interest that necessarily trumps any and all commitments to a shared political life; the good of your fellow citizens will always necessarily be secondary to the good of your own salvation. Of course, Rawls intended to block this outcome through having the core principles of liberal democracy be themselves derivable from the core principles of belief. But this just pushes back to Habermas's original worry: without presupposing either the operation of an autonomous practical reason or some version of a rational learning process leading toward the ideal of the liberal state, to assume that the diversity of religions will converge on one form of life is as likely as assuming the possibility of a pre-established harmony among isolated monads.

Democratic liberalism does not follow from pluralism; there can be an actual plurality of worldviews only if believers acknowledge that other believers are *entitled*, within political limits, to regard their competing worldviews as authoritative. By itself the sheer fact of conflicting conceptions of the godhead no more yields an actual plurality of worldviews than the circumstance of competing empirical beliefs yields an actual plurality of empirical beliefs. Pluralism as a substantive acknowledgment of irresolvable but equally authoritative conceptions of the world as a whole is an artifact or product of the historical learning process that is realized in democratic liberalism. Because believers qua believers finally have no fundamental reason to adopt pluralism – except political weakness – then pluralism can only be a consequence of adopting the overriding perspective of liberal democracy with its battery of rights and duties, its shifting but emphatic separation of private from public, and its governing commitment to politics as a perpetual form for registering the permanent contingency of the grounding of human life. But this is to say that liberal democracy is essentially a commitment to a wholly secular form of life whose central tenets necessarily exclude religion as such from the region of the bonds through which we perpetuate our life together. Religion is privatized not in the sense that it is excluded from public voice, but in the deeper sense that its political legitimacy requires that religious acts occur only between consenting adults.[2]

Habermas's secularist orientation becomes explicit, first, in his contention that "*Only* the ideologically neutral exercise of secular governmental authority within the framework of the constitutional state can ensure different communities of belief can coexist on a basis of equal rights and mutual tolerance" (*BNR*, 2–3, italics mine). Second, in his oft-reiterated set of three requirements for religious reasonableness: (i) religious citizens must develop a reflexive stance toward their own beliefs that sufficiently acknowledges the existence of competing comprehensive worldviews whose claims from a third-person perspective are equally demanding; (ii) religious citizens must accept the findings of modern science as, in their own domain, not to be challenged by religious dogma; hence the meaning of religious statements must be adjusted so as not to conflict with scientific theory or practice; (iii) religious citizens must make the same concessions to practical reason in the domain of morals and politics as (ii) requires them to make in the domain of science. Requirements (ii) and (iii) are the theoretical and practical versions of the same claim to the priority of secular reason. Hence, believers "must embed the egalitarian individualism of modern natural law and universalistic morality in a convincing way in the context of their comprehensive doctrines" (137). While condition (iii) can be given a narrow purely legal and/or policy reading, Habermas intends more; he requires that believers accept the constitution of the secular state "for good reasons," that is, reasons other than of a modus vivendi kind (129).

I take the satisfaction of the three conditions for the reasonableness of religious beliefs in a secular setting to jointly constitute the idea of "religion within the limits of democracy alone." For believers who have come to their religious orientation in the context of a lifelong exposure to the secular state, or where the work of the Reformation has already fitted their religious beliefs for a multi-faith setting, these conditions might not be felt to be too burdensome. But because they amount to giving modern autonomous reason in its theoretical and practical forms emphatic hegemony over truth and morality, they accomplish a brutal de-valuing of the standing and worth of religious beliefs. By making the normative authority of the secularly established plural world overriding, they functionally transform faith from being constitutive of a subject's relation to self and world to being an addendum, an addendum that may feel deeper, more significant, more abiding than the bonds to family and state, but functionally an addendum nonetheless. As Habermas tacitly acknowledges, from the perspective of, say, a small town in the Texas panhandle, these requirements might appear as not only burdensome but as in themselves sacrilegious or blasphemous.[3]

How, given the almost strident defense of a secular modernity legiti-mated through the lens of Kant's three critiques, can Habermas claim his position is postsecular? As even he concedes, the three conditions that are burdensome to the believer will be second nature to her secular counterpart; those conditions are embraced and espoused by the secular citizen. The only basis for calling his position postsecular is because the liberal framework does not impose "an *asymmetrical* burden on reli-gious traditions and religious communities" (*BNR*, 138) – the epistemic and attitudinal burdens on secular and religious citizens are, Habermas contends, in some sense, equal. Given the secular grounding of religious plurality, I cannot see why an equality-of-burdens thesis will be sufficient to position Habermas's account as postsecular; after all, the burdens on the religious believer are denaturing to faith, while, whatever the burdens on the secular citizen, they do not denature her secular commitments. In this respect, it could be argued that the equality-of-burdens thesis simply hides what is most troublesome in Habermas's view. Ignore this thesis; Habermas is still not entitled to his postsecular claim since the contention that there is an equality of burdens is patently false.

As implied by the idea of locating his philosophical position as "between naturalism and religion," and as is explicit in the phrasings of the Yale lectures, at least part of Habermas's strategy is to depict the secular citizen as a narrow reductive naturalist and thence to require him to adopt a more sensitive and open approach to religious beliefs, say the kind of dialogical stance that Habermas's own version of communica-tive reason proposes (*EFK*, 33–40). By beginning with an implausible conception of who the secular citizen is – as if Hegel had never written his chapter on "Faith and Pure Insight" or as if every secular citizen was a version of Richard Dawkins – Habermas can pretend that something substantial has been accomplished by requiring more than the beliefs and procedures of a reductive naturalism. I assume that, in reality, most secularists view secular modernity as having evolved, in part, from an effort to make the moral and political ideals embedded in the teachings of the monotheistic religions the framework for everyday living in the modern world. For almost all secularists, modernity in its moral and political outlook is, at least in part, the inheritor and realization of its Judaic-Christian past. Unbeknownst to themselves, most secularists are thus good left-Hegelians. Now, what is it that Habermas thinks will be burdensome to us left-Hegelians in the way that the three conditions are burdensome to religious citizens, given that we left-Hegelians are unqualified secularists?

Habermas's most consistent way of stating the burden is to say that we are required to adopt an agnostic attitude to religious beliefs. The demand for agnosticism is either empty or false. It is empty if all it requires are the procedures of Hegelian appropriation, that is, seeing if, against the background of the idea that the history of religions belongs to the history of reason, there is some wholly immanent and secular translation possible of an otherwise dogmatic belief. However, nothing stronger than this can be required since otherwise the demand would involve forsaking theoretical or practical reason in their secular self-understanding. The secularist can thus be asked to see if there is a wholly immanent rational kernel to religious beliefs, but cannot be required to give up the determining authority of secular reason over cognitive worth. This is not to deny that there is an existential excess to religious belief that defies the translation procedure; but, for us, that excess is not simply unavailable to philosophical reflection, for it is what is permanently lost in the transition to modernity. Habermas's analogy between religion and art – each possessing a hermetic core "proudly alien" to discursive thought – is thus untenable (*BNR*, 143); while aesthetic judgments cannot be discursively justified and artworks cannot be hermeneutically unlocked without remainder, the philosophical defense of aesthetic reflective judgment that begins with Kant and runs through Merleau-Ponty, Adorno, and Cavell, for example, has aimed to demonstrate the emphatic rationality of aesthetic judgments. Aesthetic judgment and artistic modernism are as much a part of rational secular modernity as mathematical physics and the liberal state.

Sometimes Habermas appears to want to interpret the agnosticism requirement as demanding that we withhold judgment concerning traditional religious beliefs like the existence of God and life after death. One does have to be a reductive naturalist to reject this claim. Even from the position of the softest possible naturalism, and acknowledging that negative existential claims can never be finally verified, it is simply implausible that traditional theistic ideas about God and the afterlife could be true; to be agnostic here would require the forfeiture of the very reason Habermas demands we affirm. Again, translations are more than possible: the experience of being absolutely dependent on a wholly other being – which is routinely regarded in the West as the paradigmatic religious experience (as Habermas notes in *FHN*, I, III)[4] – is certainly true, only that being is not God but Spirit (Hegel) or its sociological equivalent, society (Durkheim); and while no one actually survives their biological death, we are inevitably a community of the living and the dead; and in acknowledging that dependence on past ancestors it is true that, in some sense, the dead are with us and hence alive (Hegel).

Pace Habermas, serious secularism about religion is intended to save it from blunt irrationalism by regarding "religious communities as archaic relics of premodern societies persisting into the present" (*BNR*, 138). Even if something more is demanded of the broadly tolerant secularist, and I am claiming that Habermas has not really shown that more is, it is still the case that burdens on the secularist are as nothing compared to the burdens on the believer; the burdens are not only asymmetrically distributed, but wildly and obviously so. I do not see how Habermas could think otherwise. There is nothing in his account as it stands that should lead us to consider it as even remotely a part of a postsecular orientation.

But the philosophical and hence political situation is worse than this. Habermas simply again and again helps himself to the *duality* between faith and knowledge, the secular and the religious. But, as he must know, this is not a dualism the way the division between minds and bodies or the sensible and the intelligible are dualisms. Nor is the situation of faith like that of its objects. In the case of God as the wholly other, he is sublated or absorbed in the idea of *Geist*, just as life after death is sublated in the idea of our being a community of the living and the dead. But faith is not sublated by reason; rather, reason, and the other as the indissoluble fact of reason, first emerge in their secular sense through the explicit and historically necessary denial of faith.

Faith is Self-Sacrifice

Faith gets a good deal of its rational acceptance through its contrast with reason, as if the only "other" to reason were faith, even reason requiring faith, at least in itself. Worse, the "reason needs faith" view presumes that if reason is left to its own devices it becomes totalitarian, transforming all ends into means. This is non-sense. There are numerous others to reason: trust, love, commitment, loyalty, courage, et al. Commitment to reason does not entail a wholly rationalized, calculating view of the world: reason can be in the service of the love of others, of children and friends. Reason can orient trust in neighbors and strangers (doctors, teachers, politicians, plumbers, second-hand car salesmen). It can inflect our commitment to causes and ideals. What distinguishes these others is that they are not absolutely other to reason since each carries within itself norms of appropriateness and inappropriateness that make it available to rational evaluation. Trust, for example, can be earned or unearned, excessive or insufficient, sensitive or insensitive to evidence. Trust is indeed an attitude of acceptance; but, for all that, it can be rational or irrational. Faith is otherwise; by definition it exceeds the parameters of reason and evidence. That excess is constitutive of (modern) faith.

Descartes is an appropriate first guide in these waters since our situation is uncannily analogous to the one he faced, namely, a world in which there were three fiercely competing certainties – the deliverances of the senses; mathematical and logical truths, with the sciences that followed from them; and religious faith.[5] These three were complemented by a sophisticated skepticism that insisted that none of these certainties deserved allegiance. Mathematical physics contradicts the immediate evidence of the senses. The Church's condemnation of Galileo for holding the doctrine that the earth moves – in June 1633, just as Descartes was about to publish his *Treatise on the Universe* – made evident that there was a fundamental conflict between reason and faith. The writings of Montaigne give powerful expression to the skeptical tradition that holds that all human beliefs are partial, limited, and rationally open to refutation.

Descartes' goal is not to reconstitute the field of knowledge from the bottom up, but to provide a foundation sufficient to ground the structure of the sciences;[6] and for this purpose, given the nature of the crisis, a plausible, indeed compelling, skeptical procedure is to examine just "those principles upon which all [his] former opinions rested."[7] Those principles, finally, correlate exactly with the three domains of certainty: sense, reason, faith. It should not go unmentioned that placing faith in this list tacitly makes it a kind of mental faculty, a source of object-relations. In reality, faith is an attitude (like trust), or a feeling (like conviction), or an act (like believing or willing), rather than a separate faculty of mind; but as the effort is made to separate faith from sense and reason, on the one hand, and these other attitudes, on the other, it begins to take on faculty-like qualities, as if it were via this faith faculty that the human mind contacted God, apprehending if not comprehending him. Given its setting and treatment not just in Descartes, but generally, the faith versus reason opposition is routinely construed as analogous to the senses versus reason opposition. Faith marks the relation of the believer to God; faith is how the God of the Jews and the Christians is beheld.

The stunning strategy of the first *Meditation* involves bringing the three competing domains of certainty and their skeptical refutation into an orderly conversation in which the method of skepticism is employed to overcome skepticism and reason's opponents: sense-knowledge and faith. The first arguments from illusion establish that the senses never were autonomous claimants; sense awareness is always under the control of reason. Sensory cognition is always a matter of judgment; hence, the doubt concerning the senses does not imply the senses being corrected by reason, but reason as the power of judgment "in the process of self-correction."[8]

The catharsis of sensory knowing via the dream doubt leaves the meditator with only the sciences that deal with the simplest and most general things, namely, arithmetic and geometry. Even dreaming, we cannot doubt that a square has four sides. Descartes must now find a way to throw into doubt even the most irresistible of the deliverances of reason. His difficulty in doubting mathematical reason derives from the fact of it instantiating the rule of reason: what is clearly and distinctly perceived is indubitable. Hence, any doubt that could question mathematical reason would have to be supra-rational, non-natural, or metaphysical, since any such doubts would necessarily run contrary to the nature of mind. The questioning of reason originates from a domain beyond reason, but not from a domain external to the certainties governing our belief system generally. On the contrary, the third source of certainty, namely, faith in the Creator God of traditional revealed religion, appears immediately as a source of beliefs not subject to the rule of reason. Could not an all-powerful God lead me to be deceived about even the simplest calculations? To imagine he could not would be equivalent to denying his omnipotence. The claim that such a God is necessarily supremely good, and that it would be incompatible with his goodness to have made me constantly deceive myself, is no response: "it would," Descartes says, "also appear to be contrary to His goodness to permit me to be sometimes deceived, and nevertheless I cannot doubt that he does permit this."[9]

If I am right in postulating that the precise stakes and region of Cartesian doubt is the crisis of reason besetting the framework of beliefs in the light of the incommensurability among competing sources of certainty, then the original metaphysical doubt and its extension into the doubts arising from the thought of an evil demon attempting to deceive me is a reflective staging of the strife between faith and reason which exhibits, precisely, the disjunction between the demands of religion (the acceptance of an authority beyond reason) and the requirements of the new science. That metaphysical doubt arises at just the moment where reason is reassuring itself with mathematical intuitions, thus focusing the faith versus reason conflict where the latter becomes necessary for the former to carry out its self-critical examination. Faith demonstrates that it is logically possible to doubt reason; faith becomes the doubt of reason. The metaphysical doubt makes reflectively explicit what was already implicit in the cultural crisis of the time.[10]

Descartes' procedure documents the specific conditions in which faith could be rational for us moderns, namely, if having faith were the necessary condition for a binding relation to the world because it was the sole means available for overcoming a culture-wide skeptical crisis concerning the conditions of world-relatedness. If faith does not concern a binding relation to the world, then it cannot be in any sense authoritative for the believer since it would have no leverage in relation to what does bind and orient existence. Said differently, if faith is not what grounds or founds the self-understanding through which the "I" determines her way through the world, then it becomes simply optional, but if optional then without sufficient authority to provide overriding grounds for the believer to base her decisions about her life and her treatment of others on it. Non-binding faith can be an inkling or passionate hope; either way, its claims are satisfied by the principles governing moral and legal respect-based tolerance. Conversely, if faith were shown to be a necessary condition for relating to the world, then the deliverances of faith about, say, the age of the world and how it came to be or about the moral worth of embryos could, at least in principle, trump other sources for determining them. What would give faith its power to trump the self-correcting common sense of everyday reason with its scientific supplement would be the skeptical discovery that reason lacks binding authority. This is exactly the possibility the demon doubt raises. And if that doubt could not be answered, then it would be radical faith that was necessary: only a leap of faith, that is, a surmounting of the claims of intellect and sense and the according of an unconditional trust in a benevolent as opposed to malevolent omnipotent deity, could now render the subject's relation to herself, others, and the world coherent and tenable.

What the threat of an evil demon attempting to deceive me fully shares with the idea of faith is that both involve the effort to doubt the immanent authority of reason and judgment. The idea of the evil demon thus brings *self-doubt* to the highest pitch conceivable. If the defeat of reason would require faith to answer skepticism, the defeat of the faith-based doubt would demonstrate that faith is impossible. And this is the profound meaning and point of the *Cogito*: I cannot hand over or surrender my conscious existence to the other, consider it a gift, for in order for that to be possible *I* would have to do the handing over, the very act of so doing affirming what the intentional content of the act denies.

A simple objection to what I have just argued might run like this: from the fact that an act of suicide is a result of my agency that destroys my agency, it does not follow that I cannot destroy my agency. Descartes cannot be claiming that faith, as the mind's self-repudiation of its own primacy and authority, is impossible: in actively accepting the absolute authority of another, believers do that every day. The argument is rather twofold: first, that the act of faith is not what believers suppose it to be, namely, a founding of myself on the authority of another, but rather a perpetually disowned "I think," a disowned judgment that necessarily depends for its occurrence and effectiveness on granting to our powers of judgment the authority to judge what is or is not authoritative; this is the sense in which the content of the act opposes its formal conditions of possibility. But given that is the case, then, second, the act can only be one of intellectual suicide.

One last variation on this idea: If every act of faith depends on a suppressed "I think," "I take," "I judge," then faith is simply another wholly human act of judgment. As an act of judgment it is not certain, but derivative, mediated, a work of reflection. But if faith is finally an act of judgment, then it is not what it has traditionally been conceived to be and what Kierkegaard will say it is, namely, an absolute relation (= faith) to the absolute (= God), hence something irreducibly singular, immediate, and grounding. Religious spirituality depends on the idea that there is an irreducible type of mental attitude that distinguishes my relation to God from my relation to ideas and sensuous particulars. What Descartes demonstrates is that there is no such attitude – there has never been and there never could be a mental posture of faith, only a judgment, but an awful judgment because it is one that is performatively contradictory, self-repudiating, and self-denying. Once one understands the *Cogito*, faith is finished.

Faith as Sacrificing the Other

Arguably, the Abraham–Isaac narrative stands very near the center of Western religious spirituality, and certainly so since the seventeenth century; it is, perhaps, even more central than the Moses narrative.[11] While the latter introduced a new content to religious belief – both the idol destroying invisibility of the one, unique God, and his moral commandments – the Abraham narrative introduces and clarifies the necessary conditions for the reception of that content: faith. Faith is the propositional attitude necessary for the existence of religious meanings related to a certain kind of deity, the one circulating in the monotheistic religions.

Fear and Trembling presents an elaborate meditation on the sacrifice of Isaac. The work provides Kierkegaard's most explicit account of the nature of faith; it is not a complete account of faith because the episode belongs to the Old Testament, and the character and content of Christian belief is not identical with Jewish faith. Nonetheless, Abraham's ordeal does represent the paradigm case of what it is to have faith; one might even say that Abraham's faith reveals the meaning of faith – for Jews and Christians alike. The effort of *Fear and Trembling* is, through a series of failed analogies and failed contrasts, to make that revelation more available, more inspiring and terrifying, more spiritually compelling.

In broad terms, Kierkegaard's approach focuses on the two most obvious aspects of Abraham's ordeal: the quality of his faith, and the fact that he was prepared to transgress the unshakeable center of human morality by sacrificing his son. If his faith is stirring and remarkable, his willingness to murder his son is appalling. Our ordinary feelings of admiration and disgust are what any reading of this moment must address.[12]

The *Cogito* marks the absolute limit of self-dispossession. Kierkegaard, rather than denying this, makes it the hallmark of faith: the transcendental impossibility of faith is the necessary condition of its spiritual possibility. Kierkegaard underlines this gap between philosophical intelligibility and spiritual possibility by considering faith in terms of "the paradox," "the absurd," and "the incommunicable." Each of these terms attempt to both guarantee that faith remains beyond the precincts of unaided human understanding, and turn that impossibility of comprehension into an affirmative characteristic. The issue here is not any particular religious content but the character of faith itself.

The absurd will bring us quickly into the center of Kierkegaard's thought: "He [Abraham] believed on the strength of the absurd, for there could be no question of human calculation, and it was indeed absurd that God who demanded this of him should in the next instant withdraw that demand."[13] The absurd is the connection between two beliefs: that God has demanded the sacrifice of Isaac, and that God will give Isaac back. The position of faith is the unflinching, resolute acting on both those beliefs at the same time. Abraham believes – despite the fact that God is demanding him to sacrifice Isaac, and despite the fact that he intends to unflinchingly carry out God's demand, and hence despite all the evidence that Isaac is going to die, right up till the very moment that he holds Isaac's head in his hands and draws out his knife – that nonetheless Isaac will not die. The former set of beliefs, the ones based on intention and empirical evidence, is what human reason requires; the latter belief is what faith licenses.[14] Abraham must be *certain* that Isaac will not die. And it is this certainty that Kierkegaard is targeting with his conception of the absurd with its emphasis on receiving Isaac back here and now, in this life. Without certainty that Isaac will not die, Abraham's state would be something like a hope or wish that he not die, a desperate needing to believe that he will not die. But if Abraham's cognitive state were that of a mere hope, then his act would be worse than appalling. If it were a question of mere hope, we could not believe that Abraham truly, utterly, and perfectly loved Isaac. Faith is necessarily a form of certainty, a movement of making certain what can never be certain. It is the quality of certainty adhering to religious beliefs – faithing them – that makes faith operate like a mental faculty. Because faith is a making of the necessarily uncertain certain, then faith will routinely appear as dogmatic, fanatical, crazed. Kierkegaard's effort in part involves the attempt to make the apparent pathology of faith disappear.

The fundamental question raised by the Abraham narrative, a question both acknowledged and voided by Kierkegaard, is: must the very idea of faith be placed in relation to the sacrifice of a beloved other? The drive and determining energy of Kierkegaard's study is to prevent acknowledgment of the relation to sacrifice from collapsing into a literal requirement. Nowadays no one believes in sacrifice; it is thus natural to suppose that the actual human and animal sacrifices of the Old Testament are a long superseded stage of religious practice. This raises a second question: if sacrifice cannot intelligibly be thought of as actually demanding blood sacrifice, what is the meaning of sacrifice such that Kierkegaard feels compelled to place faith in relation to it as a necessary step in the elaboration of its meaning?

Because faith is an absolute relation to the absolute, it cannot be communicated. This is certainly part of what is at stake in Kierkegaard's contention that faith is beyond comprehension: what can be comprehended can be communicated, and what is communicable is comprehensible; if faith is an existential relation of my putting myself into an absolute – direct, unmediated – relation to the absolute, then it cannot be comprehended, and therefore cannot be communicated. *Fear and Trembling*, whose subtitle is "Dialectical Lyric," is presented as written by Johannes *de silentio*. While in some contexts, silence can be a form of communication (as in giving someone the silent treatment), generally silence is conceived as the opposite of communication, and keeping silent is a refusal of communication. Silence is all over *Fear and Trembling*: first, because faith itself cannot be discursively communicated, but only exemplified, shown – the text itself is an indirect communication; second, because the relation between Abrahamic faith and Christian faith remains unsaid throughout; third, because Abraham cannot communicate his faith; and therefore, fourth, because an explicit theme of the text, as taken up in the third of the "Problemata" – "Was it ethically defensible of Abraham to conceal his purpose from Sarah, from Eleazar, from Isaac" – concerns the ethical status of religious silence. Silence is the empirical reality of incomprehension: a severing of human communication.

What forces silence on Abraham in exact terms is that at the communicable, human level his direct intention is that he intends to

murder Isaac. What is the difference between murder and sacrifice? Here
is Kierkegaard's explicit meditation on this question.

> The moment he is ready to sacrifice Isaac, the ethical expression for what
> he does is this: he hates Isaac. But if he actually hates Isaac he can be
> certain that God does not require this of him: for Cain and Abraham are
> not the same. Isaac he must love with all his soul. When God asks for Isaac,
> Abraham must if possible love him even more, and only then can he *sacri-
> fice* him; for it is indeed love of Isaac that in its paradoxical opposition to
> his love of God makes his act a sacrifice. But the distress and anguish in the
> paradox is that, humanly speaking, he is quite incapable of making himself
> understood. Only in the moment when his act is in absolute contradiction
> with his feeling, only then does he sacrifice Isaac, but the reality of his act
> is that in virtue of which he belongs to the universal, and there he is and
> remains a murderer.[15]

Why must Abraham love Isaac all the more if his act is to be one of
sacrifice and not murder? Because Abraham's love of Isaac is his unconditional love of the world, his love of life, and hence constitutes his binding
to the world as such. In order to have faith, Abraham must be willing to
surrender everything that directly binds him to life and the world. Hence
faith is necessarily the sacrifice of the other, which is to say, the sacrifice
of love of the world as orienting our being in the world. In human terms,
faith is world hatred; in human terms, Abraham's sacrifice of Isaac is the
murder of Isaac – something that Kierkegaard never disputes.[16]

The requirement of world hatred is, Kierkegaard insists, just as present
in Christianity as it is in Judaism. This is clearest in Luke 14:26, where
what faith requires is expressed thus: "If any may come to me, and hate
not his father, and mother, and wife, and children, and brethren, and
sisters, yea, and his own life also, he cannot be my disciple." Kierkegaard
refuses any reading of this passage that would soften the hardness of
its demand. This demand should not be confused with a demand for
asceticism. By focusing on family attachments, Christ is focusing on what
provides for love of the world in general. For nearly all parents, children,
especially in those years when they are most needy and most vulnerable, become the anchor of their world-relation: I have a world and care
about the world because I love this child; I would happily sacrifice myself
for this child. And when this child is the promise that the earth shall
have a future worth having, the promise that is the explicit content of
Abraham's child and implicitly the content of every newborn, then one's
willingness to sacrifice everything for the child is not an act of selfishness,
but truly the exposition of love of the world. Kierkegaard knows this: the
third of his sub-Abrahams – those all too human Abrahams Kierkegaard
creates whose lack of faith helps reveal the actual Abraham's faith[17] –

who could not go through with the sacrifice of Isaac, feels he has sinned by simply having formed the intention to sacrifice Isaac, knowing full well that his love for him was such that he would have "many a time have gladly laid down his own life."[18] There is no religious faith unless the child is sacrificed.

The sacrifice of the child to faith also means that the point of view of the child, of Isaac, is necessarily excluded. Terrifyingly, Abraham and Isaac share the ordeal even though every account portrays the events as if they were Abraham's alone. And in a sense, the events are Abraham's alone because it is his faith that is being tested and perfected, and because he remains silent. The act of faith is *logically private*, beyond communication; hence, the very act which will determine forever the relation between Abraham and Isaac is one from which Isaac is excluded, yet done in his full presence and demanding his participation. Isaac's role in these events makes him an object whose own subjective life is discounted. The work of faith can only include Isaac as sacrificial victim by excluding him as subject.

Inevitably, when Kierkegaard does consider the possibility of the actual Abraham directly addressing Isaac, he does so only to demonstrate that were Abraham so tempted it would be because of weakness, not strength, and worse, because addressing Isaac would amount to feeling a need to justify himself before Isaac, then in so doing Abraham "would fall out of the paradox,"[19] out of faith altogether, and collapse back into the tawdry world of the ethical. If Isaac's understanding becomes the ethical measure, then God is displaced as ground, and faith proper evaporates. From the point of view of faith, the desire to justify oneself humanly becomes a temptation to not do one's duty to God, and hence exposes a failure of faith. What dignifies Abraham, Kierkegaard argues, is that he is not so tempted.

The argument here is circular: from the perspective of faith, any falling away from the demands of faith will appear as weakness, temptation, vacillation, a wanting and needing to justify oneself in the eyes of the world rather than before the eyes of God. In a dismissive gesture, Kierkegaard claims that such temptation "isn't even [that befitting] a tragic hero."[20] This dismissive gesture reveals something that has been implicit from the outset: much of what is at stake in the praise of Abraham is the creation of a certain *image* of Abraham – how else did we suppose that Abraham's actions might exemplify faith? In this particular case, it is just that image of silent steadfastness as a form of uncompromising virtue that is, finally, doing most of the work. Kierkegaard must make Abraham appear as neither dogmatic nor fanatical, but rather as noble; and his nobility, because it requires silence, an impossibility of intelligibly communicating with others, thus requires more than what is asked of the tragic hero. To gather all this up demands constructing an image conveying superlative virtue, a virtuousness that is akin to but emphatically more magnificent than the highest ethical virtue. And in order for this to happen, then the ethical ideal of communication must be demoted, demeaned, come to be seen as something shabby and unworthy. And that is just the image Kierkegaard works to construct. Much of the glory of Abraham, and by extension the worthiness of the very idea of faith, derives from his silent image, the image of his carrying an impossible burden that is impossible to communicate with calm determination and unbending authority. If Abraham is so calmly sure, so noble in demeanor in the face of the unspeakable action he is about to do, then how can his faith be anything other than the highest virtue, a virtue beyond ethical virtue? Such is the image of Abraham. This is how we forget Isaac.

Justifications by faith alone are incommensurable with worldly ethics, and Abraham's silence is a certain acknowledgment that before the eyes of humanity he is forever guilty. And he is forever guilty at a higher level: he does not simply keep hidden from Isaac his intention of sacrificing him, but in the unbending of his intention *Abraham does sacrifice Isaac.* And this is the reason why the angel of the lord comes down and stays his hand: "Lay not thine hand upon the lad, neither do thou any thing unto him: for now I know that thou fearest God, seeing thou has not withheld thy son, thine only [son] from me."[21] Abraham was not required to complete the action because, given the complete nature of his intention, he had already sacrificed Isaac, giving his life totally over to God. Nothing was withheld; Isaac was killed, killed in the very heart of Abraham. In de Silentio's praise of Abraham's faith, this is conceded when, in attempting to capture the relation between faith and the absurd, he presses the issue: "We let Isaac actually be sacrificed. Abraham had faith. His faith was not that he should be happy sometime in the hereafter . . ."[22]

One can only be reborn in faith if one first dies to the world. In order to die to the world one must slaughter one's living attachments to the world, one must murder one's love of the world and offer it to God. One must sacrifice Isaac. Abraham's silence is the silence of the severing of the bonds of love as what constitutes the very nature of his relation to Isaac. And the condition of this: that the point of view of Isaac is forever excluded.

Remembering Isaac: The Claim of the Other

Above, I suggested that a not inconsiderable feature of Kierkegaard's presentation of the Abraham narrative involved a work of image creation in which Abraham's faith is sublimed into a picture of ethical-religious beauty, a sublime beauty because always pointing to an inwardness and transcendence exceeding the ordinary capability of discursive communication and narrative representation. It is hence no accident that the opening sections of the text after the "Attunement" are a "Speech in Praise of Abraham" followed by (as a preface to the "Problemata") a "Preamble from the Heart." In the "Preamble" the focus is on the double movement of infinite resignation and, let's call it, infinite affirmation, on the severing of the bonds of love with the sacrifice of all worldly passion, and the simultaneous conviction that nothing will be lost. So the "whole earthly form" that Abraham presents

> is a new creation on the strength of the absurd. He resigned everything infinitely, and then took everything back on the strength of the absurd. He is continually making the movement of infinity, but he makes it with such accuracy and poise that he is continually getting finitude out of it, and not for a second would one suspect anything else.[23]

The giveaway here is the phrase "and not for a second would one suspect anything else" since that is what Kierkegaard must convince us of in order to have the violence of infinite resignation, the violence of world hatred and world negation become resolved in the invisible perfection of having everything returned – the love of the world is now affirmed as God's gift of the world. And there is only one condition for this to be possible: sacrifice Isaac. The image of Abrahamic faith lives off the invisibility of Isaac's ordeal; hence the narrative of the sacrifice of Isaac is both the account of Isaac being sacrificed and, through the narrative itself, enforcing that sacrifice, repeating it. It seems that every telling of the sacrifice of Isaac thus becomes another sacrifice of Isaac, another exclusion of him from the ordeal of his life and death.

Not every telling: we do have one depiction of the sacrifice of Isaac that interrupts the movement from infinite resignation to the absurd receiving everything back that places Isaac, terrified, screaming in an infinite agony of betrayal and loss, at the exact intersection of those two movements – Caravaggio's 1603 *Sacrifice of Isaac* (to be found in the Uffizi Gallery). In order to lodge his moral protest against sacrificial faith, Caravaggio had, in effect, to reconstruct the meaning of painting, to destroy what painting had been and give it a new, secular disposition. So André Félibien writes that "Poussin could not bear Caravaggio and said that he had come into the world in order to *destroy painting* . . . Yet his aversion for Caravaggio is not surprising. For where as Poussin sought to foreground the nobility of his subjects, Caravaggio allowed himself to be carried away by the truth of nature as it appeared to him."[24] In commenting on the Poussin–Caravaggio opposition, Louis Marin states that "the choice is between the nobility of the subject [Poussin] and the vitality of the object [Caravaggio], between bringing the dead to life – as a story is told through figures that are carefully interwoven within a scene – and simply seeing what appears in the here and now before one's eyes."[25] The issues here are immensely complex, a complexity that is densely elaborated in Marin's remarkable study, *To Destroy Painting*. Still, it seems right to say that at the core of Caravaggio's achievement is the de-sublimation, or better, a de-transcendentalizing of painting, a turning away from the narrative idealization of the dead and toward the incorrigible sensuous density of what presents itself in re-presentations. What Caravaggio set out to destroy was what Gombrich has called "the classic solution" in which the claims of order – of ideality, conceptuality, and narrative – are "balanced" by fidelity to nature. Order provides the vertical axis of classic Italian painting whereby a single image takes on the authority of an ideal meaning, a world-transcendent meaning that is but temporally and imperfectly incarnated in a physical image.[26] Let's say that in classical Italian painting, world images are sacrificed to transcendent meanings in a manner consistent with the Christian disposition of that art. The resolution of figures within a finally transcendent narrative order is, one might argue, the source of the immense pleasure, the *jouissance* proper to Renaissance art.[27]

In opposing this, Caravaggio sought a means of painting whereby the scene would not be sacrificed to its ideal meaning, in which rather than retrospectively gathering the image before our eyes we are wrenched from our position of being spectators, of being somehow outside and above, the masters of what we see, becoming ourselves present to the scene being represented. Caravaggio wanted a painting that would not be the bearer of ideas and meanings existing independently of it; rather, meaning would be fulfilled and exhausted by paint matter, by the work of color, light, and shadow in their articulation of figures. And all this was to be accomplished directly in relation to the great tradition of narrative art.

In order to accomplish this task, Caravaggio sought mechanisms for folding a painting back into the scene represented, for de-narrativizing the events depicted in order that they might take on a wholly immanent, sensuous intelligibility. If pressed, I would want to argue that Caravaggio was the first of the Southern painters to fully take on the burden of secular modernity, of finding meaning and the loss of meaning in the direct experience of persons and objects. Because his concern was with fidelity to the object, a secular notion of truth in painting, Caravaggio did not seek to make his pictures agreeable, a source of uplifted pleasure.

That notion of pleasure presumes that paintings are for the sake of the viewer, and in that they betray the objects represented. Fidelity to nature for Caravaggio meant letting the power of what was re-presented make a claim against the viewer, a sensuous claiming we would turn away from if we could. In our inability to avert our eyes, there emerges a sensuous authority relying on nothing other than the material means of its depiction and the expressive features of the objects represented.

A premise of my argument so far has been that the Abraham narrative stands near the center of Western religious spirituality because it elaborates faith as the relation proper to the God-relation. If I am right in posing Caravaggio as attempting to forge a wholly secular method of representation, then his engagement with the paradigmatic account of faith can succeed only by posing itself against that form of world-relation by destroying a central mechanism for its reproduction: the sublime aesthetic of the classic solution that had been the main bearer of the ideal binding of virtue and beauty.

The overriding condition for destroying the Abraham image is to let Isaac in; letting Isaac into the narrative is a matter of content and a matter of form. The content question and the form question are interrelated: in order to destroy the Abraham image one must not only let Isaac in, but transfigure the account so that it is not also about Isaac, but fundamentally *about Isaac*. And this is a formal question because it involves more than re-centering the image, so to speak, in order that we have Isaac constantly in view; in order to have Isaac constantly in view, in the appropriate sense, the narrative movement in which he is a constantly disappearing moment in the resignation and affirmation of Abraham's faith must be not just interrupted, but forever blocked. And this means that we require a narrative representation in which the narrative arrives as always broken, always interrupted, always failing the moment that would be its fulfillment. It is just this that Caravaggio manages.

The account of the painting I find most persuasive is Louis Marin's.[28] Let me rephrase Marin's interpretation in my own words. Although we know the Abraham story fully, this painting consistently seeks to undermine the possibility that it be finally told. Everything about the painting concerns a freezing of action, the creation of a monumental stasis, and hence a breakage in its grand narrative. Abraham's eyes that look back toward the angel are opposed by the angel's finger pointing to the lamb. Or we can follow the descending light falling from the angel's shoulder to his hand, to Abraham's hand, to the shoulder and face of Isaac. Or there is the left to right movement of the angel's finger pointing to the ram that is to replace Isaac on the stone, with his other hand staying Abraham's hand. And notice how the heads of Isaac and the ram are set one atop the other, with the peaceful ram's head, eye lifted, its look ascending, directly above the horizontal, abjected face of Isaac. These series of formal, pro-spective and retrospective movements do not add up to one story – one coherent temporality – but rather cancel one another, move toward an immobilization. And this might be thought appropriate since the *narrative center* of the picture is the immobilized hand of Abraham, forcibly being restrained by the angel, the knife fiercely gripped in his right hand, his left hand around the neck of Isaac, his thumb pressing harshly against the boy's cheek in order to hold his head firmly to the stone. The fact that the sacrifice will not take place is, so to speak, contradicted by Abraham's hands: they are the hands of a murderer. How else did we imagine those hands? But the immobilized hands that are the painting's narrative center are not what hold our visual attention; it is rather Isaac's single eye staring out at us, the painting's expressive core, that draws our looking back again and again until we are transfixed.

In staring out at us, Isaac's look breaks through the narrative formal-ity of the painting in order that we become present to him: a witness to his suffering. Isaac's pleading eye performs a searing iconoclastic shat-tering of the Abraham image, leaving just his suffering, his brutalized becoming animal, a sacrificial ram, to be witnessed. In our being petrified before that eye, Marin conjectures, we spontaneously see the fulfillment of Abraham's intention: Isaac dead. We perceive the true internal con-nection between the symbolic sacrifice and the literal one. In becoming witnesses to Isaac's brutalization and terror, his death, we leave behind the mythos of faith and enter the cold reality of a loveless world whose ruin derives solely from the fact that there have been those who have had faith.

The authority of this canvas is finally not painterly, not aesthetic at all. The painting wrenches itself out of being a representation, an object to be beheld, and by addressing the viewer makes her into a moral witness. One cannot view the painting without witnessing Isaac's ordeal. In forcing the viewer to witness Isaac's ordeal – or turn her back on the painting altogether – Caravaggio has the painting perform, in its being viewed, the moral *cogito*, that is, it performs the actuality of the other as having a claim against me that is not mine to dispose of but rather places me, situates me, in a moral space in which I must either acknowledge the full destiny of that demand – say, to perceive Abraham's irredeemable guilt – or forfeit the possibility of seeing as such. What is meant to be sublime about the Abraham narrative is that it is emptied of all meaning, all content apart from what belongs to faith itself; it gives us faith as absolute (an absolute relation to the absolute). This Caravaggio under-stands and contests. What faith means is the death of Isaac; what faith means is murder.

Caravaggio's image of Isaac is posed precisely between the two moments of Kierkegaard's dialectic of faith, precisely between the moment of infinite resignation and infinite affirmation in which everything is returned. In Kierkegaard, the "movement of infinity" is done with such "accuracy and poise" by Abraham that he keeps getting finitude out of it. Caravaggio, in destroying Abraham's accuracy and poise, makes the movement of infinite affirmation impossible. There is only finitude here. Between the glittering knife and Isaac's neck, between the angel's pointing finger and the ram that will replace Isaac, between the loss of everything and the getting it back, there is Isaac's pleading, anguished eye blocking the movement from left to right, blocking the narrative, destroying the dialectic and its message, dissolving the scene and its meaning. No more image; no more faith.

One of the motivations for Habermas's conception of the postsecular is to somehow reconcile secular reason with its religious other. There are different ways of configuring the meaning of religion, for example, the distinction between cult-based and salvific practices. One fundamental way of distinguishing the secular from the religious has been the distinction between reason and faith. These cannot be reconciled: secular reason cannot coherently disavow itself, sacrifice itself to faith; secular reason emerges in the affirmation of itself and of the claim of the other against faith. Faith is sacrifice of self and other; secular reason is the protest against sacrifice. Of course, Habermas never does explicitly urge that secular reason be sacrificed; but if secular reason is intrinsically a critique of faith, then how could there be a postsecular society that was not a repudiation of reason?

Part III

World Society, Global Public Sphere, and
Democratic Deliberation

8

A Postsecular Global Order?

The Pluralism of Forms of Life and Communicative Freedom

JAMES BOHMAN

Like the other "post" terms, the term "postsecular" marks the end of one way of thinking: it challenges the sociological thesis that the modernization of society brings about the secularization of its population. Perhaps more than anything else, the increasing salience of religion in political conflict has cast doubt upon this view, making Europe now the exception rather than the rule. In his recent work, Habermas has taken up the issue of religion and public life in a new way, giving a potentially much greater role for religion in political deliberation and in the obligations of citizens toward each other in democratic political community. For Habermas, modern democracies should not be thought to be primarily secular or based in mere toleration, but rather are better thought of as "postsecular," where religion is not merely an obstacle to democracy but a resource whose truth contents can play a role in public deliberation. Implicit in this argument is not only a radical re-evaluation of the role of religion in democracies, but also about pluralism in general. Contrary to his previous view of pluralism, which he shares with Rawls, "postsecularism" implies that religious pluralism is no longer simply a constraint upon the possibilities of democracy. While this account is developed primarily in terms of democracy within states, the idea of a postsecular order also clearly applies to the global order. However, the idea of postsecularism at this level ramifies through the global order and demands a clearer "transnational" level in his understanding of global institutional architecture. A postsecular global order depends on significant social interaction among various peoples and religions, so much so that it would suggest that the glue that holds together any cosmopolitan order is something akin to the idea of a transnational society. Transnational society is thus a site on which conflicts may become transformed through introducing democratic features into previously undemocratic arrangements. A postsecular transnational society suggests that changes in social reality through globalization and interdependence can lead to new democratic forms that do not rely solely on independent juridical constraints. A postsecular order is successful when it is capable of supporting more, rather than less, pluralism.

For my purposes, postsecularism has two sides; it is both a social fact given changes in the global patterns of migration and the equally global resurgence of political religion. As a hypothesis, secularization marks Europe as the exception rather than the global rule. However, postsecularism is for Habermas not only a social fact of the current historical period, but also a critical norm for evaluating deliberative responses to the challenges of pluralism in all of its dimensions and aspects. This normative dimension is highlighted by Richard Bernstein in a recent discussion of Habermas's work on religion: rather than calling for a new liberal modus vivendi, he argues that Habermas's discussion of postsecularism calls for "something far more demanding – a change of mentality in which religious believers and nonbelievers open themselves up to what they can 'cognitively' learn from each other."[1] It is demanding for both secular and religious citizens, requiring that all become more self-reflexive about the limits of their own perspectives and be open to the "truth contents" of other views. "Democratic citizenship," Habermas argues, "assumes a mentality on the part of secular citizens that is no less demanding than the corresponding mentality of their religious counterparts."[2] While this takes discussions of public reason in the right direction, Habermas's insistence that the issue is a conflict between secular and religious citizens misstates the fundamental issue as a hindrance overcome by reconciliation. It is rather only one instance of the kind of pervasive pluralism that now applies at all levels, from the state to the global level. When the fact of pluralism is seen in this more general way, it becomes clear that Habermas's institutional discussion of postnational institution is inadequate precisely because it fails to address the forms of interaction that are needed to deal with pervasive pluralism in every part of his cosmopolitan multi-level system. Habermas's account is decidedly not postsecular in the absence of a discussion of the conditions for communicative freedom in a world society. His account focuses entirely on the interaction between transnational publics and global institutions, and leaves out their associative basis in communicative freedom across diverse ways of life.

For Habermas, "a postsecular mentality" is a requirement of "democratic citizenship" and not simply of toleration. While this term would seem to define our postnational condition, Habermas restricts the term "postsecular" to very few states, "the affluent societies of Europe or countries such as Canada, Australia and New Zealand, where people's religious ties have steadily or rather quite dramatically lapsed in the post-World War II period" (*EFP*, 59). Here it is clear that he is referring to the *social fact* of postsecularity rather than to the normative achievement of this change in mentality in the face of specific global challenges. A closer consideration of this social fact seems to imply that "postsecularity" is a matter of the decline of the political importance of religion. But, in transnational society, postsecularity is to be found in emerging zones of social and religious conflict rather than in the relations of secular and religious citizens in liberal democracies. Instead, it designates places where the fact of pluralism has led to conflicts that have been carried out and resolved without secularization, as is the case for Northern Ireland or in struggles between Israelis and Palestinians. In what follows, I want to argue for a global fact of postsecularity which marks a fundamental change in the broader fact of pluralism, which does not simply apply to this small set of Western countries and their elites. The fact of pluralism does not somehow hinder the emergence of democracy in its mature form. Indeed, pluralism is neither inherently good nor bad for democracy; it is not an obstacle to be overcome via postsecularity. Instead, it is a fact in the sense that it is a practical context that transnational actors must address in order to achieve their democratic projects. These problems are not simply related to the cognitive demands of citizenship in a global era, but also to the fundamental requirements of communicative freedom in order for Protestants and Catholics, Jews and Muslims to live together and build peace. As Habermas puts it, in discussing the emerging form of immigrant society as a ubiquitous feature of modern societies, the practical and not merely cognitive or ideational challenges of a pluralism of ways of life "extends beyond a pluralism of denomination" (65). This practical sort of pluralism marks changes in social reality, the response to which cannot be the purely cognitive obligations of translation or even of a change in mentality that Habermas makes central to his account of the obligations of postsecular citizenship. To the extent that these practical changes in the social world have also become transnational, they cannot be accounted for in this statist frame. It is also necessary to see the pluralism of ways of life in a more practical dimension, including the significance of the many religious conflicts around the world for a transnational order.

The upshot of my criticism of Habermas's conception of postsecularism is that it is neither descriptively nor normatively rich enough to take up the challenges of pluralism in ways of life, in particular understanding religious conflicts and how they might be resolved by transnational society. In order to develop such an alternative, I turn first to an account of postsecularity as a ubiquitous and unavoidable feature of all complex modern societies. Second, when it is problematic it is because of the lack of communicative freedom among all those affected by such conflicts. Of course, I borrow the concept of communicative freedom from Habermas, although I argue that it can be achieved in civil society and other locations apart from the modern state. Habermas speaks of communicative freedom primarily in terms of "enabling rational opinion and will formation" and eventually issuing in "the legal institutionalization of various forms of communication and the implementation of democratic procedures" (*BFN*, 127, 147). With an eye to the problem of conflict, it is important to analyze communicative freedom less with an eye to formal institutionalization than on a more basic and practical level as the recognition of persons or groups as having a *communicative status*, that is, as people who are able to address others and be addressed by them in turn. This recognition of the basic status of communicative freedom across such conflicts requires a new mentality and new transnational modes of interaction and deliberation, so that the institutional structure of a global world society must make this sort of freedom possible as a universal status. In the absence of transnational communicative freedom, religious networks in civil society have developed in response to religious conflicts and to the lack of pluralism among those Western elites who are currently most influential in structuring global politics and policies. One consequence of this absence of communicative freedom is the pervasive domination of religious minorities throughout the world, as well as the persistence of other forms of religious violence. Third, a more robust account of transnational deliberation made possible by wider communicative freedom will be able to deal with these problems, notably through processes of transnational peace-building. In particular, transnational communicative freedom must make possible various forms of multi-track deliberation among the groups involved in conflicts as well as macro-level deliberation at a society-wide level. In order that transnational society may become more deliberative and capable of adjudicating among conflicting interests, certain preconditions are necessary: first, communicative status in the public sphere and, second, a status sufficient to enable access to global civil society so that the pluralism of ways of life becomes a resource rather than an obstacle to a form of democracy that emerges from international society.

The Fact of Pluralism: From Minority Rights to Transformative Democracy

Does the pluralism of ways of life in immigrant societies undermine the possibility of democracy? Or should we think that pluralism promotes rather than constrains democracy? Certainly, religious pluralism has often been an enduring source of social conflict. Habermas cautions us that "opening parliaments to conflicts over religious certainties" could make governmental authority "the agent of a religious majority that imposes its will in violation of democratic procedure" (*BNR*, 134). Such pluralism is democratically self-defeating and must be constrained by institutional procedures. At the same time, multiculturalism has developed as an affirmative conception of cultural diversity, which under the right circumstances could be democracy promoting. Will Kymlicka sees pluralism so understood as presenting a fundamental challenge to democracies, dependent as they are on shared national identities on the one hand and a universal conception of citizenship on the other. The difficulties of self-rule that he addresses derive from the messiness of the world, in which some nations become national minorities within states, the solution to which is not separate states, but differentiated citizenship and minority rights, including cultural accommodation and, where necessary, some form of partial self-government. This accommodation can be accomplished through "polyethnic rights," which permit differentiation in the rights that various citizens enjoy. Nonetheless, like Habermas's requirement that a postsecular order depends on the acceptance of a constitution by all groups, Kymlicka thinks such diversity must be institutionally constrained, in that differentiated self-governing groups must still "take the authority of the larger polity for granted" in order to avoid destructive conflict (181). But is this the peace of a Leviathan, the continued monopoly of the means to violence at the state level as a constraint on pluralism?

Seen through the lens of a postsecular mentality, it is neither cultural nor religious diversity as such which is problematic, but rather the attempt to cut the world at national joints. This simply re-creates the same structural dynamic of constrained pluralism. If Rawls is correct, "the fact of pluralism" (or the diversity of moral doctrines in modern societies) is just one such permanent feature of modern society, so that a fact is permanent to the extent democracy makes it more rather than less likely to continue.[3] This fact of pluralism thus should change the way we think of religious pluralism and its permanence in democracies; because of the permanence of pluralism a common identity or shared societal culture is hardly an unalterable requirement for democracy as such. Without locating a necessary connection between its relations to feasibility and possibility, describing a social fact as "permanent" is not entirely accurate. It is better instead to think of such facts as "institutional facts" that are *entrenched* in some historically contingent, specific social order that is the result of relatively long-term social processes, whose consequences cannot be reversed in a short period of time – such as a generation – by political action. Practical theories thus have to consider the ways in which such facts become part of such a process which might be called "generative entrenchment."[4] All institutions, including democratic ones, entrench some social facts in realizing their possibility, and thus not all social facts should be regarded as already given because they are fixed conditions of possibility for democracy or some other ideal. Pluralism is not the only such permanent fact; we should also expect that in a globalizing world any society that does not incorporate the pluralism of ways of life into its self-understanding of democracy is likely to become less rather than more democratic. This is because of the structural tendency of democracy to promote more rather than less pluralism, even if this leads to unintended consequences of various sorts over the long term. At the same time, democratically entrenched pluralism may also lead to innovative forms of self-government divided among the various units and sub-units of any multi-level system that seeks to distribute popular sovereignty in order to promote democracy. The idea behind Habermas's conception of a postsecular understanding of the role of religion is to seek some way of entrenching religious pluralism within the functional constraints of the democratic process in order to constrain its potentially negative effects. In fact, since secularization is no longer a plausible description of the historical process of the disappearance of religion as such, Habermas seeks to preserve its "semantic potential" and "truth contents" for democratic deliberation (*BNR*, 113–31).

When seen in light of the requirements of the generative entrenchment of social facts and conditions by institutions, constructivists are right to emphasize how agents themselves produce and maintain social realities such as religious pluralism, even if not under conditions of their own making. In this context, an important contribution of pragmatism is precisely its interpretation of the practical status of social facts as potentially obstacles and constraints as well as resources and opportunities. Thus, Dewey sees social facts always related to "problematic situations," even if these are more felt or suffered than fully recognized as such. The way to avoid turning problematic situations into empirical-normative dilemmas is, as Dewey suggests, seeing facts themselves as potentially transformative: "facts are such in a logical sense only as they serve to delimit a problem in a way that affords indication and test of proposed solutions."[5] Thus, Dewey saw the solution in a transformation both of what it is to be a public and of the institutions with which the public interacts. Such interaction will provide the basis for determining how the functions of the new form of political organization will be limited or expanded, the scope of which is "something to be critically and experimentally determined" in democracy itself, as a mode of practical inquiry about social facts as both obstacles and resources for realizing its ideals.[6]

With respect to increasing conflict in postsecular societies, the publics that are formed in democracies and effectively organize social peace are now postsecular and transnational. We can clearly say that so long as countries in Europe and North American remain democratic, the diversity within their countries will only increase. Attempts to limit this diversity very often fail to pass legal muster, as when in Germany repeated attempts by Baden Württemberg and other *Länder* to ban headscarves among teachers have been found unconstitutional to the extent that all religious symbols would then have to be banned. Religious minorities in Germany are clearly dominated within Germany when Christian parties enact legislation that bans Islamic dress by teachers, and the attempt to institute forms of religious domination makes Germany less rather than more democratic. Instead, what is required is not only a change to a postsecular mentality, but also the de-centering of the assumptions about democracy so that it becomes genuinely postsecular and internally more transnational in its understanding of citizenship in such a way that it enhances pluralism.

Given that Habermas has argued that the facts of social complexity and pluralism require that we "de-center" democracy, it is clear that such facts not only condition democracy but can also transform it. Many democratic norms and mechanisms are indeed "de-centered" when they are made more inclusive: deliberation, representation, group membership and identity, the public sphere, the relations of the local to the regional and the global, and so on. As a metaphor, de-centering suggests that there is no one favored level of democratic organization, such as the state, or that democracy as such requires the existence of some prepolitical "people" it organizes. A pragmatic approach to current global realities would suggest that democratic practices are now becoming increasingly transnational even in states, including new migrations of peoples, civil society, and governance. As issues related to mosques and head scarves show, the new pluralism of forms of life cannot be so easily escaped by retreating behind territorial boundaries. This internalized transnationality is a new social reality that may function as a constraint and an opportunity, as institutions could make the problems of pluralism in forms of life more (or less) tractable. They do so by promoting shared communicative freedom as a necessary condition for non-domination.

Democratization, Communicative Freedom, and Communicative Power

One of the main motivations for Habermas's postsecular turn has to do with an equitable distribution of the burdens of citizenship. A democratic polity that protects the religious liberty of its citizens "cannot expect all citizens in addition to justify their political positions independently of their religious convictions and worldview" (*BNR*, 128). Such state neutrality is for Habermas a requirement for the equal guarantee of religious freedom for all. But these rights should not be thought of only in institutional terms; it is not only a matter of religious liberty but also of citizens' communicative freedom. In more or less fully realized, existing democracies, citizens exercise a variety of freedoms and powers in virtue of their membership in the polity. Such freedoms and powers derive from having a particular mutually recognized legal status of being a citizen within a state. For this reason, civic republicans often think of citizenship as constitutive of freedom, as when they argue that the freedom of non-domination requires not just citizenship but the capacity for effective contestation of policies and decisions that undermine their basic interests. This communicative status is not simply given with citizenship, but rather allows its bearers to address others as full participants in the political process, with reasons and opinions that are their own. Kant and others have given this idea of status and membership a distinctively cosmopolitan and normative twist, as when Hannah Arendt refers not to a specific set of civil rights, but "the right to have rights" that applies to all persons.[7] This republican turn to cosmopolitanism indicates that this free status must be shared, ultimately by everyone; in this way all have the power to express their own interests in their own terms, without subordination to those who speak for them.[8] Without some such status, Kant argues, human beings would be persons without personality, "beings who have only duties and no rights," and thus "slaves or serfs"[9] dominated by those who have the power to assign those duties, while the citizens lack the standing to address them and in turn be addressed by them.

In order to avoid the great evils of domination, such communicative status is required in order that duties are not simply imposed upon us. It is this capability that enables citizens to avoid the great ills of being dominated by others. Legal status brings with it specific kinds of normatively exercised powers, the most important of which is the reciprocal power over rights and obligations exercised with others who have the same powers and control over their legal status, and it is these powers which are constitutive of civil freedom. Or, as Kant put this condition of freedom, "no one can bind another, without also being bound in the same way by the other."[10] While we need not endorse a specific version of this fundamental status here, these arguments point out that whatever status it is that assures non-domination, it is a status that must be shared with others. For democratization, a complex set of statuses and freedoms is required to enable a measure of shared freedom that would provide the reciprocal basis for us to make claims upon others and upon institutions, and for them to make claims upon us. Call this communicative status, a status that permits the exercise of communicative freedom. Universal legal status must then be further unpacked in order to understand how it contributes to making democratization possible.

In existing democracies, citizenship consists of statuses that make it possible to exercise self-rule and not to be under the control of any given individual or group of citizens. But even in a democracy with well-developed protections from political domination, a central precondition for such non-domination is the existence of the public sphere, a space in which communicative freedom can be exercised. Without the open structure of publics, transnational interactions across various political communities could very well surpass existing civil and legal statuses. Communicative freedom is tied to a particular, reciprocally recognized informal communicative status that is the necessary condition for having a public sphere at all. Participants create a space for communicative freedom to the extent that they regard themselves as a public and interact with each other accordingly. As members of a public, persons can regard each other as having at the very least the capacity and standing to address and to be addressed by each other's acts of communication. However important translation is for religious citizens, it is still an activity done by others, rather than the joint exercise of communicative freedom. Rather than thinking of a compensation to offer religious reasons in terms of burdens of the requirements of institutional neutrality, it would be better to see the obligations of religious and non-religious citizens in terms of communicative freedom and communicative status.

In his *Structural Transformation of the Public Sphere*, Habermas gives an historical account of the creation of the distinctly modern public sphere that depends upon just such a free exercise of the creative powers of communication. In contrast to the representative public of the aristocracy for whom non-participants were regarded as spectators, participation in a democratic public is fundamentally open. "The issues discussed became 'general,' not merely in their significance but also in their accessibility: everyone had to be able to participate" (38). This is the "communicative freedom" of publics, a form of freedom that may take on a constructive role by which members grant each other rights and duties in their roles as participants in the public sphere. This freedom emerges from the interaction between the communicative freedom of participants in the public sphere and statuses to enter into decision-making processes within various institutions. By acquiring such communicative freedom beyond the control of even a disaggregated authority, membership in a public uses the creative and constructive powers of communication and public opinion to reshape the operations of authority and thus often plays a role in democratization, or the transformation of democratic institutions for the sake of more and better democracy.

When such institutions are transformed, communicative freedom can become communicative power exercised under new circumstances of politics. As important as the offer of secular translations might be for the recognition of communicative freedom, such a process hardly changes the institutional basis for authoritative decision-making in the neutral state. In other words, it does not address the social realities of increasing pluralism in democracies, and thus is unable to transform communicative freedom into communicative power. By contrast, we might consider the crucial role of religious discourse in the Civil Rights Movement in the United States, where communicative freedom was exercised with the aim of a transformative effect on basic institutions though the formation of a new transracial public. The injustice of segregation was expressed powerfully in the movement, often in religious terms, and the movement created the vocabulary and concepts that expanded the scope of communicative freedom and led to the exercise of communicative power in the reshaping of many legal and political institutions. The Civil Rights Movement did not just mobilize a new public, but rather created the social basis on which certain institutions from schools to the judiciary could be changed. The force of the Fourteenth Amendment's requirements of equality was given a salience that it had not had before.

From Communicative Freedom to Communicative Power

In states, the transformation of communicative freedom to communicative power is apparent in the transformative effects of various movements and catalyzing events. In the latter category, we might include the formation of the European Union in the wake of the massive destruction of World War II. The desire to make such events less likely to occur requires rather large shifts in the organization of political power away from states and toward new forms of democracy and accountability. A truly transnational political movement led to the abolition of the chattel slave trade in the early nineteenth century. Without much political support from states, this institutional change was clearly brought about by transnational rather than international deliberation. Even if such cases of large-scale change of unjust institutions are relatively rare historically, several historical and current examples illustrate the process of transforming communicative freedom into communicative power, including very successful attempts to influence the formation of international and transnational institutions, particularly surrounding the issues of whether such institutions will be oriented to states, individuals, or publics. This was not an achievement of the League of Nations, but of the Women's International League for Peace and Freedom (WILPF), who formed one of the first publics around an international institution. In effect, they were among the first to see that non-governmental organizations could be a means to expand the democratic character of formal international institutions.

In this regard the Women's International League for Peace and Freedom, founded in the aftermath of World War I, illustrates how communicative status can be transformed into decisional status at the international level. The League had a long history of advocacy around issues of peace and opposition to war. But, as Molly Cochran has pointed out, the League transformed itself from a weak public that attempted to shape world public opinion, in order to influence various independently constituted actors such as states and the League of Nations, to a "strong" international public that sought to shape decisions made by institutions such as nation-states and League of Nations officials, in order to make them accountable to world public opinion. They sought to realize this goal through three mechanisms of normative leverage. First, they saw themselves as representative of women, roughly half the world's population; second, they claimed a unique epistemic perspective in light of which they represented; and, third, they saw themselves as purveyors of "publicness"[11] in the sense that they sought to establish a distinctly transnational public sphere and achieve a definite communicative status for women within it. Thus, the League did not seek to become another interstate actor, but a self-conscious international public that realized the conditions for communicative freedom and the epistemic advantages of its plurality of perspectives for solving problems in the international sphere. With the emergence of the League of Nations, the WILPF saw liberal international institutions as providing the means by which publics would achieve access to influence, so long as the League could be reshaped so as to be responsive to world public opinion, not simply from the outside, but precisely because of its own internal commitments to potentially transformative, democratic criteria of legitimacy. While the League of Nations eventually failed because it did not have the capacity to make effective decisions, during its existence the WILPF transformed its communicative freedom as a public concerned with world public opinion into communicative power, where the League of Nations began to take concrete steps to shift from the focus on states to the rights of individuals, such as the trafficking of women and children, among many other endeavors. While never fully completed, this marks a shift from a purely international organization, oriented to states, to a transnational one that can address and be addressed by individuals' claims. The second shift the WILPF enacted had to do with introducing claims to representation, so that part of its legitimacy was as representative of women, children, and humanity in general.

Similar publics have been formed by women's groups in other, more recent, contexts, for example, publics formed by women to establish the communicative freedom of publics to address issues of the consequences of Islamic regimes and laws for women, such as Women Living Under Muslim Laws. These are clearly postsecular in orientation, in that they have this same dual status in bringing a transnational public to bear upon the enforcement of Islamic law by the state, and they also conceive of their task more in terms of establishing transnational networks that provide the basis and organization for the exercise of communicative freedom, which in turn create the conditions for a postsecular public sphere in which to advocate for interpretations of Islamic texts and changes in various Muslim practices across the range of cultural, religious, and national backgrounds of their members.[12] With similar commitments to democratic norms as in the WILPF, such an organization shows that religiously oriented organizations can function to promote democratization by creating a broad set of addressees in transnational civil society. This organization has not yet taken the step to communicative power, but instead remains a weak public that seeks to raise world and Muslim public opinion to promote more equitable treatment of women and children under Islamic law. Nonetheless, these women's organizations promote communicative freedom by fostering plurality in transnational civil society, and by addressing claims against the domination of women within existing Islamic law. The institutional location for transforming communicative freedom into communicative power could only emerge with the achievement of greater pluralism in the Islamic public sphere.

Consider another example in which the communicative freedom of a public did attain communicative power in a previously closed set of practices that lacked the deliberative benefits of diverse perspectives. It could be argued that in the early days of the HIV epidemic, when patients had no say about the regime for testing experimental drugs, that they were dominated by medical authorities. In particular, the epistemic weakness of homogeneity among deliberators is apparent, when deliberators consisted solely of experts. From the perspective of patients, the highest possible standards of statistical significance in random controlled trials were simply unacceptable as a social policy. In deliberation that included the perspectives of patients (who also make up the pool of participants in tests and as such must restrict their use of other possible remedies), doctors, researchers and policymakers, standards of validity were balanced with other values such as quicker availability of drugs, safety, and effectiveness. The communicative freedom to show the epistemic injustices of the medical regime led to communicative power once patients and their representatives came to share decisional authority in scientific and medical institutions, including grants and various treatment protocols.

In a similar case of the epistemic benefits of pluralism, Bina Agarwal has studied the effects of the exclusion of the perspective of women from deliberation on Community Forestry groups in India and Nepal.[13] Because women had primary responsibility for wood gathering in their search for cooking fuel, they possessed greater knowledge of what sort of gathering was sustainable and about where trees were that needed protection.

We might think that NGOs and other civil society organizations strongly influence the conduct and nature of such struggles and thus are not genuine sources of diversity and transformation. As Neera Chandhoke points out, they often fail to be genuinely global and formulate problems in their own terms rather than in terms which those affected could accept; to the extent that this paternalism is true such groups may fail to realize communicative freedom.[14] In this sense, they are not creating transnational society, and in so doing fail to meet the demands of postsecularity as taken to be also a critical standard for deliberation in transnational settings. At the same time, other civil-society actors are more successful in fulfilling these standards, as in the successful efforts of a broad range of civil-society actors to achieve a multilateral response to debt relief for Highly Indebted Poor Countries, something that would not have been achieved without the communicative freedom that has emerged from the broader public sphere.[15] It is particularly striking that publics were able not only to initiate deliberation on this particular issue, but also to mobilize communicatively generated power to change the decision, thereby changing the self-understanding of the World Bank that had led to vicious circles of fruitless debt recycling. These examples clearly show that one way to improve the democratic practices of international institutions would be to incorporate novel institutional designs and procedures that would be better able to promote such interaction with global publics and citizens. But it also shows that when communicative power is attained, it is because shared communicative freedom is exercised in the proper institutional location and changes the self-understanding of important international institutions. Communicative freedom depends on this communicative status, which then under the right institutional circumstances can become communicative power, or decisional status shared with others. In cases of deep conflicts, as was the case in Northern Ireland and is still the case between Israelis and Palestinians, attaining communicative status is difficult even if it is also the basis for the society-wide deliberation that is necessary to resolve the conflict. In these difficult cases, transnational actors can make a difference.

Beyond a Multi-level Functional System: The Ends of Transnational Society

My final example of this section will consider one of the main mechanisms for achieving important ends of transnational society: *peace-building* through transnational deliberative process. With respect to the transformation of transnational society in the problematic situation of long-term violence among various groups, peace-building is a quintessential postsecular practice of deliberation, now at the macro level of a whole society. This concept refers to just one sort of transnational deliberative process aimed at creating norms of trust among long-time enemies, such as the Protestants and Catholics in Northern Ireland or Israelis and Palestinians in the Middle East. Such processes may take a long time to accomplish these ends, if they succeed at all. By peace-building, I mean the deliberative process by which transnational publics generate communicative freedom by becoming internally pluralistic, and in so doing eventually create the conditions under which communicative power can emerge and change the social reality of the conflict in question. Thus, peace-building seeks to restore the basis for communicative freedom. In such cases, the chief differences among the conflicting parties, such as the claim to a particular territory in Northern Ireland and Israel and Palestine, the status quo ante becomes transformed through communicative freedom exercised across these differences, and communicative power that changes the norms that otherwise undermine the possibility of peaceful coexistence in transnational society. This is a difficult and long-term task, but without a public and deliberative peace process the legitimacy of negotiated settlements requires a public dialogue among citizens and among various civil-society organizations and associations. While peace is the prominent end of transnational society, it is only one end among many that aim at non-domination, that is, at an end state of affairs in which domination of one party over another is no longer structurally possible post ante. Attempts at peace-building and non-domination often depend on fortunate circumstances to bring conflicting parties to consider it even possible to pursue changes in their behavior toward each other, to enable restoring their ties and reconciling relationships to each other.

While peace processes are often thought of as negotiations by both participants and observers alike, they are not best thought of in terms of bargaining, which often simply rearranges rather than changes the set of feasible alternatives. Very often, the same underlying conflict and unresolved problems simply reappear. Indeed, such processes also demand deliberation and have a highly deliberative goal: the transformation of situations of conflict. Typically conducted in relatively small groups, peace processes that create the official agreements are kept from public view and carried on among the elites of the conflicting parties. While such forms of secrecy are useful when the parties in a conflict already trust each other, even then the deliberating parties cannot assume that the legitimacy internal to the deliberating group will transfer easily to the members of the larger public sphere who remain in conflict with each other.

The need to somehow transfer legitimacy requires more than increasing the amount of better micro-level deliberations among representatives or states parties, useful as these might be in situations of conflict. Rather, macro-level deliberation needs to enter into the picture. Macro-level deliberation is multi-track and thus includes a variety of forms of communication from everyday talk to formal parliamentary debates, from informal to empowered public spaces, all of which aim at producing mutually recognized communicative statuses. Such a macro public space might house a variety of various civil-society groups, designed citizen forums, or transnational activist groups, and more; but to enable transmission at least some of them must think of themselves (as did the WILPF) as "purveyors of publicity" and "intermediaries" for macro or society-wide deliberation if there are to be successful public capacities to build peace. In the case of Northern Ireland, many different non-state actors helped to create multi-level deliberation and dialogue through the creation of a peace network that cut across the lines of conflict so as to exert a significant influence over the official process. While asymmetries of power remained between state and non-state actors, this network "connected local, regional, national and global actors into a powerful constituency and a driving force for peace."[16] It is important to see, then, that within this regional conflict such actors were able to introduce forms of novel political cooperation and argument, and in this way influenced the situation by seeing the conflict from a distinctly transnational perspective.[17]

Peace-building of this deliberative sort creates a transnational, postsecular society, however narrow or wide, with an eye to converting the communicative freedom of publics into communicative power of stable shared institutions. It is important to remember that many of the persistent conflicts throughout the world are still often directly or indirectly religiously motivated, making peace-building over time in transnational society more effective than formal negotiation. To put it in a phrase, it creates legitimation through macro-deliberation among all the members of transnational society. Accordingly, peace can be built when people organize themselves and promote common aims from that perspective. New accounts of "second" or "multi-track" diplomacy aim at transforming divisions through dialogue. Or, as I have described it, such a possibility could create the conditions for a macro-deliberation in a transnational society. A feasible peace depends on the social ties of shared norms and trusts created in the first instance in mutually recognized communicative status and ongoing deliberation.

The attempt to create peace by transnationalizing solutions to the deep local conflicts has long characterized Northern Ireland. As Daniel Wehrenfennig argues, what is distinctive about the Northern Ireland peace process was that "a continuous, multilevel dialogue process has been a key factor in the successful peace process" and its aftermath.[18] By contrast, the Israel/Palestine peace process has achieved no such stable framework or continuous, multi-level dialogue process in the absence of cross-cutting peace networks that form a transnational perspective. Peace networks created in the Northern Ireland case aimed at such a multi-level dialogue and formed networks with strong links across local, regional, national, and global actors. What is distinctive in this case is the forging of a networked public with a transnational perspective, so that new forms of political cooperation and new types of campaigning and arguments emerged in the context of shared values and aims. Even in the case of the Oslo Accords, this kind of multi-level process was missing. Even if officials agree about various interests, ordinary citizens on both sides of a conflict realize peace by changing their behavior toward each other and restoring relationships to overcome endemic conflict. The goal of citizen or public peace-building is thus not to address issues, but rather "to seek innovative ways to address, integrate and embrace the painful past and the necessary shared future as a means of dealing with the present."[19]

As this example shows, the fundamental condition for creating a transnational society is communicative freedom; without it, there is no possibility for interaction across borders. Communicative freedom is itself exercised in a non-state form of membership, the membership in a public or civil society that if free is precisely a matter of mutual recognition tied to communicative and social status as a member of society. Who are the purveyors of publicity today? Given how dispersed global governance institutions are, it is not surprising that this role is occupied by a wide variety of organizations and groups, many of which attempt to influence a particular domain or policy issue. Here I will offer a broader example that accomplishes many of the goals of the WILPF. The World Social Forum emerged primarily out of protests over the consequences of the world financial system, but shifted from a defensive strategy of protests to creating a space for global deliberation and organizing around the broad issues of global justice. As Smith et al. point out, the annual meeting, which acts as a forum to many different groups, is not an end in itself, but part of an overall process, in which there is an exchange of ideas, the mobilization of networks, and the global expansion of deliberative spaces in which people can reflect upon and try to realize alternatives to neo-liberalism.[20] These forums provide the basis for the creation of further forums and networks at the local, national, and regional levels. Thus, the World Social Form seeks to organize an enduring public sphere that creates transnational social bonds in which learning can take place across various levels of time and place. As in any attempt to create a transnational society, innovative norms and forms of communication are necessary in order to create democratic legitimacy for this dispersed task of deliberating about alternatives to the present order. Thus, as a communicative space and as an ongoing process, the organizers of the World Social Forum see themselves as creating the necessary conditions for interconnecting local and global dimensions of justice. Much like the WILPF, the World Social Forum realizes conditions of communicative freedom and basic communicative status as participants in discussions of global justice in an imagined community, even while aiming to secure the epistemic benefits of diversity.

As in the Northern Ireland case, networks also serve the cause of peace as purveyors of publicity and facilitators of communication. Certainly, some such groups exert pressure on state actors, such as in the International Campaign to Ban Landmines. But more than pressuring state actors and their diplomacy, non-state actors extend the conditions of social space through the creation of mutually recognized communicative status out of which norms and solidarity emerge in transnational society. The WSF does not attempt to achieve the specific goals as one of many civil-society organizations, but rather to create the communicative and social space in which new forms of interaction and goals might emerge. Besides the WILPF and the WSF, networks such as the International Campaign to Ban Landmines also generate political legitimacy through peace-building, creating the transnational ties and relationships that make such a peace more resilient and long lasting. Citizen dialogue and communicative diplomacy are significant not instrumentally, but constitutively in building a common society and generating social norms that provide the basis for a shared future. Given the nature of the dialogue, communication is directed not only at the conflicting parties, but also at establishing wider, transnational relations.

In both the WILPF and the WSF, the role of a transnational intermediary takes shape along with the social transformation of an international society among states into a transnational society of individuals and publics. In the case of the Northern Ireland peace networks, the same concerns for establishing the conditions of publicity also provide the basis for forming a transnational society within a divided state. They are all concerned with norms of communication that are the basis for an inclusive dialogue about social justice, including, of course, religious identities. But, even in a democracy with well-developed protections from political domination, two central preconditions for such non-domination are the existence of the public sphere and of civil society as spaces for the exercise of shared communicative freedom. Communicative freedom is tied to a particular, reciprocally recognized informal communicative status that is the necessary condition for having a public sphere at all. Participants create a space for communicative freedom to the extent that they regard themselves as a public and interact with each other accordingly. It establishes a two-way power to address claims to others and to be so addressed by them. In the first instance, a public sphere institutionalizes a particular kind of relationship between persons and makes it possible to achieve a similar relation between the public and political authority. As members of a public, persons can regard each other as having at the very least the capacity and standing to address and to be addressed by each other's acts of communication. The exercise of such freedom requires the existence of not just civil society as such, but the emergence of an international society concerned with publicity. The common ground that makes international society possible is an achievement, not something that can be specified in advance except in general terms of realizing peaceful spaces for communicative freedom.

With respect to peace-building, a transnational approach has two levels. The first is to see peace-building as the product of reconstructing political society so that it is transnational. One task of constructing a transnational society is to create the ties of communicative status across the borders that undermine peace. In Northern Ireland, these borders were religious, and the multi-track processes of creating ties across the boundaries of conflict help to produce the ties that supported the settlement. In many cases, the construction of a transnational society with norms and forms of interaction and communication is facilitated by various intermediaries, such as the peace networks in Northern Ireland that cut across religious difference. Second, on this same model, a global multi-level dialogue about peace and justice also seems possible, especially as transnational public spheres expand the scope of interaction in a variety of ways. It will certainly also take place against the background of new intermediaries such as the World Social Forum; however, there are also other formal institutions that will act as forums, such as various international courts in which debates about the scope and applications of various norms of international criminal, humanitarian, and human rights are worked out by institutions empowered to make decisions about particular cases and thus about the scope of application of various norms. These institutions are in large part international institutions, developed in the context of treaties and organizations consisting of states. Without transnational society, however, such decisional publics cannot achieve many important ends, including peace and other forms of freedom from domination in the broader public.

Non-domination and Postsecular Pluralism: Habermas on Transnational Society and Government without a State

As I have described communicative freedom thus far, it typically operates to establish communicative status in a generic modern public sphere, that is, one that combines both face-to-face and mediated communication. If that is the case, then it would be better not simply to rely on publics forming around institutions, whatever they may be, in order to exercise their communicative freedom, but also to design institutions to be deliberative and democratic so that they will be open to and locations for communicatively generated power. If there are many different levels of institutions at different scales, publics would on this account interact with various institutions in order to ensure their communicative freedom, but only if such a multi-level system promotes such freedom. In so doing, publics would have to expand their communicative and decisional statuses so as to be able secure non-domination at each level. Taking his orientation to existing structures, Habermas argues for a "political constitution of a world society as a multilevel system that lacks the character of a state as a whole." It does this by dividing functions across levels, where the supra-national level secures peace and promotes human rights; at the intermediate, transnational level, "major powers address the problems of 'global domestic politics'." In the latter, the democratic legitimacy of states is "progressively extended upwards."

This approach has a number of distinct advantages, including the extension of the United Nations beyond the idea of member states as "the exclusive subjects of international legal treaties" but can become "the constitutional pillars of a politically constituted world society" (*DW*, 161). Such a world organization "is already a community of states and citizens," where the latter refers to individuals "as the bearers of the status of world citizen" (135–6). This status would have to be sufficient to assure protections not just from genocide and grave human rights abuses, but also from domination within the new transnational realities of migration and economic integration. If democracy is not feasible beyond the national level and achieved only indirectly, as Habermas claims, where does the legitimacy of "global domestic politics" come from? Only two possibilities remain: the source of legitimacy must be either transnational or supra-national. The first horn of the dilemma quickly runs into the inherent normative weaknesses of global domestic politics. If embracing this horn of the dilemma, he is left with a deficit of legitimation, given the difficulties of securing the conditions of "fair bargaining" and leaving decisions up to policy networks with little connection to publics. If he accepts the other horn, then supra-national organizations have universal negative duties related to human rights and their enforcement as their sole justificatory bases. While recent developments in the United Nations have called for a more expansive conception of security to include global redistribution, such an agenda cannot be fulfilled by the United Nations since it is currently structured in such a way as to be unable to engage in the constructive tasks of global politics and bargaining. In fact, Habermas emphatically rejects such political functions for supra-national institutions, since they would be overburdened and potentially de-legitimated in their essential and functionally appropriate tasks of constitutionalizing human rights. The establishment of the International Criminal Court means for Habermas that the diffuse global public sphere is given "an authoritative voice" when it is stirred by moral reactions to political crimes and unjust regimes. Judged under a different rubric, it does not seem likely that this institutional architecture would be sufficient to solve such pressing problems as global warming given the need for states to have the decisional power to decide such issues of global domestic politics. This leaves open the constant possibility of domination within this sort of political structure.

For our purposes, the main structural difficulties with Habermas's settled account of a cosmopolitan political order are thus twofold. First of all, Habermas (much like Kymlicka and Miller) now accepts the limits of the scope of democratic legitimacy to the borders of nation-states, where a people can be authors and subjects of the laws. The deepening of democracy in the European Union could not be based on such a de-centered form of democracy. This gives rise to a transnational legitimation deficit, even for the institutions of international law narrowly conceived as fundamentally judicial. The issue should be to secure universal statuses of communicative freedom and decisional powers rather than to enforce sanctions for human rights violations. This differentiated institutional order thus needs a richer transnational counterpart if publics are to play a deliberative role in the multi-level system. According to the argument that I have been making about the democratizing role of pluralism in transnational society, this possibility is central to a legitimate deliberative multi-level system. While Habermas mentions the role of publics and of transnational society, they do not have any role as bearers of communicative freedom and power in his understanding of the constitutionalized world order. Yet, as a matter of social fact, they are ubiquitous, present at every level with democratic legitimacy from the national to the regional to the supra-national. Without them, there is no basis for the generative features of communicative freedom of trans-national society. At the same time, the emphasis on law in a multi-level system has the potential to give deliberative supremacy to supra-national juridical authority even when it lacks political legitimacy. The functional differentiation of tasks does not relieve the problem of legitimacy, and this problem has no easy solution since the decision-making procedures of many of the institutions within a multi-level world society are not democratic. Moreover, any solution is made more difficult because international law is not jurisgenerative in the same way as domestic law. Moreover, legal experts and judges, as important as they are, are not necessarily agents of democratic change. Rather, it is the political actors in the publics of transnational society who are jurisgenerative in making transformative rights claims in a variety of contexts.[21]

It is on terrain that cuts across the national and supra-national that transnational society could be the location for an ongoing dialogue about peace and justice. Habermas rightly thinks that such an order would be postsecular and make demanding claims on its participants, so that they would have to fulfill certain normative requirements necessary to maintain such a pluralistic endeavor, including the acceptance of consti-tutional essentials for a world society promoting such human rights and religious freedom. Of course, many religions throughout the world do not now accept these norms, and some of those who do not see them-selves as challenging the political consequences of Western secularism. If there is to be a dialogue on global justice, its procedure would have to accept something like universal inclusion of all religions, if the opposi-tion between secular Western elites and the religiously motivated and impoverished of the South is not to undermine its benefits. Maeve Cooke provides the proper grounds for rejecting content-restrictive conditions on entry into a global dialogue on deliberative grounds, when she argues that religious contributions to deliberation cannot be confined to the informal public sphere, nor can demands for inclusion and the accessibil-ity of reasons be decided prior to deliberation without deliberation losing its point. The same argument for inclusion can be made as a require-ment of political equality as a necessary condition for the acceptance of pluralism of ways of life.[22] These problems look quite different when we consider forms of deliberation that emerge through the exercise of com-municative freedom in transnational society, quite apart from states and international institutions.

When thought of in the strategic terms of standard realism, the absence of any overarching political authority means that international society, whatever it is, is in anarchy; but if it is organized as a society that gener-ates norms and statuses, even if initially a society of states, it is then ruled by shared norms, discourses, and practices that have developed over time to regulate interactions and various domains of action. Using a method of civilizing conflict by regulating through norms, international society puts a high premium on reaching understanding and shared deliberation. For example, many international regimes give a greater role to transnational participation and transparency than do formal international institutions, precisely because decisions within them must be oriented to the whole public.[23] But this means that deliberation is not confined to the micro-level of global domestic politics, but rather generates legitimacy by macro-level, transnational, and society-wide deliberation. According to John Dryzek, this macro-deliberative situation marks a shift away from predetermined norms to the sort of open exchange needed for engaging in discourse (such as in discussion of sustainability), which has now become "the means to coordinate and structure actions and interactions."[24] Absent a global sovereign or a global organization that has supremacy over all political decisions, such deliberation does not always aim at making an authoritative decision, even if over time discursive processes have shaped the norms of international society, such as in debates that led to international agreements to abolish the slave trade or that now press for sustainability and solutions to climate change. In these cases, there is certainly communicative status, and decisional status comes from the slower development of norms over time rather than their legislation. The same is true for lasting peace-building processes that are concerned not just with conflicts of interests but with establishing the conditions for sharing a peaceful and sustainable future.

Having such a space is the first step for the beginning of democratic control over such membership and the discourses that go on within it. Any postsecular and pluralist conception of the global order must include a stronger republican component, manifested not just in communicative freedom, but when such freedom can be transformed into communicative power. The condition of pluralism here is important; likeminded people do not constitute a public as such, since to remain likeminded is to exclude many from communicative status. Communicative freedom is thus generative, when tied to a particular, reciprocally recognized informal communicative status that is the necessary condition for having a public sphere at all. Participants create a space for communicative freedom to the extent that they regard themselves as a public and interact with each other accordingly. In the first instance, a public sphere institutionalizes a particular kind of social relationship between persons and makes it possible to achieve a similar relation between the public and political authority. As members of a public, persons can regard each other as having, at the very least, the transnational capacity and standing to address and to be addressed by each other's acts of communication.

When a transnational public helps to transform a situation of conflict, as did Catholic and Protestant marchers in Northern Ireland who met together on the streets of Belfast and took form in the open network of postsecular publics, communicative freedom can become the communicative power of macro-deliberation that generates inclusion and sustains peace. This possibility requires that it takes itself to be trying to realize the necessary conditions of publicity that make it possible for conflicting parties to grant each other a shared communicative status, as members of the public, and then on this basis convert communicative freedom into communicative power in order to achieve non-domination.

Conclusion: Postsecularism and Transnationalism

My argument has focused on the preconditions for successfully dealing with the increasing pluralism of ways of life. What we discover is that such pluralism is no longer exclusively a matter of how states should deal with phenomena such as the massive migration of peoples daily across borders, but also with the emerging transnational spaces within states, where we find the transnational at home as it were. So long as states are democratic, we can expect this kind of internal transnationalization to continue. While I have raised some criticisms of Habermas's model of the constitutionalization of international law, my arguments in many ways adopt the postsecular solution that he proposes for the problems of increasing religious pluralism: that is, I have argued for the necessity of shared deliberative processes in which publics and civil society act as intermediaries, much as those who do the work of translation of religious claims act as intermediaries in the political public sphere. Here, postsecularity functions as a social fact and as a critical standard for living with the permanent fact of increasing diversity of forms of life at all levels of international society. My argument has used an inclusive postsecular world society as a critical standard for evaluating international institutions and proposals for a multi-level world order. Such norms demand that the situations of conflict be resolved by multi-level macro-deliberation that cuts across these divides and involves transnational actors and organizations.

Absent the benefits of formal democratic institutions at the transnational level, many theorists have turned to the emerging global civil society as the main location for democratization. To the extent that civil society can be a means to create a space for plurality and communicative freedom, it is also a precondition for democratization. Here, peace-building as a long-term deliberative and postsecular process of resolving conflicts of ways of life provides a model for the role of transnational society. Ultimately, the task of democracy at any level is to connect communicative freedom to institutionally realized communicative power against the background of shared communicative and decisional statuses. In order for this to occur, democratic institutions are necessary to provide processes through which communicative freedom realizes the joint exercise of such freedoms and powers. Transnational macro-deliberation is essential to this process. As political communities become more transnational, pluralistic and complex, democratization requires both postsecular civil-society intermediaries to generate communicative freedom across borders, as well as transnational institutions in which the status of individuals as citizens in a world society have decisional status. Without this dimension, functional and territorial accounts of a multi-level global political order could serve to enable the achievement of human rights and permit the exercise of communicative freedom that is generative of the communicative power to transform institutions, so as to become a means to non-domination. As all levels of political organizations become increasingly pluralistic and transnational, our understanding of democracy and its aims will also change with it.

9

Global Religion and the Postsecular Challenge

Hent de Vries

The idea of the "postsecular" has no clear historical reference, demarcating a before and an after; nor, I would like to argue, does it have any particular normative valence in and for itself. As a new concept with inflating currency in contemporary debates in the social sciences, philosophy, and cultural criticism, it is increasingly appealing precisely because of its contrasting and corrective function – undoing some of the central assumptions and pretensions of the modern Enlightenment as well as of its accompanying political liberalisms, reductionist naturalisms, and the like – not as the proclamation of yet another epoch which would somehow follow or bury the "secular age" and its so-called "immanent frame," per se.[1] And yet, it is equally undeniable that the postsecular, together with what I take to be its main instigator and rationale, namely the resurgence of "global religion," presents a major challenge and, we should add, opportunity for Western-style democracies and the ideological and cultural no less than economic, political, and, indeed, military influence that they wield across the world.

It is against the self-perception and, more often, self-stylization of an outworn secularism and over-confident naturalism that an emerging "postsecular" thinking and practice protests, even though it harbors few original thoughts, political principles, and juridical precepts of its own. In a sense, therefore, postsecularism can be seen as an extension or expansion of secularism. Postsecularism is secularism *all the way down* (*or up*) – that is to say, *zu Ende gedacht*, and that means also, as Theodor W. Adorno might have put it, *immanently critiqued*.

We might just as well say that, if the postsecular breaks new ground at all, it will be in the measure that it forces the age-old concept and

modern articulation of the secular, including the institutional arrangements and constitutional backup of secularism as a political formation,
to *loosen and lighten up*. Among other things, this would mean that
the postsecular invites the secular to historicize and contextualize itself,
and, where at all possible, to venture beyond its narrowest formulation
and its juridical confines. As a matter of fact and compromise, a *relaxed
and cool* – or, as Jürgen Habermas might say, *de-transcendentalized* and
fallible – secularism, one that rids itself once and for all of its reductionist
and "fundamentalist" assumptions, might well be the most and best we
can aim and hope for at the present juncture in time.

Secularism, thus refined and, perhaps, redefined, would therefore
reign in the more overheated of its own historical ambitions to neutralize
and constrain religious expression, whether of its discourse or its so-
called "ostentatious signs" (such as dress, ritual practice, the building of
places of worship, etc.) in the public domain. But then such self-reflective
and self-critical secularism moves beyond the original and dominant
interpretations of its theoretical principles and practical politics, thereby
becoming "postsecular" along the way.

In the following contribution, I will first attempt to explain why the
recent resurgence of so-called "global" religion entails a particularly
urgent challenge for secularism and its philosophical corollary (i.e., naturalism). I will then revisit some of the most telling passages in Habermas's
latest writings and interviews, which diagnose and evaluate these contemporary trends, and which, in my eyes, further confirm the inevitable
slippage from formal, not to mention transcendental, pragmatics in the
direction of what, for lack of a better word, I call *deep pragmatism*.[2]

This observed slippage is by no means unprecedented and can be
traced throughout Habermas's earlier oeuvre as well, but it is, I claim, his
more than merely episodic – indeed, most explicit, rigorous, elaborate,
and consistent – turn to religion to date, in writings and interviews, collected notably in *Religion and Rationality* and *Zwischen Naturalismus
und Religion*, which allows us to discern the contours of what a genuine
"postsecular" thought might – at very minimum – mean and call for.
Along the way, Habermas teaches us, nothing short of a "new orientation," perhaps even a "new form of consciousness," is called for. We will
come to that.

Should we speak of a secular or postsecular age then? And, if the latter,
what relationship does the current scholarly turn to the postsecular bear
to the revisiting of that other important category of a more philosophical and historical sociological origin, namely, that of the so-called axial
age? Or should we eventually substitute the concept and practice of
(what I call) deep pragmatism for the formal and quasi-transcendental
pragmatics of old, enriched as it now is by the renewed encounter with

a phenomenon – the archive and political role of global religion that it, perhaps, all too long held at bay – and let the somewhat tedious, at times, repetitive secularism–postsecularism debate finally wither away? It would seem that Habermas himself has made decisive steps in the latter direction, and this, I would claim, nowhere more explicitly than in his latest essays on faith and knowledge, religion and the public domain.

Globalization and Beyond

It is by now a commonplace that the latter part of the twentieth and the opening decennium of the twenty-first century saw an explosion of new markets and media that effected profound changes in the human forms and categories of perception and judgments, and not just a wider variety and greater intensity of commerce and communication. Simultaneously and, perhaps, not accidentally, a remarkable *resurgence of* "religion" occurred on a worldwide scale, in roughly "global" fashion. Instead of "public religions in the modern world" (to use José Casanova's well-known title) and well beyond the modern "transformation of the public sphere" that Habermas was the first to describe in its full measure and import, the phrase "global religion" evokes a set of altogether novel problems, whose depth and tenacity call for a different conceptual apparatus just as its phenomenon requires us to address and, perhaps, mobilize a much broader range of sensibilities and responses, of affects and effects, than come commonly into view in procedural theories of deliberative democracy and political liberalism.

Leaving the precise meaning of the aforementioned "turn" and its philosophical assumptions, which I have attempted to analyze else-where,[3] aside for the moment, what exactly does the term "global," as in the current expression "global religion," mean here? And what does it tell us about this relatively recent phenomenon's overall implications and consequences, not to mention ultimate grounds and wider ramifications, that still largely escape us (and do so for what are, no doubt, structural and, I would venture to say, "essential" reasons that elude both histori-cal explanations and rational reconstruction, precisely, because of their "depth")?

Turning to Habermas's recent observations on the role of religion and "world society," I would like to distinguish and oppose two different yet related meanings of the "global" in the expression "global religion," both of which shed light on the conceptual and practical distinctions between the secular and the postsecular in ways that need to be brought out more clearly than has been done before (and than I will be able to do here). Needless to say, compared with the enormity of the challenge that so-called global religion poses to the historical, political, cultural, and institutional alignment of secularism and liberal democracy, some of these questions concerning the exact nomination of trends, not to mention ages and epochs, seem among the less urgent tasks that confront us here and now, precisely due to their abstractness or, indeed, "depth." But that is not to say that they are of lesser importance or may not come to eventually haunt us in the more profane and prosaic matters of everyday life and practical policy that worry us most.

"God and the World"

To indicate what is at stake here, it may be worthwhile to recall a summary sketch that Habermas gives us in his informative interview with Eduardo Mendieta, aptly entitled "A Conversation About God and the World." Here, Habermas starts out from a noteworthy differentiation and contrast between the ideational-cultural and the social-institutional aspects and developments of Western modernization, suggesting that religion – its archive or, as he says, "legacy" – has left indelible traces in the first and not necessarily in the second. Thus, to speak of globalization in our day and age must mean something quite different depending on whether we speak of "global religion" (and, hence, supposedly of "God") or, on the contrary, of global politics, commerce, and communication (that is to say, of the "world"). Their respective processes and structural developments are not strictly parallel, let alone identical. Expansion and accumulation in the one may mean retreat and deflation in the other. And even where the two processes of globalization (i.e., of religion, on the one hand, and of markets and media, commerce and communication, on the other) go hand in hand, their respective specific – at times, phenomenal, indeed, special – effects and general causes are rarely the same.

As a consequence, the "play" (the "*Spiel*," or "*Spiegel-Spiel*," that is, "mirroring game," of "heaven [*Himmel*]" and "earth [*Erde*]," to use a late Heideggerian idiom that Habermas himself would rather avoid, is all but a zero-sum game, as if "God" and "world," and everything these names or concepts stand for, were taken as belonging to virtually opposed poles and categories of analysis whose respective magnitudes cancel each other out. Instead, for all we know, they may well be co-originary and co-extensive realities, forces and powers, whose historical and cultural logic nonetheless operates completely differently in each case, depending in part on particular situations that might favor the one but frustrate the other. It is not clear at this point whether Habermas would admit as much.

In the passage I am about to quote, he insists that at the level of cognitive and normative structures, clearly "the Judeo-Christian heritage" (more indirectly, also the "impetus of Islam") was "more than a precursor or a catalyst" of the construction and then deconstruction – in any case, "challenge" – of Western modernity in all of its aspects, while steering clear from ascribing any mono-causal account of things that would take this "heritage" as the single explanatory factor. Apparently, the cultural and social logics of the historical developments of, say, Christianity and capitalism (but the argument for other religions and other economic systems would, *mutatis mutandis*, be the same) do not fully map on to each other:

> The themes of the Judeo-Christian heritage help to explain the cultural, but not the social, modernization of the West ... From the sociological point of view, the modern forms of consciousness encompassing abstract right, modern science, and autonomous art ... could never have developed apart from the organizational forms of Hellenized Christianity and the Roman Catholic Church, without the universities, monasteries, and cathedrals. This is especially true for the emergence of mental structures ... In the West, Christianity not only fulfilled the cognitive initial conditions for modern *structures* of consciousness; it also demanded a range of *motivations* that were the great theme of the economic and ethical research of Max Weber. For the normative self-understanding of modernity, Christianity has functioned as more than just a precursor or a catalyst. Universalistic egalitarianism, from which sprang the ideals of freedom and a collective life in solidarity, the autonomous conduct of life and emancipation, the individual morality of conscience, human rights and democracy, is the direct legacy of the Judaic ethic of justice and the Christian ethic of love. This legacy, substantially unchanged, has been the object of a continual critical reappropriation and reinterpretation. Up to this very day there is no alternative to it. And in light of the current challenges of a postnational constellation, we must draw sustenance now, as in the past, from this substance. Everything else is idle postmodern talk. (*RR*, 147–9)[4]

The passage reiterates all the ingredients and guiding themes that have formed part and parcel of Habermas's writing and express his earliest intuitions since his classic 1961 study *Strukturwandel der Öffentlichkeit* (*The Structural Transformation of the Public Sphere*), even though it re-evaluates the significance of the traditional "substance" in remarkably different ways, assuming, quite explicitly, that there is, so far, no serious "alternative" to it. Yet the citation leaves somewhat unclear why and how it is especially "now" that we can and must "draw sustenance" from a "substance" whose relentless formalization and linguistification (indeed, "liquefaction [*Verflüssigung*]"), modernization and secularization have undeniably and effectively executed, and that the more recent expansion of markets, propelled by the diffusion of technological media and informational networks, has only accelerated, diversified, and intensified.

But the quote also gestures in the direction of another intuition that is, perhaps, even more illuminating, namely, the insight that globalization – and, *before, alongside with*, and *through* it, global religion – generates a distinctively "global" rather than merely individual or personal consciousness and conscience (call it a "global soul"), whose public and almost cosmic orientation and novelty are quasi-mystical *and* down-to-earth, extraordinary, and quotidian. Their wider and more intense probing or deeper reach have important implications for our understanding of the pragmatic conditions and restraints, opportunities and challenges, under which all of us (albeit in different degrees, at variable moments, and from distinct locations) must operate in the world of global commerce and communication today. Habermas highlights the moral no less than cultural and political chances that such empirical necessities favor in turn:

> Today, globalization, mass tourism, worldwide migration, in the fact the growing pluralism of worldviews and cultural life, have familiarized us all with . . . experiences of exclusion and marginalization of outsiders and minorities. Each of us can now imagine what it means to be a foreigner in a foreign country, to be regarded as different by others. Such situations awaken our moral susceptibilities. (*BNR*, 16–17)

And this happens all the more in the measure that so-called networks of social interaction and their peculiar forms of exchange and interactivity, propelled by new technological media and economic investments, expand either exponentially or through revolutionary quantum leaps (each time affecting private and public life in ways that can hardly be underestimated and that go largely unmeasured). The net result is a mixture of extensive and intensive growth, which simultaneously generalizes and inflates certain historical givens ("religion" among them) and thus diffuses or disseminates and waters them down or empties them out with the very same gesture. Hence, the modifier "global," as in "global religion" and "global soul," which connotes the dual aspects of this – *no longer simply dialectical or paradoxical* – process of modernization as it transitions from the secular and immanent frame into the postsecular and its, as of yet unknown and untested, framing of minds and hearts, souls and bodies.

The unprecedented scale and pace at which such networks are created, mediated – and, indeed, mediatized – explains why their alternatively articulated vehicles of authority, together with their innovative modes of exchange, commerce and communication, should be distinguished from the more familiar "systems" of state sovereignty (or "power") and economic market value (or "money"), on which so much of modern social theory's analyses (including much of Habermas's own dual conception of "system" and "lifeworld") had remained centrally focused. The new networks' symbolic, yet also deeply political, capital is produced, accumulated, and circulated along different lines of distribution and consumption, whose operating logics call for a new, non-Marxist critique of ideology, according to which "interests" may yet again have ceded their place and role to "passions" or, more precisely, "passionate utterances" (to use Stanley Cavell's term) altogether differently structured in their origination and orientation.

Genuinely global networks operate under the aegis of a "solidarity" that is differently structured in *its* transformation of modern public spheres, not least because this "solidarity" moves beyond the better known forms of social interaction and communication which are familial and cultural, legal and civic, discursive and embodied. And the new "solidarity," if we insist on keeping this Durkheimian term, is not just based on de-localized identities, still culturally or multiculturally defined, but is increasingly "virtual," although its affects and effects in real life can be all too material, at times even deadly.

Yet the global dimension, role, and impact of contemporary religion in both its individualist and communal forms is, at least in part, an expression of this same "virtuality" (just as ever newer media and the sensibilities they enable or convey are, in part, an expression, if not extension, of the very archive to which the history and current phenomenon of religion holds the key). The televangelism of the former Moral Majority in the United States and the "virtual Ummah" (to use Olivier Roy's term) of worldwide – or, perhaps, especially European – Islam are cases in point, but they definitely do not stand on their own. Nor are they merely reacting against the modernity with which it is often said that they "clash," out of a lack of "existential security," due to the "economic and social conditions of life," to the "comparatively high rates of immigration from countries whose societies are still deeply shaped by tradition" (*BNR*, 117 n.6).

On the contrary, if anything, they are the products (and themselves productive) of an alternative modernity – indeed, of multiple modernities, which invite us to reconsider the concept and practice of the secular as we know it. They force us to radically rethink the presuppositions and descriptive value of the so-called modernization and secularization theses, almost irrespective of the question which data support them. Again, the problem raised by global religions in the modern world is not merely empirical or even historical, psychological, or cultural. It marks a shift in perspective and orientation that is not so much borne out by the facts as it places all facts in an altogether novel light. As Habermas notes, such a "revisionist perspective" forces one to understand Max Weber's theory of modernization, premised as it is on an idea and practice of so-called "Occidental Rationalism," as a temporally and geographically restricted "deviation," rather than the matrix for cultural development worldwide:

> From this revisionist perspective, religious traditions appear to be sweeping away with undiminished strength the thresholds hitherto upheld between "traditional" and "modern" societies, or at least to be leveling them. The West's own image of modernity seems to be undergoing a gestalt switch as if in a psychological experiment: what was assumed to be the normal model for the future of all other cultures suddenly becomes the exception. Even if this suggestive image of a gestalt switch will not stand up to closer sociological scrutiny and the explanations of secularization offered by modernization theory can be brought into line with the countervailing evidence, there can be no doubt concerning the evidence itself and above all concerning the symptomatic aggravation of the political mood. (*BNR*, 116–17)

The acceleration and intensification of a certain "political mood" is thus revelatory of a larger and, I suggest, deeper historical trend, though it is not even "historical," strictly speaking, insofar as it effaces the "thresholds" between temporal and cultural demarcations, such as those between the "traditional" and the "modern," and contracts them in the simultaneity of the then and now. But, if this is the case, it cannot just be tradition – here, "religious traditions" – that does the "sweeping away" of these normal and increasingly normative distinctions. There is also an *unprecedented* force that draws the past into the present, to say nothing of the future. Have we understood how (when this is possible), let alone what its philosophical and political consequences are or still might be?

Postsecular or Postmetaphysical?

The passage from "A Conversation on God and the World" cited earlier also reveals some of Habermas's more recent philosophical concerns, which interest me even more here. This is particularly clear from its continuation, which I will quote here extensively, not least since it introduces the very questions on which I concentrate in the remainder of this chapter:

> Surely, the globalization of markets – the rise of electronically intercon-
> nected financial markets and the acceleration of capital mobility – have
> led to a transnational economic regime, markedly diminishing the leading
> industrialized nations' capacities for action. But the intensification and
> expansion of communication and commerce creates only a new infra-
> structure, and not a new orientation or a new form of consciousness. This
> new stage in the development of capitalism takes place *within* a horizon
> of social modernity that has remained essentially the same, and within the
> normative self-understanding developed in that horizon since the end of
> the eighteenth century. As I said, religion and Church served an important
> role as pacemakers for this mentality. But the same cannot be said for the
> emergence of globalized commerce and communication. Christianity is far
> more deeply affected and challenged by the unforeseen consequences of
> this new infrastructure, as are other forms of "objective Spirit." (*RR*, 149)

Needless to say, one might well wonder what, exactly, is quantita-
tively and qualitatively new in the phenomenon Habermas describes here
so suggestively. And, again, why does this new phenomenon reveal such
a sharp discrepancy between the development of markets and media (the
social logic), on the one hand, and the life of the mind and of "objective Spirit" (the cultural logic), on the other? Further, why do the "new
orientation" and "new form of consciousness" that would be adequate
to this novel dispensation now (or still) seem to be lacking? Finally, why
does the globalization of economic markets, together with the invention
of technological media that accompanies or drives them, prove a far
greater challenge for Christianity and "other forms of 'objective Spirit'"
than was presumably the case in the past, when religion ("religious tolerance") was actually a "pacemaker" for modernity and its cultural rights,
or now that the "forms of objective Spirit" (not least Christianity) have
widely taken the form of global, commercialized and mediatized, phenomena themselves?

Must we necessarily assume that Christianity, although "far more
deeply affected and challenged" by the "emergence" and "infrastructure" of the new orders of "global commerce and communication" than
by the "social modernity" of old, had no hand whatsoever in bringing
the new – distinctively global – dispensation about (however indirect or
interrupted this causal nexus or hidden effect may further have been)? Is
religion, including public, and now global, religion, merely a free-floating
superstructure out of sync with the realities of the socio-economical,
mediatic, and political "infrastructure" of a society of networks, based
on the flow of information – indeed, as Manuel Castells has reminded us,

of time and space – into which religion finds itself steeped only after the fact? If this is Habermas's suggestion, it is hardly a convincing one.

Even though he stresses the current (and accidental or temporary?) disconnect between the innovative "infrastructure" of markets and media that make up the processes of globalization, on the one hand, and the "orientation" and "consciousness" of which religion, notably (Protestant) Christianity, was once expressive (following Max Weber's classical thesis), on the other, Habermas leaves no doubt, in different contexts, that religion and the globalized world operate, if not in tandem, then at least along similar lines. Analytically and empirically distinct, the markets and media of the networked society, on the one hand, and contemporary religious imagery, practices and institutions, on the other, function in a comparable mode and complement, rather than contradict, each other. More strongly put, the respective trends and upheavals that characterize and punctuate modern and, especially, contemporary society intersect and interweave with each other to the point of becoming virtually indistinguishable.

Habermas is right, therefore, when he writes in "Faith and Knowledge" that the relationship between global religion and the market of goods and ideas in the systems of knowledge and power and the technologies that drive, mediate, and mediatize their overall and special effects, is not that of a "zero-sum game [*Nullsummenspiel*]." It is a "mistake," he adds, to "construe secularization as a kind of zero-sum game between the capitalistically unbridled productivity of science and technology, on the one hand, and the conservative forces of religion and the church, on the other hand" (*EFK*, 104). After all, he continues, it is simply not the case that "[g]ains on one side can only by achieved at the expense of the other side, and by liberal rules which act in favor of the driving forces of modernity" (104).

If this seems accurate, it nonetheless leaves an important set of questions wide open: what, exactly, is the relationship between global religion and global media? And what are the events or effects that are generated and produced, invited and enabled (rather than simply "caused") by them? These questions, I would submit, are far from simple ones, nor are their answers, and they will have to be the subject for a different occasion.

Instead, my major claim in the following will be simply this: if my characterization of "global religion" in terms, not so much of a diminishing yet abiding, but rather ever expanding yet increasingly elusive and virtual – now maximal, then minimal – "presence" of the metaphysical and its "irreducible element" (Claude Lefort) in the public realm of the political and of politics no less than in the private space of personal convictions is at all plausible, and if, moreover, this "presence" is all the more felt and effective the less it relies on traditional conceptions of "substance" and "essence," say "onto-theology" (or the more it releases those notions from their stereotypical associations), then it is hard to see how "postsecular" thinking could tap into the most immense and (again, formally speaking) deepest of archives while, at the same time, aligning itself with a "rational" and "formal-pragmatic" understanding of "post-metaphysical thinking" (in the precise definitions Habermas has given to these terms). Yet this is precisely what Habermas claims when he writes that "the secular awareness that one is living in a postsecular society finds expression at the philosophical level in a postmetaphysical mode of thought" (*BNR*, 119).

But "postsecular" thought, if it can pretend any specificity of its own (*concesso non dato*), can hardly be reduced to – let alone form a simple subsection of – "postmetaphysical" thinking, per se. The former assumes and explores a far wider horizon – as it reaches deeper down and further back toward words and things, gestures and powers, sounds and silences – than the latter. Indeed, postmetaphysical thought, as the explicit discursive form of shared cultural and political presuppositions and modes of reasoning, must of necessity bracket or completely block such postsecular (which are also age-old, traditional and classical) elements and forms of contemporary experience (in its very re-engagement of the past and at the invitation of a different future) out of sight, allowing it no *public*, much less *global*, role to play.

Habermas claims as much when he writes that "[s]ecular and devout citizens can fulfill the normative expectations of the liberal role of citizens ... only if they likewise satisfy certain cognitive conditions and ascribe to each other the corresponding epistemic attitudes" (*BNR*, 119). Yet the whole difficulty resides in the circumstance that "the liberal state faces the problem that devout and secular citizens can acquire these attitudes only through complementary 'learning processes,' whose status as learning processes remains controversial, and over which the state cannot in any event exercise influence by the legal and political means [or media; *Medien*] at its disposal" (ibid.). If I am not mistaken, one can find further proof of this wide-ranging claim in Habermas's remarkable exchange with the then Cardinal Ratzinger, later Pope Benedict XVI.[5] But this opens a whole new chapter and leads us too far in this context.

In yet another recent interview with Eduardo Mendietta on this subject, Habermas addresses a "terminological lack of clarity" by stipulating that the postsecular indeed does not fully map on to the postmetaphysical: "Postmetaphysical thinking remains secular even in a situation depicted as 'postsecular'; but in this different situation, it may become aware of a secularistic self-misunderstanding."[6] In other words, postsecular thinking ventures into territory that postmetaphysical thinking stays clear of.

Whatever the former discovers or rediscovers does not affect the latter in the slightest, or so Habermas seems to claim. But then, was not precisely this assumption that postmetaphysical thinking could ignore or avoid, explain and contain, the other, postsecular element – perhaps, *its* other element, but in any case, the "irreducible element" of which Claude Lefort, following Adorno, speaks so compellingly – the very core of post-metaphysical thinking's "secularistic self-understanding"?

All this is another way of saying that the give and take of reasons, like the "unforced force of the better argument [*den zwanglosen Zwang des besseren Arguments*]" (*BNR*, 16), remains exposed to, if not embedded in, an ever mobile web of suppositions, meanings, and forces – that is to say, of motifs and motives, modes and moods – whose mobilizations will often carry the day or, in any case, may very well matter more than we realize or care for. Where these suppositions are religious – or, what comes down to the same, are best understood against the foil and in light of religion's immense historical archive(s), its political theologies, and the like – we are dealing with a remarkable juncture in time that, in recent scholarly and public debate, has been alternatively characterized as a "turn to religion" and a worldwide resurgence of "global religions," both of which represent nothing short of a "postsecular" challenge. Taken together, these two fairly recent developments force us to re-evaluate the secular, its "formations" (Talal Asad) and "age" (Charles Taylor), its constitutional and institutional arrangements, its sense of self and conception of citizenship, its past, present, and future. Last but not least, these developments urge us to analyze our increasing exposure to a "world-" or rather "global" consciousness, of which religion and technological media are important vehicles, and whose very energies and orientation, promises and risks, secular or postmetaphysical naturalism (whether reductionist or not) can no longer predict or contain.

In a nutshell, then, I am making a simple but, if plausible, wide-ranging claim, namely, that tapping into the traditional religious no less than theologico-political archive – and, indeed, to do so with a more than merely documentary, but analytical-theoretical and *deeply pragmatic* interest – is a necessary condition for our becoming (and remaining) attuned to models of reasoning and imagining, acting and judging, whose resources and repertoires have been far from exhausted, in spite of all modern secularist and naturalist claims to the contrary, and that only *now* seem to release their most vital conceptual and affective, rhetorical and visual, practical and political force.

What is being inaugurated in front of our very eyes is, perhaps, a "postsecular" dispensation, although this term remains problematic enough for reasons I detail below. It is fair to say that the contours, dimensions, and depths of this "new" and, indeed, "postnational constellation" have, so far, not yet been given their due. And yet its internal tensions and potentials, dangers and opportunities, become more apparent by the day.

A "New Orientation" and "New Form of Consciousness"?

A different concept of rationality, then, a more paradoxical, perhaps, aporetic mode of giving and accepting reasons – beyond or before "yes" or "no" positions on the validity claims one makes or responds to, beyond or before the aim of reaching agreement about something in and of this world – is more and more called for. Yet the alternative to "postmetaphysical thinking," including the one that has been able to rid itself of its "secularist self-understanding" (no easy call, since how does one differentiate between the secular stance in public matters that postmetaphysical thinking espouses and its alleged secularist distortion?), is hardly the metaphysics, let alone the natural or dogmatic, philosophical or systematic theology, of old. Rather, it is a conception of thinking and acting that accounts for the historical and, especially, current elements and forms of *an at once minimal and global religion*, whose public and political roles – and political theologies – have become ever more prominent on the very grounds (such as the proliferation of markets and media, the alteration of mental structures and further transformations of the public domain) we have indicated above.

No "idle postmodern talk" is intended here, and the challenge is no small one either, for how does one adopt a reflexive, even critical, stance – as all philosophical thinking and acting must – while at the same time keeping the total archive of religion and metaphysics, but not necessarily its supposed onto-theological distortions and confessional shortcuts, if not intact, then at least in circulation, indeed, in play (as any *Spiel* or *Spiegel-Spiel* must)? Can one simply discard the conceptual and, worse, material idolatries of natural theology as if these were accidental errors of a naturalist kind that a more genuine, say, "reflective" or "existential" faith and "dialectical" theology (under the inspiration of a Kant, Kierkegaard, or Karl Barth) has no business with? In one word, it may not be so easy to occupy an intellectual, practical, or affective space in-between naturalism and religion, after all.

Call it an unreconstructed Adornian insistence on "negative metaphysics" or whatever you like, but, if I am not mistaken, it is precisely the "minimal" and, in the present context, perhaps, even more remarkable "global" – inflated and hyperbolic – implications and aspects of the concept of theology and everything it stands for that lead us to the very heart of our topic, namely, the role of contemporary religion in the public and increasingly worldwide domain. Is this, then, why the much-discussed dialectic of modernization and rationalization, together with its *deeper-*seated dialectic of Enlightenment and mythology – as, in different ways, Max Weber and Georg Lukács, but also Max Horkheimer and Adorno, analyzed them in the by now classical writings from which the early Habermas would eventually depart – has been succeeded and, for the moment and in all fairness, superseded by what seems an ever more para-doxical (or, at least, no less aporetic) "dialectic of secularization"? Again, this would become the heading under which Habermas and Cardinal Ratzinger offered their sharply contrasting views, with neither overlap-ping consensus nor, to be sure, any comprehensive doctrine easily in sight.

On Habermas's more recent view, "modern reason can understand itself properly only if it clarifies its relation to religious consciousness" (*AWM*). And the reverse, he leaves no doubt, holds true as well. In agreement with Ratzinger, Habermas insists that faith requires, if not presupposes, reason and knowledge, argumentation and deliberation, whenever it wants to make itself heard in the public square, where it need not be speechless or retreat from sight. But this fundamentally complementary – and, we are led to assume, symmetrical – relationship between "faith and knowledge" (the title of one of Habermas's essays, just as it was for Hegel and Jacques Derrida) has, for all its mutual respect and openness, specific implications and overall effects that, from the moment they enter into "dialogue" with each other, affect the very meaning and integrity (i.e., intactness and, as it were, integrality) as well as the pretensions of both. This simple fact already challenges the meaningfulness of the terms "secular" and "postsecular." After all, there was never a time when "faith" and "knowledge," "religion" and "public reason" did not already converse in some form or other and, conversely, there will not be any time soon when we will have translated what one term stands for into the next (and thus have "salvaged" it in one register or another). Nor, again, will we ever be able to name or inhabit a mental space, spiritual terrain, or public domain that is situated in between these two poles of traditional societies no less than modern ones, for whose institutions and modes of discourse we have found no alternatives yet.

The reasons for the predicament of contemporary attempts to theorize the most elusive, yet often most "effective," religious phenomena are multiple, but it may suffice here to mention just one. Religion and the theologico-political (like so many historical and social, cultural and political words, things, gestures, and powers) tend to show a Janus-face. Religion, at least in its present-day public manifestations, reveals a *dual aspect and double potential*, for good and for ill. Moreover, it does so at once intelligibly (for reasons that we can make perfectly transparent by way of causal explanation) and obscurely, almost miraculously (that is to say, inexplicably, driven by forces or affects that escape us, whether in principle or just for now).

A potential source of inspiration and democratic openness, religion and the theologico-political instance simultaneously – and inevitably? – present a danger of dogmatism and, hence, of closed societies and regressive mentalities. As Derrida, in his meditation on faith and know-ledge, rightly suggested, its striving toward perfection (or perfectibility) and its tendency toward perversion go hand in hand.

Religious orthodoxies of all stripes seek to interpret this last possibility, potentiality, or virtuality, as *external* to their authoritative texts, ecclesial traditions, ritual practices, institutions, and ulterior aims. By extension, they consider such perversion as inessential to their theologico-political project as well. They portray these aberrations in terms of idolatry and blasphemy, apostasy and heresy, scandal and offense, all of which, they claim (or imply), could be *in principle* avoided even where they abound *in fact*.

But what if one tendency belonged to the other and did so necessarily or structurally, that is to say, as a standing possibility, in other words, as a danger that must – and, perhaps, ought to be – risked? If this is the case, it is of importance to ask how this double, potentially duplicitous and often deeply contradictory, even treacherous – violent, "terrorist," or "rogue" – tendency emerged in the first place. What historical articu-lations and interpretations did it receive? What chances and perils does it (still or yet again) hold in store for us? Finally, what new options and optics might it, on the contrary, set free, create, or open up, for us or for others, known and unknown?

If the "postsecular" means that we have come to assume and live through a "continuing process of secularization," without telos or end-term, then neither "faith" (religion) nor any of the past forms of "reason" (knowledge) that were imbued with it (call them metaphysics, but also magic and myth) can ever fully lie behind us. And to even suggest that they can may be to make a fateful mistake. Everyday experience – indeed, an hour of zapping or surfing of whatever network or new medium of communication – suffices to confirm the point.

It would be a performative contradiction for any formal pragmatics, premised on the assumption that in an open horizon of deliberation fal-lible claims can continue to be made *and* revoked (and be brought up yet again), to intimate that certain – past, present, or future – options are no longer on the table, that is to say, somehow, in some contexts and at other moments, no longer at play and available to us so that we could still or yet again discuss and consider them *in good faith*. Learning processes are not straightforward or unilinear, let alone irrevocable (as recurring, and often quite worthy, subjects for rational and democratic deliberation, such as the ongoing and increasing role of religion in the public square, show all too clearly).

But, as Habermas also points out, translating and salvaging motifs and motivations from the religious past or from present traditions that (still or once again) surround us affects them (i.e., their understanding and self-understanding) just as much, thus effecting a change in two directions at once. Modernization and secularization (if we insist on keeping these terms), like globalization and the coming of age of the post-secular (if we are more inclined toward substituting these latter terms for the former), work their way back and sideways, retroactively and later-ally, just as they compress and intensify, highlight and dramatize, stretch themselves out to different futures and, inevitably, wear themselves thin.

The very idea of *globality* (over against the *publicness* on which Habermas concentrated in his earlier work) indicates that the sheer dimension, by which I mean the extensiveness and intensity (or density) of the religious archive – taken in its virtual presence no less than its pure, or absolute, pastness (as Henri Bergson, the author not only of *Matière et mémoire* (*Matter and Memory*) but of also of *Les deux sources de la morale et de la religion* (*The Two Sources of Morality and Religion*) would have said) – undercuts claims that the future or outcome of religion's resurgence is certain by any standard. On the contrary, what makes religion "global" may well be that its dissemination and overall impact circumvents, if not contravenes, all causal determination or, in any case, the very proportionality of effects with respect to their putative causes. This, and nothing else, explains the – by all accounts, sudden and surreptitious – availability of religion's archive, often at times and places where one would least expect it, indeed, where all the odds are against it. In that sense, the undeniable role of ever newer technological media and the feverish rise of scientistic-naturalistic explanations and new atheisms, far from denying religion a role in secular modernity, may well be an indirect instrument – and, perhaps, indirect proof – of its undiminished, even greater prominence as well as of its limitless adaptation to novel conditions in whose creation it may very well have had a first hand.

Such an account supplements Habermas's own assessment of moder-nity's "wide-spread push toward reflection" that he credits with having contributed to the "progressive disintegration of traditional, popular piety." In his view, there have emerged two distinct yet related "specifi-cally modern forms of religious consciousness":

> on the one hand, a fundamentalism that either withdraws from the modern
> world or turns aggressively toward it; on the other, a reflective faith that
> relates itself to other religions and respects the fallible insights of the insti-

tutionalized sciences as well as human rights. This faith is still anchored in the life of a congregation and should not be confused with the new, deinstitutionalized forms of a fickle religiosity that has withdrawn entirely into what is subjective.[7]

Yet to supplement this account means to doubt that these three cited options exhaust the range of possible manifestations of public and, especially, global religion in the present day and age (or that they are even accurate descriptions of the three apparent reactions – resistance, accommodation, and evasion – that they would seem to address).

Of course, according to Habermas, the emergence and "genealogy" of modern thought reveals that, in its wake, "a differentiation took place to which the strong, metaphysical claims fell victim." He characterizes this "differentiation process" as the "sorting-through of reasons that alone still 'count'" under conditions that we must call "postmetaphysical" on the very ground that in it "statements concerning essences [*Wesensaussagen*] that are typical of the metaphysical thinking of the one unity [*Alleinheitsdenken*], and the categories of reasons that metaphysical thinking could mobilize, have been *prima facie* devalued."[8] But this qualification, already, should make us pause. After all, can we truly exclude the not so theoretical possibility that claims concerning "essences" or even hypotheses regarding totality – or, in our context, globality – can be recast and rephrased so as to retain their pertinence or acquire a new one? True enough, such claims and statements would, perhaps, need no longer direct themselves to, say, the "glassy essence" of which Richard Rorty spoke in his genealogy of modern epistemology, in *Philosophy and the Mirror of Nature*, or to the All-in-One, One-in-All that forms the *alpha* and *omega* of onto-theological thought, from, say, Parmenides to Hegel and well beyond. But they may speak to deep-seated needs, desires, and compulsions that form such an integral part of our natural histories as well as our cultural make-up that it makes almost no sense for us to (want to) dispel them by one stroke or more. To the extent that they have at times been made explicit and that words and images, gestures and powers, sounds and silences have been found to name or invoke them, they make an archive whose historical – and more than simply historical – weight we would be hard pressed to lift from our shoulders by mere intellectual or moral effort alone.

There are no historical or conceptual means for deciding, then, whether modern tendencies toward rationalization, differentiation, secularization, and even privatization do not, in the very process of minimizing – in the sense of reducing, neutralizing, and trivializing – religion in its public manifestation, do not in fact realize and, indeed, maximize or inflate its remaining potential in an even more fundamental, threatening no less than promising way, much more so than would have been the case if it would have been left uncharted, unchallenged. Religion, on this view, gained and gains by losing. In other words, it cannot be excluded that religion's apparent retreat and greater leniency, often to the point of what would, at least traditionally, have constituted its heterodoxy and betrayal, do not turn out to be a final consequence, even an apotheosis, of orthodoxy: a new intransigence and dogmatic fixation, of sorts. Again, examples abound (and have little to do with a "fundamentalist" reaction or resistance to modernity, as should now be clear).

The question of religion in the public sphere and "world society" is not whether its phenomenon (still or once again) matters or not, but *when* and *where*, as well as *how*, it does. That these moments and locations of religion's public manifestation may be fleeting, easily effaced, and quickly forgotten – also, that there may be times and places at which what is recognized as religion matters no longer or is not quite the same – does not imply that *the virtual presence of its total archive* and, hence, the significance of its *fait social total* (as Marcel Mauss would have said) could ever be lost (even though it will sometimes be lost on us). Nor does it mean that some of its elements and forms (words and things, gestures and powers, sounds and silences) are intrinsically more ill-fated, that is, doomed to irrelevance or cultural violence, than others. As a matter of principle, if not fact, everything can become available and useable anywhere, anytime, and for anyone; the important question, then, is to "know" where and when this is the case, that is to say, to read the signs, the writing – *Menetekel* – on the wall, so as to discern if and how, with what purpose and what unintended effects, something does.

There is no reason why any single one of religion's truth claims or contents – the very "substance" which modern critical thought tends to relegate to a premodern past and present obsolescence – would gradually diminish or for that matter increase in importance, value, or relevance, per se, or that, even if it does, it must thereby lose its potential semantic, normative, and, more broadly, expressive power of creation and imagination to move us in opposite directions as well.

Deep Pragmatism

To speak of "global religion" one need not refer to some self-evident historical phenomenon, nor make a merely abstract assertion about modernity, let alone the world as a whole, that would ignore relevant empirical facts or cultural trends. Rather, one might simply pick up on a recognizable and compelling problematic in twentieth-century thought, one that makes itself heard, most notably, in Habermas's longstanding arguments concerning the possible reconstruction of formal and pragmatic features of modernity and its philosophical discourse. De-mythologization and disenchantment, each with its respective countermovements, such that they produce their own dialectical reversals (as Weber and the early Frankfurters knew all too well), but also differentiation, meaning the de-centering and de-subjectivization of Western consciousness of which the de-Europeanization and, hence, provincialization of Europe seems a logical consequence or, at least, corollary effect – these are the historical, intellectual, and political tendencies that have facilitated, if not produced, "global religion."

As I have argued elsewhere, with reference to the very writings that preceded and, I would claim, led up to, his recent direct engagement with religion – and, more particularly, its role in the constitution of modern reason, together with its continued, indeed, increased relevance in the public debate and the shaping of the postsecular condition – Habermas's formal pragmatics forms a necessary and extended prolegomenon that lays bare the structural principles that have made the historical and discursive arrangement between faith and knowledge, theology and reason, religion, the state, and the postnational constellation, the public sphere and now the global world, or "world society," into what they are and may yet become.

Habermas, basing himself in large part on the theory of rationalization detailed by Weber, while taking stock of the so-called linguistic-intersubjective turn in hermeneutics and much of post-analytic Anglo-American thought, keeps circling around the fact that there was something deeply precious in modernity's universalizing tendencies, however violent their effect or side effects may further have turned out to be. Despite the apparent monologism of Kant's critical project and the conceptual pitfalls of the early dialectic of Enlightenment that some of Kant's critics (from the young Hegel and the young Lukács through early Horkheimer and later Adorno) took to task, but also often exaggerated or rhetorically dramatized – or, indeed, sought *either* to overcome in a totalizing, idealist, or materialist perspective and practice (in the case of Hegel, Lukács, and, at times, Horkheimer) *or* to merely diagnose in a quietist-therapeutic, or, in any case, negative-metaphysical meditation (in the case of Adorno) – Habermas continues to insist on the potential or virtual "unity of reason in the multiplicity of its voices" and the theoretical and normative as well as legal and political contributions it might still be able to make. And this especially at a time when many of its central premises and promises are more and more challenged, not least by the resurgence – and further transformation – of religion in the public sphere.

According to Habermas, modernity has from its first beginnings been characterized by a "linguistification [*Versprachlichung*] of the sacred" that comes down to a "liquefaction [*Verflüssigung*] of the basic religious consensus." The rationalization of worldviews and the lifeworld was marked by an irreversible development and learning process "in which the more purely the structures of universal religions [*Universalreligionen*] emerge, merely the kernel [*Kernbestand*] of a universalistic morality remains." In other words, a certain globalization – an expansion, generalization, universalization, and, perhaps, profanation, if not trivialization – of the religious took place *in tandem*, indeed, in elective affinity with, first, the systematization, and, second, the secularization and eventual formalization of its historical (i.e., revealed, positive, and ontic) content.

Habermas posits that in this – by and large unlinear and irrevocable – historical process, a procedure of rational (and, in part, historical materialist) reconstruction as well as quasi-transcendental (and, in part, phenomenological) reduction *empties* or *thins out* the original substance and metaphysical referents of religion, revealing its "kernel" to be morality – more precisely, an intersubjectively constituted consensus, of which traditional Jewish and Christian currents of mysticism formed a first, if vague and intuitive, impression and anticipation. Yet the result, as Kant anticipated, is a "purely moral religion," but one whose features are now naturalized, albeit in non-reductionist fashion, that is to say, reformulated in formal – interactive and communicative, i.e., formal-pragmatic – terms.[9]

What strikes me as deeply significant and, indeed, fully consistent with the overall line of argument I am pursuing here, in the footsteps of *Minimal Theologies*, is the fact that, in Habermas's reassessment of the ongoing, or, rather, growing relevance of the religious heritage, it is not just "elements and forms" of religious life, past and present, that continue to inform the mental structures and motivational resources that sustain the modern lifeworld and its democratic institutions, but nothing short of a *catholicity* of thought, an "essence" of Judeo-Christianity, if you like.

"Postsecularism" and Beyond

What political forms do religion and its functional equivalents and successor beliefs or rituals assume in a world where the global expansion of economic markets, technological media, and informational networks has contributed to radically *loosening* or, at the very least, virtually *suspending* the very links that once tied the theologico-political instance of its authority to a social body determined by geographic territory, national sovereignty, cities and empires, peoples or ethnic communities, familial identities or brotherhoods, parties or movements? Is a consequent transformation of the very concept and practice of religion and the theologico-political – of its idea and body politic – thinkable, possible, viable, or even desirable? In other words, could one eventually altogether *dispense* with the reference to the theologico-political instance and the religious archive on which it, for all its transformations and translations, rationalizations and secularization, has continued to rely for genealogical, conceptual, no less than rhetorical, imaginary, and affective *reasons*, of sorts?

In the idiom of the French philosopher Emmanuel Levinas, what "curvatures of social space" would religion or its structural analogues impose upon the outlines, limits, and enabling conditions of our present modernity, in which the "secular age" and its "immanent frame" seem, in the eyes of some (I am thinking of Taylor and others), to give way to a manifestly new dispensation, namely that of "postsecular societies"? The answer to these questions is far from clear, even upon reading the latest reflections Habermas has devoted to this contentious subject (and recurrent topic in his lifelong oeuvre).

Whatever shape a postsecular "world" – and not merely "lifeworld" – may take, its intellectual contours (its guiding concepts, categories, and general terminology) as well as moral or political futures are far from obvious and, as we have seen, relatively independent from, perhaps, even adverse to, the "postmetaphysical thinking" with which Habermas nonetheless identifies it time and again (as if the former were merely the becoming exoteric and public, manifest and "global," of the latter and nothing more, nothing less). But, then, if we no longer wish to understand the term "postsecular" as yet another attempt at historical periodization (following upon such equally unhelpful designations as the "postmodern," the "posthistorical," "posthuman," the "postmetaphysical," etc.), and instead take it as just a timely and topical indicator of a theoretical and pragmatic problem to be defined and responsibly, practically dealt with, then a whole new horizon of interpretation and application of its meaning and use must open itself up.

By now it is commonly accepted that so-called fundamentalisms of a religious nature – and there are other (e.g., secular) fundamentalisms which are merely a variety of this political religion as well, not unlike the nationalisms that preceded them – are not so much a reaction against modernity as an important exponent and offshoot of it. The political dimension and success of religious fundamentalism is, if not its logical outcome, then at least its paradoxical side effect.

But this apparent success also accumulates possibilities for undermining itself, making it potentially weaker as it grows stronger, increasingly marginal as it becomes more and more dominant, allowing it minimal influence in the very moment that it maximizes its presence. And, needless to say, the logic of this inverse proportionality of its at once intensive and extensive meaning and force or import can be reversed in turn, which is why religion is an ambiguous phenomenon through and through in the public domain and globalized world: at once powerful and feeble, omnipresent and intangible, full of consequence and inconclusive.

In his provocative *Brauchen wir Religion? (Do We Need Religion?)*, Hans Joas provides a helpful characterization of the – at once abstract and concrete – problem of "postsecular religion" and "postsecular thought," while aiming throughout to "repudiate all purely functional arguments with respect to faith."[10] Instead, Joas insists on a concept and experience of "self-transcendence," which he had first explored in his earlier work, *Die Entstehung der Werte (The Genesis of Values)* and of which the recent *Glaube als Option: Zukunftsmöglichkeiten des Christentums (Faith as an Option: Possible Futures of Christianity)* is the latest offshoot.

Joas starts out from what he calls the "rousing new concept of the 'post-secular' society"[11] that Habermas had introduced in his October 2001 Peace Prize acceptance speech, entitled "*Glauben und Wissen [Faith and Knowledge]*" (*FHN*, 101–15), a speech that took friends and foes more or less by surprise, even though its argumentative thrust seems largely consistent with several of his earlier – indeed, his earliest – intuitions and expositions. Habermas makes the observation that the unanticipated event of 9/11 imposed the need for a far more complex reflection upon questions that he had up until then mostly held at bay, namely, those of the relations among religion, politics, and the public domain. More specifically, he claims, we were recently violently reminded of the imperative to think and work through the still "incomplete dialectics of our own, Western process of secularization" (103). To prevent a "clash [or war, *Krieg*] of cultures" (102–3) at all costs, nothing less would be required than a revisiting of modern premises as well as of the foundations upon which they now seem to rest (or, more indirectly, draw and rely), in turn. At the very least, what the "bridge between systematic thought and current events [*Zeitgeschehen*]"[12] calls for, Habermas notes, is the fact that both modern reason and religious consciousness – knowledge and faith – remain unintelligible when analyzed in isolation. In other words, they acquire their respective past, present, and future shapes only in light of – and contrast with – each other.

By the same token, in a postsecular society, "tolerance" would have to mean a "two-way street,"[13] that is to say, a virtue expected, not just from either religious worldviews or the secular, neutral state (or both), but from the philosophical discourse of modernity and its ineradicable tendency toward dialectics and secularist, naturalist and, as it were, immanentist overreach. Only a reason that knows and acknowledges its other is worthy of the name and can stand the test of time. Yet the olive branch thus offered religion, its intellectual traditions, systematizations, rituals, and, not least, its regained voice in the public sphere, was, in Habermas's view, far from a unilateral gesture. For one thing, it was a gesture that expected – in fact, critically demanded – believers' acknowledgment of and submission to the rule of law and the forum of public reason, both within the context of liberal-republican democracy.

This said, the postsecular remains ill-defined in its central features and supposed contrast with (and historical departure from) the secular, unless one were to take it as, at once, its apotheosis and its exhaustion. Perhaps this is what the dialectics of rationality and secularization meant to express all along?

As Joas writes:

> neither Habermas's diagnosis, nor his offer of dialogue, are entirely free of deficiencies. After all, the term *post-secular*, if it is to be meaningful, must refer to a change vis-à-vis an earlier phase. But it is not clear when this earlier *secular* society is supposed to have existed and what one can actually mean by the term . . . [Secularization] might refer to religion's loss of significance but also to the emergence of modern, religiously neutralized statehood. By no means do these two always coincide. From a global perspective, it would be quite wrong to say that religion is declining in importance. Despite the further spread of industrialization, urbanization, and education of the past few decades, all world religions have retained or increased their vitality . . .
>
> But if the assumption that modernization necessarily leads to the retreat of religions is losing its plausibility, the term *post-secular*, together with the notion that Islam is out of sync with technological advances, is also beginning to look shaky. *Post-secular* now expresses not a sudden increase in religiosity following its epoch-making decline – but rather a shift in the consciousness of those who had felt justified in regarding religions as moribund. For Habermas, a society that "adapts to the fact that religious communities continue to exist in a context of ongoing secularization" is *post-secular*. But who exactly had failed to adapt to this continued existence? It would perhaps have been better to admit in self-critical fashion that one had underestimated religion – rather than dressing one's mistake up in a term redolent of epochal change.[14]

What undergoes or requires transformation, on Joas's view, is not so much the nature of the secular state, let alone its constitutional arrangements guaranteeing, say, a wall of separation between Church and state, as the "secularist self-understanding"[15] – nothing more, nothing less – of the state's functionaries, subjects, and citizens.

Habermas, too, for his part, warns against confusing the "secularization of the state" with that of "civil society," urging that the concept of the postsecular has only relevance in the latter, whereas the former remains founded on solid – if fallible – postmetaphysical premises. Postsecular "faith" is thus, first of all, an empirical given, a *de facto* reality that we had better acknowledge and respectfully deal with, while secular "knowledge" retains all its privilege and prerogatives *de iure*, as long as it restrains its tendency toward intellectual overreach and cultural arrogance. And yet it is clear that the faith that invades global society – and does so globally – has an effect on practical and political as well as juridical matters of state and, hence, does not limit itself to "curving the social space" (to once more adopt Levinas's expression) of civil society alone:

> As long as religious traditions and organizations remain vital forces in society, the separation of church and state in the context of a liberal constitution cannot result in a *complete* elimination of the influence that religious communities may have upon democratic politics.[16]

For Habermas, "postsecular" thus designates the situation in which a national state, on all of its (juridical, political, and cultural) levels – and in spite of the seemingly undeniable and unstoppable tendency of modernization, which accords religion a less and less prominent historical (and, at times, seemingly exclusively private) role – must count on the *diminishing but abiding* existence and role of the religious in all of its facets. The postsecular nation is a state "which adapts to the fact that religious communities continue to exist in a context of ongoing secularization [*die sich auf das Fortbestehen religiöser Gemeinschaften in einer sich fortwährend säkularisirenden Umgebung einstellt*]" (FHN, 104). Postsecular religion, then, is an increasingly elusive, yet also resistant, implicit and recalcitrant phenomenon, *as if its absencing fueled its presencing* and vice versa.

This is not to deny that such permanently retreating – that is, quite literally, indeed, etymologically, *ab-solute* – religion, precisely as it loosens itself from historically given contexts and, as it were, *disestablishes* itself institutionally may not, therefore, play an ever more prominent role as a "motivational" resource and political force to be reckoned with. And it is here that it fills a lacuna that procedural models of democratic deliberation, like formal pragmatics and political liberalism, must leave for what it is and, indeed, choose to remain blind and deaf to (unlike their counterparts in contemporary theorizing, such as moral perfectionism and so-called deep pragmatism, which, as I have claimed elsewhere, put such concerns on the forefront of their investigations).

In Joas's words: "The more we ascribe merely weak motivational power to any consensus amenable to rational generation, the more vital it is to look into sources of greater moral motivation and more intensive human commitment."[17] But then, to supplement the formal-procedural model with a dose of "ethical life" (*Sittlichkeit*, as Hegel said), or with the "conversation of justice" that Cavell attributes to the tradition of moral perfectionism, is not to propose or require any significant change in institutional arrangements (such as the "wall of separation," even the state's "neutrality" in matters religious or laic and public), per se. If anything, it might be a way of letting the latter flourish more, or, somewhat paradoxically, of finally bringing them into their own.

If "postsecular" no longer designates an "epochal change," then it becomes possible to attach a more modest and deeply pragmatic meaning to it, focusing on the "image" it projects (or, rather, that is projected onto it). From here on, "postsecular" signifies, for Habermas, the different governmental or public perception – and hence general effect – of the appreciation and rational evaluation, deliberation or contestation, of religious motifs and motivations, traditions and arguments, in the public domain and the global arena alike. As Joas concludes:

> Here, *post-secular* does not mean that religion is becoming increasingly important or that people have begun to pay more attention but that the secular state or the public has changed its attitude toward the continued existence of religious communities and the ideas generated by them. Once again, though, the question is whether *post-secular* is the right word for such a transformation. It is not the secular state that is being overcome but merely a secularist self-understanding [*Selbstverständnis*]. And again, we might ask to whom such a self-image is in fact applied.[18]

Needless to say, it is far from evident what kind of "self-understanding," exactly, might come to substitute for the secularism (or "secular fundamentalism") of old, not least because the phenomenon on which the "postsecular" condition reflects – namely religion's diminishing yet abiding public and, more broadly, societal, cultural, and mediatic role – is increasingly difficult to grasp conceptually, let alone to determine empirically (i.e., sociologically, anthropologically, or even statistically).

Salvaging Secularization

Habermas's suggestion is that of a "salvaging," rather than merely "destructive," secularization of the religious heritage by way of translation and transformation of the traditional substance (whose remnants, he asserts, still sustain us). Needless to say, along these lines, religion all too easily "appears as nothing more than an aspect of cultural heritage that should not be forgotten or as a relic" and is hence no longer considered and respected as "a living presence [*lebendige Gegenwart*]"[19] as such. Yet it was precisely as a living presence – or as the reliving of a presence – that the "revitalization of world religions [*Revitalisierung der Weltreligionen*]" (*KV*, 387–407), as Habermas calls it, has been assumed and reclaimed throughout.

This much is clear, then: just as there is no "postsecular" (or, for that matter, "secular") age consonant with any rigorous definition of these terms, so also is there no "postmetaphysical" condition, or thought, whose distinctive features we could firmly establish, recognize, pursue, and celebrate or foster. And to reserve the category of the "postmetaphysical" for a more limited, sociological use – that is to say, as descriptive of the political and more broadly institutional advancements and compromises that characterize the modern democratic state, its legal traditions and public cultures – seems to play down the wide-ranging claims with which this term was originally introduced and whose implications are hard to ignore, even though we now know that they are neither borne out by the historical facts nor philosophically as convincing as they may have seemed at first.

After all, the so-called metaphysics of presence, with its purported substantializing, essentializing, idealizing, subjectivizing or totalizing pretentions and attributes, was, perhaps, never present – or even presented – as such. Nor could it have been. Hence, there is no need or conceptual room for some postmetaphysical thinking to inaugurate, let alone seal, its long-awaited end. As is the case with religion more widely, its virtual archive has retained all its suggestive force and seems more relevant now than ever before, thus undermining at least one of modernity's central suppositions (the *querelle des anciens et des modernes*, Arthur Rimbaud's *il faut être absolument moderne*, etc.).

And if the current globalization of markets and media has made one thing clear, it is that the temporal and spatial logic of before and after, far and near, left and right – but also transcendence and immanence, the ideal and the real, the impossible and the possible, and even cause and effect – can no longer be assumed with certainty or, indeed, in good intellectual faith. This is not to say that these categories and dichotomies could or should be avoided, but only that the task of thinking and acting or judging – in short, of the whole gamut of human expression and agency – requires a far greater perspicuity and, indeed, *deeper* responsibility or answerability than can be guided by rules and laws, criteria and norms, alone.

The religious archive, with its political theologies and much more, no longer lies behind us (if ever it did), but, at least virtually, surrounds and precedes, or advances, us every step of the way. In fact, it could well be that some of the greatest promises and threats from its remotest recesses and resources have never been realized – i.e., thought and worked through, put to use or laid to rest – *so far*. Further, it may well turn out that, precisely as standing, if *global*, possibilities, they are closer to the surface of modern consciousness and its institutional arrangements and, hence, much nearer and more imminent than we hoped and/or feared. This uncertainty and the intellectual, moral, and political attentiveness or alertness that it calls for is what characterizes the "postsecular" more than anything else. Whether this is sufficient definition to guarantee this term – or its more current corollary "global religion" – a place in a pantheon of critical terms for the study of modern society at its deepest pragmatic level remains, of course, an open question.

10

Religion and the Public Sphere

What are the Deliberative Obligations of Democratic Citizenship?[1]

CRISTINA LAFONT

During the past few decades the role of religion in the public sphere has received increasing attention, both in academic circles and in the public sphere itself. The topic is extremely complex and involves too many issues to be discussed in a short essay. Thus, I would like to focus on some specific difficulties in the attempt to provide a plausible account of the role of religion in the public sphere by those conceptions of democracy that ascribe a crucial normative role to political deliberation among citizens in democratic societies. Concern over the proper role of religion in political deliberation increases as more normative weight is given to public deliberation for the legitimacy of political decisions in a democratic society. Consequently, such concern is at its highest among defenders of the ideal of a deliberative democracy. Indeed, the plausibility of this ideal essentially depends on the ability to provide a plausible account of political deliberation in the public sphere under the pluralistic conditions characteristic of liberal democracies in which citizens hold a wide variety of religious and secular outlooks. I will not try to defend here the virtues of the deliberative ideal or its superiority vis-à-vis other conceptions of democracy. Assuming that the deliberative conception is at least intuitively attractive, the question I would like to pursue here is whether it can actually provide a plausible account of political deliberation in a public sphere that includes religious and secular citizens.

In order to do so, I will first briefly explain what I see as the main challenge that such an account must face (I). In a second step, I will focus on the specific proposals to meet that challenge offered by two prominent defenders of deliberative democracy, J. Rawls and J. Habermas (II). After analyzing some of the criticisms and difficulties that their proposals face,

I will briefly sketch an alternative proposal that in my opinion can avoid these difficulties without giving up the ideal of a deliberative democracy (III).

I

Although there are many different conceptions of deliberative democracy, they all share the basic assumption that coercive policies can claim legitimacy only to the extent that they can meet with the assent of citizens in an inclusive and unconstrained process of public deliberation. According to this criterion of democratic legitimacy, citizens owe one another justifications based on reasons that everyone can reasonably accept for coercive policies with which they all must comply. Only in this way can citizens see themselves not just as subject to the law but as authors of the law, as the democratic ideal requires. However, in view of the pluralism characteristic of liberal democracies it can hardly be expected that citizens generally agree on most political issues prior to deliberation. Thus, the plausibility of the ideal of a deliberative democracy stands or falls with the ability to explain how public deliberation can bring about agreement without exclusion under conditions of pluralism.

But here lies the main difficulty. In order to give their reasonable assent, citizens must be able to judge the policies under discussion strictly on their merits. This in turn is possible only if they are allowed to adopt their own cognitive stance, whatever it may be, when they participate in political deliberation in the public sphere. For, only if they provide the arguments and counter-arguments they sincerely believe are right regarding the policies under discussion will they then be able to follow the "unforced force of the better argument," to use Habermas's term, and reach a conclusion in good faith on the acceptability of those policies. However, allowing citizens to provide reasons and justifications on the basis of cognitive stances that are not shared seems directly incompatible with the democratic obligation of providing generally acceptable reasons to justify coercive policies with which all citizens must comply. This suggests that the deliberative obligations of citizens who participate in political advocacy in the public sphere are potentially in conflict. Whereas the cognitive obligation of judging the proposed coercive policies on their substantive merits requires citizens to examine all reasons they consider relevant and give priority to those that support the better argument, whichever they may be, the democratic obligation of providing reasons acceptable to others requires citizens to give priority to generally acceptable reasons, whether or not they are the most compelling in any given case. Seen from this perspective, the challenge for a defense of deliberative democracy under pluralistic conditions is to come up with a design of political deliberation in the public sphere that recognizes the right of all democratic citizens to adopt their own cognitive stance in deliberation, whether religious or secular, without giving up on the obligation to provide reasons acceptable to everyone that justify coercive policies to which all must comply. If one looks at the debate on the role of religion in the public sphere from that perspective, it can be interpreted as a debate between the liberal emphasis on the citizen's obligation to provide reasons acceptable to everyone in support of coercive policies to which all must comply, and the critic's insistence on the right of religious citizens to adopt their own religious stance in public deliberation about such policies.

II

According to the liberal account of the obligations of democratic citizenship articulated by J. Rawls in his *Political Liberalism*,[2] citizens who participate in political advocacy in the public sphere should limit themselves to the use of publicly acceptable reasons in support of the coercive policies they advocate and vote for, instead of appealing to reasons based on religious or otherwise comprehensive doctrines about which citizens fundamentally disagree. According to Rawls's famous proviso, religious reasons can be included in public deliberation on fundamental political questions, but only provided that "in due course" proper political reasons are offered in support of whatever policies the religious reasons are supposed to support.[3]

One of the strengths of Rawls's proposal in comparison to other liberal defenses of the neutrality of the state and the priority of non-religious reasons in politics is his specific account of the notion of public reason.[4] Whereas liberals like R. Audi,[5] for instance, identify the pool of "generally acceptable reasons" with secular reasons, Rawls's account is more specific and, in my view, better suited for the task at hand.[6] Although religious reasons can be considered a paradigmatic case of reasons that are not generally acceptable to secular citizens and citizens of different faiths, it does not follow that all non-religious reasons can be considered generally acceptable just by virtue of being secular. Non-religious reasons that are based on different and conflicting comprehensive doctrines and conceptions of the good cannot be expected to be generally acceptable to all citizens under conditions of pluralism, whether or not they are secular. Only a much narrower subset of non-religious reasons, what Rawls calls "public" or "properly political" reasons, must be endorsed by all democratic citizens. These are reasons based on those political values and ideals that are the very conditions of possibility for a democracy: the ideals of citizens as free and equal, and of society as a fair scheme of cooperation, which find expression in the constitutional principles to which citizens are bound in liberal democracies. To the extent that an overlapping consensus around basic political values and democratic ideas of freedom and equality can be expected among citizens, these values and ideas provide the needed reservoir of generally acceptable reasons from which all citizens can draw to justify the coercive policies they advocate for to their fellow citizens.[7] Although citizens can include their religious (or otherwise comprehensive) reasons in public deliberation, they must also provide corroborating public reasons, since only those reasons count in determining which coercive policies should be enforced when fundamental political questions are at stake.[8]

Now, many critics have objected that the obligation of providing non-religious reasons in support of coercive policies imposes an undue cognitive burden on religious citizens. As N. Wolterstorff puts it, "it belongs to the religious convictions of a good many religious people in our society that *they ought to base* their decisions concerning fundamental issues of justice *on* their religious convictions. They do not view it as an option whether or not to do it."[9] Rawls's proposal may seem plausible if one assumes that citizens will always have at their disposal two parallel pools of reasons to draw from. However, in cases of conflict between religious and non-religious reasons, it seems that being religious consists precisely in giving priority to religious over non-religious reasons in forming one's own convictions. If this is the case, so the objection goes, Rawls's proviso threatens the political integration of religious citizens in liberal democracies.

In his essay "Religion in the Public Sphere," Habermas offers a proposal that aims to give its due to what he considers the correct insight behind each side of the debate: the need to meet the liberal criterion of democratic legitimacy, on the one hand, and the need to secure the political inclusion of religious citizens that democratic legitimacy also requires, on the other. He agrees with the liberal position in defending the separation of Church and state, and thus the institutional priority of non-religious reasons in politics. Consequently, he accepts the Rawlsian proviso regarding political deliberation at the institutional level of parliaments, courts, ministries, and administrations, that is, in what he calls the *formal* public sphere. But he proposes to eliminate the requirement of providing corroborating non-religious reasons in political deliberations in the *informal* public sphere whenever such reasons are not available. Religious citizens who participate in political advocacy in the informal public sphere can offer exclusively religious reasons in support of the policies they favor in the hope that they may be successfully translated into non-religious reasons. But the obligation of translation should not fall exclusively on the shoulders of religious citizens, like the Rawlsian approach suggests. Instead, this obligation must be shared by all citizens involved in public deliberation, secular citizens included. This proposal is supposed to yield a more even distribution of cognitive burdens among citizens. On the one hand, religious citizens, like all citizens, must accept the neutrality of the state and thus must accept that only non-religious reasons count for determining coercive policies with which all citizens must comply. On the other hand, secular citizens, like all citizens, must share the burden of translating religious into non-religious reasons. In order to do so, according to Habermas, all citizens have to take religious reasons seriously and cannot deny their possible truth from the outset.

At first, this proposal may seem less restrictive than Rawls's and thus more able to warrant the political inclusion of religious citizens. However, unlike Rawls's approach, Habermas's proposal admittedly relies on the development of very specific and demanding epistemic attitudes on the side of both religious and secular citizens. According to Habermas, the normative expectations of democratic citizenship can only be met after some crucial "learning processes" have actually taken place among both religious and secular citizens. On the one hand, religious citizens must develop a self-reflective epistemic attitude towards modernity. This involves accepting the possible truth of other religions, the authority of scientific knowledge, and the institutional priority of non-religious reasons in politics. On the other hand, secular citizens must develop a self-reflective epistemic attitude toward the postsecular society in which they live. This involves transcending a secularist understanding of modernity, according to which religions have no cognitive substance. Severe restrictions on the types of reasons that may legitimately be used in political discussions in the public sphere seem to follow from this approach. For example, religious citizens should not appeal to religious reasons that deny the authority of science or the possible truth of other religions, and secular citizens should not appeal to secularist reasons that deny the possible truth of religious beliefs.

In sharp contrast with Habermas's friendly amendment to the liberal policy of restraint, most critics of the liberal view argue in favor of eliminating all restraints in political debates in the public sphere. The reasons adduced in favor of such policy vary widely. Communitarians, for example, propose a completely open debate on political issues as a way to avoid cultural fragmentation and to increase solidarity among the citizens of a political community,[10] while defenders of agonistic models of democracy argue for unrestrained debate simply as a way to recognize the essentially conflictive nature of politics.[11] As the debate stands, it appears that either imposing severe restraints or eliminating all restraints exhaust the possible approaches to structuring political deliberation in the public sphere.

However, in my opinion, a more attractive, third alternative can be derived from the ideal of a deliberative democracy. The key is to cash out the liberal criterion of democratic legitimacy in terms of a policy of *mutual accountability*. According to this policy, citizens who participate in political advocacy in the informal public sphere can appeal to any reasons they sincerely believe in, which support the coercive policies they favor, provided that they are prepared to show (against objections) that these policies are compatible with the basic democratic commitment to treat all citizens as free and equal, and thus can be reasonably accepted by everyone. Since it is essential to the ideal of a deliberative democracy that there be a pervasive pressure of justificatory scrutiny in the public sphere, allowing citizens to appeal to reasons that are not shared in support of the policies they favor is only possible if they are also obligated to address objections based on reasons that are shared among democratic citizens in order to check whether they can debunk them. According to this proposal, the only element of *restraint* involved in meeting the liberal criterion of democratic legitimacy is that citizens must refrain from imposing a coercive policy until any objections based on reasons generally acceptable to democratic citizens have been successfully defeated. In order to meet this criterion, some arguments need to be offered that show the specific way in which the objection that the coercive policy under discussion is incompatible with treating all citizens as free and equals is actually incorrect. But before I try to explain the specific features of my proposal in detail, I would like to analyze Habermas's approach in order to highlight some of the difficulties that it involves and that my proposal aims to avoid.[12]

According to Habermas, the most serious objection that authors such as Wolterstorff[13] and Weithman[14] have articulated against the liberal account of democratic citizenship as articulated by Rawls[15] and Audi[16] is that the obligation to provide generally acceptable reasons for political decisions imposes an undue cognitive burden on religious citizens, threatening the integrity of their religious existence. In his opinion, the fact that many citizens may not be able to find non-religious reasons to justify their sincere beliefs suffices to make the objection compelling "given that any 'ought' implies a 'can'" (*RPS*, 8). From that perspective, the main problem with Rawls's proposal is that it may force religious citizens to be *disingenuous* in their political advocacy. Admittedly, Rawls's account of the "duty of civility" requires citizens to argue in good faith when they follow public reason. However, the fact that any "ought" implies a "can" indeed poses a serious challenge. Given that we cannot take an instrumental attitude toward our own beliefs or cognitive stances – in other words, given that it is not up to us to *choose* what reasons we find convincing and what reasons we do not – the requirement to provide corroborating non-religious reasons may leave citizens no option but to argue for something other than what they actually believe. But, beyond this cognitive difficulty, there is a normative dimension to the objection as well. Habermas approvingly quotes Wolterstorff's claim against Rawls that "it belongs to the religious convictions of a good many religious people in our society that *they ought to base* their decisions concerning fundamental issues of justice *on* their religious convictions."[17]

If this objection is compelling, as Habermas claims it is, the problem with the liberal proposal seems to be that religious citizens cannot take on the required "division within their own mind" precisely because the reasons they have to support or oppose many policies are religious reasons. As I see it, the main problem here is not so much that those who rely on religious reasons may lack sufficient imagination to come up with corroborating secular reasons, but rather that *there is no guarantee that such reasons are available*. Wolterstorff's objection can be best understood in the context of a genuine conflict between religious and secular reasons. It is relatively easy to imagine a scenario in which certain policies that are morally objectionable to religious citizens (e.g., liberalizing abortion or gay marriage) are accepted on the basis of secular reasons. In such a case, the only reasonable way they can fulfill their moral obligation to express opposition to such policies is through the use of the reasons available to them, which may be exclusively religious. Under these circumstances, the "duty of civility" understood in Rawlsian terms may seem to them unacceptable *to the extent that it rules out this possibility*.[18] Since the policies at issue concern constitutional essentials and matters of basic justice, the stakes are likely to be too high to ask citizens to simply go along with what they think are deeply immoral policies.[19]

In light of this difficulty, Habermas's proposal may be more appealing. He proposes to interpret Rawls's proviso in the narrower sense of an "institutional translation proviso." Accordingly, the duty of providing "secular translations" (i.e., "public reasons") does not apply to ordinary citizens, but only to officials

> beyond the institutional threshold that divides the informal public sphere from parliaments, courts, ministries and administrations ... Religious citizens can well recognize this 'institutional translation proviso' without having to split their identity into a public and a private part the moment they participate in public discourses. They should therefore be allowed to express and justify their convictions in a religious language *if they cannot find secular 'translations' for them.* (*RPS*, 9–10; my italics)

Thus, in contradistinction to Rawls's account, this proposal releases ordinary citizens from the obligation to justify the policies they favor with corroborating non-religious reasons whenever such reasons cannot be found.

Among the virtues of this proposal, the most obvious is that it does not demand restraint from religious citizens or any exclusion of religious reasons from the deliberative agenda of the *informal* public sphere. In this way, the informal public sphere is left open to possible learning processes, cultural changes, and so forth. Moreover, due to its elimination of additional constraints, Habermas's proviso highlights the central constraint it shares with Rawls's proviso, namely, that "only secular reasons count beyond the institutional threshold" (*RPS*, 9).

For all its virtues, however, I am not sure whether Habermas's proposal actually provides a solution to the objection that it is meant to address. My impression is that what fuels this objection runs deeper and cannot be solved by simply moving Rawls's proviso up one step, so to speak, from the informal public sphere to the institutional framework of the formal public sphere. To be sure, Habermas's proposal offers a solution to ordinary citizens confronted with a situation in which they cannot find any public reasons in support of the policies they favor, while Rawls's proviso may seem to ignore that possibility.[20] However, once we contemplate a situation of genuine conflict between religious and public reasons, the requirements of Habermas's "institutional translation proviso," though certainly less demanding than Rawls's, would be equally impossible to meet. Translation *presupposes* that it is possible to come to the same results by different epistemic means. Thus, in cases of genuine conflict between secular and religious reasons, officials would not be able to fulfill their translation obligation simply by virtue of the proviso. Here too "ought" implies "can." So, how can officials generate the required translations in cases of conflict? Where could such translations come from? In cases of genuine conflict between secular and religious reasons Habermas's "institutional translation proviso" leads to the same exclusion of religious reasons as does Rawls's proviso. Adding that the exclusion only operates "beyond the institutional threshold" can hardly silence the objection, given that this is precisely *when it matters most*.

To its credit, Habermas's revised account of the ethics of citizenship does not impose a *direct* burden of cognitive dishonesty on religious citizens below the institutional threshold. In the public sphere ordinary citizens are *allowed* to make use of any reasons they sincerely believe in, even if those reasons are exclusively religious. In that sense, they are not obliged to come up with secular reasons that do not correspond to their sincere beliefs. They are only obliged to do so *if they want their reasons to count in the legislative process*, since, according to Habermas's "institutional translation proviso," only secular reasons count beyond the institutional threshold. I wonder whether the conditional character of the latter obligation makes the burden of cognitive dishonesty more bearable (or the dishonesty more acceptable, for that matter), but I will leave this issue for later. What I want to consider first is the complementary question concerning the acceptability of the cognitive burdens imposed on secular citizens.

According to Habermas's proposal, the corollary of allowing citizens of faith to use exclusively religious reasons for political advocacy in the informal public sphere is that secular citizens must exercise restraint concerning their "secularist attitudes." Surprising as it may be, it turns out that they should not publicly adopt an epistemic stance toward religion according to which religion has "no cognitive substance." Thus, in contradistinction to religious citizens, they should not make public use of their sincere beliefs, if these beliefs happen to be of a secularist type that contradicts the possible truth of religious claims. In such cases they have no alternative but to be disingenuous and come up with alternate reasons that are independent of their authentic beliefs in order to participate in public deliberation. However, if disallowing democratic citizens to publicly adopt their own cognitive stance is unacceptable, it seems that this would be so whether those citizens have a religious or secularist stance. This problem is also aggravated by what is likely to strike many secular citizens as a disquieting additional obligation, namely, the obligation to open their minds to the possible truth of religious beliefs and reasons as a precondition for finding out whether they can be translated into secular ones. Beyond its doubtful feasibility, this obligation seems to deprive secular citizens of the very same right to publicly adopt their own cognitive stance that the proposal aims to recognize to religious citizens. It seems to me that by imposing such additional burdens Habermas's proposal opens itself to similar objections as those facing Rawls's proposal.

As already mentioned, an important advantage of Habermas's proposal is that it does not demand restraint from religious citizens or censorship of religious reasons in the informal public sphere. But precisely in view of this ideal of openness, it seems pretty arbitrary to claim that religious views should be allowed in the informal public sphere for the sake of possible learning processes, but that secularist views (whatever those may be) should be singled out for exclusion from the deliberative agenda of the informal public sphere. Habermas does offer a reason to justify this peculiar feature of his approach. According to him, it is an unavoidable consequence of allowing citizens to include religious reasons in the informal public sphere. After all, what would be the point of doing so if citizens refuse to take those reasons seriously? I totally agree that it would be rather meaningless to recognize the right of citizens to include their religious views in the informal public sphere, if it cannot be expected that other citizens will take those views seriously. However, this plausible assumption does not grant the much stronger conclusion that Habermas draws from it, namely, that "the admission of religious statements to the political public sphere only makes sense if *all citizens* can be expected not to deny from the outset any possible cognitive substance to these contributions" (*RPS*, 15). Whereas it seems obvious that the inclusion of religious (or any other) reasons in public debate only makes sense if it can be expected that they will be taken seriously by *some* citizens, it is far from obvious why they would need to be taken seriously by *all* citizens.[21] Although Habermas does not provide a specific justification for the stronger assumption, his proposal crucially depends on it, for it is what justifies his controversial claim that "secular citizens *must* open their minds to the possible truth content of these contributions and enter into dialogues from which religious reasons then might well emerge in the transformed guise of generally accessible arguments" (11; my italics).

Leaving aside the doubtful feasibility of such an obligation, it is hard to see why deliberation on contentious political issues should become meaningless among citizens who maintain their respective secular or religious cognitive stances, as Habermas's argument suggests. Let's take the example of the current political debate on gay marriage. It is hard to see why a serious engagement in this debate would require secular citizens to open their minds to the possible truth of religious claims against homosexuality. It seems to me that a perfectly serious way of engaging in that debate is to offer the objections and counter-arguments needed to show why the proposed policy is wrong, if one thinks it is. Objecting to the unequal treatment involved in denying the right to marriage to a group of citizens or appealing to anti-discrimination laws to justify opposition to this policy seem perfectly appropriate ways to participate in such public debate. Since the discussion of the ethics of citizenship concerns political obligations, it seems to me that the obligation to "take seriously" the views of our fellow citizens on contentious legislative decisions has a specifically *political* rather than merely cognitive meaning. It is the obligation of democratic citizens to provide one another with justifications based on reasons that everyone can reasonably accept for the coercive policies with which all must comply. Therefore, the obligation to engage the proposals and views of other fellow citizens in order to provide arguments, evidence, justifications, etc., for or against them does not derive from the cognitive possibility that they may be true. Secular citizens may very well be cognitively closed to the possible truth of creationism, the perversity of homosexuality, or many other religious views. Nonetheless, they owe their fellow citizens the cognitive effort of providing arguments to show why they think that the policies they propose are wrong. What their fellow citizens happen to believe tells them what they have to "take seriously," that is, it tells them *what belongs to the deliberative agenda of the informal public sphere*. Thus, it is because no particular group has the right to determine a priori or once and for all what is in need of justification and what is not, that citizens have to take views seriously that they might otherwise have disregarded.

Let's now take a look at the deliberative obligations of democratic citizenship from the perspective of religious citizens. According to the cognitive objection, the obligation to engage non-religious reasons imposes an undue cognitive burden on religious citizens to the extent that it may force them to follow an argumentative path that does not correspond to their own religious stance. This threatens the integrity of their religious existence. In light of this objection, critics like Weithman offer the contrary proposal, namely, that "citizens of a liberal democracy may offer arguments in public political debate which depend upon reasons drawn from their . . . religious views, *without making them good by appeal to other arguments*."[22] Notice that what is at issue here is not so much whether religious citizens have the right to *include* their sincere beliefs and reasons in the informal public sphere, but whether they have the right *to do nothing more*. The main issue behind the cognitive objection is whether they can be released from the obligation to check whether their arguments *can be made good in view of all other arguments available*.

Now, as became clear in the previous discussion of what it means to seriously participate in public deliberation with other citizens, the obligation to engage generally acceptable reasons by no means requires giving up one's own cognitive stance. It certainly does not require religious citizens to open their minds to the possible truth of secularist views that deny religion has any cognitive substance. According to my proposal, their political obligations only extend to engaging reasons based on basic democratic principles and ideals which are generally acceptable to all democratic citizens, in order to justify to those with a different worldview *why they should comply*. Religious citizens cannot justify the policies they favor on the basis of exclusively religious reasons for the simple reason that they happen to live in societies with secular citizens and citizens of conflicting faiths. If they want to fulfill their democratic obligations, they cannot remain "mono-glots" in their political advocacy. What their fellow citizens happen to believe also tells religious citizens what reasons and arguments they have to "take seriously." But, since seriously engaging the public reasons provided by other citizens does not require giving up one's own cognitive stance, the objection of cognitive dishonesty is not compelling against this proposal. In light of this interpretation of the deliberative obligations of citizenship, there seems to be no argumentative path from the right to *include* in public political debate whatever views and reasons one honestly believes to the *right to be released from the obligation to engage reasons generally acceptable* to democratic citizens in order to check whether the coercive policies one favors can be justified to all citizens who must comply with them.

Now, to the extent that Habermas does not draw this important distinction, it is hard to evaluate the exact meaning of his proposal, for it all depends on which of the two aspects of the "cognitive objection" it is supposed to address. If what is compelling in that objection is that religious citizens, like all citizens, should be able to adopt their own cognitive stance in public deliberation, his proposal would have to be understood as granting only the first right. Doing so, however, would require granting it to all citizens and thus a fortiori also to those with a secularist stance. Alternatively, if what is compelling in the objection is not the issue of cognitive dishonesty, but the alleged right of religious citizens to protect the integrity of their religious stance from erosion through public deliberation, then the second right would have to be granted as well. As a consequence, religious citizens would have the right to exercise whichever political influence their religious reasons may have on other (similarly minded) citizens *without* the reciprocal obligation of making such advocacy responsive to the scrutiny of generally acceptable reasons and objections brought to bear by other citizens. Obviously, granting such a right to "mono-glot" political advocacy would be tantamount to giving up any serious commitment to deliberative democracy. It is essential to the ideal of a deliberative democracy that the pressure of justificatory scrutiny in the public sphere be pervasive. Only under such a condition is it plausible to claim that public deliberation has an "epistemic dimension" that "grounds the presumption of rationally acceptable outcomes" (*RPS*, 9). Granting to any group of politically active citizens a special right to immunization from justificatory pressure would directly undermine such a presumption.

As I see it, the ambiguity inherent in Habermas's proposal is due in part to the ambiguity of his position regarding the cognitive objection to the liberal conception. Habermas seems to accept the central premise that underlies this objection, namely, that citizens of faith are obliged to let religion shape their most important convictions in the search for a religiously integrated existence. According to Wolterstorff, this religious obligation entails a further political obligation that is directly incompatible with the liberal proposal, namely, that citizens of faith "*ought to base* their decisions concerning fundamental issues of justice *on* their religious convictions." As mentioned before, Habermas approvingly quotes this passage from Wolterstorff's critique of Rawls. However, it is important to notice that this obligation implies that citizens of faith ought to give priority to religious over non-religious reasons in making political decisions. To that extent, it is not only incompatible with the specifics of the Rawlsian proposal. It is incompatible with the liberal criterion of democratic legitimacy itself, that is, with the obligation to give priority to reasons acceptable to everyone for coercive policies with which they all must comply. Now, to the extent that the Habermasian approach accepts the democratic criterion of legitimacy, it seems incompatible with accepting the alleged political obligation of religious citizens pointed out by Wolterstorff.

Now, Habermas's overall argument may seem to contain a way out of this difficulty. He admits that the ability or willingness to develop an epistemological stance compatible with democracy (i.e., a stance that supports the institutional priority of non-religious over religious reasons, the authority of scientific knowledge, etc.) cannot be forced from the outside on religious citizens, but must instead be undertaken as a genuine learning process from within religious traditions. His main contention is that the successful endpoint of such a learning process would allow religious citizens to understand the relationship of dogmatic and secular beliefs in such a way that the autonomous progress in secular knowledge will not contradict their faith. This, in turn, could eliminate the potential for conflict involved in accepting the democratic obligation to give priority to secular reasons over religious reasons in coercive political decisions. At that point, the potential incompatibility between religious and democratic obligations of citizens of faith would simply disappear. Needless to say, this view of the future seems highly desirable. But, unfortunately, political action belongs to the realm of the *here and now*. If an ethics of democratic citizenship is needed at all, it is needed precisely to answer the question of *what citizens should do in cases of conflict* before such an ideal endpoint is reached. It must determine whether citizens of faith should follow the alleged religious obligation of giving priority to religious over non-religious reasons in their decisions concerning fundamental issues of justice, as Wolterstorff argues, or whether they should follow the democratic obligation of giving priority to generally acceptable reasons over religious reasons in such political decisions, as the liberal criterion of democratic legitimacy prescribes.

Habermas's position on this central question is problematically unclear. Although he does not address the issue of how ordinary citizens should cast their votes on fundamental political questions, his acceptance of the political obligation pointed out by Wolterstorff seems to lead him to accept as a correlate that religious citizens ought to cast their votes on the basis of their religious convictions. Habermas states:

> We cannot derive from the secular character of the state a direct obligation
> for all citizens personally to supplement their public statements of religious
> convictions by equivalents in a generally accessible language. And certainly
> the normative expectation that all religious citizens when casting their vote
> should *in the final instance* let themselves be guided by secular consider-
> ations is to ignore the realities of a devout life, an existence led *in light of*
> belief. (*RPS*, 9)

However, it should be obvious that allowing a majority of religious citizens to cast their votes on fundamental political questions on the basis
of exclusively religious reasons would directly undermine the central
normative claim of Habermas's approach, namely, that only secular
reasons should count in determining coercive political decisions. There
is no easy way out of this difficulty. If the Habermasian proposal allows
citizens to vote on the basis of exclusively religious reasons, it collapses
into Wolterstorff's and Weithman's proposals against the neutrality of
the state. If it excludes this possibility, then it collapses into the Rawlsian
approach it aims to modify. It lets religious citizens include religious
reasons in political debates in the informal public sphere, but when it
comes to casting their votes it does not let them base their political decisions on religious reasons if corroborating secular reasons cannot be
found. To the extent that it does so, it does not provide *any* answer to
Wolterstorff's and Weithman's objection.

III

The dilemma that Habermas's proposal seems to face brings the central
question into focus. Is it possible to recognize what seems right about
the cognitive objection to the Rawlsian proposal without having to give
up on the liberal criterion of democratic legitimacy? In my view, the
answer is yes. As I will try to show in what follows, a proper account
of the ethics of citizenship must recognize *the right of all democratic
citizens to take their own cognitive stance in public deliberation*. This
is the most compelling element of the cognitive objection, since leaving
any politically active citizens no other option but to be disingenuous is
certainly an undue cognitive burden. However, this right by no means
includes an additional right to the *protection of the integrity* of such cognitive stances, as the objection also suggests. It seems obvious that public
deliberation, as a collective enterprise, would be pointless if citizens had
a right to include their own views and reasons in public deliberation, but
no subsequent obligation to check whether they can be made good in

view of other available arguments. Consequently, a successful policy of *mutual accountability* requires combining the right to include the cognitive stances of all democratic citizens with the need to secure reasons acceptable to everyone for the coercive political decisions with which all citizens must comply. But is it at all possible to organize public deliberation in such a way that none of the tasks involved require democratic citizens to adopt a disingenuous cognitive stance, while at the same time meeting the liberal criterion of democratic legitimacy?

I think that the possibility of an affirmative answer crucially depends on how one interprets the rationale behind the liberal claim that only reasons generally acceptable to everyone count for determining coercive policies with which all citizens must comply. Rawls interprets that claim as entailing the obligation of providing public reasons to justify each policy proposal that citizens make in public debate, regardless of what their sincere beliefs may happen to be in any given case.[23] Habermas interprets that claim as entailing the obligation of engaging in a translation into public reasons of any religious reasons introduced in public debate, however implausible or foreign to the citizen's own cognitive stance the latter reasons may be. In contradistinction to both, I think that an alternative way of explaining the priority of public reasons in determining coercive policies is by singling out these reasons as the only ones toward which no one can remain indifferent in their political advocacy. Whereas public reasons, that is, reasons based on basic democratic values and ideals, need not be the source from which a rationale in support of each proposed coercive policy must be crafted, they are the kind of reasons that cannot be ignored, disregarded or overridden once they are brought to public deliberation by any citizen. They are the reasons that all politically active citizens must engage *in their own terms* if they are offered as objections to the coercive policies under discussion. Such objections must be defeated with compelling arguments before any citizens can legitimately support (or vote for) the enforcement of the policies at issue. It is important to notice that the element of "restraint" that follows from my interpretation of mutual accountability is substantively different from the type of restraint contained in the Rawlsian proposal. Whereas, according to Rawls's proposal, citizens who participate in political advocacy on fundamental political questions must exercise restraint (i.e., must withhold support and cast their votes accordingly) whenever they can discern no public justification for the coercive policies they favor, according to my proposal they must exercise restraint only in a much more specific case, namely, when they can find no convincing way to show (against objections) that the coercive policy they favor is in fact consistent with the democratic commitment to treat all citizens as free and equal.

According to this view, citizens who participate in political advocacy in the informal public sphere can appeal to any reasons they sincerely believe in, which support the policies they favor, provided that they are also prepared to address any objections, which are based on reasons generally acceptable to democratic citizens that other participants may advance against such policies. Citizens have no obligation to provide either public reasons or translations in terms of public reasons for each policy proposal they support or criticize, but they do have the obligation to address any such reason that is introduced by others against their proposals. Whenever citizens manage to cast their objections to a proposed policy in terms of reasons generally acceptable to democratic citizens (i.e., reasons based on the basic democratic principles of freedom and equality, etc.), other citizens have the obligation to address and to defeat them with compelling reasons before such a coercive policy can be legitimately enforced. For example, citizens can adduce religious reasons against homosexuality in support of a ban on gay marriage, provided that they fulfill the correlative obligation of addressing any objections based on public reasons that other citizens may advance against such policy. Whereas citizens may not feel compelled to address objections based, say, on the intrinsic value of homosexual lifestyles or of cultural diversity, which they may not share, they must feel compelled to address objections based on the political value of equal treatment that they do share as democratic citizens. Unless next time around they are willing to accept unequal treatment themselves, before their proposal can be legitimately enforced they must come up with a convincing explanation of how is it that "separate but equal" is an acceptable policy regarding this group of citizens but not others. Similarly, secular citizens who participate in that debate do not have to open their minds to the possible truth of religious claims concerning the perversity of homosexuality as a precondition for finding out whether they can be translated into secular claims. A perfectly appropriate way of engaging seriously in that debate is to offer counter-arguments in order to show why the proposed policy is wrong if they think it is. Objecting to the unequal treatment involved in denying the right to marriage to a group of citizens seems a perfectly appropriate way to participate in such public debate.

Needless to say, citizens may disagree as to whether or not the reasons offered against the objections are compelling as much as they can disagree on whether the objections themselves are compelling, and such disagreements will typically be settled (at least temporarily) by majority rule. But, according to this proposal, the cognitive significance of the majority vote should be that it reflects the judgment of the majority as to whether or not the policy at issue is consistent with treating all citizens as free and equal, and not simply that it reflects their judgment as to whether or not it is the substantively right policy (i.e., the policy that enforces what they believe is the morally right way to act). This distinction can help to illuminate what is problematic in Wolterstorff's contention that religious citizens ought to base their decisions about justice on their religious convictions. This claim seems to imply that religious reasons that explain why, say, homosexuality (and thus gay marriage) is wrong, whatever they may be, are at the same time appropriate (and sufficient) to justify something totally different, namely, imposing coercion on others who have the right to be co-legislators. Once the distinctiveness of both questions is recognized, it becomes clear why reasons geared to prove the compatibility of the proposed policies with the constitutional principles of freedom and equality should have priority in determining the mutual acceptability of coercive policies, even by the citizens' own lights. These reasons are: (1) acceptable to all democratic citizens; (2) always relevant when coercion is at stake; and thus (3) should not be ignored or disregarded by any citizens. And to the extent that objections based on these reasons may be sufficient to rule out any proposed coercive policy, even if there are other considerations in its support, it is plausible to claim that they ought to be (4) the reasons that count in determining the legitimacy of coercive policies. Thus, if this proposal is plausible, Wolterstorff's contention would need to be qualified accordingly: religious citizens ought to base their decisions concerning fundamental issues of justice on their religious convictions, *provided that those decisions are compatible with treating all citizens as free and equal.*

Now, it is important to indicate that the interpretation of the priority of public reasons that I propose does not require endorsement of Rawls's additional (and contentious) claim regarding the completeness of public reasons. Thus, I concede that public reasons may be sufficient to rule out some coercive policies, but may not be sufficient to determine which coercive policy to adopt in cases in which both alternatives either are considered equally compatible with treating all citizens as free and equal or are equally contested as incompatible. The abortion debate can be seen as an example of the latter case in which both sides to the debate have managed to articulate their objections to the opposite view in terms of the basic political values of freedom and equality (i.e., basic rights, in one case of women and in the other of fetuses). They just disagree on their non-political views on what constitutes personhood, whether fetuses are human beings, and many such comprehensive issues. So, although the priority of public reasons is indeed reflected in the way the debate has been structured, it does not help to resolve it. In view of the possibility of a stand-off, the political resolution of those types of cases may just have to be a compromise that both sides can live with (at least for so long as there are basic metaphysical or comprehensive disagreements which are relevant to the issue but irresolvable). Even so, the priority of public reasons does explain why accommodation can be considered a reasonable (even if temporary) solution in such cases by citizens on both sides. To the extent that the objections based on public reasons have not been successfully defeated by either side, there is a serious possibility that some basic rights of citizens are violated by the policy enforced. This gives citizens on both sides of the debate additional reasons to accept a policy that minimizes the putative violation of such rights to the highest extent possible as the best temporary solution.

It should also be clear that my claim that public reasons are the only reasons that all politically active citizens *must* engage in their own terms (if they are offered as objection to the coercive policies under discussion) is perfectly compatible with the claim that citizens are *free* to engage each and all of the reasons introduced in public deliberation in their own terms. So, in the example of gay marriage mentioned above, citizens of other religious persuasions may disagree with the religious claims against homosexuality advanced by some citizens on the basis of, say, a different biblical reading or some other type of religious reason. Thus, they may engage in a debate on these issues too, and may end up convincing one side or the other to change their minds after closer scrutiny. Equally so, secular citizens are free to engage religious reasons in the search for possible translations into secular arguments whenever they can discern a common core from within their own secular stance. But the point of my proposal is that no one has the *obligation* to engage in a way of thinking entirely foreign to their own cognitive stance, whether religious or secular, to seriously participate in public deliberation about coercive policies.

To the extent that this proposal accepts the liberal criterion of democratic legitimacy and the inclusion of religious reasons in deliberations in the informal public sphere, it is similar to the Rawlsian and the Habermasian proposal. Nevertheless, it differs from theirs in important ways. It differs from the Habermasian proposal insofar as its interpretation of the requirement of accountability imposes an additional deliberative obligation: citizens who actively participate in political advocacy have the right to offer exclusively religious reasons in support of the policies they favor, provided that they fulfill the correlative obligation of showing (against objections) that the policies they favor are compatible with treating all citizens as free and equal and thus can be reasonably accepted by everyone. But precisely because this proposal recognizes that citizens cannot take an instrumental attitude toward their own beliefs or cognitive stances in order to choose what reasons they find convincing and what reasons they do not, it does not rely on any additional constraints on the epistemic stances (toward religions, science, etc.) that are appropriate for democratic citizenship, as the Habermasian proposal does. The accountability proviso entailed in this proposal is perfectly compatible with letting democratic citizens adopt whatever epistemic stance they actually have when they participate in political advocacy.

It is at this point that my proposal differs significantly from the Rawlsian proposal as well. Although the accountability proviso is similar in spirit to the Rawlsian proviso, it is based on an *interpersonal* interpretation of the nature and the rationale of the obligation in question. By interpreting accountability in interpersonal instead of intrapersonal terms, it can avoid some of the objections that critics have pointed out against the Rawlsian proviso. Whereas it seems at best unfeasible and at worst disingenuous to ask religious citizens who participate in political advocacy to come up with non-religious reasons in support of the policies they favor, regardless of what their sincere beliefs happen to be in each specific case, it does seem both feasible and legitimate to ask them to address any objections offered by other citizens against these policies which are based on reasons generally acceptable to democratic citizens. Since, according to this proposal, religious citizens, as much as any other citizens, are only obligated to address objections based on reasons acceptable to all democratic citizens (i.e., reasons based on basic democratic principles and ideals), they are perfectly capable of understanding and engaging them without being cognitively dishonest. But since the challenge is driven by those who offer the objections, religious citizens do not have to artificially generate a foreign or insincere rationale based on such reasons to support each of the policies they favor, as Rawls's proposal suggests. This task is fulfilled by those who oppose such policies on the basis of their sincere beliefs. All that religious (as well as non-religious) citizens have to do is to come up with compelling reasons to show why these objections are wrong, if they think they are. Their public debate must show that the policies they favor are indeed consistent with treating all citizens as free and equal and thus can be reasonably accepted by everyone. Only the outcome of such a debate would allow citizens to know what their considered political convictions should be. Consequently, and contrary to Wolterstorff's contention, democratic citizens cannot determine in advance of actual public deliberation the reasons upon which their political decisions ought to be based. In order to be legitimate, their decisions ought to be based on those reasons that have survived the scrutiny of political deliberation in the public sphere.

11
Violating Neutrality?

Religious Validity Claims and Democratic Legitimacy

MAEVE COOKE

Jürgen Habermas holds the view that permitting religious contributions to democratic law-making and decision-making violates the liberal
principle of neutrality in the exercise of political power. This in turn
undermines the liberal principle of legitimacy. As he puts it in his essay
"Religion in the Public Sphere": "[. . .] by opening parliaments to conflicts over religious certainties, governmental authority can become the
agent of a religious majority that imposes its will in violation of the
democratic procedure" (*BNR*, 134). From the essay as a whole, it is clear
that he wants to prevent not just conflicts over religious certainties, but
any thematization of religious convictions in the formally organized,
democratic public sphere.

Habermas does not expect *all* religious believers to be able to justify
their political positions independently of reasons arising from their religious commitments.[1] Rather, his expectation holds only for those who
occupy public office (for example, politicians operating within state
institutions) or who are candidates for such office (*BNR*, 128).[2] More
generally, his insistence that religious reasoning should be prohibited in
the democratic political process holds only for the formal public sphere.[3]
With this insistence, he distances himself from Nicholas Wolterstorff,
who rejects the traditional liberal view that citizens should not base
their decisions and debates concerning political issues on their religious
convictions.[4] Wolterstorff argues for a "consocial" position that imposes
no moral restraint on the use of religious reasons and interprets the
neutrality requirement as requiring impartiality rather than a rigorous
separation of Church and state.[5] In his view, the exclusion in principle
of religious reasons from public law-making and decision-making is at

odds with liberal commitments to equality and impartiality. This does not imply that the liberal democratic state may not exclude religious reasons; it means only that it should have a strong rationale for doing so. In the following, I examine Habermas's violation thesis to see whether he provides a sufficiently strong rationale for his prohibition.

My discussion builds on criticisms I have made elsewhere of Habermas's arguments for excluding religious contributions from democratic law-making and decision-making.[6] One of my main points in these critical discussions is that he conflates religious arguments with *authoritarian* arguments. In my view, this is too hasty. A related point is that if arguments are excluded from parliamentary debates and legislative processes, it should be on grounds of their authoritarianism and not simply on grounds of their religious character. Although I briefly discuss the authoritarian question in the present essay, my strategy overall is somewhat different. My aim is to show that it is the particular conception of democratic legitimacy he favors, combined with a particular understanding of religious validity claims, which calls for an exclusionary position. In order to make my case, therefore, I will discuss both his conception of religious validity claims and his conception of democratic legitimacy.

A key element of Habermas's violation thesis is his view that religious validity claims lack the general accessibility possessed by secular validity claims.[7] This is the prima facie reason he offers for prohibiting the use of religious arguments in democratic processes of legislation and decision-making; it is also the backdrop to his "translation proviso": the requirement that religious arguments be transposed into a secular language by way of cooperative processes of translation undertaken by religious believers and non-believers alike (*BNR*, 131–2).

In the context of Habermas's theory of communicative action, and the discourse theories of morality, law, and politics he builds on this, lack of general accessibility means lack of openness to unconstrained debate in public processes of deliberation. From the following passage, it is evident that he sees religious contributions as not open to such debate:

> Religiously rooted existential convictions, by dint of their if necessary rationally justified reference to the dogmatic authority of an inviolable core of infallible revealed truths, evade that kind of *unreserved* discursive examination to which other ethical orientations and worldviews, i.e. secular "conceptions of the good", are exposed. (*BNR*, 129)

This passage makes clear that he sees no barriers in principle to public discussion of non-religiously rooted *ethical* convictions,[8] but holds that religiously based convictions are immune to thoroughgoing argumentative evaluation of their validity claims, at least in the final instance.[9]

Presumably, this is the basis for his remark that public deliberation on religious matters can reasonably be expected to end in *disagreement* (*BFN*, 139). This contrasts with his view of public deliberation in general, in which participants are oriented toward the idea of a rational agreement.

It seems, therefore, that Habermas's main objection to including religious contributions in democratic deliberations is that they are not open to unrestricted argumentative assessment. Three interconnected reasons for this may be extracted from the passage cited above: (a) they refer to a *dogmatic* authority; (b) this authority is *authoritarian*; (c) they appeal in the final instance to *revelation*, thereby rendering argumentative assessment of their claims to validity epistemically unproductive. My principal concern in the following is with the third component of his objection: his assertion that religious validity claims – in contrast to ethical (and moral) ones – rest on an "inviolable core of infallible revealed truths." My main point is that his view of religious validity claims is connected with a conception of practical validity that is too heavily focused on argumentation. Here, I refer in particular to his conceptions of moral validity and legal/ political validity.[10] As a preliminary to my discussion of the argumentative bias in his account of practical validity, I offer some remarks on each of the other two components of his objection.

Habermas distinguishes religious validity claims from ethical claims (and other kinds of practical validity claims) on the basis of their reference to a "dogmatic" authority. To this, it can be objected that all fundamental insights of practical reason are *in a sense* dogmatic, including those that are not formulated in religious language. They are dogmatic in the sense that they are the fundaments – the "bedrock" – of processes of practical deliberation that, at any given time, in any particular sociocultural context, cannot be challenged on the basis of good reasons. In *this* sense, the Kantian moral principle, which rests on the conviction that the dignity of every human being is inviolable, is as dogmatic as the Christian idea that human beings are made in the image of God. Habermas himself acknowledges that such dogmatism is unavoidable. In the last paragraph of *Between Facts and Norms*, he ascribes a core that is dogmatic "in a harmless sense" to the paradigmatic understanding of law he develops in his book. Its dogmatic core is the idea of autonomy, according to which human beings act as free subjects only insofar as they obey just those laws they give themselves in accordance with insights they have gained intersubjectively (*BFN*, 445–6).

The language of fundaments and bedrock recalls the now famous words of Ludwig Wittgenstein: "If I have exhausted the justifications I have reached bedrock, and my spade is turned. Then I am inclined to say: 'This is simply what I do.'"[11] However, the bedrock metaphor may wrongly suggest that the fundaments of deliberation are unshakeable. In response to Wittgenstein (but, I think, in the spirit of Wittgenstein),[12] I want to say that "my spade is turned" merely temporarily and contingently. Furthermore, I want to say that even the concept of autonomy can become dogmatic in a pernicious sense, when it is held to be immune to rethinking and re-articulation. Habermas would certainly accept this. My point against him in the present instance is that core convictions of the kind mentioned, which underpin every deliberative process in the domain of practical reason and may prevent participants from reaching agreement as to the truth content of the validity claims under discussion, are never in principle beyond critical scrutiny. To be sure, at any given point in time, and in any given socio-cultural context, the speaker and hearer may not share the same evaluative vocabulary; as a result, the speaker will be unable to provide the kinds of reasons that would make her utterance intelligible, and hence potentially justifiable, to her addressees.[13] In such instances, a common reservoir of reasons is lacking. But it is a mistake to see this either as a shortcoming of language in general or of a specific vocabulary, be it religious or secular. Rather, it is a difficulty that may arise at any time and in any context, due to the dependency of reasoning on what could be called collective lived experience or a socio-cultural vocabulary.[14]

Reasons are inherently intersubjective.[15] To treat something as a reason is to treat it from the point of view of its validity for others. If reasons are to be capable of being accepted by others as valid (or rejected as invalid), they first have to be intelligible to others. But intelligibility, too, requires knowledge of validity, in the sense of acceptability conditions. This idea is central to Habermas's pragmatic theory of meaning.[16] As he puts it: "to understand what a speaker wants to say with [a speech] act, the hearer has to know the conditions under which it could be accepted" (*OPC*, 142). This involves knowing the *kinds of reasons* that someone could adduce to support the validity claim raised for what she says (340). I take this to mean that understanding a linguistic expression entails knowing how to use it in a discussion with other persons who may challenge its validity; this requires knowledge of the kinds of reasons that could be provided in support of the claims raised for the utterance in which it is used. However, as addressees, we can only know the relevant kinds of reasons when we share, or come to share, a vocabulary with the speaker. In cases where a common vocabulary is lacking, there is an at least temporary failure of intelligibility and, hence, no possibility of justification.

In *A Secular Age*, Charles Taylor gives a striking example of such a situation. This is Tocqueville's account of his visit to America in 1831. Traveling in the Michigan territory, Tocqueville, as a young Frenchman of the Romantic era, wanted to see the wilderness. "But when he tried to explain his project to the local frontiersmen to enlist their help, he met a wall of incomprehension. Somebody wanting to enter the primeval forest just to *behold* it; this made no sense. He must have had some undeclared agenda, like lumbering or land speculation.'[17]

As collective lived experiences change (which they do for multiple, complex reasons), old kinds of reasons lose currency and new kinds gain it, with the result that different kinds of reasons stock the existing socio-cultural reservoir of meaning. Taylor's discussion of Tocqueville in Michigan helps to illustrate this point too.[18] Cautioning against too hasty comparisons between Tocqueville's encounter with the frontiersmen and, say, a clash between ecological militants and loggers in British Columbia, he observes: "loggers today are all too familiar with ecological militants and no longer need to have explained to them that such people exist."[19] Although Taylor does not pursue the point, his observation draws attention to a difference between the two gaps in sensibility just mentioned. In the case of the Michigan frontiersmen, Tocqueville's reasons for wanting to see the wilderness were not collectively available; the frontiersmen did not *oppose* his wish to see the wilderness, but were simply unable to make any sense of it. In Habermas's formulation, they did not know the kinds of reasons Tocqueville would have had to provide in order to justify this wish. By contrast, the British Columbia loggers are able to oppose the ecological militants precisely because their utterances are intelligible to them. They understand them in Habermas's sense of the term: they know the kinds of reasons such ecologists would have to provide in justification of their position. However, it is one thing to understand "the kinds of reasons" in question; it is another to *accept* them. A distinction between two levels of understanding is called for here:[20] understanding as *general intelligibility*, which is contingent on a particular socio-cultural vocabulary, and understanding as *rational affirmation*, which presupposes general intelligibility and is contingent on contextual and subjective factors specific to the individuals addressed.[21] Collectively available reasons are always merely potential reasons for the persons to whom they are addressed. Contingent factors relating to their life-history and psychic-affective constitution determine whether a potential reason becomes a good or a bad reason for specific individuals. Below, I draw attention to one such factor: I argue that, in certain cases, a new way of seeing is required before validity claims can be accepted rationally by their particular addressees. Taylor's example of the loggers gives a sense of what I mean: if the loggers, as particular persons, were to be able to *accept the validity* of the ecological militants' reasons, they would have to first undergo a *shift in perception*.

So far I have challenged Habermas's view that a distinguishing feature of religious validity claims is their reference to a "dogmatic" authority; my counter-argument is that all fundamental insights of practical reason are dogmatic *in a certain sense*. I have emphasized, however, that the dogmas underpinning practical beliefs (religious or otherwise) are not unshakeable, but always in principle open to rethinking and re-articulation. Sometimes such rethinking and re-articulation involves fundamental changes in the prevailing socio-cultural vocabulary, sometimes it involves a shift in perception on the part of particular individuals. In either case, the changes, when they occur, are normally due to multiple, complex factors.

In the passage cited, Habermas not only claims that their reference to a "dogmatic authority" distinguishes religious convictions from ethical ones; he implies, furthermore, that this authority is authoritarian. To begin with, the accusation of authoritarianism needs to be rendered more precise. In my terminology, assertions are open to the objection that they are *epistemologically* authoritarian when they lay claim to privileged access to truth or validity in a practical sense; authoritarianism of this sort is typically connected with appeal to an absolute, final truth that is deemed to be attainable by human beings.[22] I refer to such views as authoritarian because they privilege the insight of certain categories of human beings and also assert the indisputable validity of particular, historically conditioned utterances regarding the truth of a state of affairs or claims about the right conduct of life. In doing so, they disregard important elements of the modern, Western self-understanding, such as belief in the equal dignity of all human beings and in the linguistically mediated character of human knowledge, together with its historicity and context-dependency. In the areas of human knowledge that involve practical reasoning (principally, ethics, law, politics, art, and religion), this authoritarian attitude to knowledge typically goes hand in hand with an *ethical* authoritarianism. I refer to ethical views as authoritarian when they call upon human beings to act in certain ways irrespective of whether they could accept or reject them (or temporarily abstain from passing judgment on them) on the basis of reasons they call, or could come to call, their own. In other words, an authoritarian view of the right conduct of life sees the validity of ethical assertions as essentially independent from the insight of those for whom they are supposed to obtain. Thus, it too disregards key elements of the modern, Western self-understanding, in particular, belief in individuals' freedom to form and pursue their own conceptions of the good.

Habermas seems to assume that the "dogmatic" core of religiously rooted convictions inevitably leads to epistemological and ethical authoritarianism. Doubtlessly, many religious believers – not to mention religious institutions – do lay claim to privileged access to truth and regard their knowledge of truth as infallible. Doubtless, too, religious believers and religious institutions issue pronouncements on the right conduct of life that they hold to be unquestionably valid. Nonetheless, this authoritarian attitude toward knowledge is not a *necessary* ingredient of religious faith. Nor is it an essential feature of religious belief that religious instructions to live one's life in a certain way must be accepted as valid, irrespective of the reasoning powers of those to whom they are addressed. Habermas himself acknowledges the considerable degree of reflexivity that is compatible with religious belief. He points out that in the encounter with modern science and the humanist Enlightenment, Christian theology was able to reconcile religious beliefs with the authority of the sciences and the secular foundations of morality and law; moreover, that the encounter made possible a transformation of religious traditionalism in belief and conduct. Thus, he does not see any "insurmountable cognitive dissonances between an enlightened religious understanding of the world, on the one side, and the rational modes of modern thought and action, on the other" (EFK, 14). At the same time, as we have seen, he holds that the process of reflexivity stops at the point where reason runs up against the core of revealed truths underpinning religious convictions. This, presumably, is the point where "dogmatism" threatens to turn into epistemological and ethical authoritarianism. The danger is real but, as I showed in the foregoing, it should not be overstated. The "dogmatic" core underpinning religious convictions is not forever resistant to change, even from the point of view of religious faith. The capacity for reflexivity that Habermas ascribes to post-Enlightenment religious believers applies not only to particular religious propositions but to the fundaments of religious belief itself. Religious believers, like postmetaphysical philosophers, can acknowledge that vocabularies change, and with them the collectively available stock of reasons, shaking up what had hitherto counted as fundamental convictions, including religious ones.[23] Just as the "bedrock" metaphor is misleading for core philosophical beliefs, it may evoke the wrong picture of fundamental religious convictions. It would be better, therefore, to use a different metaphor. Drawing on another famous Wittgensteinian image,[24] we could say that both philosophical and religious arguments appeal to "dogmas" in the sense of core convictions, which constitute riverbeds of thought (and experience); these change over time, sometimes almost imperceptibly and sometimes more obviously, due to more or less intentional human intervention.[25]

I have attributed to Habermas an over-hasty view of religious validity claims as epistemologically and ethically authoritarian, arguing that religious believers, too, are capable of the kind of reflexivity that helps to avoid such forms of authoritarianism. In the next part of my discussion, I turn to his worry about religious validity claims and revelation.

For Habermas, it is not just their reference to a "dogmatic authority" that distinguishes religious validity claims from other claims in the domain of practical reason; a further distinguishing mark is their dependency on infallible *revealed* truths. This is supposed to account for their dogmatic core, which in turn prevents them from being examined unreservedly in discourse. He makes his position quite clear in a footnote: "Only conflicting religious beliefs teach us *a fortiori* that a justified consensus cannot be reached" (*BNR*, 129 n.35). My remarks on "dogmatism" have cast initial doubt on his position: I suggested that, in the domain of practical reason at least, many validity claims are based on core convictions that at any given time, in any given socio-cultural context, are not easily opened to unreserved critical scrutiny; however, although this core may appear as unshakeable "bedrock" when we run up against it in deliberation, it is in fact a "riverbed" that changes over time as a result of multiple complex factors and is in principle always open to revision and renewal. But this is unlikely to make Habermas shift position. Quite apart from their alleged dogmatism and implied authoritarianism, he holds that there is something special about religious validity claims that has to do with their revelatory aspect; moreover, that this is a reason to exclude them from formal public deliberation. This merits closer consideration.

Why should Habermas find the dependency of religious convictions on *revealed* truths problematic? My diagnosis is that this is due to two interconnected aspects of his account of practical validity. First, to insufficient appreciation of the ways in which the rational acceptability of practical validity claims *in general* is tied to non-argumentative "world-disclosure" or "revelation." Second, to an account of epistemic quality that is defined in exclusively argumentative terms and (linking up with the first point) an over-inflation of the power of arguments to effect cognitive transformation in the domains of politics and morality.

Let me start with his insufficient appreciation of the ways in which the rational acceptability of claims to validity may depend on kinds of "world-disclosure" or "revelation" that are non-argumentative, in the sense that they do not happen within argumentation.

In the domain of practical reason, coming to accept the validity of a particular perspective or position may require a shift in perception. In other words, accepting the validity of a particular perspective or position may require us to come to see the world in a new way. Furthermore, coming to see the world in a new way involves *disclosure*: an opening of one's eyes to new ways of looking at things. A person who changes her perception of her need for a certain income level, for example, must have had her eyes opened to the importance of doing so. Some process, some event, some argument or some person(s) must have opened her eyes. For instance, her eyes may have been opened by the example of a neighbor, who lives well on a much smaller income, or by powerful arguments from someone who made her see that her need for a certain level of wealth can be satisfied only at the expense of the well-being of other persons; or by the combined weight of arguments from a number of participants in a discussion or by a combination of her neighbor's example and arguments from one or more persons. Habermas would surely be willing to accept this. But disclosure in this sense is not very different from revelation. Although traditionally both terms have had metaphysical connotations, this is no longer true of their everyday use, at least in the English language ("she revealed to me that she lives on the north side of the city"; "he disclosed his plans for restructuring the university"). Admittedly, the German term used by Habermas in the passage quoted at the start of our discussion is *Offenbarungswahrheiten*, in which the word *Offenbarung* [revelation] certainly evokes the idea of a divine presence manifesting itself to human beings. But, as indicated, revelation can also be used in ways that do not commit the speaker to belief in any such presence. I want to *leave open* the question of whether the revelation involved in practical reasoning has its source in some kind of divinity. As a reminder that this question is being kept open, I substitute the term "disclosure" for "revelation," since in current usage, the former is, perhaps, less metaphysically inflated. By "disclosure," I mean simply the opening of one's eyes that precedes new ways of seeing in the domain of practical reason.

I am referring to situations in which the rational acceptance of validity claims calls for a new way of seeing the world. Such shifts in perception are epistemically significant, for they have an important impact on assessment of the epistemic quality – the rationality or truth – of the validity claims in question. (They are also existentially significant, but I cannot pursue this aspect here.) Thus, such changes in ways of seeing may be described as "epistemically significant shifts in perception."

I have contended that coming to accept the rationality of a validity claim in the domain of practical reason sometimes presupposes an epistemically significant shift in perception. Not all such shifts happen in the same way. For analytic purposes, we may distinguish between shifts in perception that are brought about due to the exchange of reasons in argumentation, and shifts in perception that happen for reasons independent of argumentation.

In the first case, the exchange of reasons *brings about* the shift in perception: the factors determining the adoption of the new perspective or position are purely internal to the argumentative situation. In the second case, by contrast, the new perspective or position comes about independently of the argumentative situation: although argumentation is needed to assess the rational merits of the new perspective, only persons who have undergone the relevant change in perception prior to the argumentation will be able to weigh up the merits of the validity claims in question.

To illustrate the first case, we could take Habermas's account of democratic deliberation. He clearly attributes a transformative power to deliberation in the democratic public sphere.[26] To begin with, he insists that all perceptions of needs, interests, and evaluative concerns are in principle open to critical examination in public deliberation, and thereby to modification or transformation (*BFN*, 312–13). His twin-track theory of democracy is designed to enable such transformation. It allows for the dynamic interplay between particular perceptions of needs, interests, and evaluative concerns, which are thematized in the informal public sphere, and general laws and policies, which are the subject of deliberation in the formal public sphere (418–27). Prevailing laws and policies must always be open to challenge, review, and possible transformation by objections formulated in "anarchic" processes of opinion formation, while particular perceptions of needs, interests, and evaluative concerns must always be open to challenge, review, and possible transformation by the laws and policies that emerge from formal processes of political decision-making and law-making. Valid bases for objection include demonstration of prejudice, bias, and blinkered ways of thinking but above all, and especially in the formal public sphere, evidence of lack of impartiality (neutrality).[27] Laws and political decisions lose their claim to legitimacy when they fail to treat all citizens impartially. As we shall see in more detail in the final section, Habermas makes agreement on the general acceptability of laws and decisions the yardstick of impartiality and, hence, of legitimacy. Under conditions of modern pluralism, citizens tend to have conflicting perceptions of their needs, interests, and evaluative concerns. If agreement is to be achieved, therefore, citizens must be prepared to revise them in light of the needs, interests, and evaluative concerns of other citizens. The process of mutual revision calls for the public exchange of arguments in which the objections of others compel participants to look critically at their own perceived needs, interests, and evaluative concerns, and to change them if necessary. In Habermas's account, in sum, transformation of perceptions through the exchange of reasons in formal or informal processes of public deliberation plays a key role in the process of democratic legitimation.

To illustrate the second case, we could take situations in which a vegetarian way of life is to be justified rationally. Arguments for vegetarianism often involve non-argumentative forms of disclosure and transformation. In such cases, those to whom the arguments are addressed will be able to accept them on the basis of good reasons only if

they undergo, or have undergone, a change in perception prior to participation in argumentation. Of course, a change in perception is not always
necessary in order rationally to accept the arguments for vegetarianism.
Someone can be raised a vegetarian, for example. My point is merely that
a shift in perception may be a precondition of the rational affirmation of
the arguments in favor of it. In such cases, their addressees will be able
to accept the arguments rationally only if, suddenly or gradually, they
have come to see the world in a way that makes these reasons speak to
them personally. We could say the mode of transformation is *internal*
to the argumentative situation when the change in perception is a direct
result of the act of articulating certain points of view (for instance, when
someone hears an impassioned plea for vegetarianism and is immediately convinced of its rightness), or as a result of the to-and-fro of the
argumentative exchange. (I am using the concept of argumentation in a
broad, Habermasian sense to refer to the activity of raising and responding to validity claims.) We may speak of transformation *external* to the
argumentative situation when the change in perception comes about as a
result of things that happen independently of that situation (for instance,
as a result of a specific experience such as a visit to an abattoir or as a
result of behavior practiced over an extended period, such as the adoption of a meat-free diet for health reasons for a number of years).

The same holds for religious convictions. In some – perhaps in many
– instances, disclosure and transformation is a precondition of their
rational affirmation. In such cases, the addressees will be able to accept
the reasons on which the claims to validity rest only if they undergo, or
have undergone, a change in perception. Sometimes the transformation
is internal to the argumentative situation, the change in perception occurring, for example, when someone is moved by the power of the words of
a preacher and comes to see the world in a different way. Sometimes the
transformation is external to the argumentative situation, the change in
perception occurring, for example, as the result of an existentially significant experience such as the death of a loved one or a practice of attending
church services for many years.

My sketch of the factors at play in epistemically significant shifts in
perception calls for a number of qualifications and clarifications:

(i)   The internal/external distinction is analytic. Since the causes of per-
        ceptual shifts are multiple and complex, such a distinction is rarely
        possible in practice.
(ii)   My immediate concern here is with individual shifts in percep-
        tion. I leave aside the question of the role of argumentative and
        non-argumentative factors in bringing about shifts in what I earlier
        called a socio-cultural vocabulary.

(iii)   The transformative power of the rhetorical features of the argument should not be over-dramatized. From the point of view of transformation of perceptions, the content of the argument is at least as important as its rhetorical force. Furthermore, as indicated, this force may not be attributable to a single act of articulation; the to-and-fro of the argumentative exchange – the dialogue – is often the crucial factor.

(iv)   The transformative power of arguments may be cumulative: it may be their weight over time that brings about a new way of seeing things. A related point is that the rational acceptability of validity claims is not an all-or-nothing affair. As a result of a shift in perception, we may come to see *some* truth in an argument or point of view, without being entirely convinced by it. This may be a first step to further shifts in perception that lead to us accepting the argument fully.

(v)   Translation can play an important role in facilitating such shifts in perception.[28] It can help us to see some truth in arguments or points of view, even in cases where they are embedded in worldviews that are initially alien to us. This kind of translation does not require formal training or special gifts. Nonetheless, a poetically gifted translator can enable us to gain imaginative access to vocabularies that are not readily accessible to us.[29] It seems to me that even apparently untranslatable religious validity claims – say, Paul's words concerning resurrection in the Christian New Testament – might be re-articulated creatively in a way that allows people with no religion to see *some* truth in them. Paul writes: "This is how it will be when the dead are raised to life. When the body is buried, it is mortal, when raised, it will be immortal [. . .] When buried, it is a physical body, when raised it will be a spiritual body."[30] Non-believers might, for example, come to see connections between Paul's dictum that the "raised body" will be a "spiritual body" and the secular view that the spirit of a dead person outlives her physical body in a material way, in that it has a real impact on those who survive her.

(vi)   Empirically based arguments are also important in changing perceptions. In the case of a person who comes to find arguments for vegetarianism compelling, for example, the required shift in perception might be triggered by empirically based arguments about the ecological effects of the mass production of animals for human consumption. Similarly, an empirically based study of the negative social effects of imprisonment could be the crucial trigger for a person who comes to see some truth in the Christian view of compassion, which calls into question punishment and retribution as appropriate responses to serious wrongdoing. As with changes to socio-cultural vocabularies, the factors at play in individual shifts in perception are multiple and complex; empirically based arguments are always potentially transformative factors.

(vii)   Disclosure and transformation are not purely cognitive: as a rule, they impact on how we behave and on our conduct of life in general. When we undergo a shift in perception, becoming newly convinced by a particular point of view, we are subsequently likely to live our lives differently. However, exactly how we will proceed to live our lives is an open question. For example, someone who becomes convinced that human beings owe respect to dogs on grounds of their inherent dignity might still have reasons for continuing to eat meat. Or, again, someone who becomes convinced that Jesus is in some form divinely ordained may have reasons for objecting to worshiping God in community with other Christians. The implications for behavior and action of individual shifts in perception are context-specific, in the sense that they cannot be specified in advance of particular situations.

(viii)   Finally, the changes in perception that are, on occasion, the precondition of an utterance's rational affirmation have to *prove* their rational acceptability in public deliberation. An *experience* of disclosure, whether it is argumentation-internal or external, is not sufficient to *justify* the resulting shift in perception: justification is rational and tied to argumentation. I come back to this in the final section.

Notwithstanding these (and possibly other) qualifications, it seems to me useful to distinguish analytically between argumentation-internal and argumentation-external modes of disclosure and transformation, for it shows that, in many cases, the factors relevant in assessing the rationality of validity claims are not purely internal to the argumentative situation. In the final section, the significance of this point for our understanding of democratic legitimacy will become apparent. Here, we may note that the dependence on argumentation-external factors that Habermas attributes to religious validity claims – their dependence on "revelation" – is not peculiar to such claims, but rather something shared in principle with all other kinds of practical validity claims and, in particular, by (what he calls) ethical ones. We may also note that, contrary to what Habermas implies, in the case of religious validity claims the crucial transformative factors may well be argumentation-*internal* ones.

I have suggested that Habermas's account of practical reasoning neglects the "world-disclosing" or "revelatory" dimension of rational acceptability *in general* and overemphasizes its dependency on the exchange of reasons in argumentation. Connected with this is an argumentation-internal conception of epistemic quality in the domain of law/politics and morality. This conception is problematic for reasons independent of the question of disclosure and transformation. I will come back to this shortly. At this point I want merely to note that the dependency in certain instances of rational acceptability on non-argumentative factors – on non-argumentative forms of lived experience – undermines any purely argumentation-internal account of epistemic quality; by the same token, a purely argumentation-internal account of epistemic quality leaves no space for non-argumentative forms of lived experience as possible co-determinants of rational acceptability.

Habermas not only privileges the exchange of reasons in argumentation when it comes to explaining *how* epistemically significant shifts in perception come about; in addition, he makes the exchange of reasons in argumentation the determining factor in accounting for the *epistemic quality* of such shifts in perception, at least in the case of democratic and moral deliberation.[31] More precisely, his criteria for determining whether or not the new way of seeing counts as a cognitive gain are specified in terms of the procedure and outcome of argumentation. This contrasts with his view of the epistemic quality of the outcome of religious deliberations. In the case of religious deliberation, he holds that a source external to the argumentative procedure determines whether the result of the deliberation is valid – that is, rational or true. For, as we have seen, he holds that even self-reflexive, discursively inclined religious believers appeal to an argumentation-*external* authority – a divine authority that reveals itself to human beings. Let us take a closer look at this part of his account.

I have argued that non-argumentative forms of lived experience may be relevant in accounting for *how* a shift in perception comes about. I now want to say that they may also be relevant in explaining why the shift in perception is epistemically significant. Broadly speaking, we can distinguish two positions vis-à-vis epistemic significance. According to the first, the epistemic significance of a shift in perception is attributable ultimately to something external to human deliberation (indeed, to human communication); according to the second, its epistemic significance can be explained entirely in terms of human communication, for example in terms of an idealized procedure of argumentation.

The first position is held by many religious believers. Indeed, if their religious belief entails belief in a god that transcends human practices and, furthermore, the belief that God is truth, they are committed to such an explanation of the epistemic quality of the outcome of argumentation, at least in the domain of practical reason: they cannot attribute it *solely* to the exchange of arguments within an argumentative situation.

This means in turn that they make the question of whether the change in perception is an epistemic gain – whether it is a qualitatively better view of things – *ultimately* dependent on something outside of the deliberation. It is important to note that the first position is not exclusive to religious believers. It is held by anyone who asserts that truth in the practical sense is logically independent of the outcome of intersubjective deliberation. That is to say, the first position entails only a rejection of the view that the epistemic quality of particular arguments is attributable entirely to the exchange of arguments in intersubjective deliberation; although it posits an explanation of this quality that refers to something outside of the deliberation, it does not require experience of, or belief in, a divine source of validity that transcends human practices in general (or at least not in any conventional, monotheistic or personalized sense of the divine).

The second position is held by all those who affirm an epistemic-constructivist conception of truth in the practical sense. Habermas is an example of someone who does so, at least with respect to legal/political and moral validity claims. His constructivist stance is most clearly evident in his account of moral validity (*TJ*, 237–75, esp. 266–75). In his view, moral reality – the moral world – is "made by us": the realm of morality is itself generated in discourse. As he puts it: in the case of moral validity, the very domain of validity has to be *produced*.[32] Moral validity is defined as the outcome of a discursive procedure, universal in extent, in which participants reach agreement that a particular norm or principle is equally in everyone's interests. The discursively generated agreement is conceived of as the "single right answer" to the question at hand; moreover, as an answer that is arrived at by everyone for the same reasons. This is what lends moral validity its unconditional character and makes it analogous to truth (*TJ*, esp. 247–9). Here, we see the first noteworthy feature of Habermas's conception of moral validity: it attributes to human beings the power to produce knowledge that is valid in an unconditional sense. A further noteworthy feature is that it implies a purely argumentation-internal view of how we arrive at moral knowledge. In stipulating that the right answer must be arrived at *for the same reasons*, it implies that only those shifts in perception that are brought about by way of the exchange of reasons within moral argumentation are epistemically significant. Thus, when he attributes to moral deliberation a transformative power in the sense of a potential for changing perceptions, he means that the participants, who are concerned to find norms or principles that are equally in everyone's interests, come to see their own interests differently when confronted argumentatively with the interests of other participants; further, that this transformation can be fully explained in terms of the exchange of arguments in a context in which the guiding concern is to find "the single right answer."

This account of moral deliberation is troubling for a number of reasons. To begin with, it rules out the moral salience of arguments whose rational affirmation depends in part on argumentation-external factors; as we have seen, this over-inflates the power of arguments to make shifts in perception happen. Second, it leaves no room for an understanding of epistemic quality that is non-argumentative: it makes the epistemic significance of shifts in perception entirely dependent on finding "the single right answer" by way of an argumentative procedure. My distinction between two views of the sources of disclosure was intended to show that this is not the only way of accounting for epistemic quality moreover, that it is at odds with the account offered not just by religious believers but by anyone who grants (practical) truth some logical independence of argumentation. But this does not mean that Habermas's way of accounting for epistemic quality is not the right way. The fact it competes with other approaches is hardly an argument against it. Our discussion in the previous section suggested one objection: its neglect of the non-argumentative dimension of rational acceptability in the domain of practical reason. But there are other reasons for objecting to it.

My other objections, in a nutshell, are that Habermas's argumentation-internal (epistemic-constructivist) account of epistemic quality is finalistic, counter-intuitive, and hubristic. In order to see this, we can employ a thought experiment that plays an important role in Habermas's theory: the idea of the ideal speech situation.

The ideal speech situation is described by Habermas as a methodological fiction or projection that permits thought experiments (*BFN*, 322–3). As we have seen, he attributes a moment of unconditionality to moral claims. It should also be noted that he offers a postmetaphysical interpretation of this moment of unconditionality. Such an interpretation aims to avoid referring to "otherworldly" – metaphysical – ideas by understanding transcendence in purely immanent terms: as a movement beyond existing human practices that can be made sense of entirely in terms of human practices (*FHN*, 10–11). Habermas's postmetaphysical interpretation of the unconditional moment attaching to moral validity claims is in terms of an inclusive "we-perspective" that is brought about by participants in moral argumentation who seek to establish the universality of a norm: the norm counts as morally valid in an unconditional sense if everyone, everywhere, would agree for the same reasons that it is equally in everyone's interests. Moral validity thus depends both on the satisfaction, under ideal conditions, of certain demanding procedural conditions of argumentation (in particular, inclusivity and fairness) and on the achievement of a rational consensus among all concerned that the norm satisfies the principle of universalizability.

In short, a moral consensus generated under ideal communicative conditions defines moral validity. However, as commentators such as Albrecht Wellmer have pointed out, the projected ideal communicative situation is one of complete inclusion, perfect fairness, total transparency of meaning, and complete information, in which participants in deliberation would be concerned only with the common pursuit of the right answer and would be equipped with the requisite powers of understanding and imagination.[33] Note that in the ideal speech situation, moral validity is construed as a matter of *constructing* the single right answer to a moral problem, as opposed to finding it. Participants in deliberation are given the powers of understanding and imagination required not for recognizing the single right answer but for *producing* it. This is why perfection of the procedure of intersubjective deliberation, combined with application of the principle of universalizability, is held to result in perfect moral knowledge. In this thought experiment, therefore, human beings are granted the power to generate moral validity in an unconditional sense. I see this thesis of the coincidence of human knowledge and (moral) truth as worryingly hubristic. I also think it runs counter to some of our deepest intuitions, for it eliminates the moment of receptivity to the unanticipated and to the new that we associate with the best human achievements. Furthermore, I regard it as finalist, in the sense that it postulates a possible endpoint to the process of historical learning and creative human thinking, thereby denying the finitude of human knowledge, the contingency of human life and history, and the creativity and freedom of human will.[34] For, while Habermas's discourse ethics certainly allows for the thematization and critical assessment of new experiences, new needs, new interests, new ideas, and so on, it rules out reflection on the *moral* validity of the procedural framework within which such matters are thematized and critically examined. In other words, it rules out moral objections to the definition of justice as the outcome of an idealized deliberative procedure in which participants agree that the norm or principle in question is equally in everyone's interests. This opens it to the accusations that it immunizes a historically and culturally specific conception of justice against attempts to rethink it in light of new experiences, events, and ideas, and implies that no further learning as regards the very idea of justice is necessary.[35]

Let us turn now to democratic legitimacy.[36] Habermas formulates the principle of democracy, which embraces the idea of democratic legitimacy, as follows: "[O]nly those statutes may claim legitimacy that can meet with the assent of all citizens in a discursive process of legislation that in turn has been legally constituted" (*BFN*, 110).

There is evidence to suggest that his conception of democratic legitimacy is truth-analogous in just the same way as his conception of moral validity, and hence open to similar objections that it is hubristic, finalist, counter-intuitive, and neglectful of the non-argumentative dimension of rational acceptability.

There is no doubt that Habermas sees democratic politics as oriented toward truth. By "truth," he means a context-transcending conception of validity, in this case legal/political validity. This is evident in his criticism of Rawls for suspending the truth question and adoption, instead, of the category of the "reasonable" (*IO*, 49–73). Further evidence is his interpretation of the principle of majority rule in terms of a search for truth among citizens.[37] It is apparent, too, in his observation that a post-truth democracy would no longer be a democracy (*BNR*, 143–4). The crucial question is whether he holds an argumentation-internal, epistemic-constructivist, account of truth in this sense of legal/political validity. My contention is that he does. For one thing, an epistemic-constructivist account is in tune with his concern to maintain a conception of validity that is at once context-transcending and immanent to social practices of using language communicatively, making no reference to "other-worldly" authorities of any kind; Habermas calls this "innerworldly transcendence" (*BFN*, 5) or "transcendence from within" (17). As already indicated, epistemic-constructivist accounts of validity avoid any such reference. For another, as we shall now see, the analogy he draws between moral autonomy and legal/political autonomy and, by extension, between moral validity and legal/political validity, strongly suggests an epistemic-constructivist account.

Following Rousseau and Kant, Habermas ties moral autonomy to moral insight: the moral autonomy of the individual resides in binding herself freely to the insights of practical reason.[38] He goes beyond Rousseau and Kant in making insight something that is *discursively* achieved. Importantly, as we have seen, in addition to giving it a dialogical character, he construes moral insight as discursively *constructed*: as generated by way of an idealized procedure of moral deliberation.

Habermas defines legal/political autonomy in the same terms as moral autonomy. The legal/political autonomy of citizens resides in binding themselves freely to formal principles regarding the exercise of power, understood as the insights of practical reason (*BNR*, 77–97). These insights are to be achieved by way of discursive processes of will-formation in which citizens agree on which principles are rationally acceptable. Recall the idea of autonomy that he sees as the "dogmatic" core of the understanding of law he develops in *Between Facts and Norms*: [political] autonomy is held to consist in obedience to just those laws we [citizens] give ourselves in accordance with insights we have gained intersubjectively.

It seems clear, therefore, that in Habermas's conception, legal/political autonomy, like moral autonomy, has an epistemic component: it is internally linked with insight, understood as knowledge that claims validity (truth) in a context-transcending sense. Moreover, as in the case of moral autonomy, insight is construed both discursively, as something to be achieved dialogically, and as constructed, as something generated by way of (an idealized) discursive procedure. This epistemic conception of legal/political autonomy complements Habermas's epistemic conception of democracy: just as he construes legal/political insight as discursively generated insight, he gives a dialogical and constructivist interpretation to the idea of truth orienting democratic politics.

The epistemic dimension fulfills two important functions in his legal/political theory. To begin with, it serves to guarantee the freedom-constituting character of the democratic constitutional state, which makes the democratic bond more than just a modus vivendi (*BNR*, 134–5).

In addition, it secures the context-transcending, critical moment of the democratic deliberative process that is an essential element of his theory. He distances himself from radically contextualist approaches to validity, which reject the universalist orientation of claims to truth and moral rightness and restrict their putative validity to the inhabitants of a historically specific, local context.[39] Against such approaches, he asserts a concept of situated reason that raises its voice in validity claims that are at once context-dependent and context-transcendent (*PMT*, 139). Furthermore, he gives the concept of context-transcendence a strong, universalist interpretation that involves a moment of unconditionality (*TJ*, "Truth versus Normative Rightness").[40] In his account of moral validity, as we have seen, this moment of unconditionality is secured by way of the idea of a discursively achieved consensus that is deemed to be "the single right answer" to the problem at hand and accepted as such by everyone for the same reasons. We have also seen that unconditional validity is held to be discursively generated (under idealized conditions); in my terms, it is given a purely argumentation-internal, epistemic-constructivist, interpretation. How should we understand the context-transcending force he attributes to legal/political validity claims? On the reading of his position I have proposed above, moral autonomy and legal/political autonomy, and by extension moral validity and legal/political validity, are analogous in depending on "insights of practical reason," whereby such insights are to be understood as discursively generated. If this interpretation is correct, it makes sense to understand the context-transcending force of legal/political validity claims, too, in a strong universalist, argumentation-internal, sense.

While Habermas cannot lightly dispense with the epistemic dimension of his legal/political theory, he does not have to construe it in argumentation-internal terms. Recall my objections to his argumentation-internal interpretation of moral validity: that it is hubristic, counter-intuitive, finalist, and neglectful of the non-argumentative dimension of rational acceptability. In the case of legal/political validity, we can add hostility to the inclusion of religious contributions to (formal) democratic deliberations. For, as we have seen, constructivism interprets the epistemic quality of the outcomes of deliberation in purely argumentative terms, leaving no room for interpretations that account for it in terms of a source external to argumentation. Insofar as religious believers favor argumentation-external interpretations of epistemic quality, therefore, his constructivist conception of political legitimacy is hostile to religious arguments. For these and other reasons, it is worth exploring alternative interpretations.

I suggest that an alternative interpretation can be extracted from Habermas's own writings on law and politics. Whereas the epistemic-constructivist conception of democratic legitimacy fits best with the analogy he draws between moral and legal/political autonomy concerning their shared dependency on "insights of practical reason," and is consonant with his emphasis on "transcendence from within," the alternative conception builds on his remarks on the differences between moral validity and democratic validity, and corresponding distinction between moral discourses and democratic discourses.

From *Between Facts and Norms* onwards, Habermas has emphasized the differences between moral validity and legal/political validity (104–18, 157–68; see also *BNR*, 77–97). Whereas in his writings up to the end of the 1980s he made no clear distinction between these categories of validity, in this book he introduces a discourse principle, which explains in a general way the point of view from which action norms can be justified impartially (*BFN*, 107). This general principle is held to provide the basis for a differentiated account of types of practical argumentation, in which discourses are distinguished from bargaining procedures and in which various subtypes of discourses are specified. The relevant specification for our present purposes is that in the case of moral norms, the discourse principle takes the form of the principle of universalizability outlined earlier in our discussion, whereas in the case of legal/political norms it takes the form of the democratic principle (as cited earlier in the present section). The principal differences between the two kinds of norms are that they have different reference groups and regulate different matters (*BFN*, 451–2). The moral universe is unlimited in space and historical time, encompassing all natural persons in their life-historical complexity; a legal/political community, by contrast, protects the integrity of its members only insofar as they acquire the status of bearers of individual rights. Moral norms regulate interpersonal conflicts from the point of view of impartiality and are strictly bound by the principle of universalizability; legal/political decisions and norms, by contrast, draw on moral, pragmatic, and ethical considerations in order to give binding force to collective goals and programs.

For our present purposes, the latter aspect of legal/political decisions and norms is especially important. By contrast with moral discourses, in which the sole relevant consideration is universalizability of interests, Habermas characterizes democratic processes of will formation as an interplay of diverse dimensions of validity: moral claims are not the only – or even the primary – kind of validity claim raised by participants in formal processes of democratic deliberation: pragmatic and ethical validity claims also come into play (*BNR*, 93–4; cf. *BFN* 166–8).[41] Thus, he rejects what he calls moralistic misunderstandings of the democratic principle of legitimacy on account of their subordination of law to morality (See *BFN*, 229–32; *BNR*, 77–97).[42] Against such moralistic misunderstandings, Habermas insists that: "The democratic lawmaking procedure must exploit the rational potential of deliberations across the full spectrum of possible aspects of validity, and by no means merely under the moral aspect of the universalizability of interests" (*BNR*, 93). To be sure, in this passage Habermas is referring to democratic *law*-making – to specifically legal validity – as opposed to the validity of democratic processes of will formation in general. However, he consistently emphasizes the plural dimensions of validity that come into play in general processes of democratic will formation, as well as in strictly legal deliberations.

This difference between moral and democratic discourses is reflected in a difference between the criteria appropriate for determining epistemic quality in each case. In the case of moral validity, the appropriate criteria are both procedural and substantive: we must assess whether the procedure of argumentation meets conditions such as inclusivity, fairness, sincerity, and rejection of all force except that of the better argument, and *also* whether the outcome satisfies the principle of universalizability of interests. In the case of democratic legitimacy, by contrast, the procedural requirement remains the same, but the universalizability requirement is replaced by a requirement of general acceptability – the requirement that all citizens must be able to assent to the outcome. As indicated, the latter requirement – the requirement that the outcome be acceptable to all citizens – involves taking into account ethical and pragmatic as well as moral considerations. This considerably complicates satisfaction of the requirement of general acceptability for, in democracies in which citizens have different and often conflicting ethical convictions and commitments, it is unlikely that they will ever reach agreement as to the general acceptability of substantive democratic decisions.[43]

Thomas McCarthy formulates the difficulty as follows:

political discussions about matters of justice will typically encounter disagreements stemming from divergent conceptions of the good. Hence, even when there is widespread agreement at the level of basic principles and procedures, there may well be persistent disagreements at all more substantive levels of discussion. And the generally accepted political processes designed to deal with such disagreements – for example, majority rule – may well produce outcomes that violate some members' deeply held ethical beliefs about the meaning and value of life. Those members may be said to cooperate "willingly" with those outcomes only in the indirect sense that they had a fair chance to convince a majority of what they believed was right, but failed, and will now abide by the rules. They have not simply succumbed to the force of the better argument; nor need they anticipate that what they consider to be the better argument will some day convince all.[44]

McCarthy's point clearly applies to actual discourses in legal/political reality. In democracies in which citizens have different and often conflicting ethical convictions and commitments, it is quite unlikely that they will ever reach agreement as to the general acceptability of substantive legal/political decisions. Think of controversies about proposals to ban private motor vehicles from the city center, to increase public spending on medical care, or to allow shops to open on Sundays. But the point is not just that agreement is unlikely in practice. My discussion of the non-argumentative dimension of rational acceptability helps us to see that it applies even to *idealized* democratic deliberations.

I have proposed an account of practical validity in which argumentation-external factors may be involved in bringing about the changes in perception required for the rational affirmation of validity claims. For our present purposes, it suffices for this to hold for just *one* of the three kinds of validity claims that are in play in democratic discourses. Ethical validity claims are the most obvious candidate here.[45] Recall my example of the arguments for vegetarianism; this was intended to show that the rational acceptability of ethical validity claims may require a shift in perception that comes about for reasons independent of an argumentative situation. If this is so, the reasoning powers of participants in even a perfect procedure of democratic argumentation would not suffice for finding the single right answer. In other words, if the rational acceptability of ethical validity claims may depend on shifts in perception that are not attributable primarily to the exchange of arguments, there can be no guarantee that citizens would agree on the rational acceptability of substantive democratic decisions *even under conditions of the ideal speech situation.*

In sum, as soon as we allow for subjective experiences in non-argumentative contexts as possible co-determinants of rational acceptability, the conditions for generating unconditionally valid knowledge ("truth") no longer obtain. No matter how perfect the argumentative conditions, in any given instance the rational acceptability of a particular argument might depend on argumentation-external factors missing in that instance. This would mean in turn that even perfect argumentative conditions could not guarantee a consensus and, hence, that an argumentatively achieved consensus could not *produce* truth. As we have seen, Habermas's account of moral validity makes moral insight depend essentially on the exchange of reasons in argumentation. Even if we grant him this account, his account of *ethical* validity claims clearly leaves room for argumentation-external factors as co-determinants of their rational acceptability. Admittedly, Habermas's account of ethical validity is far from straightforward. In some of his writings, he attributes to it a cognitive moment, moreover one that is tied to the idea of discursively achieved consensus (*JA*, "On the Pragmatic, the Ethical, and the Moral Employments of Practical Reason"; *PMT*, "'Individuation through Socialization.' On George Herbert Mead's Theory of Subjectivity").[46] At other times, he seems to offer a more subjectivist account of ethical validity.[47] In any case, it is clear that he sees ethical arguments as context-specific, experientially based claims relating to the good life and the good society. By admitting such claims into the democratic process, therefore, he allows for the possibility that even a perfect argumentative procedure would not generate agreement, in the sense of a "single right answer" reached by participants for the same reasons. If he does so, accordingly, he cannot consistently maintain an epistemic-constructivist conception of democratic legitimacy.

This means that if ethical considerations are at play in democratic discourses, and if argumentation-external factors are taken seriously, Habermas's theory itself calls for an alternative conception of democratic legitimacy to the epistemic-constructivist one he apparently favors. The latter's three core ingredients of construction, consensus, and (strong) cognitivism would have to be abandoned or modified. Since rational agreement cannot be brought about purely by way of the exchange of arguments, the deliberative procedure could no longer be thought of as a procedure of epistemic construction: as designed to *produce* an outcome that is generally acceptable. For the same reason, no *consensus* as to an outcome's general acceptability could be envisaged, under even ideal justificatory conditions. Importantly, however, this does not deny the idea of consensus a cognitive status.[48] The proposed alternative conception retains the cognitive-consensual component of Habermas's epistemic-constructivist conception, but interprets it differently in two key respects. First, whereas the epistemic-constructivist conception sees human beings as the makers of unconditional validity in the domain of practical reason, the alternative conception sees them as capable of *recognizing* truth in the practical sense. The relationship between consensus and (practical) truth is inverted: whereas in the epistemic-constructivist conception, a discursively achieved, rational consensus *produces* (practical) truth, in the alternative conception, truth *commands* a rational consensus. The intuition here is that if something is true, every rational person who had undergone the requisite shifts in perception would have to agree to it.[49] The second important difference is that the requisite shifts in perception do not have to come about purely argumentatively. Whereas the epistemic-constructivist conception defines practical truth as the *result* of the exchange of reasons in an idealized procedure of deliberation, in the alternative conception, the ideal conditions necessary to recognize truth are not exclusively deliberative, but involve a complex mix of argumentation-external and argumentation-internal factors, which are contextual and subject-related and hence cannot be specified in advance.

This raises the question of the relationship between truth and justification; or, to put it slightly differently, of how the exchange of arguments in public deliberation contributes epistemically toward (practical) truth. For if, in the alternative conception, argumentation did not contribute epistemically to truth, it would be open to the objection that it uncouples democratic legitimacy from public deliberation (given that legitimacy, for Habermas, has an epistemic connotation). While there are, of course, many other – non-deliberative – ways of thinking about democracy, there are good reasons why some kind of deliberative-democratic model should retain its central place in Habermas's theory.[50] It is important to show, therefore, that the alternative conception is not open to this objection.

I think it is possible to do so. My argument rests on a number of normative assumptions that I see as constituting the evaluative horizon of Western modernity, in the sense that they profoundly shape its institutions, identities, and practices. They can be traced back to processes such as the de-sacralization of knowledge, secularization of authority, and democratization of political power. In the wake of such processes, the inhabitants of Western modernity have come to hold that the strengths and weaknesses of claims to validity cannot be determined independently of individual and collective human reasoning. This is why I observed earlier that although shifts in perception are (on occasion) *preconditions* for the rational affirmation of validity claims, they are not in themselves *justifications* of such claims.

One central assumption underpinning my argument for connecting democratic legitimacy with public deliberation is that human knowledge is temporal, subjective, and partial. Our perceptions of the ways things are, or of how they should be, are unavoidably influenced by the historically specific, socio-cultural context in which we live our lives as finite, embodied human beings. All access to reality, or to validity in a context-transcending sense, is mediated by history, context, and embodied subjectivity. There are no absolute, ahistorical, and disengaged standards for determining validity in a context-transcending sense. Disputing this amounts to what I earlier referred to as epistemological authoritarianism, and leads easily to the ethical authoritarianism. As mentioned, this assumption is part of a cluster of normative ideas that constitute the evaluative horizon of Western modernity. Other central assumptions include the views that the individual human agent is free to form and pursue her own conceptions of the good and that human beings are essentially equal by virtue of some capacity such as reason or freedom, and are entitled to respect on grounds of that capacity. Taken together, these assumptions provide a strong basis for the further normative idea that assessing claims to validity should take place in open-ended, inclusive, and fair practices of evaluating reasons in public spaces.[51] Thus, not only do experiences of disclosure and transformation call for rational justification; such justification should involve the exchange of reasons in public processes of deliberation.

If, for the inhabitants of modernity, the justification of validity claims is tied to intersubjective deliberation, then such deliberation evidently fulfills an epistemic function. However, this general point tells us neither which specific features of argumentation improve the epistemic quality of the outcomes nor how exactly they do so. Any attempt to give a normative account of the relationship between public deliberation and legal/political validity in an epistemic sense must address these questions on a micro-contextual level. The kind of micro-analysis called for here would have to use case studies of actual practices of democratic deliberation to show that greater inclusiveness, for example, improves the epistemic quality of the outcomes of public deliberation and to explain precisely how it does so.[52] I can only flag the need for such an analysis here.[53]

Showing why public deliberation contributes epistemically toward legal/political validity is just one side of the challenge facing the alternative conception of legitimacy I advocate. The other side is to show how legal/political validity, as a context-transcending idea of validity ("truth"), manifests itself in political deliberation. I have argued for a conception in which legal/political validity is not constructed in legal/political deliberation, but is rather a justification-transcendent idea *orienting* such deliberation. As such, it may be described as a regulative ideal.[54] But regulative ideals serve not just to guide human practices, they also serve to *motivate* them. In order to have motivating power, they must project the idea of a condition that is desirable (one of Wellmer's objections to the ideal speech situation, we will recall, was its lack of desirability). But what is projected as desirable must also be tangible,

however ephemerally. If the exchange of arguments in public deliberation did not open up spaces in which truth was present at least fleetingly
for those engaged in such an exchange, it would be hard to see why they
would continue to pursue it by way of argumentation. In other words,
the search for truth presupposes subjective experiences of truth. To be
sure, it is important to bear in mind that subjective experiences are not
epistemically reliable. Again, here, I can only flag the need for further
consideration of this question.

I have argued that Habermas's account of legal/political discourses,
when taken together with my discussion in the foregoing, pushes
us toward a conception of political legitimacy that relinquishes the
epistemic-constructivist component Habermas attributes to it. According
to the alternative conception I advocate, the epistemic component of
democratic legitimacy is not constructed in democratic deliberation, but
is rather a justification-transcendent, regulative ideal that orients public
deliberation on legal/political matters and manifests itself in such deliberation. Construed in this way, legal/political validity is granted a logical
independence of the argumentative procedure; in the terms used earlier
in our discussion, it is construed as an argumentation-external source of
epistemic quality. Thus, the alternative conception of legal/political validity is not only more consistent with Habermas's account of democratic
deliberation as an interplay of ethical, moral, and pragmatic factors, but
has a number of additional advantages: it avoids the objections of hubris,
counter-intuitiveness, and finalism that I raised against his constructivist
conception; it acknowledges the importance of the non-argumentative,
experiential dimension of practical reasoning; it is congruent with the
argumentation-external idea of truth to which many religious believers
appeal; and it places no barriers in principle to the inclusion of religious
arguments in processes of democratic legislation and decision-making.[55]

Part IV

Translating Religion, Communicative
Freedom, and Solidarity

12

Sources of Morality in Habermas's Recent Work on Religion and Freedom

Matthias Fritsch

Introduction

This chapter argues that the secularization of the divine standpoint in a moral context yielded two different aspects, one universal-egalitarian and another personal-individuating, and traces their appearance in Habermas's recent work on religion and freedom. The first aspect seeks to translate a transcendent god into the impartial viewpoint of reason from which ego and alter are equally called to responsibility. The second role God played, that of generating a moral subject aware of its irreplaceable responsibility by way of loving concern for each soul in its very uniqueness, surfaces more strongly in Habermas's more recent, explicitly "Kierkegaardian" concern with protecting singular authorship from liberal eugenics and reductionist naturalism. I seek to show that the very impersonality of reason cannot take over this second role of the transcendent god, and so confront Habermas with Levinas's opposite translation. In the latter, God's singularizing and concernful gaze is replaced by the mortal vulnerability of the other, which commands to responsibility in asymmetry and beyond reason. Seeking to secularize the divine standpoint, I conclude, requires doing justice to both equality and asymmetry in the intersubjective relation, a double demand that renders secularization constitutively incomplete.

I

In the European tradition, at least, the emergence of the ideas of free will and accountability has often been seen as requiring passage through the peculiarities of the monotheistic heritage. The reason for the distinctive (for some, even indispensable) monotheistic contribution to the notion of accountability seems to be twofold, relating both to its universal-egalitarian and its personal-individuating aspect. On the one hand, and opposed to mythical worldviews, the notion of a creator God represents a privileged point of view from beyond human society and nature alike. As such, he can address all human beings at the same time and in the same way, calling them to responsibility before his commands. In his recent emphasis on the similar dependence of modern science and European religions on the "cognitive shift" of the "Axial Age," Habermas has, perhaps unsurprisingly, emphasized this universal aspect above all (*EFK*, 2.3 *et passim*). Assuming a transcendent standpoint, prepared in history by monotheistic faith, renders possible both objective science and moral universalism, to the point that "postmodern" contextualism must be seen as a "neopaganism" (*RR*, 149, 159; *BNR*, 246).[1] Already in an interview with Eduardo Mendieta published in 2002, Habermas had put it this way:

> Unlike the range of early mythic narratives, the idea of God – that is, the idea of the unified, invisible God the Creator and the Redeemer – signified a breakthrough to an entirely new perspective. With this idea, finite spirit acquired a standpoint that utterly transcends the this-worldly. But only with the transition to modernity does the knowing and morally judging subject appropriate the divine standpoint, insofar as it assumes two highly significant forms of idealization. On the one side, the subject objectifies external nature as the totality of states of affairs and events that are connected in a law-like manner. On the other, the subject expands the familiar social world into an unbounded community of all responsibly acting persons ... For the normative self-understanding of modernity, Christianity has functioned as more than just a precursor or a catalyst. Universalist egalitarianism, from which sprang the ideals of freedom and a collective life in solidarity, the autonomous conduct of life and emancipation, the individual morality of conscience, human rights and democracy, is the direct legacy of the Judaic ethic of justice and the Christian ethic of love. (*RR*, 148f.; cf. *KV*, 387–407)

The universalist "ethic of justice," then, requires the abstraction from particular social relations in which human beings inevitably find themselves thrown. For while the modern subject assumes the divine standpoint, the latter remains a third standpoint beyond all subjects, pointing at the same time to an impartial point of view yet to be reached. On the other hand, the "ethic of love" of which Habermas speaks may be taken to refer to a different aspect of responsibility: I have in mind the assumption that the god so construed not only addresses all equally from a transcendent point, but calls each one to singular responsibility. This call is addressed to each personally in such a loving way that, paradigmatically in St Augustine, God's benevolence first of all enables the care of the self for its freedom from sin in its constant struggle with temptation and its concern for its own salvation. It is this side of responsibility that has dominated the phenomenological reflections on moral agency, from Augustine to Kierkegaard, Heidegger, Patočka, Levinas, and Ricoeur.[2] For instance, Patočka writes:

> The transcendent God of antiquity combined with the Old Testament Lord of History becomes the chief personage in the inner drama which God makes into the drama of salvation and grace. The overcoming of everydayness assumes the form of the care for the salvation of the soul which won itself in a moral transformation, in the turn in the face of death . . . Implied, though never explicitly thematized and never grasped philosophically as a central question, is the idea that the soul is by nature wholly incommensurate with all eternal being . . . and that an essential part of its composition is responsibility, that is, the possibility of choice and, in this choosing, or arriving at its own self.[3]

"European" responsibility, for Patočka, thus emerges only once the merely transcendent god of the Greeks merges with the biblical "Lord" whose personal relation to the self institutes an inner drama and moral transformation that renders the self essentially responsible in choosing its own life, the groundless ground removed from the world of being and its causal connections.[4]

It seems to me that it has been difficult to translate the origin of morality into a secular context precisely because the concept of God combines the two aspects in such a felicitous but next to impenetrable way: God's gaze addresses all equally, but at the same time each one with infinite care for the individual soul. In hindsight of a still ongoing process, it may not be so surprising that the various translations tended to emphasize one aspect at the expense of the other. While the perhaps dominant Western philosophical tradition (especially the Kantian) tends to bring out the universalistic aspect of the transcendent standpoint, it has been the distinctive trait of the phenomenological tradition to emphasize the irreducibility of the first-person standpoint. Accordingly, the latter plays up the individuation and self-care that the call to responsibility must also accomplish, at times to the unfortunate neglect of the egalitarian aspect. Despite this tendency, it seems to me that in an age of the increasing instrumentalization of action and the resulting collective action problems, when individual responsibility seems to drown in the avalanche of larger forces, reflection on morality today should attend to what leads agents to the sense of irreplaceable and uncircumventable authorship. I think that what makes the recent work of both Habermas and Derrida so fascinating is the attempt to do justice to both aspects, Habermas from within the universalist-egalitarian and Derrida from within the phenomenological tradition. I want to focus on Habermas's attempt at reintegration here, though I think his questions and solutions may at times profit from a confrontation with the phenomenological appropriation of the idea of God. To this end, I will bring in Levinas at a crucial juncture of Habermas's account of personal moral responsibility, and return to Derrida briefly at the end.

II

As always, it might be good to begin with agreement: both the phenomenologists in question and Habermas argue that the origin of responsibility, similar to the idea of God, precedes the self. The phenomenological account of agency, from Heidegger to Levinas and Derrida, agrees with Habermas that we should think the self not as first free, to then ask whether and to what extent moral obligations may or may not be binding upon it. Rather, if autonomy originally comes with obligations, the conditions of freedom are at the same time those of responsible subjectivity. In his earlier work (from the 1970s and 1980s), centered as it is on developing a universal and egalitarian morality starting from the presuppositions of language use, Habermas stressed the rationality of these conditions as those of communicative action in general.

For Habermas, only socialization by way of communicative action, that is, use of language oriented to reaching understanding, generates typically human agency with its communicative competences. These latter alone allow both language use and, as a result, rational reflection. In this way, communicative action makes selfhood possible. However, as a social practice governed by norms, this type of action comes with ineluctable "higher order" or transcendental-pragmatic norms, such as honestly aiming at the truth, truth-telling sincerity, and normative rightness. Thus, the self has to already have submitted to these norms before it can even become a self. If communicative action is prior to strategic action, these higher-order norms reflect a basic and irrevocable action orientation to give priority to normative over strategic reasons for action. The upshot is that, to reflect upon one's socialization into prioritizing the basic moral action orientation, one must already engage this action orientation; this is the sense in which it is *nicht hintergehbar* or *unverfügbar* (cannot be gotten around to dispose over it) (*TCA*; cf. *PDM*, chs XI and XII; *MCCA*, ch. 3). In this sense, then, the "divine standpoint" is translated into communicative reason, whose impartiality is extrapolated toward the idealized version of an infinite community of arguers. The standpoint can ground equality among agents by remaining transcendent to them all, thereby preserving a sense of preceding and obligating alterity.

What Habermas and, for instance, Levinas thus share is the claim that normativity precedes the free self so as to call it into being: no autonomy without responsibility.[5] Furthermore, the ineluctable normativity in question, the call to become responsible, is in part a call for justification, asking the self to justify itself before the other or others. In this sense, selfhood consists first of all in a response to a prior demand for justifications for one's egoism, one's actions, and one's assertions. In contrast to Levinas, however, for Habermas the other person asking for reasons is equally and reciprocally under the demand for justification. Given the emphasis on a third element beyond the intersubjective relation, namely the medium of communicative language in which ego and alter meet, both come equally under the normative demands of communicative action, including the demand to justify their assertions lest they become meaningless.[6] In other words, the source of the call to justify oneself here is thought to lie in communication, language, or reason itself. For this reason, the call is equally binding upon each, in such a way that, if ego is bound to justify her assertions to alter, alter is equally obliged to respond with a "yes" or "no," and to justify this response (*OPC*).

Habermas's original normativity, as discussed up to this point, addresses those conditions of responsible agency under which rational exchange is possible. However, in response to recent projects aiming at the wholesale "naturalization of the mind" and the biogenetic intervention in the human genome, he has become concerned with, not irrational, but a-rational or "natural" conditions of freedom, which he now distinguishes from the rational ones of communicative action (*BNR*, 160). These natural conditions lead Habermas to pose the question of responsibility anew, and in such a way that both the individuating power and the alterity of the preceding and obligating standpoint gain momentum, to the point where the standpoint's historically "divine" origin – and that means the question of "translating" God – resurfaces.

III

Shortly after the terrorist attacks of September 2001, Habermas reflected on the tensions between "Faith and Knowledge" in the West, noting, on the one side, the fear of "a crude naturalism of a scientistic belief in progress supposedly undermining morality" and, on the other, the fear of a religious obscurantism (*FHN*, 101). The recent virulence of this tension between science and religion indicates the incompletion of secularization. Only if the West, he suggests, comes to terms with its own, and to date unfinished, history of secularization, may it have a chance to understand the risks of a misfired secularization elsewhere, a misfiring among whose consequences we must count fundamentalist terror. As a focal point for the conflict between secular society and religion, Habermas then chooses not only the issue of religious fundamentalism as a response to overhasty secularization and immoral capitalization around the world, but the questions posed by the new possibilities of genetic engineering, in part the result of a "crude" naturalism Habermas wishes to overcome. As his argument has it, a wholesale "naturalization of the mind" not only cannot explain normative practices of justification, including those of science itself, but in its eugenic manifestation would undermine "the core of our self-understanding," to wit, "the awareness of authorship and responsibility" (*FHN*, 106).

In brief, Habermas's argument concerning the dangers of liberal practices of eugenic enhancement is this. A self that has to think of itself as having been purposefully designed by other human beings (i.e., by nominal equals) cannot understand itself to be free, and hence accountable. To avoid a situation in which a child cannot transform her parents' designs for her into her own, autonomy must be understood to emerge from a source inaccessible to autonomous manipulation.[7] Here, Western societies have "not yet" been able to accomplish what Kant did accomplish in the case of unconditionally valid duties, which he, according to Habermas, successfully translated from the authority of divine commands. Hence, the task is to once more critically assimilate the monotheistic concept of a creator God, a God who effectively symbolizes the inaccessible origin of free humanity.[8] Recalling the traditional problems of theodicy, the task is subtle, as the origin must be entirely other and unmasterable, but at the same time not predetermine, not master action to the point of denying autonomy again. In Habermas's words, "God remains a 'God of free human beings' only as long as we do not level out the absolute difference between the creator and the creature": the concern for freedom motivates the denial of equality between the free agent and her origin (*FHN*, 114). What results is a double bind: God "enables" [*befähigt*] but at the same time "obliges" [*verpflichtet*] us to be free (115).

To see more clearly how this double bind imposes itself on Habermas's otherwise fundamentally egalitarian moral theory, one must first appreciate Habermas's recent insight that his earlier "Kantian theory of justice" must be "complemented" by way of a "Kierkegaardian ethics of subjectivity" or of "being oneself [*Ethik des Selbstseins*]" (*FHN*, 7). For Kantian morality and politics, given its concern with post-traditional and post-conventional norms, cannot prescribe how we are to live our lives, and so loses the motivating force that it must now expect to come from the domain of ethics, understood as addressing not questions of justice (these being the province of universal morality), but who we want to be and how we want to live our lives, individually and collectively. Modern, secular philosophy thus has a double relation to "ethics" understood in this way: it must refrain from legislating it, yet needs to theorize how morally motivated, responsible agents may emerge out of the ethical webs of the lifeworld. As for Kierkegaard, central to ethics thus understood is the way in which individuals leave behind the "aesthetic," fragmented and irresponsible mode of existence in favor of the being-oneself that renders one capable of "assuming responsibility for his or her own actions and entering into binding commitments to others" (*FHN*, 6, translation modified). In Kierkegaard, however, such responsibilization can only occur in the face of an (interpersonal) alterity to whom the famous "leap of faith" submits. Freedom depends on conditions of possibility that are withdrawn from its control and must remain "unavailable" (*unverfügbar*) to manipulation as the "wholly other" (10).

At this point, an agnostic stance on the vexed issue of an interpersonal but still radically other source of morality may seem to recommend itself. In this sense, Paul Ricoeur – whose interest in non-reductively situating the self in both the physical and the intentional worlds shares crucial features with Habermas's recent efforts at a "soft naturalism" that preserves both the authority of science and autonomy by way of the inescapability of the objective and the subjective perspectives[9] – wrote in *Soi-même comme un autre*:

> Perhaps the philosopher as philosopher has to admit that one does not know and cannot say whether this Other, the source of the injunction, is another person whom I can look in the face or who can stare at me, or my ancestors for whom there is no representation, to so great extent does my debt to them constitute my very self, or God – the living God, the absent God – or an empty space.[10]

By contrast, Habermas's postmetaphysical stance, with all its recent attempts to accommodate religious sentiments, will not remain agnostic.

For he continues the appropriation of Kierkegaard's ethics of subjectivity:

> Under the premises of postmetaphysical thinking, however, the power beyond us – on which subjects capable of speech and action depend in our concern not to fail to lead worthwhile lives – cannot be identified with "God in time". The linguistic turn permits a deflationary interpretation of the "wholly Other" . . . The *logos* of language embodies the power of the intersubjective, which precedes and grounds the subjectivity of the speakers. (*FHN*, 10f.)

In agreement with his earlier work on communicative reason, Habermas thus argues that we can, and under postmetaphysical conditions must, translate Kierkegaard's "wholly other" – the monotheistic God who demands responsibility "unconditionally" – into the "logos of language" as a "transcending power" that, while no longer as "absolute" as God, nonetheless retains the "fallibilist as well as the anti-skeptical meaning of the 'unconditioned,'" i.e., the normativity whose origin we are seeking (*FHN*, 11; cf. *PMT*, 153). It is then the unconditionality of truth and morality, as demanded by communicative action and its transsubjective, transcendental presuppositions of argumentation, that constitute not only the bare bones on which public morality can be based, but also allow responsible freedom to emerge (*MCCA*). This reading of the responsibilizing otherness then allows for a philosophically defensible "ethics" (i.e., a discourse of identity rather than justice) after all, but this time not at an individual or a national-collective level: rather, an "ethics of the species" (*Gattungsethik*) is to identify human persons as free and equal, and thus may prohibit the biotechnological enhancement of humans (*FHN*, 11; *FHN*, 37ff.).

In some other recent texts, however, it seems to me that Habermas does not quite rest content with this solution to the new conditions of responsibility brought to light by the possibilities of bioengineering. For, in renewed reflections on freedom and responsibility, he realizes that the "logos" embodied in communicative practices may be too "impersonal" to accomplish what was central to Kierkegaard: the process of singularization that alone leads to the emergence of responsible agents. In reconsidering the "phenomenology of the consciousness of freedom" from the first-person perspective, he writes:

> this first aspect of the consciousness of freedom – namely, the rational character of the will as the foundation of accountability toward others – does not exhaust the meaning of freedom. As an impersonal faculty, reason could shape the wills of an arbitrary number of subjects in an anonymous way without allowing each individual room for *his own* action. But

someone who acts in an awareness of freedom understands himself as the author of his actions. On closer inspection, two different moments are linked in this sense of *authorship*, namely, that I take the *initiative* and that it is *I alone* who take the initiative. (*BNR*, 186, Habermas's emphases)

Hence, Habermas feels the need to account for a second, more radical singularization by way of care for oneself, which he in fact now situates temporally prior to the intersubjective concern for others:

Linked back to bodily existence, a far-sighted ethical will projects the individual self-understanding within whose horizon the moral concern for the equal interests of others is then first supposed to be integrated. The at first self-related ethical will that is open to moral considerations is the character-forming force that, together with the personal understanding of self, constitutes the self who can address itself as "I." (*BNR*, 188)

As in some of the phenomenological tradition, then, but here mediated by way of Habermas's re-reading of Adorno, the care of the self emerges as a necessary moment in the process of singularization. For a subject "constitutes himself as a responsibly acting subject on the basis of his lived bodily mode of existence and through the individuating power of the ethical concern [*Sorge*] with his own life history" (189).

It seem to me, however, that this account faces the objection, reminiscent of Levinas's famous criticisms of Heidegger, that it severs singularization from other-regarding moral concern, be it singular or universal.[11] If the other-regarding orientation emerges on this account only later (and then in a universal-egalitarian form), it is hard to see how the self-regarding care for one's own well-being is to be integrated with "the moral concern for the equal interests of others." It seems question-able that self-care without an interpersonal relation can, sufficiently and in the right way, singularize the agent in view of the moral demands of others. It seems as if normatively structured intersubjectivity is here not located deeply enough in the self, as if it could come about, perhaps not without others, but without their demands, as if the self established its agential capacities first and only then confronted the demands of others in a way that would allow it to bypass the later stage at which they are to be integrated with care for oneself. Habermas himself is concerned with avoiding an ontological account of the self as a kind of "narrow-minded self-empowerment" (*FHN*, 10), reminiscent of the criticisms, based on a concept of relational autonomy, directed at Foucault's claim that care of the self is "ethically prior" to care for others given that he holds it is "ontologically prior."[12]

There should be no doubt that Habermas wishes to avoid this kind of ontology. That is why we cannot supplement the account of responsibility to others with an unrelated notion of self-care. In reading Kierkegaard, Habermas himself alludes to the possibility, even necessity, of retaining the interpersonality of the relation between the preceding otherness that calls to responsibility and the self to be responsibilized:

> [E]ven Socratic thinkers who cannot invoke revealed truths can follow [Kierkegaard's] suggestive phenomenology of the "sickness unto death" and can agree that finite spirit depends on enabling conditions beyond its control. The ethically conscious conduct of life should not be understood as narrow-minded self-empowerment. They could also agree with Kierkegaard that we should not understand this dependence on a power beyond our control in naturalistic terms, but above all as an interpersonal relation. For the defiance of a rebellious person who finally in despair wills to be herself is directed, as defiance, against a second person. (*FHN*, 10)

In his postmetaphysical appropriation of Kierkegaard and the attending reading of the wholly other as intersubjective reason, then, Habermas asks us to remember that the *logos* that is to replace God is still "'our' language," and so intrinsically interpersonal (11). The normative demands of reason do not address the self without mediation, as if *logos* had its own *locus* separate from human speaking; rather, these demands are always articulated in intersubjective relations. On the other hand, this helpful reminder is here intended to play its role in a developmental account that is to explain how responsible adults emerge; it assumes that, once the formative process has been completed, the dependence on the second person need not subsist. In response, we should recall Habermas's warning that mature ethical self-care may always turn into a "narrow-minded self-empowerment" that we should be careful not to see as preceding from the ontological constitution of selfhood. It seems, then, that if the call to responsibility is addressed to the self by another person (without, of course, being exhausted in that address, as if the second person wholly owned it), and if that call precedes a narrow-minded or egotistic self-care, we may ask whether it is not the vulnerability of the other person that singularizes the self, in particular in continuing to address mature adults. For we should also recall what members of underprivileged groups know only too well, namely, that the dependence of individuation on communicative socialization in terms of intersubjective reason continues to render the self highly vulnerable to lack of recognition, to the point at which such lack undermines the agency even of adults. This suggests that agency indeed owes itself to interpersonal relations, and the normative demands that come with it, so that agency has always already been called to responsibility, even prior to and after reaching mature adulthood. Identification with my body and life-history in self-care, however necessary, need not result in moral responsibility to the other's needs.

If the other human being in her mortal vulnerability, both physical and symbolic, can play the role of singularizing gaze calling on the self to be herself, we would then have to see how we can preserve both the otherness of the origin of the call and the equality of the intersubjective human relation. I think we must follow Habermas in thinking the origin of the call as both transsubjective and interpersonal, as both a preceding alterity and emerging with the gaze of the vulnerable other. However, it remains an open question in his recent work how "impersonal" reason can integrate both of these aspects in claiming the postmetaphysical legacy of God. For it would seem that "translating" God into secular reason alone is insufficient, as the origin of responsibility, despite its otherness, must be sufficiently personal and singularizing to call the subject to responsibility without allowing for evasive tactics, that is, without blaming one's parents, genetic designers, or the like. There is thus reason to attempt the translation once more. In what follows, I wish to briefly present Levinas's work on this question, and not primarily because Habermas has referred to Levinas's work as an indication that postmetaphysical thinking not only may still learn from religion, but will continue to do so, thus placing philosophy between the sciences and religion.[13] Rather, the more topical point is that, of all the phenomenologists mentioned above, Levinas is the one who most consistently takes the opposite route: that of sacrificing intersubjective symmetry and universal equality in order to be able to retain the asymmetrical alterity and the interpersonal gaze in the origin of normativity. Thus, I will begin my account of Levinas with what Habermas's secularizing translation seems to account for only insufficiently but points to nonetheless, namely, singularization in relation to the other, and construe Levinas's account as an argument for asymmetry that Habermas would thus have to confront.

IV

Let us turn to Levinas, then.[14] The very "subjectivity" of the responsible subject, Levinas argues, consists first and foremost in the "traumatic" sense of being irreplaceable. What characterizes a responsible subject above all is the sense that its responsibility, whatever it may concretely consist in, cannot be evaded, excused, or delegated to another. Although it may of course be responsible to call on others for help in fulfilling one's duties, or even of charging others with their execution, responsibility rests inevitably in a singular subject. If we agree with Levinas that such a sense of irreplaceability does not come naturally, that it has to be produced, as it were, on top of merely organic, "economic" or egoistic life concerned with self-preservation or enjoyment of the world, then the call to responsibility resounding in this economic life generates subjectivity only by way of singling out the subject of responsibility. In Levinas's words, this first aspect of responsibility (P1) demands that I come to know that "no one can replace me,"[15] such that responsibility is not a merely accidental "property" of the ego but that "it is, on the contrary, as responsibility and in responsibility that the 'me' gains its uniqueness,"[16] the uniqueness we saw Habermas claim is indispensable for authorship.[17]

The next premises of Levinas's argument, as reconstructed here, go on to state that this sense of singular irreplaceability can be gained only by the call from another singular being who must, at the very least, be capable of expressing suffering (by way of her or his "face"). In the language of transcendental philosophy, the ethical relation to the other, the other's demand, is a condition of possibility for subjectivity.[18] As is well known, Levinas argues that the demand is best captured by the biblical commandment "Thou shalt not kill," which means a bit more for him than it literally says, in that not murdering the other is here taken to imply a more thoroughgoing (and not merely negative) responsibility for the mortality, and hence vulnerability, of the other. We may distinguish two crucial aspects here: the call to or demand for responsibility must be (P2) a command, and (P3) must issue from another singular, potentially suffering other (for Levinas, of course, another person, *l'autrui* rather than just *l'autre*, so that, controversially, animals can issue the command only derivatively). Let us look at the command first, then ask further why one might think that only another person, qua other, can issue it.

The second premise (P2) states that the call to singularizing responsibility cannot be a request that an autonomous agent could refuse. The call must be non-negotiable or unconditional. It must not allow itself to be reasoned with, for if the subject-to-be-responsibilized sought to negotiate with it or even just ask for its grounds, for its justifying reasons, the subject *in spe* could then also evade it, for example, by finding the reasons for it wanting or inapplicable to its situation. And by thus excepting itself, responsible subjectivity would not even be able to become established in the first place. In this sense, the call to responsibility must be a command that does not tolerate exceptions.[19] As a command, it must further emerge from a source that, as Kant knew well, is quite different from the self in the sense of not being accessible to, or manipulable by, the latter's demands and interests.[20]

The call to responsibility thus not only precedes the responsible self so as to call it into being as responsible, but does so while commanding without possibility of justification by reason or by the self. While the call is essentially a call to justify myself ethically before the other, a *"right over (my) egoism"* that demands justification,[21] this liability to justification, already emphasized by Steven Hendley as shared in Levinas's and Habermas's accounts,[22] is for Levinas not (as Hendley does not stress) reciprocal: the demand for justification does not extend to the call itself. This is no doubt one of the major conceptual (non-historical) reasons why Levinas, despite the obvious risks, insists on referring to the demanding and responsibilizing aspect of the face as "God": on a monotheistic conception, God sees me without being seen; he singles me out and charges me with moral burdens; his infinite power tolerates no disagreement; he calls to responsibility in general but remains irrevocably other to me, so that my asking for his reasons would be entirely out of place. Dissymmetry in the ethical relation means then that the call comes from a preceding alterity that despite its otherness looks without being seen; the gaze cannot be returned in some form of economic exchange. If the self to be responsibilized could return the gaze, could see the other, it could disclaim, disown, or dispute the claim, and reason or negotiate with it (in a manner that Kant calls "ratiocination," [*Vernünfteln*]) so as to dodge the call and evade being singled out by it.

To move to the third premise (P3), according to which the call comes from another singular other, we must remember that "God" is here, as in Habermas of course (*FHN*, 10), not thought of as an entity actually existing separate from the call. Rather, for Levinas, the call can be borne only by the embodied other vulnerable to being murdered, and for whose mortality responsibility is to be taken. Despite the otherness of the command's source, it cannot remain strictly anonymous or impersonal but must appear on the face of the other human. Even more radically, for Levinas, the call cannot appear in the first instance on the face of more than one other, but addresses me from and as alter's singularity. The other is unique and irreplaceable, and the call's authority in its link to vulnerability in part depends on this uniqueness: for the call to command, it must express the mortality of an irreplaceable being. As essentially unknowable, death is that which renders the other person both supremely vulnerable (namely, exposed to an uncontrollable future) and unique (namely, having its own finite but unfinished history of alterations). Further, and again viewed in relation to the genesis of the moral agent, a third party (*le tiers*) would allow evasion as ego could always refer to it as the one in the best place, or rightfully called upon, to help. Hence, the ethical relation is, for Levinas, first and foremost one that obtains between singularities, without for all that being egalitarian.

On the basis of (P1)–(P3), we may then conclude that the ethical relation is fundamentally asymmetrical. To sum up the argument, a responsible agent must know itself to be irreplaceable (P1), and the singularizing call bringing about this awareness and grounding ethics must be a command (P2) that can only come from another singular other (P3) preceding the self temporally, logically, and normatively. Thus, "morality comes to birth not in equality."[23] Asymmetry comprises at least three aspects: first, a temporal distance, a coming before the subject; and second, the fundamental otherness in the source of the moral call, that is, its not being grounded or justifiable, its being an order (P2). Third, for Levinas, asymmetry also involves, perhaps most controversially, the infinity of the moral obligation that he claims follows from the otherness of its call: if I cannot give back to the preceding singular other, precisely on account of her otherness, then I must instead give endlessly to the future beyond my death. Combining the elements of commandment and of infinity, Levinas writes that "The basic intuition of moral growing-up perhaps consists in perceiving that I am not *the equal* of the other. This applies in a very strict sense: I see myself *obligated* with respect to the Other; consequently I am infinitely more demanding of myself than of the others."[24] As he says elsewhere, "with the other, one is never paid up."[25]

The asymmetrical intuition thus expressed may be explained in this way: any grounding of ethics on a general law or on universally shared traits, on sameness, whether of sentiment ("they can suffer, too") or of reason ("they, too, are rational and hence autonomous"), abandons the factual starting point of moral responsibility in the first-person perspective from which I find myself obligated by the needs of a concrete other. As Levinas puts it:

> one habitually begins with the universality of the moral law: the great Kantian idea . . . My manner of approaching the question is, in effect, different. It takes off from the idea that ethics arises in the relation to the other and not straightaway by reference to the universality of a law. The "relation" to the other man as unique – and in this way, precisely, as absolutely other – would be, here, the first significance of the meaningful.[26]

For reasons of this abandonment, approaching ethics from a universal, third-person standpoint renders the account more vulnerable to evasion than one grounded on otherness, for the simple reason that sameness and equality are qualities that can easily be, and have often been, denied to others.[27] For instance, Levinas explains racism as resulting from a conceptual approach to the other in terms of genus and specific differences: the other's uniqueness may then be overlooked in favor of qualitative differences to which values are attributed.[28]

To this we must add the insight into what I have called the command-structure of ethics: if we could say that we should be obligated to the other because of x, then we can also deny or weaken x. The ground of ethics must be other than reason and escape the principle of sufficient reason. The naked fact of moral obligation must precede all ethics of reciprocity. Taking together unjustifiable otherness and its order or commandment gives us what Levinas calls the "height of the other" as the source of ethics.[29]

This view can more easily explain the singularization of the responsible agent by way of the singular other whose mortality and vulnerability (rather than my own dying, as Heidegger had it)[30] "looks" at the agent demandingly. Thus, one might conclude on the above reading that Levinas has precisely accomplished what Habermas thinks philosophers largely still have to do: to find secular analogues for the role the God of the monotheistic tradition plays in accounts of responsibility while preserving his preceding otherness, his authority to command, and his singularizing gaze.

However, what Levinas's translation arguably misses is what we saw Habermas stress above all: the transcendence of the "divine standpoint" which addresses all equally and thus grounds universal morality precisely from its transcendence. Let me briefly indicate the disadvantages connected with this neglect of the egalitarian dimension. First, as Derrida argued as early as 1964, Levinas fails to explain sufficiently why, if it is alterity that obligates, that alterity can only appear on the face of the *human* other.[31] It appears that what obligates the self is, for Levinas, not just the alterity of the other, but also generic features, such as common humanity; in fact, Levinas at times calls his ethics "anthropological,"[32] for it argues that "the human consists precisely in opening itself to the death of the other," that "around the death of my neighbour is manifested what I called the humanity of man."[33] An account of the ground of obligation would thus have to make room for the significant role that generic categories play in the basis of obligation that Levinas tries to rethink. To account for this role seems to require constructing and assuming a third-person perspective from out of intersubjective relations, as for instance discourse ethics does. For even if the call to responsibility must emerge with a unique face, it is never exhausted in this singularity. However, conceptualizing as alterity that which the face, in Levinas's terms, "expresses," that is, thinking it merely as an utterly inaccessible god, bars us from accounting for the role this transcendent moment plays in morality.

Second, by restricting the call to responsibility to the otherness of the other human being, Levinas renders asymmetrical not just the relation between that call to responsibility and its recipient, but also the "intersubjective" relation between ego and alter – for Levinas, precisely a "relation without relation" in which the other looks at ego from "on high."[34] Thus, staying in the first-person perspective, Levinas cannot explain the obligations of others toward the self. It is not so much that this interpersonal asymmetry downplays the co-originary presence of the third party (the fact that there are always already other others on the moral scene as well), for we may grant Levinas that he does not understand the priority of the face-to-face to the third party in a temporal, genetic sense[35] – though even Derrida's generous reading felt the need to insist on the co-presence of the third, and with arguments that seem to go beyond Levinas's own.[36] Rather, by not theorizing the construction of a third-person perspective from which not only the first and the second other, but the self as well, can be seen as both an agent and the object of moral concern, Levinas cannot explain that alter is *also* originally obligated by the preceding alterity, that is, is equally under the obligation to justify himself to the self. While it may be productive to think equality as emerging out of a primordial inequality,[37] and then to evaluate political institutions with a view toward the extent to which they allow both equality and singular responsibility,[38] it will be crucial to include the self under the demands for equal treatment, for instance, to ground a system of subjective and reciprocal rights. In fact, it is doubtful that a sense of authorship can emerge without the self not only being exposed to interpellation by another, but by learning to take the perspective of the second person on itself, so as to grasp and internalize imputations of responsibility.[39] A third-person standpoint begins to emerge when both ego and alter realize that they are, reciprocally, seeking to assume the other's standpoint. This realization of reciprocity, however, requires ultimately superseding a unilateral relation in which the other implores the self from "on high."

Finally, that the other regards the self from on high suggests that the destitute other, in the vulnerability only a mortal can express, is heir to the God whose gaze and goodness singularizes the self. However, if the asymmetry is not conceived as merely a moment in the moral relation, and equality is not also established from a third-person perspective transcending both, the other is not just barred from being a potential perpetrator, as a frequent criticism has it, but cast in the role of victim rather than equally free agent, as Levinas himself indicates.[40] Failing to inherit and translate the equally transcendent aspect of the "divine standpoint" may then lend itself, inadvertently, to a sense of superiority over the other, a sense that played such an unfortunate role in the history of monotheistic religion: one thinks of the European newcomers to North American shores, for instance, who, while initially dependent on the largely tolerant natives for supplies, nonetheless felt unshakeably superior, in part on account of their religion and the responsibility for the other's salvation it imbued in them.[41] It seems hard to disentangle this entirely unjustified asymmetry from the utter disregard for native ways of life, land use and claims, and the like. A genealogy of religion, as Amy Allen argues in this volume vis-à-vis Habermas – and we should add: in the face of Levinas – would have to take this history of colonial expansion into account.

V

With these shortcomings in mind – deficiencies that result from a consistent but perhaps one-sided attempt to stress the dissymmetrical singularization in the ethical relation without access to a third-person standpoint – we may return to Habermas's account to see where we could supplement it with Levinasian insights. For Habermas, as we have seen, the secularizing translation is to preserve the fundamental equality between alter and ego, so that the injunction to responsibility be addressed from another source (*logos*) to both ego and alter at the same time. This independent status is of course quite capable of preserving the transsubjective, inappropriable, anterior alterity and, perhaps with greater difficulty, the power to command unconditionally. However, its very "impersonality," "anonymity," and "arbitrariness" easily misses the singularizing gaze (*BNR*, 186). Following Habermas's suggestion that the *logos* as heir to "God in time" must also be thought of as interpersonal (*FHN*, 10), we may claim of the *logos* what Levinas said of God, namely, that his commandment appeared only on the face of and in the speech of the singular other – without, of course, ever being exhausted in that appearance. The source of the fundamental moral injunction would thus precede subjects in an alterity beyond ego and alter that, despite being without reason, is articulated communicatively in the normative demand for reasons and accounts for one's actions. We thus conceive the ground of obligation to emerge with a transindividual and a-rational call for justification and accountability that, however, can only appear with vulnerable individuals. Thus, we retain the transsubjective status *and* the singular gaze of the obligating, preceding otherness.

Apart from being able to account for the sense of singular authorship without which we cannot speak of responsibility, associating the origin of responsibility with the gaze of the other is also motivated by that which Habermas conceded in another context: that the equal dignity of the other demands that her singularity be taken into account as a value independent from, yet necessary for, the equal consideration of all, and this beyond being merely an exemplar of reason or of autonomy. For what equal treatment means depends, in particular according to the discourse-ethical principle of universalization, on what that treatment looks like from the perspective of the singular other, her interests and value orientations.[42] The focus on the singular other, however, gives way to the universal, in that there is no non-contingent reason why this other should be preferred over the other others, and the singular other's moral status *also* depends on participation in a genus, for otherwise it is hard to see why only *human* others have a face: as indicated, one may argue that this is what Levinas overlooks.

On this understanding of personal moral responsibility, an understanding that agrees with discourse ethics, the call to responsibility originates for Habermas both in the general other – that is, the other as considered from the point of view of what is "equally good for all," as determined in a moral discourse (that is, by *logos*) – and in the "concrete" other.[43] Regarding the concrete other, Habermas at times stresses, in a manner akin to Levinas, that it is not only the other's moral competences that generate obligation, but her or his "extreme vulnerability" (*MCCA*, 199). In the past, Habermas typically associated this vulnerability with the need for recognition of ego-identity, and so with a symbolic vulnerability, precisely because individualization requires socialization. There are some indications that Habermas's recent concern for the bodily "substrate" of moral agency, as well as his attempt to rethink the notion of human dignity, move him closer to Levinas's understanding of vulnerability as a bodily exposure grounded in mortality, in the death of the other.[44]

In closing, I would like to draw four conclusions, telegraphic indications for further explorations, from this double-sided account of responsibility in the context of religious sources.

(1) The well-known tension between the general and the concrete other on the object side of moral concern is now, according to the present argument, mirrored by a similar tension on the subject side, on the side of the agent called to moral responsibility.[45] For responsibility, it seems, requires a double movement in opposite directions. On the one hand, responsibility demands a movement toward the public, universal standards of moral accountability, for it is before these norms (transcendental-pragmatic, but also the contingent ones that are the output of moral discourses as well as political and legal ones) that an agent must justify herself. On the other hand, responsibility in the sense not of public accountability, but of singular authorship, calls for a move away from the public, toward the solitude of the moral self.[46] As with the general and the concrete other, we may also look at this double movement as a shift of perspectives from the third-person standpoint that moral agents seek to assume when justifying their acts in terms of what is equally good for all, to the first-person perspective that agents must be able to take over when seeing their choices and actions as the ones for which they are singularly responsible.

Levinas's emphasis on asymmetry in the self–other relation – his claim that, as we have seen, "I am infinitely more demanding of myself than of the others"[47] – may then be seen as his attempt to show the ultimate inescapability of the first-person perspective,[48] an inescapability that makes assuming the other's standpoint, however necessary, so fragile and fraught with dangers.[49] Stressing the asymmetrical moment also warns of the dangers of irresponsibility that come with the facile adoption of a third-person perspective.[50] For from the latter, all are equally responsible, allowing each one to hide from her original "election" as the one singled out to respond. Levinas calls this a "permanent danger which threatens goodness and the originary compassion of responsibility for the other man," the "danger of being extinguished in the system of universal laws."[51] For example, when I stand before a drowning child, the presence of another person able to help does not reduce my responsibility to save the child, despite the fact that, from the third-person perspective, the second onlooker, all other things equal, is as obligated as I am. Levinas's point, we could say, is to show that this problem of motivation, the very one that motivated Habermas to supplement discourse ethics with a Kierkegaardian ethics of subjectivity, comes with a one-sided emphasis, discourse-ethical or not, on attaining an impartial point of view.

The evasiveness of the third-person standpoint may lead to well-known collective action problems – for example, those around climate change[52] – problems that are particularly pronounced in an age of the increasing instrumentalization of action diagnosed so well in Habermas's *Theory of Communicative Action*.[53] On the one hand, one may say that, if what is collectively rational does not translate into what is rational to pursue from the individual's perspective, as in a prisoner's dilemma and the tragedy of the commons, then we must insist all the more that individuals adopt the perspective of what is good for all. On the other hand, each can rightfully point to the other to start taking responsibility for what is good for all. In this way, the universal-egalitarian perspective systematically fails to address each one first of all, and requires a different account to motivate the inescapability of responsibility. This seems to be one of the reasons why Habermas insists that the public morality of liberal, secular states cannot do without resources of meaning, such as those of religion, that provide moral motivation for individual action.[54] I have indicated that we can learn from Levinas how to "translate" – a process Levinas sees as necessary as well[55] – the religious sources of personal responsibility once more.

(2) As we have just noted, moral action requires a movement back and forth between the third-person standpoint, from which action is justified with reference to what is equally good for all, and the first-person perspective, from which agents take responsibility for an action. It may be

possible, of course, that these two perspectives do not come to overlap. In fact, one may argue that they cannot. On the one hand, a responsible act requires accountability to others, not just to another singular self, but justification in terms of public norms, both transcendental and conventional. On the other hand, if a responsible act was entirely justifiable by public norms, as if by anonymous reason acting like a machine or protocol beyond the self, the agent could not make it her own, as the norms themselves would already have decided and the agent could at most discover the pre-existing solution.[56] The second conclusion here then points to what Niklas Luhmann calls the paradox of decision, expressed by Heinz von Foerster, in a manner akin to Derrida, in the following way: "Only *those* questions that are in principle undecidable, *we* can decide."[57] If a decision was not undecidable, but rather ranked by criteria outside of (though at the disposal of) the deciding agent, the criteria would decide for the agent, and the agent could not make the decision her own. In addition to its reference to norms of accountability, there must be an unpredictable and subjective moment in a decision qua decision.[58] We may say that Habermas discovered this paradox precisely in the attempt to reclaim authorship by avoiding programmed decisions, in particular the life choices of free agents that genetic engineers threaten to predetermine: I have in mind the point in Habermas's argument against liberal eugenics and prenatal design in which "the deontological shell which assures the inviolability of the person, the uniqueness of the individual, and the irreplaceability of one's subjectivity" come to depend on an "open future" (*FHN*, 82).

The double movement of moral consideration, then – from the obligation vis-à-vis the singular other toward all the other others, and back again – is reflected in the double movement of the responsible agent: toward the public and back again toward the secrecy and solitude (Heidegger spoke of authenticity) of the moral self. This is, as it were, the paradox of agency revealed by the attempt to inherit the "divine standpoint" as the source of morality. For in combining both the universal-egalitarian and the personal aspects in that which is ultimately only accessible to faith, not to reason, the *mysterium tremendum* covered over the paradoxical relation between them. Moral action originates from a source that is other to both the self and to reason, as it is neither simply subjectively arbitrary nor fully justifiable. The trans- and intersubjective status of *logos* does not fully capture the alterity of morality's source, a source of which we said above that it recalls the problems of theodicy. We may ask, then, whether personal moral responsibility can do without a moment of faith, in particular if we do not rush to understand it in narrow religious terms.

(3) The historical origin of responsibility in monotheistic religion

may provoke a new reflection on the meaning of faith and its place in what Habermas calls the "postsecular" world: a world in which religion has learned to accept the authority of the sciences over truth and of the liberal state over justice, but also a world in which reason has learned something, namely, to accept the continuing vitality of religions that provide resources of meaning not accessible to and fully translatable into reason (see *BNR*, chs. 4, 5, 8).[59] For one may speculate that, if faith in a divine standpoint helped the emergence of personal responsibility, and this standpoint cannot without remainder – that is, without unresolved tensions and conflict-ridden movements back and forth – be translated into secular and rational terms, then perhaps some form of faith continues to attend and enable personal moral responsibility. If we agree that, as I have suggested, an agent is committed both to the singular other and to all equally, and that discharging this obligation is strictly speaking impossible in the paradox of decision, then the agent must, as it were, put her trust in the source of morality without knowing that she will be able to discharge her obligations; she must have faith in her abilities as depending on circumstances beyond her control, on an alterity she cannot fathom. As Kant already argued in the antinomy of pure reason, "the real morality of our actions, their merit or guilt, even that of our own conduct, remains entirely hidden from us," so that "no perfectly just judgment [*völlige Gerechtigkeit*] can be passed" upon the imputability [*Zurechnungen, Zuschreibungen*] and responsibility of oneself or another: we must also have faith in our freedom as in that of others.[60]

This faith and trust, about which we make countless judgments in everyday life, is both a self-relation and a social relation, for it asks the other to trust the self. Indeed, as we have just seen, for Habermas (as well as for Levinas) no responsible agent can come about without normative commitments to the other. The individuation-through-socialization thesis stipulates that any individuated agent capable of singular authorship from her point of view, and of imputability from the other's point of view, be constituted in communicative action with its ineluctable higher-order norms of sincerity, truth, and normative rightness (*PMT*, ch. 7). In preceding autonomy as unchosen commands; in preceding while enabling rationality in their own ungroundedness; and in their origin beyond but in and through the personal other, these norms introduce into sociality and individuality what we may consider a faith-like commitment: the commitment to the other to speak the truth sincerely and with a trust in normative rightness, a commitment that asks the other for trust in her abilities to discharge her inevitably context-transcending validity claims.

The commitment is faith-like both from the first-person point of view of agents and from the second-person standpoint to which responsible actors must be committed. Regarding the first, agents must trust that they can discharge the obligations of the transcendental-pragmatic norms, although they not only cannot know for certain that they can, but in fact are unable to do so, as we can see from a third-person standpoint. This follows from the high demands that these norms place upon speaker and hearer, demands that point in an ideal and universal direction despite the fact that agents remain localized in specific lifeworlds. For instance, the claims to context-transcending truth and normative rightness can only be redeemed under ideal conditions of argumentation. However, due to the necessary insertion in lifeworlds – without whose contextually taken-for-granted background assumptions no consensus is possible either – the conditions are factually presupposed (as constitutive, not just regulative ideals) but remain empirically unavailable.[61] A brief look at Habermas's evolving views on what he, with good reason, no longer calls the ideal speech situation, could confirm that he now sees the final agreement to which communicative agents are committed as paradoxical.[62]

In short, aspiring to be personally responsible involves implicitly uttering "Believe me, have faith in me as I do in myself," just as a speech act is underwritten by an inadvertent promise "Believe me, I sincerely speak the truth with a commitment to a background of normatively well-regulated interpersonal relations." The structure of agency is like a promise, and a promise requires faith in its future realizability on the part of the one making the promise as well as by the other accepting it.

(4) Arguably, this kind of basic faith underwrites both reason and religion. Perhaps we may say that it is the reason why we find ourselves, as Habermas's felicitous title has it, "*between* naturalism and religion." The sciences, as Habermas has pointed out against reductionist scientism and "hard" or "radical" naturalism, cannot reduce the normativity of social relations to the "view from nowhere" (*BNR*, 2, 140). Extending objectified nature to the social world misses the first- and the second- person perspective of individuals who see themselves as free and equal. To the extent that science remains a social enterprise, a cooperative search for truth that requires intersubjective verification as much as adequacy of data, the faith in the other remains irreducible. Every scientist who puts forward a truth claim in sincerity must have faith in himself and his findings that are (not yet) fully backed by knowledge. A wholesale naturalization of the mind, the attempt to extend the observer's perspective on nature to science's own justificatory practices, is bound to fail.

Coming to religion, one may argue that the experience of a faith that is indissociable from sociality and responsible individuality is one of its enduring sources. I have suggested that moral agency depends on a source anterior to the time of the subject and other than rational justification, a source to which a faith-like commitment is in order. Habermas encountered it in particular in his attempt to protect the organic substrate of freedom from manipulation by nominal equals, insisting on the gulf that separates autonomy from its source, and thus recalling the usefulness of the distinction between the creator and the created. If the call to responsibility comes from an inexplicable but commanding source, it is perhaps natural to hypostasize, to represent and perhaps to anthropomorphize it in terms of a supreme being capable of uttering it.

If it may be granted, then, that a faith-like structure attends and enables both science and religion, we may argue, with Derrida, that this structure is their common (though non-exhaustive) origin. The uncircumventability of intersubjective normativity even in science, I would venture, motivates Habermas's question whether modern science is comprehensible on its own terms, and the corresponding attempt to re-situate it in one genealogy of reason to which world religions also belong (see *BNR*, 146ff.). The common origin of science and religion that Habermas seeks genealogically in the Axial Age may then be helped along by the common origin that Derrida locates in the ineluctable transcendental commitments of responsibility, in the promise to tell the truth that "is always at work" in every social relation as a "commitment before the other from the moment that I address him." Thus, there can be "no responsibility without a *given word*, a sworn faith [*foi jurée*], without a pledge."[63] From this promise and "originary faith" Derrida wishes to draw a conclusion at which, certainly with differences of emphasis and ultimate destination, Habermas also aims. Rather than "naively" opposing "Reason *and* Religion, Critique or Science *and* Religion, technoscientific Modernity *and* Religion," Derrida recommends we leave behind "a *certain* tradition of the Enlightenment" – one that is characterized by what Habermas deplores as the unwillingness of "secular" reason to learn from religion, and, in Derrida's terms, its unwillingness to recognize that "religion and reason have the same source" in "the testimonial pledge of every performative."[64]

The common origin of reason and religion, sought by both Habermas and Derrida, thus points us not only to a cognitive breakthrough, accomplished in history by attaining a transcendent standpoint. Rather, the sources may also be contemporary with every speech act in the transcendental-pragmatic promise to speak the truth sincerely. Of course, we should not overdraw the contrast between Habermas's genealogy and Derrida's reference to an originary faith at the heart of religion and science or reason. While Habermas, as we know, has analyzed what Derrida calls the testimonial pledge ("I promise the truth, believe me") as a transcendental constraint always already presupposed, so that it, precisely, cannot be gotten around (it is *nicht hintergehbar*, inaccessibly anterior to the subject thus constrained), Derrida demands (though does not deliver) a genealogical investigation of the forms and sources of the promise that is also a faith.[65]

Both projects, the transcendental and the genealogical, supplement one another in pointing to a source that is anterior to (older but also other than) the time of the subject and the time of history, in which alone it nonetheless can be heard.[66] While we may not, as Habermas says, dodge the alternative between an anthropocentric and a theo- or cosmocentric worldview, in its alterity this source points perhaps beyond it.

13

Solidarity with the Past and the Work of Translation

Reflections on Memory Politics and the Postsecular

MAX PENSKY

In the notes for his never-completed magnum opus the *Arcades Project*, Walter Benjamin quoted a letter from his colleague Max Horkheimer, sent from the United States on March 16, 1937. Horkheimer had written to Benjamin complaining of the attempt, in the latter's essays, to develop a theory of historiography that held interruption and shock, rather than scientific explanation, as a methodological first principle.

Horkheimer accused Benjamin of holding an ideological view of history, according to which the past remained open and incomplete, and where the suffering of those unjustly killed was not yet finished. Responding to this incompleteness, critical historiography would then be motivated by a moral injunction to satisfy a debt to the dead, in the medium of remembrance. The unfinished narrative linking the suffering of past generations to an embattled present conflated science (historiography) and theology (hope for the past), which Horkheimer saw as an inexcusable residuum of philosophical idealism. "The determination of incompleteness is idealistic," Horkheimer insisted, unless "completeness is not comprised within it [. . .] Past injustice has occurred and is completed. The slain are really slain . . . If one takes the lack of closure entirely seriously, one must believe in the Last Judgment."

In the notes recovered after his suicide, Benjamin comments on Horkheimer's claim:

The corrective to [Horkheimer's] line of thinking may be found in the consideration that history is not simply a science but also and not least a form of remembrance [*Eingedenken*]. What science has "determined," remembrance can modify. Remembrance can make the incomplete (happiness) into something complete, and the complete (suffering) into something incomplete. That is theology; but in remembrance we have an experience that forbids us to conceive of history as fundamentally atheological, little as it may be granted us to try to write it with immediately theological concepts.[1]

But how should atheistic "science" – or philosophy, for that matter – approach such an experience as this? The standard response to this question would be that it should not. The thesis of the postsecular challenges this option. History (and, I would add, social and political philosophy) finds itself obliged to accommodate an experience of the past whose normative weight seems to demand the application of theological concepts which fall outside the legitimate terrain of postmetaphysical thinking. This experience can be called a debt to the past, specifically to members of one and the same historical society who perished in conditions of injustice.

What would the discharge of such a debt require, and how might social and political theory clarify these requirements? One way to answer this question refers to the familiar panoply of policies and measures that Jeffrey Olick refers to collectively as "the politics of regret," encompassing reparations programs, monuments, memorials and official acts of apology and mourning, revision of state-approved history texts, and so on.[2] No theological conceptions about the relation to the past are required to justify such measures on moral and political grounds, since presumably the source of the moral claims addressed by such measures are not the dead but their survivors, and in an extended sense the contemporary society working to come to terms with an unjust collective past. Therefore the problem of accommodating a theological conception of the normatively unfinished past does not arise. Memory politics are by and for the living.

But if this secular response fails to satisfy (and I will argue that it does), the converse response disturbs for the reasons that Horkheimer identifies. Our moral duties and political obligations ought not to require theological claims as a condition of their intelligibility. Ought implies can, and a moral ought in relation to currently non-existent persons thus requires such claims for the intelligibility of the normatively unfinished past. Hence, what Benjamin calls the use of "immediately theological concepts" is unattractive not only because it violates the conditions of postmetaphysical thinking. In doing so, the "skyhook" (to use Rorty's phrase) of theology offends our moral sensibilities insofar as it presumes to deprive from the dead the finality or completeness of their suffering.[3] Since neither consistently secular nor immediately theological concepts appear to offer satisfactory responses to the question of the normative status of the unjust dead, the search for a third alternative is warranted.

At least since Kant, that alternative has consisted in the attempt to change the form and nature of theological concepts to tailor them for philosophical use; to translate, in other words, theological into secular concepts. Religion within the bounds of reason saves theological concepts for morality by restricting their cognitive use, while attempting to preserve their practical indispensability. Kant thought of the transformation of theological ideas into practical postulates of reason as serving two related interests. Critical philosophy was both entitled and obliged to refuse reason the illegitimate use of certain metaphysical ideas, notwithstanding the possibility that they are indispensable for a range of experiences that we would not wish to lose. And the progress of Enlightenment depended on the general accessibility of rational ideas whose intelligibility and applicability were universal, rather than limited to the bounds of sectarian religions.

This Kantian project is vividly present in Habermas's writings on religion. Both as a critical philosopher and as a participant in ethical-political discourses in the democratic public sphere, Habermas has struggled for a language and method to transpose – transform, translate – theological ideas into postulates suitable for the discursive nature of human reason, and the deliberative structures of the democratic polity. This chapter describes how this project has handled the Benjaminian question of the normative character of the present's relationship with those who have died under circumstances of injustice for which the present remains liable. Habermas recognizes, I argue, that we can be satisfied with neither a consistently secular nor an immediately theological answer to the question of the normative status of the unjust dead – that solidarity with them requires, as Benjamin puts it, concepts neither fundamentally a-theological nor immediately theological.

Philosophy, Politics, and the Work of Translation

Simone Chambers has argued that Habermas's reflections on religion require two quite distinct translation projects, whose relationship with one another is complex and dynamic.[4] In one, philosophy attempts to translate the core epistemic and practical meaning of religious concepts into a secular language, aware of the inevitable losses and distortions involved. In the other, equally situated members of one and the same political public sphere struggle to generate secular equivalents for religious reasons as part of an ongoing project of self-governance through the means of public deliberation. In the question of the normative status of the unjust dead, this double act of translation is, as I hope to show, crucial.

Compared with the more familiar religiously inflected political controversies in the public sphere (the civic responsibilities of the devout, the religious neutrality of the liberal state, the political status of theological concepts such as salvation), the status of the dead can seem an oddly archaic and speculative issue, and perhaps one of a lesser political urgency. One of the goals of this chapter is to argue that this is not so. While all religiously inflected political debates must grapple with the general accessibility, intelligibility, and inclusivity of religious concepts, the question of the normative relation to the dead bears upon ethical-political discourses in a specially powerful and merciless way, for what is at issue is the responsibility (and potentially the guilt) of the living, the proper means for distinguishing amongst victims, perpetrators, and "innocent bystanders" as a society comes to terms with its own recent history, and, ultimately, the most trenchant of all the ethical and existential questions that can motivate a collective debate: who are we, and what have we done?

Indeed this familiar formulation, which Habermas often uses to characterize the hermeneutic, existential character of ethical-political debates, may be misleading. For if it's true that such debates are public attempts to come to grips with contested sources of identity, with troubled traditions and sources of shared meaning that can no longer be taken for granted, then the force and seriousness of such debates would be most clearly at work in memory politics: in struggles over the present significance of a morally disastrous history.

Memory politics, in other words, is the quintessential form of collective ethical-political discourse. And memory politics has less to do with who or what a society is and who or what it wishes to be, than with who it has been; what it has done, or allowed to be in its name or with its tacit consent; what facts about its past it would prefer to forget but finds it cannot or ought not; how its unavoidable past compels it to transform or jettison its cherished norms as bankrupt or failed; who or what, given what has happened, a society wishes *no longer* to be.

As an influential participant in the ethical-political discourse that fundamentally reshaped Germany's national self-understanding in the postwar half-century, Habermas was already actively practicing a crucially postsecular philosophical reception and transformation of the "semantic potential" of religious language, a fact that comes out most clearly in his reflections on the Benjaminian idea of a solidarity with the annihilated victims of injustice. In his participation in the "Historians' Debate" of the 1980s, the dual nature of Habermas's translation work –

the participant role in an ethical-political discourse in a fraught political public sphere, *as well as* in the observer role, offering translation possibilities between secular and religious languages – is most fully realized. Habermas refuses in *both* of these roles to settle definitively for either an unambiguously religious or a wholly secular reading of solidarity with the victims of past injustice. It is this refusal and the maintenance of just this tension that can help us to understand the nature of the double translation that Habermas exercises.

Postwar Germany is the paradigm case of a wrenching and protracted ethical-political debate over the future of national memory, and has served as a constant reference point for subsequent memory-political debates in post-conflict democracies.[5] In fact, no other national society has had such a sustained politics of regret, a memory politics that comprised the basis of (West) Germany's political culture. In the Historians' Debate, Habermas argued against a loose group of "conservative historians" such as Ernst Nolte, Michael Stürmer, and Andreas Hillgruber that Germany's postwar legacy was incompatible, on normative grounds, with the kind of re-appropriation of prewar traditions of German political culture that could provide robust sources of patriotic, particularistic national identity.[6] In a now-famous series of interventions in newspapers and journals, Habermas excoriated his conservative opponents for their cynical maneuvers to rehabilitate bankrupt cultural traditions.[7] For reasons quite different than for "normal" post-conflict democracies, Germany was under a number of normative obligations for self-criticism. And the explanation of this distinctiveness brings him, and us, to the problem of a duty toward, and solidarity with, the victims of the Holocaust, a problem that Habermas pursues in a profoundly non-consequentialist way.

In the Historians' Debate, Habermas deliberately broke with the discourse of collective guilt, and thus also with this long tradition of collective psychological (or crypto-religious) language. He replaced it with the proceduralist vocabulary of democratic politics. For those who were born after the civilizational break, Habermas insisted, liability [*Haftung*], rather than guilt, best captured the continued basis of a collective, social obligation or debt (*NC*, 233).

Unlike guilt, with its panoply of psycho-religious connotations, Habermas intends *Haftung* in an initially juridical sense, as the rough ethical-political correlate of the concept of the intentional tort, where a wrongdoer may not be criminally guilty but is nevertheless liable to pay compensation for damages: liability names a status of standing in a position of public responsibility to redress a wrong, even when culpability for the wrong can no longer be the matter at hand. But Habermas, an author whom we do not normally think of as inclined to indulge in etymological-genealogical reveries, also means to evoke the connection between the legalistic sense of *Haftung* as legal *Belangbarkeit*, and the literal, physical connotation of being attached [*gehaftet*] by an injured party, of a kind of bond or glue holding two parties – victims and the descendants of perpetrators – tightly together, in a way that bears powerfully on the way that perpetrators' descendants experience their room for action, their freedom for certain forms of relationship to their own political culture. In this sense, one might think of *Haftung* as a peculiar form of social-political solidarity, one that registers the inadequacy of the ethical presentism of solidarity and gestures instead to a form of solidarity generated from lacks or absences.

This double sense of *Haftung* refers the thick *ethical-political* bonds that tie consociates to their collective history and memory. This ethical-political memory envisions the ongoing practices of collective self-governance, and the underlying social network of everyday communicative interactions, as the relevant subject of collective normative attention, rather than the vision of a "community of fate" tied together by substantive and exclusive traditions.

"Liability" thus means that Germans of the second and third postwar generations (and by now the young fourth) can reasonably expect their relationship to national traditions to be subject to demands for justification in ways not the case with members of other societies, at least in regard to the break in civilization of 1933–45. Their German citizenship entails a legitimate expectation that they be prepared and willing to offer justificatory reasons to one another as to whether, and if so why, any national tradition can pass, or has passed, through a self-critical filter. Far from the description of a psychological state, "liability" is thus a procedural, deliberative term. As such, it serves as the basis for a form of political solidarity (German constitutional patriotism) no longer based on the content of national traditions themselves, but instead on expectations concerning the public use of critical reasoning that all *legitimate* traditions are subject to. Memory politics links ethical liability with a specific form of memory politics. Any national society can be thought to have a collective political duty to maintain a critical, reflexive relationship to its traditional sources of identity. But Habermas implies that the nature, the extent, and the motivational basis of such a duty change dramatically where specific national traditions and forms of life arise from massive, historically proximate injustices. Liability is a political comportment motivated and justified by a massive, ongoing *normative* rupture in the transmission of shared social life. The ethical-political justificatory discourses that liability warrants are at bottom discourses about *who is missing* from a society – who, or whose descendants, are visible as a negative space or gap in the fabric of intersubjective relationships of social existence. This orientation to the negative is also the work of commemoration or remembrance, the proper relation to what or who is not, but ought to be, present. And *Haftung*, as a politics of memory, rests on the normative relationship to the posthumous victims, rather than appealing to the posthumous victims rhetorically, to bolster consequentialist reasons for compensation of their present survivors. What gives the term its normative force is that a relationship to the dead can at once be both binding, adhesive, too close for comfort, and also one constituted by an absence.

> There is the obligation [*Verpflictung*] incumbent upon us in Germany – even if no one else were to feel it any longer – to keep alive, without distortion, and not only in an intellectual form, the memory of the sufferings of those who were murdered by German hands. It is especially these dead who have a claim to the weak anamnestic power of a solidarity that later generations can continue to practice only in the medium of a remembrance that is repeatedly renewed, often desperate, and continually on one's mind. If we were to brush aside this Benjaminian legacy, our fellow Jewish citizens and the sons, daughters and grandchildren of all those who were murdered would feel themselves unable to breathe in our country. (*NC*, 233)

Elsewhere, Habermas leaves no doubt that he views this Benjaminian legacy as an instance of the *secularizing translation* of a theological claim, in sharp contrast to Horkheimer's contemporary reading:

> After the breakdown of civilization of National Socialism, Benjamin's concept of "anamnestic solidarity" with past injustice. . . – a concept that manifestly tries to fill the gap left by the lost hope in a Last Judgment – recalled a form of collective liability beyond moral obligation. The idea of approaching the kingdom of God, assimilated within the boundaries of mere reason, does not direct our gaze toward the future alone. This idea inspires a general awareness of collective responsibility for failures to offer help and failures to cooperate in averting imminent disaster or even simply to cooperate in improving shameful social conditions. (*NC*, 241)[8]

Horkheimer thought Benjamin's claim of the *incompleteness of history* could be justified only with an immediately theological concept – the Last Judgment, and the survival or resurrection of the souls of the dead to be present at it. Habermas, by contrast, sees the legacy of Benjamin's claim as a normatively obligatory *solidarity with the missing victims* of history. This is a philosophical-political translation. But it is hardly a simple or unproblematic one. What could it mean, for instance, to claim that the solidarity with the missing dead underlies an obligatory collective liability that is "beyond moral obligation?"

Solidarity without Justice

In Habermas's discourse theory of morality, justice (equal consideration for all) and solidarity (inclusion of each in the sphere of moral recognition) are mutually interdependent concepts. As Habermas puts it, solidarity is the "reverse side" of justice, insofar as the perspective of the absolute or irreplaceable value of *each* individual person that is obligatory for adopting a moral point of view is codependent with a corresponding insight into the equal value of all persons understood as reciprocally situated, mutually constituting partners (*JS*). The discourse-theoretical version of moral deontology instructs us to adopt simultaneously the view that every human being bears an infinite hence equal worth simply by virtue of being a moral being and thus fitted to justice, while our solidarity with each person rests on her unique and irreplaceable place in a web of interpersonal relationships which constitutes, sustains, predates, and survives each of us. Precisely because of her situatedness in an extended, enduring, continuously evolving web of communicatively constructed intersubjective relationships,[9] extended indefinitely into past and future, each person is a *moral* person just because her claims for justice are so deeply connected with her claims for a role in a solidary form of inter-subjective life. Moral claims are claims for justice and solidarity *together* within discourse theory. They are claims arising from the interconnected character of persons, a fabric of social life that reconciles otherwise contradictory intuitions: the extreme vulnerability of the person and the remarkable durability of the social lifeworld.[10]

Solidarity means that we *include* others within the sphere of all those to whom we acknowledge actual or potential debts and obligations for justification and recognition, and for care, consideration, and respect.[11] The concept registers the full implications of the thesis that individuals are individuated only through a socialization process (see *PMT*, 180ff.).

In this way, the argument for solidarity as the "reverse side" of justice fulfills the Kantian demand for a translation of the omnipotence and transcendence of divine justice, and the temporally and socially unbounded nature of the soul as a subject of this justice, into the exceptionless and unbounded character of moral recognition. The theological-metaphysical ideas of the immortal soul, extending moral personality beyond the contingent and brief span of biological existence, guaranteed that the unconditional character of morality would be intelligible. But the ideas of posthumous spiritual survival, and of a final judgment where historical wrongs are righted, do not imply that the dead can safely be left to God's future justice. It is the historical relationship between the dead and the living, the solidarity over generations that links them, and that makes intelligible the *ongoing* character of past injustices, which are but one part of a comprehensive vision of a morally charged human narrative history. The pastness of past injustices is mitigated by the theological conception of a collective human history sustained in its meaningfulness, its tendency toward justice, at every moment by God. Kant's postulates of pure practical reason of course abandoned this vision as the object of a possible cognition. But they retained the function of presenting God as the guarantor of the ultimate convergence of the biological life-history of the individual human being and the spiritual fate of the immortal soul – only if we think the possibility of justice as unfinished in the span of biological life can we act on the basis of our own self-conception as fully moral persons.

Physical death, on this view, is an alteration of, but not necessarily an end to, one's moral personhood, since the sphere of all those included as fitting subjects of moral concern is not without further argument isomorphic with the natural category of all those now (biologically) living. For Kant, the practically necessary commitment to an endless moral progress in history, underwritten by a providential God, ensures the moral incompleteness of historical time. The future highest moral state of the species commands the adoption of the point of view of the mitigated or unfinished fate of those whose historical existence ended in injustice. Violating this command is incompatible with practical reasoning: despair is, for Kant, *practically* unthinkable.[12]

What *post-metaphysical* translation of this family of related terms is offered in the idea of a solidarity with the dead? The next section explores the implications of Habermas's use of this term in the context of the Historians' Debate, focusing on the very noteworthy fact that while Habermas vigorously champions, indeed demands, the practice of such a solidarity, he does not make a parallel claim for justice. This fact gives us an insight into the tension and ambivalence that must characterize translations of this kind.

Solidarity with the Dead and Moral Asymmetry

Dead people fail to meet what would appear to be a minimum requirement for moral personhood. They don't exist. It would appear to be simply analytically true that no further justice or injustice can be done to them, and this being the case, they are beyond our moral remit. Indeed, there is something preposterous, even objectionable, in the argumentative maneuvers required to recognize them as the subjects of obligations – as the fitting sources of any positive or negative duties, since no such duties could conceivably result in acts or omissions that could benefit or harm them.

But Habermas argues that there is *some* form of obligation entailed by the collective task of remembering victims of past injustice. If posthumous persons are not possible subjects of *moral* obligation (they are "beyond" such obligations), and further if there is an obligation "incumbent on us" Germans to the dead, then the conceptual interdependence between justice and solidarity breaks down. This collapse in the otherwise reciprocal and interdependent conceptual relationship between justice and solidarity suggests that our solidarity with the unjust dead arises not *despite* but precisely *because* of this asymmetry, because of the tear in the web of mutual recognition in which justice and solidarity reciprocally support one another. The unjustly dead are situated in the solidary relations of an ongoing social project in a radically different way from those whose lives and deaths can be assimilated as part of the ordinary succession of generations. While the latter are *gone*, the former, like their never-to-be-born descendants, are *missing*. Solidarity with the unjust dead is a *sense of someone missing*. The question is whether this sense is itself a kind of experience whose explanation and justification demand a translation of theological concepts, or whether this sense of someone missing is a political and ethical phenomenon that can be adequately explained in entirely secular, "atheological" terms, without any translation process.

The second option, which Habermas refuses to take, is well illustrated by some recent thoughtful work by the political theorist Pablo de Greiff, whose intriguing account of the duty to remember in post-conflict transitional societies attempts to determine what this duty actually consists of. De Greiff begins by laying out the possible conditions for the legitimate claim that the present has a duty to remember its own past victims. "Future-oriented" arguments for a collective duty to remember entail a simplistic consequentialist claim, in the form of the hypothetical imperative familiar as a cliché from Santayana: we have a duty to remember past suffering insofar as doing so is the best, or one of the best, available means for avoiding the repetition of similar suffering in the future, a goal we have good reason to pursue. While not without merits, de Greiff rejects this "prophylactic use of memory" as resting on dubious assumptions about causation. More substantially, it inevitably instrumentalizes our relationship with past victims. For if we are obliged to remember only on the prudential grounds that we ought to "inoculate" ourselves by these means against future transgressions, both the specificity and the intrinsic value of the memory of the victims appear compromised.

Stronger for de Greiff is a "past-oriented argument": the duty to remember is owed to the dead themselves, their present non-existence notwithstanding. De Greiff suspects that the emotional appeal of this argument, however understandable, is largely rhetorical in practice, and the argument itself cannot withstand critical scrutiny, largely due to the intuitively obvious problem that "[t]he dead are not normally held to be appropriate lien-holders." Our available moral concepts cannot establish the kind of moral standing that would permit us to recognize them as sources of duty.

Not surprisingly, given these alternatives, de Greiff argues for a third option – what we might be inclined to see as a duty to the dead is in fact a duty to one another *in light of* posthumous victims. Assuming that a post-conflict democracy will entail a plurality of social groups, that these groups will include perpetrators and the survivors or descendants of victims, and that the historical fact of injustice will be relevant to the maintenance of the identity of these groups, like it or not, de Greiff's "presentist" account clarifies the duty to remember with a strikingly simple and powerful formula: *"we have an obligation to remember whatever our fellow citizens cannot be expected to forget."*[13]

In an important respect, de Greiff offers a deflationary account. He clarifies the sense of duty to the dead with the explanation that such a duty does not, strictly speaking, exist, since the dead are not to be regarded as rights-bearers. His account thus debunks the often overblown rhetorical dimension of memory politics while preserving the core meaning of a political norm that cannot be trumped by purely pragmatic political considerations. Given the relevance of the past of injustice for a democratic polity, and given the potential for dissent, conflict, and the destruction of political solidarity in conflicts over the legacies of injustice, the rhetorical appeal to a debt to the dead recommends a set of civic virtues that responsible members of pluralist societies have good reason to adopt and practice if they are to live in decent political solidarity and trust with one another.

This deflationary account is also, certainly, an entirely secular one. And one important entailment of this is that it also must regard solidarity with the past – the sense of someone missing, and a set of political obligations arising from this sense – as a kind of displacement or mistake. Solidarity with the past, that is, is on de Greiff's account either a rhetorically displaced political obligation to one's fellow citizens, or an inference from a false premise regarding the moral standing of posthumous persons. I do not believe this deflationary account is warranted.

Regret or remorse can powerfully motivate forms of political comportment, but this is distinct, I would argue, from the motivational force generated by the actual recognition of a missing part of a social whole. After all, part of what such solidarity with the past means is that there are not in the present those who would and should have been born, but for the unjust elimination of their forebears from the collective. While any society generates ample opportunities and incentives for its diverse members to express remorse and regret, it is only in extreme cases, where the unjust destruction of a class of persons opens up a wound or gap in the social fabric that continues to be perceived in the present day, that we speak of a solidarity with the dead. And this kind of experience is not captured, I would insist, by the presentist account. This parallels the earlier feature I identified in Habermas's writing in the context of the Historians' Debate, to the effect that the impossibility of retroactive justice does not entail the impossibility of retroactive solidarity. In other words, our inability to conceive of posthumous persons as rights-bearers does not suffice to conclude that they are beyond the relevant, practicable sphere of our moral attention; this is what I suspect Habermas means when he describes such solidarity as "beyond moral obligation" but nevertheless obligatory.

Solidarity with the Dead as a Religious Experience

What sort of older, presumably religious, form of experience does the notion of solidarity with the dead, and its implied liability, attempt to translate? One remarkable fact that emerges in this connection is that such an experience does not really correspond to the set of theological-metaphysical concepts and categories that modernity inherited from the "Axial Age" of monotheistic religion and Greek metaphysics. To the extent that we can get some conceptual handle on the origins of the intuitions underlying this kind of solidarity, it would appear far older.

Pre-axial religion does not generally regard the community's dead as "gone" in the sense of having no further normatively relevant relationships with that community at the point of their deaths. If anything, the frequent problem is the reverse. Death imposes a change in membership status (reassignment to ancestor) that, in the absence of a metaphysics of the immortal soul as the essence of personhood, is more akin to a change in location relative to the sum total of all other community members.[14] The construction of a worldview linking living and dead in a single spatially conceived net of relations is a classic example of what Habermas, citing Jaspers, terms a "narratively linked surface phenomenon" (*FWL*, 9). Without a metaphysical Beyond denoting an essential transformation of the dead, and without the corresponding metaphysical account of a corruptible body and a soul that stands outside of perceptible reality and lived time, the relation between living and dead is rendered in terms of (what for us is) a radical immanence. The dead *remain*, under changed membership terms. The causality of their wills is undiminished, even heightened, as their membership status changes. Social time is isomorphic with the generations capable of being incorporated via ritualized remembrance in the self-image of the collective. The dead ancestors must be constantly appeased, propitiated, consulted, and honored through a suite of ritual practices.

On these terms, the advent of metaphysical worldviews solves a problem of contingency by introducing a Hereafter where the dead remain well and truly dead – even if this Hereafter is deferred according to an eschatology in which physical death is a temporary status in anticipation of a mode of living (immortality) with no precise correlative experience in the world of appearances. Metaphysically inspired monotheism, in the case of Christianity, establishes robust barriers to keep the dead and the living from interaction – only one Ghost, no ghosts in the plural. This eliminates the troubling liminal zone between the dead and the living in which shades, specters, ghosts, spirits, and other sorts of emanations are in constant motion as emissaries between the dead and the living. In eliminating this liminal zone, Jesus was never more clear and trenchant than his command (Matthew 8:18–20) to "let the dead bury the dead," which in this context seems less an unfeeling order to abandon a former life with all its attachments, than a metaphysical doctrine of the highest order.

Religions of the Axial Age, most clearly Christianity, encoded this rejection of the pre-axial entwinement of living and dead, elevating the category of death into a metaphysical event while simultaneously insisting on the denial of death's metaphysical finality. Death taboos are transformed into commentaries on the ontology of the gap separating the essential realms. In both Judaism and Christianity, the resulting ambivalence about the status of the dead tends to repeat the older, mythic ritual practice in which ritualized memory both submits to the wills and interests of the dead while simultaneously controlling and mastering the dead through the very institutionalizing of a ritual practice of submission – in a word, the dialectic of Enlightenment.

If solidarity with the dead expresses an archaic (or at least pre-axial) social experience in which living and dead remain intertwined in normatively relevant ways, then we have at least a provisional answer to the question of the sort of religious experience or idea whose translation into secular concepts is required. Of course, the sense of the proximity of the lives, interests, desires, and hopes of those community members no longer alive is a "religious experience" only in a sense broader (and for us moderns stranger) than the usual understanding of transcendent religious experiences familiar from the monotheistic religions. In this sense translation demands the recovery of an uncanny and archaic cognitive content. What would be required, in order to translate this older and more capacious sense of a religious experience of the continuity of past and present, would be a deliberate *bracketing off* of what now appears to be the distraction of axial metaphysical religious concepts. Translation would be a project of recovery of a lost or occluded, archaic dimension of religious meaning, an attempt to rediscover the diachronic character of ethics beyond and before its Hellenization.

This might also converge at least in part with the intentions of the German Catholic theologian Johann-Baptist Metz. Earlier, our brief look at de Greiff's version of an entirely secular account of solidarity and memory was meant to show the dimensions of solidarity that secular reason alone cannot cover. Conversely, Metz's project, recovering a form of remembering solidarity as an explicitly religious experience, illustrates the limitations of the other side of the postsecular.

Over four decades, Metz has developed a political theology that is no longer inspired by the eschatological promise of future justice. Instead, Metz offers a renewed appropriation of what he terms "anamnestic reason," a mode of reason derived from the Jewish tradition of memory of suffering and oppression, in which the long succession of generations of the oppressed, held fast in ritual memory, have not given way to a Greek (Platonic) imperative for forgetting and temporal presence.

A near-exact contemporary of Habermas, Metz is something of an intellectual alter-ego for Habermas's reflections on the relation of memory, politics, and religion. Rejecting the intellectual history that distinguishes between Greek rationality and Judaic memory, Metz argues that memory itself constitutes a form of rationality just as foundational and as rich as the Greek *logos*. Against this *logos*, anamnestic reason is the primary mode for thinking political theology, a rediscovery of Christianity's radical origin and heart that rejects the quietism and satisfaction with the status quo that Christianity bought with its logocentrism.

Anamnestic reason proceeds in narrative rather than discursive form;[15] constantly negotiating the presence of the past, mining the strange unstable force-field between present and past to insist on the actuality of past injustices, the unfinished character of historical oppression, and the openness of the narrative construction of this tradition of oppression.[16] Metz thus argues for a post-European, post-Hellenic, and post-bourgeois Christianity. Elements of doctrinal teaching serve as inspirational models for the Church's global missionary project of addressing root causes of injustice and suffering, a radical politics that Metz has consistently championed against a "bourgeois theology" that wields metaphysical categories largely as a conservative ideological exercise.[17]

For Metz, the two tasks of recovering Christianity's Judaic, anamnestic core, and embracing its global mission of social justice over its metaphysical concerns, converge. Both draw their power and their urgency from the scandal and shock of Christianity's (in particular, Roman Catholicism's) silence – at best – in the face of the Holocaust. Above all, the German Catholic Church, for Metz, has no other choice but to find its own self-understanding "in the face of" Jews, an expression he does not mean metaphorically. Theology is not an abstract intellectual exercise, but can only take the form of the kind of ongoing, vigorous, and courageous dialogic process of self-criticism and encounter with others that Habermas would almost certainly accept as a cognate meaning of the liability of a national society for a mass crime.

Only by a vigorous, honest, and relentless process of self-confrontation and interfaith dialogue with Jews, Metz insists, can German Catholicism claim the moral authority to work toward a postnational, postmetaphysical, genuinely ecumenical Christianity – a polycentric world Church – based on the struggle against social inequity and injustice.[18] And Metz observes that even the resurgence of German theology in the wake of World War II, in figures such as Bonhoeffer, Rahner, and Barth, has done little to confront the significance of Auschwitz directly in theological terms.

The significance of anamnestic reason for this practical, post-theodicy engagement is what Metz refers to elsewhere as the "productive non-contemporaneity" that the faithful must confront. With this loosely Blochean term, Metz means the refusal of the progressivist, meliorist, and ultimately conservative-bourgeois view of historical time that modern capitalism had superimposed upon the Christian vision of eschatological time. To recover anamnestic reason, the religious person must confront the time of faith in a way similar to that which Benjamin had seen as the explosive messianic temporality encoded within the most minute and ignored features of bourgeois material culture: unexpectedly interruptive, discontinuous, unstable, jagged, filled with strange gaps and lags, rifts and recapitulations. Memory for the "materialist critic," or for the political theologian, appears as a field seeded with bits of uncontrollable and unexpected, suddenly contemporary elements from a collectively shared past of suffering and injustice, of demands for justice that refuse to sit quietly in their assigned historical niche but intrude into the social present in a myriad of de-stabilizing ways.

For this reason, Metz describes the anamnestic structure of a living faith as a series of "dangerous memories." If German Christians are to come face to face with Jews in post-Holocaust Germany, at any rate, they will need to abandon a specific kind of metaphysics, to renounce even virtually and counterfactually the advantage that history has bestowed on those born after, who owe their postwar existence to contingencies of which they could not possibly morally approve. Dangerous memory is therefore also the rejection of memory as re-collection, as narrative reconstruction of a settled past in its relation to a stable present. Memory is "dangerous" precisely in its capacity to unsettle the cognitively comfortable but morally intolerable relation between a past of injustice and a present of undeserved survival. Clearly, this is a view very close to Habermas's conception of liability.

Anamnestic reason is the deliberate sustained effort to resist seeing past suffering as inhabiting a temporally safe and secure relationship with the present. It is a conception very like (and indeed derived from) Benjamin's, in the latter's evocation of the enraging image of enslaved ancestors. "Dangerous memories," Metz writes, are those "in which earlier experiences break through to the center point of our lives and reveal new and dangerous insights for the present. They illuminate for a few moments and with a harsh steady light the questionable nature of things we have apparently come to terms with, and show up the banality of our supposed 'realism.'"[19] They are thus "memories with future content."

Memory works in opposition to "a purely historical relationship with the past that not only presupposes that the past is past; it also works actively to strengthen the fact that what has been is not present ... Remembrance is transformative, not in the existential sense of reforming ourselves, but going out to transform the world. This is what issues from solidarity with the dead. We are made responsive to that suffering by the imitation of Christ, the suffering God. Christianity is the tradition and religion of the sufferer, the loser, the victim, the oppressed."[20]

Metz's conception of anamnestic reason clarifies in what sense a "debt to the past" is compelling as a rationally justifiable commitment, yet not entirely capable of clarification given the language of moral reasoning that has been handed down to us through a long tradition of logocentrism. Conceiving of memory as a mode of reasoning rather than a mere adjunct to the form of rationality proper for philosophy illuminates both the liberating and morally encumbering sides of the relationship to historical time.

But Metz is a theologian, not a philosopher. His translation project must therefore keep within strict limits that philosophy need not acknowledge. In fact the translation runs in a direction precisely opposite to that of Habermas's postmetaphysical thinking. The eschatological horizon of hope in God's justice is not replaced by memory. Rather, the hope for the advent of absolute justice in a Last Judgment and the obligation to keep alive the memory of unjust suffering are brought together in the single event that for Metz is the Passion of Christ. For this reason, the *memoria passionis* is not just exemplary for how the faithful are to conceive of solidarity with the dead. The memory of Christ's suffering generates anamnestic solidarity's very possibility. It is the fulcrum point around which past, present, and future entwine and interpenetrate. But this also means that the disruptive memory rediscovered before or beyond the Hellenization of Christianity derives all its power from its orientation to the Passion of Christ, the exemplar and archetype of all the logocentric denials of historical diachrony and the very quintessence of metaphysics. Christ's redeeming suffering renders the theological vocabulary of political theology into the general vocabulary of political action, spurred by remembrance, but striving toward present-day emancipation from oppression and injustice.[21] Only the *immediacy* of this untranslated and untranslatable event is open to the theologian.

In a critical aside against Habermas, Metz dismisses the very idea of a postmetaphysical philosophy, by which he means, in essence, a philosophy refraining from all transcendent concepts that offer consolation in the face of an unjust world. The *memoria passionis* is a "dangerous memory" that transforms the idea of historical suffering by appealing to a compassionate community of the faithful. But this religious transformation also relieves the idea of historical suffering from what is arguably its most genuinely dangerous dimension – not the prospect that suffering will never be redeemed through a Last Judgment, but the possibility that there is no exemplary instance in the tradition of suffering by which past suffering can be recognized as meaningful, as interpretable according to a narrative construction of the span of human history. As the sacrificial moment of historical time, as the *kairos* making chronological time capable of receiving narrative significance, Christ's suffering galvanizes the Church by offering a familiarly non-negotiable, metaphysical moment of pre-established meaning, a very vivid and in this case almost literal example of Rorty's skyhook.

Absent this metaphysics, Metz fully acknowledges that he cannot quite see the point of an emancipatory promise made good in the medium of reason. This is why the "transcendence from within" that Habermas ascribes to the procedural dimension of a universal pragmatics of speech holds such little appeal for him:

> For me memories are not just the objects of a testing discourse, but rather the ground of discourse, without which they would collapse into a vacuum. They can not only launch discourse or illustrate it, but also interrupt and halt it. I know of really only one absolutely universal category: it is the *memoria passionis*. And I know of only one authority which cannot be revoked by any Enlightenment or emancipation: the authority of those who suffer.[22]

What had seemed a rich and influential attempt to make good on the shortcomings of a presentist, synchronic, and secular account of anamnestic solidarity turns out, ultimately, to take the form of a translation project whose central term remains triumphantly untranslated. Indeed, the redemptive passion of Christ demands a translation *from* philosophy and *back to* theology as the only way to rescue the disruptive normative potentials inherent in the "dangerous memory" of historical suffering.

And this conceptual translation is, of course, in the context of a *political* theology. Therefore, the broader, public mode of translation from a secular to a postsecular (and in this case post-postmetaphysical) public idiom is at the center of Metz's project as well. Given this dynamic, it is no wonder that Habermas's few published responses to Metz's work have been cautionary at best. The question for Habermas in his critical response to Metz's version of political theology is therefore whether a translation project "in the right direction" can nevertheless say something more substantial about solidarity with the past than de Greiff's synchronic version.

In his only sustained response to Metz, the short essay "Israel or Athens: To Whom Does Anamnestic Reason Belong?," Habermas points to the limits of translation between religious and philosophical language that Metz's project illuminates. Metz's appeal to the corrective of historical memory, however normatively attractive, cannot alter the fact that theology itself is ultimately in no position to determine unilaterally where the borderline between the religious and the philosophical dimensions of the concept of reason is to be drawn. Not surprisingly, Habermas bristles at Metz's suggestion that communicative reason still exhibits the loss of memory and the uncritical championing of the present so typical of metaphysical philosophy.

For Habermas, the history of reason itself already contains all the content and resources it needs to recast its historical genealogy in a way that would recover, on postmetaphysical terms, the subterranean memory of suffering and loss. Such a recovery could also serve as a corrective for philosophy's own overweening self-confidence in its explanatory powers, and its own tendencies to collude with social domination. Religious traditions certainly can and should *make available* to philosophy those "semantic contents" that philosophy finds indispensable but inaccessible, and that a self-critical philosophy can attempt to extract relatively intact. But religion cannot take on this kind of translation work on its own.

Habermas rightly refuses Metz's theological claim of ownership over anamnestic reason, even if he does not entirely respond to the (largely undefended) claim that anamnesis can be regarded as a (primordial) form of reason in its own right. Philosophy, Habermas maintains, has already worked through the tension between the supposed anamnesis of Hellenic metaphysics and the diachrony of the Jewish tradition of the oppressed, even if this work happened largely in the long development of a burdened moral philosophy that Metz chooses to ignore.

> [T]he idea of a covenant which promises justice to the people of God, and to everyone who belongs to this people, a justice which extends through and beyond a history of suffering, has been taken up in the idea of a community tied by a special bond. The thought of such a community, which would entwine freedom and solidarity within the horizon of an undamaged intersubjectivity, has unfolded its explosive force even within philosophy. Argumentative reason has become receptive to the practical experiences of threatened identity suffered by those who exist historically. (*RR*, 132)

Postmetaphysical philosophy, unencumbered by even the most well-intentioned political theology, will pull this rope on its own and take on the translation work that Habermas has in mind.

Translation is a process of analogical thinking. It searches for imperfect equivalents. The religious vision of a past, present, and future unified in an all-embracing historical solidarity, grounded through the single unique moment of Christ's sacrifice, finds its equivalent for Habermas only in the claim of a trans-historical solidarity in suffering that can be distilled from the inclusionary dynamic of speaking and hearing subjects, a thin foundation for a community and one that must take suffering in proceduralist terms:

> Philosophy, too, pits the force of anamnesis against a historicist forgetting of forgetting. But now it is argumentative reason itself which reveals, in the deeper layers of its own pragmatic presuppositions, the conditions for laying claim to an unconditional meaning. It thereby holds open the dimension of validity claims which transcend social space and historical time. In this way it makes a breach in the normality of mundane events, which are devoid of any promissory note. Without this, normality would close itself hermetically against any experience of a solidarity and justice which is *lacking*. (*RR*, 134)

The "methodological atheism" that Habermas first proposed for philosophy, in response to the challenge by Metz and Helmut Peukert,[23] insists on appropriating theological concepts while holding aloof from the context of ritual and religious experience in which those concepts were living. Philosophy has access only to "the universe of argumentative discourse that is uncoupled from the event of revelation" (*RR*, 233). This translation work presupposes that the relation between philosophy and theology is not one of symmetry and equivalence, as a translation between two natural languages. Philosophy proceeds on the assumption that theological concepts maintain their semantic meanings even after they have been removed from their living contexts, and that those meanings still capture aspects of the human experience without any dependence on the transcendence of ritual, or overtly religious or metaphysical language.

Theological concepts, in other words, are not just translatable: they are *in need* of translation. Such a need can sometimes remain unmet. A philosophical approach to translation must develop a clear-eyed understanding of the severe limits, indeed the inevitability of failure and loss, that all translation invites. In any effort to transfer the semantic meaning of a concept from a religious to a secular mode, philosophy must remain sensitive to the desire to wrest meaning from concepts regardless of the kind and degree of violence required. The sensitivity of philosophical translation also requires a finely honed sense of when to desist.[24]

Religious language is, as Habermas has recently put it, still capable of articulating "an awareness of what is absent or lacking. It keeps alive a sensitivity to failure and suffering. It rescues from oblivion the dimensions of our social and personal relations in which advances in cultural and social rationalization have caused utter devastation" (*BNR*, 6). While religious language is in need of translation, translation of course always betrays, and always fails. But it's also true that this very failure can become part of an expressive effort to articulate not just a sense of what is missing, but a sense of who is missing as well.

Another way of making this point about the *untranslatable* dimension of religious language, this time derived from Habermas's reading of Kant's rational religion, is that religious language – redemption, sacrifice, Last Judgment – gives us semantic resources for what is at bottom a deeply non-rational act: the passionate cry of protest at a world in which individual persons exhibit such remarkable vulnerability and where extreme suffering seems to have no discernible relationship to our most cherished views of justice. Kant's conception of the constitutive use of postulates of pure practical reason, Habermas observes, was meant in large part to acknowledge, rather than to compensate for, the semantic lack that opens before us once the imagery-rich semantics of religious traditions are replaced by the abstract concepts of moral universalism.[25]

Translations from religion to philosophy *always fail*, in an important sense: the affirmation of articles of religious faith is metaphysics pure and simple, and it is precisely in this affirmation that religion, unencumbered by secular criteria for validity, can offer forms of consolation that philosophy cannot and should not. In fact, Habermas's arguments about religious language generally make a direct connection between the capacity to make non-falsifiable metaphysical assertions and the capacity to offer various modes of consolation for the generally bad news of human existence: bodily and psychic fragility, the consignment to dumb chance and contingency, our remarkable capacity for cruelty, the susceptibility to suffering, failure to find a meaningful mode of living, loss, and death. Translation work into secular terms is therefore just as important for the blank spaces and discontinuities that register in the "target language." This is the postsecular equivalent of negative theology, and has to be borne in mind in any assessment of a "successful" translation project.[26]

Solidarity with the perished victims of injustice offers no consolation, even if we can affirm some possibility of past suffering and past injustice as having a mode of redress. This mode of redress doesn't extend to the full-blown claim that a divinely ordered global history of salvation will render individuals' physical death less than absolute and that each individual has at least the possibility of resurrection. As Lutz Wingert has argued, moral personhood for the generations of the unjust dead becomes visible *also* as a negative space, as the sum of all those whose justified membership in a moral community extended indefinitely in both historical time and social space was cut off, denied, annihilated.[27] To regard oneself as obligated by norms whose context of justification transcends the parochial limits of the here-and-now is also to regard oneself as obligated to attend to the massive exclusions from moral community.

For Wingert, as for Habermas, it is the *missing* or lacking inclusion, the gap or tear that massive injustice opens in the fabric of such a community, that is the object of a solidarity with victims. While Wingert acknowledges the counterfactual, virtual, indeed symbolic character of remembrance as a posthumous re-inclusion into moral community, he also touches upon the necessary failure of a translation from religious to moral language. Offering no consolation, solidarity also does not repair the gap in the social fabric, any more than it returns those who are missing. But it can bring to collective awareness a sense of *what*, and not just who, is missing.

For Habermas, neither a-theological nor immediately theological concepts are truly at our disposal for coming to terms with the experience of who, and what, is missing in the wake of massive injustice, violence, and death.[28] Between the theological and a-theological is a form of experience that we can neither interpret satisfactorily nor ignore. Solidarity arising from the experience of radical loss and infinite responsibility cannot be taken even symbolically as restitution or as a repair of the gaps that violence opened in the social fabric. But the liability that we take on in confronting this lack is not merely a moment of melancholy. It also calls upon the best and strongest that societies are very occasionally capable of, expressed in a language strange and broken, and therefore beautiful.[29]

14

What Lacks is Feeling

Hume versus Kant and Habermas

JOHN MILBANK

I Introduction

Was Fehlt?, asks Jürgen Habermas, in the course of his now famous debate about postsecularity, faith, and reason with the Munich Jesuits (*AWM*), itself held in the wake of Pope's Benedict XVI's still more famous (and infamous, for some) "Regensburg address." *What lacks* to us today, in an age supposedly governed by reason? Here, Habermas takes up the post-religious lament of Brecht and Adorno: how do we supply the role that religion once fulfilled?

But he takes it up in a very different key, because he is newly aware, in the early twenty-first century that, far from going away, religion is if anything returning – in terms of numbers in the third world, and in terms of public influence in the West. This return is by no means always benign: religious extremism is returning also. Yet in a new combination, secular extremism has reached a new pitch of intensity and we are also seeing the rise of an increasingly militant naturalism. Both these phenomena Habermas understandably regards as threatening to a reasonable humanism. In the face of this threat, he wishes to defend and re-fortify its neutral, secular ground. However, he continues to be haunted by the Brechtian lack. And, in the face of this lack, he no longer suggests merely a novel substitute for lost faith, but rather that reason must continue to draw upon faith's resources. Religion is not going to go away and we need not only reasonable forms of religion, but also a rational respect for faith, if human beings and the planet are to have a sane future.

This seems immediately compelling. However, I shall argue below that what is problematic about Habermas's proposals is the sharp divide that he assumes between faith and reason, on the basis of a presumed non-surpassability of the postmetaphysical era inaugurated by Kant. He understands both Pope Benedict's revival of a metaphysical mediation between faith and reason *and* newly over-extended ontological naturalism to be violations of the "limits of pure reason."

In what follows, I shall further contend that Habermas is already outdated in the face of a manifest revival of metaphysics and that both a revived blend of Greek reason with biblical faith and an ambitious naturalism are coherent, though rival programs. Either idiom, I shall suggest, permits a much greater mediation between faith and reason than Habermas allows, and does so especially in terms of the role given to *feeling*. Morever, if we read David Hume aright (which is to say in a drastically revisionary fashion), we shall see that such a perspective is by no means entirely alien to the Enlightenment legacy, to which Kant need not, after all, be regarded as the primary witness.

I shall try to show how, when faith and reason are mediated by feeling, they are actually less likely to take sinister forms than when they are corralled against each other. Finally, I shall suggest that Habermas's own pragmatized transcendentalism, far from being a bulwark against anti-humanist reduction, is entirely subject to such reduction. By contrast, the right sort of naturalism can lend itself to a spiritualizing elevation.

Was fehlt?, I shall therefore claim, in an inter-linguistic play on verbal affinities, is "feeling," a notion imbued with a sense of our experience of "the other," both as lack and as presence.

II Habermas and the Lack within Reason: The Debate with Ratzinger and the Munich Jesuits

Habermas's approach to our current global dilemmas is sensitive, even anguished, and highly acute. As he observes: "At the level of elementary interactions, a gap seems to be opening up between a prickly moral consciousness and impotence in the face of the structurally imposed switch to strategic conduct" (*AWM*, 74).

Exactly so: one has here a kind of sterile oscillation between a ruling ruthlessness, on the one hand, and impotent moralistic whining, on the other. The ruthlessness is the result of the ever-greater submission of more and more spheres of human life to an instrumentalist and capitalist logic, which Habermas fears is increasingly driven by a revived social Darwinism. In the face of this ruthlessness, moral reserve retreats into the private domain and takes the form of a stuttering series of complaints that too often are merely about the supposed restriction of certain individuals and groups from full participation in the mass instrumentalizing process.

It is a considerable tribute to his intellectual integrity that Habermas sees that perhaps the greatest exception here is that of religious groups, who continue to foster impulses toward moral action on a collective scale. For this reason, one has to ask what it is they provide that is otherwise "lacking." Habermas's answer, broadly speaking, is that they provide vivid pictures and motivating stories for individuals, and above all that they provide images of community which are compelling ("the body of Christ" and so forth), but which exceed the bounds of the mere nation-state – thereby opening up a universal and global loyalty.

Habermas is clear that human solidarity now needs these religious resources if it is to fight both religious and naturalistic fanaticism. However, he asks to what extent it is legitimate for religious people to speak in terms of their religious visions in the public domain – and at times his questioning here is in excess of his answering. Yet, on the whole, he supplies a rather uncompromising kind of reply: although secularity must continue to draw, like Hegel, on religious resources, it must eventually translate these resources into strictly rational terms for the sake of official legislative debate and usage. And by rational terms, Habermas means the terms of Kantian critical reason, which render out of court any totalizing and cosmological metaphysical claims.

In order to sustain such a demand, two more protocols must be observed. First, religions must be required to accept this need for translation, along with the secular neutrality of the state, the monopoly over "fact" of scientific discourse, and the monopoly on public morality of the norms of communicative action in terms of free access to conversation and the intention of publicly verifiable truth. But, second, this acceptance must be no mere reluctant resignation. To the contrary, religions must be required so to modify their dogmas (if they are not already so compliant) as to find specifically internal, theological ways of embracing the absoluteness of these secular norms (*AWM*, 15–23).

Yet, correspondingly, secular reason must be required to admit that it has no remit when it comes to determining the truth or otherwise of faith. So the trade-off, one might say, for outlawing the metaphysics of Joseph Ratzinger, would be that we would equally outlaw the scientism of Richard Dawkins.

A question, of course, arises about the dubious practicality of such proposals. But, more theoretically, questions arise about their coherence. Everything, in fact, depends for Habermas upon the absoluteness of the Kantian revolution, which, by banishing metaphysical mediation, finally gave secular consecration to the Protestant separation of reason and faith. But, in that case, is Habermas covertly engaging in a new sort of *Kulturkampf?*

One could argue that this is indeed so. He is prepared to admit that the great metaphysics of East and West are of a single axial birth with the world religions. However, he wishes to say that later "a division of labour" between metaphysics and Christian theology was worked out. Yet this is immediately to admit that what we are faced with here is an explicitly Christian event, and the question arises as to its possible ideological contingency rather than logical necessity. Habermas chides Ratzinger with a deficient historicism, and yet it is concerning just this issue that Ratzinger is the far more prodigious historicist. For the previous Pope would ascribe to the view that the dogmatic separation of philosophy from theology is the paradoxical result of the dubious creation of a category of "pure nature" by a theology concerned for theological reasons sharply to divide nature from grace. Equally, he would ascribe to the view that a metaphysics independent of all theology is the result of a specifically theological establishment after Duns Scotus of being as univocal and so as comprehensible outside the Neoplatonic logic of participation in God.[1]

The fact that the issue between Habermas and Ratzinger turns in part on this question of genealogy is clearly confessed by Habermas himself at the end of his essay in the Munich debates (*AWM*, 22–3).[2] There, he alludes to the contingent shifts just mentioned, but says that: (1) Scotism and nominalism were preconditions for the rise of modern science; (2) that Kant's transcendental turn was required for "our modern European understanding of law and democracy"; (3) that historicism was the precondition for a proper cultural pluralism, besides an improper relativism. Finally, and crucially, he identifies these three stages as ones in a progressive "de-Hellenization."

But all these claims are historically dubious. First, the medieval rebirth of Greek science preceded the advent of univocity and nominalism, and one could even argue that they led physics initially in an over-mechanistic direction that more Neoplatonic and hermetic influences later corrected, beginning with Isaac Newton. Second, the French and American, to say nothing of older British, Scandinavian, and Swiss contributions to European constitutionalism, have got nothing to do with Kant. In the third place, historicism only implies an irreducible pluralism if one disallows the more radically historicist idea – as admitted by Ratzinger – that events can uniquely disclose truths.

Meanwhile the approbation of "de-Hellenization" is revealing. For this phenomenon cannot be prised apart from a claimed (but arguably spurious) greater fidelity to the biblical legacy, sundered from Greek metaphysics, which is traceable through Scotus, nominalism, and the

Reformation. Clearly, Habermas cannot rationally be seen to be assenting to this tendency in theological or a fortiori Protestant theological terms. Yet here arises most acutely the question about the status of his proposed "translation" of theological into secular terms.

For evidently the above cited remarks show that at least some of the theology he wants to translate is Scotist, Ockhamist, and Protestant. But, in that case, do the secular variants really struggle entirely free of a specifically religious origin? And is it not strange that the translations that *all Christians* are asked by Habermas to sign up to are translations of positions at variance with those of most mainstream Catholic intellectuals? Thus, in order to ascribe to these translations, they would have first to switch their allegiance from theologically metaphysical positions, which, according to Habermas, are *not translatable into the terms of reason at all.*

In order to make such a drastic requirement of Catholic Christians, Habermas would have to show that, far from his Kantian philosophy being rooted in certain older theologico-metaphysical assumptions, these assumptions were rather initial adumbrations of a truly critical philosophy. This would be to accord with the position of the fine intellectual historian Ludger Honnefelder, for whom Scotus' writings were the beginning of a critical turn which asked first about the capacities of human reason as an instrument rather than first about the division of being.[3]

However, the suspicion must lurk that Ratzinger might be able to trump Habermas metacritically at this juncture. Is Scotus the anticipator of Kant's new reason, or is Kant still the prisoner of Scotus and Ockham's theology? It is after all clear to historians that univocity of being, nominalism, and voluntarism were all taken up for reasons that were as much theological as philosophical. And all three positions can and are contested within perfectly respectable contemporary theology and (more decisively) philosophy. So if, as many historians of philosophy (Honnefelder included) have now claimed, the Kantian critical turn assumes the validity of these positions, then its absolute historical *hiatus* can be questioned.

The point is not to adjudicate here on this issue, but rather to throw into doubt Habermas's rather blithe (and surely now rather provincial) assumption that those who cannot accept our "postmetaphysical" situation have somehow failed to follow certain inelectable arguments. But, to the contrary, it is rather the octogenarian ex-Pope who (unusually amongst contemporary Germans) now looks "cool," who seems "to get" the post-postmodern zeitgeist, without trying, like Habermas, to retreat into a modern humanist comfort zone that is no longer sustainable (see the following section). Hence Ratzinger might well counter to Habermas that to embrace "de-Hellenization" from a secular vantage point is to fall victim to a theologically exegetical error that is outright factually wrong. For Hellenic influence is indeed present within the New Testament from the outset; nor do contemporary biblical critics (outside Germany, at least) any longer subscribe to nineteenth-century Lutheran delusions about a vast gulf between the Hellenic and the Hebraic.

Therefore, it must remain highly doubtful as to whether Habermas has succesfully shown that the Pope's alternative premodern model for the mediation of faith and reason is no longer critically viable. Is genuinely objective reason just a matter of conforming to pragmatically normative criteria for communication, as Habermas teaches? Or is our "communication" of reason true to the degree that it participates in the infinite communication of the *Logos* by the divine Father who created finite reality, as Ratzinger suggests? There is great prima facie plausibility in the latter's claim that this idea alone rendered reason coterminous with being itself and suggested an unlimited diversity and scope for its reach.

How ironic indeed that we are therefore faced with a debate between a religious rationalism, arguing for the limitless sway of reason, and a secular rationalism, arguing for the limits of reason and yet a sublime respect for a faith that lies ineffably outside reason altogether! Is it the limitation and yet confinement of reason to formal checkability that guards against terror, or is it rather the advocacy of a generous extension of reason both in reach and kind?

I shall argue below that the latter position of Ratzinger is the better safeguard. In arguing it, he is perhaps, as a contemporary German, somewhat unusual. But besides exhibiting many French influences, Ratzinger in addition draws upon longstanding traditions of German Catholic Romanticism that were deeply critical of Kant in the ultimate wake of the Lutheran pietists Jacobi and Hamann – who drew much inspiration from David Hume.[4] For comprehending part of the reason why I have singled out Hume in this chapter, it is important to bear this "romanticism" of Ratzinger in mind.

For what it implies is that it is not enough simply to try to "reinstate" a pre-critical (pre-Scotist, pre-nominalist, pre-Kantian) outlook, since one has to ask just how it was possible for the latter to arise. What I think can be argued here is that the "critical" view emerged because of an increasing sundering of reason from the emotive and the aesthetic, and a corresponding sundering between reason and a will increasingly viewed as pure "choice" and "decision." In order, therefore, to recover, as Ratzinger desires, a "broader" reason, it is necessary to insist, in a "Romantic" fashion, upon the embedding of reason in the emotive, the aesthetic, the linguistic, the social, the historic, and the natural, far more explicitly than did even the "high metaphysical" synthesis of faith and reason that preceded the Scotist rupture.

In choosing (it might seem perversely) Hume to make this point, I am deliberately trying to show how the "Romantic" current, far from being marginal (or dependent upon the Kantian shift) begins well back in the "Enlightenment" or arguably the "pre-Enlightenment," which already entertained doubts about both the consequences of the late medieval Christian legacy and the naturalist reaction against it. In this way, I hope to show that "an alternative to Kant" is neither eccentric, nor in any simplistic way "counter-modern."

As both Augustinian and Romantic, Ratzinger differs markedly from Habermas's Jesuit Munich interlocutors who are mostly themselves far too Kantian, trying somewhat incoherently to combine Kant with pre-modern Catholic philosophy.

However, the one non-Jesuit interlocutor in the collection – Michael Reder – makes important critical points.[5] These are threefold: first, Habermas's rejection of religion's public right to speak in its own voice is a subcategory of his insistence that public virtue is a matter of Kantian *Moralität* and not Hegelian *Sittlichkeit*. In other words, Habermas will not allow that there can be any publicly rational adjudication as to the common good and the shared ends of human flourishing. Reder rightly notes that this seems to take no account of the revival of the claims of virtue-ethics. Second, Reder suggests that Habermas also ignores the idea that reason can speak negatively of the infinite by realizing that in the face of the infinite the usual logic of non-contradiction breaks down, as suggested by Nicholas of Cusa. Yet here Reder also presents Cusa anach-ronistically as a Kantian who asked epistemological questions about the possible reach of our intellect and so as articulating a sublime gulf between its positive finite and its negative infinite reach. But, in reality, Nicholas was still situating the human mind metaphysically within a fini-tude that he newly grasped as paradoxically extending of itself, as finite, into the infinite. Accordingly, his idea of contradictory utterance does not express an impassable barrier so much as an analogical mediation that can be mystically traversed. He was more the Renaissance renewer of Neoplatonic tradition than an advance articulator of the postmetaphysi-cal.[6] And were he but the latter, then his example would be of little use in qualifying Habermas, because it would still leave reason sundered from faith. The former would merely sketch out a space for faith to fill with its own exclusive content.

Reder's third point is the most crucial: that, following Schleiermacher, we can understand "feeling" as a category intermediate between faith and reason. Once more, however, Reder puts things in an overly nega-tive "critical" fashion, presenting Schleiermacher's "feeling of absolute dependence" in terms of a failure of autonomous self-grounding reaching out to a Kantian sublime, rather than as a mode of cognitive relationship to the whole of immanent reality, as Schleiermacher actually articulated it, following Spinoza's "third kind of knowledge." All the same, it is true that Schleiermacher did not ultimately escape the Kantian lure, and so increasingly presented this experience of cosmic dependence and interdependence as specifically "religious," rather than being the entire horizon of our human condition, both cognitive and practical, as the *Speeches on Religion to its Cultured Despisers* originally intended.[7] The trouble with Schleiermacher was that, when he cleaved to this more interesting vision, he lost the subjectively personal in the pantheistically immanent, but when he later confined feeling to "a religious category" he lost the sense that all reason is a mode of feeling.[8]

I shall argue below that such a thesis had already been presented in a far more comprehensive fashion by David Hume, and in a manner that does not evidently reduce the personal since it does not necessarily lose its guarantee by the transcendent.

Reder is only able to put forward feeling as offering a kind of bridge to faith, in a manner that still leaves faith and reason profoundly divided. But (a retrieved and genuine) Humean model, I shall argue, allows us to see that reason and faith are always thoroughly entangled, and also provides a social model that allows for this entanglement.

But before invoking Hume against both Kant and Habermas, I shall try to suggest reasons why the latter's notion of public discursive neutrality is philosophically incoherent.

III Questioning Discursive Neutrality

As already stated, Habermas is acutely aware that we live in a period where the humanist consensus is being challenged both by naturalisms and by more militant forms of faith. In the face of this circumstance, he proposes that we need to reinstate a firm Kantian distinction between what belongs to discursive reason, on the one hand, and to ineffable faith, on the other (*BNR*). Discursive reason should recognize that it operates within strict limits and therefore is not competent to pronounce against either metaphysically naturalist or religious positions. Both must be allowed to speak in their own voices in the public domain (and one should welcome Habermas's step beyond Rawls in saying this), and yet – problematically from the point of view of democratic inclusion – official constitutional debate and decision-making must be conducted within the terms of "neutral" discourse. The latter is notably an emotion-free discourse, following Kant's views about the moral law. For, despite the contortions that Kant went through in relation to the role of feeling with respect to the ethical, this played for him either a negative role as the feeling of the emptily sublime ushering us into the presence of the moral law, or a subordinate role in terms of our "feeling" that the moral should be harmonized with the sensorily pleasurable and the emotionally satisfying.[9]

It might be questioned, however, whether this adherence to a basic Kantian principle really does justice to the double novelty of the cultural situation in the twenty-first century, of which Habermas is so acutely aware. Essentially, there is nothing new about his Kantian proposal to sustain an agnostic neutrality in public discourse, free of metaphysical commitments of either a naturalistic or a spiritualistic kind. Such "transcendentalist" neutrality was already often the norm (explicit or implicit) in the official assumptions of the preceding century. All that Habermas does, in effect, is to call defensively for the reiteration of a now threatened status quo. But this may be to underestimate the way in which the seemingly contradictory return of naturalism and religion at one and the same time puts both intellectual and sociological pressure upon the very possibility of a "neutral" discursive space. In contrast to Habermas, the young French (and atheist) philosopher, Quentin Meillasoux, whose work follows somewhat in the wake of that of Alain Badiou, has suggested two reasons for the current collapse of methodological agnosticism – reasons which it would be hard critically to surmount.[10]

The first reason is intellectual: the terms of "transcendentalist" neutrality have been deconstructed within both analytic and continental philosophy, and therefore "postmetaphysical" philosophy is collapsing – ironically because it has been exposed as the very consummation of the metaphysical as a supposedly autonomous and non-theological discourse about being. This is because the quest for certainty about being must inevitably collapse into the quest for certainty about knowledge, and therefore a methodologically secular metaphysics mutates into a foundational epistemology. The latter relies upon showing how there is a proper fit between our minds, when critically regulated, and reality as it appears to our understanding. Yet it no longer seems plausible that there is a "correlation" between the way our minds work and objectively given appearances. Instead, philosophy (again both analytic and continental) is proposing full-blooded accounts of nature that incorporate (with various degrees of reduction) an account of the human mind. Kantian anthropocentrism and finitism now appear to be unscientific and, indeed, to revert to the pre-Copernican. Conversely (one might add to Meillassoux), if one wishes to defend the spiritual character of mind, it is not possible to appeal to some supposedly "given" transcendental circumstances: one would need instead a speculatively metaphysical account of the reality of mind and soul.

Hence, if naturalism and religion are squeezing out the agnostic middle, this is not because the bounds of reason are being transgressed; it is rather because reason (with good reasons) no longer tends to credit such bounds, since if there is no demonstrable "correlation" between intellectual category and phenomenal content, it is no longer possible to set the Kantian critical test of "schematisation" in order to distinguish between those concepts which do and those which do not violate our finitude.

So Reason is being once more infinitized – but this occurs from two opposite directions: by either a naturalistic or a spiritualist metaphsysic. In either case, it is argued that a claim for limits is paradoxically self-refuting, as one must exceed a limit in order to know that it is absolute. In the naturalist case, it is further suggested that our post-Cantorian ability to think the mathematically infinite suggests also an ability to think the natural infinite, if it is true that mathematics is the language of nature In the spiritualist case, it is suggested that since limits cannot be shown, we must assume that a God-given soul can aspire somewhat outside their bounds. This does not at all mean, however, that such bold speculative programs can be exhaustively justified from a rational point of view. To the contrary, their best practitioners admit that a certain stance of "faith" is involved in their pursuit.

The second reason is sociological. Speculative metaphysics is not a leisurely pastime – to the contrary, it is directly linked to people's pragmatic need to direct their life by certain definite beliefs about reality. Metaphysically agnostic philosophy, one can argue, has allowed religious extremism to fill a certain void, because it fulfills a hunger that is as much for a meaningfulness of reality as for an emotional and expressive dwelling within reality. Moreover, a situation of simply formal discursive conditions for politics and formal respect for rights does not deal with the fact that certain substantive choices and views have necessarily to prevail. Hence, if one restricts reason to the formal and insists that it operates only within knowable boundaries, one will encourage entirely irrational and purely emotive political movements to take centre stage by exploiting procedurally rational norms against the intentions of those who set up those norms in the first place. This is what the Nazis did: Weimar was thoroughly "Kantian" and Habermas repeats the error of Weimar, even though he imagines that his philosophy guards against any resurgence of totalitarianism. For the culture of Weimar was notoriously characterized by a drift of negative freedom toward decadence and nihilism. Nazism at once esoterically perpetuated this drift and exoterically put an end to it.

The sharp separation of reason and faith is therefore dangerous for a politics that is "liberal" in the sense of constitutional. It implies that faith at its core is "non-rational" and beyond the reach of any sort of argument, while also implying that reason cannot really have a say on issues of crucial substantive preference. But, in reality, reason and faith are always intertwined in a beneficial way, even if this is hard to formulate theoretically. Reason has to make certain assumptions and has to trust in the reasonableness of the real – as indeed Kant himself acknowledged. Faith has continuously to think through the coherence of its own intuitions in a process that often modifies those intuitions themselves. So, if critical faith has to become a more reflective mode of feeling, then reason has always to some degree to feel its way forward. What reason at first seeks to know, it already knows obscurely, as Plato taught in the *Meno* – which is to say that it feels it: Plato says through the reach of *eros*.

The mediating role of feeling gives the lie to the Habermasian idea that one requires a content-neutral formal framework in order that arguments between apparently incommensurable positions may take place. For all arguments short of tautology have to assume an area of given agreement in a merely ad hoc fashion, and to win an argument usually means (following Socrates) that one shows someone that something he imagines he thinks contradicts something that he thinks more habitually and fundamentally. Outside a horizon of shared faith, no arguments would get off the ground, and shared faith means something like "common feeling."

IV   From Kant to Hume: The Alternative Mediation of Feeling

The Kantian agnostic notion of public space is feeling-neutral, yet this is not the only "enlightened" model to hand. Both the Scottish and the Italian Enlightenments saw the public sphere as primarily one of "sympathy."[11] Often this just meant imaginative projection or animal instinct, and this predominantly Stoic perspective tended to neglect questions of teleology or of shared "ends" and shared attitudes as to substantive human goods. Such a pluralism of emotion would seem to suggest that the play of sympathy still requires a formal regulation, or else publicly relevant sympathy must be restricted to a utilitarian concern for the maximization of sensory pleasure and the diminution of sensory pain. For this reason, the lingering Roman cast of much eighteenth-century ethical thought inevitably drifted toward subjective rights in one direction and toward utilitarianism in the other. But where this is the case, then "the feeling of sympathy" provides no real alternative to formalist neutrality save in terms of a crudely materialist reduction that would simply deny the pertinence of all faith-commitments, of whatever kind.

Here, though, one can argue that David Hume was (to some degree) an exception, and that the centrality of sympathy in his thought is somewhat guarded against a displacement in primacy by subjective right and egoistic happiness. The key to this difference is a certain marrying of sympathy with teleology. For, in the case of Hume, in the long-term wake of Benjamin Whichcote through the Earl of Shaftesbury, "sympathy" at times seems to be a self-grounding end in itself, and the sympathetic links between people to be something that reason itself cannot really grasp. While we are to "sympathize" with public "utility," the "public" is itself only composed through the reciprocal bonds of sympathy, which are irreducible to any mere "original instincts of the human mind," or, in other words, any projected egoism.[12] Hence, Hume's human "sympathy" remains (extraordinarily enough) a kind of "occult" sympathy, in continuity with the inscrutable binding powers within nature: "the coherence and apparent sympathy in all the parts of this world."[13] (By historical derivation, "sympathy" in Platonic, Stoic, and Hermetic thought meant the secret power that binds together the cosmos, the body, and human society.)[14]

One can link this with the entire nature of Hume's philosophy and suggest that our current situation is "Humean" and not Kantian, both in intellectual and sociological terms. But in order to make this claim, and fully to show how sympathy as irreducible goal is consonant with Hume's entire philosophy, one must briefly sketch out a revisionist account of the nature of this philosophy, which rescues it from the usual empiricist, egocentric, and materialistic construals.

Intellectually speaking, Hume, unlike Kant, attempted a full-blooded "experimentalist" approach to human nature and the human mind. This meant that he was prepared to account for human thinking in terms of pre-human natural processes. At the same time, he was prepared to think nominalism, with which much of modern science had long been linked, through to its very limits.

It might be thought that Hume's naturalism is in natural harmony with his nominalism. However, this turns out not to be the case. For, in order to explain human nature scientifically, he must do so in terms of "atomic" individual substances and efficient causality. Yet Hume shows that nominalism is as fatal for individual substance as it is for universals and real relations; and for efficient as it is for formal, teleological, and material cause. In this way, he turns Ockham's minimizing rationalist instrument deployed against Aristotle, against even Ockham's legacy itself. Hence, he says that there are, rationally speaking, only bundles of qualities and no "substance," and that any inherent "link" between cause and effect is just as occult and merely nominal as scholastic ideas of specific form – which had frequently been derided as obscurely tautologous (a tree is a tree because it has the form of a tree, etc.) ever since the seventeenth century.

Given this circumstance, Hume has been read in three different ways: (1) as a positivist, who reduces science to observation of constant conjuncture; (2) as someone implicitly calling for a Kantian transcendentalist solution; (3) as someone so ultramodern that he indicates a new "nocturnal," proto-Romantic entry to a traditional realist metaphysics. For this third and highly revisionary perspective, it is as if he knocked over all the furniture inside the Western intellectual house and then exited into the sunlight through a front door marked "reason," with a triumphantly complacent skeptical smirk on his face ... but then, when no one was looking, sneaked round to the back where the garden lay in shadows, and was conducted by a Jacobite servant through a back door marked "feeling," and then proceeded to put back in place at least some of the furniture he had earlier abused ...[15] In fact, on this view, Hume rescues modern scientific rationality only through linking it once more (albeit obscurely) to a traditional metaphysic by ascribing a new, ontologically disclosive role to "feeling."

The first two views assume that Hume was only a skeptical rationalist. The third claims that he advanced beyond skepticism in the name of feeling and the view that feeling not reason (reason being but a variant of feeling) is what *truly* reveals to us the real. We require politically this irreducibility of feeling if we are not once more to surrender to either a formalism of reason or a reductionism of the senses – neither of which will be hospitable to the presence of religious, or even substantively ideal, reasonings within the public realm.

Any truly attentive reading of Hume suggests strongly that the third reading is the correct one.[16] The positivist reading is false because Hume is clear that even constant conjuncture is something ineffably experienced and established according to habitual imagination and not something rationally known. This mode of empirical connection is for him in the end extra-rational. It is emotionally sensed and not *merely* "imagined," precisely because the imagination performs a mysterious work in excess of rational probability by assuming that an absolutely novel instance will fall into the same "historical" sequence of cause and effect as instances have been taken to so fall in the past: thus, we "feel" the link of cause and effect and do not merely "speculate" that what is constantly conjoined might be in some way connected.[17]

It is, of course, this sense of a "connection" that Kant elaborated into a rational a priori, and yet the Kantian rendering of Hume is also false, because there is simply no warrant to suppose that the biases of our mind are anything other than natural, or that the phenomena we know are not the things themselves – as they explicitly are for Hume. "Correlationism" in Kant between rational category and sensory information remains a mode of pre-established harmony, and the unsophisticated core of Kant's (astonishing) surface sophistication is that it is only his own variant on a speculative monadology that contradictorily permits the "banishing" of speculation.[18] This is because one requires the idea of a noumenal (monadically spiritual) realm in order first to be able to declare that phenomena do not disclose noumena ("things in themselves"), and, second, to be able to suppose that the human spirit, as noumenally self-determining beyond the sphere of natural causality, can stand outside and so perceive the "bounds" of the phenomenal and the categories supposed to apply only to the phenomenal.

Hume, by contrast, never denies the full ontological ("noumenal" as well as "phenomenal") reality of causation, substance, personal identity, or the soul:[19] he doubts them all, but in the end finds a new way to affirm them. In a Baconian tradition, he sees knowledge as to do with experience and making, but insists (in a Socratic-Platonic lineage as he indicates)[20] that what we most experience and make is ourselves. Even though he takes it that we are but part of a chain of natural causation,[21] he says that the best clue to the nature of the latter lies within our own self-experience. But within ourselves the experience of our own consecutive causal action is a matter of feeling, habit, and imagination. One might say that "we are led according to a consistent pattern to make ourselves up."

In one place in the *Treatise*, Hume indicates quite clearly that we have to assume that causality in nature is something analogous to this human process:

> I do not ascribe to the will that unintelligible necessity which is suppos'd to lie in matter. But I ascribe to matter, that intelligible quality, call it necessity or not, which the most rigorous orthodoxy must or does allow to belong to the will. I change nothing, therefore, in the receiv'd systems with regard to the will, but only with regard to material objects.[22]

In other words, Hume insists in an "intellectualist" manner that the will never exercises pure "free choice" but is always in some fashion "compelled." Yet this cannot mean that he reduces the will to determination by efficient causality, because he has already deconstructed the latter. So, even though he is arguing for a naturalistic account of willing, it is still in terms of our experience of willing that we must try to decipher causality and not vice versa. Therefore, he is a revisionist *not* with respect to orthodox psychology, but with respect to the philosophy of nature: in nature herself there must reside something analogous to "will." It follows that the primacy of feeling in Hume entails also a species of vitalism, as the *Dialogues Concerning Natural Religion* in several places indicate.[23]

This therefore reverses not only his skepticism as regards causation but also as regards constitutive relation. Reason can only make sense of individual items that are shifting and unstable but utterly isolated, and in no way intrinsically connected with anything else. The same must be true, rationally speaking, of our "impressions"; yet we "feel" certain unshakeable links between them in various ways. The feeling of association that sustains the link between cause and effect in our experience of thoughts then leads to a legitimate projection of intrinsic association also into the world of things, since we are otherwise unable to make sense of our experience of causality and the way in which its constantly conjoined elements seem to involve an emotive coinherence that is in excess of rational constant conjuncture, as already explained.[24] Hence, while the denial of internal relation lies at the heart of Hume's thought insofar as it is a merely rational empiricism, a certain "internal" (or better, "constitutive") relation *returns* within his thought insofar as it is an extra-skeptical empiricism of feeling that even points us back toward a metaphysical realism in the broad sense of affirming a structure to objective reality that is independent of our perceptions of that reality.[25] Significant in this respect is the fact that Hume declares that the crucial difference between mere fictions, apparitions, dreams, and reality is nothing other than the strength of feeling we have in the face of the real, despite the fact that every experience of the real is only conveyed by a series of impressions that we *imaginatively* put together.[26] It is as if Hume is saying that reality is simply a very convincing and continuous story that frames all the other stories because we feel it does so with an unshakeable degree of intensity. A story that we have to take to be true, like Vico's *vera narratio*.[27]

Hume, then, is saying that all thought is feeling (and reason is tempered feeling); that we must trust at least some of our most constant feelings and that there may be something "like" feeling already in pre-human nature. (This concurs with the fact that he affirms and does not at all deny "design" in nature, while seeing this as far more immanent that did the Paleyite approach.)[28] Clearly, Hume parted company with rationalism by empirically observing that reflection cannot seriously break with habit, and that even the most basic assumed stabilities (substance, the self, causation) depend upon dispositional consistencies and not upon sheer intuited "givenness." But he also began to break with empiricism by allowing (albeit in a highly reserved fashion) that, in being slaves to habit, human beings must acknowledge the workings of a natural power constituted through time that *exceeds* our capacity to observe it.[29] This is why Jacobi argued that Hume was effectively showing that all reason requires faith, and why Maine de Biran and then Félix Ravaisson developed Humean insights regarding causality and potency in a more specifically vitalist direction which eventually led variously to Bergson and Blondel.[30] Nature is a matter of sedimented habits and not laws: on this assumption, it became possible for Ravaisson to reconcile Hume with Aristotle and restore a "classical" metaphysics in terms of the view that all reality is a matter of mutually affective (passive and active) response, in which habit is both degeneration (as identical repetition) and elevation (as non-identical repetition). Ravaisson (who was close to Schelling in certain respects) in effect brought Jacobi and Biran's Humeanism together. He did so by suggesting that one can only explain how habit is fundamental even though it must be established, or why there is "a habit of contracting habits," if we invoke theological notions of grace within cosmology itself. This is because it is *theology* that, in terms of grace, thinks the paradox of "a habit at the origin." Thus, for Aquinas, grace was a "supernaturally infused habit" or *aliquod habituale donum* (ST I.II Q. 109, a. 9 resp; 110 a. 2 resp), and he subverted Aristotle by proclaiming that our only genuine, uncontaminated good, including, besides charity, also perfectly authentic justice and prudence involves, through the arrival of supernatural grace, the seeming impossibility of a habit that can "suddenly" begin and as suddenly be lost. Ravaisson deploys this model to conclude that, if all temporal, evolutionary being is habitual, then its deepest character must be that of "grace," which implies for him at once both "gift" and "beauty."[31]

With respect to Aristotelian metaphysics, there are certain indications in Hume that one can, after all, "feel" the operation of formal and final as well as of efficient causality.[32] This is a logical development of his view that efficiency has to do with a repeated pattern. For, if there is a pattern, then there is a substantively constituting form and if there is a groundless passion, then it must at least "presume" a teleological direction in order for it to be operative. Indeed, since it is our sympathies that would attune us to natural reality, and since the teleological establishment of the community of sympathy is irreducible to interest, instinct, or projected egoism, then it would appear that (as Gilles Deleuze argued in 1952) Hume thought that nature teleologically fulfilled itself in the human *civitas*.[33]

Moreover, Hume effectively re-establishes "substance" in terms of the view that infinite divisibility is not really thinkable for the feeling intellect and therefore should not be taken as real. There is no endorsement of an atomism here, much less any exaltation of "difference," as Deleuze at times argues, since we only think at all and only make sense of the world in terms of constitutive relations, despite the fact that the cold emotion of an abstracted pure reason must conclude to a strict nominalism that recognizes relations only of an accidental, external kind. Hume indicates, rather like Aristotle, how in any *genus,* in order for it to be a *genus,* we have to suppose ultimate stable constituents – as, for example, geometry *must* presuppose indivisible points and lines, even though this indivisibility is not rationally thinkable and must even be rationally negated.[34]

Within the terms of this genuinely Humean perspective (properly developed in terms of a Jacobian-Biranian hybrid), one can see how "feeling" operates as the crucial third term in two respects. First (as Bergson saw), between matter in motion and mind that experiences "meanings." It is not that mind "represents" an external world; it is rather that natural habits in us turn reflective, more intense, and more adaptable. In a footnote on the second page of the *Treatise,* Hume actually *rejects* Lockean "ideas" and his favored term "impression" for patterned or structured cognitive content is initially agnostic about the origins of these impressions.[35] They are *not* sense impressions or representations, even though they are assumed to be of sensory origin: they are rather more like "phenomena" in Husserl's sense, though without his subjectivism, since they are not sharply distinguished from external "objects." (Indeed, it was the influence of Hume which allowed Husserl to break with neo-Kantianism.)

In this context, Jerry Fodor's neo-positivist use of Hume to support a "representationalism" of the brain is completely erroneous and shamelessly deploys only the first part of the *Treatise.*[36] For Hume is *not* a skeptic about metaphysics and a dogmatician about morals. Instead, he is a skeptic concerning reason in both domains, but a trusting affirmer of feeling and "sympathy" in both domains also. Sympathy retains for him both Stoic and Platonic connotations, and we fail to note that he was a self-declared "academic skeptic" like Cicero – this means a skeptic *of the Platonic school.* A kind of incredibly apophatic Platonist, one might almost say.[37] Hence, in his account of philosophies, which is clearly *in order of merit,* Hume put skepticism at the top followed by Platonism and then Stoicism, with Epicureanism at the bottom.[38] Like Vico and Doria in Naples, he incorporates elements of Hobbes and so of Epicurus, but finally rejects this mode of materialism as "uncivil" – as too linked with a selfish individualism.[39]

This academic skepticism has its political equivalent in his "speculative Toryism" and support for the ancient if not the modern House of Stuart. Hume thought that human society only exists through the ability of monarchic or aristocratic families to combine particular with general sympathy – otherwise the range of human sympathy is too restricted to accommodate justice.[40] Hence, Hume, unlike Locke, Rousseau, or Kant, considers that the core of political society is a matter of substantive feeling – no mere formality could ever at bottom move human beings to collective action. It follows that a Humean response to Habermas would include the point that political order depends always less on any formal procedure than on a "political class," however constituted or to whatever degree dispersed – that is, a class of people able to link their personal destinies with the destiny of the whole of their society: local, national, or global.

For Hume's rejection of contract theory entails the view that any merely procedural set of norms, such as Habermas's protocols of free communication and tacit aiming toward publicly recognizable truth, provides no basis on which the necessary content of such communication and truth-proposing can arise. Equally, it provides no guarantee that human beings, normally bound within local circles of prejudice, will in fact embrace such protocols. To mend these lacunae, from a Humean perspective, one must invoke sympathy twice over. First, a shared sympathetic horizon must arise, whose substantive content will alone provide an adequate framework of binding social norms, even though it cannot be established through the formal rules of communicative action. Second, such a horizon can only emerge if a group of people (however small or large) is able imaginatively to extend their immediate sympathies toward a much larger social group. In this way, Hume – in a no doubt over-Stoicized fashion – still retained an antique and "aristocratic" virtue-perspective upon the political which Kant abandoned.

Feeling is, in the second place, a middle term between reason and faith. Hume, the defender of Church establishment, took it that the unity of interest between monarch and people has to have sacred sanction if people are really to feel its force.[41] Likewise, in his ethics, the comparison of promise as fiction to transubstantiation as fiction (he actually says that the latter is a *more* rational notion as less "warped" by the exigencies of perpetual public interest) is not meant merely skeptically.[42] Rather, by carrying the skeptical critique of religion in a proto-Nietzschean fashion through also to ethics, and to aspects of our belief in cause and substantial unity, Hume is at once chastening our all too human assumptions and yet at the same time indicating how religion as "natural" is in continuity with the rest of human natural and cultural existence. It secures our sense of the diversity, unity, order, and mystery of life in terms of the polytheistic, the monotheistic, the extra-humanly designed, and the apophatic – all of which aspects of religiosity Hume explicitly affirms.[43]

V   Feeling Against Fanaticism

It follows from the above that the Humean view that what binds us together is shared sympathy cannot possibly make any easy discriminations (à la Habermas) between what belongs to the realm of reason and what belongs to the realm of faith. For just as, in some sense, political society at its core must always be monarchic/aristocratic, so, also, religion must always be established: in Europe, we disallow public bloody sacrifice and we tend to ban scientological offers of high-cost chemical salvation not simply because we are "enlightened," but because at bottom our mode of "enlightenment" still retains a Christian coloring.

If the risk then seems to appear that fanaticism could win through the democratic process if the latter is not "transcendentally" bound to the formal use of reason, then one needs to reflect further. First, how could one ever legislate for this without in reality suppressing freedom of speech, and forever excluding those perfectly rational voices who do not accept the Kantian terms of settlement? Although Habermas talks in the voice of dry reason, he actually puts forward the outrageously provincial view that the basis for global human association forthwith must be universal acceptance of the Kantian critique of metaphysics! Quite apart from the intuitively unjust character of this proposal, how does it make pragmatic sense of the fact that Habermas can enjoy a respectful conversation with Joseph Ratzinger, even though the latter (unrepentently wedded to a pre-Kantian metaphysical synthesis of faith and reason) does not accept the only basis upon which, according to Habermas, they can be having a proper conversation.

Second, and more crucially, I have already pointed out how formalism gives substantive claims the license to be unreasonable and unaccountable, precisely because something substantial *always* rules in the end. In this way, Habermas encourages rather than guards against a dangerous positivity. Faith placed behind an unpassable sublime barrier is encouraged to be dangerous faith – as much to be fanaticism as to be a Wittgensteinian fideism or an Iris Murdoch-style agnosticism, and for just the same reason, which is that its claims have been declared to be utterly ineffable from the point of view of public, philosophical reason.

Habermas indeed allows that religious claims can be "translated" into public terms, but few religious people will accept the adequacy of such translation, since it leaves the rational aspect of specifically religious content redundant and suggests that faith makes no difference at all to the shape of genuine human action. (It is, of course, no accident that one exception here might be certain currents of German Lutheranism which reduce the religious sense to an inner feeling of assurance of extrinsic justification.) However, if religious people are not encouraged to explicate their own specific faith-based logic in the public domain, then their sense that their faith makes "all the difference" may take on a virulently fideistic and fundamentalist form.

Moreover, if "translation" means merely into the terms of the norms governing fair communicative discourse, this translation must always mean the loss of substantive "ethical" content as well as of religiosity. And it remains patronizing to both religious *and* secular people to say that the only humanly "shareable" aspect of religious truths must be a non-religious one – as if, for example, an agnostic could have *no sense whatsoever* of the specific mode of solidarity generated by the Eucharist and the idea of "the body of Christ." It is simply not the case that people of other faiths or of none can only embrace the insights of, say, Judaism, in a purely non-religious guise. This disallows the fact that they might well allow certain intimations of transcendence to be involved in their act of partial appropriation.

For to define reason quite apart from faith is to place it also quite apart from feeling, since it can be convincingly argued after Hume that reason, as much as faith, arises only as a specific variant upon the experience of feeling which is always to do with reciprocal recognition of an "other." If this is the case, then reason partakes of the obscurity as well as the clarity that is always involved in any experience of emotion. The latter presents itself as a horizon to be explored and as something which has to be reflexively sifted in terms of how far it is to be trusted. Reason cannot therefore escape being situated within a prospective horizon; nor be exempted from the requirements of trust and risk that require a certain exercise of faith, as Jacobi argued. Because discursiveness is always inextricably bound up with emotions, and is not austerely trapped within a series of apprehensible procedural criteria (Habermas cleaves all too closely to Weber here), there can be *partial* degrees of assent as to religious perspectives: for example, in terms of the feeling that "the good" is rather more than a mere human fiction. Many people both feel and articulate a sense inherited from both Platonic and biblical tradition that "goodness" is a reality not reducible to the natural, and is yet not simply another "thing" in the way that a stone or a building is a thing. At the same time, they draw back (inconsistently or otherwise) from the full affirmation of a transcendent or supernatural realm.

Of course, the kind of Humean perspective which I am suggesting nonetheless *can* favor naturalism as much as it can favor religion. The habituated and the vital might be sheerly immanent, somehow not requiring grace. This means that, if transcendentalism is both false and dangerous, that we must now accept that the public space is one of a clash of rival metaphysics and not one of polite agnostic neutrality and humanism undergirded by transcendental philosophy. We live now in the era of Dawkins versus Ratzinger, not of agnostics and clerics equally savoring the novels of Iris Murdoch; nor of a continued Teutonic compromise (ever since Kant and Hegel) between the legacy of the French Revolution and the spirit of Christianity.

However, this does not condemn us to a future of unmediated violence, and I have already offered arguments as to why the return of metaphysics can temper violence on the side of religion, since it requires the worldviews of faith also to express themselves as worldviews of reason – a possibility that Habermas *dangerously* disallows. But the reason for optimism is also because the shared horizon of feeling with its inherent fluidity permits of many substantive shared outlooks and actually fosters *less* conflict than a situation where we will endlessly debate (as in the history of the United States) whether formal barriers between faith and reason have been transgressed or not.[44] In the face of the arrival in the West of Islam, we now see far more clearly how our shared modern Western ethos is both an extension of a Christian ethos and a radical departure from it. The horror of Muslim critics of the West is often a horror at both these aspects. Thus, we cannot have a genuine debate with Islam unless we allow the porosity of faith and reason and try to assess the ways in which the content of Islamic faith and reason both is and is not compatible with that of Western faith and reason, or ways in which it might become more so.

VI　The Elevation of the Natural

To these sociological considerations one can add psychological ones. Here also, I would argue that Habermas's strictures on both naturalism and metaphysics are somewhat misplaced, and that both can offer a better barrier against terror than the humanistic critical philosophy which he persists in promoting.

In certain ways (going completely counter to Habermas and his Munich Jesuit interlocutors), naturalism is less problematic for religion than is transcendentalism. For the a priori categories of understanding can in principle be themselves psychologized with the advance of brain science – especially if they have been *already* pragmatized, as by Rawls or Habermas.[45] The norms of communicative action can thereby be reduced to evolutionary purposiveness. All that would then hold out against such reduction is the issue of freedom: the freedom of human discourse to construct the language that denies even the force of the evidence that the human person is predetermined; the freedom of the "last experimenter" upon the human brain whose own decision to experiment can never be neurologically explained without an infinite series of experiments being carried out. These arguments defending freedom are valid, but all they defend is a freedom to experiment or a bare freedom to refuse the force of the evidence (the freedom of the crank which nonetheless oddly auto-validates his crankiness) without any practical upshot that would incarnate freedom itself as something that makes a real difference in the "real" realm of matter in motion.

Therefore, no truly substantive freedom, linked to the reality of a wide range of human emotional and ethical categories is here established. This is because rationalism, of which transcendentalism is a mode, is unable to attribute any teleology to the will other than bare self-assertion. No choosing, outside the range of formal reason, can be defined by that reason as anything other than mere subjective predilection. Thus, in relation to neural science, all it can do is indicate a bare and contentless transcendence of the brain by a supposed human mind.

As to both formal and instrumental reasons themselves, precisely because they can be publicly and exhaustively expressed in linguistic structures, they are somewhat subject to a reductionist view as regards consciousness, because we could imagine all instrumental and cooperative uses of reason as taking place unconsciously. It is at this point that the quasi-transcendental status of governing pragmatic norms (like Habermas's rules for a perfect speech community, or Rawls's "neutral" principles of justice derived from the supposition of the "veil of ignorance") slide back toward mere empirical generalization, in such a way that they no longer protect the dignity of human freedom as such, and become instead mere utilitarian accounts of how to coordinate the clash of inevitably differing animal perspectives. Hence, within the bounds of mere rationalism one can propose, with more or less plausibility, that consciousness is mere epiphenomenon or even, in some sense, illusion.

If the quasi-spiritualism of the transcendental approach is subject to such reduction, then conversely it is possible for naturalism to undergo a perfectly coherent elevation. For, if we acknowledge "feelings" in Hume's sense as always accompanying "impressions" and supplying them with their relative weight and significance, then we do not have any "bare consciousness" with which one could possibly dispense – in the way that a camera does not need to be conscious in order to take a picture. When emotion is brought into consideration, then consciousness is always rather a "modification of consciousness" in such a way that its *qualia* belong to a "language" (external as well as internal) that is entirely incommensurable with the discourse of firing neurons. Even the bare experience of consciousness is thus incommensurable,[46] but in the case of feelings one has more than an irreducible spectator, but rather an entirely irreducible realm of "actors" who are emotionally inflected and active states of mind which find expression in the evaluative register of human discourse.

So far was Hume from pointing in the direction of the reduction of mind to brain that he actually says that purely physical explanations of feelings should *only* be invoked when these feelings are pathological.[47] This means that he sustained not only the soul, but also a certain teleology of the soul. Even though he could give no rational defense of subjective unity, his affirmation of this inexplicable unity in terms of feeling involves far more of a narrative and teleological register than the Cartesian or the Kantian model of self-awareness.[48] Indeed, for Hume, we make ourselves up as fictions, but since he denies the reality of any purely self-sustained will, it follows that for him we are obscurely compelled within our very own fictioning toward certain ends, such that we are also "made up" by forces not under our command. Nor is freedom here quite denied, because will is for Hume but a more intense manifestation of the adaptability of natural habit which at bottom he appears to see as a kind of spontaneity.[49]

Feelings, for Hume, are in some sense, and to a crucial degree, trustworthy: we can distill true from false feeling through long processes of experience, comparison, interacting, and rational analysis – which is yet itself for Hume but a further feeling about feeling, since he sees ideas as merely reflectively doubled impressions, intensifying their crucially accompanying emotions.[50] And as trustworthy, we can say, they are therefore not reducible to brain-processes. But this does not mean that they are "yet more interior" than the brain itself. To the contrary, since feelings are for Hume prior to identity – identity being a kind of patterning of feelings – they at first impinge from "without," or rather they impinge as our insertion within the very stream of passing reality.

In this way, Hume concurs in advance with the views of modern philosophers who claim that we think with our bodies and even our whole natural and social environment rather than with our brains alone.[51] For to imagine, with Fodor, that we think only with our brains, is to remain the victim of the Lockean "mirror of nature." It is to think of the brain as a repository of representing ideas or "evidences" of things, just as Locke thought of the mind as "taking pictures" of things rather in the way that the eye reflects visible realities. This is oddly to "anthropomorphize" the brain, which is only a physical organ! All the brain does is encode signals from the senses and the body in neurological connections. Hence, the reason why researchers discover that there is never any perfectly predictable one-to-one correlation between thoughts and observably firing neurons, and that the networks of neurons seem spontaneously to re-order themselves in parallel to thoughts, is because what goes on in the brain is *not* the only, or even the prime, material instantiation of thinking. For if thoughts as feelings and reflected feelings are in any sense real, the brain can only be the *occasion* for the arising of these things which we should more properly say are caused by our entire insertion in our environment and our active reception of this environment – just as every physical reality constitutes a "prehensive" active reception of its temporal antecedents and spatial surroundings.[52] Because neither the brain nor the mind primarily "mirrors," we can see how the crucial aspect of thought is to do with "feeling" other realities in such a way that one is both responding to them and asserting oneself in relation to them – in terms of a rather more ecstatically inflected version of Spinoza's *Conatus*. Thought is reciprocal – it establishes a real relation, precisely because it is a species of feeling.

And far from this being an "irrational" conclusion, it is in fact what alone saves metaphysical realism, and a realist basis for science. For in terms of pure reason it is impossible, as Hume saw, to understand why there are regular links within nature, and hence one will tend to become skeptical about their reality. Moreover, the reduction of the mind to brain processes must invite skepticism as to whether the brain truly mirrors anything objective, and skepticism as to the very existence of reason itself or the rationality of reality, once reason has been so denatured that one no longer considers it to be a spiritual category.

It is perfectly possible and indeed more logical for naturalism to entertain the view that we do not think merely with our brains but also with our bodies and with our environment. However, if consciousness somehow "reaches out to things" in this rather Aristotelian way, then does one not have to speak of some sort of "spiritual exchange" between action and response taking place, however rooted this may be in materiality? Is not my thinking the tree as the tree where the tree is, also my being really moved by the tree in an ontological dimension of emotion in which the tree is situated alongside myself? Would not this be the precondition of the idea that meaning is "out there" in things, as John McDowell has half-suggested?[53] Otherwise, one would have to espouse the "direct realism" of the Francisan Peter John Olivi as revived by Thomas Reid: but, as explicitly with Reid, this involves a vicious mode of correlationism that necessitates some sort of pre-established harmony. Actually, Hume is curiously nearer to Aristotle, as Ravaisson eventually (in effect) realized: his "feelings" which seem to migrate from things in order to shape "selves" can, not implausibly, be seen to play in a more affective mode the rational role of Aristotelian species which is abstracted from the hylomorphic compound to become pure form within human cognition.[54]

This defense of the "outwardness" of cognition and meaning in terms of the priority of feeling can also readily concur with the advocacy of panpsychism by various recent analytic philosophers.[55] If other things besides ourselves belong within the space of meaning, then, in order to avoid idealism, this will be because something already approximating to mutual feeling (without necessarily being fully conscious as we experience consciousness) exists within the physical world and is indeed its most primary ontological characteristic – responsible for shaping the sedimented habits that then constitute the regular shape of the universe, and with which human "culture" is in essential continuity. This "culture" *is* our nature, because the more variegated and yet steadier character of human habit is only possible through an equally heightened consistency of habit that is both the manifestation of, and the condition of possibility for, the exercise of "free will." Both the variety and the consistency are but an intensification of the very nature of habit that one can take to be the heart of the natural order.

In the light of these considerations, one can see how the clash of naturalistic and religious visions is a clash that is amply capable of mediation. For the fact is that *a certain Enlightenment* (and indeed the most sophisticated and crucial one; the one that engendered political economy) – however ultimately unsatisfactory it may be from a Christian perspective – was already concerned to restore that supra-political space that had been "the Church" under the new name of "civil society." And its goal of binding together in "sympathy" was at least a distorted echo of the earlier binding together in charity (eschewing any merely unilateral gesture). Once one has grasped this double point, one can then see that Habermas's alternative between the postmetaphysical and the metaphysical, and between the modern secular and the postmodern "freely theocratic,"[56] is not an exclusive one after all, even for genuinely modern times. For the idea of a "community of feeling," extended from society to nature and back to society, is both a Christian and a post-Christian one. Indeed, it is our most crucial European legacy – which lies in essential continuity with the trajectory of Plato, Aristotle, Augustine, and Aquinas, rather than the deviant path of Scotus, Luther, and Kant – which we must now both defend and elaborate.

Reply to My Critics

JÜRGEN HABERMAS (TRANSLATED BY CIARAN CRONIN)

I am indebted to the editors, Craig Calhoun, Eduardo Mendieta, and Jonathan VanAntwerpen, for their initiative in inviting a select group of outstanding colleagues to engage in an informed discussion of my scattered works on *Postmetaphysical Thinking and Religion*. The results of a vibrant conference are helpful to me as an author because the interesting objections and proposals, coming in the midst of my work on a pertinent project, confront me with new ideas, alert me to over-hasty assumptions, and force me to clarify my thoughts. On the other hand, the fortunate circumstance that a birthday with a zero provided an occasion for discussing ideas *that are still in flux* also has a drawback. The participants had to refer to a position that is not yet sufficiently developed. Thus, the need for explanation, which I would like to meet as far as is possible within the scope of a brief response, is entirely my responsibility. I owe a major debt of gratitude to my colleagues for their attentiveness and their patient reading, and above all for their (in certain cases renewed) willingness to engage in a detailed debate. The sequence in which I present my responses is a reflection of the need to impose a certain systematic order on the different objections. The length of a reply reflects the opportunity that the corresponding objections present for clarifying my thoughts, not the importance that I attach to individual contributions.

I "Stages" of Religious Development

The contemporary developments that have provoked a two-decades-long controversy over the relation between religion and social modernization are not the focus of, though they are an important stimulus for, my renewed engagement with the prominence currently enjoyed by religious movements and traditions. José Casanova is among the most inventive among those sociologists who from an early date argued forcefully for revising the hypothesis, long dominant in the discipline (and to which I at the time also adhered), that there is a zero-sum relation between the progressive modernization of society and the continued viability of religious communities. I find his theses, which he recapitulates here, as impressive as his responses to critics. But I lack the expertise to offer more than this impression of this learned dispute.

I use the expression "postsecular" as a sociological description of a shift in consciousness in largely secularized or "unchurched" societies that by now have come to terms with the continued existence of religious communities, and with the influence of religious voices both in the national public sphere and on the global political stage. In the present context, Casanova is not so much concerned with the empirical claim that the secularistic self-understanding is on the wane in such societies. He is more interested in the empirical refutation of the secularistic conception as such and denies that religious convictions and practices are essentially expressions of a historically obsolete stage of consciousness. He also finds me suspect in this respect. For he understands my philosophical use of the concept "postmetaphysical" as an attempt to justify a form of secular thought, which, even though it rejects naturalistic reductions of the human mind and its cultural objectifications, nevertheless refuses to recognize religion as a contemporary intellectual formation. This misunderstanding can be explained by the fact that José Casanova is critical of the "consciousness of stages" (*Stadienbewusstsein*) that *also* finds expression in secularistic consciousness. But not *every* attempt to uncover learning processes and advances or "stages" in the genealogy of worldviews leads *eo ipso* to a questionable de-valuation of religious forms of thought.

For me, whether religious communities will remain viable in the future is an open question, and in this regard I find Casanova's extrapolations, presented under the heading of "global secularizations," entirely plausible.[1] In my view, those religious interpretations of the self and the world that have adapted to modern social and epistemological conditions[2] have an equal claim to recognition in the discourse of modernity to the competing approaches of postmetaphysical thinking. Religious traditions differ from philosophy in their mode of belief and their way of justifying taking-to-be-true, but above all in the stabilizing anchoring of faith in the ritual practices of a religious community. It is precisely the historical simultaneity of the forms of secular thought and of religious consciousness, which have now diverged into polar opposites, that leads me to explore the shared genealogy of postmetaphysical thinking and the major world religions. For the self-referential question about how we as human beings should understand ourselves continues to set philosophy apart from the objectifying sciences.

I want to mention at least why I take an evolutionary perspective in terms of "stages" in the development of worldviews to be fruitful. In Casanova's view, contingent changes in the external "conditions of faith" suffice to explain historical thresholds such as the emergence of the major world religions in the Axial Age or that shift in the religious self-perception of European societies that Taylor locates in the Reformation era. I do not believe, however, that the structural transformation of religious worldviews and of the corresponding ritual practices can be explained entirely in terms of *accommodations to changed social environments*. They can be traced back also, and perhaps in the first instance, to *internal* learning processes that respond to cognitive challenges while being triggered by social upheavals. At the turn to the third millennium of the pre-Christian era, literate cultures emerged within the first state-organized societies and put the oral traditions of tribal origin under considerable pressure to change.[3] The organization of religious worship became the preserve of the state and was made to serve the legitimation of royal rule. At the same time, the mythical narratives were brought into conformity with the political hierarchies in such a way that the centralized pantheons of the gods mirrored political reality. In spite of the pressure that these profound ruptures in social development exerted on traditional myths and tribal rituals, neither the cognitive structure of mythical worldviews nor the magical mode of thought and ritual underwent significant change during the subsequent two millennia.

It was only the well-known metaphysical worldviews and world religions, which arose around the middle of the first millennium in China and the Indus Valley and in Israel and Greece, that made the breakthrough to a transcendent point of view, whether in the guise of a monotheistic deity or of a cosmic law. This cognitive advance (to which Robert N. Bellah has devoted a comprehensive study)[4] cannot be adequately explained in terms of an accommodation to changes in the social conditions under which religious communities deal with forces of salvation and perdition (*Mächte des Heils und Unheils*). The new worldviews instead represent productive answers to cognitive challenges. Only the moralization of "*Heil*" and "*Unheil*," propitious and unpropitious forces, which had hitherto appeared *within* the world, into a God or godhead who *transcends* the world as a whole could satisfy the minds of prophets, monks, hermits, and wise teachers whose moral consciousness was revolting against the irresponsibility of capricious gods. They had in the meantime developed new moral sensibilities and standards in the face of the suffering of the broader population from the repressive and belligerent authorities in the ancient empires. At the time, a historical consciousness and a reflexive approach to texts had evolved within the educated classes of the first literate civilizations. These intellectuals had also accumulated technical and organizational expertise as well as mathematical, astronomical, and medical knowledge. This mundane knowledge inevitably came into conflict with mythical explanations and magical practices. The cognitive dissonances could be resolved only within the more encompassing theological or cosmological conceptual framework of one or the other of the Axial Age worldviews. Moreover, the sublimation of the sacred into a transcendent power went hand-in-hand with distinct paths to salvation, which in turn involved an ethical reinterpretation of the traditional rites and the abolition (or later on the inversion)[5] of the magical meaning of sacrifice.

With his insightful remarks on conceptual history, José Casanova traces the Occidental path taken by the subsequent development through which Pauline Christianity entered into a symbiosis with Greek philosophy during the Roman Empire. I found only one aspect of his terminological clarification of the expression "secular" problematic. In reference to the late Roman imperial period, when the majority of the population continued to make sacrifices at the numerous altars to their deities, while the Christian minority refused to observe the official political rites that were binding for all, Casanova describes their perception of each other as follows: "The Christian sacred was the pagan profane and vice versa." Aside from the fact that those who had a Greek education and who as Epicureans or (as in Cicero's case) Stoics made fun of the popular religion, constituted a third party,[6] that description implies a symmetry between Christians and pagans that did not exist. The Christian category of "heathenism" not only reflected a rejection of "idolatry" and polytheism; it betrayed the radical repudiation of a concretistic mode of thought that in the religious domain, too, remained fixated on natural events in the world. On the other hand, for the pious worshipers of the Roman gods it was utterly incomprehensible why the God of the Jews and Christians should not be identified with Jupiter, just as the other Oriental high gods were taken to be an equivalent for Zeus.[7] This asymmetry is an example of the cognitive transformation undergone by the mode of faith and by devotional practice in response to cognitive challenges that cannot be adequately explained in terms of *changed social conditions of belief*. It is the Christians themselves who exhibited something akin to a consciousness of stages by comparison with the "heathens." Perhaps the dubious sense of superiority felt by secularists toward religious faith even represents a continuation of the attitude of the early Christians toward paganism. In order to criticize this stance, however, one need neither deny nor play down the importance of stages in the development of religious consciousness.

Along the Western path of religious development, the transition to modernity constitutes a similar juncture to the Axial Age. Here, too, the internal dynamic of knowledge played an important role. For, in the High Middle Ages, the Church and theology set off a legal development with the "papal revolution" in canon law,[8] and a scientific development with the "nominalistic revolution"[9] that escaped their control and in the end exploded the framework of both Christian natural law and Aristotelian natural philosophy. With the stubborn moral orientation of the modern legal system and the stubborn empirical orientation of the modern sciences, profane forms of knowledge developed that reacted back on their theological and metaphysical origins. At first sight, it seems as though the autonomy of morality, rational law, and modern science, and the secularization of political authority triumphed with the philosophical assault on the waning authority of the Church and of religion in general. On a closer inspection, however, these complex developments involved just as many cognitive challenges for the secular philosophical as for the theological side. It is certainly true that theology gradually broke the connection between the message of redemption and the cosmological worldview of the Greeks and absorbed the results of the philological critique of biblical sources, while the Church had to learn to make its peace with the secularized constitutional state. But philosophy underwent an equally profound transformation when it entered into an alliance with the sciences and the secular state. For its part, it had to revise the metaphysical heritage in the light of an all-pervasive fallibilism and it had to distance itself from the "strong" theoretical claims of the teleological view of Greek metaphysics.

The religious consciousness that "reformed" itself ("reformed," that is, in a non-confessional sense) and the postmetaphysical thinking that developed a "critique of reason" (in both senses of the genitive case) without becoming defeatist (see *KV*, "Introduction") are in the final analysis *complementary* answers to *the same* cognitive challenges of the Enlightenment, which was nourished by secular sources of knowledge. This complementarity establishes a contemporaneity between the two intellectual formations that excludes a secularistic devaluation of religion as long as theology is able to understand itself as the interpretation of a vital faith rooted in some form of worship of a religious community. For in this way it maintains the connection to an archaic source of social solidarity under modern social conditions to which secular thought no longer has access.

For secularly minded individuals like ourselves, only aesthetic experience retains trace elements from this largely dried-up source. On the other hand, postmetaphysical thinking can claim the advantage that it operates in a universe of the unrestricted quest for justification *that is equally open to all*. Understood in this way, postmetaphysical thinking does not fit the phenomenologically rich, but insufficiently differentiated, picture of a philosophical understanding of the self and the world "devoid of transcendence" that Charles Taylor sketches under the heading of the *immanent frame*. With the moral law, Kant had already explicated a moral point of view that ties the judgments of practical reason to a *transcendence from within*.[10] The theory of communicative action de-transcendentalizes the Kantian ideas of reason when it explains the success of linguistic communication in terms of the discursive redemption of validity claims; these claims, although they are raised locally, point to a *context-transcending* validity, however.[11] I am convinced that human forms of civilized social life cannot be maintained without this kind of self-transcendence that creates a distance from anything occurring within the world.

II   Why a Secular Translation of Religious Potentials at all?

María Herrera Lima is so well acquainted with my work and develops such a judicious and multifaceted critique that I will be able address only a couple of aspects here. Moreover, her remarks on social evolution and on the legacies that we discuss under the heading of "secularization" concern a topic to which I will return in the commentaries on other contributions.[12] I, too, prefer to use the expression "profane" in a neutral sense to refer to the "worldly," that is, non-religious, spheres of life, for the simple reason that the development of religious worldviews was repeatedly driven forward by the assimilation of pragmatic knowledge. Here, I must confine my remarks to the issue raised by María Herrera Lima with the wonderful quotation from Adorno, which affords me an opportunity to clarify the underlying issue. Adorno's ambiguous formulation that "Nothing of theological content will persist without being transformed; every content will have to put itself to the test of migrating into the realm of the secular, the profane"[13] (see note 1 in Herrera's chapter) touches on several issues. One is whether religion "survives"; another is whether from religious traditions a semantic substance can be released and acquire independent significance for the social integration of democratic societies as such. Without being able to make predictions, I assume:

- that under the premises of postmetaphysical thinking, we have no reason to deny the possibility of a *continued* "migration of theological contents into the secular, the profane"; and
- that it depends on our (admittedly tentative, empirically more strongly or weakly supported) diagnoses of the present whether we regard such a transformative assimilation or translation as desirable.

The first part of this statement presupposes a Hegelian perspective on the history of philosophy, albeit a deflationary one corrected in the light of Jaspers's concept of the Axial Age. We have to be able to draw on past examples of the migration of theological contents into profane cultural domains. However, the source of María Herrera Lima's misgivings is more the substance of the claim. If I am not mistaken, she interprets Charles Taylor's description of the state of religious consciousness in our secular age[14] as asserting that modernity only encounters itself in what appears as "the other" (although it has in fact long since been assimilated). But if faith had also become a mere option in the wake of the expressivist turn "from obedience to pleasure," there would be no reason to assume that *not yet exhausted* semantic potentials remain valid in such assimilated religious communities. I certainly cannot contribute much to the empirical assessment of the relevant phenomena. Yet the impact that the most recent stage of the "individualization" of religiosity has, according to María Herrera Lima, on the evaporation of religious substance will be relativized if we choose a somewhat broader historical horizon.

The differentiation in the development of religion into the public worship of the gods, on the one hand, and the privileged relation of individuals to particular deities, on the other, can be traced back to the era of the Babylonian and Assyrian Empires and to ancient Egypt. The next stage of individualization is reflected in the moralization of the sacred and in the corresponding routes to salvation of the Axial Age religions. Finally, a further advance in the subjectivization of piety was accomplished in the West by Protestantism, especially by the Pietist movements from the end of the eighteenth century onwards. Thus, when it comes to an evaluation of the "new" kind of de-institutionalized religiosity, it is difficult to distinguish between a continuation of this trend, and thus a deepening and spiritualization of religiosity, and the opposite, trivializing trend toward mere self-realization and innerworldly "human flourishing." María Herrera Lima reserves the term "internal secularization" for this trend toward a self-centered ethos. Only by sufficiently differentiating between these trends and measuring their relative weights could one gauge María Herrera Lima's objection that the religious potentials are "used up," as it were. If this assumption were correct, religious tradition would forfeit precisely the solidarity-founding element of a communal practice of religious worship that sets it apart from all other cultural formations in the modern era. A religion that had lost the capacity to organize the encounter with the sacred in ritual forms and survived only in the fleeting shape of religiosity[15] would be indistinguishable from other ethical forms of life. So far, I can see no convincing evidence for a direct development in this direction.

More interesting is the doubt about the second part of the above statement. Even assuming that religious traditions contain buried semantic contents that, in the modern age, have not yet been absorbed by critical reasoning on crises, by conceptions of moral universalism, and by various ethical interpretations of autonomy, ego-identity, individuation, and so on, why should we, as secular members of contemporary societies, take any interest in this heritage at all? The general diagnosis of the times, according to which the resources of social solidarity are drying up in tandem with the accelerated functional differentiation and increasing autonomy of social subsystems, is far from providing new and startling insights. This diagnosis is as old as the rise of sociology. The associated suspicion has motivated programs in social theory from Émile Durkheim and Max Weber up to Talcott Parsons, and definitely needs to be qualified in ways that I cannot address in the present context. This much seems plausible, however: the systemic problems of the emerging multicultural world society, with its intranational upheavals and international conflicts, have not yet been mastered. For the time being, they outstrip the integration and steering capacities of the nation-states and especially the established forms of cooperation in democratic countries, and thus suggest that an old topic has acquired renewed relevance. Moreover, history teaches that in modern societies only social movements bring the relevance of new challenges to the attention of a broader public. They force new issues on to the political agenda and implicitly shift the parameters of the range of values defining the spectrum of what can be perceived as topics that call for political treatment. As not only the first half of the twentieth century demonstrates, social movements are certainly ambivalent; but new normative patterns do not emerge without the pressure for innovation that they exert either. Where did their motivations come from? Looking back over the century of the progressive and socialist movements to which Western countries ultimately owe the containment of class conflicts by the welfare state, authors like Norman Birnbaum discover the *unacknowledged* motivating role played by a religious socialization that was still taken for granted at the time.[16]

Even in highly individualized societies that primarily reward the economic success, opportunistic competition for power, and self-realization – and thus the egocentric mindsets – of their "achievers" and consumers, most children have the good fortune to grow up in families in which they acquire a finely tuned moral sensibility. María Herrera Lima correctly observes that, in moral matters, religious citizens behave no differently from members of non-religious groups. But the question that interests me is not situated at the level of actions and their motives. At the level of cultural resources, the normative self-understanding of modernity is expressed primarily in the scientific orientation to truth, in the egalitarian universalism of law and morality, and in the autonomy of art and criticism. The question I want to ask is the following: is the potential of this admirable and, let's hope, resilient Enlightenment culture sufficient under conditions of rapidly increasing social complexity to motivate the kind of collective action, of action *in social solidarity*, which is required in times of crisis for the formation of social movements?

I am far from being able to answer this question, but I do have doubts. María Herrera Lima is quite right to focus on this, but she does not address exactly the point I have in mind. Assuming that the Kantian ethics of duty (however this is interpreted) reconstructs the intuitive kernel of conceptions of political justice that are justified "from reason alone," and thus that it captures what we can legally and morally expect from each other in terms of self-criticism and understanding in cases of conflict, then the *political* deficiency of that kind of individualistic approach toward rational morality becomes apparent.[17] We should not confuse this with a general deficiency in motivation. In an attempt to avoid this error, I would first like to distinguish the two deficiencies more clearly, beginning with the *motivational deficiency* usually bemoaned by critics of Kant.

Ideally, a person who acts responsibly is aware that she is situated within a culturally circumscribed "space of reasons" and that she should be equally receptive to reasons *pro* and *contra*: she should form her practical judgment by weighing up relevant reasons (in the moral case, those based on universalizable interests). Then the judging person must *make her own* the reason that tips the scales in cognitive terms. If the will is to be determined by reasons, the volitional element of agency must be added. "I could have acted otherwise," but it is "up to me" whether I act on the better reasons. Because Kant had rather too much confidence in the motivational force of good reasons and attached rather too little importance to the volitional moment of making good reasons one's own, the deontological approach is exposed to the objection that rational will-formation "lacks the power to motivate." I am not at all convinced by this objection. The role of philosophy is to explain what it means to examine something from the moral point of view. But it cannot take responsibility for the cultural traditions and processes of socialization, or for the institutions, that must *anchor* the moral point of view in the hearts of acting subjects.

The *political deficiency* I have in mind is rather a consequence of the individualistic orientation of all of modern ethics. There are good reasons why rational morality only recognizes duties that are addressed to the conscience of the individual person and require him or her to act responsibly. In a well-ordered democratic polity, this orientation to duties is completely sufficient as long as it is a matter of routinely responding to problems through reforms. But in times of crisis, when the existing institutions and procedures are no longer able to cope with the pressure of problems, the parameters of the established range of values must first undergo a change.[18] Achieving this calls for collective action in Hannah Arendt's sense, namely, joint action that gives rise to communicative power. An ethics of justice is not tailored to this kind of solidary action, however; thus, it cannot make solidarity per se into a duty, but can only hope that solidarity will arise as a consequence of individuals fulfilling their duties. I don't want to be misunderstood on this subtle point: there are good reasons why rational morality appeals only to the subjective mind of the individual and to the capacity to bind one's will by moral insight; no rational morality can *extend* this appeal to pluralistic collectivities as such, that is, to collectivities composed of individuals who must remain capable of taking independent "yes" or "no" stances.

To be sure, with every supposedly valid moral norm we associate the presupposition of rational consensus that could be achieved among all of the potential addressees of that norm; but the act of making good reasons one's own, that is, the moment of moral agency, could be *socialized* only at the cost of the autonomy of the individual. Interestingly, the practice of religious communities bridges this *fault line of the individual facilitation* of solidarity in advance through the shared faith in the promise of a "*redemptive*" or "*liberating*" justice. Since the Axial Age, this faith has found expression in religious traditions and in corresponding practices of encountering the sacred. This additional dimension of justice must not be confused with the eudemonistic dimension of an ethics of the good or the good life. The redemptive moment of the impending kingdom of God, or the liberating moment of release from the cycle of rebirths, is not exhausted in individual happiness; rather, *against the background of a widespread awareness of crisis*, it acquires the significance of a collective fate that concerns human beings as such. In this regard, the sense of crisis was more the triggering condition than itself the force for social integration.

Under the heading of "Progress versus Providence," Karl Löwith interpreted the philosophies of history of the Enlightenment and the nineteenth century as attempts to appropriate the religious way of dealing with crises in secular terms.[19] These speculations, including the underlying assumptions of the Marxist philosophy of history, have long since been exposed as a transposition of the teleology of traditional natural law out of the natural sphere into the dimension of history. And there can be no doubt about the rather ambivalent political potential of this approach. However, this has not dissuaded contemporary philosophers, for example, Jacques Derrida, from attempting to recuperate the religious motif of "critique and crisis" at a different level of reflection.[20] Taken literally, Derrida's proposal for a "fiduciary administration" of religious contents by a "reflected faith" is a contemporary version of the old idea of a "religion of reason" on which the numerous "positive" religious traditions are supposed to converge. By contrast, Adorno's proposition that any theological content that is to achieve universal acceptability in modern pluralist societies "must migrate into the secular, the profane" calls for strict observance of the boundary between the discourses of faith and knowledge (*BNR*, 209–47, esp. 243ff.). I can reassure María Herrera Lima that, from a postmetaphysical point of view, a "translation" can by no means be purchased at the cost of returning to the unity of a "substantive" concept of a reason that is embodied in history or nature. And I regard it as an open question whether the political deficiency of rational morality in fact *can* be counterbalanced by a continuation of the philosophical appropriation of unexhausted religious contents.

III The "Secularization Debate" of the Humanities in Postwar Germany

Under the heading of "Political Theology" to which Carl Schmitt lent currency, María Pía Lara takes up a topic that recalls the historical connection between religion and politics. This tradition gave rise to the strong concept of "the" political that certain contemporary postmodern theorists, following Claude Lefort, contrast with constitutional "politics" and the "policies" pursued by the actors within the "political system."[21] The dissolution of the symbiosis between religion and politics by the secularization of political authority set this religiously connoted concept free, as it were, for a quite different constellation. Today, the term is used in connection with Hannah Arendt's concept of communicative power to refer to those spontaneous and inspiring countercurrents that emerge, in opposition to a highly bureaucratized politics, within civil society and the political public sphere. The political-theological heritage of the concept raises the question of the religious traces that "the" political has left behind in the postsecular society. I do not want to take up this issue here once again.[22] María Pía Lara mainly addresses a debate that touches on Carl Schmitt's theory of the "transposition" of theological concepts into concepts of modern political theory, but basically concerns another topic, namely, the self-interpretation of Western modernity in relation to ancient European traditions, whether Greek or Christian. This controversy does not concern how "secularization" is understood in social theory; it focuses on the contribution of the humanities to the question of whether monotheism has bequeathed anything at all to modern thought, and if so what. This controversy discussed by María Pía Lara provides a suitable backdrop for a rough sketch of my own interpretation of these legacies.

Karl Löwith (1897–1973) initiated the debate with the first German edition of his work *Meaning in History* (1949), which was published in 1953 under the title *Weltgeschichte und Heilsgeschehen* – one of the most influential books for my generation. Carl Schmitt (1888–1985) had published his *Politische Theologie* already in 1922, but with his *Politische Theologie II* in 1970 he garnered renewed attention for a position he continued to develop during the 1920s and 1930s. Both authors dramatized the interpretation of modernity as a history of decline from a perspective they shared with conservative thinkers of the same generation, such as Leo Strauss and Martin Heidegger. For all of them, "secularization" was a pejorative term – though, of course, this was all that they shared (quite apart from their sharply contrasting political biographies). The diagnoses of the present offered by Karl Löwith, the emigrant, and by Carl Schmitt, the Führer's "crown jurist," focus attention on different periods in the history of ideas from different perspectives.

Löwith regards the kind of historical thinking that began with the eschatological thought of Judaism and became secularized, via Christian world-ages speculation, in the Enlightenment philosophies of history, on the whole as a calamitous deviation from the proper cosmological thought of classical Greece. On this interpretation, the very notion of progress exposes those secularized versions of the history of salvation in general as the fatal turn to the erroneous historical consciousness of the modern mind. It is not secularization as such that points the development in the wrong direction; but secularization first reveals the dire consequences of the monotheistic belief in a "God in history." By comparison, "secularization" is something more than a mere catalyst for the committed Catholic Carl Schmitt. For him, the expression acquires its pejorative connotation from the unjust expropriation of the legal power of the Christian ruler by the revolutionary forces of the liberal bourgeoisie and socialism. From the perspective of the history of salvation adopted by political theology, the Roman-Christian imperial rule since Constantine and the Christian kingdom of the early modern European states amalgamate into a *saeculum*; and the continued existence of the Christian saeculum had been placed in question, from the French Revolution onwards, by the secularization of political authority, hence by the dissolution of the divinely ordained symbiosis between politics and religion. Carl Schmitt was sympathetic to Donoso Cortes's radicalization of the counter-revolutionary interpretation of history, according to which atheism congealed into sheer violence, especially in the anarchism of a Bakunin.

However, in Carl Schmitt's view, a supposed structural similarity between basic concepts of theology and the conceptual frame of public and international law in the early modern period lend the term "secularization" the additional, but in this case conservative, meaning of the transformative preservation of a Christian continuity. From the twentieth-century nostalgic historical perspective of a constitutional lawyer on the disintegration of the early modern system of sovereign territorial states, the secularization of divine omnipotence into the conception of state sovereignty in classical international law had also acquired a redemptive significance. On Carl Schmitt's interpretation, the unity of "the political" preserved in the sacred aura of the medieval emperors had had a chance of surviving under modern conditions only in the guise of the absolutism of Christian kings to which Hobbes erected a monument with his *Leviathan*. The redemptive continuity was supposed to have come about through the secularizing assimilation of the medieval pattern of legitimacy into the divine right of absolutist rulers. For a thinker of the younger generation, Hans Blumenberg (1920–96), precisely this alleged continuity represented a prime example of the "delegitimation of the modern age." Blumenberg vehemently opposed Carl Schmitt's view on secularization. In his work *The Legitimacy of the Modern Age*,[23] he argued against the traditionalist Catholic reading for a sharp discontinuity between religious and secular thought. Against Schmitt (and in contrast to Löwith), he affirmed the independent legitimacy of a modern age that draws upon its own resources in overcoming the traditions of ancient Europe.

The controversy turns on the recognition versus the rejection of the anthropocentric turn during the early modern period. Concerning the "transfer" of eschatology into the profane "ledger" of progress, for example, Blumenberg asserts: "the crucial question is still whether this situation [i.e., the *eschaton*] is to be brought about immanently or transcendently, whether man can achieve it by the exertion of his own powers or has to rely for it on the grace, which he cannot earn, of an event breaking in upon him."[24] In response to the traditionalist critique that the self-empowerment of a finite mind goes too far and should be brought back under the sway of divine authority, Blumenberg appeals to the self-consciousness of an autonomous mind, backed by scientific and technological successes, which relies exclusively on rational self-preservation. According to Blumenberg's interpretation, the appearance of continuity is merely a function of the unsatisfied interest in solving philosophical problems with which the modern mind has to wrestle once again under different premises because it inherited them unsolved from theology. At the semantic level, secularization is not reflected in a "conversion" of theological contents into secular ones. Instead, the backlog of still smoldering problems leads simultaneously to the systematic de-valuation and a merely metaphorical employment of a theological vocabulary that brings the new answers under the sway of the old questions. And because Blumenberg fears that this involves the danger of obfuscating the new, he prefers to speak in terms of a "reconfiguration" (*Umbesetzung*) rather than of a "conversion" (*Umsetzung*) of inherited concepts.

The debate on secularization in postwar Germany continued to be shaped by the polarizing controversy over the "value" or "worthlessness" of modernity mentioned by María Herrera Lima. The controversy over the "legitimacy" of the modern age was by no means confined to the political sphere to which Carl Schmitt attached primary importance. Blumenberg more generally resists the idea of a "cultural debt" that modernity supposedly has to discharge to its religious past. Today, this dividing line has completely lost its relevance. One can instead identify cognitive and moral-cognitive learning processes reflected in cultural traditions and worldviews without having to claim superiority for the actual moral behavior or the ethical forms of life of later generations. I cannot discern anything like "progress" in a personal moral conduct that is always tied to particular contexts, not to speak of the complex dimensions of the "not-misspent life," and I would regard it as absurd to try to make descriptive comparisons between such factors over broad ranges of time. The claim that there is progress in the de-centering of our perspectives when it comes to viewing the world as a whole, or to making considered judgments on issues of justice, is a different matter. Examination of the long rhythms of such learning and progress in knowledge will reveal cognitive developments that bear on changes in the patterns of valid argumentation, in the standards in terms of which propositions are justified, and generally in the dispositions to respect the "burdens of reason" (Rawls).

These changes have become so natural for later generations that they are assumed to be irreversible. Blumenberg appeals to this characteristic of learning processes when he insists, contra Carl Schmitt, that the rationalism of the Enlightenment is no longer in need of justification.[25] This is why, when translating semantic contents from religious traditions into secular language, the question doesn't even arise whether the secular side in its claims to validity makes itself dependent on the theological side. If Blumenberg had not been negatively fixated on the monotheistic doctrines, he could have responded in a more relaxed manner to Schmitt's and Löwith's narratives of decline. But none of the three parties to the debate considered Jaspers's concept of the Axial Age, which was based on the co-originality of monotheism and Platonism and the structural similarity between them. Otherwise, Löwith and Schmitt would scarcely have propagated the wholesale return to either the cosmological thought of the Greeks or to the eschatology of the Church Fathers, and Blumenberg would have felt no need to wrestle with the objection that theology in fact accommodated itself to the advances of modern sciences without having to join with modern philosophy in making the anthropocentric turn. Blumenberg misunderstood the nature of the learning processes out of which modern philosophical thought and a "reformed" religious consciousness evolved simultaneously. This *simultaneity* enables them to enter into a dialogue in which postmetaphysical thinking can aspire to "translate" theological contents without having to confront the question of the relative "value" of the one or the other side.

It is odd, by the way, that Blumenberg did not address the issue of the secularization of political authority, since this is the core of the process that goes to the heart of Carl Schmitt's denial of the legitimacy of the modern age. Morality, law, and politics remain blind spots in Blumenberg's justification of the independence of the modern age.[26] The fact that the constitutional revolutions of the late eighteenth century were inspired by ideas of social contract theory is an example of the dialectical appropriation of a religious heritage that gainsays Blumenberg's alternative, according to which modernity is either the heir of tradition and remains dependent on it or it repudiates tradition and thereby achieves its independence. On the one hand, human rights owe their egalitarian universalism (in addition to Stoic sources) to the secular translation of Jewish and Christian ideas of the equal worth of every person in the eyes of God; rational natural law could not have developed without the anthropocentric reversal of the world-transcending viewpoint of the Last Judgment into the moral point of view which transcends all partial standpoints *from within* the world. On the other hand, without this transformation it would not have been possible to overcome the limits placed on the mutual toleration of religious communities wherever the believer's perspective remains centered on the absolute truth of the teachings of his own community. Blumenberg shut his mind to the fact that the legitimacy of the modern age, conceived as a result of learning, reaches beyond the achievements of modern science to include the moral justification of the principles of the constitutional state. The insight into the twofold character of learning processes as both "extending" and "overcoming" also prepares the ground for the modernized concept of "the" political to which María Pía Lara appeals to ensure that religious voices are accorded a legitimate place in the postsecular civil society of constitutional states.

IV   What is Meant by a "Genealogy" of Postmetaphysical Thinking?

The postwar debate just discussed is fundamentally hampered by its narrow focus on free-floating connections in the history of ideas taken in isolation from their broader social and cultural contexts. Both the Axial Age revolution in worldviews and the separation between secular and religious thought in modern Europe represent at the same time caesuras in the genealogy of postmetaphysical thinking and stages in social evolution. The urban centers of the state-organized and highly stratified societies of the ancient empires first made possible the emergence of forms of profane knowledge that provided, during periods of social upheaval and in more peripheral regions, the impetus for critically overcoming the mythical worldviews. And it was only under the conditions of the emergence of the modern administrative state and of the capitalist mode of production that, propelled by the de-centralizing effects of the functional differentiation of social subsystems, the impetuses toward an increasing autonomy of law and politics, of science and philosophy, and of art and criticism from the Church and theology gained momentum (whereupon the new forms of knowledge reacted back on religion).

Amy Allen offers a useful clarification of that concept of "genealogy" from which I take my orientation in the attempt to reconstruct the prehistory of postmetaphysical thinking. From the standpoint of *rational reconstruction*, the aim is to represent this history as a sequence of solutions to problems, whereas the *genealogical perspective* reveals the contingent historical constellations that made the actual learning processes possible. Imre Lakatos, for example, attempted to reconstruct paradigm shifts in the history of science in a similar way.[27] This program differs in a variety of respects from Nietzsche's understanding of "genealogy." In the first place, it is not guided by the *subversive intention* of undercutting the repressive features of a dominant mode of thought. From my point of view, today there is no alternative to the postmetaphysical mode of doing philosophy. However, the genealogy that leads from the modern age back, via the symbiosis of Greek metaphysics with Christianity, to complementary origins in the Axial Age should serve as a corrective to a particular self-understanding of philosophy that is dominant in the profession, and by no means only among hardcore naturalists. Thus, it is guided by the *problematizing intention* of enlightening *secular* thought concerning the Enlightenment's blinkered secular*istic* self-understanding.

Amy Allen is right to focus on the question of the sense in which this undertaking belongs to the category of *vindicatory*, and hence justifying, genealogies. It is certainly not vindicatory in the apologetic sense that the validity of the accepted postmetaphysical patterns of argumentation should be justified *genetically* in terms of its *origin* in unquestionably valid religious and metaphysical conceptions of the world. For then we would have *learned* nothing as regards our philosophical understanding of ourselves and of the world since the nominalist revolution. On such a false premise, it would not be possible (as Pope Benedict XVI suggests in his Regensburg Address) to identify any learning processes in those discourses on epistemology, rational natural law, and morality that began at that time. In this respect, I agree with Blumenberg that the postmetaphysical thinking to which these discourses gave rise operates in a "bottomless" fashion insofar as it *creates* the building blocks of its "ground of validity" from its own resources, instead of *borrowing* them from some traditional authority. An act of *insight* that arises from working through good reasons and is not, for the time being, contradicted by better arguments does not need an *additional* genetic justification.

The intended genealogy does not have a justifying, but a critical function; it is supposed to foster a reflexive awareness of the contingency of the context of emergence of the background premises of the kind of theoretical and practical knowledge that at present may claim rational acceptability. This contextual awareness is generally expressed in the fallibilistic self-interpretation of science and philosophy, because it reminds us of the possible context-dependence of prima facie universal propositions. This fallibilistic consciousness seems to be especially relevant in intercultural discourses. The genealogy of one's own pre-understanding fosters the willingness to de-center this background and to engage in mutual perspective-taking, a disposition that every party must bring to such a discourse. Over and above this fallibilism, the contextual awareness acquires a special importance because the genealogy of worldviews alerts postmetaphysical thinking to shared roots of philosophy and religion. Insofar as the genealogy throws light on the divergence between the secular and the religious intellectual formations – and on the complementary relation between the two that evolved in the course of this differentiation – it can present philosophy with a balance sheet of its learning processes and foster an awareness of what one side might still gain from a dialogue with the other.

The *problematizing intention* of the undertaking focuses historical attention on the internal cognitive dynamic on the basis of which the complementarity between postmetaphysical thinking and "reformed" religious consciousness can be understood, where appropriate, as the outcome of learning processes. In this context, portions of the political and social context play the role of contingent boundary conditions. The fact that the *countervailing* processes of the repressive influence of theology and Church on culture and society are excluded from this spectrum of topics may give rise to the suspicion of a trite "Whig" history of progress. Only a perspective on social evolution that is sensitized to the dialectic of Enlightenment would also reveal the reverse process, which, as Amy Allen rightly warns, should at least not be forgotten. Before I address the question posed in the title of her contribution, I would first like to offer a brief clarification of two terminological misunderstandings.[28]

"Neo-paganism" is the name given itself by an intellectual current in the Weimar period whose adherents followed Nietzsche in identifying the origins of the alienated present in monotheism and an emancipation from the present malaise in a return to the healthy sources of mythical thought. During the 1930s, this reading of Nietzsche also inspired Martin Heidegger, who had earlier turned his back on the "system of Christianity."[29] From that time onward, Heidegger sought to return to the pre-Platonic origins of onto-theology with the aim of recovering an "original truth" from Presocratic sources.[30] My critique of "neo-pagan" thought is directed against the leveling of the cognitive advance from "myth to logos" that occurred not alone in Israel and Greece during the Axial Age, and against an "originary thought" that seeks to reanimate supposed mythological "truths" from the reflective standpoint of modernity.[31]

My second remark concerns the expression "context-transcendent." In reference to validity claims, it was meant to have the gerundive meaning of *transcending*; Maeve Cooke's proposed emendation captures the performative meaning of the act of exceeding all contexts that is *performed* when making such claims. In science (as already in everyday communication), we cannot avoid raising within local contexts claims to truth or rightness that assert a validity for declarative or normative propositions that exceeds, and thus is independent of, all contexts.[32] However, thematizing such contexts, which at first remained in the background, can reinforce the participants' awareness of fallibility, because making explicit potentially qualifying background assumptions broadens the spectrum of objections against the claimed universal validity. Bringing implicitly qualifying contexts of emergence to awareness leads to the enlargement of the previously accepted perspective. Jaspers's concept of the Axial Age, for example, which asserts that comparable cognitive achievements led to the emergence of similar metaphysical and religious worldviews in China and India to those which emerged in Greece and Israel, stimulates the de-centering of Europe's long-dominant view of itself. This teaches us something about the limitations of our view of the world.

Whereupon one can, of course, ask whether "one" *always only* refers to the "we" of a particular group, or whether "we," when we assert that something is true, must adopt the standpoint of "everyone" and hope that the reasons that convince us also in the final analysis convince everyone else. Who has the final say? The objectifying (in this case, self-objectifying) gaze of the scientist or the performative perspective of the philosopher who knows that the self-referential process of forming a self-understanding cannot be re-objectified without slipping into a meaningless and endless regress? This brings me to Amy Allen's *principled contextualism*. Her proposal is that we should subject the results of our genealogically reconstructed learning processes to a further contextualization at a meta-theoretical level. Adopting a bird's-eye perspective, we should, for example, relativize the methodological atheism of postmetaphysical thinking or the egalitarian universalism of rational law and morality into something that is binding *only* "for us" in our historical context. This supposed objectivity misunderstands the *irreducible* self-referentiality of genealogy. We cannot have good, and hence context-independent, reasons for taking the knowledge produced by our learning processes to be true while *simultaneously* relativizing the scope of their validity for *additional* genealogical reasons. My objection is directed against the postulate of an unsurpassable "view from nowhere." The whole thrust of postmetaphysical thinking was to deconstruct the divine standpoint which has, by definition, the last word. Its place is taken by the impartiality of the practice of argumentation among participants. Abstracting from the participant perspective that we adopt with every truth claim is required in the case of the objectifying sciences, but it is not allowed in the case of the self-referential philosophical process of contributing to the best available and most reasonable self-understanding.

Forgoing self-reflection for the purposes of objectification is even less an option for a genealogist who knows that she is situated in and speaks from contexts when she defends what she has learned from her reconstructive descriptions – for instance, the premises of postmetaphysical thinking – against objections. On the other hand, not to assume for the time being that, in justifying her reconstructions, she had liberated herself from all contexts that could limit the validity of her statements would be to fail to take these reconstructions seriously. Her fallibilistic consciousness tells her that this *assumption* is not without risk, because she cannot immunize her convictions by appeal to a divine standpoint. The appropriate meta-level for testing the premises of postmetaphysical thinking further is not provided by an "observer perspective," however neutral, but only by the horizontal exchange of *pro* and *contra* arguments, first within the discipline and then if possible also in intercultural debates that may compel "us" to adopt an enlarged "we-perspective." Such discussions will be more productive the greater the cultural distances are between the background assumptions of participants (and the more successfully they in turn have been in similar attempts to reconstruct the history of the origins of their own cultural background).

Finally, with her point about having one's cake and eating it, Amy Allen addresses the problem that changes in religious consciousness that we describe from a secular point of view as learning processes might appear completely differently in the self-description of religious communities. Wouldn't even a, let us assume, successful genealogy of postmetaphysical thinking describe the modern relation between faith and knowledge in an asymmetrical fashion, that is, only from the perspective of one side? This question cannot be dismissed by appealing to the shared roots in the Axial Age. But the latter offer both parties a common starting point for dialogue even if they arrive at different interpretations of their relation to each. However, we must pay close attention to the difference between the stances we adopt when we ascribe something to another person from the observer perspective of a third person and when we communicate with a second person as a first-person participant. As for the complicated relation between postmetaphysical thinking and religious interlocutors from whom we may be able to learn something, even though we reject their theocentric view of the world, the discussion of the following two contributions may take us a step further.

V   Methodological Atheism and Agnosticism

Whereas J. M. Bernstein is a forceful advocate of the laicist self-understanding of philosophy, Matthias Frisch attempts to recuperate a strong religious motif from our philosophical discourses. With my combination of methodological atheism and agnosticism, I am located somewhere between these two positions. Bernstein defines methodological atheism as follows (p. 160): "The secularist can thus be asked to see if there is a wholly immanent rational kernel to religious beliefs, but cannot be required to give up the determining authority of secular reason over cognitive worth." I agree with this, but J. M. Bernstein rejects agnosticism when he continues: "This is not to deny that there is an existential excess to religious belief that defies the translation procedure; *but for us that excess is not simply unavailable to philosophical reflection, it is what is permanently lost in the transition to modernity."* What does "perma-nently lost" mean here? The agnostic only asserts that these semantic contents are *inaccessible* and refrains from making judgments concern-ing the truth claim that believers associate with them. In leaving a truth claim *undecided*, the agnostic expresses his failure to understand a form of discourse. For, from his perspective, religious "truths" are formulated in concepts that are prior to the usual differentiation into descriptive, evaluative, and normative statements.[33]

I share J. M. Bernstein's adherence to methodological atheism and argue (against John Rawls, for example) that the practical reason of political philosophy, rather than the truths proclaimed by religious communities, must have the final say when it comes to the rational acceptability of secular constitutional essentials. But that does not prevent me from adopting an agnostic stance on the dogmatic founda-tions of the validity claims of a religious interlocutor. J. M. Bernstein correctly describes us both as "young Hegelians," which means that as a postmetaphysically minded student of Hegel I am aware of the long process of mutual assimilation of concepts of Greek and Judeo-Christian origin, though I cannot know whether this process can also be continued. And as a social scientist I respect the conspicuous fact that conditions the present-day asymmetry between the two sides: while the philosophi-cal side derives its vitality from a purely academic tradition of research, the other side relies on the theological explication of the teachings of a *religious community founded on ritual practices*. Both sides share the intention of elaborating an explicit understanding of oneself and of the world. But, in religious dogma, the *cognitive* dimension is combined with the *social* dimension of membership in a worldwide association that (from the secular perspective) preserves a connection with archaic sources of solidarity (which are buried beyond the reach of the secular side).

On the other hand, I share with Matthias Fritsch the agnosticism that allows for a receptive dialogue with theology and thus keeps open access to potentially unexhausted semantic contents of the religious tradition. But I am not sure whether the specific proposal he presents can be justi-fied from the anthropocentric perspective of methodological atheism.

(1) The equanimity of the agnostic stance has overcome resent-ment. There were good reasons for the militancy of the Enlightenment at one time. It is a testimony to struggles for emancipation against the secular clerical power of a religious authority that long enough lent its seal of approval to outrageous political repression and social exploita-tion. We could *also* recall that, in more recent times, the clergy was engaged on both sides. But it appears that some wounds are still fresh. J. M. Bernstein makes the surprising claim that the Old Testament story

of Abraham and Isaac is central to Western religious spirituality.[34] Appealing to Kierkegaard, he develops a reading of this episode according to which Abraham's blind obedience to God's command to offer up his beloved son as a sacrifice – a human sacrifice! – reveals that the masochistic character of faith in God is a general trait of religion. The theological justification for this reading is somewhat more interesting: "One can only be reborn in faith if one first dies to the world. In order to die to the world one must slaughter one's living attachments to the world, one must murder one's love of the world and offer it to God. One must sacrifice Isaac" (p. 170). Although Bible interpretation is not my specialty, this ahistorical and biased interpretation, which purges religious belief as such(!) of any cognitive or moral import, incites me to four brief observations.

(a) The sacrifice required of Abraham is untypical for Judaism, which abandons the pagan practice of sacrifice and condemns it as "idolatry." Sacrifices were performed for magical purposes in order to propitiate a god or a divine power. But the Hebrew Bible is as hostile to sacrifice as it is to divination, the interpretation of observable happenings as signs of future events, and to magic, which flouts the natural causality governing events in the world. For, from the perspective of Judaism and Christianity, this "superstition" fails to comprehend the transcendent sublimity of a God who is removed from the world while governing everything that takes place within it.[35]

(b) The Hebrew Bible incorporates traditions from different periods of Jewish history; thus, the compilation of texts preserves traces of earlier practices, pagan residues such as the practice of trial by ordeal or the ceremony of the scapegoat, the magical use of incense, etc. But, as in the case of Abraham's sacrifice, these remnants of popular belief are *reinterpreted* from the perspective of exile or post-exile Judaism. The story of the patriarch was among the most ancient traditions of Israel and its neighboring peoples. The unembellished literary form of the dry relation of the episode already stands in sharp contrast with, for example, the elaborate poetry of Job's lament, which approaches the problem of the devotion of a "servant of God" from a different direction. The question of how God could issue such an immoral command could not have been posed in the same form for the members of the tribes of Israel of the pre-kingdom period as it must have under the assumption of a full-fledged monotheism. For an editor around the year 500 BCE, reworking the ancient Israeli teachings from the monotheistic perspective of a Deutero-Isaiah, therefore, the cognitive dissonance may have been blunted by the fact that his readers could be expected to accept God's moral integrity as a matter of course. They would have assumed from the outset that the problematic command would be revoked, and they would have read the story only from the actually thematic perspective of an experimental testing of Abraham's devotion to God.

(c) The history of the reception of Genesis 22 in Western art and literature reflects a profound disquiet mingled with fascination over the biblical traces of the long since surmounted archaic power of human sacrifice. Given the current controversy with Islam, this revulsion even leads Christian theologians to plead for a "taking leave of" Abraham.[36] In contrast, a Romantic spirit like Søren Kierkegaard immersed himself in Abraham's torn state of mind in an attempt to recover the dimension of the promise of salvation that was lost with the transition to a secular and purely rational morality. As in the doctrine of stages of *Either/Or*, in his interpretation of the story of Abraham in *Fear and Trembling*, Kierkegaard is concerned with the pivotal difference between moral consciousness and religious faith. The moralization of the demonic forces of good and evil and the move toward a transcendent deity overcame myth and magic, but did not dissolve into the binding power of mere morality that which forms the proper core of religious experience, namely, the ambivalent dread inspired by the immediate presence of the sacred. The complex idea of God's *redemptive* justice is a synthesis in which the impersonal justice of morality represents just *one of two* moments. *Law-abidingness* (*Gesetzestreue*) – obedience to the moral legislator – is founded on *devoutness* (*Glaubenstreue*): trust in and loyalty to the omnipotent savior. *But they are not identical.* Kierkegaard's point is that devoutness must not be absorbed entirely by law-abidingness, as it is in Kant: "The story of Abraham contains . . . a teleological suspension of the ethical," because there is "no absolute duty *to* God" if the latter, in his primary role as a *power of salvation*, calls on the patriarch to commit a prima facie immoral action.[37]

(d) J. M. Bernstein argues too superficially when he reads into this episode the immoral call to "hatred of the world" and confuses this with the *liberating* distancing from the capriciousness of the mythical gods and spirits. Monotheistic thought does in fact break with the fixation of mythical thought on natural processes in the world, as the cosmo-ethical worldviews of the Axial Age, Buddhism in the first instance, do in a different way. The Bible passes judgment on a disenchanted world from which the many immortal, but corruptible, deities have withdrawn because all natural processes in the world are now entirely subject to the will and the laws of a power that is prior to and underlies this world as a whole, namely, the transcendent creator of the universe.[38] Through the existential relation to that

God, the believer also achieves cognitive distance from all natural processes in the world, which enables him to judge his life and that of everyone else according to the same moral standards. Even the notorious saying in Luke 14:26 acquires a positive meaning in this context.[39] Moral universalism shatters the ethnocentric bonds of familial morality: Jesus preaches the repudiation of a life that is completely absorbed *in and by the world*.

(2) The recognition of the cognitive advance that took place during the Axial Age and the openness to the possibility of continuing a process of translation of religious contents into a secular language must not mislead philosophy into adopting a mystifying imitation of religious pretensions, as in the case of Heidegger's "remembrance" (*Andenken*) of being. Methodological atheism commits us to a rigorous form of discursively justified discourse that resists the surreptitious rhetorical importing of theologoumena. On the other hand, translating difficult texts, such as Celan's poetry, itself requires a literary effort. This is why the terrain bordering on religion is mainly reserved for the writers among the philosophers, like Benjamin and Derrida. They develop innovative concepts and leave their contemporaries in the dark as to how suitable they are for discursive purposes. An interesting case in point is the figure of the "other" that Levinas uses to introduce an asymmetry into the relation between *ego* and *alter*.

Matthias Fritsch explores the suitability of this figure of thought for recovering a neglected aspect beyond the egalitarian-universalistic obligations of rational morality, as expressed in the second part of the following statement: "God's gaze addresses all equally, but at the same time each one with infinite (!) care for the individual soul" (p. 279). An intersubjective version of Kantian ethics that includes everything that one person owes to another person, and is based on symmetrical and reciprocal relations of recognition, does not fully recuperate the theological import of such a conception. It does not take into account the demand that ego should show *overriding* concern for the well-being of alter *in her singularity*. For this devotion presupposes a kind and degree of empathy that cannot be made into a universalistically grounded duty. From a secular perspective, in the morally grounded expectation of others I encounter the authority of a universal norm that can be violated and that others who are affected can require me to obey. This authority is based solely on the correct application of a reasonable norm – that is, one that deserves universal recognition, including my well-considered assent. The binding force of these norms is not yet limited (as in contractualism) by the narrow constraints of rational egoism imposed by the *do-ut-des* rationality of parties to a contract; however, the strict deontological

nature of duties reflects the structure of a process of justification steered
by the *reciprocal* perspective-taking and the autonomous "yes" or "no"
of participants who enjoy equal rights in deliberation.

Matthias Fritsch quite rightly agrees with Levinas that the justification of a solidarity that *goes beyond this* "must" or "ought" must appeal
to a different authority. Here, my encounter with the concrete other is
embedded in the asymmetrical relation to something *entirely* other hiding
behind the second person before my eyes. But does this Other with a
capital "O" derive his or her appellative force from an experience that
can justifiably be universalized to all human beings? A detailed response
to the careful arguments of Matthias Fritsch would take me beyond the
limits of the present discussion.

VI   The Role of Religion in the Public Sphere

How philosophy should interpret its relation to religion is one issue;
another is how the role of religious communities in the public sphere of
secular constitutional states appears from the postmetaphysical perspective of political theory. The credit for highlighting this issue goes to John
Rawls with his Kantian concept of the citizens' "public use of reason."
The starting point of the discussion is the assumption that citizens in a
democracy should offer each other reasons for their political stances.
The problem is that liberal constitutions exude an air of paradox in this
regard. Although they are designed to guarantee all religious communities an equal freedom to participate in civil society, they simultaneously
shield the public bodies that make collectively binding decisions from
religious influences. The same persons who are expressly authorized to
practice their religion and to lead a pious life are supposed, as citizens, to
participate in a democratic process whose results must remain free from
any religious "contamination."

The laicist answer to this problem is to banish religion from the
public arena entirely. But as long as religious communities play a vital
role in civil society, censoring the voices of religious citizens already at
the source of the democratic process is inconsistent with the spirit of a
liberal constitution. What restrictions must religious citizens accept? My
proposal is that the polyphonic babble of voices cannot and must not be
subject to regulation already at the level of the political public sphere.
Religious contributions have to be translated into a generally accessible
language, however, before their content can enter into the deliberations
of political institutions that make legally binding decisions. Contrary
to John Rawls's proposal, this institutional filter has the meaning of a

translation proviso that is not imposed on each religious citizen individually but, when necessary and possible, should be satisfied cooperatively. For some, this proposal goes too far; for others, not far enough. Cristina Lafont's insightful objections, on the one hand, and Maeve Cooke's friendly doubts, on the other, provide an opportunity to respond to both sides. These problems of religious and metaphysical pluralism arise not only at the national level, however, but have precise counterparts at the supra-national level. This is the focus of Jim Bohman's remarks, which I can address only briefly.

(1) Cristina Lafont's central objection is directed at one of the two obligations that follow, according to my conception, for the secular as well as for the religious side from the ethics of citizenship implicitly recognized by all loyal citizens. Whereas religious citizens might feel the translation proviso as a burden, secular citizens, *in their role as citizens,* face the burden of another obligation, namely, not to deny a priori that public utterances, even ones formulated in religious language, could have a cognitive content susceptible to translation. Obviously, opening the democratic process up to religious utterances would be meaningless unless each citizen acknowledged that all of her fellow citizens could make potentially meaningful contributions to the political debate in principle. For a *public practice* of pure secularism would mean that secular citizens could treat certain groups of their fellow citizens at best as species in need of protection because of their religious outlook. To do so would be to fail to take religious citizens seriously as modern contemporaries and thereby to discriminate against them in their capacity as citizens. This attitude is as incompatible with the requirement of reciprocal recognition as it is with the willingness to adopt the perspectives of others in the give and take of arguments and positions.

Cristina Lafont rejects the expectation that secular citizens should exhibit such a postsecular self-understanding in exchanges with religious citizens as normatively unacceptable. She believes that this would amount to denying secular citizens the very right that religious citizens are granted when religious utterances are admitted into the public arena, namely, the right "to adopt their own cognitive stance."[40] I believe, on the contrary, that this expectation is a direct implication of the ethical (not legal) requirement that citizens endowed with equal rights should mutually recognize one another as *participants in the joint venture of co-legislation.* And secular citizens can meet this obligation without denying their own disbelief in any kind of religious teaching. They are only asked not to exclude the possibility that religious speech might contain traces of a lost or repressed, or otherwise unavailable, normative intuition that is compelling and still awaits a saving translation.

However, this controversy only touches on the content of an *ethics* of democratic citizenship. Even more important is the cognitive structure underlying the required self-reflexive attitude of tolerance. Both the secular and the religious side can only *hope* that a complementary learning process will result in those cognitive attitudes that are necessary for satisfying the demanding obligations on either side. These attitudes cannot just be prescribed by political theory. That was my point in the relevant essay (*BNR*, 146f.).

Cristina Lafont's own proposal – "it is the obligation of democratic citizens to provide one another with justifications based on reasons that everyone can reasonably accept" – has no bite. On the one hand, it is trivial, because it boils down to the obvious requirement that every citizen, when contributing to public political debates, should respect the limits laid down by the principles of the constitution. On the other hand, the proposal is empty because it does not speak to the interesting point, namely, whether religious fellow citizens must be taken seriously *as such* in their contributions to the democratic formation of public opinions, and whether their religious utterances *can* possess a cognitive potential that the secular state must not ignore.

(2) Maeve Cooke's objections are the precise opposite of those of Cristina Lafont. In Maeve Cooke's opinion, the controversy over how best to exercise political authority in a religiously and metaphysically neutral way is pointless because it is impossible to make a clear distinction between secular and religious contributions to the formation of a political will from the start. If I understand her correctly, the argument goes as follows: all normatively substantive contributions to political discourse are embedded in some religious or metaphysical context; thus, secular utterances in the public sphere pose the same interpretative problems as those we are familiar with from communication between religious believers, members of different faiths, and non-believers. Thus, secular contributions should not claim the presumptive advantage of being generally accessible. If religion loses its supposed special status in this regard, however, the secular character of the state enshrined in the constitution cannot be protected by channeling flows of public communication into a secularized space of supposedly neutral reasons. At the same time, Maeve Cook does not share the kind of strong contextualism defended by Nicolas Wolterstorff in the same context. She argues for the moderate position that, in the public sphere, all background premises must be exposed to *unrestricted* discussion, so that bargaining between incommensurable religious universes does not get the final word. Even when Wittgenstein's "spade is turned," it must be possible for a discourse to continue: "both philosophers and self-reflective believers are likely to engage in processes of creative reimagining and rearticulating of even their core – dogmatic – convictions."[41]

Since deductive arguments merely make explicit the relevant implications of propositions, substantial controversies always rest on reasons that are embedded in widely ramified contexts. But normally such non-thematic background assumptions, if they *can* be thematized, do not represent a barrier to the continuation of discourses. The "spade bends" only when it reaches paradigm-constituting networks of concepts that establish a view of the world *as a whole*. But the spade does not break when dialogue continues even at the bottom. For then it can transpire which assertions have an evaluative character or are so bound up with a metaphysical cluster of validity claims that they can meet with agreement only within the framework of particular cultures or religious communities. Maeve Cooke is right to attribute a world-disclosing character to religious languages in particular. This world-disclosive function can be beneficial when positions expressed in a rich religious language call attention to forgotten or repressed aspects in public debates over morally sensitive issues, and cast a new light on until now inadequately described conflicts. This is why I am also against over-hastily reducing the complex polyphonic diversity of voices within the political arena. Otherwise, democratic states are at risk of cutting the democratic process off from meaning- and identity-generating resources on which it can draw in the search for imaginative solutions to problems.

However, these correct observations do not support the problematic blurring of the boundary between secular and religious utterances. Let us recall the point of departure. Historically speaking, the upheavals caused by the clashes between militant "powers of belief" necessitated the secularization of political authority. Until then, the conflicting parties had not been able to find a shared basis within their political community for resolving the pressing problems in ways convincing to all. It was only with the translation of the universalistic core of each religious community's fundamental convictions into the principles of human rights and democracy that they discovered a shared language bridging irreconcilable religious differences. It was only under the assumption of a "natural" human reason shared by all that the parties to the dispute were able to adopt a shared standpoint in political controversies beyond the social boundaries of their respective religious communities. This *transgression of limits* marked a shift in perspective that later generations – ourselves included – can no longer ignore. Religious claims to validity are tied to the thick experience of membership in a religious community and remain particularistic even in the case of proselytizing creeds that aspire to worldwide inclusion. In this respect, the presumptively universal claim to validity of the major world religions resembles the *centered* universalism of the ancient empires; they sought to extend their political and cultural claims to domination outward, looking outward from the capital city to fluid frontiers that almost fused with the horizon.

Whereas rational morality and rational law sketch a formal standpoint of an inclusive "we" that obliges *all* parties equally to engage in *mutual* perspective-taking without prejudicing the outcome, a dogmatically fixed religious standpoint only permits the *incorporation* of assimilated others into the perspective of one's own religious community. The key issue in discursive will-formation processes, however, as in all processes of reaching an understanding, is the willingness to de-center one's own perspective. The point is not to convert others, but to engage in a process of reciprocal learning in which each participant's particular view becomes fused with that of everyone else in an ever more enlarged and shared horizon (Gadamer). Of course, secular citizens must also learn to distinguish their conceptions of the "good life" (Rawls), that is, their personal existential life projects and value orientations, from *generalizable* interests and *universal* standards of justice. But religious citizens bear a particular burden in addition to this. For what is of vital importance for religious citizens are not "values" but "truths"; whereas values are ordered transitively, truths obey a binary code. This is why religious citizens face the twofold task of justifying the secularly grounded constitutional principles once again within the context of their faith[42] and, what is more onerous, of recognizing the difference between fallible public reasons (that is, those which can be accepted by everyone in principle) and infallible truths of faith.

For the boundary that Maeve Cooke, like Charles Taylor, wants to level turns on this difference. The point is not the difference between the ways of taking-to-be-true that must be described in phenomenological terms; it is rather the difference between the twofold, *incorporating* and *de-centering*, meaning of "universality": we claim universal validity for propositional truths in a different sense than we do for certainties of faith. Granted, "truths of faith" are not *sui generis* truths from the point of view of the believer. Nevertheless, as a citizen of a democratic polity, there is an institutional expectation that the believer must recognize the political relevance of the distinction between these two kinds of truth claims. For the customary kinds of empirical, pragmatic, legal, ethical, and moral validity claims, the epistemic contexts of public discourses are sufficient to bring their persuasive power to bear. By contrast, as long as a religion retains its specificity – namely, its anchor in the sacred complex combining a specific interpretation of man in the world with the practice of communal worship – membership in a religious congregation remains relevant for faith itself: the cognitive dimension is not separate from the social dimension. For all of the world religions associate with ritual practices their own epistemic paths to the sacred, be it revelation, meditation and ascetic exercise, or prayer. These particularistic ties explain the need, in the context of the political will-formation of a pluralistic society, to test the generalizable content of religious assertions independently of their epistemic context of origin. This is the point of the translation proviso.

Maeve Cooke attributes this requirement to a one-sided cognitivist conception of legitimation. This objection touches on the important question of whether a political community of free and equal persons can be content with a modus vivendi. On this, I agree with Rawls that the constitutional state is a political system founded on principles whose legitimacy must be recognized by the citizens *for good reasons*. Quite apart from the fact that a form of rule that is only accepted de facto or that rests on a mere compromise is unstable, in such cases there could be no question of a political community of *autonomous* citizens. Regardless of how the background consensus on constitutional principles comes about, in pluralistic societies it must be renewed in each subsequent generation on generally acceptable grounds. Therefore, its stability cannot depend on religious reasons that owe their persuasive power to the epistemic context of particular communities.

(3) With the emergence of a multicultural world society, religious pluralism is also increasingly playing a role at the international level. As the 2008 financial crisis brought home, at least temporarily, to the overtaxed nation-states, the scattered international organizations are not able to meet the growing need for coordination of the globalized markets (and of social subsystems in general) in spite of their dramatically increased numbers. This led me to reflect on a constitutionalization of international law and on the design of a global multi-level system (*PC*, 113–29; *DW*, 115–93; *EFP*, 109–30). The long-term goal for the world society rocked by crises should be a political constitution without a world government. But how could the international community acquire the ability to act politically even if it does not assume the character of the state? What is required, among other things, is the satisfaction of a political-cultural condition that philosophy can help to clarify: whatever shape a global system assumes in the future, if it is to be stable it must rest on a worldwide normative consensus on standards of justice. The signatures of 192 states under the UN Charter are a beginning, but nothing more than that. The realization that the cultures of the major world civilizations – in the first instance, those of the West, China, India, and the Arab world – are profoundly shaped by the religions that originated in the Axial Age makes it clear that the problems we are discussing at the national level reappear in an exacerbated form at the international level.

However, the disagreement between Jim Bohman and me turns less on the role of religions in the global public sphere than on the fundamental problem of how our notions of democratic legitimation could even find a foothold in the domains of transnational politics. From the perspective of a *civic republican* like Jim Bohman, my reflections on a *politically constituted* world society are clearly unnerving. How is it supposed to be possible to extend the channels of legitimation of democratic processes of opinion- and will-formation beyond the boundaries of nation-states? It may be difficult for a citizen of the world's oldest democracy, of a self-sufficient republic of continental dimensions, to relate to such an idea. Be that as it may, Jim Bohman ignores institutional proposals entirely and focuses on the global communicative network formed by an internationally enlarged civil society. Taking the historical example of the Women's International League for Peace and Freedom (WILPF), he advocates the "soft" communicative power that actors of civil society can also exercise beyond national boundaries. Far be it from me to downplay the global influence of the World Social Forum, for example, which mobilizes the oppositional forces to the capitalist World Economic Forum in Davos. The activists congregate in Brazil while the heads of government and economics ministers rush to meet with the managerial class of global capitalism in Switzerland. This example already reveals how what the forces of civil society scattered throughout the global public sphere lack, namely, an institutional counterpart on which they could exercise pressure. Jim Bohman is right to pose the question "Where does the legitimation of global domestic politics come from?" But if we content ourselves with the thoroughly asymmetrical global economic regime that developed in a haphazard, quasi-natural way, and do not even attempt to institutionalize decision-making procedures at the supra-national level, there will never be a global domestic policy that would then have to withstand the pressures exerted by a many-voiced globalized public. The transition from the debating society of the G7 to the summit of the twenty economically most powerful nations, which met for the first time in London in May 2008, was necessitated by the international financial crisis. In the meantime, the solemn declarations of intention to regulate the financial markets are no longer even worth the paper they are printed on. If we persist in consigning the destiny of a global political system to the cunning of economic reason, we can only docilely await the disastrous consequences of the next crisis.

VII Political Background Consensus under Conditions of Social Complexity

Over the decades, I have learned almost as much from my friend Tom McCarthy as from my philosophical mentor Karl-Otto Apel, albeit in opposite directions. Whereas for Apel I have succumbed too much to the, as he sees it, fashionable trend toward a de-transcendentalization of the Kantian concept of reason, McCarthy allies himself increasingly insistently with the pragmatist urgings of Richard F. Bernstein and Richard Rorty that I should pursue the path of contextualizing reason further. Faced with this quandary, I try to keep a clear head. The philosophical convictions that I have shared with Tom McCarthy from the beginning, through *Ideals and Illusions* up to his magnificent work *Race, Empire and the Idea of Human Development*, may have distracted me from a clear perception of the differences now under discussion.

With customary aplomb, Tom McCarthy (pp. 116–18) presents an accurate synopsis of my arguments to date in support of the postmetaphysical self-interpretation of a philosophy that is open to an exchange with religious traditions. In the process, he may have overlooked that these prolegomena only serve to clarify the self-understanding of the philosophical side. In order to begin a dialogue, it is neither necessary nor probable that the theological interlocutor will share the self-interpretation of his philosophical partner. Here already I would like to point out the differences, not just between the roles, but also between the cognitive attitudes that a philosopher must adopt when he participates in religious conversations, or, more generally, in intercultural discourses, as opposed to those that he must adopt when he defends his understanding of postmetaphysical thinking against the objections of professional colleagues. In the one case, he is *engaging* in a difficult dialogue, regardless of the unclear or controversial boundary between faith and knowledge; in the other, he is taking part in a normal expert discussion. Why should such a dialogue, which has to overcome deep differences between the respective background texts, function better without such an internal clarification of preliminary philosophical questions?

Within the ambit of this complex of issues, we continue to meet with a series of questions that, whatever their intended effects, can be dealt with in social scientific or philosophical terms. For the moment I need not concern myself with whether academic controversies over concepts of political justice, the ethics of citizenship, cultural and social modernization, faith and knowledge, secularization, the hermeneutic presuppositions of intercultural discourses, the metaphysical and religious pluralism of potential participants, and so on, could one day influence the mindset of the political actors. As regards my general line of thought, however, my starting point is the *political* assumption that the era of nation-states is coming to an end and that the creation of institutions of a global domestic policy must be opened up for discussion. These institutions cannot achieve stability without a transnational background consensus on principles and procedures conducive to reaching legitimate decisions. Philosophers, too, can agonize over this issue. Skeptical objections can only have the positive meaning of guarding against underestimating the disagreements that must be reasonably expected to accumulate in this regard *at the level of the object.*

The thrust of Tom McCarthy's objections is not altogether clear to me. In what context does the complexity of differences of opinions, which needless to say exist at all of these levels of discussion, play a special role? Tom McCarthy's intention is certainly not to dissuade anyone from attempting to bring their professional expertise to bear on one or the other discussion. In other contexts, the awareness of fallibility does not prevent us from going about our business either. Thus, I understand the tenor of his objections more as a methodological warning against over-hastily abandoning the required reflection on conceptual distinctions that fail to deliver in practice what they promise at the conceptual level. Tom McCarthy is dissatisfied with analytical distinctions, which I will review in what follows, because they forfeit their supposed clear-cut character in contexts of application.[43] Notwithstanding these problems, I will first address the two theoretical objections. In the process, I will recapitulate arguments, at the risk, in Tom McCarthy's case, of revisiting old debates, in (A)–(B). In conclusion, the three specific objections provide an oppor-tunity for returning to the question of the location from which each of us speaks, in (C).

(A) Philosophers certainly disagree over whether it is possible to adopt an impartial point of view in moral-political questions (as all Kantians, including John Rawls, affirm). When examining the hermeneutic presup-positions of intercultural discourses, I start from the assumption that universalistic issues of justice can be distinguished from particularistic questions of the good. Whereas the former are geared to answers that can command universal agreement, the latter can be answered only relative to the values of the reference persons or reference groups in ques-tion. Tom McCarthy doubts whether these analytical distinctions can be upheld in practice. He summarizes a series of arguments developed elsewhere in the assertion: "'good' cannot be an inherently contestable concept without 'equally good for all' being so as well."[44] I understand his point to be that the participants in practical discourses, even with the best will in the world, cannot agree on what is presumptively *equally good for all*, because they can use the concept "good for X" *only* with reference to interests that must be interpreted and evaluated relative to the cultural background and lifeworld horizon of the affected person or group in question.

This objection seems to me to miss the feature that distinguishes questions of justice from ethical questions. Questions of justice can also arise for the members of a collectivity embedded in specific social and historical contexts; but even then, as moral questions, they differ from questions of the good life not in virtue of the *social and historical reference to something particular* as such, but in that they accord *equal* consideration to the interests of *all* those affected. Equal and complete inclusion calls for a shift in perspective: all those involved must abandon the perspective from which they judge what is good for me or for us in favor of a uniformly inclusive "we" perspective. This impartial point of view is not that of an ideal observer; it is a first-person plural perspective that includes all members of a collective or, as ultimately in the case of moral judgments presumed to be unconditionally valid, the ideally extended universe of all responsible persons. The *key point is the social-cognitive shift in attitude.* In the transition from the self-centered ethical perspective to the impartial perspective of justice, we leave behind the egocentric or ethnocentric viewpoint and thereby *break* the continuum of questions of the good life asserted by Tom McCarthy.

Every participant in practical discourse must seek to *enlarge* his understanding of himself and his situation through reciprocal perspective-taking to include the relevant aspect of all others' understandings of themselves and their situations. This must go so far that, within the enlarged, and thus de-centered, horizon of interpretation on which all positions converge from different sides, one proposal, or one family of proposals, is acceptable for all. The orientation to the "single right" answer is already prescribed for practical reason by the context in which it operates: in the end, it should be conducive to social cooperation founded on intersubjectively recognized behavioral expectations. The pragmatic pressure to coordinate action bars the route to skepticism, that is, the luxury of idle reflection. *The extent of the empirically ascertained differences of opinion is not an objection against the orientation to a justified consensus.* Contradiction and the orientation to consensus already go hand-in-hand in everyday communication. The coordination of practical goals in straightforward interactions must pass through the risky thresholds of the implicit "yes" or "no" positions on criticizable validity claims, while the ever-present risk of disagreement is absorbed by the shared lifeworld background. So, too, in complex social domains where establishing discursive procedures means mobilizing objections and multiplying religious and metaphysical differences, on the one hand, though it fosters learning processes and the recognition of procedurally correct results, on the other. When systemic mechanisms are lacking or break down in conflict-ridden domains, the need for coordination is met by institutionalized consultation and decision-making procedures.

(B) Tom McCarthy doubts further, whether truth claims raised in the human sciences for interpretations of cultural and social modernity can be assumed to be more reliable than claims raised for religiously grounded alternatives. In his opinion, the one is as good as the others. But does the relatively weak status of the genealogies and theories of development in the social sciences really justify erasing the boundary between philosophy, the social sciences, and the humanities, on the one side, and competing religious views, on the other? Before I address the sobering and disciplining character of organized academic research, I would like to recall the place from which each of us argues. The interdisciplinary controversy over the correct dialectical understanding of the "achievements" of modernity is conducted in accordance with the usual academic rules and without any regard to whether it will ever affect the cultural background understanding of political actors. The strong or weak status of social theories capable of clarifying implicit presumptions about the context of application of principles of distributive justice is of little concern to participants in G-20 negotiations over a global regime for financial markets. Of course, this does not apply to social scientists who compare theories, or to philosophers who follow this controversy. At this level, I would like to defend the controversial distinction between religious interpretations "of the present age" and corresponding secular interpretations that process the expert knowledge of various scientific disciplines.

To be sure, the human sciences differ from paradigmatic natural science in their hermeneutic mode of access to their object domain of symbolically embodied meanings. They do not gain this access from the perspective of an *observer* who collects and processes the physically measured data, but instead from that of an interpreter who must at least virtually *participate* in the relevant practices and language games, as it were, before he can objectify them, that is, convert them into data, describe them, and process them analytically. I agree with Tom McCarthy that the performative attitude of the interpreter ties the findings of historians and sociologists in a different and more intimate way to the time and place of the hermeneutic situation than even the findings of quantum physicists are tied to the context of the physical measurements. Historical representations regularly become "obsolete" in ways that can be dated, whereas physical theories are "superseded" by explanatorily more powerful theories. Representations in the humanities and social sciences always also express the inevitably unreflected features of a preunderstanding that is constitutive for the cognitive access. Nevertheless, these practices also merit the title of a scientific discipline. They observe methodological standards of objectivity in the light of which all results are exposed to critical examination. Otherwise, we would not be able to distinguish between the academic enterprise of historical research and the pedagogical or political use of history: *Geschichtspolitik* is not the same thing as *Geschichtswissenschaft*.

On closer inspection, not even the question of which side merits the title of greater objectivity is as easily answered as appears at first sight. The hermeneutically refracted claim to objectivity of the human sciences is at least less naive than the "view from nowhere" to which the natural sciences lay claim. For them, eliminating any reflection on what the knowing subject contributes to the construction of the data found is certainly necessary; but the hidden purpose of processing only data that fit physical measurements, for example, technical mastery of natural processes, could at the same time involve a functional restriction of the cognitive perspective. Be that as it may, philosophical theories are even more liable to the verdict of context-dependence than are the human sciences. Here, all that remains is the "infinite conversation." Today, philosophy still understands itself as a scientific activity; however, attaching the predicate "scientific" to philosophical argumentation no longer means that philosophy is reducible to science, or that it is one of the "normal" academic disciplines. If an academic discipline is judged to be normal by the fact that it has *settled* on a method and an object domain defined in terms of a fixed conceptual frame, then the difference between philosophy and science can be determined by the fact that philosophy is "non-settled thinking." By distancing itself in a further stage of reflection from any knowledge acquired *intentione recta*, philosophy makes as it were "uninhibited" use of a basic feature of human cognition.

Philosophy promises to provide us with a very abstract kind of enlightenment about ourselves. At any rate, the reference point that rescues the choice of philosophical problems from arbitrariness is the "self" of a process of reaching a *self-understanding*. While all scientific disciplines focus their attention on one object domain alone, philosophy attends at the same time to the self-referential impact of the corresponding learning processes, that is, to what the knowledge acquired means "for us." It operates in a dimension where a link is maintained between growth of knowledge about the world and changes in our self-understanding. In contrast to the sciences, however, philosophy has no need to be ashamed of this self-reference. It secures the objectivity of its fallible reflection not by obscuring but by *universalizing* the self-reference to an *inclusive* "we." The "self" of the philosophically enlightening self-interpretation is not a particular nation, a particular era, a particular generation; nor even an individual, unless it be this person qua *person*. The philosophical meaning that something has "for us" is subject to the abstraction proviso that it is meaningful "for us in our human existence as such."

This perspective is also instructive in view of the origins of critical social theory in the critique of reason from Kant to Hegel. At the end of the eighteenth century, philosophical thought faced the challenge of a new and radicalized time-consciousness, which is accompanied by the emergence of the social sciences and the humanities. This experience imposed an entirely new topic on a by now postmetaphysically deflated philosophy, namely, the self-understanding of a modernity apparently uncoupled from tradition. Philosophy became all the more aware of the growing need for orientation the more forcefully it rejected the search for metaphysical answers. With the growing intensity of needs for practical orientation, the new issue of "comprehending its time in thought" was assigned to philosophy, in addition to the agenda of its classical disciplines. Philosophy pursued this task of arriving at a self-understanding of modernity in collaboration with other disciplines, initially political economy. After Hegel's death this role devolved to sociology;[45] thus, social theory is the result of a relatively contingent constellation. This explains the hybrid character of the peculiar symbiosis between an emerging social science and the philosophical legacy of a self-referential discourse of modernity. Moreover, it throws light on the controversial status of the "universal interpretations" that Tom McCarthy ascribes to the diagnoses of the present informed by social theory.

This sketch of the relation between the human and the natural sciences in general, and between philosophy and social theory in particular, is intended to suggest a perspective from which the various claims to objectivity converge on one feature they all depend on, namely, the discipline of research governed by methods and rules of argumentation. In each of those domains, we can achieve as much objective knowledge as the corresponding questions permit. The different degrees of *achievable* objectivity do not prevent us from *correcting* each other *in the search* for a single right answer. What sets the scientific character of the projects of social theory apart from approaches to the same issues in theology is the unconditionality of this fallibilist search without reservation. There is no kernel of an infallible truth left which is immune against any objection whatsoever. It is the unreserved openness and rationality of the approach that grounds the claim to scientific status, however weak the status may be. No interpretation by theologians, however liberal, can ultimately meet this procedural requirement. No theology can embrace the unconditional openness to critical self-revision as long as it has to administer the means of salvation and must be nourished by the lived faith of a practicing community and does not shrink into just another academic discipline.

(C) Tom McCarthy turns, in conclusion, to the issue of the role of religion in national public spheres. He supplements his skeptical assessment of the possibility of reaching a cross-cultural understanding of the meaning of "Justice among Nations" with arguments against particular analytical distinctions that supposedly lose their force in practice, so that reasonable disagreements become perpetual. When exercising their right of freedom of speech, secular citizens are, of course, allowed to expose not only religious utterances, but also religion as such, to the sharpest critical scrutiny. Tom McCarthy asks how this *cultural* public sphere, in which colleagues like Daniel Dennett and Richard Dawkins present their books for discussion, can be demarcated from the *political* public sphere in which the ethics of democratic citizenship enjoin these *same* citizens to exhibit a certain restraint regarding the persons and utterances of their religious fellow citizens. There is a simple answer to this question. All parties should and could be aware of the consequences when they, in their role as citizens or potential voters, engage in political opinion- and will-formation on matters that call for legal regulation; *political* utterances are simply contributions to discussions that in one way or another issue in the *legally binding*, hence *officially sanctioned*, decisions of the authorized institutions.

Tom McCarthy identifies a further difficulty with demarcating the normative substance of a rich religious metaphorical language or allegorical discourse, which under certain circumstances can remind agnostic fellow citizens of forgotten or suppressed aspects of their own *moral intuitions*, on the one hand, from those descriptive religious statements or existential presuppositions (on God, the creation of the world, etc.) whose consequences potentially clash with the mundane knowledge of generally accepted *facts*, on the other. I would suggest, however, that this analytical distinction is less relevant for the *process* of the translation of religious contents than for its *result*: after all, only the normative contents can acquire importance for evaluating existing or constructing new alternatives to the regulations at stake.

Finally, there is a confusion concerning the requirements of the "universal acceptability" and the "universal accessibility" of proposed norms. The secularization of political authority is supposed to ensure that the means of legitimate force held in reserve, with which collectively binding decisions are sanctioned and enforced, do not fall into the hands of any particular religious community (or of any other ideologically based group). Establishing democratic and constitutional procedures serves this purpose. Democratic procedures can generate legitimacy through a combination of deliberation and inclusion because they justify the presumption that the results are in the equal interest of all, and hence are *universally acceptable*. However, the inclusion condition – that is, the requirement that all those potentially affected should be assured appropriate access to the procedure – would be violated if the collectively binding decisions were not formulated *and justified* in a *universally accessible language*. Religious languages, in particular, would violate this condition because they involve a category of reasons (for example, revealed truths) that prima facie cannot claim universal acceptability outside of the corresponding religious community.

VIII   Difficult Discourses

The difficulties posed by the discourses that now follow seem to put Tom McCarthy in the right after all. I fail to take up the generous offer of two theologians who confront me with philosophical arguments, or that of a philosopher who keeps open the frontier to religious thought, and take advantage of the opportunity they present for a productive exchange. Insofar as this inability is due to a lack of hermeneutical sensitivity on my part, I apologize in advance to these three colleagues.

(1) Some academic discourses prove to be difficult because a simple hermeneutic condition is not met, namely, the familiarity with a background of argumentation that guards against trivial misunderstandings. The unfortunate distortions afflicting the situation of discussion between me and such an interesting and astute colleague as Nicholas Wolterstorff cannot be repaired through retrospective clarifications of differences between our respective uses of expressions such as "postmetaphysical"[46] or "reasonable,"[47] for that would simply amount to rejecting the premises on which the objections rest. However, I would like to address at least one contentious issue and one confusion:

- Nicholas Wolterstorff declares the controversy over the distinction between religious and non-religious utterances to be pointless because he thinks that the appeal to dogmatic sources, such as revealed truths, is not relevant. But without the appeal to revelation or to some form of contact of the believer with the divine, be it through prayer, ascetic practice, or meditation, "faith" would lose its specific character, namely, its rootedness in religious modes of dealing with *Heil* and *Unheil*.[48] The cultural Protestantism that shaped the environment in which I myself grew up is aware of the danger of the disintegration of religion into a *mere* worldview, which portends the end of religion as such.
- In several places Nicolas Wolterstorff confuses the levels of discussion: the cognitive attitudes actually adopted by citizens in the public sphere are a subject for empirical study; the political ethos that a liberal constitution demands of its citizens is a subject for normative political theory; the cognitive presuppositions that are required to satisfy such a demanding ethics of citizenship, and the learning processes that would be needed to fulfill these cognitive presuppositions, are subjects for epistemology, whereas the arguments with which a "soft" naturalism can be defended against a reductionist or "hard" naturalism are situated at a different philosophical level. Only the latter topic is directly related to the attempt to clarify the status of postmetaphysical thinking.

(2) John Milbank presents the unusual conception of a revived Humean Platonism as a refreshing alternative to the anemic "postmetaphysical thinking" indebted to Kant. He claims that this fallback position is squeezed out by the clash between the only two vital intellectual forces of the present day, namely Christian religion, on the one side, and hard naturalism, on the other: "We live in the era of Dawkins vs Ratzinger." This diagnosis leads Milbank to the conclusion that an agnostic conception of philosophy and a formalistic conception of democratic politics and a liberal constitution open up a void into which the fundamentalist movements stream. As historical evidence for his thesis, he cites the political destiny of the Weimar Republic. Against all empirical evidence, he puts forward the bold proposition: "Weimar was thoroughly Kantian and Habermas repeats the error." In fact, the reason for the failure of the Weimar Republic was surely the failure of the bourgeois elites to understand the liberty-promoting character of constitutional and democratic *procedures*. If only the Kantian conception of the staunch constitutionalist Hans Kelsen had prevailed over the substantialist conception of the clerico-fascist Carl Schmitt! As Heidegger's case demonstrates, the "deep" philosophical thought of the academic elite, which Milbank invokes against the dangers of the jejune Enlightenment, played a disastrous political role.

However, the political argument merely serves John Milbank as rhetorical support for the daring thesis in the history of philosophy that Hume's theory of the emotions, with the central role it reserves for sympathy, opens the door for recovering a Platonizing Christianity. This original thesis – and here I must confess that I am not sufficiently acquainted with Milbank's philosophy – is puzzling for the conventional reader of Hume; but the strategy of exploiting Humean skepticism for the purposes of a metaphysical renewal of Christian faith has its appeal. I assume that Hume experts have long since tested whether the alleged Stoic and Platonic connotations of Humean "sympathy" can in fact establish a stable bridge to the ingenious hybrid of emotivism and speculation on the "world soul." As it happens, in a quite different way Friedrich Schleiermacher had introduced feeling as the systematic connecting link between faith and knowledge in the architectonic of Kant's transcendental philosophy.

The few places where John Milbank refers to my own positions call for a reply. First and foremost, I fail to understand why a secular concept of communicative rationality, hence one introduced independently of "faith," implies that no internal relation exists between rationality and feelings (see p. 334). The rich vocabulary of evaluative expressions encountered in every natural language is an expression of the emotional life of the language community. And every evaluative statement expresses an emotional stance. Since Strawson's famous essay on "Freedom and Resentment,"[49] it is a commonplace in analytic philosophy, too, that moral judgments express a certain kind of emotional attitude. The propositional content of feelings features not only in moral discourse but also in aesthetic discussion and in therapeutic talk on repressed emotions that are excluded from communication. I am a bit baffled by Milbank's assertion that a procedural understanding of practical reason purged of substantive content assigns the free will no other orientation besides one to self-assertion (p. 343). No less perplexing is the construction of a regression of deontology into utilitarianism and the thesis that there is an intellectual complicity between transcendental philosophy and physicalism.

(3) The position of Hent de Vries presents a challenge of a different sort. It oversteps the boundary between postmetaphysical thinking and religion and seeks to replace the philosophy of religion with a "religious philosophy."[50] Hent de Vries expresses this intention in the question: "How does one adopt a reflexive, even critical, stance ... while at the same time keeping the total archive of religion at least in circulation, indeed, in play?" This is supposed to be accomplished through aporetic figures of thought and paradoxes that extend the concept of rationality beyond merely "giving and asking for reasons." Without a doubt, the rich literature extending from Kierkegaard to Benjamin, Lévinas, and Derrida has achieved exemplary results in translating religious contents. In contrast, Heidegger's "remembrance of being" is a veiled borrowing, not a translation. This example highlights the dangers of mere gestures toward transcending the limits of *Verstandesdenken*. The pathos of "depth" that claims for great thinkers privileged access to truth has no place in a sober mode of philosophizing. Philosophy may not be a scientific discipline in the conventional sense, but it nevertheless understands itself as a scientific activity.

Hent de Vries offers some thought-provoking sociological observations on the relation between the globalization of markets and electronic communication, on the one hand, and, on the other, the virtual realization of the long-standing claim to worldwide inclusion in the shape of religious communities that are now globally networked via these media. With these empirical processes, he associates the philosophical interpretation of a supposedly new form, not of religion, but of religiosity. The latter is supposed to be purged of metaphysical contents, being on the one hand "weak" in the sense of having minimal impact on everyday secular life, yet on the other hand "strong" enough in virtue of its maximal proliferation and vague omnipresence. It may be that these rather vague descriptions of contemporary developments are consistent with the "postsecular" transformations in the consciousness of largely secularized societies.

IX   What We Owe to the Murdered Innocents

It is all too easy to lose one's footing on the slippery terrain of religious philosophy. Perhaps my suspicion of a mode of philosophizing that degenerates into religious kitsch has prevented me from being sufficiently adventurous. Max Pensky, at any rate, ventures on to black ice, but without slipping. He does not shy away from *spelling out* theologoumena in postmetaphysical terms. His impressive essay also presents my own reflections on coming to terms with our National Socialist past much more clearly than I managed to do myself. This is especially true of my complex relation to the theology of Johann Baptist Metz who advocates anamnestic solidarity as a means of answering the question of theodicy radicalized in the light of Auschwitz. In the context of the present volume, I find it gratifying that Max Pensky *performatively* silences the abstract debate over the possibility or impossibility of translating contents from religious traditions. He uses an example to show how this can be done: "Translation is a process of analogical thinking. It searches for imperfect equivalents."

The essence of a political culture of remembrance, which has by now spread to many countries, is the question of how later generations should cope with the legacy of the atrocities committed by a past violent regime that enjoyed the support of the native population, and on what such a public practice of commemoration can draw. That members of a political community are also *liable* for one another *across generations* because they belong to the same traditions and are connected by threads of socialization is a pretty awkward idea, one that Karl Jaspers developed after 1945 in his famous text "On the Question of German Guilt." According to present-day moral standards, which are tailored entirely to individual personal responsibility, it makes no sense to speak of collective *guilt*. A duty toward the victims of past political crimes in the *strict moral* sense can be justified only in the case of those who participated in these crimes *in propria persona*. Nevertheless, the anguish over the mass crimes committed in *one's own country* gives rise to a gnawing feeling that the descendants of the perpetrators also owe something to the murdered innocents – and to their descendants. But what do they owe? This indeterminate, in the broadest sense moral, obligation can be interpreted as *collective liability* (*Haftung* is the term introduced by Jaspers). The legal connotation of the concept points to compensation payments, insofar as material reparation (which necessarily remains incongruous) is even possible. But what kind of liability exists beyond that? Can the legacy of "poisoned" social conditions found a special responsibility – and, if so, for whom?[51]

That question concerns the level at which citizens, who have to clarify their attitude toward the criminal past of their own nation, form their ethical and political self-understanding. However, this commemorative practice does not seem to be able to break out of the circle of concern over one's own political identity and future. The practices of the politics of memory have something narcissistic about them even when they are not exhausted in prophylactic invocations of a "never again." Max Pensky is not satisfied with the more far-reaching interpretation of Pablo de Greiff either. On the latter reading, the descendants of the generation of perpetrators owe those who were tormented and murdered the public gesture of recognition of past injustice, because otherwise the descendants of the generation of victims would not be able to breathe freely in the land of the perpetrators. Even this plausible reference to the reconciliation of the descendants of the one and the other side does not eradicate the reference of the nation of citizens to itself. Drawing on the famous correspondence between Max Horkheimer and Walter Benjamin, Max Pensky would like to see more than that in the commemorative practice, namely, an expression of solidarity with the victims *themselves*. This runs up against Horkheimer's objection: "the slain are really slain." In contrast to God's judgment on the Last Day, the weak anamnestic force of collective remembrance cannot exercise any retrospective effects. It cannot atone for the injustices inflicted on the dead. The justice that is possible on earth is not a *redemptive* justice. Nevertheless, a vague moral sense tells us that closing the file on such a process would be wrong *for the sake of the victims themselves*.

In the case of Auschwitz, Max Pensky proposes a non-deflationary interpretation: "While any society generates ample opportunities for its diverse members to express remorse and regret, it is only in extreme cases, where the unjust destruction of a class of persons opens up a wound or a gap in the social fabric that continues to be perceived in the present day, that we speak of a solidarity with the dead." The commemorative political practice in the country of the perpetrators should call to mind *the gap* in the social fabric of the polity opened up by the crime. Recognizing the wound that refuses to heal[52] prevents the presentism that consists in subsuming the past entirely into the present. Commemoration should preserve what happened in the past in the imperfect tense, that is, in the mode of *a past that continues to have a normative impact on the present*. The public act of remembrance should reinforce the mourning for those who are missing by making present the void they have left in the cultural fabric of the political community.

However, this *perspective of grieving over those who are missing*, which is natural, as it were, for mourning relatives, is more appropriate for the survivors and for the descendants of the victims than for those of the perpetrator generation. The starting point for the latter is different, namely, the anguish over the violent exclusion of a part of the population of one's own country who were stigmatized as a whole, and the consternation over the incomprehensible fact that extreme brutality could coexist with the continuance of normality in everyday life. On this side, the path leading to empathy with the victims passes through this threshold of consternation over the perpetrators and through a hermeneutics of suspicion toward those cultural ties that connect "them" with "us." The gulf separating the perpetrators from the victims is continued in the invisible, but in the final analysis unbridgeable, distance between the descendants of the one side and those of the other. The spontaneous grief over those who are missing contrasts with the distraught conscience that first provokes an awareness of what is missing. The gulf between these perspectives is unbridgeable, as is shown by the failure of obscene psychological, or even social, attempts to switch sides. Furthermore, how future generations will behave is an empirical matter. If things are to go well, it must be left up to the grandchildren and great-grandchildren to decide for themselves. But, for the time being, they should not be permitted to avoid the decision.

Appendix

Religion in Habermas's Work

EDUARDO MENDIETA

Jürgen Habermas's work spans over half a century. Its impact has been monumental as his productivity has been prodigious and simply exorbitant. When we try to survey and assess what Habermas has written and contributed to our understanding of religion, therefore, we have to be mindful of the sheer vastness of his work.[1] Additionally, we have to attend to the fact that, in a uniquely distinct way, Habermas is a social theorist and philosopher who has always worked in teams, through extensive dialogues and thoughtful replies in which he has not shied away from acknowledging that he may have overstated or understated a certain position. In addition, since his earliest works, Habermas has adopted the practice of preparing *Literaturberichte* (reports on the status of the literature), which provided him with an opportunity to become thoroughly familiar with the latest developments within different disciplines. These *Literaturberichte*, however, were also the building blocks of Habermas's own system. In them was manifested an omnivorous theoretical appetite but also a master builder and synthesizer. Already, in an essay from 1969, the great English Marxiologist George Lichtheim had written about Habermas:

> He seems to have been born with a faculty for digesting the toughest kind of material and then refashioning it into orderly wholes. Hegel, whom he resembles at least in his appetite for encyclopedic knowledge possessed this capacity in the highest degree, but he was cursed with an abominable style and a perverse fondness for obscurity, whereas Habermas writes as clearly and concisely as any empiricist.[2]

Indeed, if we follow on Lichtheim's comparison, Habermas's *Theory of Communicative Action* is to Hegel's *Phenomenology of Spirit*, as the former's *Between Fact and Norms* compares to the latter's *Philosophy of Right*. But, most importantly, while Hegel wrote only for those who could hear the whispers of *Geist*, Habermas has always written for the general public, academics, and philosophers across many different traditions. Habermas's modus operandi and his philosophical style embodied the key idea that guides his entire *oeuvre*, namely, communicative rationality. For these reasons, it would be unrealistic and absurd to approach Habermas's work without attending to its transformation over the last five decades. As we look at the evolution of this thinking over these five decades, we can divide Habermas's work into four distinct periods or phases of the evolution of his thinking.[3]

I   The Philosophical Anthropological: The Critique of the Philosophy of Consciousness and Positivism (1952–1971)

This period extends from the time of his first doctoral dissertation *Das Absolute und die Geschichte. Von der Zwiespältigkeit in Schellings Denken* in 1954,[4] through to *Knowledge and Human Interests* (1968). This is the period in which he is still deeply influenced by Erich Rothacker, Helmut Plessner, Arnold Gehlen, Hans-Georg Gadamer, and even Martin Heidegger. During this period, he wrote *The Structural Transformation of the Public Sphere* (1962), the numerous essays that were collected in *Theory and Practice* (1963), *On the Logic of the Social Sciences* (1967), and *Philosophical-Political Profiles* (1971, 1st edn). Under the influence of Rothacker, his teacher in Bonn, and his close friend Karl-Otto Apel, he undertook a critique of the transcendental, merely epistemic subject (see *LPS*, 66–77). Appropriating elements of historical materialism and hermeneutics, he rejects the philosophy of consciousness that disregards social and natural evolution. Consciousness emerges from specific historical and material conditions that reflect a process of social learning. *The Structural Transformation of the Public Sphere* has to be read precisely as a critique of de-historicized, de-materialized approaches to the emergence of individual and social consciousness. This period is also characterized by Habermas's work on the critique of positivism, in particular, as it had come to permeate the social sciences. The mid-sixties were also the years of the *Positivismustreit* (the Positivism debate) in which Adorno, Habermas, and Wellmer confronted Hans Albert and Karl Popper as the main representatives of a form of critical positivism that in Habermas's view still remained enthralled by the ideology of value-neutral science. In particular, Habermas rejects the naive notion that the social sciences can model themselves after the natural sciences and obtain something like "objectivity." Above all, the social sciences reflect the specific societies that they aim to comprehend. In that case, social science has to engage in a critical self-reflection about how it relates to its own contemporaneity.

There are thus three themes running through this period that culminate in *Knowledge and Human Interests*. First, there is the confrontation with the philosophy of consciousness that found its highest expression in Husserl's phenomenology, which de-historicized the human subject and de-historicized knowledge. Second, there is the critique of positivism in general, but most especially positivism that aligned itself with technocracy, thus contributing to an idolatry of science that entailed the suppression of deliberation and public participation in the political decision-making processes. Third, there is the concern with what Habermas called an "emancipatory knowledge interest," that guides the development of the social sciences. The core of Habermas's thinking during this period involved the development of a philosophical anthropological analysis of knowledge interests. Knowledge and the structures that condition it are not immutable, but both are determined by the fact that knowledge is guided by some basic interest, goals, or *telos*. Habermas identified three knowledge-constitutive interests: technical, practical, and emancipatory. The technical knowledge interest is oriented toward nature and it proceeds by way of objectification and instrumentalization. This knowledge interest has allowed humans to survive by managing nature. The practical interest is oriented toward understanding other human beings; its goal is the coordination of human interaction and behavior. The third knowledge-constitutive interest, that of emancipation, aims at the liberation of humans from conditions of subjugation and "unnatural" constraint.

These three themes were developed in his Goethe University inaugural lecture from 1965, when Habermas was named professor of philosophy there. The Goethe University is in Frankfurt am Main, and it is the university with which the Institute for Social Research is affiliated. In this lecture, simply titled "Knowledge and Human Interests," Habermas formulated five theses, which merit a brief discussion because they exhibit the extent to which Habermas's work has been guided by a series of key themes. The first thesis read: "The achievements of the transcendental subject have their basis in the natural history of the human species" (*KHI*, 312). Evidently, this natural history of the human species must also include humanity's break from nature. For we are the creatures whose very natural history includes the creation of culture, which both links us and separates us from the mere realm of nature. The second thesis read: "knowledge equally serves as an instrument and transcends mere self-preservation" (313). Knowledge which helps us cope with nature is at the same time a tool pregnant with utopian tendencies. All tools also prefigure their overcoming and sketch a better condition beyond mere self-preservation. The third thesis reads: "knowledge-constitutive interests take form in the medium of work, language, and power" (313). These three media relate to the three possible ways in which we apprehend reality: information that enhances our control of our natural environment; interpretations that enable and facilitate interactions with others and cultural traditions; and analyses that liberate consciousness from "hypostatized powers." The fourth thesis reads: "in the power of self-reflection, knowledge and interest are one" (314). Why? Because: "Reason also means the will to reason. In self-reflection knowledge for the sake of knowledge attains congruence with the interest in autonomy and responsibility." Knowledge is thus configured internally by what Habermas calls the emancipatory knowledge interest. Thus, the fifth thesis proclaims: "the unity of knowledge and interest proves itself in a dialectic that takes the historical traces of suppressed dialogue and reconstructs what has been suppressed" (315). Self-reflection is thus also the reconstruction and redemption of past repression.

There is, however, a formulation that captures all these five theses in one thought, a thought that is the life vein of Habermas's entire system of thought: "What raises us out of nature is the only thing whose nature we can know: *language*. Though its structure, autonomy and responsibility are posited for us. Our first sentence expresses unequivocally the intention of universal and unconstrained consensus" (314). Already, here, we find the core of his theory of communicative rationality. When we think about Habermas's engagement with the question of religion, it is not difficult to immediately note that he considered the phenomenon of religion predominantly from a philosophical standpoint, that is, from the standpoint of how religion prefigures philosophical concepts or philosophical categories. Noteworthy pieces from this period are Habermas's essay from 1961, "The German Idealism of Jewish Philosophers," in which he paid tribute to the incredibly important contribution of German Jewish philosophers to the development of German idealism, as well as his essay from the same year, "Dialectical Idealism in Transition to Materialism: The Philosophical Historical Consequences of Schelling's Idea about the Contraction of God," included in the German edition of *Theory and Practice* (1963). While there are some scattered remarks about secularization, the dominant tone in Habermas's early work is of a deep concern with the ways in which religious ideas are a source of philosophical insight, a source that is neither exhausted nor to be dispensed with, if only because, as he put it in his essay on the Jewish philosophers, "we are now forced into the historical irony of taking up the Jewish question without the Jews" (*RR*, 58).

II From the Reconstruction of Historical Materialism toward a Theory of Communicative Action (1971–1982)

This period is one in which the philosophical-anthropological reconstruction of knowledge interests, developed in *Knowledge and Human Interests*, becomes a project about rescuing, transforming, and updating Marxism by infusing it with systems theory, developmental psychology, and social theory in general. *Legitimation Crisis* (1973) belongs to this period. The Gauss Lectures, delivered at Princeton University in 1971, announced this new project in terms of the call for a "linguistification of social theory."[5] The shift from the epistemic subject, to the linguistic structure of both action and understanding becomes the core stone of Habermas's new programmatic orientation. It could be posited that the project of the "reconstruction" of Marxism ends when Habermas writes the 1976 "Was Heisst Universal Pragmatik?" ("What is Universal Pragmatics?"), which was published in a volume edited by Karl-Otto Apel, titled *Sprachpragmatik und Philosophie* (*Language Pragmatics and Philosophy*).[6] Here, it must be noted that the English translation of this essay was published in a book titled *Communication and the Evolution of Society* (*CES*), which takes essays from *Towards the Reconstruction of Historical Materialism* and fuses them with independent essays that will become the foundation for *Theory of Communicative Action* (1981). The shift from the pre-1970s period to the 1970s is the abandonment of philosophical anthropology and hermeneutics, and a shift toward a theory of social rationalization in terms of systems theory and a theory of linguistic competences that allow us to track the evolution of societies, on the one hand, and the socialization of competent moral and acting subjects, on the other. The core of this shift, however, is the abandonment of the project of the reconstruction of knowledge interests for a reconstruction of the "universal conditions of possible understanding [*Verständigung*]" and more concretely, at least since 1976, the project is to reconstruct the "general presuppositions of communicative action" (*CES*, 1).

   The task that Habermas took up during the late 1970s, then, was to reformulate social theory as a general theory of the evolution of communicative action that could explain both individual communicative competencies and how social structures both enabled and passed on such competencies that could at the same time explain modernity with its paradoxes. As Habermas put it, the two-volume work had three distinct tasks; first, to develop:

> a concept of communicative rationality that is sufficiently skeptical in its development but is nevertheless resistant to cognitive-instrumental abridgements of reason; second, a two-level concept of society that connects the "lifeworld" and "system" paradigms in more than a rhetorical fashion; and finally, a theory of modernity that explains the type of social pathologies that are today becoming increasingly visible, by way of the assumption that communicatively structured domains of life are being subordinated to the imperatives of autonomous, formally organized systems of action. (*TCA*, 1.xlii)

TCA, then, is an attempt to offer us:

1 A theory of social evolution as a theory of social rationalization that can allow us to distinguish between pathological and normal or benign forms of rationalization. It is a theory of social evolution that conceptualizes the social order as being enabled through two distinct central mechanisms of integration: on the one side, we have the mechanisms of social integration, and on the other, the mechanisms of systemic integration. While the former refer to the symbolic structures of the lifeworld, the later refer to instrumental securing of the material substratum of society. Thus, society must be conceived as a system that achieves both systemic stabilization and the social integration of social agents by decoupling the lifeworld from the system. This differentiation or decoupling is an evolutionary achievement obtained through learning processes.
2 In conjunction, thus, *TCA* aimed to offer a theory of the ontogenesis of social agents that links both mental and action competencies in terms of communicative competencies. For Habermas, social theory should be able to not just map phylogenesis, but also ontogenesis. Social evolution is also about providing subjects with the competencies to flourish in new levels of social complexity.
3 Finally, *TCA* is a meta-theoretical critique of both philosophy and social theory, in that if a theory of social evolution is about a theory of societal rationalization, then this theory should also provide a criteria by means of which we can evaluate the claims of that theory. In this last aim, Habermas is following his long-time philosophical partner and friend, Apel, who formulated what he called *Selbseinholugnsprinzip* (principle of self-accountability, or self-recuperative principle), which states that any adequate reconstruction of history must "take account of the possibility of the historical development of its own presupposi-

tions."[7] From this perspective, then, *The Theory of Communicative Action* is at the same time a normative reconstruction of the possibility and necessity of critical theory. In Habermas's work, the critique of ideology, which becomes tangled in performative self-contradictions, is turned into a critique of reason that includes self-reflection on the normative grounds of that very same reflection.

As we think about Habermas's treatment of religion in this period, we notice an increased attention to religion, but now from an almost predominantly sociological perspective. As Habermas became mainly concerned with rethinking social theory as a theory of communicative action, he assimilated questions of religion to questions of the rationalization of worldviews and social practices. The most important statement of Habermas's views on religion during this period are to be found in volume two of *TCA*, in the chapter intriguingly titled "The Authority of the Holy and the Normative Background of Communicative Action." In this chapter, Habermas is preoccupied with elucidating, with the aid of George Herbert Mead and Émile Durkheim, the religious sources of the normatively binding power of social systems. Habermas aims to show how religious worldviews, which in the early stages of human evolution provided for an analogical coordination among humans, nature, society, and God, would in turn unleash a power of rationalization that would be the source of social solidarity and the power of moral authority. A key passage from this chapter merits lengthy citation:

> The core of collective consciousness is a normative consensus established and regenerated in the ritual practices of a community of believers. Members thereby orient themselves to religious symbols; the intersubjective unity of the collective presents to them in concepts of the holy. This collective identity defines the circle of those who understand themselves as members of the same social group and can speak of themselves in the first-person plural. The symbolic actions of the rites can be comprehended as residues of a stage of communication that has already been gone beyond in domains of profane social cooperation. (*TCA*, 2.60)

This is a remarkably pregnant passage. As I argued in my introduction to a volume of Habermas's writings on religion, he is here formulating a new way to understand religion, for the core thought here is: religion linguistifies the world through its elaboration of symbols that are embedded in ritualistic practices. This linguistifying symbolization (symbols establish certain semantic and syntactic relations) catalyzes the very distinctions and opposition (God vs World, God vs Us, God and Us vs Others, etc.) that in turn bring about the linguistification of the sacred.[8] This linguistification of the sacred is itself the heart of the logic of secularization.

Before secularization becomes a social-political process, it is first and foremost a mode of making sense of the world through symbols that frame a matrix of subjectivizing, objectifying, and socializing relations. The linguistification of the sacred, the result of the linguistifying symbolization of religion, results in the disempowerment and disenchantment of the sacred, which in turn unleashes the normatively binding power stored in ritualistically achieved fundamental agreements. Both the cowering fear and the uplifting love of the terrifying and spellbinding omnipotent God are sublimated into the *binding/bonding* power of communicative action. In this analysis, however, it is not clear whether religion itself has become a mere archaic source of the normatively binding power of communicative action, or whether, inasmuch as religion continues to be nurtured and transformed in ritual, it continues to nourish the sources of social solidarity. Has religion been totally absorbed into norms of social interaction, leaving nothing behind but the memory of ecstatic rituals and the empty pedestals of exiled gods?

III   Postmetaphysical Thinking and Deliberative Democracy (1982–2000)

This is the period in which Habermas's theory of communicative rationality, qua a theory of rationalities and their social embodiments, is turned into two distinct areas of reflection. On the one hand, Habermas focuses on the ways in which philosophy, qua critique of reason, has either failed or succeeded at grasping the nature of modern society. *TCA* had already announced that one of the goals of social theory should be to comprehend modernity; in this third period, Habermas turns to philosophy itself. If philosophy is reason reflecting on itself, especially of reason as it is embodied in social systems, then the task became to understand to what extent philosophy had either succeeded or failed to grasp modern societies as embodiments of successful or pathological processes of rationalization. In this sense, Habermas took on modern philosophical developments from the standpoint of how they contributed to the self-clarification of society's own rationalization. In other words, in what sense has modern philosophy contributed, or measured up, to the task of understanding the processes of rationalization of society, while also making evident the ways in which such understanding presupposes that clarification? This task is taken up in his *The Philosophical Discourse of Modernity: Twelve Lectures* (1985), a book that should be read as the philosophical sibling of *TCA*. What Habermas had done for social theory in *TCA*, he now sought to achieve for modern philosophy, beginning with Hegel and culminating with Foucault, with whom he was supposed to have a dialogue in 1984, the year of Foucault's untimely death. In tandem, if reason could only now be conceived as embodied in communicative rationality – that is, if reason was now only to be conceived as thoroughly linguistified – then what would be the consequences for philosophy as reason reflecting on itself? Two major consequences followed for Habermas. On the one hand, philosophy has to be conceived as a *platzhalter* or "place holder," that is, as a form of reflection that can merely adjudicate among different scientific theories. Philosophy cannot stand either above or below the other sciences. As a critique of reason or, more precisely, as reason reflecting on itself, philosophy can only relate itself to the different theories or proposals put forward by the various sciences that attend with their distinct expert cultures to different dimensions of human interaction. On the other hand, following through on the theoretical claims established in *TCA*, Habermas had established that social theory should be a theory of modernity, that is, a theory about how society should be conceived as a system of differentiated integration that presupposes the differentiation between the lifeworld and the system level. Now, during this period, Habermas took the next step: what are the consequences for philosophy if reason is to be conceived as embodied in communicative action? Modern philosophy that kept pace with society, with the emergence of new social institutions and a cultural lifeworld, would need to be linguistified, and this meant for Habermas that its point of departure would be different from most classical paradigms in philosophy. Modern philosophy would have to depart from "postmetaphysical thinking." As against the philosophy of origins, or the philosophy of subjectivity, modern philosophy would have to begin from more humble and precarious points of departure. The linguistification of reason meant that philosophy would have to recognize that reason had become historicized, become procedural, and that it had been de-transcendentalized and thus dispossessed of exorbitant claims about the extraordinary or transcendent. In *Postmetaphysical Thinking: Philosophical Essays* (1988), Habermas profiled what he called "postmetaphysical thinking," the only type of thinking that is now possible for any philosophy that aims to remain contemporaneous with the type of society we have achieved, and the self-reflection of reason in its mundane embodiment in communicative action.

At the core of this, Habermas's new theoretical model is the dichotomy of the lifeworld and systems level (taken over from Luhmann and Parsons). As already noted, social evolution is conceived as social learning, learning that is sedimented and crystalized in social systems and mechanisms of the socialization of social agents. While the system level preserves lessons learned from successful instrumentalizations of nature, the lifeworld preserves a reservoir of meanings and cultural institutions through which social agents are socialized into their individuation as they become members of their specific cultural tradition. The lifeworld, which is the hermeneutical horizon in which subjects are socialized and individuated, obeys a logic of rationalization that is guided by interaction that aims at mutual understanding. The lifeworld is a fluid, historical horizon of expectations that is the amniotic medium that nourishes social agents as they become mature. The work from this period thus focuses on the most striking paradox of modern society, namely: the more the system's level is rationalized, the more subjects are unmoored from traditions, the more they are required to seek their orientation by norms rather than unquestioned values. The more action is oriented by instrumental systems, the more the individual is required to make more abstract choices that erode the cohesion and socializing power of background convictions in the lifeworld. The rationalization of the systems comes along with a consequent request for even more rational agents. This unleashes the colonization of the lifeworld by a system's level to the detriment of the former. The challenge is met by new personality structures and the emergence of new psychological orientations. Indeed, the more the subject is unburdened of historically frozen traditions, the more they are required to take normative orientations vis-à-vis their acts or behavior. This is what is called the postconventional moral and psychological orientation. Modern subjects are those that can distinguish questions of the good life from questions about justice. While the former are individual and private, the latter are generalized and concern our interactions with other subjects. For this reason, Habermas turned toward moral philosophy, which is the subject of two of his books from this period: *Moral Consciousness and Communicative Action* (1983), and *Justification and Application* (1991). It could be said that if *The Philosophical Discourse of Modernity* and *Postmetaphysical Thinking* sought to articulate what a thoroughly linguistified reason would mean for philosophy in general, his books on moral theory from this period sought more specifically to render a linguistified version of Kantian deontology. Now, Kant's categorical imperative was reformulated from the perspective of communicative action as the principle of universalization (U) and the discourse principle (D):

> *All* affected can accept the consequences and side effects its *general* observance can be anticipated to have for the satisfaction of *everyone's* interests (and these consequences are preferred to those of known alternative possibilities for regulation). (MCCA, 65)

This principle in turn already entails the fundamental principle of Habermas's discourse ethics, which proclaims:

(D) Only those norms can claim to be valid that meet (or could meet) with the approval of all affected in their capacity *as participants in a practical discourse* (66)

It can be shown, however, that the great accomplishment of this third period is yet another of Habermas's magnum opuses, namely *Faktizitaet und Geltung* (translated with the title *Between Facts and Norms*) (1992). In this work, Habermas develops a theory of democracy that links a procedural theory of law with his discourse ethics. The central idea of this massive work is to show how deliberation among citizens generates a communicative power that translates moral intuitions into administrative power through law. In other words, the process of juridification is a process that links a postconventional moral orientation to the rational regulation of society through the law. Law, in this perspective is Janus-faced. It has one face turned toward moral consciousness, while the other is oriented toward the administrative coordination of agents. But the processes of juridification are rooted in the public deliberation of citizens who actively participate in their self-legislation through democratic participation. If *TCA* raised the specter of the colonization of the lifeworld by the system, the subordination of social integration and interaction to instrumental goal, *Between Facts and Norms* delineates clearly and forcefully the ways in which engaged citizens can and do direct the systemic imperatives. Learning processes occur at two levels, the system and lifeworld; but both obey two different imperatives, and both generate different forms of power. From the lifeworld, through socialization into cultural traditions that are regenerated and transmitted through this very process, agents also get to engage in a process of cultural, or hermeneutical, learning processes. Cultural traditions, thus, are themselves reservoirs of societal accomplishment that require continuous preservation and unleashing. This preservation and unleashing of cultural traditions takes the form of the translation of normative contents that are both buried and deciphered in the very structure of social interactions. To become a competent modern subject whose moral and cognitive orientation is postconventional requires that they become good translators of semantic contents, and preserve the cultural traditions they have been socialized into as individuals and their own individuality. Culture is always a system of translation: it links generations as it transfers and unleashes the moral learning from one community to another. In other words, political systems, and more specifically the background beliefs of a cultural tradition, are not simply instrumental and technical systems for the coordination of action; they also already embody normative contents. It is this growing attention to moral norms and normative contents that led Habermas during this period to pay closer attention to religious issues. Particularly significant in terms of this growing concern with religion are two essays. One essay is from 1988 and was written as a reply to a conference with theologians held at the University of Chicago Divinity School: "Transcendence from Within, Transcendence in this World." In this text, Habermas takes up the questions of theologians, as a philosopher who declares his methodological atheism, but who nonetheless can be sympathetic to the normative questions implied by theological questions. This is a significant text, in that it contains a combination of this sympathy but also distance from theology and religion. On the one hand, religion is here more specifically discussed in terms of ritualistic practices: "Religious discourse is closely joined to a ritual praxis that, in comparison with profane everyday praxis, is limited in the degree of its freedom of communication in a specific way. If a functionalist description is permitted, then it could be said that faith is protected against a radical problematization by its being rooted in cult" (*RR*, 75). Theological discourses that sought to explain these practices did not threaten religious discourses so long as the theological discourses operated on unquestioned metaphysics. Yet, as Habermas points out, metaphysics has been dissolved in the acids of modernity. For this reason, even theological discourses must refer to expert culture in which its claims are adjudicated. Theology itself has succumbed to the logic of postmetaphysical thinking. On the other hand, Habermas affirms against religious philosophers and theologians who claim the indispensability of a transcendent Other as a guarantee for the normativity of our lifeworld that such a claim to unconditionality is present in language itself:

> As agents of communicative action, we are exposed to a transcendence that is integrated in the linguistic conditions of reproduction without being *delivered up* to it. This conception can hardly be identified with the productivist illusion of a species that generates itself and which puts itself in the placed of a disavowed Absolute. Linguistic intersubjectivity goes beyond the subjects without putting them *in bondage* [*hörig*]. It is not a higher-level subjectivity and therefore, without sacrificing a transcendence from within, it can do without the concept of an Absolute. (*RR*, 91)

Language is neither what replaces God conceived as a metaphysical background that unifies everything, an onto-metaphysical substratum, nor something that determines absolutely subjective relations. Communicative action and its corresponding linguistic intersubjectivity are the site of a non-coercive subjection that commands while liberating. Even as postmetaphysical thinking dispenses with God as an onto-metaphysical referent, it retains the insight of a normative claim that constrains as it frees, for, as created creatures, we nonetheless remain utterly free.

The other relevant essay was published in 1991 in a Festschrift for

Alfred Schmidt, which dealt with Max Horkheimer's late work, specifically the work after his so-called religious turn. In this essay, Habermas takes up Horkheimer's claim that the "critical task of philosophy consisted essentially in salvaging the truth of religion in the spirit of the Enlightenment" but that such a task was a pyrrhic one, as the secularization of religion cannot be accomplished without at the same time giving it up (*JA*, 133). The secularization of religion meant its extinguishment. On the other hand, Horkheimer celebrated the dark and skeptical thinkers of the bourgeoisie because they "trumpeted far and wide the impossibility of deriving from reason any fundamental argument against murder."[9] Habermas reads this and similar remarks as entailing that it is "vain to strive for unconditional meaning without God." In response to Horkheimer's skepticism about the task of salvaging religion, Habermas affirms that this task remains philosophy's challenge, but at the same time he rejects Horkheimer's linkage of the unconditional to a transcendent God. In fact, such unconditionality can be discerned in the very structure of language: "Whoever employs language with a view to reaching understanding lays himself open to a transcendence from within. He is left without any choice because he masters the structure of language through the intentionality of the spoken work. Linguistic intentionality outstrips subjects without *subjugating* them."[10] And it is here where religion and philosophy part ways, for it is the distinct characteristic of "postmetaphysical thought" that it differs "from religion in that it recovers the meaning of the unconditional without recourse to God or an Absolute."[11] This "unconditionality," however, is of a different character from the one Horkheimer may have meant, namely, the type of unconditional meaning that grants consolation and perhaps even reprieve: "philosophy cannot provide a substitute for the consolation whereby religion invests unavoidable suffering and unrecompensed injustice, the contingencies of need, loneliness, sickness, and death, with new significance and teaches us to bear them."[12] Morality sublimates the demand for unconditionality, as postmetaphysical thinking reveals it to be implicit in the structure of language. Yet religion retains a function or meaning that can neither be usurped nor replaced by philosophy, namely, the need for consolation and even reprieve in the face of unmerited suffering and anguish.

IV   Postsecular Consciousness and World Society (2001)

A thinker like Habermas, who is so attuned to the spirit of the times, would not be one to have either over-reacted or under-reacted to the terrorist attack of 2001. He certainly would not have been the slowest John

Wayne among intellectuals to have shot a response, which he did on the occasion of receiving the German Booksellers' Association "Freedom Prize." Yet, notwithstanding the bellicose metaphor, Habermas's own response was far from a war cry. In this speech, simply titled "Faith and Reason," Habermas took the terrorist attack in the US as an opportunity not to pile accusations or vilifications upon alleged enemies, but rather to reflect on the West's own tense relationship with the process of secularization: "Orthodoxies exist in the Western world as well as in the Middle or Far East, among Christians and Jews as well as among Muslims. Who wants to avoid a clash of civilizations must call to mind that the dialectic of our occidental process of secularization is not yet closed" (*FHN*, 102, my trans.). He had, as we have chronicled thus far, been profoundly concerned with the role of religion in Western society. He had thus far approached the question of religion from philosophical, sociological, and ethical perspectives. But by the end of the 1990s, as he continued his engagement with John Rawls's work, he had began to consider the challenge of religion from the standpoint of deliberative democracy. In fact, I visited Habermas during the summer of 2001 at Starnberg, and had several hours' conversation and dinner with him that was taken up by discussion of his current work: what should be the proper response of a constitutional democracy to the religious belief and claims of society in such a way that they are not adversely disadvantaged in relation to secular citizens? Essentially, these were the ideas that would be articulated in a series of essays now published in *Between Naturalism and Religion*. One of these essays was presented at a colloquium where Habermas entered into dialogue with then Cardinal Ratzinger, now retired Pope Benedict XVI, in which he articulates the relationship between postmetaphysical thinking and postsecular society, terms that he appropriated from his long-term collaborator Klaus Eder. His other substantive contribution from this period, the long essay "Religion in the Public Sphere," takes up where the essay from the dialogue takes off, namely from the imperative call that "A liberal political culture can even expect of its secularized citizens that they participate in efforts to translate contributions form the religious language into the publicly accessible one."[13] In "Religion in the Public Sphere," Habermas aims to show how secularization cannot be seen as a zero sum in which gains in secularization are losses for religion, for both secular society and religion are caught in a dialectic, one in which the former continues to translate semantic contents of moral and ethical value, while religions themselves enter into a process of both protection and self-clarification.

In the fall of 2012, Habermas published another collection of essays, titled very tellingly *Nachmetaphysisches Denken II: Aufsätzen und Repliken* (*Postmetaphysical Thinking II: Essays and Replays*). It is telling because of the II, clearly aligning this book with his 1988 book of the same title. That book gathered all those essays that deal with the rethinking of philosophy in light of the linguistic turn. This new collection, which is divided into three parts, opens with three essays on the lifeworld as the background against which we as communicative agents are always under the expectation and burden of having to give reasons. The first essay returns to one of Habermas's old preoccupations, how to think through a lingustified phenomenology about the relationship between world pictures and the lifeworld. World pictures arise from lifeworlds, but they have an impact on how that lifeworld is structured. This line of analysis is expanded by the development of some hypotheses about the way in which ritual may have been indispensable for the emergence of myths and mythical worldviews. The second section of the book is eponymously titled "postmetaphysical thinking" and is made up of two very lengthy replies to engagements with his working manuscript on religion. One of the replies in the German book is the one that closes the present book. This section also contains a long interview I conducted with Habermas while he was a visiting professor at Stony Brook University, and which is available in English at the website of the Social Science Research Council, under the blog "Immanent Frame."[14] These three texts, as the title of the section indicate, are predominantly concerned with offering a genealogy of a postmetaphysical approach to religion, or rather, why postmetaphysical thinking cannot and should not continue to share the "secularist" bias that most Enlightenment thinking has seemed to presuppose and defend. In these texts, Habermas is working assiduously to demonstrate how respectful but critical engagement with religion has been fruitful and can continue to be fruitful. The third section, titled "Politics and Religion," is made up of four shorter essays that through engagement with John Rawls's thinking – which includes a lengthy review of Rawls's recently discovered and published senior thesis at Princeton[15] – explores the distinctly political challenges of religion to constitutional democracies, global and national religious pluralism, as well as in what sense neo-Schmittian and neo-Straussian discussions of "the Political" cannot be an appropriate philosophical-political response to the economic crises of globalized financial capital and the growing political deficit of rule-of-law democracies.[16]

This latest book offers us a wide lens into Habermas's theoretical laboratory, and anticipates generously the manuscript he has been working on during the last few years. This manuscript, already over five hundred pages, carries for the moment the titled "Versuch über Glauben und Wissen: Zur Genealogie nachmetaphysischen Denke" ("Essay on Faith and Knowledge: On the Genealogy of Postmetaphysical Thinking"). The manuscript is so far divided into five chapters. The first two were presented as lectures at Yale in the fall of 2008. Chapter 1 deals with the "revitalization of the world religions as a challenge for the secular self-understanding of modernity." This chapter takes as its point of departure debates about the viability of the secularization thesis, which was and remains central to most modern social theory.[17] This chapter in fact aims to rethink the foundations of sociological theories about modernity in light of a necessary uncoupling of the secularization of political power from the non-secularization of social life, due precisely to the obvious persistence of religion at the social and cultural levels. Chapter 2 focuses on the "sacred roots of the Axial Age traditions." The theme is, however, the "cognitive breakthroughs" that were embodied in the monotheistic and universalistic axial religions. This chapter ends with a lengthy discussion of the origins of language out of ritual and myth. The next chapter deals with the transformation of religious consciousness itself through the cognitive breakthroughs embodied in these universalistic axial religions. These two chapters can be read as attempts to explain religion and philosophy, out of their common axial roots, as thematizing and crystallizing the acquisition of cognitive competencies and orientations that were the result of learning processes unleashed by new forms of social and political organization. Chapter 4 offers a comparison among some of the Axial Age world pictures. There are analyses and discussions of Buddha's teachings, Confucianism and Daoism, Socrates's "Natural Philosophy," and Plato's doctrine of ideas. The fifth chapter closes, for the moment, on an analysis of the configuration of a distinct constellation of forces among faith and knowledge as a "result of the convergence and conjunction between Christianity and Platonism." This manuscript, frequently interrupted due to Habermas's commitment as a European public intellectual to speaking about the effects of the financial crisis on the European Union, reveals that his concerns with religion are neither faddish nor superficial. As it stands, the text is already a major statement on the need to rethink both the Eurocentric and "secularist" foundations of modern social theory in light of contemporary trends and the fact of the emergence of a global society, which have made such biases and prejudices anachronistic and self-deluding. The work is also a re-articulation and re-tracing of philosophy's own engagement with faith and religion, ongoing since its christening by Socrates and Plato in ancient Greece. But something else has already been made very clear by Habermas about his growing *oeuvre* on religion – that this work on how we have to re-articulate social theory and philosophy's own self-understanding in the modern age has unequivocal and obvious political relevance and efficacy. These are not idle speculations by the living giant of philosophy, but are pointed and eloquent interventions in the global public sphere concerning how we ought to deal with the fact of religious pluralism in the midst of the failure of economic and political systems, alongside the growing global inequalities that have become fuel for religious violence and political intolerance.

Notes and References

Editors' Introduction

1 See the exchange between Habermas and Charles Taylor in Eduardo Mendieta and Jonathan VanAntwerpen, eds, *The Power of Religion in the Public Sphere* (New York: Columbia University Press, 2011), pp. 60–9.

2 This book is the product of a workshop held at New York University's Institute for Public Knowledge, and co-sponsored by the Social Science Research Council and Stony Brook University. As editors, we are particularly grateful to Charles Gelman for assistance with both the organization of the workshop and the compilation and editing of the volume. We should note that since the workshop at NYU, Habermas has revised and published some of the work-in-progress that was originally distributed to workshop participants.

3 See Craig Calhoun, ed., *Habermas and the Public Sphere* (Cambridge, MA: MIT Press, 1992).

4 See David Zaret, "Religion, Science, and Printing in the Public Spheres in Seventeenth Century England," in Craig Calhoun, ed., *Habermas and the Public Sphere* (Cambridge, MA: MIT Press, 1992), pp. 212–35; and Craig Calhoun, "Introduction: Habermas and the Public Sphere," in Craig Calhoun, ed., *Habermas and the Public Sphere* (Cambridge, MA: MIT Press, 1992), pp. 1–48.

Chapter 1 Exploring the Postsecular: Three Meanings of "the Secular" and Their Possible Transcendence

1 Robert A. Markus, *Christianity and the Secular* (Notre Dame, IN: University of Notre Dame Press, 2006).

2 Charles Taylor, *A Secular Age* (Cambridge, MA: Harvard University Press, 2008). My analysis in the following section draws upon my review of Taylor's work: José Casanova, "A Secular Age: Dawn or Twilight," in Michael Warner,

Jonathan VanAntwerpen, and Craig Calhoun, eds, *Varieties of Secularism in a Secular Age* (Cambridge, MA: Harvard University Press, 2010).

3 Peter Berger, Grace Davie, and Effie Fokas, *Religious America, Secular Europe? A Theme and Variations* (Burlington, VT: Ashgate, 2008).

4 Peter Berger, ed., *The Desecularization of the World* (Washington, DC: Ethics and Public Policy Center, 1999); David Martin, *Has Secularization Gone into Reverse?* Occasional Paper 13 (Malta: DISCERN, 2010), p. 28.

5 Taylor, *A Secular Age*, p. 269.

6 Marcel Gauchet, *The Disenchantment of the World: A Political History of Religion* (Princeton, NJ: Princeton University Press, 1997).

7 "A Postsecular World Society? On the Philosophical Significance of Postsecular Consciousness and the Multicultural World Society," An Interview with Jürgen Habermas, by Eduardo Mendieta. *The Immanent Frame,* Posted February 2010 at: <http://blogs.ssrc.org/tif/2010/02/03/a-postsecular-world-society/.

8 José Casanova, *Public Religions in the Modern World* (Chicago, IL: University of Chicago Press, 1994).

9 Rodney Stark, "Secularization RIP," *Sociology of Religion,* 62/2 (1999); Rodney Stark and William S. Bainbridge, *The Future of Religion* (Berkeley, CA: University of California Press, 1985).

10 There is empirical evidence of some progressive decline in the last decades in the number of those who declare never to attend religious services in the US. But one should take into account that it is a decline from unusually extraordinarily high level of religious practice, so that even now the proportion of those who declare never to attend religious services hovers in the upper teens, a percentage which is well below the one that one finds even in the least secularized societies of Europe, namely, Poland, Ireland, Portugal, or Greece. Defenders of the European paradigm of secularization have fastened on to this declining trend in religious practice, and upon the empirical evidence of increase in the proportion of those who declare "no religion" from 8 percent to 12 percent of the American population since the 1990s, as evidence that at long last American society is also undergoing a process of secularization similar to the European one. I think one can offer more persuasive explanations for the latest religious trends in America than to argue that American society at last is also following general European patterns of secularization. See the 2007 US Religious Landscape Survey. Pew Forum on Religion and Public Life, available at: <http://religions.pewforum.org/reports>.

11 R. Stephen Warner, "Work in Progress Toward a New Paradigm for the Sociological Study of Religion in the United States," *American Journal of Sociology,* 98/5(1993): 1044–93.

12 Theodore Caplow, "Contrasting Trends in European and American Religion," *Sociological Analysis,* 46/2(1985); Rodney Stark and Laurence Iannaccone, "A Supply-side Interpretation of the 'Secularization' of Europe," *Journal for the Scientific Study of Religion,* 33(1994); Roger Finke, "The Consequences of Religious Competition: Supply-side Explanations for Religious Change," in L. A. Young, ed., *Rational Choice Theory and Religion: Summary and Assessment* (New York: Routledge, 1997).

13 Steve Bruce, "The Supply-Side Model of Religion: The Nordic and Baltic States," *Journal for the Scientific Study of Religion*, 39/1(2000).

14 José Casanova, "Beyond European and American Exceptionalism: Towards a Global Comparative Perspective," in Grace Davie, Paul Heelas, and Linda Woodehead, eds, *Predicting Religion* (Burlington, VT: Ashgate, 2003).

15 Berger, Davie, and Fokas, *Religious America, Secular Europe*.

16 Pippa Norris and Ronald Inglehart, *Sacred and Secular: Religion and Politics Worldwide* (New York: Cambridge University Press, 2004).

17 Unpublished manuscript, distributed to symposium participants in 2009.

18 Pippa Norris and Ronald Inglehart, *Sacred and Secular*, p. 5.

19 There is, moreover, significant evidence of various kinds of religious revivals within contemporary China (*qigong* movements as well as evangelical Christianity, Taoism as well as folk religion, Confucianism as well as Buddhism) as it experiences dramatic rates of economic growth and increasing levels of socio-economic development across large sectors of the Chinese population, which are similar to developments associated with South Korean and, to a lesser extent, Japanese modernization.

20 Actually, the most disprivileged decile of the American population seems to be less religious than economically more secure sectors.

21 José Casanova, "Immigration and the New Religious Pluralism: A EU/US Comparison," in Thomas Banchoff, ed., *Democracy and the New Religious Pluralism* (New York: Oxford University Press, 2007), pp. 59–84.

22 José Casanova, "Spanish Religiosity: An Interpretative Reading of the Religion Monitor Results for Spain," in Bertelsmann Stiftung, ed., *What the World Believes: Analyses and Commentary on the Religion Monitor 2008* (Gütersloh: Verlag Bertelsmann Stiftung, 2009), pp. 223–56.

23 Danièle Hervieu-Léger, *Religion as a Chain of Memory* (New Brunswick, NJ: Transaction Books, 2000).

24 José Casanova, *Europas Angst vor der Religion* (Berlin: Berlin University Press, 2009).

25 As quoted in Jürgen Habermas, "Versuch über Glauben und Wissen. Nachmetaphysisches Denken und das säkulare Selbstverständnis der Moderne," unpublished manuscript, 2009, p. 1.

Chapter 2 The Anxiety of Contingency: Religion in a Secular Age

1 Radio interview with Eugen Kogon, published in the *Frankfurter Hefte*, 13/6 (June 1958): 494. In English: *Critical Models, Interventions and Catchwords*, transl. Henry Pickford (New York: Columbia University Press, 1998), pp. 135–42 (translation modified).

2 T. Adorno, "Reason and Revelation," in Adorno, *Critical Models: Interventions and Catchwords* (New York: Columbia University Press, 1998), p. 136.

3 In Habermas's words: "I assume that the constitution of the liberal state can satisfy its need of legitimation in a modest way by drawing on the cognitive sources of a set of arguments that are independent of religious or

metaphysical traditions; however, even granting this premise there remain doubts from the motivational side" (*BNR*, p. 104).

4 As when he says that: "This diagnosis cannot be dismissed out of hand; but it should not be understood in such a way that the learned defenders of religion derive an unearned benefit from it, as it were," (ibid., p. 102).

5 That he was developing during those same years, as in his crucial essay "What is Universal Pragmatics?" (1976), which was also published in *CES* and *PSI*.

6 In an unpublished manuscript, "Essay on Faith and Knowledge: Postmetaphysical Thinking and the Secular Self-Interpretation of Modernity" (delivered as Lectures at Yale University, 2008), he states this explicitly in the context of the discussion of the alternative conception of modernity of J. P. Aranson: "The assumptions of the theory of civilizations can serve as a correction to a certain evolution-theoretical narrowness of *The Theory of Communicative Action*" (p. 26, n. 51).

7 See David Zaret, "Religion, Science, and Printing in the Public Spheres in Seventeenth Century England," in Craig Calhoun, ed., *Habermas and the Public Sphere* (Cambridge, MA: MIT Press, 1992), pp. 212–35. And, in the same volume, Thomas McCarthy, "Practical Discourse: on the Relation of Morality to Politics," pp. 51–72.

8 On this distinction, I follow Thomas McCarthy; see "Legitimacy and Diversity: Dialectical Reflections on Analytical Distinctions," *Cardozo Law Review*, 17/4–5 (March 1996): 1083–1125.

9 See, for example, the kind of historical reconstruction undertaken by Stephen Toulmin, in *Cosmopolis, The Hidden Agenda of Modernity* (Chicago, IL: University of Chicago Press, 1992), where he also criticizes some simple-minded historical narratives in the history of philosophy, but, at the same time, offers reasons to pay attention to the concrete historical situation of the writing of philosophy: "Each new philosopher presents theses to an audience that lives, with him, in a situation different from those of his predecessors. Their *contexts* of writing often differ in major respects; and by ignoring these differences, we impoverish our understanding of the *content* of their ideas" (pp. 86–7, emphasis in the original).

10 See Steve Bruce, ed., *Religion and Modernization: Sociologists and Historians Debate the Secularization Thesis* (Oxford: Clarendon Press, 1992). See also José Casanova, *Public Religions in the Modern World* (Chicago, IL, and London, University of Chicago Press, 1994), p. 163.

11 See Hans Blumenberg, "Status of the Concept," ch.1 in *The Legitimacy of the Modern Age* (Cambridge, MA, and London: MIT Press, 1983), pp. 3–11.

12 See "Rethinking Secularism and Religion in the Global Age" (a discussion with Robert Bellah), posted by Mark Juergensmayer, *The Immanent Frame* (SSRC Blogs, 08/09/2009), available at: <http://blogs.ssrc.org/tif/2009/09/08/rethinking-secularism-and-religion-in-the-global-age/> (accessed March 3, 2013).

13 J. Casanova, *Public Religions in the Modern World*, p. 214.

14 Celebrations held in ancient Rome (which originated with the Etruscans) to

mark the commencement of a new *saeculum* or generation, a pagan ceremony (an expiatory offering for the past and on behalf of the coming generation) recovered later by Pope Boniface VII, who changed their name to *Papal Jubilees*. See *The New Encyclopedia Britannica*, Micropaedia, vol. 10, 15th edn (Chicago, IL: University of Chicago, 1990), p. 592.

15 See Bryan R. Wilson, "Reflections on a Many Sided Controversy," in S. Bruce, ed., *Religion and Modernization,* pp. 195–210.

16 As presented by Lucien Goldmann, in *Le Dieu caché* (Paris: Gallimard, 1955).

17 According to H. Blumenberg, this implied a supplementary theory in which there is a re-valuation of the process of secularization as providential: "Thus a loss of power, influence, occupied positions, and cultural ambience can be understood 'as a providential process with a purifying effect on Christianity,'" Cfr. Hellmut Gollwitzer, in Hans Blumenberg, *The Legitimacy of the Modern Age*, transl. Robert M. Wallace (Cambridge, MA: MIT Press, 1983), Note 2, Part I, p. 7.

18 See, on this topic, William Connolly, *Capitalism and Christianity, American Style*, (Durham, NC, and London: Duke University Press, 2008).

19 See *The Immanent Frame* (SSRC Blogs, 08/09/2009).

20 As reported by Roy Wallis and Steven Bruce, in S. Bruce, ed., "Secularization: The Orthodox Model," *Religion and Modernization* (Oxford: Clarendon Press, 2001), p. 20.

21 R. Wallis and S. Bruce, commenting on Hugh McLeod's contribution to the same volume: "Secular Cities? Berlin, London and New York in the Later Nineteenth and Early Twentieth Centuries," in *Religion and Modernization*, p. 21.

22 For example, in the Bible we could find textual support for an egalitarian and cosmopolitan morality: "There shall be one law for the citizen and for the stranger who dwells among you" (Exodus 12:49). Quoted in a letter to *The New York Review of Books* by Avishal Margalit and Michael Walzer (October 8–21, 2009, vol. LVI, no. 15, p. 46). Or grounds can be found for justifying fixed hierarchies and forms of social inequality (based on gender, class, and other differences), as has been the case in the history of Christianity.

23 See Norbert Brieskorn, in Habermas, *AWM*, p. 33.

24 Ibid.

25 For the use of the media and political accommodations of fundamentalist Christian movements in the US, see Steve Bruce, "Modernity and Fundamentalism: The New Christian Right in America," *The British Journal of Sociology*, 41/4 (December 1990): 477–96.

26 Charles Taylor, *A Secular Age* (Cambridge, MA, and London: Harvard University Press, 2007), pp. 429–30.

27 Charles Taylor, *A Secular Age*, Part V, pp. 539–72.

28 Ibid., pp. 19–20.

29 Ibid., p. 488.

30 Cf. Philip Reiff, *The Triumph of the Therapeutic: Uses of Faith After Freud* (New York: Harper and Row, 1966); Taylor, *A Secular Age*, p. 618.

31 Charles Taylor, *A Secular Age*, p. 21.

32 Ibid., pp. 711–27.

33 John Rawls, *Political Liberalism* (New York: Columbia University Press, 1993), and *The Law of Peoples: The Idea of Public Reason Revisited* (Cambridge, MA: Harvard University Press, 1999).

34 See Susan Meld Shell, *Kant and the Limits of Autonomy* (Cambridge, MA, and London: Harvard University Press, 2009).

35 Ibid., p. 193.

36 Ibid., chapter 5, pp. 186–211.

37 Ibid., p. 338.

Chapter 3 Is the Postsecular a Return to Political Theology?

1 I wish to thank the reviewers for their suggestions, as well as those made by Chiara Bottici, Alessandro Ferrara, Craig Calhoun, and Eduardo Mendieta.

2 Charles Taylor, *A Secular Age* (Cambridge, MA, and London: Harvard University Press, 2007).

3 See Mark Lilla, *The Stillborn God: Religion and Politics, and the Modern Western* (New York: Alfred A. Knopf, 2007). For a very careful study about the relationship of religion in political conceptual building, see Ronald Beiner, *Civil Religion in the History of Political Philosophy* (New York: Cambridge University Press, 2011). For a sociological discussion about the importance and dependence of religion, see Hans Joas, *Do We Need Religion? On the Experience of Self-Transcendence* (Boulder, CO, and London: Paradigm Publishers, 2008).

4 This was the title of the book written by Hans Blumenberg, who argued against the theory of secularization as an eschatological translation by Karl Löwith. See Hans Blumenberg, *The Legitimacy of the Modern Age*, transl. Robert M. Wallace (Cambridge, MA: MIT Press, 1991). See also Karl Löwith, *Meaning in History* (Chicago, IL, and London: University of Chicago Press, 1949).

5 See Jürgen Habermas, "Religion in the Public Sphere", *European Journal of Philosophy*, 14/1 (2006): 1–25.

6 See Cristina Lafont, "Religions in the Public Sphere: Remarks on Habermas's Conception of Public Deliberation in Postsecular Societies," published in the journal *Constellations*, 14/2(2007): 239–59. See in the same volume of the journal the articles by Maeve Cooke and Simone Chambers.

7 See Reinhart Koselleck, *Future Past: On the Semantics of Historical Time*, transl. Keith Tribe (Cambridge, MA: MIT Press. 1985), p. 74.

8 Ibid.

9 Carl Schmitt, *Political Theology: Four Chapters on the Concept of Sovereignty*, translated by George Schwab (Cambridge, MA: MIT Press. 1988), p. 36.

10 Habermas has written a piece about this subject recently, which I will also be citing and using. See Jürgen Habermas, "'The Political': The Rational

Meaning of a Questionable Inheritance of Political Theology Revised" (I am citing directly from a manuscript given to us at the Workshop).

11 In effect, Kant argues "I am left with the *formal attribute of publicness*. For every claim upon right potentially possesses this attribute, and without it, there can be no justice (which can only be conceived of as *publicly knowable*) and therefore no right, since right can only come from justice," in Immanuel Kant, second section: "On the Agreement Between Politics and Morality According to the Transcendental Concept of Public Right," in *Perpetual Peace*, transl. H. B. Nisbet (New York: Cambridge University Press. 1991), pp. 93–130, and p. 125.

12 Key in this regard is how he conceptualized the notion of the public opinion. See Immanuel Kant, Appendix I to *Perpetual Peace*, transl. H. B. Nisbet (New York: Cambridge University Press, 1991), p. 116, and p. 125.

13 It could also be defined as the other way round, namely, as immanent practices that inspire the theoretical conceptual building into coining a concept that then transforms itself into a new path of legitimate action.

14 Reinhart Koselleck, *Critique and Crisis: Enlightenment and Pathogenesis of Modern Society*, transl. Berg Publishers (Cambridge, MA: MIT Press, 1988).

15 Ibid., p. 2.

16 See Koselleck, *Critique and Crisis*.

17 Koselleck, *Critique and Crisis*. As in n. 13 of this chapter, it could also be defined as the other way round, namely, as immanent practices that inspire the theoretical conceptual building into coining a concept that then transforms itself into a new path of legitimate action.

18 Ibid., p. 2.

19 See Koselleck, *Critique and Crisis*.

20 Löwith argues that "'The future of Christianity' is, as Rosenstock-Huessy recently pointed out, no casual combination of two words, like the future of motoring. The living toward a future *eschaton* and back from it to a new beginning is characteristic only for those who live essentially by hope and expectation – the Jews and the Christians. To this extent future and Christianity are synonymous. A basic difference between Christianity and secular futurism is, however, that the pilgrim's progress is not an indefinite advance toward an unattainable ideal but a definite choice in the face of the eternal reality and that the Christian hope in the Kingdom of God is bound up with fear of the Lord, while the secular hope for a 'better world' looks forward without fear and trembling. They have in common, nonetheless, the eschatological viewpoint and outlook into the future as such. The idea of progress could become the leading principle for the understanding of history only within this primary horizon of the future as established by Jewish and Christian faith, against the 'hopeless, because cyclic, world view of paganism'," in Karl Löwith, *Meaning and History* (Chicago, IL, and London: University of Chicago Press, 1959), p. 84.

21 Ibid., p. 5.

22 Ibid., p. 4.

23 Hans Blumenberg, *The Legitimacy of the Modern Age*, transl. Robert M. Wallace (Cambridge, MA: MIT Press, 1991).

24 Ibid., p. 136.

25 Blumenberg argues that "the converted Gnostic had to provide an equivalent for the cosmic principle of evil in the bosom of mankind itself. He found it in inherited sinfulness, as a quantity of corruption that is constant rather than being the result of the summation of individual faulty actions," in Blumenberg, *The Legitimacy of the Modern Age*, p. 53.

26 "The concept of the bad in the world had been displaced and continues up to the present to be displaced further and further: the bad [Bösse] aspect of the world appears less and less clearly as a physical defect of nature and more and more (and with less ambiguity, on account of the technical means by which we amplify these things) as the result of human actions," Blumenberg, *The Legitimacy of the Modern Age*, p. 56.

27 Hans Blumenberg, *The Legitimacy of the Modern Age*, p. 126.

28 "Self-assertion [. . .] means an existential program, according to which man posits his existence in a historical situation and indicates to himself how he is going to deal with the reality surrounding him and what use he will make of the possibilities that are open to him" (Blumenberg, *The Legitimacy of the Modern Age*, p. 138).

29 Blumenberg, *The Legitimacy of the Modern Age*, p. 214.

30 Ibid.

31 Hans Blumenberg, *The Work on Myth*, transl. Robert M. Wallace (Cambridge, MA: MIT Press, 1990).

32 Ibid.

33 Only the religions based on "the Book" – as Bottici argues – "are fundamentally hostile to myth" because the "written word became the means through which God revealed himself as a unique God, the *biblos* became the bearer of an absolute claim to truth that was alien to myth," in Chiara Bottici, *A Philosophy of Political Myth* (New York: Cambridge University Press, 2007), p. 48.

34 Blumenberg, *The Work on Myth*, p. 274.

35 In Löwith's view, Marx is interpreted as a prophet; his theory of historical progress is seen as mere eschatology. See Löwith, *Meaning in History* (Chicago, IL, and London: University of Chicago Press, 1949), pp. 33–51.

36 This position is also the one taken by Jan Assman in his book *The Price of Monotheism*. He says that the written tradition of monotheistic religions are part of the "Scriptural Turn" and he explains it as: "the shift from primary to secondary religious experience [which] can be understood as a shift from ritual to text. Whereas, in primary archaic religions, the text is embedded in ritual and subordinate it to it, in monotheism the text (in the form of canonized writings) assumes cardinal importance, and ritual is reduced to a supporting and supplementary role. The turn from one to the other acts as a watershed, separating two types of religion, which could be contrasted as cult religions and book religions. The latter include the three Western monotheisms of Judaism, Christianity, and Islam, as well as Buddhism, Jainism, and the Sikh religion. *All secondary religions are religions of the book. They are based on a canon of sacred texts like the Hebrew Bible, the Christian*

Bible, The Koran, the Jaina Canon, the Pali Canon, and the Adi Granth. The monotheistic turn has its correlate in a change of medium. Writing and transcendence belong together on the side of the secondary religions, just as ritual and immanence belong together on the side of primary religions" (italics are mine), in Jan Assman, *The Price of Monotheism*, transl. Robert Savage (Stanford, CA: Stanford University Press. 2010), p. 104.

37 Blumenberg cites Shakespeare as his main example.
38 His work on myth in the political domain begins with how Hobbes first used the myth of Prometheus in order to deal with the question of order and chaos. The social contract was the device used by Hobbes to restore the order among beastly men. He also reconstructs how Rousseau took up the myth of Prometheus to envision dangers within the gift of fire (culture). His analysis goes on to interpret Marx not in the eschatological version that Löwith had presented before, but rather, by making explicit how Marx used the device of Prometheus to explore his own project of writing a theory for human liberation from the chains of capitalism. According to Blumenberg, Marx later proposed the proletariat as a collective actor that took up the Promethean enterprise of becoming the collective actor of political emancipation. See Blumenberg, *The Work on Myth*, p. 586.
39 Koselleck argues that "a central target of the critical offensive, the Christian religion in its manifold divisions, prepared the charismatic-historical heritage that was subsumed into the future-oriented worldview, in the most varied ways. We know the process of secularization, which transposed eschatology into a history of progress. But, likewise, consciously and deliberately, the elements of divine judgment and the Last Day were applied to history itself, above all in the exacerbated situation," in Koselleck, *Critique and Crisis*, p. 11.
40 Koselleck argues "insofar as conscience participated in the political world it became the controlling authority of the duty to obey," in *Critique and Crisis*, p. 37.
41 Ibid., p. 54.
42 Ibid, p. 55.
43 Organizations that Koselleck says were the places "where philosophers, for instance, devote themselves especially to the investigation of the moral laws," in *Critique and Crisis*, p. 55.
44 "In the secret Masonic organizations, religious and political elements entered into a new kind of union. Rationalistic resurgences of the myths and mysteries of Antiquity and the unfolding of a dominant indigenous hierarchy characterized the leagues; as a whole, however, they were part neither of the Church nor State but a form of organization peculiar to the new bourgeois society. In essence, Freemasonry is as old as bourgeois society – if bourgeois society is not indeed a mere scion of Freemasonry" (ibid., p. 71).
45 Koselleck argues that "In England and France the word group associated with the concept of criticism was incorporated into the national languages from the Latin around 1600. The terms *critique* and 'criticism' (and also 'criticks') established themselves in the seventeenth century. What was meant by them was the art of objective evaluation – particularly of ancient texts, but

also of literature and art, as well as of nations and individuals," in *Critique and Crisis*, p. 105.

46 This position bears many similarities with the one developed by Carl Schmitt, who argues about how concepts such as "humanity" are ideological instruments of "imperialist expansion, and in its ethical-humanitarian form it is a specific vehicle of economic imperialism." He adds: "humanity is not a political concept, and no political entity or society and no status corresponds to it," in Schmitt, *The Concept of the Political*, transl. George Schwab (Chicago, IL, and London: University of Chicago Press, 1996), pp. 54–5.

47 Ibid., p. 119.

48 Indeed, Koselleck argues "The philosophy of history substantiated the elitist consciousness of the Enlightenment. This was the power that the Illuminati possessed, a power they shared with the whole of Enlightenment. This was the threat: it revealed the plan of conquest to those under attack," in *Critique and Crisis*, p. 130.

49 Ibid., p. 137.

50 Maeve Cooke has analyzed the problematics of critical theory versus utopian theories in her book *Re-Presenting the Good Society* (Cambridge, MA: MIT Press, 2007), pp. 129–88.

51 Hannah Arendt, *On Revolution* (New York: Penguin Books, 1990).

52 Hannah Arendt, "What is Authority?," published in the volume *Between Past and Future* (New York: Penguin, 1977), p. 92.

53 Ibid., p. 108.

54 Maeve Cooke defines this authoritarian position as the "position appeals to a transcendent, final authority . . . the crucial feature of this position, which sets it off from the preceding one, is that correct perception entails the acceptance of the unquestionable authority of some transcendent power or idea. Thus, appeals to authority of a divine will, or to natural necessity, or to the logic of history, are typical," in her *Re-Presenting the Good Society* (2007), p. 15.

55 Hannah Arendt, "What is Authority?," p. 115.

56 Hannah Arendt, "Foundation I: Constitutio Libertatis" and "Foundation II: Novus Ordus Saeclorum," in *On Revolution* (New York: Penguin Books, 1990), pp. 115–78 and 179–214.

57 Arendt, "Foundation I: Constitutio Libertatis," p. 157.

58 Ibid.

59 Jürgen Habermas, "'The Political': The Rational Meaning of a Questionable Inheritance of Political Theology Revised" (I am citing from the manuscript).

60 Reinhart Koselleck, *Critique and Crisis: Enlightenment and the Pathogenesis of Modern State* (Cambridge, MA: MIT Press, 1988), p. 39.

61 See, for example, *STPS*, p. 272 nn.8, 9, 11, 77, where he cites this work by Koselleck.

62 Habermas argues that "Kant's concept of publicity held good as the one principle that could guarantee the convergence of politics and morality. He conceived of the 'public sphere' at once as a principle of the legal order and as the method of the enlightenment" (*STPS*, p. 104).

63 See Nancy Fraser's essay – among others – first published in Craig Calhoun, ed., *Habermas and the Public Sphere* (Cambridge, MA: MIT Press, 1996), 109–42.

64 Habermas claims in this reply that: "I must confess, however, that only after reading Mikhail Bakhtin's great book *Rabelais and His World* have my eyes become really opened to the *inner* dynamics of plebeian culture. This culture of the common people apparently was by no means only a backdrop, that is, a passive echo of the dominant culture; it was also the periodically recurring violent revolt of a counterproject to the hierarchical world of domination, with its official celebrations and everyday disciplines. Only a stereoscopic view of this sort reveals how a mechanism of exclusion that locks and represses at the same time calls forth the countereffects that cannot be neutralized. If we apply the same perspective to the bourgeois public sphere, the *exclusion of women from this world dominated by men now looks different than it appeared to me at the time*" (italics are mine), in Habermas, "Further Reflections on the Public Sphere," published in Craig Calhoun, ed., *Habermas and the Public Sphere* (Cambridge, MA: MIT Press, 1996), pp. 421–61 and p. 427.

65 He argues in this work that "the political public sphere can fulfill its function of perceiving and thematizing encompassing *social problems* only insofar as it develops out of the communication taking place among *those who are potentially affected*" (italics are mine; *BFN*, p. 365).

66 Habermas argues "I have described the political public sphere as a sounding board for problems that must be processed by the political system because they cannot be solved elsewhere. To this extent, the public sphere is a warning system with sensors that, though unspecialized, are sensitive throughout society. From the perspective of democratic theory, the public sphere must, in addition, amplify the pressure of problems, that is, not only detect and identify problems but also convincingly and *influentially* thematize them in such a way that they are taken up and dealt with by parliamentary complexes" (*BFN*, p. 359).

67 See, especially, Nancy Fraser's article "Rethinking the Public Sphere: A Contribution to the Critique of Actually Existing Democracy," in Craig Cadhoun, ed., *Habermas and the Public Sphere* (Cambridge, MA: MIT Press, 1996), pp. 109–43. Also published in Nancy Fraser, *Justice Interruptus: Critical Reflection on the "PostSocialist" Condition* (New York and London: Routledge, 1997), pp. 69–99.

68 Feminism is key in this regard as can be seen at *BFN*, p. 381.

69 I found Maeve Cooke's study about Habermas's conception of the good society very illuminating. She claims that "Habermas' idea of the ideal speech situation or, more generally, of a communicative rationalized life-world, do not merely evoke a picture of a (more or less) specific social condition; they conjure a picture of society that transcends the contingencies of human life and history and in which human finitude would have been overcome," in Cooke, *Re-Presenting the Good Society* (2007), p. 166.

70 Cooke argues that Habermas's postmetaphysical notion of the good society possesses two features which are important for our discussion: (1) "the projected good society expresses a potential already contained within existing

reality"; (2) Habermas seeks to avoid the accusation of finalism (Koselleck's critique of philosophy of history) because Habermas's views of the good society "must avoid teleological conceptions of the historical process. Instead, it must keep open the process of history by making emancipation a contingent matter, dependent on the perceptions, interpretations, and interventions of concrete, historically situated, autonomous agents who respond to specific experiences and exigencies," in *Re-Presenting the Good Society*, p. 165.

71 Indeed, as Habermas argues, "the labor movement and feminism, for example, were able to join these discourses in order to shatter the structures that had initially constituted them as 'the other' of a bourgeois public sphere" (*BFN*, p. 374).

72 Habermas argues, "political and social actors would be allowed to 'use' the public sphere only insofar as they make convincing contributions to the solution of problems that have been perceived by the public or have been put on the public agenda with the public's consent" (*BFN*, p. 379).

73 By "redemption," Maeve Cooke argues, "making good of present (and possibly past) deficiency: the idea of redemption refers to a condition in which all relevant obstacles to human flourishing would finally be removed," in *Re-Presenting the Good Society*, p. 166.

74 Maeve Cooke, *Re-Presenting the Good Society*, p. 167.

75 Jürgen Habermas, *Between Facts and Norms*, trans. Wilhelm Rehg (Cambridge, MA: MIT Press, 1996), p. 146.

76 Ibid., p. 147.

77 Ibid., p. 148.

78 Ibid., p..149.

79 Ibid., p. 147.

80 Habermas suggests that Julius Fröbel "has recourse to the communicative condition under which opinion formation oriented to truth can be combined with majoritarian will-formation", and, thus, "Fröbel's position shows that the normative tension between equality and liberty can be resolved as soon as one renounces an overly concrete reading of the principle of popular sovereignty" (*BFN*, p. 475).

81 See Plato, *The Republic*, Book 2, 79a. (Plato, *The Republic*. In 12 volumes; volumes 5–6, trans. Paul Shorey. Cambridge, MA: Harvard University Press, 1969–70).

82 Claude Lefort, "The Permanence of the Theological-Political?," published in its English version, transl. David Macey, in Hent de Vries and Lawrence E. Sullivan, eds, *Political Theologies: Public Religion in a Post-Secular World* (New York: Fordham University Press, 2006), pp. 148–87 and p. 187; emphasis mine.

Chapter 4 An Engagement with Jürgen Habermas on Postmetaphysical Philosophy, Religion, and Political Dialogue

1 Habermas observes that "this missing worldview character" of postmetaphysical philosophy does not constitute a defining difference between

postmetaphysical philosophy and religion. "For theology in the West responded to the modern conditions of life with an accommodation of religious traditions and practical articles of faith to the challenge of the monopoly of the sciences over secular knowledge, to the challenge of religious pluralism, and to the challenge of the secular foundation of the constitutional state. The metaphysical substance of the faith has by now become so emaciated that these secular achievements give rise to cognitive dissonances only among fundamentalist circles" (*EFK*, 2.7).

2 Cambridge: Cambridge University Press, 2001.

3 Cf. *EFK*, 1.39: "The self-understanding of the Enlightenment as critical of religion is an expression of a constellation of philosophy and religion that precludes a *dialogical relation* between autonomous reason and religious traditions. Philosophy reserves the right to define the rational content of religious traditions, insofar as one can speak of such at all. A dialogue, by contrast, presupposes a symmetrical relation between the two sides and demands from both the reciprocal readiness to learn from one another if possible – albeit in accordance with the standards of their respective language games. A form of postmetaphysical thinking that wished to engage in such a dialogue would have to find reasons to revise the secularistic self-understanding of autonomous reason that has prevailed since the eighteenth century. Reasons that could prompt secular reason to approach religion *in both a receptive and an agnostic spirit* could follow only from a transformed constellation of science, postmetaphysical thinking, and religion."

4 "Postmetaphysical thinking is prepared to learn from religion while at the same time remaining agnostic. It insists on the difference between the certainties of faith and publicly criticizable validity claims; but it eschews the rationalist presumption that it can itself decide which aspects of religious doctrines are rational and which irrational. The contents that reason appropriates through translation must not be lost for faith" (*BNR*, p. 143).

5 Cf. p. 141: "The secular counterpart to reflexive religious consciousness is an agnostic, but nonreductionist form of postmetaphysical thinking. It refrains, on the one hand, from passing judgment on religious truths, while insisting (in a nonpolemical fashion) on making a strict demarcation between faith and knowledge. On the other hand, it rejects a scientistically truncated conception of reason and exclusion of religious doctrines from the genealogy of reason."

6 For another passage in which Habermas speaks out in opposition to a purely naturalistic philosophy, see *BNR*, pp. 140–1.

Chapter 5 The Burdens of Modernized Faith and Postmetaphysical Reason in Habermas's "Unfinished Project of Enlightenment"

1 Immanuel Kant, *Critique of Pure Reason*. Preface to first edition.

2 Ibid., Preface to second edition.

3 D. S. Browning and F. S. Fiorenza, eds, *Habermas, Modernity, and Public Theology* (New York: Crossroad Publishing, 1992).

4 T. McCarthy, *Race, Empire, and the Idea of Human Development* (Cambridge: Cambridge University Press, 2009), Part Two.

5 J. Habermas, *Versuch über Glauben und Wissen. Nachmetaphysisches Denken und das säkulare Selbstverständnis der Moderne, Kapitel II*, "Der Mythos im Verhältnis zum Ritus" (manuscript, 2009).

6 Ibid.

7 T. McCarthy, *Ideals and Illusions* (Cambridge, MA: MIT Press, 1991); T. McCarthy (with D. Hoy), *Critical Theory* (Oxford: Blackwell, 1994).

8 *Ideals and Illusions*, ch.7; T. McCarthy, "Legitimacy and Diversity: Dialectical Reflections on Analytical Distinctions," in M. Rosenfeld and A. Arato, eds, *Habermas on Law and Democracy* (Berkeley, CA: University of California Press, 1998), pp. 115–53.

9 T. McCarthy. *The Critical Theory of Jürgen Habermas* (Cambridge, MA: MIT Press, 1978), ch. 3.

10 Ibid., 261ff.; *Race, Empire, and the Idea of Human Development* (2009), Part Two.

11 I. Kant, *Critique of Pure Reason*, transl. N. K. Smith (New York: St Martin's Press, 1961), p. 100.

12 Ibid., p. 533f.

13 Ibid., p. 299f.

Chapter 6 Having One's Cake and Eating It Too: Habermas's Genealogy of Postsecular Reason

1 I borrow this tripartite typology from Colin Koopman, *Genealogy as Critique: Foucault and the Problems of Modernity* (Bloomington, IN: Indiana University Press, 2013), chapter 2. Koopman is, in turn, building on Bernard Williams's distinction between vindicatory and subversive genealogies in his *Truth and Truthfulness: An Essay in Genealogy* (Princeton, NJ: Princeton University Press, 2002).

2 Friedrich Nietzsche, *On the Genealogy of Morals*, trans. Walter Kaufmann and R. J. Hollingdale (New York: Vintage, 1967), p. 20.

3 Ibid.

4 For an eloquent defense of Nietzsche on this point, and others, see Alexander Nehamas, *Nietzsche: Life as Literature* (Cambridge, MA: Harvard University Press, 1985).

5 Williams, *Truth and Truthfulness*, p. 263. Cited in Koopman, *Genealogy as Critique* p. 67.

6 Koopman, p. 60. Koopman draws on this notion of genealogy as problematization to argue that Foucault is able to escape the charge of genetic fallacy leveled against him by critics such as Nancy Fraser. Questions could certainly be raised about the interpretive claims that Koopman makes vis-à-vis Foucault, but for purposes of this discussion, I shall set those issues aside.

7 Thanks to Jay Bernstein for prompting me to think more about this issue.

8 William Rehg, *Insight and Solidarity: The Discourse Ethics of Jürgen Habermas* (Berkeley, CA: University of California Press, 1994), p. 67.

9 Thomas McCarthy, *Race, Empire, and the Idea of Human Development* (Cambridge: Cambridge University Press, 2009), p. 231.

10 Michel Foucault, "Space, Knowledge, Power," in Paul Rabinow, ed., *Power: Volume 3 of the Essential Works of Michel Foucault* (New York: The New Press, 2000), p. 358.

11 Michel Foucault, "Afterword: The Subject and Power," in Hubert Dreyfus and Paul Rabinow, *Michel Foucault: Beyond Structuralism and Hermeneutics*, 2nd edn (Chicago, IL: University of Chicago Press, 1983), p. 210.

12 See McCarthy, *Race, Empire, and the Idea of Human Development*, for a trenchant analysis.

13 I discuss Habermas's response to the charge of ethnocentrism in more detail in Allen, "Discourse, Power and Subjectivation: The Foucault/Habermas Debate Reconsidered," *The Philosophical Forum*, 40/1 (spring 2009): 1–28.

14 Maeve Cooke, *Re-Presenting the Good Society* (Cambridge, MA: MIT Press, 2006). I discuss Cooke's work more fully in Allen, *The Politics of Our Selves: Power, Autonomy, and Gender in Contemporary Critical Theory* (New York: Columbia University Press, 2008), pp. 137–43.

15 See Cooke, *Re-Presenting the Good Society* (2006), p. 20.

16 Ibid, p. 147.

17 Ibid.

18 I argue for this in more detail in chapter 6 of Allen, *The Politics of Our Selves* (2008).

19 For these latter two formulations, see David Hoy and Thomas McCarthy, *Critical Theory* (Oxford: Blackwell, 1994), pp. 74–5. I discuss McCarthy's contextualized version of Habermasian critical theory in Allen, *The Politics of Our Selves*, pp. 143–9.

20 I am not hereby suggesting that when we raise validity claims in the course of moral, political or truth discourses, we should bracket them with the further claim that we are only claiming their validity for us. Rather, the point is a meta-theoretical one, and it concerns the status that Habermas claims for the normative idealizations that undergird his theory, not the status of validity claims that are themselves raised in discourse.

21 Thanks to Colin Koopman for suggesting this formulation.

Chapter 7 Forgetting Isaac: Faith and the Philosophical Impossibility of a Postsecular Society

1 Ronald Dworkin, *Is Democracy Possible Here? Principles for a New Public Debate* (Princeton, NJ: Princeton University Press, 2006), ch. 3.

2 Although there is no space to discuss it here, this view, which I take to be at one with Habermas's, requires that it is a necessary condition for a good to be conceived of as choice-worthy that it be chosen autonomously – that is the substantive, non-neutral meaning of the priority of the right over the good.

3 John Rawls, "The Idea of Public Reason Revisited," *University of Chicago Law Review*, 64 (1997): 781; and for Habermas's concession, *BNR*, pp. 145–6.

4 As Habermas notes in "Are There Postmetaphysical Answers to the Question: What is the 'Good Life'?" and "Faith and Knowledge," both in *The Future of Human Nature*, transl. William Rehg and Max Pensky (Cambridge: Polity, 2003).

5 On being directed toward "the whole sphere of certainty," see M. Gueroult, *Descartes' Philosophy Interpreted According to the Order of Reasons*, transl. R. Ariew (Minneapolis, MN: University of Minnesota Press, 1983), vol. I, p. 15.

6 R. Descartes, *The Philosophical Works of Descartes*, transl. E. S. Haldane and G. R. T. Ross (Cambridge: Cambridge University Press, 1967), vol. I, p. 144.

7 Ibid., p. 145. *Pace* Michael Williams, "Descartes and the Metaphysics of Doubt," in John Cottingham, ed., *Descartes* (Oxford: Oxford University Press, 1998), p. 36.

8 Hiram Caton, *Origin of Subjectivity* (New Haven, CT: Yale University Press, 1973), p. 109. My reading of Descartes has been much influenced by Caton's too little known book.

9 Descartes, *The Philosophical Works* (1967), vol. I, p. 147.

10 Caton, *Origin of Subjectivity* (1973), p. 117.

11 The question of the role of faith prior to the modern age – in which religious belief is from the outset in relation to non-belief – is complex. I certainly do not want to rule out the possibility that what we think of as faith, faith as Kierkegaard or Pascal or even the medievals saw it, could only arise when religion as an orienting form of life has died; faith might well turn out to be one of the ways that religious ideas appear when the forms of life they originally informed have disappeared. This would make modern faith-based religiosity not the return of the repressed, but the return of the dead.

12 For a powerful contrary reading of the episode, see Omri Boehm, *The Binding of Isaac: A Religious Model of Disobedience* (New York: T&T Clark, 2007).

13 Søren Kierkegaard, *Fear and Trembling: Dialectical Lyric by Johannes de silentio*, transl. Alastair Hannay (London: Penguin Books, 1985), p. 65.

14 For a nuanced discussion of the range of interpretive options, see John Lippitt, *Kierkegaard and Fear and Trembling* (London: Routledge, 2003), pp. 66–76. My reading of Kierkegaard owes the most to two former Essex colleagues, Michael Weston and Stephen Mulhall.

15 Kierkegaard, *Fear and Trembling* (1985), pp. 101–2.

16 In what is the most penetrating reading of *Fear and Trembling* available, Stephen Mulhall, *Inheritance and Originality: Wittgenstein, Heidegger, Kierkegaard* (Oxford: Clarendon Press, 2001), wriggles free from this issue by emphasizing the allegorical or analogical reading of Abraham's ordeal as pre-figuring Christ's atonement, and then urging, given that Christ is the kind of God willing to shed his own blood for the sake of others, it follows that "faith could never require the violation of ethical duty" (p. 383). Certainly the inference itself is hollow; that apart, Mulhall both stops too quickly in thinking through what the stakes of sacrifice are for Kierkegaard, and worse, as I shall show, contradicts the letter and spirit of Kierkegaard's argument.

17 Kierkegaard, *Fear and Trembling* (1985), pp. 45–8.
18 Ibid., p. 47.
19 Ibid., p. 142.
20 Ibid.
21 Genesis, 22:12.
22 Kierkegaard, *Fear and Trembling*, p. 65.
23 Ibid., p. 70.
24 Quoted from the 1725 *Entretiens sur les vies et sur les oeuvrages des plus excellens peintres anciens and modernes* by Louis Marin, *To Destroy Painting*, transl. Mette Hjort (Chicago, IL: University of Chicago Press, 1995), p. 3.
25 Ibid., p. 4.
26 For an attempt to free the claims of Dutch realism from the grip of the ideal of the classic solution, see my *Against Voluptuous Bodies: Late Modernism and the Meaning of Painting* (Stanford, CA: Stanford University Press, 2006), ch. 1.
27 On "*jouissance*," see Marin, *To Destroy Painting* (1995), p. 5.
28 Ibid., p. 141.

Chapter 8 A Postsecular Global Order? The Pluralism of Forms of Life and Communicative Freedom

1 Richard Bernstein, "Naturalism, Secularism and Religion: Habermas' Via Media," *Constellations*, 17 (2010): 161.
2 Habermas, *Between Naturalism and Religion* (Cambridge: Polity, 2008), p. 143.
3 John Rawls, "The Idea of an Overlapping Consensus," in S. Freeman, ed., *Collected Papers of John Rawls* (Cambridge, MA: Harvard University Press, 1999), p. 424.
4 William Wimstatt, 'Complexity and Organization', in R. S. Cohen, ed., *Proceedings of the Philosophy of Science Association 1972* (Dordrecht: Riedel, 1974), pp. 67–86.
5 John Dewey, *Logic: The Theory of Inquiry*, in *The Later Works*, Vol. 12 (Carbondale, IL: Southern Illinois University Press, 1986), p. 499.
6 Ibid., p. 281.
7 Hannah Arendt, *The Origins of Totalitarianism* (New York: Harcourt Brace, 1971), pp. 296–7.
8 Immanuel Kant, *Metaphysics of Morals,* transl. and ed. M. Gregor (Cambridge: Cambridge University Press, 1996), section 6.3. See also Otfried Höffe, *Kant's Cosmopolitan Theory of Law and Peace* (Cambridge: Cambridge University Press, 2004), p. 121.
9 Kant, *Metaphysics of Morals*, VI, p. 241.
10 Kant, "Perpetual Peace," in H. Reiss, ed., *Kant's Political Writings* (Cambridge: Cambridge University Press, 1970), p. 119.
11 Molly Cochran, "The Normative Power of International Publics: The Case of the Women's International League for Peace and Freedom, 1919–1925," American Political Science Association 2008 Annual Meeting, pp. 3–4.

12 See Brooke Ackerly, *Political Theory and Feminist Social Criticism* (Cambridge: Cambridge University Press, 2000), p. 164.

13 See Bina Agarwal, "Conceptualizing Environmental Collective Action: Why Gender Matters," *Cambridge Journal of Economics*, 24 (2001): 283–310.

14 Neera Chanhoke, "How Global is Global Civil Society?," *Journal of World-Systems Research* (2005) XI: 355–71.

15 Randall Germain, "Financial Governance and Transnational Deliberative Democracy," *Review of International Studies*, forthcoming.

16 On the role of transnational actors in this example, see Daniel Wehrenfennig, "Multi-Track Diplomacy and Human Security," *Human Security Journal*, 7 (2008): 84. According to Wehrenfennig, multi-track diplomacy has not been as characteristic of the Israeli/Palestinian conflict.

17 Held has already argued that this is the distinct advantage of the interaction of the global, regional, and the local, in David Held et al., *Global Transformations* (Stanford, CA: Stanford University Press, 1999), pp. 371–2.

18 See Daniel Wehrenfennig, "Conflict Management and Communicative Action: Second Track Diplomacy from a Habermasian Perspective," *Communication Theory*, 18(2008): 356–75.

19 J. P. Lederach, *Building Peace* (Washington, DC: United States Institute of Peace Press, 1997), p. 35.

20 See Jackie Smith, *Social Movements for Global Democracy* (Baltimore, MD: Johns Hopkins University Press, 2008), p. 178. Such movements aim at "an effective, coherent and more democratic global polity," by building up transnational society and its norms.

21 See Seyla Benhabib, "Claiming Rights across Borders: International Human Rights and Democratic Sovereignty," *American Political Science Review*, 103(2009): 691–704. "The neglect of social movements as actors of social transformation and jurisgenerative politics in recent theorizing has led to a naive faith in legal experts, international lawyers, and judges as agents of democratic change" (692).

22 See Maeve Cooke, "A Secular State for a Postsecular Society? Postmetaphysical Political Theory and the Place of Religion," *Constellations*, 14 (2007): 224–38.

23 Rodger Payne and Nayef H. Samhat, *Democratizing Global Politics* (Albany, NY: SUNY Press, 2006), p. 6.

24 See John Dryzek, "Soup, Society or System: On Global Democratization," presented at Conference on Democracy and the Deliberative Society, University of York, 24–6 June 2008.

Chapter 9 Global Religion and the Postsecular Challenge

1 This terminology makes reference to Charles Taylor's *A Secular Age*. See my "Tiefendimension von Säkularität," *Deutsche Zeitschrift für Philosophie*, 57/2(May 2009): 301–18, and "The Deep Conditions of Secularity," *Modern Theology*, 26/3 (July 2010): 382–403.

2 As to my use of the expression "deep pragmatism," see my "Introduction:

Why Still 'Religion'," in Hent de Vries, ed., *Religion – Beyond A Concept* (New York: Fordham University Press, 2008), pp. 1–98. For my discussion of Habermas's earlier work, see my *Minimal Theologies: Critiques of Secular Reason in Theodor W. Adorno and Emmanuel Levinas*, transl. Geoffrey Hale (Baltimore, MD, and London: Johns Hopkins University Press, 2005), pp. 108–64.

3 Hent de Vries, *Philosophy and the Turn to Religion* (Baltimore, MD, and London: Johns Hopkins University Press, 1999, 2000).

4 In addition to pointing out the role of the Judeo-Christian legacy in shaping the cultural outlook of Western modernity, Habermas writes: "Through the reception of Greek philosophy (if one thinks of Toledo, for example), these impulses are also united with the impetus of Islam. We should also remember that for all three monotheistic religions it was above all the heretical movements and schisms that preserved a sensitivity for the more radical forms of revelation" (p. 147). By contrast, he notes, "cultural and social modernization has not been completed in the regions dominated by Buddhism" (p. 148).

5 Yet another parallel might be pursued to clarify the same point. I am thinking of Habermas's take on another Brechtian motif, namely that of "*Etwas fehlt* [Something's Missing]," a trope also taken up by Theodor W. Adorno in his radio conversation with Ernst Bloch on the remarkable subject of immortality (a theme broached in Adorno's *Minima Moralia* and picked up and reframed in the French political philosopher Claude Lefort's musings on the "irreducible element" in "the political" and, hence, in "politics"). But these further contexts, although "deeply" relevant to my argument, as a metaphysical prelude or afterthought of sorts, I must leave aside here. On the background of these motifs in Lefort, see my "'The Miracle of Love' and the Turn to Democracy," in *CR: The New Centennial Review*, 8/3(2009): 237–90.

6 Eduardo Mendieta, "A Postsecular World Society? On the Philosophical Significance of Postsecular Consciousness and the Multicultural World Society: An Interview with Jürgen Habermas," transl. Matthias Fritsch, in *The Immanent Frame* (2010), p. 4. Available at: <http://blogs.ssrc.org/tif/wp-content/uploads/2010/02/A-Postsecular-World-Society-TIF.pdf> .

7 Ibid.

8 Ibid.

9 For an attempt to read Kant in a slightly different vein, see my *Philosophy and the Turn to Religion* (Baltimore, MD, and London: Johns Hopkins University Press, 1999, 2000), ch. 5, and *Religion and Violence: Philosophical Reflections from Kant to Derrida* (Baltimore, MD, and London: Johns Hopkins University Press, 2002, 2006), ch. 2.

10 Hans Joas, *Do We Need Religion? On the Experience of Self-Transcendence* (Boulder, CO, and London: Paradigm Publishers, 2008), pp. vii, 7.

11 Ibid., pp. 105–22.

12 Ibid.

13 John Micklethwait and Adrian Wooldridge, *God is Back: How the Global*

Revival of Faith is Changing the World (New York: Penguin Press, 2009), p. 138.

14 Joas, *Do We Need Religion?*, pp. 106–7 and p. 124. Cf. also Hans Joas, "Gesellschaft, Staat und Religion. Ihr Verhältnis in der Sicht der Weltreligionen. Eine Einleitung," in Hans Joas and Klaus Wiegandt, eds, *Säkularisierung und die Weltreligionen* (Frankfurt/M.: Fischer Verlag, 2007), pp. 9–43.

15 Joas, *Do We Need Religion?*, pp. 107–25.

16 Mendieta, "A Postsecular World Society?".

17 Joas, *Do We Need Religion?*, pp. 107–24.

18 Ibid., pp. 107, 124–5, transl. modified.

19 Ibid., pp. 109–26.

Chapter 10 Religion and the Public Sphere: What are the Deliberative Obligations of Democratic Citizenship?

1 An earlier version of this essay was published in *Philosophy & Social Criticism*, 35/1–2(2009): 127–50. In revising the earlier version I have greatly benefited from discussion with Mark Alznauer, Robert Audi, Jürgen Habermas, Richard Kraut, Charles Taylor, and Nick Wolterstorff, as well as with other participants in the workshop on "Religion, Public Sphere and World Society" at the Institute for Public Knowledge, New York University in October 2009.

2 See John Rawls, *Political Liberalism* (Cambridge, MA: Harvard University Press, 1993).

3 See Rawls, "The Idea of Public Reason Revisited" (1997), in Rawls, *Collected Papers* (Cambridge, MA: Harvard University Press, 1999), p. 584.

4 See Rawls, *Political Liberalism* (1993), pp. 212–54, and "The Idea of Public Reason Revisited" (1997), in Rawls *Collected Papers* (1999), pp. 573–615.

5 See R. Audi, "The Place of Religious Argument in a Free and Democratic Society," in *San Diego Law Review*, 30/4 (1993): 677–702; "Liberal Democracy and the Place of Religion in Politics," in Audi and Wolterstorff, *Religion in the Public Square* (London: Rowman & Littlefield, 1997), pp. 1–66; *Religious Commitment and Secular Reason* (Cambridge: Cambridge University Press, 2000).

6 In my opinion, Rawls's interpretation of the content of public reason in terms of basic democratic values offers the most plausible account of the kind of reasons that must have priority in public political deliberation. However, this is all that my proposal borrows from Rawls's account of public reason. In particular, it does not require the endorsing of some stronger assumptions that Rawls includes in his account, such as the completeness of public reason. I address this issue in the last section of this essay.

7 Rawls's account of public reason also includes trivial elements that belong to common human reason such as "presently accepted general beliefs and forms of reasoning found in common sense, and the methods and conclusions of science when these are not controversial" (Rawls, *Political*

Liberalism (1993), p. 224). For the details of Rawls's account of the content of an overlapping consensus, see Rawls, *Political Liberalism* (1993), pp. 133–72.

8 For Rawls, "fundamental political issues" are those related to constitutional essentials and matters of basic justice. See Rawls, *Political Liberalism* (1993), p. 137f.

9 N. Wolterstorff, "The Role of Religion in Decision and Discussion of Political Issues," in Audi and Wolterstorff, *Religion in the Public Square* (1997), pp. 67–120.

10 For an example of a defense of this view, see M. Sandel, *Public Philosophy* (Cambridge, MA: Harvard University Press, 2005).

11 For an example of a defense of this view, see C. Mouffe, *The Democratic Paradox* (London: Verso, 2000).

12 For the following analysis of Habermas's approach, I draw from Cristina Lafont, "Religion in the Public Sphere. Remarks on Habermas's Conception of Public Deliberation in Postsecular Societies" *Constellations*, 1412, (2007): 239–59.

13 See Wolterstorff, "The Role of Religion in Decision and Discussion of Political Issues" (1997).

14 See P. Weithman, *Religion and the Obligations of Citizenship* (Cambridge: Cambridge University Press, 2002).

15 See Rawls, *Political Liberalism* (1993), and "The Idea of Public Reason Revisited" (1997).

16 See Audi, "The Place of Religious Argument in a Free and Democratic Society," (1993); "Liberal Democracy and the Place of Religion in Politics," (1997); *Religious Commitment and Secular Reason* (2000).

17 Wolterstorff, "The Role of Religion in Decision and Discussion of Political Issues" (1997), p. 105.

18 For a defense of this objection articulated in terms of the Rawlsian idea of "the strains of commitment," see C. Eberle, *Religious Conviction in Liberal Politics* (Cambridge: Cambridge University Press, 2002), p. 143ff.

19 For a strong defense of the moral objection to Rawls's proposal, see Sandel, *Public Philosophy* (2005), p. 224ff.

20 In fact, I do not think that it does. On the one hand, it is true that Rawls assumes that most of the time reasonable citizens will find public reasons in support of the policies that their comprehensive doctrines support, so that a political debate (or even a political stalemate) will occur among views supported by public, but mutually conflicting, reasons. On the other hand, however, this does not mean that whenever that fails to be the case Rawls's proviso remains silent. In light of the proviso, whenever citizens cannot find proper public reasons in support of the policies that their comprehensive or religious doctrines support, they have two clear options. First, they can change their minds accordingly ("it is up to citizens themselves to affirm, revise, or change their comprehensive doctrines. Their doctrines may override or count for naught the political values of a constitutional democratic society. But then the citizens cannot claim that such doctrines are reasonable"

(Rawls (1997), p. 609). Second, they can maintain their comprehensive views and keep searching for public reasons to support them. But, of course, this implies that for the time being, far from allowing citizens to continue their political advocacy on the basis of non-public reasons, Rawls's proviso requires them to accept the implementation of the contrary decision based on public reasons "as legitimate law and therefore [to] not resist it with force" (Rawls, "Introduction to the Paperback Edition," in *Political Liberalism* (Cambridge, MA: Harvard University Press, 1996), p. lvii).

21 Strangely enough, this is precisely the argument that Habermas himself makes against the liberal proposal that obligates *all* citizens (and thus, a fortiori, all religious citizens) to provide corroborating non-religious reasons for the coercive policies they advocate for. See previous note.

22 Weithman, *Religion and the Obligations of Citizenship* (2002), p. 3.

23 Although it must be noted that in Rawls's proposal it remains unclear on whom the obligation to honor the proviso falls. See Rawls, *Collected Papers* (1999), p. 592. But, no matter how this obligation is specified, it remains the case that, according to Rawls, for each policy proposal a justification based exclusively on public reasons must be provided. This general obligation is based on Rawls's assumption that public reason "is suitably complete, that is, for at least the great majority of fundamental questions, possibly for all, some combination and balance of political values alone reasonably shows the answer" (Rawls, *Political Liberalism* (1993), p. 241). In contradistinction, my proposal does not require accepting the problematic assumption that public reasons alone are sufficient to determine most fundamental political questions. Rawls's assumption of completeness has been forcefully criticized by many authors. For two detailed versions of this critique, see Sandel, *Public Philosophy* (2005), p. 223ff., and Eberle, *Religious Conviction in Liberal Politics* (2002), part III.

Chapter 11 Violating Neutrality? Religious Validity Claims and Democratic Legitimacy

1 By contrast, Rawls seems to expect this of all religious believers – or, at least, that they should be able to find an independent justification "in due course." See John Rawls, "The Idea of Public Reason Revisited," in S. Freeman, ed., *John Rawls, Collected Papers* (Cambridge, MA: Harvard University Press, 1999).

2 This fits with his well-known distinction between the informal or "weak" public sphere, which serves as a vehicle for public opinion and fulfills functions primarily of discovering and identifying problems, and the formal or "arranged" public sphere, which serves to construct the will of the people and fulfills functions primarily of justification, decision-making, and general problem-solving.

3 In this essay, I focus on Habermas's prohibition on religious reasoning in the *formal* public sphere. Readers unfamiliar with Habermas's position might wrongly assume that he is generally hostile to public reasoning on religious

topics. But this is not the case. In his writings since 2001, Habermas has endorsed public discussion of religious validity claims in the informal public sphere. I give a brief account of the development of his position in M. Cooke, "A Secular State for a Postsecular Society? Postmetaphysical Political Theory and the Place of Religion," *Constellations*, 14/2 (2007): 224–38. See also M. Cooke, "Critical Theory and Religion," in D. Z. Phillips and T. Tessin, eds, *Philosophy of Religion in the 21st Century* (London: Palgrave, 2001), pp. 211–43, and M. Cooke, "Die Stellung der Religion bei Jürgen Habermas," in K. Dethloff, L. Nagl, and F. Wolfram, eds, *Religion, Moderne, Postmoderne* (Berlin: Parerga, 2002), pp. 99–119.

4 Nicholas Wolterstorff, "The Role of Religion in Decision and Discussion of Political Issues," in Robert Audi and Nicholas Wolterstorff, *Religion in the Public Square* (London: Rowman & Littlefield, 1997), pp. 67–120.

5 Wolterstorff, "The Role of Religion," pp. 114–16.

6 See Cooke, "A Secular State?"; Cooke, "Critical Theory and Religion."

7 Indeed, Habermas frequently uses the terms "generally accessible" and "secular" reasons as though they were synonymous (e.g., *BNR*, pp. 137, 139). See my critical comments in Cooke, "A Secular State?," esp. pp. 228–30.

8 It is noteworthy that Habermas, who distinguishes sharply between ethical validity claims and moral validity claims, here describes ethical convictions in terms he usually reserves for moral ones. For his distinction between ethical and moral validity claims, see *JA*, pp. 1–17; cf. *BFN*, pp. 157–68.

9 Habermas does allow for the evaluation of the *usefulness* of the truth content of religious validity claims from the point of view of semantic renewal: assessment of their capacity to feed valuable semantic contents into postmetaphysical philosophy and political thinking. See *BFN*, p. 142; see my critical comments in M. Cooke, "Salvaging and Secularizing the Semantic Contents of Religion: The Limitations of Habermas's Postmetaphysical Proposal," *International Journal for the Philosophy of Religion*, 60(2006): 187–207. For a more sympathetic view, see M. Cooke, "The Limits of Learning, Habermas' Social Theory and Religion," *European Journal of Philosophy* (forthcoming).

10 I leave aside the question of whether Habermas's conception of ethical validity, too, is overly focused on argumentation. As I observe in the final section of this essay, his conception of ethical validity is not straightforward.

11 L. Wittgenstein, *Philosophical Investigations*, transl. G. E. M. Anscombe (Oxford: Blackwell, 2001), §217, p. 133.

12 Recall Wittgenstein's "riverbed" metaphor in *On Certainty*, transl. D. Paul and G. E. M. Anscombe (Oxford: Blackwell, 1969), §99. Like the bank of a river, the riverbed of thoughts is held to consist partly of hard rock, subject only to imperceptible alterations, and partly of sand, which now in one place, now in another, gets washed away or deposited.

13 I discuss this difficulty as it arises in the case of "poetic" formulations and novel uses of language in M. Cooke, *Re-Presenting the Good Society* (Cambridge, MA: MIT Press, 2006), pp. 156–9.

14 Here, and earlier in the paragraph, I use the word "vocabulary" in the sense made popular by Richard Rorty (see his *Contingency, Irony, Solidarity* (Cambridge: Cambridge University Press, 1989)).

15 The following draws on Cooke, *Re-Presenting the Good Society*, p. 158.

16 See the essays in *OPC*, and my discussion in Cooke, *Language and Reason* (Cambridge, MA: MIT Press, 1994), ch. 4.

17 C. Taylor, *A Secular Age* (Cambridge, MA: Harvard University Press, 2007), pp. 349–50.

18 Indeed, Taylor's book as a whole offers an excellent sense of the kinds of reasons that have lost and gained currency in the Western world from the Middle Ages to our present "secular age."

19 Taylor, *A Secular Age*, p. 350.

20 These two levels do not exhaust the concept of understanding. For instance, there are a number of forms of non-linguistic understanding.

21 It would be important to clarify the interrelationships between the two levels. Unfortunately, I cannot address this question here.

22 M. Cooke, "Avoiding Authoritarianism: On the Problem of Justification in Contemporary Critical Social Theory," *International Journal of Philosophical Studies* 13/3(2005): 379–404. See also Cooke, "A Secular State?," pp. 234–5, and Cooke, *Re-Presenting the Good Society*, esp. pp. 16–20.

23 Habermas criticizes Karl Jaspers's assimilation of philosophical insights to religious beliefs. In my view, he does so for the wrong reasons. Jaspers's mistake is not his blurring of the boundaries between philosophy and religion, but his epistemologically authoritarian picture of religious belief in which revealed truths constitute an unshakeable core that is dogmatic in a pernicious sense. See *EFK*, p. 56.

24 See my reference to Wittgenstein's famous "riverbed" metaphor in note 12 above.

25 To be sure, Wittgenstein does not mention the impact of intentional human agency.

26 See M. Cooke, "Five Arguments for Deliberative Democracy," *Political Studies* 48/5(2000): 947–69, esp. 958–9.

27 Unlike Wolterstorff, who calls for impartiality rather than neutrality, Habermas tends to use the terms "impartiality" and "neutrality" interchangeably.

28 I see this as the valid intuition in Habermas's call for the translation of the contents of religious traditions into a generally accessible language. However, he underestimates the complexities of the work of translation. See M. Cooke, "Translating Truth," *Philosophy and Social Criticism.* 37/4(2011): 479–92.

29 In using the words "poetically gifted," I do not want to give the impression that I see the translator as *determining* or *controlling* the transfer of meaning; rather, the genius of the translator consists in her role as *facilitator*.

30 Paul, 'First Letter to the Corinthians', 15, 42.

31 His position regarding ethical validity claims is more difficult to ascertain. See n.10 above.

32 He writes: "[The] unconditional nature of moral validity claims can be accounted for in terms of the universality of a realm of validity that *has to be produced*" (. . . eines *herzustellenden* Geltungsbereichs, emphasis in original, transl. altered.) (*TJ*, p. 262; J. Habermas, *Wahrheit und Rechtfertigung*, Frankfurt/Main: Suhrkamp, 1999, p. 301).

33 A. Wellmer, "Ethics and Dialogue: Elements of Moral Judgement in Kant and Discourse Ethics," in his *The Persistence of Modernity*, transl. D. Midgley (Cambridge: Polity, 1991), pp. 113–231.

34 For some remarks on finalism, see Cooke, *Re-Presenting the Good Society*, pp. 162–4 and 177–8.

35 See Cooke, "Avoiding Authoritarianism." Habermas disputes that his definition of justice as the outcome of an idealized discursive procedure, in which everyone agrees that the resulting norm or principle is equally in everyone's interests, is historically and culturally specific. He claims that this idea of justice emerges from a formal-pragmatic reconstruction of the idealizing suppositions of everyday linguistic practices *in general*. See Habermas, "Discourse Ethics: Notes on a Program of Philosophical Justification" in *MCCA*. For some critical remarks, see Cooke, *Language and Reason*, ch. 2, and Cooke, *Re-Presenting the Good Society*, ch. 3.

36 Passing over some difficulties arising from Habermas's tendency to conflate political and legal validity, I use the term "democratic legitimacy" in a general sense to refer to the normative claim to political/legal validity raised for democratic processes and their outcomes.

37 He describes the democratic principle of majority rule as retaining an internal relation to the search for truth and representing only a caesura in an ongoing discussion (*BFN*, p. 179). The epistemic significance he attaches to majority rule is particularly noteworthy, since it indicates that his cognitive interpretation of political legitimacy is not confined to formal legal/political principles regarding the exercise of political power but extends to the substantive issues under discussion in everyday legal/political deliberations.

38 See M. Cooke, "Habermas, Autonomy, and the Identity of the Self," *Philosophy and Social Criticism*, 18/3–4(1992): 269–91.

39 One of the most prominent contemporary proponents of what I call radical contextualism is Richard Rorty. See Habermas's critique of Rorty in his "Richard Rorty's Pragmatic Turn" (*OPC*, pp. 343–82). Cf. my critique of radical contextualism in Cooke, *Re-Presenting the Good Society*, pp. 25–36.

40 Cf. M. Cooke, *Language and Reason* (1994), esp. chs 2 and 5.

41 With regard to the latter it should be noted that in his Postscript to *BFN* Habermas admits that the schema he presents on these pages is misleading because it presents ethical, moral, and pragmatic validity claims as the object of discourses that are independent of one another, whereas in fact these claims are bundled together in the process of political will formation (*BFN*, p. 565, n.3).

42 See his critical remarks on R. Alexy, in his *BFN*, pp. 229–32, and on Apel, in "The Architectonics of Discursive Differentiation," pp. 77–97.

43 McCarthy, too, reads Habermas's account of democratic legitimacy as

extending to the substantive issues under discussion in everyday legal/ political deliberations as opposed to confined to formal legal/political principles regarding the exercise of political power (see note 37 above). T. McCarthy, "Legitimacy and Diversity: Dialectical Reflections on Analytical Distinctions," in A. Arato and M. Rosenfeld, eds, *Habermas on Law and Democracy: Critical Exchanges* (Berkeley, CA: University of California Press, 1998), pp. 115–53 (here p. 128)

44 Cf. McCarthy, "Legitimacy and Diversity," p. 128.

45 In fact, I think my argument holds for moral validity claims as well as ethical ones (and religious ones), but I will not pursue this point further here.

46 However, I find no indications in his writings that an idealized discursively reached consensus *determines* the validity of ethical validity claims; thus, I consider it unlikely that he holds an epistemically constructivist conception of ethical validity.

47 For an early discussion of some of the ambiguities in his account, see M. Cooke, "Realizing the Post-Conventional Self," *Philosophy and Social Criticism*, 20/1–2(1994): 87–10.

48 Nor does it rule out the possibility of consensus.

49 I leave open the question of whether a discursively achieved consensus indicates truth, in the sense of pointing toward it. This seems to be Habermas's position with regard to empirical truth. As he puts it: "[. . .] rational acceptability [. . .] indicates the truth of a proposition" (*OPC*, p. 381 n.55).

50 See Cooke, "Five Arguments for Deliberative Democracy."

51 By appealing to the normative context of Western modernity, it may look as though I construe the relationship between argumentation and context-transcending validity as historically arbitrary. This is not my understanding of the relationship. I see it as historically *contingent*, in the sense that this way of thinking about context-transcending validity need not have emerged, but I also see it as having a stable foundation. See Cooke, *Re-Presenting the Good Society*, pp. 131–3. Moreover, I acknowledge important overlaps between the normative context of Western modernity and other modernities. Finally, like Habermas, I hold that modernity is the result of a historical learning process and should be seen as an ongoing project.

52 David Estlund, for example, argues that democratic arrangements involving public discussion improve the epistemic quality of democratic outcomes. See his *Democratic Authority: A Philosophical Framework* (Princeton, NJ: Princeton University Press, 2009). I see the need for more detailed micro-analyses of actual deliberative situations to test this – intuitively plausible – claim.

53 In the context of a discussion of argumentation in the natural sciences, William Rehg calls for such micro-contextual analysis, suggesting some interesting, context-specific reasons for the belief that improving the quality of the procedure improves the quality of the outcome. See W. Rehg: *Cogent Science in Context: The Science Wars, Argumentation Theory and Habermas* (Cambridge, MA: MIT Press, 2009). See also my review of Rehg's book, in *Contemporary Sociology: A Journal of Reviews*, 40/1(2011), pp. 73–5.

54 I discuss what it means to see legal validity as a regulative ideal in Cooke, "The Dual Character of Concepts and the Discourse Theory of Law," in Matthias Klatt, ed., *Institutional Reason: The Jurisprudence of Robert Alexy* (Oxford: Oxford University Press, 2012).

55 Thanks to the anonymous external reviewer for helpful comments and especially for encouraging me to develop and tighten my argument in the final section.

Chapter 12 Sources of Morality in Habermas's Recent Work on Religion and Freedom

1 Joe Heath has argued that, at least in the language of analytic philosophy, Habermas's own position is a kind of anti-foundationalist ("neo-pagan"?) contextualism. See Joseph Heath, *Communicative Action and Rational Choice* (Cambridge: MIT Press, 2001), in particular p. 201ff. On Heath's definition, a contextualist position is one that solves the regress problem in justification by accepting, with foundationalism, the need for terminating judgments, but sees the latter as varying from context to context. While Habermas shares this view, he adds the formal-pragmatic account of procedural rules under which all justification, necessarily dialogic, has to be conducted. As is well known, it is these rules that point at the same time to the context-transcending validity of speech acts, thereby asking us to assume and translate the, historically, "divine standpoint."

2 Cf. Fritsch, "Cura et Casus: Heidegger and Augustine on the Care of the Self," in Craig de Paulo, ed., *The Influence of Augustine on Heidegger: The Emergence of an Augustinian Phenomenology* (Lewiston, NY: Edwin Mellen Press, 2006), pp. 89–113; and Martin Heidegger, *The Phenomenology of Religious Life*, transl. Matthias Fritsch and Jennifer A. Gosetti (Indianapolis, IN: Indiana University Press, 2004). If we do not emphasize Husserlian origins too strongly, we may add Charles Taylor to this list. See, for example, Paul Ricoeur's essay on the former's *Sources of the Self* in Ricoeur, *Reflections on the Just*, transl. David Pellauer (Chicago, IL: University of Chicago Press, 2007), pp. 168–86.

3 Jan Patočka, *Heretical Essays in the Philosophy of History*, transl. Erazim Kohak (Chicago, IL: Open Court Press, 1996), p. 108f.

4 Cf. Rodolphe Gasché, *Europe, or The Infinite Task: A Study of a Philosophical Concept* (Stanford, CA: Stanford University Press, 2009).

5 Cf. Arne J. Vetlesen, "Worlds Apart? Habermas and Levinas," *Philosophy and Social Criticism*, 23/1(1997): 1–20; and Steven Hendley, *From Communicative Action to the Face of the Other: Levinas and Habermas on Language, Obligation, and Community* (Lanham, MD: Lexington Books, 2000).

6 For Habermas's connection between meaning and validity – the claim that to understand an utterance, I must be committed to the conditions of validity, including the higher-order validity claims mentioned above – see, in particular, *OPC*, ch. 4, and also *TCA*. In fact, the liability to justification in Habermas,

by contrast to, for instance, Robert Brandom's inferentialism, is so strong as to include the commitment to enter purely argumentative language games, in which even more demanding norms bind the speaker. For this difference between Habermas and Brandom, see Habermas, "From Kant to Hegel: On Robert Brandom's Pragmatic Philosophy of Language," *European Journal of Philosophy*, 8/3(2000): 322–55; and Brandom's response in "Facts, Norms, and Normative Facts: Reply to Habermas," *European Journal of Philosophy*, 8/3 (2000): 356–74.

7 To be sure, Habermas's argument must make a distinction between parental or social influence upon identity by way of socialization and by way of genetic manipulation, so as to be able to argue that only the latter leads to the make-up of a human being with which the person cannot very well identify, as required for autonomy. He does this by arguing that genetic influence is irreversible, while socialization, which takes place in communicative action, is "essentially contestable" and may be revised by the adolescent and mature adult on the basis of good reasons (*FHN*, p. 62). The argument against liberal eugenics is not only made on the basis of undermining freedom, but also equality, for genetic manipulation would constitute, for Habermas, an irreversible dependence at odds with the symmetrical recognition of equals as free beings (p. 63ff.). I should note that I am here not so much interested in the details of Habermas's novel bioethical arguments, which are not required as premises in what follows. Rather, the emphasis here lies on the hitherto unthematized conditions of autonomy that the prospect of decoding the human genome bring to light (p. 12f.): to wit, the singularization of the self in response to a preceding otherness and contingency.

8 As further monotheistic or religious resources of which secular morality could make good use, Habermas mentions the notion of radical evil and, inspired by Walter Benjamin in particular, the potential reversibility of past suffering (See *FHN*). Elsewhere, he also mentions the issue of motivation and, in reference to Kant again, the "deficiency that practical reason is unable to justify the realization of collective goals based on solidarity or the cooperative averting of collective dangers as convincingly and effectively as the individual observance with moral duties," AWM, p. 75; cf. *BNR*, ch. 8.

9 See Ricoeur, *Oneself as Another*, transl. Kathleen Blamey (Chicago, IL: University of Chicago Press, 1992), p. 35; and Habermas, *Between Naturalism and Religion*, p. 153. See also Habermas, "The Language Game of Responsible Agency and the Problem of Free Will: How Can Epistemic Dualism Be Reconciled with Ontological Monism?," *Philosophical Explorations*, 10/1(2007): 13–50.

10 Ricoeur, *Oneself as Another* (1992), p. 355.

11 Cf. Jill Robbins, ed., *Is It Righteous To Be? Interviews with Emmanuel Levinas* (Stanford, CA: Stanford University Press, 2001), p. 126; and Emmanuel Levinas, *God, Death, and Time*, transl. Bettina Bergo (Stanford, CA: Stanford University Press, 2000).

12 Michel Foucault, "The Ethics of the Concern for Self as a Practice of Freedom," in Paul Rabinow, ed., *Ethics: Subjectivity and Truth (Essential*

Works of Michel Foucault, 1954–1984, Vol. 1) (New York: New Press, 1997), p. 287. For the above mentioned criticisms, see Catriona Mackenzie and Nathalie Stoljar, *Relational Autonomy* (Oxford: Oxford University Press, 2000).

13 See Eduardo Mendieta, "A Postsecular World Society? On the Philosophical Significance of Postsecular Consciousness and the Multicultural World Society: An Interview with Jürgen Habermas," transl. Matthias Fritsch, *The Immanent Frame* (2010). Available at: <http://blogs.ssrc.org/tif/wp-content/uploads/2010/02/A-Postsecular-World-Society-TIF.pdf>; and cf. *KV*, p. 407.

14 Given Levinas's notoriously dense and even poetic style, it is hard to say whether the inevitable violence of commentary is in the following schematization stretched too far to still be called faithful (cf. Jacques Derrida, *Writing and Difference*, transl. Alan Bass (Chicago, IL: University of Chicago Press, 1978), p. 312 n.7; and Simon Glendenning, *In the Name of Phenomenology* (London: Routledge, 2007), p. 150ff.). I ask forgiveness on the basis of seeking to render Levinas's conception of ethics fruitful in a dialogue with a rather different tradition of philosophical argumentation, one which, despite the praiseworthiness of clarity, may not always sufficiently appreciate the performativity of philosophical writing. To make Levinasian points stick in that dialogue (to say nothing of economy) suggests, I believe, such schematic treatment.

15 *Totality and Infinity*, transl. Alphonso Lingis (Pittsburgh, PA: Duquesne University Press, 1969), p. 245.

16 *God, Death, and Time* (2000), p. 158.

17 Cf. *God, Death, and Time* (2000), p. 140; and *Is It Righteous To Be?* (2001), p. 110f.

18 There is a debate in the secondary literature whether Levinas's face-to-face is best understood as a possibly concrete experience or a transcendental condition. While I cannot discuss this here, it seems clear to me that Levinas construes the encounter with the mortality of the other as an enabling condition of subjectivity. See Michael L. Morgan, *Discovering Levinas* (Cambridge: Cambridge University Press, 2007), pp. 45–60; Theodore de Boer, *The Rationality of Transcendence: Studies in the Philosophy of Emmanuel Levinas* (Amsterdam: J.C. Giehen, 1997); and Robert Bernasconi, "Rereading *Totality and Infinity*," in Charles Scott and Arleen Dallery, eds, *The Question of the Other: Essays in Contemporary Continental Philosophy* (Albany, NY: SUNY Press, 1989), pp. 23–35.

19 "The recognition of the unique, the recognition of the other, the priority of the other is, in a certain sense, unreasonable" (*Is It Righteous To Be?*, p. 111). In *The Gift of Death*, Derrida puts it thus: "The Other has no reason to share his reasons with us" (transl. David Wills (Chicago, IL: University of Chicago Press, 1995), p. 41; cf. ibid., p. 56f.).

20 This sense of ethics as emerging with a heteronomic otherness and grounded in a command may conflict with a common, but mistaken, understanding of autonomy. In particular, in the modern, specifically Kantian lineage, it is often thought that morality requires an autonomous agent who freely

accepts, or even self-imposes, its dictates. Here, however, normativity is seen to precede and (in part) to ground autonomy, so that there is always some unchosen and thus heteronomic aspect to autonomy. Kant himself, it may be worth pointing out, did not understand the moral law as depending on the autonomous agent accepting it autonomously: while particular norms may be issued autonomously by way of the categorical imperative, the moral imperative itself, as the law of reason, is strictly speaking without reason and we can only "comprehend its incomprehensibility" (*Groundwork of the Metaphysic of Morals*, transl. Herbert James Paton (New York: Harper and Row, 1948), p. 132 (B 128)). Cf. Allen Wood, *Kantian Ethics* (Cambridge: Cambridge University Press, 2008), p. 106ff.; see also Bernhard Waldenfels, *Schattenrisse der Moral* (Frankfurt: Suhrkamp Verlag, 2006), p. 21f. Habermas accepts that moral development starts with commands backed by sanctions in Kohlberg's preconventional stage, though mature adults are ideally supposed to overcome this necessitation (see *PMT*, pp. 57–87; *CES*, ch. 2) For complications in this developmental account, see Amy Allen, "Systematically Distorted Subjectivity? Habermas and the Critique of Power," *Philosophy and Social Criticism*, 33/5(2007): 641–50; and *The Politics of Our Selves: Power, Autonomy, and Gender in Contemporary Critical Theory* (New York: Columbia University Press, 2008).

21 Levinas, *Totality and Infinity* (1969), p. 40.
22 Hendley, *From Communicative Action to the Face of the Other* (2000), chapter 1.
23 Levinas, *Totality and Infinity* (1969), p. 245.
24 *Difficult Freedom: Essays on Judaism*, trans. Sean Hand (Baltimore, MD: Johns Hopkins University Press, 1990), p. 21f.
25 *God, Death, and Time* (2000), p. 138. As my main point is the confrontation with Habermas regarding asymmetry, I do not have the space here to unfold the infinity of the ethical relation, which Levinas presents as part and parcel of the other's alterity. The basic claim is that since we cannot know the death that makes the other who she is – what death is and when it will come – since we cannot thus predict the future, we cannot know what more letting the other live will have required from us. In this sense, the alterity of the other renders obligation incalculable or infinite. This infinity also has an intergenerational aspect to be explored in future work: if by letting the other live, potentially beyond my death, I assume responsibility for her responsibilities, then I become responsible for her children (biological or not), and their children, ad infinitum.
26 *Is It Righteous To Be?* (2001), p. 114.
27 As we have seen, Levinas cannot quite leave it at that, either: qualifications must be added as to where the ethical call can come from (mortality, the face, and so on), and such qualifications, of course, can in turn be seen as exclusionary (for example, with respect to non-human animals).
28 See *Is It Righteous To Be?* (2001), p. 110ff.
29 *Ethics and Infinity: Conversations with Philip Nemo*, transl. Richard A. Cohen (Pittsburgh, PA: Duquesne University Press, 1985), p. 88.

30 See Heidegger, *Being and Time*, transl. John Macquarrie and Edward Robinson (New York: Harper and Row, 1962).

31 See Derrida, "Violence et métaphysique: Essai sur la pensée d'Emmanuel Levinas," in *L'écriture et la difference* (Paris: Seuil, 1967); *Writing and Difference* (1978), p. 107.

32 For example, *Is It Righteous To Be?* (2001), p. 129.

33 Ibid., p. 124.

34 Levinas, "Le trace de l'autre," in *En découvrant l'existence avec Husserl et Heidegger* (Paris: Vrin, 1974), *passim*.

35 Cf. Morgan, *Discovering Levinas* (2007), pp. 110ff., 236ff.

36 See Derrida, *Adieu to Emmanuel Levinas*, transl. Pascale Anne Brault and Michael Naas (Stanford, CA: Stanford University Press, 1999), p. 29ff. It seems to me that Levinas's position on the place of the third party in the face-to-face remains ambiguous: at times, the singular face right away charges the self with the responsibility to other others (e.g., *Otherwise than Being: Or Beyond Essence*, transl. Alphonso Lingis (Pittsburgh, PA: Duquesne University Press, 1998), p. 158), to the point where the infinity of the obligation seems in part to stem from this co-implication of the face and the third party; at other times, Levinas writes that "In the situation of the face to face, there is no third party that thematizes what occurs between the one and the other" (*God, Death, and Time* (2000), p. 161).

37 See Levinas, *Otherwise than Being* (1998), p. 159.

38 Cf. Morgan, *Discovering Levinas* (2007), p. 455ff.

39 There are a few places in which Levinas acknowledges that I am an other to my others as well, but these places do not develop this second-person standpoint or its reciprocity. For instance, in *Otherwise than Being* Levinas writes that "it is only thanks to God that, as a subject incomparable with the other, I am approached as an other by the others," but he still insists that "inequality" remains "more ancient . . . than equality" (p. 158). As a result, this idea of God as transcendent and thus mediating the relation with the other remains undeveloped as a standpoint to be "translated" for secular morality and rendered appropriable as an impartial viewpoint. The co-originariness of reciprocity, of myself as asymmetrically responsible *and* equally free, is of little consequence in Levinas's account. In a revealing passage in which Levinas comments on the Talmud, he recognizes the other's responsibility for me but insists (as we will see below, with good reason) on the ultimate inescapability of the first-person perspective, an inescapability that, I am arguing, we must also take into account: "I always have, myself, one responsibility more than anyone else, since I am responsible, in addition, for his [the other's] responsibility. And if he is responsible for my responsibility, I remain responsible for the responsibility he has for my responsibility. *Ein ladavar sof*, 'it will never end'" (*The Levinas Reader*, ed. Sean Hand (Oxford: Blackwell, 1989), p. 225f.).

40 Levinas, *Time and the Other*, transl. Richard A. Cohen (Pittsburgh, PA: Duquesne University Press, 1987), p. 72.

41 See John Dickinson and Brian Young, *A Short History of Quebec*, 4th edn (Montreal: McGill-Queens University Press, 2008), p. 22ff.; J. R. Miller,

Skyscrapers Hide the Heavens: A History of Indian–White Relations in Canada, 3rd edn (Toronto: University of Toronto Press, 2000), p. 34ff.; and Olive Patricia Dickason, *The Myth of the Savage and the Beginnings of French Colonialism in the Americas* (Edmonton: University of Alberta Press, 1984).

42 I propose such a reading of Habermas's principle of universalization ("A norm is valid when the foreseeable consequences and side effects of its general observance for the interests and value-orientations of *each individual* could be *jointly* accepted by *all* concerned without coercion" (*IO*, p. 42, Habermas's emphases), in "Equality and Singularity in Justification and Application Discourses," *European Journal of Political Theory*, 9/3(2010): 328–46); cf. Fritsch, "Equal Consideration for All – an Aporetic Project?," *Philosophy and Social Criticism*, 32/3(2006): 299–323. Apart from a direct reading of the principle of universalization, one could say that if its theory of justice needs and presupposes singularized responsible agents (at least for the sake of motivation), then that theory must in turn value the singularity of agents. For a more general account of the way in which equality implies singularity and vice versa, see Christoph Menke, *Spiegelungen der Gleichheit: Politische Philosophie nach Adorno und Derrida* (Frankfurt: Suhrkamp Verlag, 2004).

43 See Seyla Benhabib, "The Generalized and the Concrete Other," *Praxis International*, 5/4(1986): 402–25; and Habermas, "Transcendence from Within, Transcendence in this World," in Eduardo Mendieta, ed., *The Frankfurt School on Religion* (New York: Routledge, 2004), pp. 303–26.

44 It is worth noting that, with his recent emphasis on the body as required for singularization beyond impersonal reason, and the new experience of the body's potential exposure to genetic engineers, Habermas's appreciation of corporeal vulnerability has increased. In 1988, he still wrote that "Persons are symbolic structures, whereas the symbolically structured nature-like substratum, although experienced as one's own body, nonetheless as nature, remains just as external to individuals as does the material natural basis of the lifeworld as a whole" (*OPC*, p. 252). Compare this to the following words in *The Future of Human Nature*: "I conceive of moral behavior as a constructive response to the dependencies rooted in the incompleteness of our organic makeup and in the persistent frailty . . . of our bodily existence. Normative regulation of interpersonal relations may be seen as a porous shell protecting a vulnerable body, and the person incorporated in this body, from the contingencies they are exposed to. Moral rules are fragile constructions protecting both the physis from bodily injuries and the person from inner or symbolical injuries" (*FHN*, p. 33f.). Still a few years later, Habermas put it perhaps more strongly: "Not the rational will as such but the subjective nature into which it extends – its organic roots in the lived nature of my bodily existence – is the point of reference of selfhood and of the self-ascription of 'my' actions" (*BNR*, p. 188; to avoid the impression Habermas here merely paraphrases Adorno's view, cf. p. 160). Of course, the body that has now become a centre of personhood is my own seen in view of enabling its agency, that is, the body

of the "I can", not the other's body asking for food, as for Levinas (though he too writes that I experience the other's hunger by way of transference from my own; see *God, Death, and Time*, p. 171).

45 Cf. Menke, *Spiegelungen der Gleichheit*; and Fritsch, "Equal Consideration of All" (2006) and "Equality and Singularity" (2010).

46 Cf. Derrida, *The Gift of Death*, p. 60ff.; and Waldenfels, "Response and Responsibility in Levinas," in Adriaan T. Peperzak, ed., *Ethics as First Philosophy: The Significance of Emmanuel Levinas for Philosophy, Literature, and Religion* (London: Routledge, 1995).

47 *Difficult Freedom* (1990), p. 21f.

48 Cf. Levinas, *Time and the Other* (1987), p. 109n; and *The Levinas Reader* (1989), p. 226.

49 Cf. Iris Marion Young, "Asymmetrical Reciprocity: On Moral Respect, Wonder, and Enlarged Thought," *Constellations*, 3/3(1997): 340–63.

50 See Adriaan Theodore Peperzak, *To the Other: An Introduction to the Philosophy of Emmanuel Levinas* (West Lafayette: Purdue University Press, 1993), p. 26ff.; and Paul Standish, "Ethics before Equality: Moral Education after Levinas," *Journal of Moral Education*, 30/4(2001): 339–47.

51 *Is It Righteous To Be?* (2001), p. 116.

52 Stephen Gardiner, "A Perfect Moral Storm. Climate Change, Intergenerational Ethics, and the Problem of Corruption," *Environmental Values*, 15/3(2006): 397–413.

53 See Joseph Heath, "Rational Choice as Critical Theory," *Philosophy and Social Criticism*, 22/5(1996): 43–62; and "Ideology, Irrationality and Collectively Self-Defeating Behaviour," *Constellations*, 7/3(2000): 363–71.

54 See *AWM*, pp. 74–6. Of course, another way to seek to solve collective action problems is by enforcing, typically by legal means, what is collectively rational. For by its sanctioning power, law can translate what the latter demands into the rationality of strategic actors. This is why Habermas rightly emphasizes the importance of law in democratic societies whose capitalist markets encourage instrumental action (see *BFN*).

55 Cf. *Is It Righteous To Be?* (2001), p. 224.

56 One may argue that the discourse-ethical understanding of conventional public norms (that is, non-transcendental norms justified deliberatively, such as human rights) reduces this tension because these norms may be thought of as the result of deliberative processes. Given that the self has or could have participated in these fora, we may argue that it will be easier to appropriate these norms as its own (cf. *BNR*, p. 277ff.). While this points to the usefulness of the discourse-ethical construction of the third-person perspective, it cannot do away entirely with the paradox, as a decision will have to remain unpredictable. I have argued that one way in which this tension between the perspectives shows up in Habermas's discourse ethics is in the tension between universal justifiability and the standard of appropriateness to cases; the latter requirement must be inherently unpredictable (Fritsch, "Equality and Singularity" (2010)).

57 Heinz von Foerster, "Ethics and Second-Order Cybernetics," *Cybernetics*

and Human Knowing, 1/1(1992): 14. Cf. Niklas Luhmann, "Die Paradoxie des Entscheides," *Verwaltungs-Archiv: Zeitschrift für Verwaltungslehre, Verwaltungsrecht und Verwaltungspolitik*, 84(1993): 287–310; and Derrida, "Force of Law," transl. Mary Quaintance, in Drucilla Cornell, Michael Rosenfeld, and David Gray, eds, *Deconstruction and the Possibility of Justice* Carlson (New York: Routledge, 1992), p. 24. For some of the differences between Luhmann and Derrida on this question of the decision, see Gunther Teubner, "Economics of Gift – Positivity of Justice: The Mutual Paranoia of Jacques Derrida and Niklas Luhmann," *Theory, Culture and Society*, 18(2001): 29–47; and "Dealing with Paradoxes of Law: Derrida, Luhmann, Wiethölter," in Oren Perez and Gunther Teubner, eds, *On Paradoxes and Inconsistencies in Law* (Oxford: Hart, 2006), pp. 41–64.

58 See Luhmann, "Die Paradoxie des Entscheidens," (1993), p. 295.

59 While one may think Habermas came to this postsecular understanding rather recently – that is, in the wake of the terrorist attacks of 2001, or as a result of his engagement with "hard" naturalism in bioethics and beyond – he had already concluded his "Themes in Postmetaphysical Thinking," a paper published in 1988, by arguing that religion remains indispensable for permitting "intercourse with the extraordinary" and for its "inspiring semantic content" (*PMT*, p. 51). Habermas clarifies the relation between postmetaphysical thought and the postsecular (sociological) condition in a recent interview (Mendieta, "A Postsecular World Society?").

60 Kant, *Critique of Pure Reason*, transl. Norman Kemp Smith (New York: St Martin's Press, 1965), p. 475 (A 552/B 580). One may compare this affirmation of the self's "I can," "I am free," to Heidegger's notion of *Bezeugung* (see *Being and Time*, especially §54) and Ricoeur's development of it as *attestation* (in *Oneself as Another*). Arguably, Heidegger stresses the self-relation in this attestation at the expense of its co-originary intersubjectivity, a sociality on which both Habermas and Levinas insist.

61 Habermas has in fact admitted that some formal-pragmatic conditions are impossible to realize on their own terms, and this not only for empirical reasons. For example, the higher-order norms of argumentative discourses include, on what Habermas names the logical-semantic level, the idealizing and counter-factual presupposition that speakers have to use expressions with the same meaning, that a predicate has to be applied to different but sufficiently similar objects, and the like (Habermas, *Moralbewußtsein und kommunikatives Handeln* (Frankfurt, Suhrkamp Verlag, 1983), p. 97). Now, if meaning is in part constituted by the *in toto* unthematizable background knowledge of the lifeworld, the conclusion hermeneutic and deconstructive theories have drawn seems inescapable: the dependence of meaning on ultimately unthematizable and shifting contexts implies the interminability of seeking understanding in transparent certainty, as well as the impossibility of the absolute identity of meaning to itself. Referring to its implications for individuality and intersubjectivity as well, Habermas put it as follows (with passing reference to Derrida): "As far back as the early sixties ... I did not treat communication so much technically as paradigmatically ... I stressed

the broken nature of all intersubjective relationships. In other words, even if these are idealized, they must still be conceptualized in such a way that their tensions remain irreducible – otherwise, the whole structure collapses: tensions, not just between subjects, but reflexively as well, between different perceptions and self-perceptions of what constitutes an individuality and which nevertheless is perpetually in flux, in change, never identical with certain presuppositions which are nevertheless necessary and unavoidable. Today, having gone through more standard cases, I would say you have to analyze idealizations in such a way that you stress both: the idealizations and the failures. For instance, there are no identical meanings in the terms in which we are now trying to communicate, from the third person's point of view there are none; it is easy for psychologists and for Derrida too (if he would analyze anything!) to show that there is only non-identity over the whole space of communication. On the other hand, we have simultaneously to realize that any human communication would break down the moment you could not presuppose that we exchange identical meanings" (Peter Dews, ed., *Autonomy and Solidarity: Interview with Jürgen Habermas* (London: Verso, 1986), p. 197f.). I think Derrida more or less subscribes to these statements regarding necessary and ideal presuppositions that cannot but fail to be realized; hence, the predominance of the notion of aporia and of the impossible in his writings. He would, however, insist that the reasons for the failures are not of the psychologist's order, as they refer to the transcendental requirement of differentiation procedures, which defer identical meaning to a future to come (see Derrida, *Margins of Philosophy*, transl. Alan Bass (Chicago, IL: University of Chicago Press, 1982), chapter 1). See also the next note.

62 Habermas feels uncomfortable with the notion of the "ideal speech situation" due to its "concretistic" connotations (*JA*, p. 163ff.). A look at the history of Habermas's statements about the empirical attainability of this ideal reveals his evolving thought on the matter as well as its difficulties: In the early 1970s, Habermas introduces the ideal speech situation as not only necessarily presupposed as possible, but as actually realizable (though only under rare institutional conditions) (see "Wahrheitstheorien," in *Vorstudien und Ergänzungen der Theorie des kommunikativen Handelns* (Frankfurt: Suhrkamp Verlag, 1984), p. 179), so that Habermas wonders whether we should consider it a "form of life to be realized in the future" (ibid., pp. 181, 126 n.94). By the time of the *Theory of Communicative Action*, and after the first in a series of objections by Albrecht Wellmer, Habermas rejects the "utopianism" that presents an ideal life form on the basis of a merely procedural rationality, for such life forms also consist of historically contingent, non-formalizable, substantial features like customary practices, group identities, cultural patterns of interpretations and socialization, and so on (*TCA* 1, 73–4). Nonetheless, the idealizations of communication and the modern, rationalized lifeworld are the "necessary conditions for an emancipated society" (ibid.) and, as such, in principle realizable (though perhaps not in fact). So in this sense, as Habermas has repeated quite recently, the ideal

speech situation can count as an ideal that we ought to strive to approximate asymptotically, an ideal that is both regulative and constitutive with regard to real argumentation (*JA*, p. 163ff.). Responding to some further criticisms by Wellmer (in particular, in Albrecht Wellmer, "Wahrheit, Kontigenz, Moderne," in Harry Kunneman and Hent de Vries, eds, *Enlightenments: Encounters Between Critical Theory and Contemporary French Thought* (Kampen, NL: Kok Pharos, 1993), pp. 25–44), however, Habermas has also conceded that the presuppositions of argumentation may not be understood as a final state that we ought to strive to attain, for this state would imply the end of all disagreement. He writes that "this entropical condition of a definitive agreement that would render superfluous all further communication cannot be represented as a meaningful goal, because in it paradoxes (such as those of a final language, of a conclusively valid interpretation, of a non-revisable knowledge, etc.) would have to occur" (Habermas, "Reply to Symposium Participants," in Michael Rosenfeld and Andrew Arato, eds, *Habermas on Law and Democracy* (Berkeley, CA: University of California Press, 1998), p. 418).

63 Derrida, "Faith and Knowledge: The Two Sources of 'Religion' at the Limits of Reason Alone," in Jacques Derrida and Gianni Vattimo, eds, *Religion* (Stanford, CA: Stanford University Press, 1998), p. 26.

64 Ibid., p. 28.

65 Ibid., p. 26.

66 In fact, at the outset of his work on religion, Derrida remarks that a transcendental analysis of the "historicity of history" must be supplemented by an empirical analysis of the "history of historicity" ("Faith and Knowledge," (1998), p. 9). I have sought to analyze the idea of a "quasi-transcendental" in reference to philosophy's inheriting from messianic religion in *Promise of Memory: History and Politics in Marx, Benjamin, and Derrida* (Albany, NY: SUNY Press, 2005), chapter 2.

Chapter 13 Solidarity with the Past and the Work of Translation: Reflections on Memory Politics and the Postsecular

1 Walter Benjamin, *The Arcades Project* (Cambridge, MA: Harvard University Press, 2000), p. 478. Translation modified.

2 Jeffrey Olick, *The Politics of Regret: On Collective Memory and Historical Responsibility* (London: Routledge, 2007).

3 Richard Rorty, *Objectivity, Relativism, and Truth*, Philosophical Papers, Volume 1 (Cambridge: Cambridge University Press, 1991), introduction, p. 13.

4 On the double nature of translation, see Simone Chambers, "How Religion Speaks to the Agnostic: Habermas on the Persistent Value of Religion," *Constellations*, 14/2 (June 2007): 210–23.

5 In the vast literature of memory politics in the divided Germany, see the now-classical work by Jeffrey Herf, *Divided Memory: The Nazi Past in the Two Germanies* (Cambridge, MA: Harvard University Press, 1997).

6 For a translated compendium of texts of the "Historians' Debate," see Thomas Knowles, ed., *Forever in the Shadow of Hitler?* (New Jersey: Humanities Press, 1993); for analyses, see Charles Maier, *The Unmasterable Past: History, Holocaust, and German National Identity* (Cambridge, MA: Harvard University Press, 1998); John Torpey, "Habermas and the Historians (Introduction to Special Issue on the *Historikerstreit*)," *New German Critique*, 44 (spring/summer 1988): 5–24.

7 Many of Habermas's longer essays on the Historians' Debate are collected in NC.

8 It has never been clear to me whether this notion of anamnestic solidarity is actually Benjamin's. For a discussion of this particular appropriation of Benjamin, see Max Pensky, "On the Use and Abuse of Memory: Habermas, 'Anamnestic Solidarity,' and the *Historikerstreit*," *Philosophy and Social Criticism*, 15/4 (1989): 351–80. It has never been entirely clear to me whether "solidarity" is the correct term to capture Benjamin's own position, however sketchily outlined, in the "Theses on History." Solidarity is in essence a process of inclusion; Benjamin seems to be advocating a far more wrathful incitement to revolutionary action on behalf of the dead, rather than an inclusion of the dead in a circle of all those from whom one may recognize a moral demand.

9 See *MCCA*, p. 200: "Since moralities are tailored to suit the fragility of human beings individuated through socialization, they must always solve *two* tasks *at once*. They must emphasize the inviolability of the individual by postulating equal respect for the dignity of each individual. But they must also protect the web of intersubjective relations of mutual recognition by which these individuals survive as members of a community. To these two complementary aspects correspond the principles of justice and solidarity respectively. The first postulates equal respect and equal rights for the individual, whereas the second postulates empathy and concern for the well-being of one's neighbor."

10 "Every autonomous morality has to serve two purposes at once: it brings to bear the inviolability of socialized individuals by requiring equal treatment and thereby equal respect for the dignity of each one; and it protects intersubjective relationships of mutual recognition requiring solidarity of individual members of a community, in which they have been socialized. Justice concerns the equal freedoms of unique and self-determining individuals, while solidarity concerns the welfare of consociates who are intimately linked in an intersubjectively shared form of life – and thus also to the maintenance of the integrity of this form of life itself" (*JS*, p. 231).

11 Max Pensky, *The Ends of Solidarity: Discourse Theory in Ethics and Politics* (Albany, NY: State University of New York Press, 2008), ch. 1.

12 For a fuller discussion of this point, see Max Pensky, "Contributions toward a Theory of Storms: Historical Knowing and Historical Progress in Kant and Benjamin," *The Philosophical Forum*, 41/1 and 2(spring/summer 2010): 149–74. For Habermas's reading of the normative significance of Kant's philosophy of history and the "unthinkability of despair," see his "On the

Reception and Contemporary Relevance of Kant's Philosophy of Religion" (*BNR*, pp. 209–48).

13 Pablo de Greiff, "The Duty to Remember: The Dead Weight of the Past, or the Weight of the Dead of the Past?, " unpublished, p. 18. Emphasis in original.

14 For an interesting recent account of the transition from a "pre-axial" to a metaphysical conception of the dead and the afterlife, see John Casey, *After Lives* (Oxford: Oxford University Press, 2009), chs 1 and 2.

15 Johann-Baptist Metz, "Erinnerung," in H. Krings, H. M. Baumgartner, and C. Wild, eds, *Handbuch philosophischer Grundbegriffe* (Munich: Koesel Verlag, 1973), p. 388.

16 Johann-Baptist Metz, "Anamnestic Reason: A Theologian's Remarks on the Crisis in the *Geisteswissenschaften*," in Thomas McCarthy and Axel Honneth, eds, *Cultural-Political Interventions in the Unfinished Project of Enlightenment* (Cambridge, MA: MIT Press, 1992), pp. 189–94.

17 Johann-Baptist Metz, "The Concept of a Political Theology as a Practical Fundamental Theology," in *Faith in History and Society* (New York: Seabury Press, 1980), p. 49ff.

18 See Johann-Baptist Metz's comments, in Johann Baptist Metz and Elie Wiesel, *Hope Against Hope: Johann-Baptist Metz and Elie Wiesel Speak Out on the Holocaust* (Mahwah, NJ: Paulist Press, 1999).

19 Metz, *Faith in History and Society* (1980), p. 8.

20 Ibid., p. 190.

21 See Johann-Baptist Metz, *Memoria Passionis. Ein provozierendes Gedächnis in pluralistischer Gesellschaft* (Freiberg: Herder, 2006).

22 Metz, in Metz and Wiesel, *Hope Against Hope* (1999), p. 24. Unfortunately, Metz expands this observation, weighty and controversial enough, with what I take as a profoundly unfortunate claim to the Jewishness of Critical Theory. Commenting on the lack of theological interest in Habermas's work (though I doubt now he could make the same comment) Metz writes, "I will risk this conjecture here: perhaps what makes Habermas appear less theological than Benjamin and the early Frankfurt School, but also in my view always more of an idealist, is the Jewish background, which is missing or only dimly illuminated in him."

23 Those familiar with the debates I am discussing here will have remarked the absence of Helmut Peukert's voice. For reasons of space, I choose instead to focus on Metz, whose potential for a truly productive debate with Habermas on the relation between religious and secular normativity is for me at least far greater. Where Metz struggles to find a new mode of thinking and speaking to describe the specific challenges of Christian faith after Auschwitz, his student Peukert seems to me to be engaging in an essentially conservative project – finding ways of generating new versions of theistic proofs appropriate to modern forms of consciousness. But these proofs generally reduce to the unimpressive argument that universal justice as offered by all modern deontic moral theories, discourse ethics among them, are aporetic unless they take on board the ontological reality of God as the thought of the ground of unity of

a history of suffering and the sum total of our peremptory moral interests. But this argument simply retreats back behind the prohibitions on the constitutive use of pure practical reason for purposes of cognition that Kant had established. For this reason, Peukert's arguments seem quaint. For a good reconstruction of Peukert's writings, and Habermas's responses to them, see Thomas McCarthy, "Critical Theory and Political Theology: The Postulates of Communicative Reason," in *Ideals and Illusions: On Reconstruction and Deconstruction in Contemporary Critical Theory* (Cambridge, MA: MIT Press, 1991), pp. 200–17, for a very thorough criticism of the premodern character of Peukert's "aporias" argument.

24 "Philosophy, even after assimilating utopian impulses from the Judeo-Christian tradition, has not been capable of mastering by means of consolation and trust the de facto meaninglessness of death in its contingency, that of individual suffering, or that of the private loss of happiness – in general, the meaninglessness of the negativity of the risks built into life – in a way that had been possible for the religious hope in salvation. In the industrially advanced societies we see for the first time as a mass phenomenon the loss of hope in redemption and the expectation of grace, which, even if no longer supported within an ecclesiastical framework, are still supported by interiorized faith traditions" (Habermas, "Does Philosophy Still Have a Purpose?," in *Philosophical-Political Profiles* (Cambridge, MA: MIT Press, 1983), pp. 17–18).

25 "Pure practical reason can no longer be so confident in its ability to counteract a modernization spinning out of control armed solely with the insights of a theory of justice. The latter lacks the creativity of linguistic world-disclosure that a normative consciousness afflicted with accelerating decline requires in order to regenerate itself" (*BNR*, p. 211).

26 "Secular languages which only eliminate the substance once intended leave irritations. When sin was converted to culpability, and the breaking of divine commands to an offense against human laws, something was lost. The wish for forgiveness is still bound up with the unsentimental wish to undo the harm inflicted on others. What is even more disconcerting is the irreversibility of *past* sufferings – the injustice inflicted on innocent people who were abused, debased, and murdered, reaching far beyond any extent of reparation within human power. The lost hope for resurrection is keenly felt as a void. Horkheimer's justified skepticism – 'the slaughtered are really slaughtered' – with which he countered Benjamin's emphatic, or rather excessive, hope for the anamnestic power of reparation inherent in human remembrance, is far from denying the helpless impulse to change what cannot be changed anymore. The exchange of letters between Benjamin and Horkheimer dates from Spring 1937. Both, the true impulse and its impotence, were prolonged after the holocaust by the practice, as necessary as it was hopeless, of 'coming to terms with the past' ['Aufarbeitung der Vergangenheit'] (Adorno). They are manifest as well in the rising lament over the inappropriateness of this practice. In moments like these, the unbelieving sons and daughters of modernity seem to believe that they owe more to one another, and need more

for themselves, than what is accessible to them, in translation, of religious tradition – as if the semantic potential of the latter was still not exhausted" (*BNR*, p. 111).

27 Lutz Wingert, "Haben wir moralische Pflicten gegenüber früheren Generationen? Moralischer Universalismus und erinnernde Solidarität," in *Babylon. Beiträge zur jüdischen Gegenwart*, 9(1991): 78–93.

28 Habermas has in fact written movingly, and in the familiar cadences of the sermon, regarding just this aspect of discourse-based solidarity: "It is the experience of an equality that does not level out difference and of a togetherness that individualizes. It is the experience of a closeness across distance to an other acknowledged in his or her difference. It is the experience of a combination of autonomy and self-surrender, a reconciliation which does not extinguish the differences, a future-oriented justice that is in solidarity with the unreconciled suffering of past generations. It is the experience of the reciprocity of freely granted acknowledgement, of a relationship in which a subject is associated to another without being subjected to the degrading violence of exchange" (*RR*, p. 232).

29 "The idea of God is transformed into a concept of a *logos* that determines the community of believers, and the real-life context of a self-emancipating society. 'God' becomes the name for a communicative structure that forces men, on pain of the loss of their humanity, to go beyond their accidental, empirical nature to encounter one another *indirectly*, that is, across an objective something that they themselves are not" (*LC*, p. 211).

Chapter 14 What Lacks is Feeling: Hume versus Kant and Habermas

1 See, for all this, Tracey Rowland, *Benedict XVI: A Guide for the Perplexed* (London: T. & T. Clark, 2010).

2 For an earlier debate between Habermas and Ratzinger, see *The Dialectics of Secularization: On Reason and Religion* (San Franscisco, CA: Ignatius, 2006).

3 Honnefelder's complex genealogy is most accessible in his short book based on lectures given in Paris, *La métaphysique comme science transcendentale* (Paris: PUF, 2002).

4 See John Milbank, "The Theological Critique of Philosophy in Hamann and Jacobi," in *Radical Orthodoxy: A New Theology* (London: Routledge, 1999), pp. 21–37, and John R. Betz, *After Enlightenment: Hamann as Post-Secular Visionary* (Oxford: Wiley-Blackwell, 2008).

5 Michael Reder, "How Can Faith and Reason be Distinguished? Remarks on Ethics and the Philosophy of Religion," in Habermas, *AWM*, pp. 36–50.

6 For an authentic reading of Cusa not through Idealist lenses, see Johannes Hoff, *Kontingenz, Berührung, Über schreitung: zur philosophischen Propädeutik christlicher Mystik nach Nikolaus von Kues* (Freiburg/Munich: Karl Alber, 2007).

7 Friedrich Schleiermacher, *On Religion: Speeches to its Cultured Despisers* transl. Richard Crouter (Cambridge: Cambridge University Press, 1988).

8 See John Milbank, *The Word Made Strange: Theology, Language, Culture* (Oxford: Blackwell, 2002), p. 167 n.20.

9 For my own understanding of Kant at this point, see John Milbank, *Being Reconciled: Ontology and Pardon* (London: Routledge, 2003), pp. 1–25.

10 Quentin Meillassoux, *After Finitude: An Essay on the Necessity of Contingency,* transl. Ray Brassier (London: Continuum, 2009).

11 See Luigino Bruni and Stefano Zamagni, *Civil Economy* (Oxford: Peter Lang, 2007), pp. 77–122. It is true, however, as Bruni and Zamagni argue, that the Scots lagged behind Neapolitans like Antonio Genovesi (who heard Vico lecture) in developing a "civil" not a "political" economy, such that the market lay *fully inside* civil society and therefore a contract could still be a matter of mutual sympathy and one *might* (*contra* Adam Smith) care about the personal well-being of one's butcher and he about yours. In either case, these thinkers deployed Epicurean and Jansenist themes (from Boisguilbert) of how order can be distilled from human selfishness and evil (Smith's "hidden hand"), but in either case, also, this was qualified by a humanist concern with disinterestedly binding sentiment and deliberate teleological orientation. However, the Neapolitans admitted the latter into the market in a way that the Scots failed to do. Thus, Hume bequeathed to Smith too strong a division between "natural" and "artificial" justice, and because of the supposed limited reach of sympathy attributed too much to the liberal individualist contractualism of the latter. All the same, Hume's invocation of the role of aristocratic identification of familial with general societal interests, his attribution of acceptance of private property to the force of inherited association, his ideas of emotional attachment to the artificial, plus his more general interweaving of the affective and the fictional in his account of cognition means that this division is arguably somewhat more qualified for him than it is for Smith. One should also mention here that Hume's appeal to "utility" was not as yet that of Bentham, but rather meant something more like the "convenient and fitting," following the Horatian and Ciceronian coupling *utile et dulce.*

12 David Hume, *A Treatise of Human Nature* (Oxford: Oxford University Press, 1978), III.III.vi, pp. 618–21.

13 David Hume, *Dialogues Concerning Natural Religion* (New York: Hafner, 1948), XII, p. 86. See also VI, p. 42.

14 The idea of "cosmic sympathy" associated with the notion of a universal "world-fire," is thought by many commentators to have originated with the Stoic philosopher Posidonius of Rhodes. For a summary of the influence of the notion up to medieval times, see Paul Magdalino and Maria Mavroudi, *The Occult Sciences in Byzantium* (London: La Pomme d'Or, 2008), chapter 2.

15 We know that when he was in France, Hume was regarded as a crypto-Jacobite and even occasionally crypto-papist opponent of Voltaire's "whiggish" view of English history in favor of a defense of the Catholic deep past (including Thomas More) and the Stuart recent past; that Catholic apologists sometimes returned the compliment of Hume's covert deployment of the Catholic skeptics and, finally, that Hume's political thought continued

to inspire the thought of the traditionalists in France up to and beyond the French Revolution. This all casts serious doubt on Macintyre's ascription to Hume of an "Anglicizing subversion." See Lawrence L. Bongie, *David Hume: Prophet of the Counter-Revolution* (Oxford: Oxford University Press, 1965), and Alasdair Macintyre, *Whose Justice: Which Rationality?* (London: Duckworth, 1988), pp. 281–99. Macintyre's reading of Hume is accurately criticized by Donald W. Livingston: see subsequent footnote. It may well be that Hume is in a certain fashion *nearer* to Aristotle than is Francis Hutcheson, whereas Macintyre has this the other way round.

16 A variant of such a reading (which I can do little more than roughly sketch in this article) is upheld by the greatest living Hume scholar, Donald W. Livingston, who has made the sadly rare attempt to read all of Hume's works (including the historical ones) together in the round. In his two crucial studies of the Scottish philosopher, Livingston validly compares him to Vico, insofar as both thinkers point out, and draw back from, the existential and political consequences of living according to pure reason and suggest that, by contrast, the emotions and the imagination may have an irreducible role in the discerning of truth. See Donald W. Livingston, *Hume's Philosophy of Common Life* (Chicago, IL: Chicago University Press, 1984), and *Philosophical Melancholy and Delirium: Hume's Pathology of Philosophy* (Chicago, IL: Chicago University Press, 1998).

17 This is why feeling tends to be always blended with the imagination in Hume. See *Treatise of Human Nature,* I.I.v., pp. 12–13: "cohesion" amongst ideas is "a kind of ATTRACTION, which in the mental world will be found to have as extraordinary effects as in the natural." Hume is *not* doing "epistemology" but experimental science of mind, which renders his perspective upon knowing both naturalistic and ontological. Just like "sympathy," "attraction" is to be found in nature as well as in the human mind. Because "cohesion" is inscrutable for Hume, it is not the case that the "constant conjuncture" of two objects causes us to engender the notion of cause and effect by virtue of probability, since this cannot apply to the absolutely new. Rather, we *imagine* a union of ideas according to an impulse which is a "principle of association," or else "certain relations" which are naturally given and cannot be comprehended, since they are the unknowable *ground* of all human comprehension. Jacobi was right to see that Hume undermined all "foundationalism." See *Treatise,* I.III.vi–vii, pp. 90–8, and also xii, p. 134; we only "transfer the past to the future" by "habit" and it is habit which informs "the first impulse of the imagination." Later, Hume affirms that human reason is but heightened animal instinct and that our assumption of temporal consistency, although it is the very foundation of our "reason," is the work of an instinctual power that thinks in excess of the rational evidence. This instinct is a "habit" that is "nothing but one of the principles of nature and derives all its force from that origin" (I.II.xvi, p. 179). It follows, then, that though the cause and effect relation is only something that we "make up," this very making up is the work of a natural causal power which is a kind of habitual flow, not a law-governed efficiency.

18 See John Milbank, *The Word Made Strange* (Oxford: Blackwell, 1997), pp. 7–35.

19 I disagree with Edward Caird that Hume's prime target is the *imago dei* in human beings. Caird bases this claim on the view that Hume attacks deductive reasoning as linked to notions of direct spiritual insight and the notion of reason as a divine spark. It is true that Hume adopts the model of Baconian inductive reason, but he also subverts it by (a) saying that the empirical knowledge of other things depends upon "Socratic" self-knowledge, and (b) saying that our self-experience is of fathomless processes. Therefore, reason is not *reduced* to feeling; rather, reason as the instrument of noumenalist reduction is humiliated and feeling gets elevated. In terms now of feeling, the idea of insight as direct intuition is sustained and, if anything, extended. Moreover, in the *Dialogues Concerning Natural Religion*, Hume is prepared equivalently to re-conceptualize *God*, following Plotinus, as supra-intellectual. See note 23 below and Edward Caird, *The Mind of God and the Works of Man* (Cambridge: Cambridge University Press, 1987), pp. 69–130.

20 Hume sees his relationship to Bacon as like that of Socrates to Thales: *Treatise*, Introduction, pp. xvi–xvii.

21 *Treatise*, I.IV.v, p. 248: "motion . . . is the cause of thought and perception."

22 *Treatise*, II.III.ii, p. 410.

23 *Dialogues*, VI, p. 42. Hume's alter ego Philo (as he surely is, by and large – and note the Platonic name!) is happy to entertain the notion that the world is like "an animal or organized body" and seems "actuated with a like principle of life and motion" which is a kind of world-soul.

24 See n.7 above.

25 I prefer the term "constitutive" to the term "internal" relation, because the former implies a relation that enters into the very substance of a thing (and is not therefore merely accidental and "external") without implying that its *relata* can be logically deduced from the nature of the thing after the fashion of idealism. For, if there is *no* element of external contingency in a relation, then all relations are in the end internal to the one monad of all reality and relationality is after all abolished.

26 *Treatise*, Appendix, pp. 623–9; 629: "An idea assented to *feels* different from a fictitious idea, that the fancy alone presents to us"; I.III.viii, pp. 98–106; I.IV.ii, pp. 193–218.

27 Indeed, Hume's historicism is more thoroughgoing than Hegel or Marx's because he denies that there is any reality beneath established habitual fiction – whether composed by nature or by humanity. In terms of human history there can therefore be no social order outside a continued allegiance to such fictions.

28 *Dialogues*, VI–VIII, pp. 42–56; XII, p. 94.

29 Clare Carlisle and Mark Sinclair well describe this sequence regarding habit that passes from Cartesian rationalist skepticism through empiricist skepticism, to conclude in affirmed vitalism. However, they fail to allow that the inklings of the third "ontological" move are already there in Hume. See their

"Editors' Introduction" to Félix Ravaisson, *Of Habit,* transl. C. Carlisle and M. Sinclair (London: Continuum, 2008), p. 7, and also their "Editors' Commentary," pp. 111–12. They rightly say, though, that Hume had already tried to explain association of ideas by habit and not vice versa, such that he was closer to Ravaisson than the latter realized. He underrated the degree to which, via Biran, he was developing a Humean lineage. See also Alberto Toscano, *The Theatre of Production* (London: Palgrave MacMillan, 2006), pp. 114–16. Toscano also denies that Hume begins to ontologize habit and sees him as concerned only with the observed "principle" of habit and not with its ontogenesis. This reading, though, is contradicted by Livingston's demonstration that Hume's fundamental thinking is "historical" or genetic in character, rather than merely psychological or proto-transcendentalist. Hume thinks that we can "compare" a present to a past sensation, and on this basis establish "ideas," because the past sensation only survives at all by always already being contained within the idea: in other words, because we remember it in "narrative connection" with a present sensation. Although this is to historicize the content of habit and not habit as such, the refusal of the primacy of "presentist" association (nearly all non-Humean empiricisms) means that habit is self-referring and deliriously abyssal: habits which arise historically are only accounted for by the habit of habit in general. This implies the ultimacy of a genetic account and the constitution of human beings through habit rather than the idea that habits reside "inside us." So, however apophatic Hume is about ontogenesis, he still gestures towards it. See Livingston, *Hume's Philosophy of Common Life,* pp. 91–105. Arguably, Toscano misreads Deleuze when he affirms that there is no "geneticism" in Hume: for Deleuze seems to line this up with psychologism and so an account of human genesis that would either be merely "internal" or cultural in character and therefore *not* an ontogenesis. Since Deleuze clearly himself favors the latter and yet also identifies with Hume's "empiricism" (while refusing the usual psychologizing readings of Hume), one has to read his saying "Genesis must refer to the principles, it is merely the particular character of a principle" to mean that there can be no "rationalistic" genealogy (not even a Nietzschean one ought to be the implication) that would seek to ground the obscure "principles" which constitute in Hume relations. However, these principles *only* act historically. An ontology of habit that goes "all the way down" is also an abyssal historicism. See Gilles Deleuze, *Empiricism and Subjectivity,* transl. Constantin V. Boundas (New York: Columbia University Press, 1991). Hume's "historicism" (which is not constrained to any determined meta-narrative as with Hegel or even Nietzsche) also casts a different light upon his distinction of fact from value. For if all thought is for him a matter of historically constituted feeling, according to an unfathomable process (whose effects we can merely observe), then *all thought* is a kind of valuation, even though it still registers realities. (One can note here that for Hume, unlike Locke, primary qualities are as subjective as secondary ones and yet both can still be taken to be in some sense extra-subjective also: *Dialogues,* I.IV.iv, pp. 225–31.) Thus, factual discourse differs from evaluative discourse for Hume only in terms of a diversity of feeling. In the one case of the observation of facts we *feel* objective difference and distance, whereas in the case of ethical and aesthetic valuation we feel both a more intense connection and yet a greater uncertainty as to what in the object occasions in us the sentiment. Yet that this is a matter of objective relating of ourselves to "outness" is not by Hume, as by later positivists, denied.

30 Friedrich Heinrich Jacobi, "David Hume on Faith" (1787), pp. 253–338, and Preface to the 1799 version, pp. 537–90; Maine de Biran, *Essai sur les fondements de la psychologie, Des Oeuvres de Maine de Biran, TomeVII/ 1 and 2*, ed. F. C. T. Moore (Paris: J.Vrin, 2001), pp. 161–8; *Influence de l'habitude sur le faculté de penser* (Paris: L'Harmattan, 2006). Maine de Biran deployed Hume's skepticism against Locke and Condillac's empiricist "way of ideas" and followed Hume in the view that we only have an "internal" clue to notions of cause and power as operating in nature. However, he attributed to Hume a complete skepticism as the existence of a mysterious "principle" of force within us and explained this in terms of the neglect of the centrality of touch in favor of the centrality of vision in the philosophies of Locke, Berkeley, and Hume (in contrast, of course, to Aristotle). However, he is clear about the way in which Hume himself invites an ontologization of habit: I would simply argue, along with Deleuze and others, that he underrated the beginning of this move in Hume. Biran, however, illustrates very well in *Influence* the logical sequence which I am advocating: (1) one tries to explain thinking in terms of motion; (2) we discover that the causality of motion cannot be thought; (3) therefore the closest we get to understanding it is through our immediate experience of mental motion as habit; (4) in consequence, in order to avoid skepticism, we are speculatively justified in projecting habit on to nature as the pre-legal reality of causality and so in developing a vitalist ontology. In *Influence*, Biran refuses any mere associationism or physicalism as inadequate to explain why sensation and action become "unconscious" as habit, and why the interruption of habitual sensing and acting is emotionally distressing. He rather accounts for this in terms of "a secret activity" that belongs to "the principle of life" and that results in a sort of sympathetic fusion or "equilibrium" of a sensing organ with the object sensed. As I argue in this essay, the ontologization of sympathy is also at times hinted at by Hume.

31 Ravaisson, *Of Habit*, p. 123 n.6, and *passim*. For the necessity of grace, however, he alludes not to Aquinas but to Fénélon. See also Milbank, "The Mystery of Reason," in Peter Candler and Conor Cunningham, eds, *The Grandeur of Reason: Religion, Tradition and Universalism* (London: SCM Press, 2010), pp. 68–117.

32 *Dialogues*, VIII, pp. 54–5. Arguing against Cleanthes' "extrinsicist" notion of design, which was typical of theo-mechanistic physics, Philo notably says, "It is vain . . . to insist upon the uses of the parts in animals or vegetables and their curious adjustment to each other. I would fain know how an animal could subsist unless its parts were so adjusted? Do we not find that it immediately perishes whenever this adjustment ceases, and that its matter, corrupting,

tries some new form? It happens indeed that the parts of the world are so well adjusted that some regular form immediately lays claim to this corrupted matter; and if it were not so, could the world subsist?" Earlier Philo has speculated that the world appears to us as if there were some kind of stabilizing principle, claiming the work of an anarchic "actuating force." Thus, alongside a kind of *élan vitale*, Hume seems to argue for the notion of a formative power at work in each substantial thing that is in excess of materiality: "Let us contemplate the matter a little, and we shall see that this adjustment if attained by matter of a seeming stability in the forms, with a real and perpetual revolution or motion of parts, affords a plausible, if not a true, solution of the difficulty [i.e., the appearance of 'design' in nature]." So, against the barbarism of Newtonian theology (though in deliberate keeping with Newton's admission of the working of unknown "active principles"), Hume, in a "neo-Renaissance" fashion, hints at a kind of vitalized Aristotelian ontology after all. In terms of reason indeed, as the *Treatise* argues, we cannot make sense of hylomorphism, yet we cannot really *imagine the stability that we see* (in nature) without this supposition: nature appears to have an occult attraction for certain patterns into which it typically falls. Likewise, in Part VII (pp. 47–51), Philo invokes the finality at work in biological generation as a model for the whole world taken as a kind of "animal" (*Gaia*, as we might now say, following James Lovelock) against Cleanthes' argument for an extrinsic finality. For more on final causality, see XII, pp. 82, 84–6. While refusing the mere external imposition of design, Hume still affirms God as the ultimate designer on the basis of something like the view that, since reason belongs to nature, God must be eminently rational as well as eminently generative in the biological sense. He invokes both Malebranche and Plotinus in the course of a truly remarkable – and remarkably theologically orthodox – refutation of an idolized God who is a mere infinitization of human reasoning power: II, p. 15; III, pp. 29–30. Hence, for Hume, if, by virtue of naturalism one must see biological generation as governing thought, and against Cleanthes Philo says it would be more natural to think of the first principle as an unconscious animal than as a knowing God, by virtue of his skepticism he has to give a certain cautious epistemological primacy to knowing over generation, since knowing is (a) the generative process into which we have the most insight, and (b) the one which, within our own experience, most achieves a spontaneity of origination. So the *most* concession to naturalism that Hume's skepticism will allow is not at all an Epicurean or even a Stoic immanentism, but rather an explicitly *Neoplatonic* view that God lies absolutely as much beyond intellect as he does beyond matter, reinforced by Hume's citation in the voice of Demea (whose mysticism Philo avowedly *shares: Dialogues* X, p. 67) of the spiritualist Malebranche's view that God is just as much eminently matter as he is eminently mind. (One can also note here that in the doctrine of the Trinity, thought and generation absolutely *coincide*.) Thus, Hume always affirms transcendence and never merely immanence, just as Philo defends against Cleanthes the (Thomistic) doctrine of the divine *simplicity* by denying that God entertains "plans" separate from his own being (*Dialogues* IV, p. 32). It is partly for these reasons that one should also question the idea that Hume is abandoning the notion of the *imago dei* rather than redefining it (see note 12 above). His reported declaration to a French host that he had never met an atheist must be linked with his view in the *Dialogues* that everyone must naturally suppose that there is some sort of vital, driving force behind the entire universe and that we must assume that this is somewhat like the different processes found *within* the universe – processes which also obscurely resemble each other. Both the vertical and horizontal analogy are therefore affirmed by Hume. In this light, he would appear to regard the "atheist" more as a minimal theist who is extremely cautious about these analogies and thereby becomes indistinguishable from a very apophatic theologian. The theist, by contrast, insists more on the likeness, but he can only do so by *faith* (as Hume stresses) because feelings vary according to degrees of intensity that cannot be strictly measured. As Frédéric Brahami argues, Hume sees this instability of feeling as a far better way of explaining how human thought shifts and develops than that provided by the Lockean representationalist model, which cannot account for how the mind is so readily able to move from the presence of one image to that of another, nor why we habitually link diverse things beyond any scope of reason. One can then argue that Hume sees the dominance of analogy in theological discourse, with its undecidabilty between "atheism" and "theism," as an especially acute manifestation of the indeterminacy of feeling. Because we have at once to affirm and to deny the likeness of the intra-cosmic to the trans-cosmic, we can never confidently know "just how like" or "just how unlike" the Creation is to the Creator. It may perhaps be this communicated circumstance which creates an hermeneutic undecidability for the reader as between Hume's religious skepticism, on the one hand, and a both apophatic and fideistic piety, on the other. See Frédéric Brahami, *Le Travail du Scepticisme: Montaigne, Bayle, Hume* (Paris: PUF, 2001), pp. 167–234.

33 Deleuze, *Empiricism and Subjectivity,* pp. 123–33.

34 *Treatise,* I.II.i–v, pp. 26–66.

35 *Treatise,* I.I.i, p. 2 fn.1; I.III.x, p. 106. Edward Caird rightly insists on this point: see *The Mind of God and the Works of Man.*

36 Jerry Fodor, *Hume Variations* (Oxford: Oxford University Press, 2003).

37 Besides Hume's citing of Plotinus in the *Dialogues,* his use of the Platonic-Ciceronian dialogue form and his speaking through the mouth of "Philo," one can cite his approving mention of the Origenist, Platonist, Freemason, and Catholic covert, his fellow Scot, the Chevalier Andrew Michael Ramsey in a footnote to *The Natural History of Religion.* See *Dialogues* and *Natural History of Religion* (Oxford: Oxford University Press, 1993), *The Natural History of Religion,* n.1, pp. 190–3. Hume's citation of Ramsey's description of the immorality of a "positivist," voluntarist theology has been taken as merely ironic. Yet this seems surely over-simplistic, because in the *Dialogues* Hume abundantly shows himself aware of how something like Ramsey's Origenism could lay claim to being a far more ancient and authentic mode of religiosity. He became friends with Ramsey during his Paris sojourn.

38 David Hume, *Essays Moral, Political and Literary* (Indianapolis, IN: Liberty Fund, 1987), XV, XVI, XVII, XVIII, "The Epicurean," "The Stoic," "The Platonist," "The Sceptic," pp. 138–80.

39 Although he breaks important new ground in his systematic comparison of the Edinburgh and Neapolitan Enlightenments, and specifically between Hume and Vico, John Robertson wrongly assimilates Vico to Hume's supposedly more explicit Epicureanism, instead of assimilating Hume to Vico's clearly more explicit Platonism. Even though Vico incorporates elements of the French Augustinian synthesis of Augustine with Epicurus (notably in his vision of feral fallen man), both his theology and his ontology are more Platonic-humanist than Jansenist or semi-Jansenist. See John Robertson, *The Case for Enlightenment: Scotland and Naples 1680–1760* (Cambridge: Cambridge University Press, 2005). And even though Hume can appear to take the opposite side to Vico in the great debate over Pierre Bayle's question about a possible society of atheists, his grounding of the ethical in feeling and imagination tends to approximate it to the religious, which Hume also (like Vico) grounds in feeling and imagination. Moreover, most of his polemic is directed against the idea of any *necessary* connection between religion and ethical goodness – the point being to discriminate between forms of religion, not to recommend a virtuous atheism. See David Hume, *The Natural History of Religion*.

40 *Treatise*, III.II.vii–x, pp. 534–67.

41 *Essays*, VII, VIII and XI, "Whether the British Government Inclines More to Absolute Monarchy or to a Republic," "Of Parties in General," and "Of the Parties of Great Britain," pp. 47–72.

42 *Treatise*, III.II.v, pp. 524–5.

43 *The Natural History of Religion, passim.* Religion, for Hume, secures our sense of the diversity, unity, order, and mystery of life in terms of the polytheistic, the monotheistic, the extra-humanly designed, and the apophatic. He argues that the ancient gods were little more than modern Scottish fairies, and in either case he contends that the recognition of such preternatural beings may be a perfectly rational acknowledgment of hidden psychic forces within nature. Polytheism has the ethical value of sustaining both social tolerance and bravery, as we can more easily imitate the heroism of the gods than the ineffability of "God." The order of the universe, however, demands monotheistic assent and, morally speaking, monotheism better sustains political unity. Yet pure monotheism, which is philosophical, is at variance with human capacities, and therefore must be qualified by the mediation of angels, daemons, saints, and sacraments. These, in turn, when they over-proliferate, become superstitiously absurd, and thus one gets an event like the Reformation. Not only does this idea of the flux and reflux of polytheism seem akin to Vico's *corso* and *ricorso* between imagination and reason in human religious and social history, but it also suggests a kind of Catholic or perhaps Episcopalian balance between the monotheistic and the polytheistic. Hume rejected both papal superstition as proceeding from an excess of melancholy, and Protestant enthusiasm as stemming from an excess of commercial

success and material well-being (anticipating Weber here!). Yet Part XI of the *Dialogues* implies clearly a still Augustinian and Baylean bias toward the "Catholic" (in Humean terms) primacy of *melancholia* in the face of overwhelming natural suffering and human iniquity. Although Philo defends traditional religion in terms of its mysticism and ontological-cosmological arguments against modern debased attempts to see God as a supreme but extrinsic and ontic designing influence, he still denies against Demea that the "proofs for God's existence" emphatically point to God rather than to a self-designing nature. So, if we "feel" the superiority of human habits and aims and suspect their elevation beyond analogous forces in nature, it is finally a certain melancholic *refusal* of nature and search for salvation which causes us to embrace the mysticism and affirm the proofs. As he is clearly represented, Philo is more skeptical than the apophatic Demea only because he is also more *fideistic*. So true religion for Hume is a melancholy seeking refuge in the *abstract sublime*, which nonetheless pulls back from Catholic superstition in the direction of the *beauty* of this-worldly sympathy, and yet then restrains in turn the self-congratulating yearning toward enthusiasm. If this sounds like Anglicanism, then there is no *entirely* conclusive reason to deny that Hume also thought it was orthodox Christianity. (With respect to miracles, the point is that there is never any convincing *reason* to affirm them.) Indeed, the only explicit Christian doctrine which Hume denied on grounds of faith as well as reason was that of the eternal punishment – objecting that fear of this does nothing to elevate human virtue and that it implies a contempt of the divine person. For this reason, he seems to endorse his friend the Chevalier Ramsay's Origenism. See note 37 above.

44 Just as, for Hume, human beings as creatures of feeling do not really know quite how atheistic or theistic they are, so also they never really know how far they are in the domain of esoteric faith and how far in that of exoteric reason.

45 On the relationship between transcendentalism and pragmatism in both Habermas and Karl-Otto Apel, see Jean-Marc Ferry, *Philosophie de la communication I* (Paris: Cerf, 1994). For a scintillating account of the way in which John Rawls's pragmatizing of Kant's transcendentalism creates fatal problems for his account of justice, see Michael Sandel, *Liberalism and the Limits of Justice* (Cambridge: Cambridge University Press, 1983), pp. 15–65.

46 As is rightly argued by Colin McGinn in his book *The Mysterious Flame: Conscious Minds in a Material World* (New York: Basic Books, 1999).

47 *Treatise*, I.II.v, pp. 60–1. Hume declares that he has normally refrained from describing the operation of thought in physiological terms. This is clearly because he sees the mind – as a faculty of the soul – as irreducible to the physiological: it is a spiritual power which interacts with the body by means of intermediate vitalistic "animal spirits." Thus, he says here that "as the mind is endowed with a power of exciting any idea it pleases; whenever it despatches the [animal] spirits into that reach of the brain, in which the idea is placed; these spirits always excite the idea, when they run precisely into the proper traces, and rummage that cell, which belongs to the idea." It is only *mistakes* that arise from sheerly physiological influences: "the animal spirits,

falling into contiguous traces, present other related ideas in lieu of that which the mind first desir'd to survey."

48 *Treatise,* I.I.vi, p. 261: "our identity with regard to the passions serves to corroborate that with regard to the imagination, by making our distant perceptions influence each other, and by giving us a present concern for our past or future pains or pleasures." Hume has just – like Plato – compared the human psyche to a "republic" containing several members who are synchronically speaking *hierarchically* arranged in "reciprocal ties," and dia-chronically speaking connected by sequences of cause and effect. The self is thus both a drama and a narrative, and its only substantial identity lies in this continuity, not, as for Locke, in any "punctuality." And see again Livingston, *Hume's Philosophy of Common Life,* pp. 91–111.

49 *Treatise,* II.III.i–iii, pp. 399–418.

50 *Treatise,* I.I.i, pp. 1–7. Hume was perhaps the first person to use the term "emotion" besides the more traditional terms "feeling" and "passion." However, little seems to hang upon this new usage. Soon, however, "emotion" in other Scottish thinkers, beginning with Thomas Brown, came to imply something definitely caused by physical "motions," such that the resultant "feelings" could not be taken to offer any clues whatsoever about reality. (See Thomas Dixon, *From Passions to Emotions* (Cambridge: Cambridge University Press, 2003), pp. 98–134.) This constitutes an abso-lutely enormous shift toward a radical subjectivism that took firm root in the nineteenth century and arguably renders even the eighteenth century "ancient" and in ultimate continuity with the preceding millenia by com-parison. For, in that century, "sympathy" was still seen as disclosive of the states of being of other persons and even of natural realities: both things remain true for Hume. In the eighteenth century, the passions still *medi-ated,* and hence the association of passion with the externality of *music* was absolutely crucial: "what passions cannot music raise and quell?" asks John Dryden in his "Ode for St Cecilia" that was set to music by many, including of course both Purcell and Handel. Arguably, music itself is de-natured when it becomes regarded merely as a physical and mechanical arouser of "emo-tions" in the later Romantic period. This may be one clue to our fascination with "early music": in it, we actually uncannily "hear" and so experience an older "participatory" ontology (in Owen Barfield's sense of an intrinsic link between meaning and objectivity, humanity and nature). Compare, for example, Michel Carette's Baroque sonata "On the Pleasures of Solitude" which, despite its subject matter, remains part of a *dance,* with Gustav Mahler's Late Romantic piece "Blue Flower" which, even though it is osten-sibly referential, sounds both sentimental and solipsistic.

51 See Alva Noë, *Out of Our Heads* (New York: Hill and Wang, 2009); Andy Clark, *Supersizing the Mind* (Oxford: Oxford University Press, 2008); Michael Tye, *Consciousness Revisited* (Cambridge, MA: MIT Press, 2009).

52 Alfred North Whitehead, *Process and Reality* (New York: Free Press, 1978), pp. 19–20.

53 John McDowell, *Mind and World* (Cambridge, MA: Harvard University Press, 1994), pp. 108–26. McDowell refuses, however, to make the ontological moves which would accommodate his insights about meaning in terms of allowing an ontology of nature in excess of the conclusions of natural science.

54 "Hylomorphic" alludes to the Aristotelian view that every terrestrial reality is composed of "form" and "matter," which as unformed is in itself a mysterious negativity. Aristotle also thought that in the process of knowledge the form appears in the space of comprehending mind as still the "same" form, but now abstracted from matter. Hence, this is generally known as a theory of "knowledge by identity."

55 See David Skrbina, *Panpsychism and the West* (Cambridge, MA: MIT Press, 2005), pp. 249–69.

56 See Vladimir Soloviev, *The Philosophical Principles of Integral Knowledge* transl. Valeria Z. Nollan (Grand Rapids, MI: Eerdmans, 2008), pp. 53–4. Soloviev explained that "free theocracy" means that "the Church as such does not interfere in governmental and economic matters, but provides for the government and district council [!] a higher purpose and absolute norm for their activities."

Reply to My Critics: Jürgen Habermas

1 José Casanova, *Europas Angst vor der Religion*, transl. R. Schieder (Berlin University Press, 2009), pp. 98ff.

2 Here I have in mind religions that, with regard to our mundane knowledge, respect what *can no longer be asserted* within the limits of a fallible, but scientifically filtered, domain of arguments.

3 Jan Assmann, *Religion and Cultural Memory: Ten Studies*, transl. R. Livingstone (Stanford, CA: Stanford University Press, 2006), p. 122.

4 Robert N. Bellah, *Religion in Human Evolution: From the Paleolithic to the Axial Age* (Cambridge, MA: The Belknap Press, Harvard University Press, 2011).

5 René Girard, *I See Satan Fall like Lightning*, transl. J. G. Williams (Maryknoll, NY: Orbis Books, 2001), pp. 103–53.

6 Paul Veyne, "Culte, piété, et morale dans le paganisme gréco-romain," in Veyne, *L'empire gréco-romain* (Paris: Éditions du Seuil, 2005), pp. 419–543.

7 Jan Assmann, *The Price of Monotheism*, transl. R. Savage (Stanford, CA: Stanford University Press, 2010), chs 1 and 3.

8 Harold J. Berman, *Law and Revolution: The Formation of the Western Legal Tradition* (Cambridge, MA: Harvard University Press, 1983).

9 Ludger Honnefelder, *Woher kommen wir? Ursprünge der Moderne im Denken des Mittelalters* (Berlin: Berlin University Press, 2008).

10 See my discussion of Rawls's posthumously published senior graduation thesis, *A Brief Inquiry into the Meaning of Sin and Faith*, in "The Good Life – A Detestable Phrase: The Significance of the Young Rawls's Religious Ethics for His Political Theory," *European Journal of Philosophy*, 18(2010): 443–54.

11 Thomas McCarthy, *Ideals and Illusions* (Cambridge, MA: MIT Press, 1991).

12 See the commentaries on María Pía Lara and Amy Allen below.

13 T. W. Adorno, "Reason and Revelation," in T. W. Adorno, *Critical Models: Interventions and Catchwords* (New York: Columbia University Press, 1998), p. 136.

14 Charles Taylor, *A Secular Age* (Cambridge, MA: The Belknap Press, 2007), pp. 594ff.

15 Martin Riesebrodt, *The Promise of Salvation: A Theory of Religion*, transl. S. Rendall (Chicago, IL: University of Chicago Press, 2009).

16 Norman Birnbaum, *After Progress: American Social Reform and European Socialism in the Twentieth Century* (New York: Oxford University Press, 2001).

17 On the following, see Habermas, "The Language Game of Responsible Agency and the Problem of Free Will," *Philosophical Explorations*, 10/1(2007): 13–50, here pp. 15ff.

18 I am not only thinking of the social crises of the transition from national societies to a multicultural world society that cannot be held together by markets and electronic networks alone but requires a political constitution. An even more profound moral-political challenge is posed by the eugenic options toward which economic interests are driving the development of "converging technologies." "Human enhancement" is being pursued under a premise for which Carl Schmitt in a different context coined a nice phrase: "*Homo homini res mutanda.*"

19 Karl Löwith, *Meaning in History: The Theological Implications of the Philosophy of History* (Chicago, IL: University of Chicago Press, 1949).

20 Jacques Derrida, "Faith and Knowledge," in Jacques Derrida and Gianni Vattimo, eds, *Religion* (Stanford, CA: Stanford University Press, 2001), p. 14: "How then to think – within the limits of reason alone – a religion which, without again becoming natural religion, would today be effectively universal? And which, for that matter, would no longer be restricted to a paradigm that was Christian or even Abrahamic?"

21 Oliver Marchart, *Die politische Differenz* (Berlin: Suhrkamp, 2010); Thomas Bedorf and Kurt Rötthers, eds, *Das Politische und die Politik* (Berlin: Suhrkamp, 2010).

22 See Habermas, "'The Political' – the Rational Meaning of a Questionable Inheritance of Political Theory," in Eduardo Mendieta and Jonathan VanAntwerpen, eds, *The Power of Religion in the Public Sphere* (New York: Columbia University Press, 2011), pp. 15–33.

23 Hans Blumenberg, *The Legitimacy of the Modern Age*, transl. R. M. Wallace (Cambridge, MA: MIT Press, 1983), pp. 89–102. This is a translation of the revised German edition that appeared in three volumes in 1973, 1974, and 1976.

24 Ibid., p. 86.

25 Hans Blumenberg and Carl Schmitt, *Briefwechsel 1971–1978* (Frankfurt am Main: Suhrkamp, 2007).

26 Blumenberg even follows Schmitt's interpretation of the political idea of

progress when he, arm in arm with Reinhart Koselleck, takes "progress" to be an expression of the political deficit of the Enlightenment's moralizing critique of history: Blumenberg, *The Legitimacy of the Modern Age* (1983), p. 31 n.7. Here he refers to Reinhart Koselleck, *Critique and Crisis: Enlightenment and the Pathogenesis of Modern Society* (Cambridge, MA: MIT Press, 1988).

27 Imre Lakatos and Alan Musgrave, *Criticism and the Growth of Knowledge* (Cambridge, UK: Cambridge University Press, 1974); on this, see Werner Diederich, ed., *Theorien der Wissenschaftsgeschichte: Beiträge zur diachronischen Wissenschaftstheorie* (Frankfurt am Main: Suhrkamp, 1974).

28 A logically misleading error has crept into the translation quoted in footnote 27. The quotation in question (*An Awareness of What Is Missing*, transl. C. Cronin (Cambridge, UK: Polity, 2010), p. 18) should read: "Postmetaphysical thinking can [not: 'cannot'] cope on its own with the defeatism concerning reason which we encounter today both in the postmodern radicalization of the 'dialectic of the Enlightenment' and in the naturalism founded on a naïve faith in science."

29 Hugo Ott, *Martin Heidegger: A Political Life*, transl. A. Blunden (London: HarperCollins, 1993).

30 Following Nietzsche and appealing to the "original" truth of the Presocratics or alluding to Hölderlin's plural gods ("only a (!) God can save us," as he put it in his final interview, published posthumously in *Der Spiegel*), Heidegger embraced nationalistic neo-pagan sentiments, or at least made use of them. From the Nazi period onward, his "mythological" conversation with Hölderlin was intended to promote the "dream" of a national religious "reconnection with the gods" of holy Germany. See Christian Sommer, "Rückbindung an die Götter: Heideggers Volksreligion (1934/35)," the *Internationales Jahrbuch für Hermeneutik*, vol. 9 (Tubingen: Siebeck, 2010), pp. 283–310.

31 Klaus Heinrich, *Parmenides und Jona: Vier Studien über das Verhältnis von Philosophie und Mythologie* (Frankfurt am Main: Suhrkamp Verlag, 1966); idem, *Dahlemer Vorlesungen* (Frankfurt am Main: Stroemfeld/Roter Stern, 1981).

32 Amy Allen explicitly endorses this reading in n.20.

33 On the analysis of religious validity claims, see Edmund Arens, *Gottesverständigung: Eine kommunikative Religionstheologie* (Freiburg: Herder, 2007), pp. 239ff.

34 I'm afraid that this accentuation has more to do with present-day Islamophobia, which inadvertently aligns Bernstein with certain Christian agitators.

35 Moses proclaims to his people: "When you come into the land that the Lord your God is giving you, you must not learn to imitate the abhorrent practices of those nations. No one shall be found among you who makes a son or daughter pass through fire, or who practices divination, or is a soothsayer, or an augur, or a sorcerer, or one who casts spells, or who consults ghosts or spirits, or who seeks oracles from the dead. For whoever does these things is abhorrent to the Lord" (Deut. 18: 9–12).

36 Troels Nørager, *Taking Leave of Abraham: An Essay on Religion and Democracy* (Aarhus, Denmark: Aarhus University Press, 2008).

37 Søren Kierkegaard, *Fear and Trembling*, in Kierkegaard, *Fear and Trembling; Repetition*, transl. H. V. Hong and E. H. Hong (Princeton, NJ: Princeton University Press, 1983), pp. 64 ff.

38 Benjamin Uffenheimer, "Myth and Reality in Ancient Israel," in Shmuel Noah Eisenstadt, ed., *The Origins and Diversity of Axial Age Civilizations* (Albany, NY: State University Press of New York, 1986), pp. 135–68, here pp. 143–9.

39 "Whoever comes to me and does not hate father and mother, wife and children, brothers and sisters, yes, and even life itself, cannot be my disciple."

40 The further objection that the proposed expectation could tempt secular citizens into insincerity has no force for a discourse-theoretical understanding of the democratic process. Aside from the fact that motives for actual voting behavior may not in any case be exposed to any form of regulation, only public utterances, hence actual contributions to the formation of opinions and consensus-building, and not mindsets, have a bearing on the legitimizing power of democratic discourses.

41 Here, I disregard the asymmetry between the interlocutors. The interlocutors of the people of faith are secular citizens, not secularly minded philosophers, who study the epistemic attitudes and the nature of the arguments exchanged.

42 This is the "stability"-conception of John Rawls's idea of overlapping consensus.

43 I suspect that lurking behind this disagreement is the more far-reaching antithesis between philosophical cultures, going back to Hume and Kant, respectively. The antagonism was initially sparked by opposed strategies concerning the best way to address the problem of the application of concepts (understood nominalistically) to the given (whatever it may be), namely, whether to proceed from the sensory input or from the concept. Pragmatism goes beyond these alternatives by appealing to the practice of employing concepts. The gap between concept and the given, when we become aware of it in the functional domain of established practices, has "always already" been pragmatically bridged. But within pragmatism, whose intersubjective approach makes it responsive to the pluralism of participants in shared practices, the problem of bridging differences reappears in the guise of a pluralism of perspectives. How do we bridge the differences between the conceptions of different participants that emerge in the process of applying the same analytical distinctions from their respective particular contexts of origin? The Kantian strategy suggests the answer that the conceptual structure of the shared practice of discourse equips the practicing participants with a sufficiently convergent *prior* understanding to enable them to clarify those differences that emerge in the course of applying the same concepts through the give and take of reasons. The most uncompromising pragmatist version of Hume's opposing nominalistic strategy is the one developed by Richard Rorty.

44 Thomas McCarthy, *Ideals and Illusions* (Cambridge, MA: MIT Press, 1993), pp. 181–99.

45 See the excellent account of this transition in Herbert Marcuse, *Reason and Revolution* (Boston, MA: Beacon Press, 1960).

46 See the relevant essays in *PMT*. In an interview, I explained the expression succinctly as follows: "In considering Kant the first 'postmetaphysical' thinker, I simply follow a convention. His 'transcendental dialectics' ends the bad habit of applying the categories of the understanding, which are cut out for inner-worldly phenomena, to the world as a whole. This devaluation of essentialist propositions about nature and history as a whole is one of the far-reaching consequences of the 'nominalist revolution' of the High Middle Ages and of early modern thought. The anthropocentric turn toward the world-constituting achievements of subjectivity or language – that is, the paradigm shift toward the philosophy of consciousness and of language – goes back to this revolution as well. Already in the seventeenth century, the objectifying natural sciences led to the separation between practical and theoretical reason. This separation in turn provoked the attempts of rational law and rational morality to justify obligations and worldviews merely on the basis of practical reason, rather than out of the 'order of things.' Finally, with the emergence of the humanities since the early nineteenth century, a historical mode of thinking, which devalues – up to a point – even the transcendental approaches, forced its way through. Furthermore, the results of hermeneutics confront us with a split in our epistemic access to the world: the lifeworld that discloses itself to our understanding only as (at least virtual) participants in everyday practices, cannot be described from the natural-scientific perspective in such a way that we are able to recognize ourselves in this objectifying description.

"The sciences emancipate themselves from the guidelines [*Vorgaben*] of philosophy in *both* directions: they sentence philosophy to the more modest business of retrospective reflection on, on the one hand, the methodologically proper advances of the sciences, and, on the other, on the presumptively universal features of those practices and forms of life that are for us without alternatives, even if we find ourselves in them contingently. In other words, the uncircumventable [*nicht-hintergehbaren*] universal structures of the lifeworld in general replace the position of the transcendental subject. Along the paths of a *genealogy of modern thought*, merely sketched here, a differentiation took place to which the strong, metaphysical claims fell victim. We can also think of this differentiation process as a sorting-through of reasons that alone still 'count' for postmetaphysical thinking. By contrast, the statements concerning essences [*Wesensaussagen*] that are typical of the metaphysical thought of the one-all [*Alleinheitsdenken*], and the categories of reasons that metaphysical thinking could mobilize, have been *prima facie* devalued." Understood in this sense, Nicolas Wolterstorff attempts to develop his own fideistic position under "postmetaphysical" premises.

47 I fail to understand the laborious attempt to construct a so-called "*Kant-rationality*" (Wolterstorff, p. 98 of this vol.). From my perspective, all that is necessary is the sufficiently explicated procedural concept of "communicative

rationality," which is intended to take the place of the traditional substantive concept of reason. For an introduction, see *PMT*, pp. 115–85, and *TJ*, pp. 83–130.

48 As it happens, that is my *general* objection against a reformed epistemology that, if I am not mistaken, wants to cancel the distinction between the modalities of taking-to-be-true involved in religious and secular assertions, respectively.

49 P. F. Strawson, "Freedom and Resentment", in *Proceedings of the British Academy*, 48(1962): 1–25.

50 The plea of Michael Theunissen, "Philosophie der Religion oder religiöse Philosophie," *Information Philosophie* 5/1 (December 2003): 7–15, points in the same direction, though, in my opinion, with stronger arguments.

51 Lutz Wingert, "Haben wir moralische Verpflichtungen gegenüber früheren Generationen?" *Babylon – Beiträge zur jüdischen Gegenwart*, 9(1991): 78–94.

52 Adorno spoke in this sense of "Heine the Wound" (*die Wunde Heine*).

Appendix: Religion in Habermas's Work

1 There is now a massive doctoral dissertation that covers all of Habermas's work as it relates to his views on religion, which I had the honor and pleasure of directing. See Javier Aguirre, *Postmetaphysical Reason and Postsecular Consciousness: Habermas's Analyis of Religion in the Public Sphere* (Stony Brook University, Dissertation, 2012).

2 George Lichtheim, *From Marx to Hegel* (New York: Herder and Herder, 1971), p. 175.

3 I developed this periodization with Barbara Fultner, who convinced me of moving some dates around to reflect more accurately theoretical shifts. See Barbara Fultner, ed., *Jürgen Habermas: Key Concepts* (Durham, UK: Acumen, 2011), pp. 3–7.

4 One of Habermas's early essays, published in *Theorie und Praxis*, which takes up and synthesizes his work from this dissertation is now available in English as "Dialectical Idealism in Transition to Materialism: Schelling's Idea of a Contraction of God and its Consequences for the Philosophy of History," in Judith Norman and Alistair Welchman, eds, *The New Schelling* (London and New York: Continuum, 2004), pp. 43–89. This essay remains key for any indepth understanding of Habermas's overall work on religion and theology.

5 These lectures are now available in English, in Jürgen Habermas, *On the Pragmatics of Social Interaction: Preliminary Studies in the Theory of Communicative Action*, transl. Barbara Fultner (Cambridge, MA: MIT Press, 2002), pp. 1–104.

6 Karl-Otto Apel, *Sprachpragmatik und Philosophie* (Frankfurt am Main: Suhrkamp Verlag, 1976).

7 Karl-Otto Apel, *Ethics and the Theory of Rationality: Selected Essays, Volume Two*, edited and introduced by Eduardo Mendieta (New Jersey:

Humanities Press, 1996), p. 178. See also Karl-Otto Apel, *From a Transcendental-Pragmatic Point of View*, ed. Marianna Papastephanou (Manchester and New York: Manchester University Press, 1998), ch. 10: "The Self-Recuperative Principle of a Critical-Hermeneutic Reconstruction of History," pp. 232–43.

 8 See Eduardo Mendieta, "Introduction" to Habermas, *Religion and Rationality: Essays on Reason, God and Modernity* (Cambridge, MA: MIT Press, 2002), pp. 23–4.

 9 Marx Horkheimer and T. W. Adorno, *Dialectic of Enlightenment* (New York: Continuum, 1972), p. 118, quote by Habermas, *Justification and Application: Remarks on Discourse Ethics* (Cambridge, MA: MIT Press, 1992), p. 134.

10 Ibid., p. 146.

11 Ibid.

12 Ibid.

13 Jürgen Habermas, "On the Relation between the Secular Liberal State and Religion," in Eduardo Mendieta, ed., *The Frankfurt School on Religion: Key Writings by the Major Thinkers* (London and New York: Routledge, 2004), p. 348.

14 Eduardo Mendieta, "A Postsecular World Society?: An Interview with Jürgen Habermas," *The Immanent Frame*. Available at: <http://blogs.ssrc.org/tif/2010/02/03/a-postsecular-world-society/> (accessed September 28, 2012). The full subtitle of our interview is "On the Philosophical Significance of Postsecular Consciousness and the Multicultural World Society." This is a very informative subtitle, one that perhaps because it is so verbose, was dropped in the German publication. In the German version, Habermas has changed the titled to "A New Interest of Philosophy on Religion: An Interview with Eduardo Mendieta."

15 This review is available as "The 'Good Life' – A 'Detestable Phrase': The Significance of the Young Rawls's Religious Ethics for his Political Theory," in *European Journal of Philosophy*, 18/3(2010): 443–54.

16 The essay that deals with "The Political" has appeared in English with the title "'The Political': The Rational Meaning of a Questionable Inheritance of Political Theology," in Eduardo Mendieta and Jonathan VanAntwerpen, eds, *The Power of Religion in the Public Sphere* (New York: Columbia University Press, 2011), pp. 15–33.

17 I discussed some of these concerns in my essay "Rationalization, Modernity, and Secularization," in Barbara Fultner, ed., *Habermas: Key Concepts* (Durham, UK: Acumen, 2011), pp. 222–38.

Bibliography of Works by Jürgen Habermas

Most of Habermas's writings are available in English and references in this volume are to English translations where available. German publication information has been included here in square brackets. Occasionally, the contents of a collection of essays varies slightly from the German original; a few collections are drawn from multiple sources and therefore do not correspond to any German editions.

Habermas, J. 1954. *Das Absolute und die Geschichte von der Zwiespältigkeit in Schellings Denken* (Bonn: H. Bouvier).

Habermas, J. 1963. "Dialektischer Idealismus im Übergang zum Materialismus: Geschichtsphilosophische Folgerungen aus Schellings Idee einer Contraction Gottes". In *Theorie und Praxis: Sozialphilosophische Studien* (Neuwied am Rhein: Luchterhand).

Habermas, J. 1970. *Toward a Rational Society: Student Protest, Science, and Politics*, transl. J. Shapiro (Boston, MA: Beacon Press). [From *Technik und Wissenschaft als "Ideologie"* (Frankfurt: Suhrkamp, 1968) and *Protestbewegung und Hochschulreform* (Frankfurt: Suhrkamp, 1958)].

Habermas, J. 1971. *Knowledge and Human Interests*, transl. J. Shapiro (Boston, MA: Beacon Press). [*Erkenntnis und Interesse* (Frankfurt: Suhrkamp, 1968)].

Habermas, J. and N. Luhmann 1971. *Theorie der Gesellschaft oder Sozialtechnologie: Was Leistet die Systemforschung?* (Frankfurt: Suhrkamp).

Habermas, J. 1974. *Theory and Practice*, transl. J. Viertel (Boston, MA: Beacon Press) [*Theorie und Praxis* (Frankfurt: Suhrkamp, 1971)].

Habermas, J. 1975. *Legitimation Crisis*, transl. T. McCarthy (Boston, MA: Beacon Press) [*Legitimationsprobleme int Spätkapitalismus* (Frankfurt: Suhrkamp, 1973)].

Habermas, J. 1979a. *Communication and the Evolution of Society*, transl. T. McCarthy (Boston, MA: Beacon Press) [from *Zur Rekonstruktion des historischen Materialismus* (Frankfurt: Suhrkamp, 1976) and *Sprachpragmatik und Philosophy*, ed. K.-O. Apel (Frankfurt: Suhrkamp, 1976)].

Habermas, J. 1979b. "History and Evolution", *Telos*, 39: 5–44.

Habermas, J. 1980. "The Hermeneutic Claim to Universality." In *Contemporary Hermeneutics: Hermeneutics as Method, Philosophy, and Critique*, ed. J. Bleicher, pp. 181–211 (London: Routledge and Kegan Paul) [Originally published in 1970, reprinted in the expanded edition of *Zur Logik der Sozialwissenschaften* (Frankfurt: Suhrkamp, 1985)].

Habermas, J. 1981. *Kleine Politsche Schriften (I–IV)* (Frankfurt: Suhrkamp).

Habermas J. 1983. *Philosophical-Political Profiles,* transl. F. G. Lawrence. (Cambridge, MA: MIT Press) [*Philosophisch-politische Profile* (Frankfurt: Suhrkamp, 1981); essays from the period 1958–79].

Habermas, J. 1984a. *Vorstudien und Ergänzungen zur Theorie des Kommunikativen Handelns* (Frankfurt: Suhrkamp).

Habermas, J. (ed.) 1984b. *Observations on the "Spiritual Situation of the Age": Contemporary German Perspectives*, transl. A. Buchwalter (Cambridge, MA: MIT Press) [*Stichworte zur geistigen Situation der Zeit* (Frankfurt: Suhrkamp, 1979)].

Habermas, J. 1984/1987. *The Theory of Communicative Action*, 2 vols, transl. T. McCarthy (Boston, MA: Beacon Press) [*Theorie des kommunikativen Handelns*, 2 vols (Frankfurt: Suhrkamp, 1981)].

Habermas, J. 1985a. "Reply to Skjei", *Inquiry*, 28 (March): 105–12.

Habermas, J. 1985b. "Konservative Politik, Arbeit, Sozialismus und Utopie heute (1983)." In *Die Neue Unübersichtlichkeit: Kleine Politische Schriften V*, pp. 59–76 (Frankfurt: Suhrkamp).

Habermas, J. 1986. *Autonomy and Solidarity: Interviews with Jürgen Habermas*, ed. P. Dews (London: Verso).

Habermas, J. 1987. "Geschichtsbewußtsein und posttraditionale Identität: Die Westorientierung der Bundesrepublik." In *Eine Art Schadensabwicklung*, pp. 161–79 (Frankfurt: Suhrkamp).

Habermas, J. 1988a. *On the Logic of the Social Sciences,* transl. S. Weber Nicholsen and J. A. Stark (Cambridge MA: MIT Press) [Originally published in 1967, reprinted as *Zur Logik der Sozialwissenschaften*, exp. edn (Frankfurt: Suhrkamp, 1985)].

Habermas, J. 1988b. "Law and Morality." In *The Tanner Lectures on Human Values,* vol. 8, ed. S. McMurrin, transl. K. Baynes, pp. 217–79 (Salt Lake City: Utah University Press).

Habermas, J. 1989a. *The New Conservatism: Cultural Criticism and the Historians' Debate*, transl. S. Weber Nicholson (Cambridge, MA: MIT Press). [Mostly from *Kleine Politische Schriften V* and *VI* (Frankfurt: Suhrkamp, 1985, 1987)].

Habermas, J. 1989b. *The Structural Transformation of the Public Sphere: An Inquiry into a Category of Bourgeois Society*, transl. T. Burger (Cambridge, MA: MIT Press) [*Strukturwandel der Öffentlichkeit* (Neuwied: Luchterhand, 1962)].

Habermas, J. 1990a. *The Philosophical Discourse of Modernity: Twelve Lectures,* transl. F. Lawrence (Cambridge, MA: MIT Press) [*Der philosophische Diskurs der Moderne: Zwölf Vorlesungen* (Frankfurt: Suhrkamp, 1985)].

Habermas, J. 1990b. "Justice and Solidarity." In *The Moral Domain: Essays in the Ongoing Discussion Between Philosophy and the Social Sciences*, ed. T. E. Wren, pp. 224–52 (Cambridge, MA: MIT Press).

Habermas, J. 1990c. *Moral Consciousness and Communicative Action*, transl. C. Lenhardt and S. Weber Nicholsen (Cambridge, MA: MIT Press) [*Moralbewusstsein und kommunikatives Handeln* (Frankfurt: Suhrkamp, 1983)].

Habermas, J. 1991. *Texte und Kontexte* (Frankfurt: Suhrkamp).

Habermas, J. 1992. *Postmetaphysical Thinking: Philosophical Essays*, transl. W. Hohengarten (Cambridge, MA: MIT Press) [*Nachmetaphysisches Denken* (Frankfurt: Suhrkamp, 1988)].

Habermas, J. 1993. *Justification and Application: Remarks on Discourse Ethics*, transl. C. Cronin (Cambridge, MA: MIT Press) [From *Erläuterungen zur Diskursethik* (Frankfurt: Suhrkamp, 1991) and *Die Nachholende Revolution: Kleine Politische Schriften VII* (Frankfurt: Suhrkamp, 1990)].

Habermas, J. 1994. *The Past as Future*, transl. M. Pensky (Lincoln, NE: University of Nebraska Press) [*Vergangenheit Als Zukunft: Das Alte Deutschland im neuen Europa?*, ed. M. Haller (Munich: Piper, 1993)].

Habermas, J. 1997. *A Berlin Republic: Writings on Germany*, transl. S. Rendall (Lincoln, NE: University of Nebraska Press).

Habermas, J. 1998a. *The Inclusion of the Other: Studies in Political Theory*, transl. C. Cronin (Cambridge, MA: MIT Press) [*Die Einbeziehung des Anderen: Studien zur politischen Theorie* (Frankfurt: Suhrkamp, 1996)].

Habermas, J. 1998b. *Between Facts and Norms: Contributions to a Discourse Theory of Law and Democracy*, transl. W. Rehg (Cambridge, MA: MIT Press) [*Faktizität und Geltung: Beiträge zur Diskurstheorie des Rechts und des demokratischen Rechtsstaats* (Frankfurt: Suhrkamp, 1992)].

Habermas, J. 1998c. *On the Pragmatics of Communication*, ed. M. Cooke (Cambridge, MA: MIT Press).

Habermas, J. 2001a. *The Postnational Constellation: Political Essays*, transl. M. Pensky (Cambridge, MA: MIT Press) [*Die postnationale Konstellation: Politische Essays* (Frankfurt: Suhrkamp, 1998)].

Habermas, J. 2001b. *The Liberating Power of Symbols: Philosophical Essays*, transl. P. Dews (Cambridge, MA: MIT Press) [*Vom sinnlichen Eindruck zum symbolischen Ausdruck* (Frankfurt: Suhrkamp, 1997)].

Habermas, J. 2001c. *On the Pragmatics of Social Interaction: Preliminary Studies in the Theory of Communicative Action*, transl. B. Fultner (Cambridge, MA: MIT Press) [Selections from *Vorstudien und Ergänzungen zur Theorie des kommunikativen Handelns* (Frankfurt: Suhrkamp, 1984)].

Habermas, J. 2001d. "Intentions, Conventions, and Linguistic Interactions" [1976]. In *On the Pragmatics of Social Interaction: Preliminary Studies in the Theory of Communicative Action*, transl. B. Fultner, pp. 105–28 (Cambridge, MA: MIT Press).

Habermas, J. 2001e. "Constitutional Democracy: A Paradoxical Union of Contradictory Principles?," *Political Theory*, 29/6: 766–81.

Habermas, J. 2002a. *Religion and Rationality: Essays on Reason, God and Modernity* (Cambridge, MA: MIT Press).

Habermas, J. 2002b. "Resentment of US Policies is Growing." *The Nation* 275/21: 15.

Habermas, J. 2003a. *Truth and Justification*, transl. B. Fultner (Cambridge, MA: MIT Press) [*Wahrheit und Rechtfertigung* (Frankfurt: Suhrkamp, 1999)].

Habermas, J. 2003b. *The Future of Human Nature*, transl. H. Beister, W. Rehg and M. Pensky (Cambridge: Polity) [*Die Zukunft der menschlichen Natur: Auf dem Weg zu einer liberalen Eugenik?* (Frankfurt: Suhrkamp, 2001)].

Habermas, J. 2003c. "On Law and Disagreement: Some Comments on 'Interpretive Pluralism,'" *Ratio Juris*, 16/2: 193–4.

Habermas, J. 2004. "The Moral and the Ethical: A Reconsideration of the Issue of the Priority of the Right over the Good." In *Pragmatism, Critique, Judgment: Essays for Richard J. Bernstein*, ed. S. Benhabib and N. Fraser, pp. 29–43 (Cambridge, MA: MIT Press).

Habermas, J. and J. Derrida 2005. "February 15, or, What Binds Europeans Together." In *Old Europe, New Europe, Core Europe: Transatlantic Relations After the Iraq War*, D. Levy, M. Pensky, and J. C. Torpey (eds), pp. 3–13 (London: Verso).

Habermas, J. 2006a. *Time of Transitions*, transl. C. Cronin and M. Pensky (Cambridge: Polity) [*Zeit der Übergänge* (Frankfurt: Suhrkamp, 2001)].

Habermas, J. 2006b. "Religion in the Public Sphere", *European Journal of Philosophy*, 14/1: 1–25.

Habermas, J. and J. Ratzinger 2006. *Dialectics of Secularization: On Reason and Religion*, transl. B. McNeil (San Francisco, CA: Ignatius Press) [*Dialektik der Säkularisierung: Über Vernunft und Religion* (Freiburg im Breisgau: Herder, 2005)].

Habermas, J. 2007a. *The Divided West*, transl. C. Cronin (Cambridge: Polity) [*Der gespaltene Westen* (Frankfurt: Suhrkamp, 2004)].

Habermas, J. 2007b. "The Language Game of Responsible Agency and the Problem of Free Will: How Can Epistemic Dualism Be Reconciled with Ontological Monism?," transl. J. Anderson, *Philosophical Explorations*, 10/1: 13–50.

Habermas, J. 2008. *Between Naturalism and Religion: Philosophical Essays*, transl. C. Cronin (Cambridge: Polity) [*Zwischen Naturalismus und Religion: Philosophische Aufsätze* (Frankfurt: Suhrkamp, 2005)].

Habermas, J. 2009a. *Europe: The Faltering Project*, transl. C. Cronin (Cambridge: Polity) [*Ach, Europa* (Frankfurt: Suhrkamp, 2008)].

Habermas, J. 2009b. *Philosophische Texte: Studienausgabe in fünf Bänden* (Frankfurt: Suhrkamp).

Habermas, J. 2009c. *Philosophische Texte, Band 5. Kritik der Vernunft.* (Frankfurt: Suhrkamp).

Habermas, J., M. Reder, J. Schmidt, N. Brieskorn, and F. Ricken 2010. *An Awareness of What Is Missing: Faith and Reason in a Post-Secular Age,* transl. C. Cronin (Cambridge: Polity) [*Ein Bewusstsein von dem, was fehlt* (Frankfurt: Suhrkamp, 2008)].

Habermas, J. 2012. *The Crisis of the European Union: A Response*, transl. C. Cronin (Cambridge: Polity) [*Zur Verfassung Europas* (Frankfurt: Suhrkamp, 2011)].

Habermas, J. n.d. *Essay on Faith and Knowledge: Postmetaphysical Thinking and the Secular Self-Interpretation of Modernity*.

Habermas, J. n.d. "From Worldviews to the Lifeworld: On the Genealogy of a Concept."

Index